NEW-ENGLAND

Historical and Genealogical Register.

PUBLISHED QUARTERLY, BY THE

New=England Historic Genealogical Society.

FOR THE YEAR 1886.

VOLUME XL.

BOSTON:

PUBLISHED AT THE SOCIETY'S HOUSE, 18 SOMERSET STREET.

PRINTED BY DAVID CLAPP & SON.

1886.

Committee on Publication

1886

JOHN WARD DEAN,   WILLIAM B. TRASK,
LUCIUS R. PAIGE,   HENRY H. EDES,
EDMUND F. SLAFTER,   HENRY E. WAITE,
JEREMIAH COLBURN,   FRANCIS E. BLAKE.

Editor
JOHN WARD DEAN.

Facsimile Reprint
Published 1996

HERITAGE BOOKS, INC.
1540E Pointer Ridge Place
Bowie, Maryland 20716
1-800-398-7709

ISBN 0-7884-0539-X

A Complete Catalog Listing Hundreds of Titles
On History, Genealogy, and Americana
Available Free Upon Request

GENERAL INDEX.

Index of Names of PERSONS at the end of the Volume.

Genealogical Gleaners, notice, 327
Genealogical Gleanings in England, 34, 158, 300, 362
German Immigrants 1752, note, 323
Gleason Family, query, 324
Green Family, queries, 407
Greenwood, reply to query, 110
Guide to English and Foreign Heraldry, 326
Guilford (Conn.) Genealogies, note, 209
Gurtley, William, query, 210

Hanbury, note, 106
Harvard, John, and his Ancestry, Part II., 362; notes on, 180, 181, 321
Harvard, John, and Cambridge University, note, 103, 207
Haslam, John, query, 108
Herefordshire Pedigrees, notice, 326
Hillyer, query, 107
Historical Societies, Proceedings—Chicago, 114, 215, 331; Connecticut, 331; Maine, 215; New England Historic Genealogical, 113, 213, 329; Old Colony, 330; Rhode Island, 114, 215, 330; Virginia, 114, 215, 331
Hitchcock Genealogy, excerpts from, 307
Horne tabular pedigree, 46
Huguenot Emigration to Virginia, note, 110
Hulen, reply to query, 109

General Index.

THE

HISTORICAL AND GENEALOGICAL REGISTER.

JANUARY, 1886.

MEMOIR OF WILLIAM A. WHITEHEAD, A.M.

BY HIS NIECE.

WILLIAM ADEE WHITEHEAD, late Corresponding Secretary of the New Jersey Historical Society, was a man of no ordinary attainments. He was born in Newark, New Jersey, Feb. 19, 1810. His father was William Whitehead, cashier of the Newark Banking and Insurance Company, and his mother, Abby, daughter of Benjamin and Bethia Coe. The attractive old-fashioned brick house in which he was born, serving both for business purposes and family home, has since been removed, and on its site are the rooms of the New Jersey Historical Society. It is a pleasant coincidence that it was on that same spot, especially during the last years of his life, that Mr. Whitehead devoted so many hours to the historical writing and research in which he took so deep an interest.

His early education seems to have been but meagre. When a small child he attended several primary schools, and when about ten years old became a pupil in the old "Newark Academy," situated where the Post Office now stands. The two Scotchmen who kept the school, Andrew Smith and his son, were extremely superficial in their method of teaching, and on the approach of the seasons for examination, special preparation, popularly known as "cramming," was resorted to for the occasion. Quiet and order were apparently unknown, and the punishment administered for offences and shortcomings was that of the "cat-o'-nine tails." After less than two years of this very unsatisfactory tuition young Whitehead graduated, being just twelve years old. To his own diligent application in after years, either alone or with comrades of like tastes, he owed that knowledge of history, science and general literature which rendered him the cultured and agreeable companion to whom so many looked for sympathy, counsel and instruction. Thorough, exact and efficient as surveyor, draftsman, merchant, banker, historian and writer, who would think that his early advantages had been so few and limited! When a youth of fifteen or sixteen the trust reposed in him was very unusual. His father had removed to Perth Amboy, where he became cashier of the Commercial Bank of New Jersey, and to his son was given the responsible position of travelling circulator of the bills of the bank. Thus he was in the habit of journeying to Woodbridge and Rahway, carrying hundreds of dollars to be exchanged at those towns for bills deposited to the credit of the Amboy Bank in New York. A short time after this he was appointed bank messenger, and made weekly journeys to New York by steamboat, there being then no railway communication between the two cities. In his leisure hours he devoted much time to the diligent study of French, Elocution and Drawing, while to his young friends in Amboy his literary work was a source of much pleasure and profit. His genial wit, keen sense of humor and affectionate disposition made him a most agreeable companion and caused him to be generally beloved.

In the autumn of 1828 he joined his elder brother in Key West, with the view of engaging in mercantile business. When he arrived, however, the knowledge which he had acquired by his own efforts was signally useful to himself and to others, and he was found to be fully competent to run the dividing lines between the lots and portions of the respective proprietors of the island. With great modesty and distrust of his powers he undertook a new survey, which was successfully completed in March, 1829, and is still considered authoritative. When scarcely twenty-one he entered upon the duties of Collector of the Port of Key West, an office which he held until July, 1838. During the ten years of his life in Key West he spent much of his leisure time in diligent study and reading, and in efforts for the promotion of the good of his fellow citizens. There he began those meteorological observations which he carried on for more than forty years. He was a member of the town council, mayor of the city, and was deeply interested in the establishment of a newspaper and the advancement of education in the island. He also united with several others in establishing an Episcopal church, of which he was a devout member, and which was the first congregation organized in Key West. In grateful recognition of Mr. Whitehead's public spirit and beneficent labor in these early days, his name was given to a point of the island and also to a street in the town.

Mr. Whitehead was married August 11, 1834, in Perth Amboy, to Margaret Elizabeth, daughter of Hon. James Parker, of that city, and with his bride returned to Florida in the autumn of the same year. Concerning his sojourn in the South he writes: "The ten years of my life, during which I considered Key West my home, laid the foundation of my future usefulness. What success in life I may have achieved is due to application to reading and study, to the responsibilities which my official position rendered it necessary for me to assume, and the fixed determination to render myself worthy, if possible, of the regard of those with whom I was connected."

In 1838 he began business as stockbroker in New York, and lived in the city for nearly five years, during which time he had access to the library of the New York Historical Society, and conceived the idea of writing the early history of New Jersey, a plan afterwards executed by him. About this time a number of contributions from his pen appeared in the *Newark Daily Advertiser*, under the title of "Glimpses of the Past." Numerous articles followed these on History, Meteorology, Biography, Political and Ecclesiastical matters, besides various other topics of local interest. His monthly weather reports began in June, 1843, and were continued until his death. After 1843 his home was in Newark, although he continued for several years to do business in New York. In 1848 he entered the service of the Astor Insurance Company. The following year he received the appointment of Secretary of the New Jersey Railroad and Transportation Company; and in 1855 that of Treasurer of the Harlem Railroad, which he held for three years, when he resumed connection with the New Jersey Railroad. His fine head and erect figure as he sat in his office gave him a military appearance, which was singularly in accordance with the spirit of the period. His keen but kindly eye will be long remembered by those with whom he had any intercourse and by the officers and soldiers of the late civil war, when the transportation of troops and supplies formed a large part of the business of the railroad. In 1871 Mr. Whitehead resigned his position on the railroad, and until 1879 was connected with the American Trust Company of New Jersey.

In January, 1845, a meeting was held in Trenton to organize an Historical Society for New Jersey. The subject had been introduced a short time previous by the Rev. D. V. McLean, of Monmouth County. To it Mr. Whitehead gave his earnest and enthusiastic attention. He was chosen Corresponding Secretary of the new organization, and held the office until his death. A large amount of valuable material had been collected by him for a history of the province of New Jersey, and at the suggestion of Mr. Charles King, afterwards President of Columbia College, these manuscripts were adopted by the Society for the first volume of its printed collections, and issued in 1846 under the title of "East Jersey under the Proprietary Governments."

In 1846 the Newark Library Association was organized. This invaluable institution originated with the late Rev. Dr. Samuel Irenæus Prime, then living in Newark. His efforts were ardently seconded by Mr. Whitehead, and their labors to obtain subscribers to the necessary capital stock were unremitting. The charter was obtained in 1847, and the Newark Library stands to-day a fitting memorial of its indefatigable founders. Mr. Whitehead was the first Secretary of this association, and for some time before his death President of the Board of Directors. The library contained in January, 1849, 1900 volumes; in January, 1855, 11,500 volumes;

in January, 1875, 21,000 volumes; in January, 1885, 26,666 volumes. Books taken out in 1884, 31,421—an increase over previous year of 3,400.

In 1860 Mr. Whitehead was elected member of the Board of Education and represented the first Ward of Newark for ten years, when he was chosen President of the Board; he declined a re-election in 1871. From 1862 till 1871 he was one of the Trustees of the State Normal School, and on the death of the Hon. Richard S. Field, became President of that board, a position which he held during the remainder of his life. His services, in connection with the Essex county Bible Society, Trinity church, Newark, and the Diocesan Conventions of New Jersey and Northern New Jersey to which he was a delegate, if not so conspicuous, were nevertheless indicative of his large public spirit and religious character.

In 1858 there appeared a most exhaustive "Analytical Index to the Colonial Documents of New Jersey in the State Paper offices of England, compiled by Henry Stevens, edited, with notes, by Wm. A. Whitehead." This work of more than 500 pages, the fruit of years of immense industry and determined zeal, is of the greatest interest and importance to the antiquarian. It could not be accomplished without laborious research in England, and aid was solicited from the State for that end; but for seven years all efforts failed, and the completion of the volume is due to the liberality of the late James G. King, Esq. Finally in 1872 an appropriation was made by the Legislature through the instrumentality of Hon. Nathaniel Niles, "for the purpose of obtaining, arranging and publishing any papers relating to the history of New Jersey." Mr. Whitehead then engaged in editing the "Documents relating to the Colonial History of New Jersey," the Index to which has just been mentioned. The first volume was published in 1880; six others followed in rapid succession, and the eighth was ready for the press in 1883. Illness prevented the completion of the ninth volume which was in preparation, and he was obliged to forego the industrious prosecution of his favorite pursuit. Declining health induced him in 1879 to resort to a European voyage in the company of his wife and son. To visit the scenes familiar to him through books of travel and correspondence with men of letters, afforded him new and enduring gratification, and it was a constant pleasure to him after his return, to recall to mind the venerable cathedrals and beautiful scenery, as well as novel and amusing experiences which he had enjoyed so much while abroad. But the journey failed to bring permanent benefit to his health; gradually he failed more and more in strength, until July, 1884. On the 2d of that month, he was borne by loving friends to his beautiful summer home in Perth Amboy, where on the 8th of August, 1884, he gently passed away. On the 11th (his Golden Wedding day), he was laid to rest in the peaceful churchyard of St. Peter's.

In his social and domestic relations, Mr. Whitehead was most affectionate and hospitable. Humble-minded and generous, to him and to his beloved wife "the cry of suffering was always the cry of Christ for help." In their early married life, when they had no money to bestow, they resolved to give their time, advice and sympathy to those who were in need. "Inasmuch as ye have done it unto the least of these My brethren ye have done it unto Me."

We may form some idea of Mr. Whitehead's industry and patience from the fact that to each of his many books on the shelves of the Society, he prepared a complete index and table of contents. Besides his larger works he wrote numerous important pamphlets, and more than six hundred articles and letters contributed to the newspapers between 1837 and 1882, chiefly historical and biographical in character. His duties as secretary of the Society demanded a voluminous correspondence for nearly thirty years, and his printed reports of the meetings give internal evidence of method and perseverance. We must not omit mention of numerous papers which have added much value and interest to the meetings, and may be found in the publications of the Historical Society of New Jersey. The subjects of these, as well as the titles of his larger works, are here subjoined.

1.—East Jersey under the Proprietary Governments. 1846. 341 pages. (A second edition revised and enlarged in 1875, 486 pages.)
2.—The papers of Lewis Morris, Provincial Governor of New Jersey; edited by W. A. W. 1852. 336 pages.
3.—Contributions to the Early History of Perth Amboy and Adjoining Country, with sketches of men and events in New Jersey during the Provincial Era. 1856. 428 pages.
4.—Analytical Index to the Colonial Documents of New Jersey in the State paper offices of England. Compiled by Henry Stevens. Edited, with notes, etc., by Wm. A. Whitehead. 1858. 504 pages.
5.—The Records of the Town of Newark, N. J., from its settlement in 1666 to its incorporation as a city in 1836. 294 pages. By Wm. A. Whitehead and Samuel H. Congar. 1864.
6.—Documents relating to the Colonial History of New Jersey. 8 volumes. 1880 to 1884.

The following is a list of his papers :

1.—A Biographical Sketch of William Franklin, Governor from 1763 to 1776. Read before the Society, Sept. 27, 1848.
2.—A Biographical Notice of Thomas Boone, Governor of New Jersey in 1760–61. Read May 17, 1849. 336 pages.
3.—The Robbery of the Treasury of East Jersey, in 1768. Read Sept. 12, 1850.
4.—The Facilities for Travelling, and the Transportation of Mails and Merchandise before the Revolution. Read Sept. 11, 1851.
5.—A Biographical Memoir of William Burnet, Governor of New York and New Jersey, 1720 to 1728. Read Sept. 8, 1852.
6.—Paper, embodying an Account of the Voyage of the Henry and Francis, 1684, with Sketches of some of her Passengers. Read Jan. 19, 1854.

7.—A Biographical Sketch of Robert Hunter, Governor of New York and New Jersey, 1709 to 1719. Read May 17, 1855.

8.—The Appointment of Nathaniel Jones as Chief Justice of New Jersey in 1759. Read May 21, 1857.

9.—A Brief Statement of the Facts connected with the Origin, Practice and Prohibition of Female Suffrage in New Jersey. Read Jan. 21, 1858.

10.—The Circumstances leading to the Establishment, in 1769, of the Northern Boundary line between New Jersey and New York. Read May 19, 1859.

11.—A Brief Sketch of the Summer-house of Cockloft Hall, &c. Read May 15, 1862.

12.—Eastern Boundary of New Jersey: A Review of a Paper on the Waters of New Jersey. Read before the Historical Society of New York by the Hon. John Cochrane; and a rejoinder to a Reply of " A member of the New York Historical Society," by W. A. Whitehead, August, 1865.

13.—A Historical Memoir of the Circumstances leading to and connected with the Settlement of Newark, May, 1666. Read May 17, 1866.

14.—An Answer and Explanation concerning certain Documents presented to the New York Historical Society, with reference to the title of New York to Staten Island. Read May 16, 1867.

15.—A Review of some of the circumstances connected with the Settlement of Elizabeth, N. J. Read May 20, 1869.

16.—The Circumstances preceding and leading to the Surrender of the Proprietary Government of New Jersey to the Crown in 1703. Read Jan. 15, 1874.

17.—Sketch of the Life of Richard Stockton, one of the Signers of the Declaration of Independence from New Jersey. Read Jan. 18, 1877.

18.—The Resting Place of the Remains of Christopher Columbus. Read May 16, 1878.

THE POTE FAMILY.

By Isaac Bassett Choate, A.M., of Boston, Mass.

THE following letter will be found to relate to a family of a name which the writer observes is "singular and not common." The Captain Samuel Pote, to whom it was addressed, was a ship-master of Marblehead at the time of the Revolution. It appears that he had before the writing of this made a voyage to Liverpool, and from the report of his arrival at that port reaching Mr. Joseph Pote at Eton, this correspondence began. Captain Pote, it seems, expected to be in London in the spring of 1776. There could not have been much intercourse between the colonies and England during those years of war; but at any rate, the letter reached the person for whom it was intended. The original is in the possession of a granddaughter of Captain Samuel Pote, Miss Dorcas Pote, a lady of advanced years now residing in Hyde Park. The " perfect impression of the family arms" is also in this lady's hands. The brother of Captain Pote, to whose changed circumstances reference is made in the letter, would seem to have been a Jeremiah Pote who had left the colony on account of his tory sentiments, and who, according to the traditions of the family, spent the rest of his life a loyalist in New Brunswick. In the will of Samuel Pote his brother Jeremiah is mentioned as "not to be come at." There is, however, among the letters of the family one addressed by Samuel to his brother, in which he entreats him to return, saying that the feeling towards the loyalists who left is far less bitter than towards the tories who remained; and he adds that he is authorized to assure his brother of the good will of Col. Orne and of Mr. Gerry. The fact of the original letter being now in New England may be taken as evidence that Jeremiah Pote returned and declared allegiance to the government of the United States of America.

Captain Samuel Pote was a proprietor, either original or by purchase, of North Yarmouth, Maine. In his will he devised his lands in that township to his sons, and one or more of these settled in that part of the town since made Freeport, near the end of the last century. It may be doubted if a descendant of Capt. Pote bearing the name is now living in Maine; and as in England so in New England, "the name is singular and not common."

To Mr. Samuel Pote,
      Sir :
            On the receipt of yours I looked into some papers that I have long had by me respecting the family. The most ancient of which is a writing on the marriage of *William Pote* and *Johanna Cheridon* in the Reign of Richard II. An. Dom. 1334. They were then settled at *Clawson, Devonshire,* and from that time continued by regular succession at *Clawson* till the year 1620, at which time there were three brothers, *John, Thomas* and *Roger.* John the eldest brother by *Richarda*, Daughter and Heir of *Thos Downe Esqr*, had a daughter named Charity, his only child and consequently his Heir. This Charity, as near as I can recollect, about the year 1660 married into the family of the Rowes of Indyllon in Cornwall, and the estate whatever it was went from the family on this marriage. Thomas and Roger the two younger brothers were now at large to provide for themselves, and took themselves, it is reasonable to suppose, into Cornwall also ; and themselves, or sons rather, continued in part to settle there, and as I have it from the tradition of my own Father, they were dispersed— some went to the West Indies, and one of the family went into Holland, and I have some reason to believe prospered in that country. You see, Sir, I now write on uncertainties, and must return to the brothers, Thomas and Roger, from whom I date that your branch of the family and my own are descended. In respect to myself I only know that my Father's Father lived at Truro in Cornwall; had some employ or station in the court of the Tin mines. His name is Ephraim ; he had several children, among whom was my Father, named Joseph, and a brother of the name of Ephraim also. My Father died now sixty years since and left me with a sister only (since dead) a youth. I should have observed that on the dispersion of the

family, my Father with two sisters came to London, where he settled and was of good Report and Employ in the trade of a stay-maker. One of the sisters named Gertrude was married and lived in good credit also. The other sister Anne lived many years in the family of the Lord Arundell of Truro (?) a noble family of Cornwall, and who was exceeding kind to the family in general (from long knowing their former estate). This Anne dying unmarried left considerable to her two brothers, Ephraim of Truro, my father and the sister Gertrude. Thus have I entered into as minute a relation of circumstances as I can recollect, and in respect to myself have been nearly fifty years happily settled in business at this college, and have many children—three sons and four daughters, all happily settled in life except one daughter who at present is with me. During this long course of life I have had regard to hear if there was any other of the family living and have made enquiry in Devon and Cornwall to that purpose, but getting no intelligence from any quarter, have for years past concluded myself the only one remaining branch, as I before mentioned, of an ancient family who lived in those western parts of the kingdom many centuries with character and station, as I find they intermarried with .... of the respectable families in those counties till the con.... chance of life dispersed them in the manner I have related. The article in the papers of your arrival in Liverpool occasioned my late letter of enquiry, as after many years fruitless attention it gave me reason to believe I was not the sole branch of the family, as I had long conceived; and as the name is singular and not common, I conclude we are equally descended from the same stock, and are one and the same family, tho' not so immediately connected in relationship. Whether the above particulars may lead you and your brothers to the same sentiment I should be glad to be informed of in due time. And as the address you give me to yourself leads me room to think your employ may some time bring you to London, I should be glad to have an opportunity to give you a meeting and with pleasure promote an acquaintance that I trust from name sake only (if no other considerations ensued) may be agreeable to both.

You mention a change of circumstances respecting your brothers in the neighborhood of Boston from the present unhappy differences with the colonies. Unhappy indeed they are, I declare farther that I deem them unnatural and destructive to this Kingdom and her interest in general. But this is a subject I would choose not to enter into. I remain in hopes of future correspondence. Sir

Your namesake and most humble servant

JOS. POTE.

Eton near Windsor
Mar, 1776.

P. S. If in the course of your employ you should come to London, as I have above mentioned, on a line I would give you a meeting being frequently there myself on business for a week or more at a time.

Let the seal should be broke I besides give you the above perfect impression of the family arms.

(Addressed)
For Capt" Samuel Pote,
to the care of Mess" Lane Son & Fraser,
Merchants in London.

GENEALOGY OF THE ANDREWS FAMILY.

By Lieut. GEORGE ANDREWS, U.S.A., of Fort Snelling, Min.

THIS Genealogy is devoted to the descendants of John and Hannah Andrews, of Boston, and mainly to the descendants of their son, Capt. John Andrews, of Taunton, Mass.

1. JOHN[1] ANDREWS, the progenitor of this family, is found in Boston, Mass., in 1656. He was a cooper by occupation. The bible record still in possession of the Providence (R. I.) branch, says, "A sea-cooper, and came from Wales to America." He died in Boston, June 25, 1679, and the inventory of his effects includes "tooles and cooper's stuffe," dwelling house and ground, and household effects. He married Hannah, daughter of Edmond Jackson, of Boston, by his wife Martha, who afterward married John Dickinson. They had children :

  i. JOHN,[2] b. 21 Nov. 1656 ; d. young.
  ii. HANNAH, b. Feb. 20, 1657.
  iii. SUSANNAH, b. Aug. 12, 1659.
  iv. MARTHA, b. Dec. 5, 1660 ; probably m. Thomas Raper.
  v. MARY, bapt. 2—4, 1661.
 2. vi. JOHN, b. Sept. 20, 1662 ; d. 1742 ; m. Alice Shaw, of Weymouth.
  vii. JAMES, b. Dec. 1, 1664 ; d. young.
  viii. EDMOND, b. Nov. 4, 1665.
  ix. JAMES, b. March 17, 1666.
 3. x. SAMUEL, b. May 18, 1668.

2. Capt. JOHN[2] ANDREWS (*John[1]*), born Sept. 20, 1662, in Boston, and was a housewright. In 1692 he purchased several tracts of land and a dwelling house in "new Bristol," Mass. (now Bristol, R. I.), of Thomas Lewis, of Mendon, and resided there. In 1701 he sold his property and purchased a farm in Taunton, Mass., including a water privilege on the bank of Three Mile River, where with Nathaniel Linkon he built a gristmill and sawmill; and the location was called "Andrews' Mills" about a hundred years—now "Westville." Here he resided the remainder of his life. Capt. Andrews held various town offices: was chairman of the board of selectmen four years ; also deputy sheriff; a man highly esteemed. He died 25 July, 1742, at the age of 80 years. He married Alice, daughter of John and Alice Shaw, of Weymouth, born July 6, 1666, and died Feb. 1, 1735, aged 69 years. He married second, Mary, widow of Jacob Barney, and daughter of Rev. Samuel Danforth, fourth minister of Taunton. His will was probated August 17, 1742. By his wife Alice he had children :

  i. ALICE,[3] m. Nathaniel Linkon, of Taunton, by whom she had : 1. *Nathaniel[4] Linkon ;* 2. *Ichabod[4] Linkon ;* 3. *Alice[4] Linkon,* m. Benjamin Briggs, of Rehoboth, Mass. ; 4. *Mary[4] Linkon,* m. Peter Pratt, of Taunton ; 5. *Constant[4] Linkon,* m. Samuel Torrey, of Taunton ; 6. *Marcha[4] Linkon,* m. Richard Liscombe, of Taunton ; 7. *Susannah[4] Linkon,* m. George Burt, of Taunton.
 4. ii. JOHN, b. 1686 ; d. 1763 ; m. Hannah Hall.
 5. iii. EDMOND, d. Jan. 14, 1750, in 58th year ; m. first, Esther Harvey ; m. second, Hannah Linkon.

6. iv.   SAMUEL, d. 1756 ; m. first, Elizabeth Emerson ; m. second, Mary Pitts.
   v.   SETH, d. Taunton, March 5, 1749, aged 46 ; m. Sarah Linkon, of Taun-
       ton, by whom he had : 1. *Sarah.*[4]
  vi.   HANNAH, m. Jonathan Linkon. He d. 1773, aged 87. They lived in
       Norton, Mass. She had children : 1. *Jonathan*[4] *Linkon,* b. 27 Janua-
       ry, 1713, m. Mary Stephens ; 2. *James*[4] *Linkon,* b. March 1, 1715 ;
       3. *Elkanah*[4] *Linkon,* b. July 2, 1718, m. Lidia —— ; 4. *Abiel*[4] *Lin-
       kon,* b. March 5, 1719, m. Sarah Fisher ; 5. *Hannah*[4] *Linkon,* b. Aug.
       29, 1723 ; 6. *George*[4] *Linkon,* b. Aug 20, 1727 ; 7. *Job*[4] *Linkon,* b.
       July 14, 1730.
  vii.   MARTHA, m. Thomas Jones, of Dighton, Mass.
viii.   SUSANNAH, single.

The records of births, deaths and marriages in Taunton were
destroyed by fire in 1838, and many dates could not be obtained.

3.   SAMUEL[2] ANDREWS (*John*[1]) was born May 18, 1668, and was a
housewright by occupation. He was in Milton, Mass., from 1707
to 1711, and in Dorchester in 1716 ; signed the covenant in Canton, Mass., in 1717, and died about 1725. He married Elizabeth,
widow of Joseph Ludden, of Weymouth, Mass. They had children :

7.   i.   SAMUEL,[3] b. Weymouth, Mass., Feb. 17, 1693 ; m. Mehitable Trott.
   ii.   ELIZABETH, b. in W. Oct. 15, 1700 ; m. John Strowbridge.
8.   iii.   JOSHUA, m. Hannah Truesdale.
9.   iv.   JAMES, m. Abigail Crane.
   v.   HANNAH, m. first, John Harris ; m. second, Shubael Wentworth, of
       Stoughton. She had one child by first husband : 1. *John*[4] *Harris,* of
       Dedham, Mass.

4.   Dea. JOHN[3] ANDREWS (*John,*[2] *John*[1]), born 1686. He was one of the
first settlers of Norton, Mass., and deacon of the first church in that
town, where he died in 1763. He married Hannah, daughter of
Lieut. John Hall, of Taunton. She died Sept. 10, 1772. They
had children :

   i.   HANNAH,[4] born in Norton, July 3, 1713 ; m. Ichabod Franklin, of Attle-
       boro'.
   ii.   JOHN, b. in N. July 28, 1714 ; d. Aug. 31, 1720.
  iii.   LYDIA, b. in N. Feb. 7, 1717 ; d. July 6, 1772, aged 55 ; m. William
       Hodges, of Taunton.
10.   iv.   JOSEPH, b. in N. January 15, 1719 ; d. 1800 ; m. Sarah Torrey.
11.   v.   JOHN, b. in N. January 12, 1722 ; d. 1756 ; m. Mary Webber.

5.   Capt. EDMOND[3] ANDREWS (*John,*[2] *John*[1]) died in Taunton, Mass.,
January 14, 1750, in 58th year ; married first, Esther Harvey, of
Taunton ; married second, Hannah Linkon, of Taunton. She died
Feb. 16, 1762, aged 70. By wife Esther he had :

12.   i.   EDMOND,[4] m. Keziah Dean, of Raynham, Mass.
   ii.   ESTHER, m. Thomas Linkon, of Taunton, Aug. 16, 1733.
       By wife Hannah he had :
  iii.   JAMES, m. Oct. 6, 1743, Mary Reed. She d. Oct. 12, 1771.
  iv.   FREELOVE, m. Capt. Samuel French, of Berkley, Mass., a man promi-
       nent in church and town affairs. They had children : 1. *Freelove*[5]
       French, b. 1747, m. in 1765 Seth Paul in Taunton ; 2. *Hannah*[5]
       French, b. 1749 ; 3 *Samuel*[5] *French,* b. 1751 ; 4. *Edmond*[5] *French,* b.
       1754 ; 5. *Cyrus*[5] *French,* b. 1756 ; 6. *Rachel*[5] *French,* b. 1758 ; 7. *Rog-
       er*[5] *French,* b. 1760 ; 8. *Matilda*[5] *French,* b. 1764 ; 9. *Abner*[5] *French,*
       b. 1767.
   v.   MARY, b. Taunton, Feb. 14, 1724 ; m. Dea. Joseph Hall* in 1749. She
       d. Dec. 21, 1814. They had children : 1. *Peris*[5] *Hall,* b. August 21,

---

* Genealogy of the Halls of Taunton.

1750 ; d. 1792 ; m. Zilpha Dean, daughter of Ebenezer Dean of Raynham, Mass. ; 2. *Mary[5] Hall*, twin of Peris, d. Dec. 1839 ; m. May 24, 1770, Capt. David Leonard, of Bridgewater, Mass. ; 3. *Elizabeth[5] Hall*, b. Feb. 17, 1752 ; d. March, 1848, aged 96 ; m. 1776, Nathaniel Dean, son of Ebenezer, of Raynham ; 4. *Josias[5] Hall*, b. April 12, 1754 ; d. July 2, 1809 ; m. Dec. 8, 1791, Susannah[5] (20), daughter of Capt. Joseph Andrews, of Norton, Mass. ; 5. *Hannah[3] Hall*, b. Nov. 23, 1755 ; d. 1847 ; m. Capt. Zebulon Field ; 6. *Sarah[5] Hall*, b. 1758, d. 1798, unm. ; 7. *Anna[5] Hall*, b. April, 1761, d. 1823, unm.

vi.   MIRIAM, not m. in 1750, when her father's will was made.
13. vii. SAMUEL, d. Taunton, Feb. 5, 1799, in 71st year ; m. Abigail Cobb.
viii. HANNAH, d. Taunton, Oct. 7, 1765, in 35th year.

6. SAMUEL[3] ANDREWS (*John,[2] John[1]*), married first, Elizabeth Emerson. She died March 14, 1724. He married second, Mary, daughter of Ebenezer Pitts, of Dighton, Mass. The exact date of his death is wanting, but in the settlement of his estate, Sept. 6, 1757, his widow Mary states that she " Paid to Capt. James Andrews (besides all the wages due to said deceased for his services as a soldier in the Crown Point Expedition in 1755) for going to Albany after deceased £0 14s. 5d." From the bible record it appears he had by Elizabeth :

  i. SAMUEL,[4]   ii. ELIZABETH,   iii. RUTH,

but no other record of them has yet been found. By wife Mary he had :

14. iv. EBENEZER,[4] b. in Dighton, Jan. 10, 1726 ; m. first, Elizabeth Shaw ; m. second, Mary Francis.
15. v. JOHN, b. in D. March 13, 1729 ; d. June, 1767 ; m. Elizabeth Talbot.
16. vi. ELKANAH, b. in D. March 4, 1731 ; d. June 8, 1787 ; m. Alice Beal.
vii. STEPHEN, b. in D. Dec. 22, 1734 ; d. Dec. 22, 1737.
viii. MARY, b. in D. Nov. 30, 1736 ; d. Nov. 30, 1737.
17. ix. ZEPHANIAH, b. in D. Feb. 9, 1738 ; d. Jan. 23, 1816 ; m. Elizabeth Eddy.
x. MARY, b. in D. August 2, 1741 ; d. in D. Oct. 3, 1813 ; m. —— Peirce.
xi. JOB, b. in D. April 2, 1744.

7. SAMUEL[3] ANDREWS (*John[2], John[1]*), born in Weymouth, Mass., Feb. 17, 1698 : died in Stoughton, Mass., January 1, 1739-40, in 42d year ; married Mehitable Trott, of Stoughton. She was baptized in Milton, Nov. 13, 1698, and was the daughter of John Trott and Mehitable Rigbye, and granddaughter of Samuel Rigbye, and great-granddaughter of John Rigbye, of Dorchester. She married second, 1744, Philip Goodwin, of Stoughton. They had children:

  i. SAMUEL,[4] b. in Stoughton, March 25, 1727 ; d. 1728.
ii. SAMUEL, b. in S. April 23, 1729 ; d. April 30, 1734.
iii. SARAH, b. in S. August 29, 1731.
iv. ELEANOR, b. in S. Sept. 16, 1733 ; m. March 5, 1752, Ephraim Jones, of S.
v. PATIENCE, b. in S. July 20, 1736 ; buried March 21, 1758, aged 21 years.
vi. ELIZABETH, b. in S. Oct. 23, 1739, bapt. Jan. 6, 1740 ; m. John Nash, of Weymouth, his third wife. She d. Dec. 10, 1795—the record says aged 90 years. ?

8. JOSHUA[3] ANDREWS (*Samuel,[2] John[1]*), probably married March 10, 1726, Hannah Truesdale, at Boston. She was of Newton, but after marriage lived in Milton, Mass. They had :

  i. EDMUND,[4] bapt. Dec. 8, 1728.
ii. WILLIAM, bapt. Jan. 25, 1729.
iii. MARY, bapt. Dec. 26, 1730-31.
iv. ELIZABETH, bapt. Nov. 4, 1733.

9. JAMES[3] ANDREWS (*Samuel,[2] John[1]*) married April 13, 1732, Abigail
   Crane, of Stoughton, Mass. He owned the covenant August 5,
   1733. They had children:
   - i.   ABIGAIL,[4] b. in Milton, July 20, 1733; m. Henry Shaller, of Stoughton.
   - ii. MARY, b. in M. Oct. 1, 1734; m. Elijah Houghton, of Milton.
   - iii. SETH, b. in Stoughton, Dec. 9, 1735; d. 1736.
   - iv. REBECCA, b. in S. Nov. 22, 1738.
   - v.   RUTH, b. in S. July 17, 1741; d. 1748.
   - vi. JOHN, b. in S. May 2, 1743.
   - vii. HEPZIBAH, b. in S. Jan. 30, 1745.
   - viii. DAVID, bapt. in Stoughton, May 22, 1748.
   - ix. MARIA, b. in Stoughton, July 22, 1751; m. Josiah Mero, of S.
   - x.   BENJAMIN, b. in S. July 8, 1754.

10. Capt. JOSEPH[4] ANDREWS (*John,[3] John,[2] John[1]*), born in Norton,
    Mass., January 15, 1719; died 1800. As executor of his father's
    estate he closed also the estate of his grandfather. He left a will.
    He married Sarah Torrey, by whom he had:
    - 18. i.   SARAH,[5] b. in N. July 4, 1756; m. Sylvanus Braman, Jr., of Norton.
    - 19. ii. JOSEPH, b. in N. Aug. 26, 1758; m. Hannah Church, of Marshfield.
    - 20. iii. SUSANNAH, b. in N. Feb. 3, 1761; m. Dea. Josias Hall, of Taunton.
    -     iv. PHEBE, b. in N. Oct. 16. 1763; m. Ichabod Leonard, of Taunton.
    - 21. v.   JOHN, b. in N. April 9, 1766; m. Rebecca Webber, of Taunton.
    -     vi. HANNAH, b. in N. Jan. 29, 1769; not married.
    - 22. vii. NATHAN, b. in N. Dec. 11, 1771; m. Abigail Soams, of Vermont.
    - 23. viii ISAAC, b. in N. Jan. 12, 1775; m. Hannah Briggs, of Taunton.
    - 24. ix. JAMES, b. in N. Jan. 23, 1778; m. Mercy Linkon, of Taunton.

11. JOHN[4] ANDREWS (*John,[3] John,[2] John[1]*), born in Norton, Mass., Janu-
    ary 12, 1722; died there in 1756; married Mary Webber. He left
    no will. They had children:
    - i. MARY,[5] b. in Norton, Oct. 26, 1752.
    - ii. HANNAH, b. in N. Sept. 19, 1755.

12. Capt. EDMOND[4] ANDREWS (*Edmond,[3] John,[2] John[1]*) married Oct. 2,
    1742, Keziah Dean, of Raynham, Mass. He purchased land in
    Easton, Mass., in 1754, and kept an inn there from 1761 to 1773.
    They had children:
    - i.   EDMOND,[5] b. July 16, 1743; d. Oct. 20, 1743.
    - ii. EDMOND, b. Aug. 9, 1744.
    - iii. KEZIAH, b. Oct. 1, 1746; probably m. William Drake, of Easton, in 1767.

13. Lieut. SAMUEL[4] ANDREWS (*Edmond,[3] John,[2] John[1]*) died at Taunton,
    February 5, 1799, in 71st year. He married Abigail, daughter of
    Capt. Thomas Cobb, iron master, of Taunton. She died in 1815.
    They had children:
    - i.   ABIGAIL,[5] m. Joseph Foster.
    - ii.   FREELOVE, m. Jonathan Ingell.
    - iii. LYDIA, m. Jonathan Macomber.
    - iv.   MARY ANN, m. Abel Franklin.
    - v.   HELEN, m. David Arnold, Jr.
    - vi.   POLLY, m. Peleg Bowen.
    - vii. SALLY, d. Dec. 5, 1839, not married.
    - viii. THOMAS.
    - ix.   LINCOLN, probably m. Mary Short in 1789.
    - x.   SAMUEL.

14. EBENEZER[4] ANDREWS (*Samuel,[3] John,[2] John[1]*), born at Dighton,
    Mass., January 10, 1726; settled in Bristol, N. Y., and died there
    May 21, 1808; married first, Elizabeth Shaw, of Dighton. She

died May 3, 1767. He married second, Dec. 24, 1768, Mary Francis, of Dighton. She died in 1808, a few weeks before her husband. By Elizabeth his first wife, he had :

    i. EBENEZER,[5] b. in Dighton, June 4, 1752 ; never married.
25. ii. MELICENT, b. in D. April 5, 1754 ; m. Seth Farrar, of Berkley, Mass.
    iii. STEPHEN, b. in D. April 4, 1756 ; d Oct. 8, 1756.
26. iv. STEPHEN, b. in D. August 26, 1757 : m. first, Deborah Williams ; m. second, Hannah Williams, both of Dighton.
27. v. LYDIA, b. in D. Sept. 3, 1759 ; m. William Gooding, of Dighton.
28. vi. SABRINA, b. in D. Feb. 4, 1762 ; m. Azariah Shove.
29. vii. CAROLINE, b. in D. March 14, 1765 ; m. James Gooding, of Dighton.

    By Mary, his second wife, he had :

30. viii. SAMUEL, b. in D. July 2, 1771 ; m. Dorcas Aldrich, of Farmington, N.Y.
31. ix. BENJAMIN, b. in D. Feb. 28, 1775 ; m. Amy Cudworth, of Freetown, Ms.
    x. MARY, b. in D. ; m. —— Nichols, and settled in Kentucky.
32. xi. SALLY, b. in D. Oct. 10, 1781 ; m. Faunce Codding.
    xii. BETSEY, b. in D., d. in Mass.
    xiii. JOSEPH, b. in D., d. at sea.

15. JOHN[4] ANDREWS (*Samuel,*[3] *John,*[2] *John*[1]), born in Dighton, Mass., March 13, 1729. He was a sea-captain and died at St. Eustatius, West Indies, in June, 1767 ; married in 1754 Elizabeth Talbot, of Dighton. They had :

    i. ELIZABETH,[5] b. in Dighton ; m. in 1782. Samuel Whitmarsh.
33. ii. HANNAH, b. in D. 1761 : m. Ephraim Hathaway, of D.
34. iii. JOHN, b. in D., drowned there Jan. 23, 1807, in 43d year ; m. first, Patience Hathaway, of D. ; m. second, Sally Pettis, of Somerset, Mass.
    iv. ICHABOD, b. in D. Aug. 19, 1767 ; d. young.

16. ELKANAH[4] ANDREWS (*Samuel,*[3] *John,*[2] *John*[1]), born in Dighton, March 4, 1731, and was a sea-captain. He made many voyages to the West Indies and South America, and died at Essequibo, British Guiana, June 8, 1787. He married Alice Beal, of Dighton. She was born Nov. 2, 1739, and died June 13, 1808. They had :

35. i. ALICE,[5] b. at Dighton, Jan. 12, 1758 ; m. Rev. John Smith, of D.
36. ii. ELKANAH, b. at D. Feb. 29, 1760 ; m Elizabeth Talbot, of D.
37. iii. JOSEPH, b. at D April 5, 1764 ; m. Nancy Talbot, of D.
38. iv. DAVID, b. at D. March 19, 1766 ; m. Phebe Smith, of Bristol, R. I.
39. v. POLLY, b. at D. Feb 26, 1768 ; m. first, Dr. George Ware, of Dighton ; m. second, Dr. William Wood, of D.
40. vi. WILLIAM, b. at D May 7, 1770 ; m. Mary Baylies, of D.
    vii. THOMAS, b. at D. Dec. 4, 1772 ; m. Mary Leonard, of Raynham.
41. viii. CLARISSA, b. at D. Feb. 18, 1775 ; m. Capt. William Richmond, of D.
    ix. JOB, b. at D. April 2, 1779 ; d. May 28, 1799 ; not married.

17. ZEPHANIAH[4] ANDREWS (*Samuel,*[3] *John,*[2] *John*[1]), born at Dighton, Mass., Feb. 9, 1738 ; settled in Providence. R. I., in 1756, where he lived the remainder of his life. He was one of the first Universalists of Providence, a man of active mind, a reader and writer. He was colonel of the Providence Marine Artillery, and died January 23, 1816. He married Elizabeth, daughter of Capt. Benjamin Eddy, of Providence. They had :

42. i. BENJAMIN,[5] b. in Providence, Feb. 19, 1764 ; m. Elizabeth Gladding.
43. ii. MARY, b. in P. Dec. 2, 1765 ; m. Peter Grinnell, of Little Compton, R. I.
    iii. CHARLES, b. in P. March 20, 1768 ; d. Dec. 29, 1797 ; not married.
44. iv. ELIZABETH, b. in P. Nov. 17, 1770 ; m. William Taylor, of Little Compton, R. I.
    v. JOHN, b. in P. Nov. 4, 1773 ; d. Aug. 17, 1776.
45. vi. SUSANNAH, b. in P. April 3, 1776 ; m. Benjamin Howland.

vii. SALLY, b. Oct. 27, 1780 ; d. April 1, 1781.
viii. JOHN, b. Feb. 2, 1782 ; d. June 6, 1783.
46. ix. JOHN, b. in P. Jan. 3, 1786 ; m. Betsey Whipple, of Cumberland, R. I.
  x. ZEPHANIAH, b. in P. July 20, 1788 ; d. 1820 ; not married.

———

The compiler is under great obligations to Capt. J. W. D. Hall, of Taunton, a descendant, for much valuable information.

Many of the lines have been brought down to the present time, and the compiler expects soon to publish it all for the benefit of those interested. Those having dates and facts of the Andrews family lines, partially given in the foregoing record, will please communicate with the compiler.

———

NOTES AND DOCUMENTS CONCERNING HUGH PETERS.

Communicated by G. D. SCULL, Esq., of London, England.

[Continued from vol. xxxix. page 378.]

NOTES.

THOMAS ROSS, who was associated with Elias Ashmole in the examination of Hugh Peters in the Tower of London,* was the " Keeper of his Majesties Libraries." Concerning the examination, Ashmole, in the preface to his Antiquities of Berkshire, says that " On June 18, 1660 the church and state being restored to its Antient Glory Mr Ashmole was introduced by Mr Thomas Chifinch to kiss the King's hand, with whom he discoursed some hours the next day and then was constituted Windsor Herald and his patent signed on the 22^d of the same month and took the Common oaths of his Office on Augt 10 following. Soon after this he was appointed by the King to make a description of his Medalls and had them delivered into his hands and King Henry VIII^ths closet assigned for that purpose. At the same time was also a Commission issued out for the Examination of that infamous Buffoon and Trumpeter of Rebellion Hugh Peters Concerning the disposal of the Pictures, Jewells &^c belonging to the Royal Family which were committed chiefly to his Care and sold and dispersed over Europe and are yet in the Closets of several Princes who then connived at, nay encouraged the depredations made on the Royal Exile and enriched their own Cabinets with the invaluable Curiosities of England at a very cheap rate which neither Generosity, Honour, nor Justice has ever induced them to restore though they well knew the invalidity of the Title upon which they purchased ; but crowned Heads have as little regard to Honour or Justice when they interfere with their Interest, as the vulgar else how shall we account for their Courting the Usurper Conceeding to the most unreasonable demands, and sacrificing all even to the most sanguine Expectations he could entertain. This Commission was soon brought to a conclusion by the obstinacy, or Ignorance of their criminall who either would not, or was not able to give the desired satisfaction. Thus was this matter drop^t and every one left, if their own consciences permitted to enjoy without molestation the Plunder they had collected." In Dr. Rich'd Raw-

———

* This examination of Hugh Peters was taken, Sept. 12, 1660, before Sir John Robinson (alderman of London), created a knight June 22d, 1660, by Charles II. The king's order to Sir John and the testimony of Peters are printed in the REGISTER, xxxix. 264.

linson's interleaved copy of Ashmole's " Antiquities of Berkshire," a note is made that " Dᵣ Rawlinson has a catalogue in Mr Ashmoles handwriting of the persons names who bought the Kings and Queens goods with the sums of money paid for them, collected out of the Contractor's register MSS."

On the 26th June, 1649, parliament passed "an Act for the sale of the Goods and Personal Estate Of the late King, Queen and Prince," " Whereas the Goods and Personal Estate heretofore belonging to the late King Charles, and to his wife and eldest son, have been and justly are forfeited by them, for their several Delinquencies ; And though the same be of considerable value yet in regard many parcels thereof are dispersed in several hands and places, they may for want of a certain accompt, probably be spoiled and imbezled, or made away without advantage to the State, if due care be not had, and some speedy course taken to prevent the same ; The Commons of England assembled in Parliament, taking the premises into their serious consideration have thought fit and resolved—That the said Goods and Personal Estate, heretofore belonging to the persons above named, and to every, or any of them, shall be inventoried and apprised, and shall also be sold, except such parcels thereof as shall be found necessary to be reserved for the uses of the State ; Be it therefore Enacted, and it is enacted by this present Parliament, and by the authority of the same, that John Humphreys and George Withers of Westminster Esqᵣ, Anthony Mildmay, Ralph Grafton of Cornhil, Michael Lampier, John Belchamp, Philip Cartwright of the Isle of Jersey, Gent. Henry Creech, John Foach, David Powel and Edward Winslow, Gentlemen and Citizens of London, shall be, and are hereby constituted and appointed Trustees for the enquiring out, inventorying, apprizing and securing of the said Goods and Personal Estate, and they or any four or more of them, shall be, and are hereby authorized, to repair to any and every house or place whatsoever, where any of the said Goods, or any part of the said Personal Estate doth lie, and to make or cause to be made a true and perfect Inventory or Inventories thereof, and of every part and parcel thereof, which they shall or may any way finde out or discover, and to make a just and equal apprizement of the same & of every part and parcel thereof, according to the true value thereof, as they in their judgments and consciences shall think the same may reasonably and probably be sold for, expressing in the said Inventory or Inventories the several sums or values at which the several parcels shall be apprized as aforesaid, and to secure, or cause to be secured, the said goods, and every part and parcel thereof, at such place or places & in the hands & custody of such person or persons as they shall finde most fit and convenient to prevent any spoil and imbezlement thereof, of which Inventory or Inventories, with the several apprizements of the premises the said Trustees or any 4 or more of them shall make three Duplicates certified under their hands and Seals, and expressing the several places where, and the persons in whose Custody the premises or any part thereof respectively are secured as aforesaid, and keeping the Originals in the hands of such Clerk register as they shall think fit to imploy, shall within fourteen days after any such apprizements make return and send one of said duplicates to the Councel of State, which shall be kept by the Secretary thereof & the other to the other Commissioner hereafter named to be Contractors for sale of the said Goods, or to the Clerk register whom the said Contractors shall imploy for that purpose, which shall by him be Registered & safe kept, and the third to the Treasurers hereafter mentioned." The trustees had ample powers given them to search, examine and issue warrants for the calling of any person before them, suspected as possessing any of the late king's effects. The agents or officers appointed by the trustees to execute the various commissions for the search and sale of the said king's effects, were to be allowed seven pence in the pound out of all such moneys made by said sales. The commissioners and contractors appointed for the sale of the goods found, were " Daniel Norman of the Isle of Jersey Merchant, John Hales of London Merchant, Clement Kinnersley, John Price, Henry Parre, and William Allen Gentlemen and citizens of London." Careful provisions were inserted in the act to regulate the sales and to dispose of the proceeds. With regard to certain goods a clause was inserted that " whereas divers of the said goods and premises are of such a nature, as that though by reason of their rarity or antiquity, they may yield very great prices in Foraign parts, where such things are much valued yet for particular mens use in England they would be accounted little worth, and so yield no considerable price, if they should be forthwith sold here, according to the foregoing directions. It is therefore further Enacted and Provided That for such particulars of the premises as the said Contractors shall find to be of that nature, they or any 3 or more of them may treat & agree with any merchant-adventurer or Foreign Merchant about transporting such of the said goods into any Foreign parts where they may be sold at the best rates, &c. &c." The agents or commissioners of the contractors in this business were to be paid by the allowance of five pence in the pound upon such sales. The treasurers to receive and disburse all moneys under the operation of the act were " Humphrey Jones and John Hunt Gentlemen and Citizens of London," and any clerks they might need to assist them were to be paid by the allowance of two pence in the pound " out of all and singular the moneys to be received and accounted for by them." Parliament made a condition that out of the first moneys raised by the sales, 30,000£ were to be " issued and lent unto the Treasurer of the Navy," which said sum before the 2^d day of May, 1650, was to be restored and reimbursed by said Treasurer of the Navy out of his receipts for the Navy." Hugh Peters was paid £100, December 24th, 1656, as " one of the Preachers in Whitehall Chappell being for $\frac{1}{2}$ a years salary for y^e same due 17th December 1655," and on January 6, 1657, the sum of £50 to " Hugh Peters one of the Preachers in Whitehall Chappell being for one quarters salary for ye same and was due unto him 7° Janij. –55." Again on April 8th, 1658, " To Mr Hugh Peters being in full of a Warr^t bearing ye 30th day of 8bre 1656 for ye paym^t of £150 unto him 100£ thereof being paid unto him as by page ye 12th appears and now more " the sum of £50. Mr Peter Sterry was one of the preachers at Whitehall Chapel associated with Mr. Peters, and his pay was also in arrears, he having been appointed in October (18), 1656, and a payment of £100 on account made the 26th December of the same year. Hugh Peters gave up his appointment as preacher at Whitehall to attend the army into France. Sir William Lockhart, who is called " His Highness's Ambassador in France," writes from Dunkerk, July 8–18, 1658, to " the Right Honble my Lord Thurloe one of the Lords of his highnesse Counsell and principall Secretary of State," that " I could not suffer our worthy friend Mr Peters to come away from donkerke without a testimony of the greatt benefitts we have all receaved from him in this place, wher he hath laid himself forth in greatt Charity and goodnesse, in sermons, prayers, and exhortations, in visiting and relieving the sick and wounded, and in all these profitably applying the singular talent

God hath bestowed upon him to the two Cheef ends propper for our awditory, for he hath not only showen the soldiers their deuty to God, and prest it home upon them I hope to good advantage, but hath likewyse acqwainted them with their obligations of Obedience to his highe government and affection to his persone, he hath labored amongst us heare in much good will and seems to enlarge his harte towards us and love of us for many other things, the effects whereof I desyre to leave upon that Providence which hath brought us hither, it were superfluous to tell your lo^{pp} the story of our present condition either as to the Civill goverment, works, or soldiery, he who hath studdied all these more than any I know heare, can certainly give the best account of them, wherefore I remitt the whole to his information and begge your lopp' casting a favorable eie upon such propositions as he will offer to your lo^{pp} for the good of this garrison." Another letter, also bearing the date from the 8th to the 18th of July, 1658, from " lord ambassador Lockhart " to Secretary Thurloe, makes further mention to Hugh Peters. " Mr Peeters hath taken leave at least 3 or 4 tymes but still something falls out which hinders his return to England, he hath been twice at bergh and hath spoak with the lord : three or foure tymes, I kept my self by and had a care that he did not importune him with too long speeches he returns loaden with ane account of all things hear and hath undertaken every mans business, I must give him that testimony that he gave us three or foure very honest sermons and if it were possible to gett him to mynd preaching and to forbear the trubling of himself with other things he would certainly proove a very fitt Minister for Soldiers. I hope he cometh well satisfied from this place, he hath often insinuated to me his desyer to stay heare. If he had a Call, some of the officers also hath been with me to that purpose but I have shifted him so hansomely as I hope he will not but be pleased for I have told him that the greattest service he could do us 'tis to goe to England and Cary on his propositions, and to own us in all our other interests which he hath undertaken with much zeal."

Many efforts were subsequently made by Charles II. to obtain the restoration of the goods belonging to his father, and to this end he had a separate clause inserted in the Treaty of Peace concluded between himself and the States General, at Breda, 21–31 day of July, 1667. The following was the clause inserted in the treaty :

" If it happen that any Tapestry, Hangings, Carpets, pictures or Household furniture of what kind soever or precious stones Jewells, with Curiosities, or other moveable goods whatever belonging to the King of *Great Britain* either now or hereafter shall be found to be in the hands or power of the said States General or of any of their subjects, the said States Generall do promise that they will in no wise protect the possessing of any moveables appertaining unto the said King which goods may be taken from them in such manner that they who shall make difficulty to restore them freely may not be dealt withall, by any means contrary to equity and Justice and the said States do promise to use their most effectual endeavours that a plain and summary way of proceeding may be taken in this affair without the ordinary formal method of Process usually observed in Courts ; and that Justice be administered whereby his said majesty may be satisfyed soe far as possibly may be without the wrong of any one."

A committee was also appointed by Charles II. "authorized for the getting in and Compounding for his late Majesty's goods, &c." John Singleton, the clerk to the committee, issued a notice 4 July, 1662, at a meeting where Mr. William Rumball, Mr. Elias Ashmole, Mr. Francis Rogers, Col. Hawley and Mr. Beauchamp were present, for a further adjournment to the next Tuesday at Somersett House. They called before them twelve persons who were suspected of possessing articles belonging to the late king. The committee met from time to time, but with indifferent results, if we may take the following as a sample. "15. October, 1662, whereas Mrs   willis of ye Starr Chamber Westminster ye relict of Mr Willis deceased was this day before the said Com^tee & called in question for 2 old leaden cesternes and other goods of small value and satisfaction demanded for ye same and for as much as the said Mrs Willis hath made it appeare that ye goods are very inconsiderable & that ye greatest part thereof are fixed to ye said tenement called ye starr chamber & there remaineing & therefore prayed that she might be acquitted and discharged thereof. It is therefore thought fitt & accordingly is ordered that the said Mrs Willis be acquitted & forever discharged of the said goods & that she be put to no further trouble for or by reason of ye same & all persons herein any waies concerned are desired to take notice of this order as occasion shall require."

The warrant for the appointment of the commission to reclaim the King's property was issued 30 June, 1662, and the first meeting was held 4 July, 1662, when the following persons were present:—Mr. William Rumball, Mr. Elias Ashmole, Mr. Francis Rogers, Col. Hawley, Mr. Beauchamp. It was ordered by the committee that the "accompts of the persons heretofore called Trustees Contractors, and Treasurers for the sale of the goods belonging to the late King of ever blessed memory" should be examined, and notices were to be served upon three of the late contractors to appear at Somerset House on the next Tuesday. The contractors were "ye worshipful Clement Kinnersley Esqr yeoman of his Majesty's removing wardrobe, Mr Henry Parr, and Mr William Allen. Trustees, Mrs Grafton, the widow of Ralph Grafton, Mrs ffoach, the widow of John Foach, and Mr Humphrey Jones as one of the treasurers." At a meeting on

8 *July*, 1662, "Humphrey Jones late treasurer for the sale of the said goods bee hereby desired and required to send in to them a p^cular acc^t of what moneys were paid to the late contractors and Trustees, &c."

18 *July*, 1662. Mr. Robert Sherley at Bromley, Kent, and Mr. Robert Mallery of Scalding Alley, London, having failed to appear when summoned before the committee, orders were given to arrest them at their dwellings and bring them to the next meeting at the Queen's Council Chamber.

3d *Oct.* 1662. Mr. Marshall, Senior, "hath some small quantity of marble and stone that did formerly belong to his Majesty for which he hath offered as a composition for ye said marble, &c. to pay the summe of 45 Shillings vizt 30^s for his maj^y & 15s. for fees," which the committee accepted of.

9th *Oct.* 1662. Mrs. ffoach, the widow of Mr. ffoach, required to bring in the following articles, in the keeping of her late husband : "1 great Chaire, 4 cushions, 2 blew chairs, 6 Stooles, a foot stoole of flowered velvet laced and fringed (all valued at)—14£., one Turkey Carpet, 3£, 6 lesser Turkey old Carpets, 2£, a long picture of many figures, 3£, 2 paire of plaine water pots, 1£ 10. 0, two little paire of plaine water potts, ten shillings."

1st *November*, 1662. The Earl of Salisbury having appropriated "50 Tunnes of flour belonging to his Majesty, to his own use, during the tyme of the late usurped power," is called upon to meet the committee at the Queen's Council Chamber.

21st January, 1662–3.   Sir Launcelott Lake " is called upon to appear and give acc^t touching severall hangings of China Sattin, Crimson and lemon colour." A letter also written to Mr. Pashall for a picture of a landscape done by Bartholomew. A letter also sent to Lady Gray desiring to be informed who Lord Gray's executor is.

Mr. Oliver Bowles, without, over against the Mermaide tavern, is notified to meet the committee on Friday, *28th Jany.* 1662–3, to give account of a bedd of crimson damask and other goods ; and Mr. Day in Lumber St. is to bring in "the aggot cup with him."

Mr. Tryham to attend, *17th Dec.* 1662, about a suit of Hangings of " Vulcan and Venus." Mr. Adrian about " 2 Christall Salts." Mr. English at Mortlake to appear on the 15 *April,* 1663, to give account of " ye disposition of divers hangings in his custody, &c." Mr. Duart to attend " ye 29 *May,* 1663, to account for a picture of the Queen by Vandyke, 30£, one of ye King & Queen with the Laurell leafe 60£, a Casket in the fashion of a Tortiss 40£." " To attend 6 *March* 1662 ffry day Mrs Mason ye late wife of Dr Mason in Doctors Commons to 2£ a lyning of a cloke or shew cause. Mrs Cogin at Greenwich to a Billiard table or shew cause, and eight others are summoned for goods not named. To attend the 13 *March,* 1663. " Mr Sergeant Glynne in Portugal Row in Lincolns Innfields, for a picture of an Italian familye done by Perdenino (*Pordenone*) to 2 pence to ye messenger," and four others summoned.

It was ordered in the Committee that as Mr. Thomas Beauchamp " hath beene at more than ordinary pains and care in discovering ye said goods belonging to her Majesty that out of the moiety of all moneys received, the said Thomas Beauchamp shall receive 2–5 part and Robert Jenkins Esquire Clerk of her Majesties Counsell, Henry Brown, Gent. and Colonel William Hawley each of them one fifth part of such money recovered."

CHURCH RECORDS OF FARMINGTON, CONN.

Communicated by Julius Gay, A.M., of Farmington, Conn.

[Continued from vol. xxxix. page 341.]

January 3, 1763	Departed this life Susannah Dr. of David Hills.
January 26, 1763	Departed this life Giles son of Ezekiel Cowles.
Jany 27, 1763	Departed this life Rhoda Dr. of Timo North
February 2, 1763	Departed this life the Wife of Stephen Andruss.
February 22, 1763	Departed this life Widow Wadsworth of Ensign Nathaniel.
April 14, 1763	Departed this life Joseph Newell.
May 1763	Departed this life David Grant.
June 11, 1763	Departed this life a child of Charles Stedman.
August 6, 1763	Departed this life Elijah son of Tim° Wadsworth.
August 21, 1763	Departed this life Thomas Couch.
August 22, 1763	Departed this life Paul Andruss.
September 26, 1763	Departed this life Lucy a Babe of Tim° Woodruff.
October 18, 1763	Departed this life Seth son of Mr Gay.
Novr. 2, 1763	Departed this life George son of Thos Norton.
Novr. 27, 1763	Departed this life a Child of James Luske.

January 16, 1764	Departed this life Nath[ll] a babe of Nath[ll] Wadsworth.
Feb'y 4, 1764	Departed this life Olive Dr. of Matt[hw] Woodruff.
February 26, 1764	Departed this life Samuel Gridley.
May 19, 1764	Departed this life Wid[o] Elizabeth Woodruff.
August 1, 1764	Departed this life Elizabeth, Dr. a babe of James Cowles.
August 5, 1764	Departed this life Joel (?) babe of Gideon Belding.
August 12, 1764	Carried from the womb to the grave a babe of Thos. Newell.
September 1, 1764	Departed this life Dorothy Dr. of Thomas Norton.
October 14, 1764	Departed this life Timothy Gridley
December 19, 1764	Departed this life Joseph Hooker Esqr.
December 23, 1764	Departed this life the Wife of Jacob Barns.
January 17, 1765	Departed this life Hezekiah Scott.
February 6, 1765	Departed this life Betty Negro Woman.
April 1, 1765	Departed this life W[m] son of Ezekiel Cowles.
April 3, 1765	Departed this life Ezekiel son of Ezekiel Woodruff.
April 21, 1765	Departed this life Asahel Merriam.
May 29, 1765	Departed this life Ephraim Smith.
July 20, 1765	Departed this life W[m] Lewis son of Elisha Strong.
August 26, 1765	Departed this life Solomon son of Solomon Mossage.
August 27, 1765	Departed this life Abigail Dr. of Doct[r] Lee.
October 6, 1765	Departed this life Esther Hawley.
October 15, 1765	Departed this life Sarah a babe of Noadiah Hooker.
October 24, 1765	Departed this life y[e] Wife of Sylvanus Woodruff.
February 20, 1766	Departed this life Stephen Andruss.
February 23, 1766	Departed this life a Child of Matt. Woodruff.
March 12, 1766	Departed this life a Babe of Capt[n] Judah Woodruff.
June 16, 1766	Departed this life Nathaniel Thomson.
July 14, 1766	Departed this life Wid[o] Woodruff.
July 18, 1766	Departed this life a Child of Sol[o] Massugg—Indian.
August 10, 1766	Departed this life Doct[r] Thomas Mather.
August 18, 1766	Departed this life the Wife of Seth Kellogg.
September 11, 1766	Departed this life Matthew Woodruff.
Oct[r] 1766	Carried to the Grave two Babes of Noadiah Hooker.
November 20, 1766	Departed this life William Porter.
November 28, 1766	Departed this life George a Babe of Timo. Marsh Jr.
December 7, 1766	Departed this life the Wife of Tim[o] Marsh Jr.
December 11, 1766	Departed this life Wid[o] Susanna Woodruff.
December 25, 1766	Departed this life Wid[o] Bidwell.
February 8, 1767	Departed this life a Daghter of Aaron Woodruff.
	[A leaf lost.]
March 19, 1770	Departed this life Erastus son of Mr. Gay.
May 11, 1770	Departed this life y[e] Wife of Deacon Portter.
May 16, 1770	Departed this life a Child of Tim[o] Woodruff.
June 30, 1770	Departed this life Dan[ll] son of Dan[l] Thomson.
July 15, 1770	Departed this life the Wife of Mr. Seth Lee.
August 18, 1770	Departed this life Eliz: Daugr. of Dea[n] Dorchester.
August 21, 1770	Departed this life a Babe of Gift Hills.
Novr. 1, 1770	Departed this life a Child of Ambrose Callins.
Novr. 18, 1770	Departed this life a Babe of Aaron Woodruff.
January 1, 1771	Departed this life Abr[m] a babe of Elijah Woodruff.

January 13, 1771	Departed this life Benjamin Hawley.
January 13, 1771	Departed this life the Wife of Stephen Hart Junr.
Feby 13, 1771	Departed this life Peg a Negro Woman.
February 21, 1771	Departed this life Mr. Thomas Wadsworth.
April 1771	Departed this life Nathl a son of Rezin Gridley.
April 12, 1771	Departed this life a Babe of Doct^r Asa Johnson.
April 12, 1771	Departed this life a Babe of Peter Curtiss.
April 16, 1771	Departed this life a Babe of Heman Watson.
May 25, 1771	Departed this life Eliz: Daugr. of Tim^o Portter Jr.
June 20, 1771	Departed this life John Strong Jr.
July 11, 1771	Departed this life Allan Merril.
July 16, 1771	Departed this life Lydia North.
July 17, 1771	Departed this life Jemima Warner.
August 18, 1771	Departed this life Chauncey son of David Hart.
Septr. 13, 1771	Departed this life a Babe of Doct^r Hosmer.
Septr. 14, 1771	Departed this life Abigail Evans.
Octr. 11, 1771	Departed this life Elizabeth Dag^r of Benjn Andruss.
Novr. 5, 1771	Departed this life Ephraim son of Tim^o Woodruff.
Novr. 17, 1771	Departed this life a Dagtr. Child of Zadoc Orvis.
December 13, 1771	Departed this life the Wife of Isaac Gridley.
January 22, 1772	Departed this life Zenas son of David Hart.
February 19, 1772	Departed this life William Cole.
February 27, 1772	Departed this life the Wife of Ens^n James Cowles.
March 8, 1772	Departed this life a Babe of Ebenezer Hubbard.
March 10, 1772	Carried to the grave a Babe of Capt. Judah Woodruff.
March 19, 1772	Departed this life ye Wife of Solomon Whitman Esq.
March 22, 1772	Departed this life a babe of Levi Clarke.
May 30, 1772	Departed this life Cyprian son of Eneas Cowles.
June 4, 1772	Departed this life a Babe of Gift Hills.
June 10, 1772	Departed this life a Child of Saml Adams—Indian.
	[A leaf lost.]
July 28, 1776	Departed this life Sidney son of Wm Wadsworth.
August 14, 1776	Departed this life Titus son of Eli Andruss.
August 22, 1776	Departed this life Col Fisher Gay at N. York.
August 24, 1776	Departed this life the Wife of Amos Tubbs.
August 26, 1776	Departed this life Theodosia Dag^r of Saml Stedman Jr.
August 29, 1776	Departed this life Sarah Daug^r of Mr. Thomas Lewis.
August 31, 1776	Departed this life ye Wife of Mr. James Judd.
Septr. 3, 1776	Departed this life Benjn Hawley, a Child.
Septr. 10, 1776	Departed this life Ruth Gridley.
Septr. 11, 1776	Departed life a Dag^r of Ebenezer Caronton.
Septr. 13, 1776	Departed life the Wife of Ebenezer Caronton.
Septr. 1776	Departed life in ye Army Ensign Solomon Curtiss, Noadiah Woodruff, Phinehas Caronton, Isaiah Post, Ira Judson, Mark Woodruff, Ebenezer Dickinson, Joel Root & Gad Brownson, Elijah Woodruff.

[To be continued.]

GENEALOGICAL GLEANINGS IN ENGLAND.

By HENRY F. WATERS, A.M., now residing in London, Eng.

[Continued from vol. xxxix. page 338.]

MR. WILLIAM RENDLE has published in the Athenæum of April 18, July 11 and Oct. 24, 1885, some communications as to the genealogy of John Harvard, and in certain quarters allusions have been made to a "controversy" on the subject. There is properly speaking no controversy at all. There is and can be no question whatever in the minds of those conversant with the facts in the case as to who discovered the parentage and ancestry of John Harvard. The credit of this remarkable discovery belongs undeniably to Mr. Henry F. Waters, and to him alone.

The facts in the case are briefly these. Mr. Rendle seems to be a local antiquary who has, I believe, lived many years in Southwark, and who has spent much time among the records there, and has undoubtedly there done good work. But unfortunately for Mr. Rendle, there is not in this case so far a single scrap of evidence to show that there is anything whatever in the Southwark records to establish the slightest possible connection between the Harvards of that Borough and John Harvard of Emmanuel College and of New England. There were Harvards in Southwark, it is true, and perhaps in other parts of Surrey, just as there were Harvards in Devonshire, Somerset, Dorset, Wilts, Middlesex, Warwickshire, and doubtless in other parts of England. The problem was to identify, among them all, the father of John Harvard. So far as Mr. Rendle was concerned, this problem might have remained unsolved to the end of time, for there was nothing in the Southwark records which would have enabled him to solve it.

The proof of this relationship Mr. Waters discovered after much research in the records of the Prerogative Court of Canterbury. There he found, among others, the wills of John Harvard's father, mother, brother, uncle, aunt, two step-fathers and father-in-law. This proved the whole family connection. If Mr. Waters had stopped there and gone not a step farther, it would have been enough to completely dispel the mystery which had so long enveloped the birth and early life of the benefactor of the noble University. After thus finally solving the problem he went to Southwark merely for supplemental evidence, not at all necessary however to substantiate his case, and there in the parish registers he found the record of the baptism of John Harvard and other collateral matter.

Information of this visit of Mr. Waters to Southwark and its successful result was communicated to several persons. That Mr. Rendle was apprised of it by one of them can be shown by evidence both direct and circumstantial.

In articles published by Mr. Rendle in the Genealogist for April and July, 1884 (N. S. i. 107 and 182), he gives the names of the Harvards found by him in the records of St. Saviour's, Southwark. But there nowhere appears in his list the name of our John Harvard. He even quotes the late Chaplain Samuel Benson as saying that " he cannot find the name of John Harvard, the founder, but that he had no doubt he was born of this family of Harvard of St. Saviour's." Mr. Rendle then adds : " After careful, I will not say exhaustive examination, of the original books and papers, I am quite of the same opinion." On page 182 he quotes the entry in the books of Emmanuel College, where Harvard is said to be of Middlesex, and in a foot-note talks of drawing the "attention of officials of Middlesex churches to the name John Harvard, and the dates *circa* 1605 and after." Mr. Rendle, although fully apprised of the fact that Harvard, Harverde and Harvye were merely different forms of the same family name, had evidently overlooked the entry of Harvard's baptism, or had failed to recognize it, or to appreciate the importance of the entry, even if his eye had ever rested upon it, and was as late as July, 1884, turning to Middlesex for the record of it, having apparently given up all hope of finding it in Southwark. The "extremely diverse spelling" of the name, being already well known to him, will by no means account for this failure.

On the 11th of April, 1885, a date, be it remembered, subsequent to Mr. Waters's visit to Southwark and his discovery of the record of this baptism, Mr. Rendle published in the South London Press a letter, which with some additions he again published in the Athenæum of April 18th.

In this letter he printed conspicuously in Italics the record of this baptism, and added, "I believe" him "to be the founder" of Harvard College, but he neither then nor has he since offered any proof of his own to substantiate his belief or to show any reasonable grounds for it. Sometime, therefore, between July, 1884, and April, 1885, Mr. Rendle saw a great light. He evidently does not mean to tell us how or when this flashed upon him. But he unwittingly, in the very letter above referred to, shows us the source of his information in these significant words : " The clue, or rather the result of the clue, is before me. I believe that some American friends, anxious to do honor to their benefactor and his birth-place, are now among us. It would have been pleasant to me to have known them; probably now I may." Of course he did not know "them." But when we consider that at the very time he penned these lines Mr. Rendle knew that the long search for John Harvard was over, that even the record of his baptism had been found and that Mr. Waters was the successful discoverer, the extremely disingenuous and misleading nature of this allusion to American friends can be readily seen. What is the "clue" the result of which Mr. Rendle had before him? Does he mean to say that somebody else had the clue and that he had only the result? The general denial made by W. D. in the Athenæum of July 11th, 1885, is altogether too vague. It should be more specific if it is expected that much weight should be attached to it.

There seems indeed to be a confusion or haziness in Mr. Rendle's mind as to what constitutes not merely legal but even genealogical proof. Mr. Waters, on the other hand, like a true genealogist, has made a scientific treatment of the subject, and shows us step by step how he reached the successful result of his search, and on what his conclusions are based. He gives us the pedigree of Harvard and the proof by which it can be substantiated. That the search was an independent one, is shown by Mr. Rendle's chief and only witness W. D., who, in the letter above referred to, kindly proves Mr. Waters's case for him by admitting that Mr. Rendle's offer of assistance was "neither acted on nor acknowledged" by Mr. Waters.

In an article in the New England Historical and Genealogical Register for July, 1885, I expressed my astonishment at what I called this "extraordinary proceeding" on the part of Mr. Rendle. That such a proceeding is happily considered as extraordinary in England as it is here, and that the standard of literary morality is at least as high there as here, is shown by the fact that I have before me, as I write, letters from several English antiquaries whose names are known on both sides of the Atlantic, and who are fully cognizant of the facts in the case, who express surprise at what they call the "strange conduct" of Mr. Rendle. As these are private letters, not intended for publication, I have no right to quote them in this matter, but the evidence thus afforded is overwhelming.

Mr. Rendle's pamphlet, a copy of which I have only lately seen, will, I understand, be reviewed elsewhere and by abler hands than mine. I will therefore not take up space to point out certain inaccuracies in it, which are patent to everyone who has given much thought to the subject. I will content myself with calling attention to the fact that it furnishes not an iota of proof of the connection of John Harvard of Southwark with John Harvard of New England, except what is taken from Mr. Waters's pamphlet on the subject. This indebtedness Mr. Rendle is, however, careful to acknowledge, and he has conspicuously marked with a W. the source of information thus obtained. It is instructive to notice how plentifully sprinkled Mr. Rendle's pages are with this initial letter.

I freely admit—now that Mr. Waters has conclusively shown that John Harvard was a Southwark man, and has put this statement in print so that all may read—that Mr. Rendle's local knowledge as a Southwark antiquary may enable him to carry on still further the investigations in that Borough, and I certainly trust that he may supplement and add to the already accumulating data concerning the early life of the benefactor of America's oldest and most famous University. Any such supplemental and corroborative material will command the attention of antiquaries on both sides of the ocean, and will deserve and receive due recognition on their part.

JOHN T. HASSAM.

EDWARD PARKS citizen & merchant tailor of London, 23 January 1650. To wife Mary Parks, in lieu of her thirds, fifteen hundred pounds (in various payments) and one third of the plate and household stuff, and all that my freehold messuage or tenement with its appurtenances, &c. which I lately purchased of William Pennoyer of London, merchant, wherein I now dwell, in the parish of Stepney, being the North western part of that great messuage formerly the possession of the Right Hon. Henry Earl of Worcester. My wife to have the education of my children.

If my son Henry Parks shall within three months, &c. and after notice given, release and quitclaim, &c. all his part of all my goods, &c. (according to the custom of the city of London) and release to George Jackson of Sandhurst in the county of Kent all his part of lands, &c. in Maidstone in the County of Kent which I lately have sold to George Jackson, then I give & bequeath unto him three hundred pounds (in various payments). And further I give & bequeath unto my said son Henry Parks and his heirs forever, in consideration as well of the release by him to be made to my brother George Jackson of the lands in Maidstone, &c. all my messuages, houses, lands, tenements & hereditaments situate, lying and being in New England in the parts of America beyond the seas.

If my son Edward Parks, within three months next after notice given him of my death and after he shall attain the age of twenty & one years, release his part of personal estate according to purport of an indenture, dated 26 June 1640, between me the said Edward Parks, of the one part, and Thomas Westby of Fresby in the county of York, gentleman, and Edward Gell of Brimington in the county of Derby Esq., of the other part, then I give and bequeath unto the said Edward three score pounds for his preferment & placing him to apprentice. To my son John five hundred pounds within three months after he attains the age of twenty-one years, and to sons William & Stephen (the same amount with the same limitation). To daughter Elizabeth Parks five hundred pounds at twenty-one or day of marriage. To sons Thomas, Dannett, Francis & Samuel (legacies similar to their brother John's above). To Mark, Francis & Susan Wilcox, three of the children of my sister Alice Wilcox, ten pounds apiece, & to Anne Wilcox another daughter twenty pounds, to be paid, the sons at twenty-one and the daughters at that age or day of marriage. Bequeaths to the widow Brewer, to Martha Wilson now wife of Thomas Wilson, being both my late servants, to my daughter Mary, now wife of Thomas Plampin and my two grand children Thomas and Edward Plampin. Reference to lands in Hadleigh in the county of Suffolk lately bought.

My son in law Thomas Plampin and cousin John Bagnall, both of London, merchant tailors, to be my executors and my brothers Dr William Forth and Dannett Forth of London, woollen draper, to be overseers. A Thomas Forth a witness.

The above will was proved 29 January 1650; but the executors having died before fulfilling their trust a commission was issued 29 March 1673 to John Parkes, a son & legatee. He also died before completing his ad-

ministration, and commission was issued 3 November, 1681, to Mary Caw-
ley als Parkes, the widow relict of said defunct, &c.　　　　Grey, 10.

[A full abstract of this will was printed in a note in Mass. Hist. Soc. Collections,
4th S., vol. vii. p. 385, from a copy obtained for me by Col. Chester. The note was
appended to several letters from Edward Parks to John Winthrop, Jr. These show
that Parks terms Henry Bright of Watertown his uncle. In the genealogy of the
Brights of Suffolk, Eng. (Boston, 1858), we find on pp. 270–71, an abstract of the
will of Mrs. Elizabeth Dell, sister of Henry Bright, in which she mentions her
nephew William Parks. She also mentions her brother Henry Bright, William
Forth and —— Blowers, her sister Martha Blowers, her cousin —— Cawby, Esq.,
and her nephew Dr. William Forth.
　　Henry Parks, son of Edward, sold in 1655, his land in Cambridge to John Stedman, and very probably came here for the purpose. This particular branch, however, then ceased to have any connection with New England. But at Cambridge
one of the early settlers was Dea. Richard Parke, 1638–1655, whose son Thomas
had a son Edward. At Roxbury was William Parke, whose will of 20 July, 1684,
mentions only three daughters and their children, brother Thomas Parks of Stonington, deceased, and brother Samuel with his sons Robert and William. Savage
says that these three were sons of Robert of Wethersfield and New London, who
died in 1665. Very probably this Robert was the man who wrote to John Winthrop
in 1629 from Easterkale in Lincolnshire (see Mass. Hist. Soc. Coll., 5th S. vol. i.
p. 194), proposing to go to New England.
　　These *may* have been relatives of Edward Parke, who was clearly allied to Winthrop through the Forths. The family name of Dannett ought also to lead to some
trace of this family.
　　The Alice Wilcox, sister of Edward Parks, recalls the William Wilcockes of our
Cambridge, who died in 1653, leaving a widow Mary (Powell) but no children, and
a sister Christian Boiden in Old England. A John Wilcox was of Dorchester,
1661, and went to Middletown. The names Wilcox, Hastings, Fox and Hall are
in the Leicestershire Visitations, and Wilcox also in Rutland.—W. H. WHITMORE.]

WILLIAM GOORE of Nether Wallop in the county of Southampton gentleman, 9 November 1587. To wife Joane, eldest son William, all my
land called Garlacks. To my four youngest sons Richard, John, Nicholas and William Goore the younger all my land in Newington, in the
county of Wilts, and in Basingstoke, in the county of Southampton, and
two hundred pounds apiece. To my four daughters Agnes, Elizabeth,
Barbara and Margery Goore two hundred pounds apiece. The executors
to be my eldest son William Gore and Margaret Reade, the supervisors
to be John Pittman of Quarley, Thomas Elie, Clerk vicar of Nether Wallop and Leonard Elie of Wonston.
　　10 May 1588. Emanavit comͥissio Willᵐᵒ Sᵗ John armigero marito so-
roris naturalis et ltiͥe dict def et Leonardo Elie generoso uni superviso-
rum &c. cum consensu Wᵐⁱ Gore filii &c. durante minori etate eiusdem
Willmi et Margarete Reade als Gore alterius executorum &c.
　　　　　　　　　　　　　　　　　　　　　Rutland, 37.

WILLIAM GORE of Nether Wallop in the county of Southampton, gentleman, 22 January 1655, proved 29 March 1656. Wife Elizabeth to be
sole executrix. To the poor of Nether Wallop three pounds to be distributed in one month after my decease. To my wife a portion of my now
dwelling house at Garleggs in the parish of Nether Wallop and part of the
orchard. To my cousin Richard Hamon. To Amy Singer, daughter of
my late sister Margaret, and Jane Singer, another daughter, and Roger
Singer, a son. To my cousin Mary Poore the now wife of John Power
thirty pounds. To Nicholas & Margaret, son and daughter of my late sister Wallingford, twenty pounds apiece in one year after my decease. To
my cousin Nicholas Gore, son of Nicholas Gore late of Farley deceased,

ten pounds in one year. To Nicholas Hatchet of Nether Wallop five pounds in one year. My brother in law Mr Robert Sadler, my cousin John Poore and my cousin Richard Miller of Broughton. To the now five children of Richard Hamon forty pounds apiece and to William Poore and Elizabeth Poore, son & daughter of my late cousin William Poore deceased, forty pounds, and to the now children of my late cousin Thomas Singer deceased, forty pounds. To my godson Richard Sherfield, son of my late brother Roger Sherfield, gentleman, deceased. If my cousin Nicholas Wallingford shall have issue of his body or Margaret Wallingford have issue of her body then, &c. To John Gore, son of my late uncle Richard Gore. To my uncle Hugh Mundy.   Berkeley, 110.

[In these Goore wills Mr. Waters is evidently probing the connections of the ancestors of our Merrimac Valley settlers. The villages of Wallop, like those of Choulderton, lie upon the edges of the Counties of Wilts and Southampton, and when Dummer, Saltonstall and Rawson, with their English associates, had arranged for developing a stock-raising town in New England, they arranged also to secure from co. Wilts and its vicinity the transfer of a colony of practical men not only accustomed to the care of live stock, but to the trades which interlaced in the products of a stock-raising community. The matter of first importance was to secure ministers with whom the community would feel at home. Rev. Thomas Parker and his relatives the Noyes family, natives of Choulderton, were secured, and with them the Wiltshire men were glad to join.

In the will, proved 28 March, 1657, the names of many of the Poore family are mentioned as cousins of the testator, and so is Nicholas Wallingford, who came in the Confidence from Southampton in 1638, with others—Stephen Kent, John Rolfe, John Saunders, John and William Ilsley, and more recruits to join their relatives who established the town of Newbury. Joseph Poore, of Newbury, married, 6 August, 1680, Mary Wallingford, daughter of Nicholas, born 20 August, 1663. Anthony Sadler was a passenger in the same vessel. In the Visitation of co. Wilts in 1623 are pedigrees of the Sadler family on p. 63. The son and heir of the family given there is Robert Sadler, born in 1608, who may have been the person mentioned as " brother-in-law " in the will given above.

The will proved in 1588 contains an instance, not uncommon at that period, but a terrible annoyance to genealogists, of two sons having the same baptismal name— *eldest* son William, and four youngest sons, among whom is William the *younger*. The name of Margaret Read recalls the fact that the Read and Noyes family intermarried in the locality of these testators.—JOHN COFFIN JONES BROWN.]

JOSEPH BLAKE of Berkley County in the Province of South Carolina, 18 December, 1750. My whole estate to be kept together until it raises the sum of two thousand pounds sterling money of Great Britain and one thousand pounds Proclamation money, or the value thereof, in the currency of this province, exclusive of the maintenance of my sons Daniel and William and my daughter Ann Blake. After said sums are cleared—to be kept at interest and the interest applied towards educating & maintaining my sons Daniel & William and daughter Ann until they arrive at full age. Then one thousand pounds sterling to my son Daniel, the same to son William and the remaining thousand pounds Proclamation money to daughter Ann. To son Daniel the plantation I now live on called Newington and a tract of land on the Cypress Swamp lying between the lands of Mr James Postell and Barnaby Brandford, part of which I purchased of Mr James Postell deceased, the remainder I took up of the King; and that part of my land on Charles Town Neck which lies between the High Road and Cooper River ; and fifteen hundred acres to be taken out of my lands on Cumbee River between Mrs Hudson's land and the land I bought of Colonel William Bull, the line to run towards Calf Pen Savanah as far back as will take in the quantity of fifteen hundred acres ; and a plantation containing five hundred & ninety-seven acres in two tracts bounding on Mrs Donings and Mrs Drake to the North East and to the North West on Mrs Donings, Mrs Sacheveralls and Doctor Brisbanes, to the South West on a tract of land which was formerly Mr Dowses but now mine and on Mr Ways, to the South East on Mr Richard Warings. To son William & his heirs forever my plantation containing more or less on Wadmelaw River and new cut, commonly called Plainsfield, lying between lands of Mr John Atchinson and Mr Fuller ; and that part of my land on Charles Town Neck that lies between the High Road and Ashly River, bounding on Mr Gadsdens, Mr Hunts & Mr John Humes ; and two tracts of land lying between Mr Atchinsons and Mr Stoboes, one tract containing two hundred & thirty acres, the other seventy-six acres ; and two tracts of land containing four hundred & forty acres purchased of Stephen Dowse by Mrs Jennis, bounding on Mr William Elliott, Mr John Drayton & Mr Graves.

I give and bequeath unto my loving daughter Rebecca Izard, to her and her heirs forever a tract of land containing eighteen hundred & seventy three acres in Granville County on the Lead of Coosaw, Hatchers and Chili Phina Swamp, bounding on James Therrs to the North West ; and an Island on Port Royal River in Granville County commonly called Cat Island, containing four hundred acres. I give and bequeath to my loving daughter Ann Blake one thousand acres of land to be laid out by my executors and executrix on the Calf Pen Savanah to be taken out of my lands on Cumbee on the head of the said tracts and an island containing two hundred and eighty-six acres of land in Granville County on the North East side of Port Royal River and on all other sides on marshes and creeks out of the said River. I give all my Real estate, not already given, devised or bequeathed, unto my two sons Daniel & William Blake, all my household goods & plate to be divided between my two sons Daniel & William & my daughter Ann Blake, to each a third. To son Daniel my coach & harness and Prime Thorn, his wife Betty Molly & all their children which they have or shall have. To son William Wally Johnny Molatto Peter Mol Juda & all their children, &c. To daughter Ann Blake Lampset Nanny Patty & Molly child of Hannah & all their children, &c. All the residue of my personal estate (not already given, devised or bequeathed) unto my four children Rebeccah Izard, Daniel Blake, William Blake & Ann Blake, to be equally divided.

I nominate, &c. daughter Rebecca Izard, son Daniel Blake and son Ralph Izard executrix & executors & guardians to my children until they attain the ages of twenty-one years, &c. & to improve the estate of my said children either by putting money at Interest, buying slaves or any other way they shall judge most advantageous.

Wit : Jacob Molte, William Roper, Alexander Rigg.

Charles Town So : Carolina Secretarys Office.

The foregoing Writing of two sheets of paper is a true copy from the Original will of the Honble Joseph Blake Esquire deceased. Examined & certified p William Pinckney Dep^{ty} Sec^{ty}.

11 February 1752 Depositions of John Ouldfield, of South Carolina, planter, & William George, freeman of South Carolina, at present residing in the city of London, gentleman.

The will was proved 20 February 1752 by Daniel Blake Esq. son, &c. &c. Power reserved for the other executors.   Bettesworth, 30.

GEORGE JONES, of the City of Philadelphia in the Province of Pennsylvania, yeoman, having a design by the Permission of the Almighty to pass over the seas, 22 September 1743. To Sarah Toms daughter of Robert Toms twenty pounds current money of Pennsylvania, to be paid her at her age of eighteen years. To Thomas Howard of the city of Philadelphia, joyner, all my right & title of & to my seat in Christ church in Philadelphia. To Mary Howard, daughter of Thomas Howard, ten pounds at age of eighteen. To Andrew Robertson, miller at Wesschicken, my horse, saddle & bridle, my watch & seal thereto affixed. To Kattrine Hinton one hundred pounds immediately after my decease, &c. provided that the said Katrine do not marry till after my decease. To Abraham Pratt, of the city of Philadelphia joyner, twenty pounds, &c. To the children of my brother James Jones deceased, of the parish of S[t] John at Brogmore Green in the County of Worcester in Great Britain, & to my sister Elizabeth Clay, of the city of Worcester, & to her children, all the rest & remainder of my estate, Real & Personal, to be equally divided.

I do nominate & appoint Jonathan Robeson of Philadelphia Esq., Lawrence Anderson, of Philadelphia merchant, and Jacob Duchee, shopkeeper in Market Street, executors.

Wit: William Cunningham, Warwick Coats John Chapman.

14 February 1752 Admon. with the will annexed of the goods & chattells, &c. of George Jones late of the city of Philadelphia, in the Province of Pennsylvania, but at the city of Worcester deceased, lying and being in that part of Great Britain called England only but no further or otherwise, was granted to Elizabeth Clay, widow, the natural & lawful sister of the said deceased & one of the Residuary Legatees named in said will, for that Jonathan Robeson Esq., Lawrence Anderson & Jacob Duchee, the executors appointed in said will, have taken upon them the execution thereof so far as concerns that part of the estate of the said deceased within the Province of Pennsylvania, but have respectively renounced the execution of the said will and their right of administration of the said deceased's estate in that part of Great Britain called England. Bettesworth, 39.

[Probated in Philadelphia, 1751, Book i. p. 404.—C. R. HILDEBURN, of Philadelphia.]

WILLIAM STOCKTON, Clerk, parson of Barkeswell in the County of Warwick, 2 March 1593, proved 17 June 1594 by Elizabeth his relict & executrix, through her attorney Thomas Lovell Not. Pub. The will mentions brother Randulph Stockton, brother Raphe Stockton, the children of cousin John Stockton, parson of Alcester, the children of cousin Thomas Gervise, son Jonas Stockton, eldest daughter Debora Stockton, wife Elizabeth & daughters Judith & Abigail, cousins John Stockton & Thomas Gervis and Thomas Benyon of Barkeswell yeoman, & John Massame of the city of Coventry, clothworker, to be overseers. Dixey, 49.

[I suppose the " cousin John Stockton, parson of Alcester," mentioned in the above will, was the father of Patience, wife of Edward Holyoke of New England, whose father, John Holliock, of Alcester in the county of Warwick, mercer, made his will 21 November 30th Elizabeth (proved 31 January, 1587) in presence of John Stockton. If this be so, then Mr. Stockton must have removed before 1607 to Kinkolt in Leicestershire, where he was living (probably as Rector of that parish), as shown by a letter from young Edward Holyoke to his betrothed, dated 21 Nov. 1607. (See Emmerton & Waters's Gleanings from English Records, pp. 57-59.)—H. F. W.]

ROBERT WILCOX, the younger, of Alcester in the county of Warwick, mercer, xiiii October 1626, proved 14 February 1626. To my father. M[r] Robert Wilcox, over and above the two hundred pounds due to him by bond, one hundred pounds within one year after my decease (and some chattell goods). To my son Robert fifty pounds to be put out for his best use at his age of xiiii years. My will is that Ann & Elizabeth Heath shall have x^{li} between them for the money I received by their brother Richard's will. To each of my sisters xl^s. To Humfry Bedowe x^s. To Joane my maid servant xv^s, to Elenor my maid servant x^s. I give x^{li} to be from time to time lent gratis to honest tradesmen at the discretion of Mr Bayliffe for the time being, with the assent of my father Wilcox, brother Bridges, brother Holioke and Mr Jeliffe, or of three, two or one of them so long as any of them shall live, and, after the death of the survivor of them, at the discretion of Mr Bayliffe for the time being. To mine apprentice xx^s at thend of his terme. The rest of my goods chattells, &c. to Martha, my beloved wife, whom I make sole executrix. The overseers to be my well beloved father in law John Halford and George Jelliffe and my brother Florisell Bovey and I give them ii^s vi^d apiece for their pains.

Wit: Samuel Hulford, Edward Holioke.   Skinner, 12.

[An article on the Wilcoxes of New England is printed in the REGISTER, xxix. 25-9, but no connection with Robert of Alcester is found. There is probably some relationship between his " brother Holioke " and Edward Holyoke, the immigrant ancestor of the Holyokes of New England, who seems to have come from Alcester (see will of Edward Holliock, 1587, in Emmerton and Waters's Gleanings, p. 57). Two other New England immigrants, William and Richard Waldern (written by descendants, Waldron), were natives of Alcester (see REG. viii. 78).—EDITOR.]

MR. THOMAS ROPER'S will. John West my servant to be set free. Alexander Gill, servant to Capt. Peirce, to be set free or else if Capt. Peirce shall refuse to release him, then that the said Alexander receive two hundred pounds of Tobacco from Capt. Peirce. I give and bequeath all tobaccoes due unto me in Virginia to my brother John Roper in England and that Mr George Fitz Jefferyes receive it to the use of my said brother. Item a pair of Linen breeches to William Smith of James City. To the said William Smith a waistcoat. To my brother John Roper three hundred and odd pounds of good & lawful money of England, in the hands of my father in law Mr Thomas Sheaperd of Moine in Bedfordshire. The residue to my brother John Roper. Fifty shillings in money to Mr Haute Wyatt, minister of James City.

Wit: Haut Wyatt, William Smith, George Fitz Jefferey.

In the letter of administration (5 February 1626) to John Roper Thomas Shepard is spoken of as the natural & lawful father of John, Elizabeth and Constance Shepard, brother and sisters of the deceased on the mother's side (*ex materno latere*), the letters of administration granted in the month of May 1624 having been brought back and renounced.

                                                        Skinner, 11.

[According to a pedigree of the Wyatt family furnished me some years ago by Reginald Stewart Boddington, Esq., London, England, the Rev. Hawte Wyatt (a younger brother of Sir Francis Wyatt, twice governor of Virginia, married 1618, buried 24 August, 1644, at Boxley) was the second son of George and Jane (daughter of Sir Thomas Finch of Eastwell, Knight, by his wife Katherine, elder daughter and co-heiress of Sir Thomas Moyle of Eastwell) Wyat (of Allington Castle, Boxley, and in right of his wife, Lord of the Manor of Wavering, son of Sir Thomas Wyat by his wife Elizabeth, daughter of Thomas Brooke, Lord Cobham, beheaded 11 April, 1554) and Jane (married 1537), younger daughter and co-heiress of Sir William Hawte of Bishopbourne, co. Kent, Knight, and to whom Queen Mary granted the Manor of Wavering) ; inducted after his return to England to the living of Boxley, 3 October, 1632, and Rector of Merston, co. Kent; died 31 July, 1638 ; buried at Boxley.

He was married twice, " *and his issue said to have gone to Virginia.*"

The following document in my possession may be of interest in connection with the immediately preceding paragraph :

"Oct. 29, 1655. This day Pindabake the Protector of the young King of Chiskoyack was at my house [punctuation mine], intending to have spoken with the Governor, then expected to be heer'd, but he came not, & therefore hee desyned to leave his mind with mee, Maior Will Wiat & divers others, as followith, viz : that Wassahickon the —— [illegible] had freely given unto Mr. Edward Wyatt and his heyres, executors, administrators or assigns, all the land from Mr. Hugh Guinn's old marked trees to Vttamarke Creeke, including all Pagan —— [illegible] high Land, being freely given, and with the consent of all the rest of the Indians, it was also agreed among them all that neither the King nor any other of his Indians should sell, alienate or dispose of any land belonging unto them without the consent of Mr. Ed. Wyatt, which was the only business that he had to acquaint the Gov'r therewith in the behalfe of Mr. Ed. Wyat, as we heere doe testify under our hands, this present 29th of October, 1655."

The marke of

Pindabake, Protector of
the young King of
Chiskoyake

Will'm Benett
John West Junior
Toby West

The marke of Wm Godfrey

The marke of John Talbutt
John King

Signed and sealed in the presence of
all whose names are here subscribed.

I find the following grants of land to the name Wyatt and Wyat of record in the Virginia Land Registry Office : Ralph Wyatt, "Gent." Book No. 1, p. 590, lease to Richard Johnson, Roger Davis and Abraham Wood, "planters," "one parcell of Islands," 1636 ; Henry Wyat, Esq., eldest son of Sir Francis Wyat, p. 757, lease for 21 years. of 50 acres in Pasbylaiers James City county for the raising of corn for the better protection of the plantation, Dec. 16, 1641 ; Thomas Wyat, p. 916, 2000 ac. on the south side of the Rappahannock river, "twenty miles up," Sept. 24, 1643 ; George Wyatt, No. 2, p. 54, 250 acres in James City county, April 12, 1642 ; Richard Wyatt, p. 154, 500 acres in Mobjack bay, Aug. 20, 1645 ; William Wyatt, No. 3, p. 4, 400 acres in Gloucester county, April 27, 1653 ; p. 354, 300 acres in New Kent county, June 6, 1665 ; Edward Wyatt and Robert Grig, 4, p. 439, 370 acres in Kingston parish, Gloucester county, April 19, 1662 ; William Wyatt, 5, p. 286, 400 acres in Gloucester county, March 16, 1663 ; Major William Wyatt, p. 439, 1940 acres in New Kent county, May 20, 1664 ; William Wyatt, p. 453, 300 acres in New Kent county, May 20, 1664 ; Anthony Wyatt, p. 510, 282 acres in New Kent county, June 28, 1664 ; Thomas Wyatt, p. 608, 500 acres in Mobjack bay, May 9, 1666 ; William Wyatt, 6, p. 322, 500 acres in New Kent county, June 20, 1670 ; Anthony Wyatt, p. 247, 398 acres in Charles City county, July 24, 1669 ; William Wyatt, p. 296, 2240 acres in New Kent county, April 17, 1669 ; p. 364, 1900 acres in New Kent county, Oct. 21, 1670 ; 7, p. 32, 850 acres in New Kent county, April 25, 1680 ; Henry Wyatt, p. 123, 649 acres in New Kent county, April 20, 1682 ; John and Richard Wyatt, p. 321, 650 acres in New Kent county, Sept. 20, 1683 ; Nicholas Wyatt, p. 510, 115 acres in Brandon parish [Charles City county ?], April 27, 1686 ; John Wyatt, 9, p. 654, 700 acres in King and Queen county, May 2, 1705 ; James Wyatt, No. 10, p. 85, 139 in upper parish of Nansemond county, May 2, 1713 ; Richard Wyatt, p. 247, 285 acres in Charles City county, Aug. 15, 1715 ; Francis Wyatt, 23, p. 635, 377 acres in Prince George county, Nov. 25, 1743 ; Francis Wyatt and Mary Hawkins, No. 28, p. 208, 100 acres in Prince George county, Aug. 20, 1747, and in same, p. 211, 200 acres in Amelia county, Aug. 20, 1747.

Anthony Wyatt was a prominent citizen of Charles City County, Virginia, 1660–70.—R. A. BROCK, of Richmond, Va.]

NICHOLAS JUPE, citizen & merchant Taylor of London, 10 March 1650, proved 13 October 1651. To cousin Benjamin Jupe, his executers & assigns, all my moiety or half part of two houses, &c. in the parish of St Buttolph Aldgate, London, in the occupation of Richard English and Edward Mott, and the house where a stone-cutter did dwell and my own dwelling house and so much of the dwelling house as is now in Mr Finch's occupation,—which I and Richard English bought of Matthew Beanes. To the said Benjamin fifteen pounds and to his brother John & his sister Margaret five pounds apiece. To Anthony and Mary Jupe, equally between them, my half of five houses which were bought by me and the said Richard English, standing in Gravel Lane in the Parish of Saint Buttolph without Aldgate, London, being in one row or rank, they to pay, out of the profits, to Christopher Jupe & Thomas Evans ten pounds apiece within two years after my decease. I give to Simeon Smith my half of four tenements granted by lease from the Hospital of Christ Church London. To Rebecca Smith, daughter of my brother Joseph Smith, my lease of tenements in the occupation of Mr Mason & Mr Harman. To the poor of Bishopsgate, to the minister, Mr Fuller, to the poor of Aldgate. To Richard English & John Euerett & to each of their wives twenty shillings apiece, to Sarah Martin & Mrs Katherine Jackson twenty shillings apiece, to Mr Dye and his wife twenty shillings apiece, to Simeon Smith forty shillings, to Sarah Wilmott ten pounds, to Rebecca Unckles three pounds & to her mother four pounds, to my brother Christopher's daughter Mary five shillings, to my cousin Evans forty shillings, to my cousin Christopher Jupe forty shillings, to cousin John Jupe twenty shillings, to cousin Margaret Jupe twelve pounds, to Anne Foster twenty shillings, to my wife's sister Denton three pounds & to her daughter twenty shillings, to Mr Hedges & his wife twenty shillings apiece, to Edward Smith the elder and Edward Smith the younger and to Elizabeth Smith (certain legacies), to William Harper forty shillings, to Thomas Jackson twenty shillings, more to Benjamin Jupe ten pounds, more to Joseph Smith & his daughter Rebecca Smith, &c. Loving friends Mr Grimes, Richard English & John Everett to be overseers. Simeon Smith to be executor. Grey, 189.

[At the time of the decease of the testator, the five houses in Gravel Lane above devised were in the occupation of "John Trigg senio^r m^{rs} oakeman; widdow Izard widdow Bocken and m^r Chambe^{rs}" and the interest of the testator's niece Mary Jupe, afterward Mary Morse, therein, was conveyed with other property by her husband John Morse of Boston in New England, salt boiler, by deed of mortgage dated Nov. 9th, 1654, recorded with Suffolk Deeds, Lib. 2, fol. 180, to Capt. Robert Keaine of said Boston, uncle of said mortgagor, to secure the payment of £32. Capt. Keaine had advanced £15 to pay for the passage of Morse, his wife and his wife's brother, Benjamin Jupe, from New England back to Old England, and the latter sum was to be paid at the Golden Crown in Birchin Lane, London, on or before April 26, 1655, out of the rents belonging to the said wife or brother Benjamin Jupe remaining in the hands of Simeon Smith of Southwark, the executor of the foregoing will, as appears by a bond and order recorded fol. 183 and 184. See also fol. 86 and 182. See note to the will of Benjamin Kaine (*ante*, xxxvii. 234). See also the abstract made by Stanley Waters of an indenture, found by him in the Suffolk Court Files, dated March 10, 1652, "between Benjamin Kayen of London Esquire, sonne and heire apparent of Robert Kayen of Boston in N. E., Esquire, on the one part, and Simeon Smith, Cittizen and Haberdasher, of London, the executor of the last will &c. of Nicholas Jupe, Cittizen & Marchant Tayler of London, deceased, of the other part." This abstract was published in the REGISTER for July, 1881 (xxxv. 277).—JOHN T. HASSAM.]

FRANCIS NEWTON of London, grocer, 24 August 1660, proved 11 January 1661, now bound out on a voyage to Virginia. To wife Mary Newton six hundred pounds within six months after my decease. The residue to my loving sisters Elizabeth and Susan Newton and loving brother Joseph Newton, equally, &c. Friends John Berry, Anthony Stanford & Joseph Wilson to be executors. Laud, 8.

[See note " Newton of Kingston upon Hull, England," REG. April, 1885, p. 194.—R. A. BROCK.]

RICHARD SMITH, of St Dunstan's West, London, Cook, 13 January 1660, proved 17 January 1661. To be buried in the parish church of St Dunstans in the West. Wife Joane, brother John Smith. To my sister Ann Hawthorne five acres in the possession of John Alley, butcher, of the yearly value of five pounds for her natural life, &c. and then to her two sons John & Nathaniel Hawthorne and their heirs equally. To my brother John Smith the reversion I purchased (after the decease of Anne Henman, widow) of William Backhouse Esq., with remainder to his eldest son Samuel Smith & his heirs male, next to Richard Smith, second son of said brother John, then to the right heirs of the body of the said John Smith.

I give and bequeath to William Hawthorne, son of Anne Hawthorne, my sister, the reversion of one pightle called Leachrye or Tan-house Pightle, containing by estimation three acres, in the possession of John Vincent. One third part of land called Welshman's (after my wife's decease) to my loving sister Mary Holloway and the heirs of her body, one third to my loving sister Rachel Horton & the heirs of her body, the remaining third to the children of John Topping begot upon the body of my sister Prudence and their heirs. To my wife the lease or leases of the two houses in Chancery Lane, &c. To my loving friend Mr Robert Hawe of Wokeingham twenty shillings to buy him a ring. To M^r —— Sedgwick, without Temple Bar, ten shillings to buy him a ring. To the poor of the town of Wokeingham twenty shillings. To the poor of the parish of Wokeingham and dwelling in the said town twenty shillings. Lands, &c. in Wokeingham in the County of Berks. Brother John Smith to be executor & Richard Palmer of Wokeingham Esq. to be overseer.

Wit: L. Astry, George Chapman. Laud, 9.

[The Salem Hathornes, as well as the Hawthornes named above, were allied with a Smith family, the immigrants, William and John Hathorne (REG. xii. 295 ; Emmerton and Waters's Gleanings, pp. 52-5) having had a sister Anne who was the wife of Hugh Smith (REG. xxxix. 201-4).—EDITOR.]

HENRY SEWALL of the parish of St Michael in the city of Coventry, alderman, aged fourscore years or thereabouts, 1 Sept. 1624, proved the last of June 1628 by Margaret Sewall his relict and executrix. To my wife Margaret an annuity or yearly rent charge of eleven pounds, eight shillings, issuing out of certain lands in Ansley in the county of Warwick, granted to me & my heirs forever, and now in the tenure of Elizabeth Throckmorton widow, and all my lands, tenements and hereditaments, with the appurtenances, &c. in the city of Coventry & in Corley and Coundon in the County of Warwick and in Radford Coundon in Urchenfield & Stoke in the county of the city of Coventry. To Henry Sewall, my eldest son, all my lands, tenements and hereditaments, &c. &c. in the hamlet of Radford in the county of the city of Coventry and in Coundon in Urchenfield in the county of the city of Coventry and in Coudon in the County of Warwick, and all my lands, tenements & hereditaments, &c. in Dog

Lane in the said city, in the occupation of Richard Baldwyn, a messuage or tenement & one garden, with the appurtenances, in Much Park Street, in Coventry, in the tenure of Henry Critchlowe, draper, and all those messuages or tenements, &c. &c. in the said city in the several occupations of John Harbert, William Heyward, Richard Heyes or Walter Wiggens, and all those three tenements in Little Park Street, in the occupation of Mr Henry Davenport, —— Thorton, Katherine West, or their assigns, after the decease of my wife Margaret, and during his natural life; then to the heirs of his body lawfully begotten, &c.; also to the said Henry, my son, a tenement & garden, &c. &c. in Heylane in the said city, in the tenure of Bryan Conigrave.

To Richard Sewall, my younger son, after the decease of my wife Margaret, lands & tenements, &c. in Corley, in the county of Warwick, which I lately purchased of Stephen Hales Esq. with the wyndell thereupon now standing, and other lands, &c. purchased of Richard Patchett, of Martin Whadocke & of Thomas Nicklyn and of Thomas Barre; also to the same Richard one messuage, &c. in Smithford Street, Coventry, in the tenure of Jefford, barber, and a tenement & certain stables called the Sextree in Coventry.

To my daughter Anne, now the wife of Anthonie Power, my messuage & tenement, &c. &c. in Corley, now in the occupation of me the said Henry, which I lately purchased of Daniel Oxenbridge, and other lands, &c. purchased of Thomas Patchet & of George & Walter Holbech, and two tenements in Bailie Lane in Coventry, one in the tenure of Theophilus Washington, and a messuage in High Street, Coventry, in the tenure of Mr William Hancock, and a messuage in the suburbs of Coventry in the tenure of John Lindon, and a messuage in the tenure of Roger Bird and a tenement in the tenure of Joyce Hobson, a widow and late in the occupation of Lawrence Armeson.

To Margaret, my youngest daughter, now the wife of Abraham Randell, tenements without Newgate in the several tenures of Francis Robinson & Edward Coles, lands, &c. purchased of John Horne of Stoke, gentleman, lands in the tenure of John Wilkinson, & of William, or Thomas, Pywall, that my messuage or tenement & garden in Bailie Lane, in the city of Coventry wherein I now dwell, tenements, &c. in Bailie Lane in the occupation of Roger Dudley, James Knib, William Miller, Edward Malpas, Johane Newland, widow, William Cumberledge & Edward Bissaker, a tenement in Earl Street in the occupation of John Wright, a garden in the occupation of Mr Richard Clarke, a tenement I purchased of John Hammond, Doctor in Physick and tenements in Darbie lane in the occupation of the widow Wothon & the widow Kinsman. Reference also made to tenements in the occupation of Richard Faulkner, Raphe Mellowes, Peter Baxter, Henry Wetton, Randall Cleaver, Clerk, Thomas Hobson and John Hill. To my loving friend Humphry Burton forty shillings, &c. &c. Wife Margaret to be executrix and friends Mr William Hancock, of Coventry, alderman, and my loving kinsman Reginald Horne, gentleman, to be overseers. To my cousin John Horne a cloke cloth.

Wit: John Brownell, James Brownell. Barrington, 63.

[The eldest son of the testator of the above will, Mr. Henry Sewall, came over to New England and was the ancestor of the distinguished family of that name in Massachusetts. In Essex County Court Papers (Book xxvi. No. 59) may be found a deposition made 10 April, 1679, by Robert Walker, of Boston, Linen webster, aged about seventy-two years, in which he testified that about fifty-six years before, living with his father in the town of Manchester, in Lancashire, within the realm of England, he did then know one Mr. Henry Sewall who lived at the same town and in the same street with the deponent's father, being his overthwart neighbor, and that afterwards the said Mr. Henry Sewall removed with his family to New England, and there dwelt in the town of Newbury, &c. &c.   H. F. WATERS.

This will furnishes another example of the wisdom of the course pursued by the associated collection and publication of material of this kind. In the introduction to the Sewall Papers, now in course of publication by the Mass. Historical Society, after stating the investigations made by Col. Chester, the main results of whose search was placed in their hands, the editors state that the Sewall family cannot be traced beyond the two brothers (Henry, whose will is here given, and his brother William, both of whom had been mayors of Coventry in England). It is to be supposed that neither the editors nor Col. Chester had the detail which Mr. Waters furnishes your readers, for in the closing paragraphs of the will here given, the mention of his "loving kinsman Reginald Horne, gentleman," who was made an overseer of the will, and the bequest to his "cousin John Horne," furnish direct guides to obtain the name of the father of Henry and William Sewall. It appears from the pedigree of the Horne family, which is given below from the Visitation of Warwickshire, 1619 (see Harleian Soc. Pub., vol. xii. p. 343),* that William Shewell married Matilda Horne, and that her brother John was the father of both Reginald and John, who are mentioned in this will of Henry Sewall respectively as his "kinsman" and "cousin."

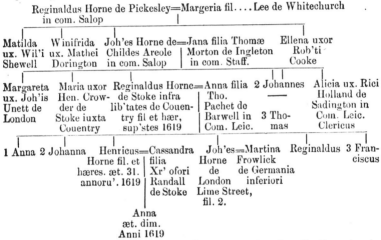

Reginaldus Horne de Pickesley=Margeria fil....Lee de Whitechurch
in com. Salop

Matilda ux. Wil'i Shewell | Winifrida ux. Mathei Dorington | Joh'es Horne de Childes Areole in com. Salop=Jana filia Thomæ Morton de Ingleton in com. Staff. | Ellena uxor Rob'ti Cooke

Margareta ux. Joh'is Unett de London | Maria uxor Hen. Crowder de Stoke iuxta Couentry | Reginaldus Horne de Stoke infra lib'tates de Couentry fil et hær, sup'stes 1619=Anna filia Tho. Pachet de Barwell in Com. Leic. | 2 Johannes ——— 3 Thomas | Alicia ux. Rici Holland de Sadington in Com. Leic. Clericus

1 Anna 2 Johanna | Henricus=Cassandra Horne fil. et | filia hæres. æt. 31. | Xr' ofori annoru'. 1619 | Randall de Stoke | Joh'es=Martina Horne Frowlick de de Germania London inferiori Lime Street, fil. 2. | Reginaldus 3 Franciscus

Anna
æt. dim.
Anni 1619

Judge Samuel Sewall was always sharp in money matters, from the time when he received the dowry upon his marriage with the mint-master's daughter until his death, and whether his visit to his relatives was one of affection of for mercenary motives, it is plain that if he could get an honest penny, he went for it. He evidently had a full copy of this will, and displayed this paragraph from it in his Diary, under date of April 9, 1689 :

" To the said Margaret during her natural Life and after her decease to the Heirs of her Body issuing, and for want of such issue of her body, to remain to the right heirs of me, the said Henry the Testator, for ever."

This extract is followed by a memorandum of the date of Margaret Randall's will, May 4, 1646. If this will could be found it might throw some light upon other relations.

The Judge saw some of the real estate which had been left to his grandfather's sister Margaret, *with the above proviso*, and she had given it to the descendants of her sister Anne, ignoring the rights of the descendants of Henry, her brother, the grandfather of the judge. He told them who he was, and offered to confirm the right (for a consideration?), and he received the emphatic answer that his relatives would not give him 3d. for it.   JOHN COFFIN JONES BROWN.]

---

* Was John Horne (otherwise Orne), of Salem, descended from this Warwickshire family ?

NOELL MEW being intended by God's permission to go to old England, 3 August, 1691, proved 4 April, 1700. To my wife Mary Mew, during her widowhood, all my estate, real and personal. But if she sees cause to marry, then she is to have out of my estate in England one hundred and ten pounds sterling in lieu of her dowry, in one year after her marriage, and all the household stuff. To my son Richard Mew all my farm Rockey Farm, &c., with the mulatta boy called George and fifty pounds sterling, he paying each of his sisters five pounds per annum to help bring them up till of age or married, and then to be acquitted of the said payment. To him also my great bible and silver tankard. To my daughter Mary Mew one hundred pounds sterling, &c., an Indian girl called Jenny, one Spanish silver cup, one round silver cup, one silver dram cup with a funnel. To my daughter Patience one hundred pounds sterling, the negro woman Bess, six silver spoons. All my land in West Jarsey to be sold and the proceeds to be equally divided betwixt my said three children. My wife to be executrix and my friends William Allen, Benjamin Newberry and Peleg Sanford to be overseers.

Wit: Richard Jones, Joseph Blydenburgh, Thomas Roberts, William Cload.

Testimony, 22 December, 1692, that the above is a true copy. John Easton Govr, John Greene Dep. Govr, Walter Clarke, Benjamin Newberry, William Allen, Christopher Almy. In the Probate the testator is called Noell Mew late of Newport in the Colony of Rhode Island and Providence plantations, in New England, deceased.   Noel, 59.

[Richard Mew, of Stepney, merchant, was one of the first twelve proprietors of East Jersey, 1681 (N. J. Archives, i. 366, 383 *et seq.*). Richard Mew, of Newport, R. I., merchant, had an action at law against Jahleel Brenton in 1708. (R. I. Colonial Records, iv. 39. See also iii. 555.)—EDITOR.]

NATHANIEL WEBB of Mountserrett, merchant ——, proved by Robert Webb, Esq., his son, 26 March, 1741. I grant full power and authority to my executors to make & execute a lease to my beloved wife Jane of all my negroes on and belonging to a certain plantation in the parish of St Anthony in the said Island, commonly called Carrolls Plantation, with the house & lands in town (and sundry movables) for her natural life, she paying to my executors in trust for my children the yearly sum of two hundred and fifty pounds sterling. This in full satisfaction of her dower, also the use of half my house in the town of Taunton one half of the furniture, &c. To my eldest son Robert my estate in the County of Somerset formerly under lease to John & Richard Barber of Taunton, and all my houses and lands in said Taunton or elsewhere in England, and five thousand pounds sterling, &c. To my son Nathaniel my plantations in Mountserratt now under lease to John Dyer of the said island, and all my houses & lands in the said island, and my house and land in the town of Bassterre in the island of St Christophers. Item I give & bequeath to my son John all my lands in the County of Connecticut in New England near the town of Seabrook, they containing about five hundred acres. To my brother John Webb of Abington one hundred pounds sterling, at the same time forgiving him what he owes me. To my brother Harry Webb fifty guineas to buy him a mourning ring. To my executors ten guineas each to buy them mourning rings. To my sisters Anne Stone & Sarah Smith twenty pounds sterling each to buy them mourning & mourning rings. The rest & residue to my five children, Robert, Ann, Ruth, Nathaniel & John.

I appoint William Gerrish, Esq., in London, Isaac Hobhouse of Bristol, merchant, John Paine of Taunton, mercer, Dominick Trant, Thomas Meade, George French and Peter Lee of this Island, Harry Webb of Antigua and my son Robert Webb executors & the guardians of my children.

Spurway, 78.

BENJAMIN PLUMMER of Portsmouth in the Province of New Hampshire in New England Esq. 7 May, 1740, proved 12 March, 1740. To my esteemed friend Mrs Mary Macphederis my gold watch, my negro boy named Juba and a ring of five guineas price. To Theodore Atkinson Esq. my saddle Horse and to him & his wife each of them a gold ring. To Mr John Loggin one suit of mourning apparel. The whole of my apparel to be sold for the most they will fetch in the town of Boston. To my honored mother one hundred pounds sterling. The residue to be equally divided amongst my brothers. My brother Mr Thomas Plummer of London, merchant & Theodore Atkinson of Portsmouth Esq. to be the executors.

Wit: Arthur Browne, James Jeffrey, Jos^h Peirce.

Proved at London by Thomas Plummer, power reserved for Theodore Atkinson the other executor.

Spurway, 73.

[I extract the following from a letter to me from Miss Plumer, of Epping, N. H., dated Nov. 1, 1885, in reply to an inquiry about Benjamin Plumer: "In a note at the end of my father's manuscript genealogy of the Plumer family, my father writes, 'Benjamin Plumer was appointed collector of Piscataway in New England. His commission, of which I have a copy in the handwriting of R. Waldron, Sec^ry, is dated Feb. 11, 1736. It was sworn to before Gov. Belcher, June 8th, 1736. He was perhaps the progenitor of the Portsmouth Plumers. There is a silver vase in the Atkinson family on which is inscribed the deaths of various persons, among the rest that of Benjamin Plumer, Esquire, who died May 8th, 1740, aged 24 years. If this was the collector he was but twenty when appointed.'"—*Com. by George Plumer Smith, Esq., of Philadelphia. Pa.*

In the New Hampshire Provincial Papers, vol. iv. p. 864, is a letter from John Thomlinson to Theodore Atkinson, dated "London, 5 April, 1737." Mr. Thomlinson writes: "Altho the Bearer Mr. Plummer his coming over Collector in your place may be some Disadvantage or Disappointment to you, yet when I tell you I dare say he will prove the most agreeable Gentleman that you could have had, in every respect, you will excuse my here recommending him to your friendship. .... He is a gentleman of good sense and of a very good family and good circumstances." I presume that Plumer was an Englishman.—EDITOR.]

Notes on Abstracts previously printed.

NATHANIEL PARKER (*ante*, vol. xxxvii. p. 376).

["My god-daughter the daughter of my nephew Bernard Saltingstall."

The pedigree of the Saltonstall family, given in Bond's Watertown, shows that Bernard Saltonstall was a great-grandson of Gilbert Saltonstall, from whom the New England family descended, through Sir Richard of Huntwicke. The Bernard Saltonstall referred to in the will was son of Sir Richard Saltonstall of North Ockenden, co. Essex. Susanna, sister of Bernard, married William Pawlett of Cottles in co. Wilts, who was a grandson of William Pawlett, first Marquis of Winchester. (See Dr. Marshall's Visitation of co. Wilts, 1623, p. 92.)

JOHN COFFIN JONES BROWN.]

RICHARD PERNE ; RACHEL PERNE (*ante*, vol. xxxviii. 311 and 429).

[It was noticed in Rachel Perne's will that she cut off Edward Rawson, our faithful Colonial Secretary, with the proverbial shilling, although she bequeathed to Rachel, his wife and her daughter, £40.

By a deed of his recorded in Suffolk Deeds, vol. iii. pp. 413 and 414, he acknowledges receipt of a marriage "portion of £300, which he long since Received with his wife." This accounts for the omission to bequeath any more of the Perne estate to him on its final distribution by will.

JOHN COFFIN JONES BROWN.]

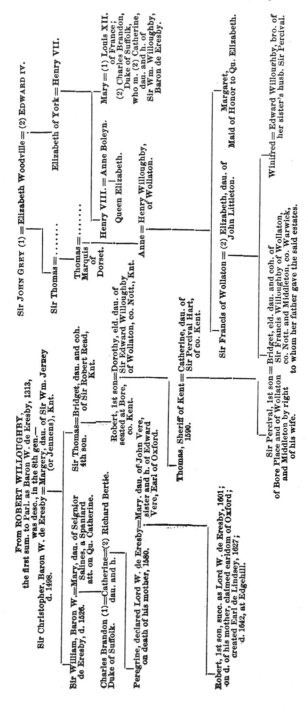

SUGGESTIONS AND INQUIRIES RESPECTING THE ANCESTRY OF COL. WILLIAM WILLOUGHBY,

FATHER OF DEPUTY GOVERNOR FRANCIS WILLOUGHBY OF MASSACHUSETTS.

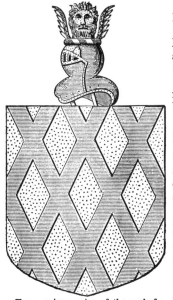

From an impression of the seal of Dep. Gov. Francis Willoughby.

AN elaborate account of Dep. Gov. Francis Willoughby and of his father, Col. William Willoughby, prepared by Mr. Isaac J. Greenwood of New York, appeared in "The N. E. Historical and Genealogical Register" for Jan. 1876.

From this and other sources of information the following particulars have been obtained.

In the "King's Pamphlets" (British Museum) it is stated that Col. William Willoughby was a native of Kent. In the Civil War, 1644, he was Colonel of a regiment of "the Hamlets of the Tower," and rendered active and successful service on the side of the Parliament. In 1648-9 he was appointed Master Attendant for Portsmouth and Commissioner of the Navy. Letters to and from him, in the "Calendar of State Papers," show that he was treated with much respect by the Government. After his death "The House referred to the Council of State to make payments to Col. Willoughby of his moneys, which, with great willingness and good affection, he laid out for defence of the river of Thames in the time of the insurrections of Kent and Essex, and of other moneys due to him from the State." He died in 1651, aged sixty-three years. He was therefore born about 1588.

I have photographs and a water-color drawing of his mural tablet in St. Thomas's church, Portsmouth. Above the inscription his arms are emblazoned: they are *Or fretty azure; crest: a lion's head couped at the shoulders, guardant Or, between two wings expanded,* mantled Gules, doubled Argent.* The helmet above the shield is that of the nobility—five gold bars slightly in profile, the helmet steel.

Mrs. Elizabeth Willoughby, widow of the Colonel, died about 1652.

His son Francis Willoughby came to New England in 1638, with his wife Mary. In 1651 he went back to England. In 1652 he was appointed to succeed his father as Commissioner of the Navy. In 1658 he was chosen Member of Parliament for Portsmouth. In 1662 he returned to

---

* These arms are the same (omitting quarterings and differences) as those ascribed by Burke in his "General Armory," ed. 1878, to Sir Francis Willoughby, born at Beauchamp Court, co. Warwick, knighted in Ireland in 1610. Sir Bernard Burke sent me a copy of the arms with description.

America, bringing with him a third wife, Margaret Locke, widow of Daniel Taylor, a wealthy merchant of London.* He became Deputy Governor of Massachusetts in 1665, and continued in office till his decease in 1671. He was one of the most influential friends of the colony, both in this country and in England. In Frothingham's "History of Charlestown" he says of Willoughby : " He is mentioned in warm terms of affection by his contemporaries. .... It is to such far-sighted men as Willoughby that New England owes its liberties." For his good services the Colonial Government voted to give him a thousand acres of land. A writer describes his funeral—" the doleful noise, the thundering volleys of shot, the loud roaring of great guns rending the heavens with noise at the loss of so great a man." " He left a large estate, of which £600 was in money and plate."

Dep. Governor Willoughby's arms, still existing on a seal upon a deed, are the same as those on his father's tablet, but drawn with more accuracy.

There have come down from the Dep. Governor several articles which still remain in the family, pieces of silver, a diamond ring, a gold snuff-box, etc. A letter written in 1864 by the wife of a descendant,† formerly American Consul in Italy, describes one of the family relics thus : " It is a tablecloth composed of fine linen, with two rows of exquisite needlework across it, said to have been wrought by Queen Elizabeth when she was confined in the Tower, in her sister Mary's reign, and given by her to Francis Lord Willoughby, who was a relative, and thus handed down." I have since learned that there is a private mark embroidered upon one end, with the initials F. M. W. at the other. A letter of about the same time from an old lady in Windham, Connecticut, a descendant, gives the tradition that the tablecloth wrought by Queen Elizabeth in the Tower was given to a Maid of Honor of hers, who was one of the Willoughbys, by whom it came down in the family. We suppose the statements need to be united to make a complete whole. The story has descended with the tablecloth, and is probably as old.

There is also a very large, massive, richly carved chest, owned by the late Mr. Theodore Raymond of Norwich, Conn., in which the tablecloth and other articles are said to have been brought from England. The carvings inside of the lid represent two scenes : one of Sir Walter Raleigh spreading his cloak before Queen Elizabeth, the other of some gay party of pleasure—boats among little islands, with a turreted castle in the background. The drawings are very quaint. Between the scenes is a coat of arms, of which the shield has either a cross or lines to make four quarterings on what is now a plain field (perhaps originally painted), and the supporters are a lion without a crown and a unicorn without a chain, in the attitude of the same animals on the royal arms of England, but with the dexter and sinister reversed. The shield is surmounted by a ducal coronet, and has apparently the rose of England in the mantlings.

The first Mrs. George B. Loring, of Salem, Massachusetts, a descendant, through another line, from Dep. Gov. Willoughby, wrote several years ago as follows : " I have heard my aunt, who lived to be ninety-two, speak of her remembrance of articles of value said to have come down from noble Willoughby relatives in England."

These are the facts, traditions and relics which have come down to the

---

* Her descent from the heraldic families of Locke and Cole is given in " The N. E. Hist. and Gen. Register " for January, 1881.
† Dr. Baker, of Norwalk, Ohio.

American descendants of Col. William and Dep. Gov. Francis Willoughby. In seeking for the ancestry of these gentlemen we naturally go to Kent; and we find that the Willoughbys of Beauchamp Court, co. Warwick, from whom came the Sir Francis Willoughby knighted in Ireland in 1610, whose arms were similar, as I have said, to those our Willoughbys bore, were from the same ancestry as the Kent family—descendants of the Willoughby de Eresby and the Wollaton Willoughby families. Searching in the Kent family, before the time of Col. William, we find two marriages between these two families—two sons of Thomas Willoughby,* the Sheriff of Kent in 1590, of the de Eresby family, having married two daughters of Sir Francis Willoughby of Wollaton ; as Sir Percival Willoughby of Bore Place, co. Kent, married Bridget Willoughby, eldest daughter of Sir Francis, while his brother Edward married her sister Winifred.†

Now I find that Margaret Willoughby, sister of this Sir Francis of Wollaton, was assigned, in 1555, to the household of the Princess Elizabeth at Hatfield, with whom she remained till her marriage, in 1558, to Sir Matthew Arundel. The Princess was a great-granddaughter, and Margaret Willoughby a great-great-granddaughter, of Elizabeth Woodville. Chambers's " Cyclopædia " states that Princess Elizabeth was sent to the Tower in 1554, and remained there some months, for some time was kept a prisoner at Woodstock, during the remainder of Mary's reign (till 1558), and, " though occasionally at Court, resided chiefly at Hatfield House, where *she occupied herself with feminine amusements* and the study of classical literature." Though Miss Margaret Willoughby was not assigned as Maid of Honor to the Princess until some months after she had left the Tower, yet, being her second cousin once removed, she may easily be imagined to have been near the Princess's person before her official appointment. She shared her captivity elsewhere, during the three years or more she was in her service before her marriage.

The coincidences will be noticed between the American family-traditions and the facts of English history. All will unite to make a complete whole, if a place can be found for Col. William Willoughby, either in the family of Bridget who married Sir Percival Willoughby, or in that of her sister Winifred who married his brother Edward. Both ladies were daughters of the Sir Francis whose sister Margaret was Maid of Honor to the Princess. Margaret might well be supposed to have given to her brother any articles received from the Princess ; and they would have been most carefully handed down in the family of one of his daughters. In regard to dates, Sir Percival Willoughby was knighted in 1603 (fifteen years after the birth of Col. Willoughby), and died in 1642. In point of time he could have been his father. In the pedigrees I have seen the names of five sons of Sir Percival and Bridget are given; among whom William does not appear. No children of Edward and Winifred Willoughby are named in those pedigrees ; perhaps Col. William was *their* son. If he could be placed in either of these families, his family-traditions would be verified.

One version of the family-tradition respecting the tablecloth embroidered by the Princess Elizabeth speaks of it as having been given to Francis Lord Willoughby, who was a relative ; the other says it was given to a Maid of Honor of hers, a member of the Willoughby family. History tells us

---

* It is stated in Hasted's Kent, vol. 3, p. 220, that this Thomas Willoughby bore for his arms *Or fretty Az.*
† " Visitation of County Nottingham for 1569 and 1614," pp. 149, 185.

that Margaret Willoughby, sister of Sir Francis and second cousin once removed of Princess Elizabeth, was her companion during most of her captivity ; and she may have been, perhaps, actually in the Tower with her. William was a frequent early name in the Willoughby family ; the name of Francis was constantly repeated. The fact that Col. William Willoughby fought on the Cromwellian side may have separated him from his father's family, and caused his name to be dropped from their pedigrees.

I add a few suggestions in regard to the arms above referred to, aided by facts furnished me in recent letters from my valuable correspondent Mr. Isaac J. Greenwood of New York, which seem to tend to confirm the relationship of which I have inferred the existence between Col. William Willoughby and the Willoughby de Eresby family.

The arms of the early Willoughbys de Eresby were undoubtedly *Or fretty Azure.* These were borne by Robert de Willugby, afterwards Lord Willoughby de Eresby, at the siege of Caerlaverock in Dec. 1299, where he attended King Edward I. The earliest crest mentioned in the collections of Glover, the Somerset Herald temp. Elizabeth, who drew up an account of the Willoughby family, is a *bat or demi-bat volant, the wings fretty.* This crest was used on the monument of Peregrine Bertie Lord Willoughby de Eresby, son of Catherine Willoughby, Duchess of Suffolk, and Lord Richard Bertie, who took his mother's name, as well as her title, and signed himself " P. Willugby." It is described as *" a bat displayed, mantled gules, doubled argent."* The bat is also found among the armorial bearings on the monument of his father and mother.

From a manuscript in the library at Canterbury we have the arms of Peregrine Bertie Lord Willoughby as borne in 1590, the crest a full, round, fierce head, as though of a lion, but the wings on either side are those of a bat and fretty. This crest, with a distinct *lion's face and a bat's wings Or fretty Azure* is engraved in Edmondson's " Baronagium Genealogicum," vol. i. p. 54, as that carried by Robert Bertie, the son of Peregrine Bertie or " Willugby," Lord Willoughby de Eresby, who succeeded his father as Lord Willoughby de Eresby in 1601, and was created Earl of Lindsey in 1627. By consulting the pedigree prefixed to this paper, it will be seen that he descended from Sir Christopher Willoughby, who was also the ancestor of that branch of the Willoughby de Eresby family which intermarried with the Wollaton Willoughbys, and to which belonged Sir Percival, who married Bridget, and whose brother Edward married Winifred, both daughters of Sir Francis Willoughby of Wollaton, and nieces of Margaret Willoughby, Maid of Honor to Princess Elizabeth.

It will be seen that the bat's *face* of the early Willoughbys had been changed to that of a lion, while the bat's wings had been retained.

This early crest seems to have been dropped by many branches of the Willoughby family who still bore the shield *Or fretty Azure.* Their crest was generally a man's bust ducally crowned. Previous to the edition of Burke's " General Armory," published in 1878, the crest *a lion's head guard. couped at the shoulders Or, between two wings expanded Or fretty Azure,* did not appear as a Willoughby crest ; but in that edition Sir Bernard Burke gives this as the crest of Sir Francis Willoughby knighted in Ireland in 1610. In a private letter to me, Sir Bernard says that this Sir Francis was from Beauchamp Court, co. Warwick. The quarterings of his arms, as well as his place of residence, show that he was of the same descent as the Willoughbys of Kent. The pedigree prefixed to this paper shows that Robert Bertie Lord Willoughby and Earl of Lindsey, was third cousin of Sir Percival Willoughby of Bore Place, co. Kent.

It is evident that, the bat's head having fallen into disuse, no care was taken to retain the exact form of bat's wings. Sir Francis Willoughby, knighted in Ireland in 1610, used the crest *a lion's head guardant couped at the shoulders Or, between two wings expanded Or fretty Azure,* the *kind* of wings not described.

On Col. William Willoughby's tablet the wings on each side of the lion's head are irregular and indistinct in their outline, and may have been those of a bat outspread, but the drawing is bad, and I have copied instead the more clearly defined, though small, design upon Dep. Gov. Francis Willoughby's seal. By reference to the description of the mural tablet it will be noticed that Col. William has not only the *lion's head Or between two wings expanded,* but even the mantlings "gules, doubled argent," described as on the monument of Peregrine Bertie Lord Willoughby.

There is however one discrepancy. On the tablet the lion's wings are painted *Gules.* But any one who in these days has had dealings with heraldic draughtsmen, knows the difficulty of securing accuracy even *now,* and can easily understand how mistakes might have been made, nearly two hundred and fifty years ago, by the original draughtsman, or by some later restorer, in painting the wings *Gules* when the mantlings which surrounded them were of that color.

Putting together all the facts and correspondences, I have not hesitated to believe that Col. William Willoughby's entire crest is the same as that used in the other instances mentioned, and that his full arms should be given as : *Or fretty Azure ;* crest : *a lion's head guardant couped at the shoulders Or, between two wings expanded Or fretty Azure, mantled Gules, doubled Argent.*

Therefore, when we find that there was used on the mural tablet of Col. William Willoughby of Portsmouth, and on the seal of his son Dep. Gov. Francis in America, the same coat-armor which was borne by Sir Francis Willoughby knighted in 1610, of the Warwickshire branch of the Kent family, and the same crest which was borne by the early Willoughbys de Eresby, and by the Bertie branch of this family, may we not believe that they had a right to it by descent? They both held high official positions, had the confidence of the Governments they served, and the respect of the people. They were both too long well known in public life to have ventured to assume arms without a title to them, and so to claim a lineage to which they had no right. Even if, after the great lapse of time, we cannot find a record of the birth of Col. William Willoughby in the pedigrees of the Willoughbys of Kent, may we not, *should no proof to the contrary be found,* trust the evidence of his arms and the coincidences between his family-traditions and the facts of history, and feel justified in believing him to have belonged to that family?

But it is with the hope of obtaining fuller knowledge that this paper is printed.

Information is also desired in regard to the family of the wife of Col. William Willoughby. I only know that her name was Elizabeth, and that she survived her husband. Her Will was witnessed in London, May, 1662, by Hen: Paman, John Parker (name of Parker doubtful), and Charles Towne. It was recorded in Boston, "2. 2. 1663." A seal attached to her signature bears a *chevron engrailed between three boars' heads.* It may or may not have belonged to her. She makes her "much respected and singular good friends Robert Thompson and John Taylor," both of London, the overseers of her Will.

She gives most of her property to her son Dep. Gov. Francis Willoughby, but leaves legacies to her sister Mrs. Anna Griffin of Portsmouth, wife of William Griffin, to her sister Jane Hammond of Virginia, and Mrs. Hammond's son Laurance Hammond.　Margaret, widow of Dep. Gov. Willoughby, married this Hammond for her third husband.　In Mr. Henry Fitz Gilbert Waters's Genealogical Gleanings, published in "The New England Historical and Genealogical Register" for April, 1885, he mentions Rebecca Saintbury of St. Olave, Southwark, co. Surrey, widow, as making in her Will, dated 30 November, 1677, a bequest to her niece Elizabeth Griffin in Virginia.　Among early grants of land in Virginia is one of 1662, Dec. 9, to William Griffin.　This is about the time when Dep. Gov. Willoughby proved his mother's Will.　This Elizabeth Griffin may have been her niece and namesake.　The Griffins may have gone to Virginia to join their relatives the Hammonds, who were there before this time.　Can the family-name of Mrs. Elizabeth Willoughby be ascertained ?

Any reader of this paper who can assist in tracing the ancestry of Col. William Willoughby, or that of his wife Elizabeth, or throw any light on any single point here presented, is requested kindly to communicate with me.　　　　　　　　Address :

Mrs. EDWARD ELBRIDGE SALISBURY,
June, 1885.　　　New Haven, Connecticut, United States of America.

PARTIAL COPY OF RECORDS OF THE TOWN OF WINCHESTER, N. H.

Communicated by JOHN L. ALEXANDER, M.D., of Belmont, Mass.

Continued from vol. xxxix. page 348.

*Births.**

Children of Caleb & Harriet (Locke) Alexander
　Gardner b Nov 1st 1794　Harriet b Apr 27th 1797　Louisa b Sept 7th 1799　Emily b Oct 11th 1800　Timothy b Feb 26th 1803

Children of Calvin & Rhoda Chamberlain
　Amos b Apr 14th 1794　Calvin b Oct 7th 1795　Melonia b Mar 24th 1798

Children of Joshua & Naomi Cook
　Zadoc b Mar 11th 1794　Clarissa b Jany 23d 1796　Chloe b Mar 23d 1798　Naomi b Decr 24th 1801　Hulda b Nov 5th 1804　Everson b Decr 7th 1807　Abel Hammond b Mar 20th 1810

Children of John & Susannah Knapp
　Lamson b Aug 13th 1794　Elijah Alexander b June 19th 1795　John b Mar 13th 1797

Children of Ezra & Caroline (Goldsbury) Parker
　John Goldsbury b May 14th 1794　Ezra Aldis b May 14th 1795　Sally b Dec — 1796　Gardner Gilman b July 21st 1798　Reuben Alexander b Mar 2d 1800　Abagail b May 9th 1804　Caroline b Decr 14th 1805　Mary Ann b Apr 21st 1807　Maria Ann Lany b Nov 21st 1809

Children of Samuel & Sophia Hill
　Eliot Ashley b Decr 6th 1795　Silas b Decr 8th 1796　Royal b Aug 20th 1798　Daniel　　Sophia　　Harry

* The heading of these records, vol. xxxix. p. 346, should be *Births* instead of *Baptisms.*

Children of Elisha & Charlotte Smith
  Horatio b Nov 3ᵈ 1795   Mary & Martha b Feb 3ᵈ 1798
Child of Daniel & Eusebia Twitchell
  Henry b Sept 14ᵗʰ 1795
Children of Elisha & Hannah Knapp
  Melinda b July 22ᵈ 1787   Clark b Apr 18ᵗʰ 1789 in Richmond N H
  Clarissa b —— 1795   Sophia b Mar 15ᵗʰ 1797   Harry b Jany 11ᵗʰ
  1799   Ora H b Jany 1ˢᵗ 1804 in Winchester by 2ᵈ wife Lucretia Al-
  exander
Children of Charles & Polly Mansfield
  Hannah Punderson (Henderson?) b May 11ᵗʰ 1795   Betsey b Oct 11ᵗʰ
  1796   Rella (Rolla?) b Apr 25ᵗʰ 1799   Charles ——
Child of Joseph & Martha Miles
  Joseph b Sept 19ᵗʰ 1795
Child of Pearley & Rhoda Hutchins
  Pearley b Oct 17ᵗʰ 1795
Children of Jesse & Olive Guernsey
  Abner b Oct 24ᵗʰ 1796   Eunice b Nov 12ᵗʰ 1798
Children of Henry & Rebeckah Pratt
  Mariah b Jany 6ᵗʰ 1796   Henry b July 6ᵗʰ 1797   Marshall b Sept 25ᵗʰ
  1799   Adison b Feb 21ˢᵗ 1802   Sophronia   Eliza   Charlotte
  Horace   Julius
Child of Levi & Elizabeth Ripley
  Mariah b Oct 11ᵗʰ 1796
Children of Noadiah & Polina Kellog
  Loisa b Nov 27ᵗʰ 1796   Mary How b Apr 11ᵗʰ 1798   Josiah b Decr
  15ᵗʰ 1799
Children of William & Keziah Ripley
  Samuel b Aug 15ᵗʰ 1796   William b June 11ᵗʰ 1797   Francis b Jan
  25ᵗʰ 1799   Elizabeth b Mar 28ᵗʰ 1802   Keziah b May — 1804   Jo-
  seph b
Children of Ephraim & Sarah Watkins
  Truman b May 6ᵗʰ 1796   Walter b Feb 10ᵗʰ 1799   Philany b Aug 3ᵈ
  1803
Child of Moses & Lucretia Cadwell
  George Washington b Decr 28ᵗʰ 1797
Children of Ephraim and Grata Hawkins
  Parmelia b Apr 3ᵈ 1797   Daniel b Aug 13ᵗʰ 1799   Pamelia b Aug 13ᵗʰ
  1802
Children of Asahel & Hepsibah Jewell
  Pliny b Sept 27ᵗʰ 1797   Hepsibah b Aug 15ᵗʰ 1799   Hepsibah b Oct
  2ᵈ 1802   Moses Chamberlain b Aug 8ᵗʰ 1804   Hepsibah Nurse b Nov.
  16ᵗʰ 1805   Asahel Leonard b Nov 16ᵗʰ 1810
Child of Luther & Olive Vary
  Olive b Feb 14ᵗʰ 1797
Child of Daniel & Sarah Burlingale
  Sally b May 29ᵗʰ 1798
Children of Gersham & Sally Brigham
  Alvin b Oct 21ˢᵗ 1798   Becca Merill b Feb 27ᵗʰ 1802
Children of Jesse & Rhoda Spaulding
  Salathiel b July 15ᵗʰ 1798   Elijah b Mar 12ᵗʰ 1800

Children of Amos & Mary Adams
   Joab F b Oct 17th 1699   Lita b Decr 13th 1801   Noah b June 2^d 1804
   Asal   Dennison
Children of John & Phebe Erskine
   Gilman b May 28th 1799   Pollina b Decr 25th 1801   George b Decr
   18th 1803
Child of Seth Hammond & Anna Morse
   John Gilman Morse illegitimate b Sept 6th 1799
Children of Porter & Hannah Wood   Samuel b Nov 24th 1801   Almena
   b Aug 31st 1805
Children of Loved & Abagail Haskins
   Nehemiah b Decr 14th 1800   Lowra (Laura?) b Mar 21st 1804
Child of Dr Joseph & Content Stowell
   Parmelia b Jany 22^d 1800
Child of Ebenezer & Lucy Copeland
   Orra b Decr 8th 1801
Child of Jesse & Mary Stowell
   Esther b Nov 13th 1802
Children of Asa & Abagail (Alexander) Alexander.
   Horace b Mar 5th 1803   Eunice b Decr 2^d 1804   John Locke b Decr
   21st 1806   Charles b Mar 8th 1810   Francis b Feb 8th 1812   Harriet
   Locke b Feb 16th 1814   Albert b Feb 13th 1817   Amos b Decr 5th 1819
   Sarah Ann b Feb 28th 1822   Henry b Mar 24th 1824   Esther Marion
   b July 1st 1827
Children of John & Abagail Bogle
   Eliza b Decr 4th 1803   John b Aug 11th 1805   Loiza b Feb 15th 1807
   Nathan Bent b Feb 25th 1809   Mary b Decr 18th 1810
Child of Shubal & Prudence Robinson
   Hannah b May 22^d 1803
Children of Samuel & Polly Goss   Polly b Mar 29th 1803   Edward b
   Decr 9th 1805   Willard Conant b Oct 19th 1807   Leonard b Sept 21st
   1811
Child of John & Christian Taylor
   Windsor b June 25th 1803
Children of Walter & Martha Follett
   Mary b Mar 26th 1806   Dexter b Sept 3^d 1808
Children of Samuel Pickering
   Ferdinand b Mar 22^d 1809   Loring b —— 31st 1812   Alcander b
   Elvira   Samuel
Child of Tertius and Hannah Lyman
   Tertius Alexander b Mar 13th 1812

THE WISWALL FAMILY OF AMERICA.

Four Generations.

By the Rev. Anson Titus, Amesbury, Mass.

ELDER JOHN WISWALL, of Boston, whom Savage says was a
brother of Thomas Wiswall, of Dorchester, married a daughter of
Thomas Smith, of London; probably had a second wife. His children
were: *John; Hannah,* married, 1st Mahahaleel Munnings, 2d William Read,

and 3d Thomas Overman. She died in 1694. *Deborah ; Mary*, married Emands ; *Esther*, married Daniel Fisher; *Martha*, married John Cutter, of Charlestown ; *Lydia*, married —— Ballard; *Ruth*, married Henry Mountfort, their son Ebenezer, H. C. 1702 ; *Rebecca*, married Matthew Johnson. Other children died young. The following is the inscription upon his gravestone: " Here lyeth buried ye body of John Wiswall, seruant of Jesus Christ, Elder of the First Church in Boston, aged 86 years. Departed this life the 17ᵗʰ day of Augᵗ Anno Dom. 1687." John Wiswall, 2d, married 1st, Mellicent ——; married 2d, Hannah ——, and had John, born March 21, 1667, who was " a young man with somewhat original objurgatory tendencies."* John, 2d, was a mariner, and died about 1700, leaving widow Mary who married a White. John Wiswall, 2d, is mentioned as " a well-known and wealthy citizen." First Report of Record Commissioners, page 40. None of the Wiswall name of to-day are of this line.

1. THOMAS¹ WISWALL, said by Savage to have been a brother of the foregoing John. He resided in Dorchester, Cambridge, Newton; was born in England ; came to New England in 1635; married 1st, Elizabeth ——; married 2d, late in life, Isabelle, mother of Edward Farmer, Billerica, and widow of John. The second wife died in Billerica, May 21, 1686. He died December 6, 1683. He was an elder of the church, aad was a useful man in every department of church, official and social life. Children :

  2. i.   ENOCH, b. 1633.
    ii. ESTHER, bapt. 1635 ; m. May 16, 1655, William Johnson, Woburn ; had nine children.
  3. iii. ICHABOD, b. 1637.
  4. iv. NOAH, bapt. Dec. 30, 1638.
    v.   MARY, m. Samuel Payson. (So stated by Jackson and Savage.)
    vi. SARAH, bapt. March 19, 1653 ; m. Nathaniel Holmes.
    vii. EBENEZER, b. 1646 ; m. Mar. 26, 1685, Sarah Foster, widow of Elisha and daughter of Giles Payson. He died June 21, 1691. His widow died in 1714.
    viii. ELIZA, b. April 15, 1649.

    The Dorchester Church records contain the baptism of Benjamin Wiswall and Mary 16. 2 mo. 49. Savage places Benjamin among the children of Elder John Wiswall, but adds that Mr. Ebenezer Clapp, " after most patient investigation," thinks that he and another child named Henry " may have belonged " to Thomas.

2. ENOCH² WISWALL (*Thomas¹*) married Nov. 25, 1657, Elizabeth daughter of John Oliver, Boston, " the scholar." She died May 31, 1712, aged 75 years. He died Nov. 28, 1706, aged 73 years. *Vide* Oliver family, *ante*, REG. 1865, p. 100. Children :

  5. i.   JOHN, b. Dec. 10, 1658.
    ii. ENOCH, b. Jan. 10, 1661 : d. young.
    iii. HANNAH, b. April 6, 1662.
  6. iv. OLIVER, b. Jan. 25, 1664-5.
    v.   ELIZABETH, b. April 28, 1667; d. April 25, 1692.
    vi. ESTHER, b. Dec. 28, 1669 ; m. Silence Allen, Jan. 20, 1692.
    vii. SUSANNA, b. Aug. 2, 1672 ; m. Edward Breck, April 1, 1698. He d. in Dorchester, Sept. 3, 1713, aged 39 years.
    viii. ENOCH, b. April 6, 1675 ; d. Oct. 8, 1676,
    ix. MARY, b. Aug. 27, 1677 ; m. Samuel Robinson, March 13, 1706.
    x.   SAMUEL, b. Sept. 2, 1679; H. C. 1701 ; ordained over church at Edgartown ; unmarried ; d. Dec. 23, 1746.
    xi. ENOCH,   } twins, b. Feb. 25, 1682.
  7. xii. EBENEZER, }

---

* Vide Bay State Monthly, January, 1884, pp. 24-7, and February, 1884, p. 128.

3. ICHABOD[2] WISWALL (*Thomas[1]*) married 1st, Remember —— ; married 2d, Priscilla Peabody, Dec. 24, 1697, daughter of William[2] (John[1]) and Elizabeth (Alden) Peabody. Priscilla was named for her grandmother Priscilla (Mullens) Alden, wife of John. Ichabod entered Harvard College, but did not graduate. He was ordained pastor of church in Duxbury, and died there July 23, 1700. His wife Priscilla died in Kingston, June 3, 1724, a. 71 years. Children :

   i.   ELIZABETH, b. Nov. 6, 1670 (by first wife) ; m. Elisha Wadsworth, Duxbury ; d. Jan. 25, 1741.
   ii. MERCY, b. Oct. 4, 1680 ; m. Dea. John Wadsworth, June 25, 1704 ; d. Nov. 12, 1716.
  iii. HANNAH, b. Feb. 22, 1682 ; m. Rev. John Robinson, her father's successor in the Duxbury pastorate. *Vide* REG. vol. viii. p. 173.
8. iv. PELEG, b. Feb. 5, 1683.
   v. PEREZ, b. Nov. 22, 1686. Not mentioned in father's will, 1700.
  vi. PRISCILLA, b. Dec. 21, 1691 ; m. Oct. 23, 1716, Gershom Bradford. *Vide* REG. vol. iv. p. 50.
 vii. DEBORAH, m. Samuel Seabury, Oct. 17, 1717 ; d. in 1776, aged 84.

4. NOAH[2] WISWALL (*Thomas[1]*) married Theodocia, daughter of Deacon John Jackson, Dec. 10, 1664. Resided in Newton. He died July 6, 1690. His widow afterwards married Dea. Samuel Newman, Rehoboth, as his third wife. Children :

9. i. THOMAS, b. April 29, 1666.
   ii. ELIZABETH, b. Sept. 30, 1668 ; m. Rev. Thomas Greenwood, H. C. 1690, Rehoboth, Dec. 28, 1693. He died Sept. 8, 1720. She died in Weymouth, Jan. 24, 1735. Had several children, among whom John (H. C. 1717), who succeeded his father in pastoral office.
  iii. CALEB.
  iv. MARGARET, b. March 1, 1672 ; m. Nathaniel Parker ; d. July 30, 1736.
   v. HANNAH, b. April 1, 1674 ; m. Caleb Stedman, Roxbury, 1697.
  vi. MARY, m. Nathaniel Longley.
 vii. ESTHER, b. April 1, 1678.
viii. SARAH, b. Jan. 5, 1681 ; m. 1702, Joseph Cheney, Newbury.

5. JOHN[3] WISWALL (*Enoch,[2] Thomas[1]*) married Hannah, daughter of Richard Baker, May 5, 1685. She died Sept. 18, 1690, aged 28 years. He married, 2d, Mary ——. Resided in Dorchester. Children :

   i.   ENOCH, b. Jan. 7, 1685.
   ii. JOHN, b. Nov. 15, 1688 ; m. 1st, Sarah Pierce, June 25, 1719. She died Dec. 31, 1747, and he m. 2d, Elizabeth, widow of John Capen, Nov. 1750. She died May 12, 1790, in her 87th year, and he died Sept. 12, 1774. Had eleven children by first wife—Hannah, Abigail, Ann, James, Esther, Lois, John, Sarah, Rachel, Lucy and Francis.

6. OLIVER[3] WISWALL (*Enoch,[2] Thomas[1]*) married Sarah, daughter of John Baker, Jan. 1, 1690. She died April 29, 1755, in her 87th year. He died March 14, 1746. Resided in Dorchester. Children :

   i.   THOMAS, b. Aug. 9, 1692 ; m. Elizabeth Jones, Oct. 17, 1717. She died July 22, 1748. He died Nov. 21, 1752. Children : *Sarah, Thomas, Mary* and *Elizabeth.*
   ii. HANNAH, b. Jan. 18, 1694-5 ; m. Edward White, Brookline, Jan. 22, 1718-19.
  iii. ENOCH, b. March 19, 1697 ; m. Susanna Cocks, Nov. 30, 1722. She died July 15, 1772, and he died Feb. 6, 1784.
  iv. EBENEZER, b. March 3, 1699.
   v. OLIVER, b. June 2, 1702 ; m. Mary Minot, March 18, 1730. She died Jan. 2, 1795, in her 90th year, and he died Feb. 13, 1791.
  vi. ICHABOD, b. Sept. 14, 1704.
10. vii. SAMUEL, b. April 13, 1707.
viii. JOHN, b. Jan. 6, 1712.

7. EBENEZER[3] WISWALL (*Enoch,[2] Thomas[1]*) married Anna Capen, of Dorchester, Nov. 30, 1721. Children :

  i.   EBENEZER, b. June 10, 1722.
  ii.   MARY, b. April 7, 1724.
  iii. OLIVER, b. Nov. 24, 1725.
  iv. NOAH, b. Nov. 25, 1727. Settled in Westminster and died there, 1801.
  v.   DANIEL, b. Nov. 26, 1729.
  vi. JOB, b. Sept. 10, 1731; d. Nov. 6, 1731.
  vii. ESTHER, b. Dec. 28, 1732.
  viii. SAMUEL, b. Oct. 3, 1734 ; m. Sarah Dyer, July 18, 1759, in Worcester.
  ix. ELIJAH, b. Dec. 22, 1738 ; d. Jan. 16, 1738-9.
  x.   ANN, b. Jan. 11, 1739-40 ; d. Feb. 10, 1739-40.
  xi. HANNAH, b. July 3, 1742 ; d. Sept. 16, 1742.
  xii. ICHABOD, b. Dec. 18, 1743.

8. PELEG[3] WISWALL (*Ichabod,[2] Thomas[1]*), H.C. 1705, married Elizabeth, daughter of Dr. Samuel Rogers, H. C. 1686, of Ipswich. Published in Ipswich, Nov. 21, 1719. She died Dec. 1, 1743, a. 47. The following is the inscription upon his tombstone in Copp's Hill, Boston : " Here Lyes buried the Body of Mr. Peleg Wiswall, late Master of the North Grammar School, died Sept. 2nd 1767, in the 84th year of his age." Mr. Wiswall became master of the Boston Grammar School early in the century. He was engaged for six months, in 1705, as per *Memorial* History, vol. ii., and invited to the North Grammar School in 1719. The Memorial History may be in error when it says that a son of the same name was given liberty for a writing school for this winter (1729) in the chamber of the Alms-house. Children :

  i.   ELIZABETH, b. Nov. 4, 1720.
  ii.   DANIEL, b. Feb. 13. 1722 ; m. Sarah Hall, April 12, 1753. She died Sept. 17, 1769, aged 33. Buried in Cambridge.
  iii. PRISCILLA, b. Dec. 17, 1725.
  iv. SARAH, bapt. in Old South Church, Boston, May 4, 1729.
  v.   JOHN, b. April 15, 1731 ; H. C. 1749; settled over parish Falmouth, 1756. In 1764 changed religious views and settled over Episcopal Church in Portland ; was a loyalist in the Revolution ; went to England in 1775, where he was a curate ; at close of Revolution he established himself at Cornwallis, Nova Scotia, where he died in 1812. He m. Mercy Minot, of Brunswick, daughter of Judge John Minot. Had family, among whom was son Peleg, Judge of the Supreme Court of Nova Scotia. Sabine's Loyalists, vol. ii. p. 448.

9. THOMAS[3] WISWALL (*Noah,[2] Thomas[1]*) resided in Newton on homestead of his father ; married Hannah Cheney, of Newbury, Dec. 17, 1696. He died 1709. His widow married Dea. David Newman, Rehoboth, June, 1719. Children :

  i.   HANNAH, b. Oct. 15, 1697.
  ii.   NOAH, b. Sept. 1699. Had a son John born 1753, who removed to Marlborough, N. H. *Vide* History of Marlborough, p. 700.
  iii. SARAH, b. March 4, 1701 ; m. John Newman, 1730.
  iv. MARY, b. Oct. 1, 1702.
  v.   ELIZABETH, b. Aug. 25, 1704 ; m. Nathaniel Longley, Jr.
  vi. THOMAS, b. 1707 ; m. Sarah Daniel, Needham, Dec. 20, 1733 ; settled in Medway, Mass.
  vii. ICHABOD, b. 1709 or 10; settled in Attleborough.

10. SAMUEL[4] WISWALL (*Oliver,[3] Enoch,[2] Thomas[1]*) married Elizabeth Franklin, Oct. 17, 1733, in Dorchester. Children :

i. ELIZABETH, b. Jan. 29, 1733-4.
ii. DAVID, b. Nov. 13, 1735.
iii. JONATHAN, b. Feb. 11, 1737-8. Settled in Holliston, where he died in 1808, leaving wife Mary, sons David, Oliver, and several daughters.
iv. MOSES, b. Dec. 15, 1740.
v. RUTH, b. Oct. 12, 1742; m. Joshua Sabin. (*Ante*, REG. vol. xxxvi. p. 57.)
vi. BENJAMIN, b. Aug. 29, 1745.
vii. LUCY, b. Dec. 29, 1749; m. Sylvanus Sabin, and from whom the compiler descended. (*Ante*, REG. vol. xxxvi. 1882, p. 57.)
viii. ——, b. Aug. 24, 1751.
ix. SARAH, b. Aug. 19, 1753.
x. SAMUEL, b. April 24, 1758.

NEW ENGLAND GLEANINGS.

[Continued from vol. xxxix. page 185.]

UNDER this head we print items furnishing clews to the English residences of the settlers of New England.

XI.

Registry of Deeds of Suffolk County— Vol. viii. *page 392.*—Philip Torrey aged fifty-nine years or thereabouts, heretofore of Combe St Nicholas in the county of Somersett within the Realme of England, there living until the yeare sixteen hundred and forty (yeoman) in that year removeing to New England, with William Torrey & Samuell his son both of the sd Comb St Nicholas with whome he lived for severall years & being arrived in New England settled and hath ever since lived in Roxbury in the county of Suffolk in New England aforesd, on his corporall oath deposed that hee well knew & was acquainted with the sd William Torrey the Father, and Samuell Torrey his sonn all the whiles hee lived in Comb St Nicholas aforesd in Old England & ever since he came to New England and to this day, beeing in their company on his oath affirms them to bee the same William Torrey & Samuel Torrey father & sonn abovesd, having several opertunities in each year to see and confer with them ever since, they being in good health this day being the fifth of March 1673-4.

(*Same paper as above.*) George Fry also of Combe St Nicholas deposes he came in 1640 in the same shipp with Wm Torrey & Sam'l Torrey his sonn—" and being arived in New England settled and ever since have lived in Weymouth."

Com. by John J. Loud, Esq., Weymouth, Mass.

[I send the following abstract from a copy of a will in my possession :

Will of John Hollister of the precincts of the Castle in the City of Bristol [Gloucestershire], cordwainer, being aged. Dated Sept. 12, 1690. To late wife's grand dau. Jone Webb ; late wife's grand son Brice Webb. The meeting house to which I usually go. Late wife's grand dau. Mary Mitten's [possibly Mibben's] two daus. Mary and Elizabeth. To my daughter Elizabeth, wife of William Taylor, a chest marked I. G. which was her mother's maiden chest. My cosen Hannah Conway wife of Mr. William Conway of Westport near Malmsbury, Wilts. My brother-in-law William Shipp of Saterby in Acton, Glouc., and his wife. My brother Shipp's two sons Daniel and John which he had by my sister. My cosen John Hollister, son of Abel Hollister late of Yeate in Glouc., dec'd. All the rest of my brothers' and my sisters' children, " excepting my cosen Samuel Alway " [query,

Conway] because as I judge he defrauded his sister Hannah Conway and her husband of a bond of £10." To my cosen Samuel Hollister of Burrington, Somerset, the management of the ground there in the parish of Huntspil, Somerset, called Catchams in the possession of Francis Seaker; " and also the Ground called Torreys (12 acres) wherein Capt. William Torrey and his son Mr. Samuel Torrey hath (*sic*) lease for their lives in it (*sic*), both lying (*sic*, query " living " ?) in New England," he to collect rents, &c., " till otherwise ordered by them in New England," and to discharge a legacy of £22-19-0 to Mr. Conway and his wife of Malmesbury, Wilts. " To 8 ministers, that is Mr. Thomas Barnes of Welles, Mr. Axell of Wootton, Mr. Barnes of James' schoolmaster, Mr. Winney, Mr. Dancey of Stabelton, Mr. Smith of Barton and Mr. Searle of Marshfield 20 s. each." To my cosen Axell of Wootton & Mr. Smith of Saford's Gate. " To 5 poor women viz w⁰ Noble in Temple street, w⁰ Peugh of the Alms house, w⁰ Hyes with out Salford's Gate, w⁰ Harris in Thomas street and Mrs. King behind St. Philips church yard." To Jane Parker. To my cosen Abel Hollister's six sons. To Mr. Thomas Scroope & Doctor Chauncy for charitable uses £2. yearly for seven years out of my house in the Castle. To my dau. in law Elizabeth Taylor's mother's grand children, Mary Mitten's [possibly Mibben's] children to have their mother's part. To my cosen Philip Hollister my house " in " the Castle ditch for life " if lease last so long," with remainder to my grandson Brice Webb. To my grand dau. Jone Webb my house " by " the Castle ditch. All the residue to my cosen Philip Hollister. Appoint him sole executor. My son in law William Taylor and friend Jonathan Allen to be overseers. *Proved* Dec. 5, 1699.—WILLIAM H. UPTON, of Walla Walla, W. T.]

XII.

John Boden aged 66 deposes at Salem Sept — 1730 that he well knew Arthur and Andrew Alger of Scarborough (REG. xxix. 270) and always understood from them that they called their place Dunstan after the place they came from in England.

Mass. Archives, xv. A. p. 11.—Elizabeth Scott, aged about 47, relict of the late Robert Scott, of Boston, deposes 4 Dec. 1663 that about 26 years ago she well knew one Robert Smith, said to be a wine cooper in London who came over with his wife to New England and brought with them his sister Mary Smith, and had sent over his sister Anne Smith the year before. That when Robert Smith and his wife went back to England, he left his two sisters behind—That Anne Smith about 25 years ago married John Kenrick then of Boston and had several children by him. That Mary Smith married Philip Torrey and has children and is still living in Boston.

[Peter Gardiner of Roxbury testifies that Mary Torrey's first husband John Scarborough was killed at Boston, shooting off one of the great guns.—H. E. W.

See Gleaning XI.—EDITOR.]

Id. viii. 92.—Joseph Cooper, of Birmingham, County Warwick, Kingdom of England, aged 75, and Thomas Guest, of said Birmingham aged 84, depose 7 Dec. 1700, that they knew old Anthony Pen a shoemaker in said Birmingham long since dead who had several children viz. Guy Pen, John Pen, William Pen, Athony Pen, and Elizabeth Pen, all which except yᵉ said William Pen these Deponents know to be dead, and say yᵗ above 50 years agoe yᵉ sd William Pen went into New England in America where he is said to be dead also. That said John Pen and Elizabeth Pen died without issue; that said Guy Pen died leaving but two children viz. Elizabeth and Mary, which said Elizabeth has been dead many years and yᵉ said Mary is now living and yᵉ wife of one James Ensor living in Deritend a vill next adjoining to said town of Birmingham, that said Anthony Pen the son left several children who are all dead without issue except his son Anthony a shoemaker whom they know and who is now living in health at Birmingham.

Id. xv. A. 269.—Alexander Stewart deposes 7 June 1764 that he was born and brought up at Belfast in Ireland and there lived until about 33 years of age, and then came over into this Province where I have lived about 30 years more.

Id. ix. 125.—Writ against Sir Robt. Robinson Knt late Lieut. Governor and Commander in Chief of Bermudas als Summer Islands at present resident in Boston—dated 12 July 1692.

Id. xv. A. 40.—3 Nov. 1749. Pierre Bellee and Julius Jacques Giraudet, two French surgeons petition for and receive permisson to settle in Massachusetts—and their permission to depart from Louisbourg is dated 20 Oct. 1749.

Id. xv. A. 59.—Mr. Joseph Crellius, a gentleman of Franconia and for divers years past a resident in the Colony of Pennsylvania.—Letter of 1 Aug. 1750.

Id. viii. 266.—Isaac Robardo and Samuel McKinnon both of St Christopher's now residing in Boston, depose 14 Sept. 1730, they were personally acquainted with Mr. George Eames of St Christopher's aforesaid, but now of said Boston.

Id. viii. 237.—30 Jany 1720. Lettuce Bedgood, wife of Capt. Edward Bedgood of Boston, mariner, deposes that about 6 years since she lived at a place called Ringwood in the County of Hampshire in Great Britain, she being born there and having always lived there till her marriage : that she knew and was well acquainted with Edward Baily of said town of Ringwood, clothier, who died about 14 years since, who had two sons named Richard Baily and Henry Baily which were the children living of said Edward when she left Ringwood : that she very well knows the said Henry Baily having on the day of the date hereof seen him in Boston—the said Henry being always reputed the lawful son of said Edward Baily deceased by Mary his wife who was living when this deponent left Ringwood.

Id. viii. 238.—Richard Baily of Dorchester in N. E. husbandman, deposes 30 Jan'y 1720 that he was the son of Edward Baily clothier and Mary his wife who was lately living—and was born in Ringwood in the County of Hampshire in Great Britain, and came over into this country about 4 years since. That he has a brother Henry Baily now living in New England—whom this Deponent saw on the day of the date hereof— and one sister named Frances, who with himself are all the children now living left by his said father and mother.

Id. viii. 238.—28 July 1718. Thomas Spencer, Master of the ship " Alexander " at the order of the Court gives bond in £25. to save the town of Boston harmless from charges for support of John Bellow an infirm passenger he brought with him in said ship.

York Reg. i. 19.—5 May 1636. Thomas Bradbury Agent for Sir Ferdinando Gorges conveys 500 acres on the Piscataqua River to Edward Johnson for the use of John Treworgy of Dartmouth.

[This Thomas Bradbury is supposed by the late John M. Bradbury, Esq., to have been a son of Wymond and Elizabeth (Whitgift) Bradbury of Wicken Bonant in Essex, baptized in that parish, Feb. 28, 1610–11; and he produces evidence that makes his conjecture extremely probable (REG. xxiii. 263-6). Elizabeth Whitgift, wife of Wymond Bradbury, was a niece of Archbishop John Whitgift (*Idem*, p. 262). Thomas Bradbury, the agent of Gorges, was in England, May 1, 1634, as he, with the noted Thomas Morton, witnessed a deed executed that day (REG. xxxii. pp. 52-4). A fac-simile of his autograph will be found on p. 54 of that volume, which may be compared with his autograph at a later period of his life, which is given in the REGISTER, xxiii. 263.—EDITOR.]

Id. i. 259; 9 May 1661.—Robert Fletton writing from " Haulborne hills Corner house going into Scroupe's Court against St. Andrews Church London " to " Mr [Sylvester?] Herbert a Taylor liveing at Pishchataqu[e] river 100 miles Eastward from Boston in New England " states—" your wife's mother in London whose name was Mis Ramsey, shee being now dead left mee her Executor & by her will . . . . £100 was to bee payd to you or your assigns by tenn pounds a yeare for the education of your daughter . . . . It was given to her as Liveing in the Barbados.

The bearer is my friend . . . . his name is Mr. Edmund Caverly."

Id. i. 91.—16 Oct. 1659. Pierre La Croix acknowledges himself indebted to Nicholas Shapleigh, of Kittery, in the sum of £40: 9s. to be paid in good " Muskavado Sugar " at the bridge Towne in Barbados.

Witnessed by Henery Barkecley, Antipas Mavericke, Jacope Tomker, Stephen Spencer.

Id. i. 89.—Certificate from the Registry of the Court of Probate at Westminster, that on the 8th day of September 1653, " letters of administration upon the estate of William Berkley late one of the Aldermen of the City of London, were granted to Henry Berkley the natural & Lawfull Sonne of the said deceased . . . . who desessed without anie will " . . . .

Id. i. 200. 1 Oct. 1660.—" Hen: Barklet " acting as Attorney for Capt. Walter Barefoot.

Com. by William M. Sargent, Esq., Portland, Me.

XIII.

Mass. Archives, xxxix. 554.—William Thompson aged about 28. May 26. 1677, lived with his uncle Mr John Cogswell of Ipswich 16 years, and when in Old England last Winter heard " my father " Dr. Samuel Thompson say that " my uncle " had a turkie work carpet there.

Id. xl. 193.—James Boaden in 1684 says he came from Ireland with John Jones on account of Mr Samuel " goukeing " of Cambridge " who transferred me to his brother Edmond Batter of Salem, who transferred me to his kinsman John Felps of Salem," &c.

Id. lix. 127.—Richard Hollingworth of Salem in 1673, says his father arrived about 40 years since with a family of twelve and a good estate and was the first builder of vessels.

Essex County Court Files, xxxv. 92.—Mary Wayte aged 40 years, June 25, 1681, testifies about Mr Farley coming over from England in 1675 and entering upon the fulling mills of Richard Saltonstall Esq at Ipswich.

Id. xliv. 28-33.—John Peach aged about 80 years says June 23, 1684, that John Bennett dec'd came with him into N. E. in the same ship in the year 1630, and his wife Margaret some years after, and they lived many years in Marblehead, where they had one daughter called Mary. No other child. John Devereux, aged about 70 and wife Ann about 62 say July 1, 1685, that Mary, dau. of John & Margaret Bennett dec'd was wife of Christopher Codner dec'd and afterwards m̄ Richard Downing & had many children, by Chris. Codner she had Joane who m̄ Joseph Bubier.

Id. xliv. 74.—John Codner deposed at Boston May 28, 1685 as witness to Letter of Attorney, executed at Sherburne, County Dorset, England by John Hudd, Mch 5, 1684, to Bartholomew Gedney of Salem.

Id. xlix. 143.—Margaret wife of John Searle of Marblehead in 1690, calls Richard Girdler a Jersey Rogue.

Id. liii. 11.—Marblehead inhabitants represent in 1667, that many came there from England New Foundland and elsewhere and some were undesirable.

Id. xxvi. 67.—Jeffrey Thissell of Abbotsbury, County Dorset, England, now of Marblehead, 1675.

Id. xviii. 82.—Elizabeth Barker of London, widow, only daughter and heiress of Hugh Peters sometime heretofore of Salem, N. E. deceased, Clerk, confirms to Robert Devereux of Marblehead, Tanner, the farm of 350 acres now in his occupation June 30, 1704.

[See REGISTER, xxxix. 373.—EDITOR.]

Id. xi. 132.—" The Testimony of John Devoreux of Marblehead aged about Eighty years,—Testifieth & Saith yᵗ about yᵉ yeare of Our Lord One thousand Six hundred & Thirty I came over from old England to New England & yᵉ place of my abode and residence has been at Salem & Marblehead Ever since & when I came hither here was an old Sqwah Called old Sqwaw Sachem yᵉ Sqwaw of yᵉ deced Sachem which had three reputed sons, viz: John James and George, whoe were yᵉ Reputed Sachems & Owners of all yᵉ Lands in these parts as Salem, Marblehead, Linn and as far as Mistick & in those dayes yᵉ Land where Salem Towne Now Stands & yᵉ Lands adjacent was Called Nahumkege by yᵉ Indians & English Then Inhabiting in these parts: Sworne, Marblehead, December yᵉ 24, 1694, before us   JOHN HATHORNE Just p̄c & Coram

BENJAMIN BROWNE ⎱
JOHN HIGGINSON   ⎰ Just. peaces."

Com. by Henry E. Waite, Esq., of West Newton, Mass.

RELATION CONCERNING THE ESTATE OF NEW-ENGLAND.—ABOUT 1634.

Communicated by HENRY FITZ-GILBERT WATERS, A.M., of London, England, with Introduction and Notes by Dr. CHARLES EDWARD BANKS.

THE subjoined document is properly to be accounted a part of the harvest of "Gleanings" made by Mr. Waters for the REGISTER, but is here treated separately on account of its length and importance. It was not first discovered by Mr. Waters, however, as a large portion of the same manuscript was copied for John Scribner Jenness, Esq., and printed by him in 1876 in his private edition of "Transcripts of Original Documents relating to New Hampshire," pp. 21–25. In that form the document was seen by but few persons to whom the limited private edition was available, and it is now believed that a complete collated reprint of the manuscript will attract the attention which it deserves, and secure for it a worthy place beside the similar Maverick MS. found by Mr. Waters and printed in the REGISTER (vol. xxxix. pp. 33–48).

It is certain that this document was considered an important collection of information at the time of its writing, as three contemporary copies have been found in the British Museum,—Sloane Collection, Nos. 2505, 3105, 3448,—by Mr. Waters,[1] as stated in his note at the end of the "Relation." It is possible that this importance might have arisen from the character of the writer, who may have been sent out officially by the Council for New England to gather material, or he may have been some well known traveller, for the authorship is anonymous. There are some few points in it, however, which help us to give it a date and possibly a habitation and a name. The writer refers to the plague which decimated the Indian tribes of New England, "wch happened," he says, "about 17 years since." This plague is by general consent assigned to the three years, including 1616–1618, and if we add the "17 years" above stated to the mean of the period occupied by the plague, we shall make 1634 the proximate date of this document.[2] The single reference the writer makes to his own personality is at the close of the manuscript where he describes himself as "noe professed Scholler," which for purposes of identification is exceedingly vague, and leaves us to infer simply that he was not a college graduate. However, he says, "my aboade was farre distant from neighbo^{rs} . . . myselfe and Colonie allwayes professinge the doctrine discipline of the Church of England." This seems to point, without much doubt, to the settlements at the mouth of the Piscataqua or in the Province of Maine, which were colonized by Churchmen. Among the prominent inhabitants of the former locality, the name of Captain Walter Neale suggests itself as a possibility because of his official connection with the New Hampshire settlements, having been in effect a "Governor" of all the territory owned by Mason and Gorges as early as 1630, by virtue of his connection with the Laconia Company. He could well say he was "noe professed Scholler," as he was a soldier by education, "having served," he says, "in all the Kings expeditions for the last twenty years; and commanded for four years the Company of the Artillery Garden," of London.[3] He returned to England in August, 1633, and December 12, following, was recommended by King Charles for reappointment as captain of the Artillery Garden.[4] After his return to London he may have drawn up the "Relation" printed below, for the use of Mason and

[1] Jenness printed a portion of No. 3448 in his "Transcripts."
[2] The original authorities on the subject of the Indian Plague are Mourt's Relation 33, 42, Gorges, Briefe Narration, lib. i. p. 12; Bradford, Plymouth Plantation, 195; Cushman, in Young, Chronicles of Pilgrims, 225, 258; Higginson, New England's Plantation, Mass. Hist. Coll., i. 123; Morton, New English Canaan, lib. i. c. 3; White, Planters' Plea, c. iv.; Johnson, Wonder-Working Providence, lib. i. c. 8.
[3] Colonial State Papers, ix. 131.
[4] Domestic State Papers (Charles I.), cclix. 76; comp., Repertory, xlviii. f. 39^b.

others, and the date of the paper, as computed above (1634), would seem to make this a plausible guess.[5]

Other names might be suggested, but it would be a mere list of names of prominent persons who could have written it, and such speculations, with not as much basis as the surmise above made, would be unprofitable.

The words in brackets appear in one or more of the copies collated by Mr. Waters, and such interpolation will be noted in the references to foot-notes with the initials II. F. W.

CHARLES E. BANKS.

A [TRUE] RELATION CONCERNYNGE THE ESTATE OF NEW=ENGLAND

[As it was presented to his Matie].

A Relation Concerninge New England

ffor the perfect understandinge the state of New England these three thinges deserue consideracõn vizt,

i   The Countrie,
2   The Comodities:
3   The Inhabitants :

THE COUNTRYE.

Scittuation and Clymate.   New=England is scituate in the North part of the Maine Continent of America included wthin the degrees of 40 and 48 of Northerly Latitude a Clymate through out all the world esteemed temperate and healthfull and by experience it is found that noe Countrie enioyeth a more salubrious aire then New-England, and though the Winter be more sharpe then ordinariely heare, yett it is lesse offensiue by reason the aire is more cleer and the cold allwayes drie

Sea Coasts and Inland parts.   The sea coast is rathe^r a lowe then a high land full of headlands or causies wch are Rocky   The Inmost parts of the countrie are mountaynous intermixed wth fruitfull valleyes and large Lakes, wch want not store of good ffish the hills are noe where barren though in some places stonie, but are fruitfull in trees and grasse

Rivers.   The Countrie is full of Rive^{rs} ffresh brookes and springes the rive^{rs} abound in plentie of excellent ffish as sturgion Basse &c. yett are they full of falls wch makes them not navigable farr into the land.

Harbours.   There is noe countrie greate^r stored of good Harbours then in New=England.

---

[5] One other piece of collateral evidence may be here considered. The writer says in the Relation, that the patents of " Cassica " (Casco) and " that granted to John Stratton were at my Cominge away forsaken." The Casco patent to which he refers is the one granting 6000 acres to Christopher Levett, who built in 1624 a fortified house on House Island, Portland Harbor. This patent was soon " forsaken " by Levett, and not till the spring of 1633 did George Cleeves settle there under this " dead and outworne title," as Trelawny styles it. Neale may not have known in August, 1633, of this settlement of Cleeves when he sailed for England, and so stated that it was " forsaken " at his " coming away." Stratton had a grant of 2000 acres, 1 December, 1631, on the south side of Cape Porpus, but never settled there. (Trelawny Papers, 102, 199; comp. Levett, Voyage into New England, *passim.*)

Seas.   The seas borderinge the shore are full of Islands and plentiful-
lie stored wth the best ffish as Codd Hake Haddock Mackerell &c :

Soile.   The Soyle of New-England is generally fruitfull abounding in
Wood of all sorts proper to this Countrie, there are besides great
plentie of Pyne ffirr spruce and some Cædar it is fruitfull in
grasse where the highnes of the woods hinder it not, the Corne
used in the countrie is the Indian Maize called Turkey Wheate,
but all sorts of English graine, where they are sowne thriue exceedinge well, the soyle naturally produces wild veynes in aboundance and some whose grapes for bignes surpasse the grapes of
ffrance and were they husbanded would questioneless excell in
goodnes there are three sorts of plants whereof Lynnen and Cordage may bee made, the coursest sort excells our hempe and the
finest may equall the coursest silke

Beastes.   The land doth nourish aboundance of deere beares and the
beasts called moose peculier to those countries, and the brookes
Rive^rs and ponds are well stored wth Beave^rs Otte^rs and mus-
quashes, there are alsoe diue^rs kindes of small beasts but those
offensiue are onely wolues and ffoxes

ffoule.   There is alsoe great plenty of all sorts of ffoule in theire seuerall
seasons especially Turkyes Geese and Ducks :

ffertilitie.   To conclude what soeuer the earth in England or ffrance doth
either nourish or produce though it may not att this present bee
found in New England yett beinge transported or planted will
thriue and growe there to more then an ordinarie perfection

COMODITYE

The most valuable comodities the Countrie will afford are theis
ffish Beaver skins wyne Pitch Tarr Lynnen Cordage Iron and
Tymber of all sorts for shippinge, what Mines or Minerall except
Iron are in the Countrie is yett unknowen for want of tryall

Off theis Comodities onely ffish and Beave^r skins are for the
p^rsent made use of

ffish and   The ffish of theis parts is noe where excelled and bringes into
Beaver.   England yearely great store of ready money from ffrance and
Spaine The Beaver likewise wch comes from thence preserues
w^thin this kingdome both money and merchandises wch otherwise
would bee exported for the same into ffrance and other countries :

The other Comodityes are to the Plante^rs as yett unusefull
nethe^r caun they wth Proffitt bee undertaken untill the Countrie
shalbee so sufficientlie stored wth Corne and Cattle as it will ffeede
the Inhabitants w^thout any dependance for supplie from England

It is most probable that salt may bee made in New England
ffor the sunn and weather are of sufficient strength to make it
And soe large a tract of land and so full of Marishes by the sea
side cannot waunt some grownds proper for that use

INHIBITANTS

The Inhabitants of New England are of two sorts the natiues
and the Plante^rs.

Natiues.   The natiues of the Countrie are att this tyme verie few in
number though heretofore populous distroyed by a great and
generall plague wch happined about 17 yeares since, leavinge

not the fortieth person liveinge since wch time they have neue^r increased, they liue nere and amonge the English but are beneficiall to them onely in the trade of Beaue^r wch they exchange for our Comodities   Theire want of people makes them not feared by us as not beinge able to doe much mischeife ; wch otherwise doubtles they would doe as was found by lamentable experience the last yeare.[6]

What the manne^{rs} and customes of these Indians are is trulie and att large related by a ffrenchman whose booke is translated into English intituled Nova ffrancia:[7]

The Plante^{rs} of newe England are of three seuerall nations, English ffrench and Dutch

Dutch plan- The Dutch are seated uppon the southwest part of New
tacon. England on the uttermost borde^r confininge Virginia they are there planted by authoritie from the Indian Companie, not acknowledging his Maties royaltie, who though they are not proffitable to theire maste^{rs} by reason of the great charge in maintenance of servants and souldie^{rs}, yett are they a great hindrance to the English Colonies in their trade of Beave^r, ffor that one Rive^r whereon they are setled yeilds as much (if not more) beaver then all the rest of New England planted by the English, and may bee esteemed yearelie about tenn thousand pounds waight of beave^r the Rive^{rs} and Countries adioyninge where they are planted is the best part of New=England onely they haue noe ffishing

ffrench. The ffrench are now possessed of that wch formerlie was the Scottish plantations beinge on the Northeast part of New Eng-land, they doe already beginn to exceede the bounds intended by his Matie for their Lymitts and doe day(lie) furnish the Indians wth armes and munition to the great dange^r and preiudice of the English they alsoe intend to prohibite the English their accustomed traffique in those parts for these reasons they are iustlie seated[8] to proue ill neighbou^{rs}.

English. The English are planted in the middest betwixt the Dutch and ffrench in a Countrie farr exceedinge that of the ffrench though somewhat inferiour to the Dutch habitacon.

This part of the countrie was manie yeares since planted by the English in the time and by the meanes of the Lord Cheife Justice Popham and some others, and especially by S^r ffirdinando Gorges knight but those plantacons prospered not through the ill choice [made] of places comodious for habitation[9]

---

[6] The "lamentable experience" which was encountered the "last yeare," that is 1633, if our date is correct, may be one of the numerous plots laid by the Narraganset Indians against the English, as told by Winthrop and other contemporary writers.
[7] Marc Lescarbot's Historie de la Novvelle France, first published in Paris, 1609. It was translated into English by Erondelle and published in London without date, and this edition is probably the one referred to.
[8] No. 3105 has "ffeared." I have inserted two words [in brackets] from that MS., viz. "made" and "since."—H. F. W.
[9] The phrase "prospered not" may be used by some advocate of the permanency of the Popham Colony to show that it was not abandoned, but merely unprosperous. This may be strengthened by a quotation from the succeeding paragraph, which says that the Ply-mouth Colony was the first plantation settled "to any purpose." On the contrary, Maverick's statement (REG. xxxix. 35) leaves no doubt that it was abandoned. See an article by the writer of these notes on "Settlements in Maine Prior to 1620," in the Maine Genealogi-cal and Historical Recorder, vol. ii. No. 4, in which the Popham case is discussed.

The Present Inhabitants of New Plymouth were the first that settled a plantation to any purpose in New England who went thither to inhibite about some 15 yeares [since][10] but the great numbe^{rs} of people wch makes the Countrie seeme now somewhat populous wth English hath been transported wthin these 9 yeares under the governm^t of Mr Indicott and Mr Winthrop :[11] who haue seated themselues in the west and more southerlie part of the countrie about the same tyme and since diue^{rs} others private Colonies haue been planted in the more Esterlie and Northern parts

Patents.		The English are planted in this Countrie by vertue of Patents granted unto them from the President and Counsell of New England wch soe farr as I can understand are in number 18 vizt

 i The Patent of New Plymouth
 2 The Patent of Massachusetts Baye:
 3 The Patent of Agawam granted to Captaine John Mason
 4 A Patente granted to S^r fferdinando Gorges
 5 A Patent of Laconia granted to S^r fferdinando Gorges and
  Captaine Mason
 6 A Patent of Pascataquacke graunted to S^r fferdinando
  Gorges and others
 7 A Patent granted Edward Hilton
 8 A Patent of Accaminticus granted to Captaine Norton wth
  othe^{rs}
 9 A Patent granted to John Stratton about Cape Porpus
  Rive^r
 10: 11 Two Patents of Sohaketocke granted to Richard Vynes
  & Thomas Lewis
 12 A Patent granted to Captaine Thomas Cam̄ock of black
  pointe
 13 A Patent granted to Mr Trelanye of Cape Elizabeth
 14 A Patent of Casico granted to Captaine Levitt
 15 A Patent of Pechipscote granted to Thomas Purchis and
  othe^{rs}
 16 A Patent granted to Richard Bradshaw of the Northeast
  side of Pechipscot Rive^r
 17 A Patent of Quinabecke belonginge to them of New Plymouth
 18 A Patent of Sagadehock granted to Crispe and othe^{rs}
 19 A Patent of Pemaquid granted to M^r: Alde^r and Mr Elbridge
 20 A Patent granted of Penobscott to Mr Sherlie, and othe^{rs}

Off theis Patents [those] granted to S^r fferdinando Gorges, and Captaine John Mason are included wthin the Patent last granted to the Inhabitants of the Massachusetts Bay

Concerninge which matte^r there hath been and still remaines

---

10 This would seem to make the date of the paper 1635.
11 This period is hard to reckon for the purposes of ascertaining the date of the manuscript. The Dorchester Company established their plantation at Cape Ann in 1623 (Palfrey, History of New England, i. 285), but Endicott did not arrive till 1628, and Winthrop two years later. Perhaps the author refers to the settlement of Conant at Salem in the fall of 1626, to which date if we add nine years we shall have 1635, near enough to 1634 for all practical purposes of determining the date.

some Controversie Sagadehock was never planted.[12] That of Cassica, and that granted to John Stratton were at my comminge away forsaken

The Patent of Penobscott is largest of extent, it comprehendinge (as is pretended) nere 40 leagues in length yett it is planted but wth one house, And is now possessed by the ffrench[13]

Extent of Patents.   The English in their seuerall patents are planted along the sea coast and haue their habitations nere adioyning to Rive^{rs} navigable ffor shippinge, or Barkes, the charge and difficultie of transportinge provision by land, ffor want of horses causes the Inland parts to bee yett unpeopled

The Plantaĉons beginninge at ye most Southerlie, wch is new Plymouth and endinge at penobscott, containe in length alonge the sea cost about 70 leagues and are peopled with more then 30000 Persons whereof new Plimouth may containe well nere 1800, the Massachusetts (more then 20000) the rest of the Patents beinge planted wth the residue

Cattle.   Att my Comeinge ouer there was estimated to bee att the least 1200 head of kyne belonging to the seuerall plantaĉons, And are now increased to : 5000:[14] or there abouts, great store of swyne and goates and some horses

The Inhabitants haue in all places convenient houses and good quantitie of cleered land ffor Corne

Difference of Patents.   The aboue menĉoned Patents are not all of one kinde, for some are in the nature of Corporaĉons and haue power to make Lawes, ffor the governinge of their plantaĉons, others are but onely as-signm^{ts} of soe much land to bee planted and possessed wthout power of governm^t.

Of the first sort are onely theis ffower vizt:

    i New Plymouth
    2 Massachusetts
    3 Pascatequack
    4 & Pemaquid

Governm^t.   The Civill governm^t of the Colonies remaine in the power of those who are Principall in the Patents of wch those wch haue authoritie to establish lawes, doe execute their Jurisdiction (soe farr as I could understand) as neere as may bee accordinge to the lawes of England, And those who haue not that legall powe^r doe governe theire servants and Tennants in a Civill way, soe farr as they are able

Defects.   The defects in theis plantations ffor the present, as I conceive, are onely theis

---

[12] This does not refer to the Popham Colony, but to the Plough colonists, who under-took to settle on the south side of Sagadahoc, probably about Cape Small Point. See an article by the annotator on the " Plough Patent " in Maine Genealogical Recorder (1885), vol. 2, p. 65 *et seq.*

[13] The Plymouth Pilgrims had a trading post at Penobscot, and the " one house " spo-ken of is probably the truck house of their trading station. The French captured this and seized that portion of Maine in 1635, and as the writer states that it " is now possessed by the ffrench," the inference is that this paper could not have been written till that year. It would seem that the paper was not composed for some time after the author left the coun-try, and that he added such sentences as the above from subsequent information. This is the only theory that will reconcile the variety of internal evidence as to its date.

[14] " And since augmented to 6000 or thereabouts," says No. 3105.—H. F. W.

i The Inhabitants (except in the Massachusetts Bay) are too farr scattered one from an other a longe the coast, soe that they cannot uppon any occasion Reunite themselues to oppose an enemye

2 There is fewe fforts[15] nor places of strength in all the Countrie

3 There are but few of those, who haue Patents granted unto them that doe obserue the Lawes, and orde[rs] of Plantation appointed unto them in their Patents and expressed in the grand Patent granted by his Ma[tie] to the President and Councell

4 When there happeneth any question betweene the Plante[rs] of seuerall Patents, those quarrells are seldome, or neuer ended because there is none in the countrie that hath authoritie to decide them; every mans powe[r] beinge limitted, wth his owne Patent

5 There wants an uniformytie in the Lawes and Customes of seuerall Patents and alsoe a generall unitie, in thinges that concerne the publique good of the Countrie

As Concerninge matte[rs] of Religion, because my aboade was farre distant ffrom neighbo[rs] and noe professed Scholler, I was therefore little acquainted wth other mens dissagreeinge opinions, and my selfe and Colonie allwayes professinge the doctrine discipline of the Church of England I was not curious afte[r] that of othe[rs] w[ch] then concerned me nott

FFINIS

NOTE BY H. F. WATERS.—The above is from MS. No. 3448 Sloane Collection, British Museum. It is in a little square volume of forty-four folios, of which the above takes up fifteen. The next (16 to 44) is in the same hand and is entitled "An abstract of the Lawes of New=England." There are two other copies in the Sloane Collection, Nos. 2505 and 3105. The three copies are all in different handwritings, all differing in some particulars, especially in numbers. I have made No. 3448 the basis, and have taken from the others such items as seemed needed to make the result correct.

WILLIAM READ.—In the deposition of John Wiswall, Jr., in 1695 (REG. xviii. 70), he states that William Read married his sister Hannah Munnings.

There was a William Read in Boston who by wife Hannah had William, born 26 March, 1665.

The inventory of William Read's estate was taken by James Johnson and Thomas Dewer, Sept. 23, 1667, to which John Wiswall. Junr,, deposed Nov. 28th following (file 476 Suffolk Probate Office). I should judge this William Read was a shopkeeper, by the number of yards of blacke, gray, "whit," plaine and Irish "frise," "linsie woolsie," &c.. mentioned.

It would seem that Hannah Wiswall married first, Mahalaleel Munnings, who was "drowned in y[e] Mill creek at Boston in y[c] night 27 (12) 59" (see REG. xxxvii. 379); second, William Read, who, if he was the one whose inventory is above mentioned, was dead in 1667; third, Thomas Overman, whom she married previous to 27: 3: 1672, at which date the Boston Town Records have this entry: "Libertie is granted to Thomas Ouerman who married with Elder Wiswalls daught[r] to wharfe before theire owne land." Report of Record Commissioners, vii. 70; REG. vii. 273, 274, Letters from Old England, 1660; present volume, page 59; Bay State Monthly, Feb. 1884, page 128.   WILLIAM B. TRASK.

[15] "There is noe ffort nor place," etc., says No. 3105. "There wants yett some store of fforts or places," etc., says No. 2505.—H. F. W.

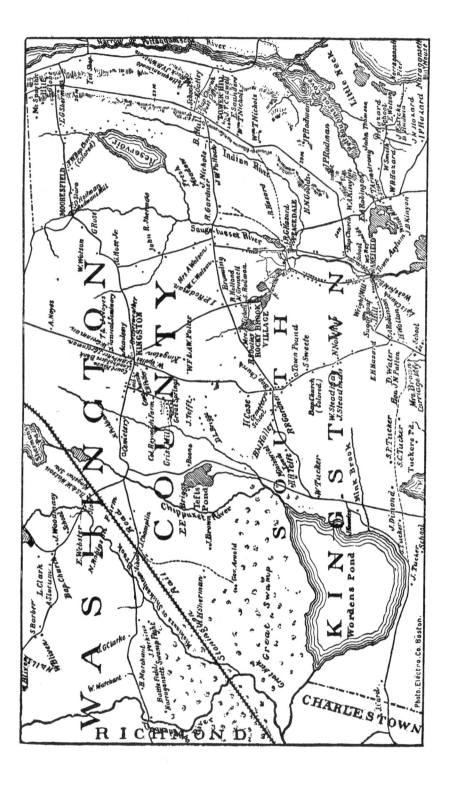

SOLDIERS IN KING PHILIP'S WAR.

Communicated by the Rev. GEORGE M. BODGE, A.M., of East Boston, Mass.

[Continued from vol. xxxix. page 383.]

No. XIII.

THE NARRAGANSETT CAMPAIGN TO THE CLOSE OF THE "GREAT SWAMP" BATTLE.

THE above picture, representing the present appearance of the site of the old "Swamp Fort" of the Narragansetts, destroyed by the forces of the United Colonies, Massachusetts, Connecticut and Plymouth, December 19th, 1675, was published several years since in a book called "Picturesque Rhode Island." Saving the changes incident upon the clearing and cultivation of contiguous land, the place could be easily identified as the battlefield, even if its location were not put beyond question by traditions and also by relics found from time to time upon the place. It is now, as then, an "island of four or five acres," surrounded by swampy land, overflowed except in the dryest part of the year. The island was cleared and plowed about 1775, and at that time many bullets were found deeply bedded in the large trees; quantities of charred corn were plowed up in different places, and it is said that Dutch spoons and Indian arrowheads, etc., have been found here at different times. There is no monument to mark this site of one of the most brilliant victories in American warfare. The place is now owned by the Hon. J. G. Clarke, of West Kingston, R. I., to whom and to John G. Perry, Esq., of Wakefield, R. I., I am indebted for confirmation of the above facts.

The accompanying map is a section—slightly reduced—of the large map of Rhode Island, made from surveys under the direction of H. F. Walling, Esq., and published by him in 1862. It takes in the line of march from Pettisquamscot (Tower-Hill) to the Fort. There is no "scale of miles" upon the large map, but by a careful comparison of known distances, it appears that it is about seven miles in a bee line, nearly west, from Tower-Hill to the battle-field; by way of McSparran Hill, in direct courses, about ten miles. The army, following the higher land, with frequent halts and probably much uncertain wandering and careful scouting, consumed the time from five o'clock in the morning to about one o'clock P.M.; and it is likely that in this roundabout march they made about fifteen or sixteen miles, the distance reported.

In the retreat, the Army probably followed back upon their morning track as far as McSparran Hill, and thence to Wickford to their quarters at Mr. Richard Smith's [106] garrison-house, arriving there about two o'clock in the morning, after a march of about eighteen miles, as was reported at the time.

The residence of Hon. J. G. Clarke, proprietor of the ancient battlefield, is about a mile north of it. Tower-Hill is the site of Jireh Bull's garrison-house at Pettisquamscot.

PREPARATIONS AND MARCH AGAINST THE NARRAGANSETTS.

After their somewhat disastrous campaign of the autumn of 1675 in the western parts of the colony of Massachusetts, the United Colonies, upon information that the hostile Indians with Philip were retiring towards the south and to winter quarters amongst the Narragansetts, determined to carry the war against this powerful tribe, who for some time had shown themselves actively hostile. The veteran troops were recalled and reorganized; small towns in various parts of the colonies were garrisoned, and an army of one thousand men was equipped for a winter campaign. General Josiah Winslow, Governor of Plymouth Colony, was appointed commander-in-chief of this Army; Major Samuel Appleton to command the Massachusetts regiment, Major William Bradford that of Plymouth, and Major Robert Treat that of Connecticut. War was formally declared against the Narragansetts on November 2d, 1675,

---

[106] Mr. Smith, called Capt. and Major by contemporary writers, was a person of wide influence in this part of the country, and held in high esteem in all the colonies. He was the son of Richard Smith, Senior, who came from "Gloster Shire" in England, and in 1641 bought a large tract of land, including the present town of Wickford, and there built the first English house in Narragansett, and set up a trading station and offered free entertainment to all travellers.

in the meeting of the Commissioners of the United Colonies held at Boston that day.

General Winslow, upon his appointment to the command of the army in this expedition, rode to Boston for consultation with Gov. Leverett and the Council. Thence on Thursday, December the 9th, he rode to Dedham, having Benjamin Church as aid, and probably the gentlemen who constituted the Massachusetts part of his staff or " guard," consisting of the ministers, among whom was Mr. Joseph Dudley, the surgeons, of whom the chief was Daniel Weld, of Salem. I presume other general officers and aids went along with him, of whom we find no mention. Commissary John Morse was probably of this number. The General assumed command of the Massachusetts forces drawn up on Dedham Plain, and formally delivered to him by Major General Denison of Massachusetts, on Thursday, December 9th. This force consisted of six companies of foot, numbering four hundred and sixty-five, besides Captain Prentice's troop of seventy-five. The full quota of Massachusetts was five hundred and twenty-seven soldiers, but there were doubtless many others along as servants to the officers, scouts, camp-followers, &c. To the soldiers a proclamation was made at this time on the part of the Massachusetts Council, " that if they played the man, took the Fort, & Drove the Enemy out of the Narragansett Country, which was their great Seat, that they should have a gratuity in land besides their wages." On the same afternoon they marched twenty-seven miles to Woodcock's Garrison, now Attleboro'. In the evening of Friday, December 10th, they arrived at Seekonk, where vessels with supplies were in waiting. And here also Major Richard Smith was waiting their arrival with his vessel, and took on board Capt. Mosely and his company, to sail direct to his garrison-house at Wickford. Some others, it is likely, went with them to arrange for quartering the troops, and Benjamin Church was sent to make ready for the General's coming. The rest of the forces " ferried over the water to Providence," and probably formed a junction with the main part of the Plymouth regiment at Providence, on Saturday, December 11th. From Mr. Dudley's letter of the 15th, it will be seen that an account had been sent the Council of their movements to the time of arriving at Pautuxet. This letter is now lost from the files. In the evening of Sunday, December 12th, the whole body advanced " from Mr. Carpenter's," crossed the Pautuxet River and marched a long way into " Pomham's Country," now Warwick, R. I.; but from the unskilfulness of their Warwick scouts (probably Englishmen, for if they had been Indians their failure would have been deemed treachery), their purpose of capturing Pomham and his people was defeated, and after a whole night spent in weary marching about, they arrived at Mr. Smith's garrison-house at Wickford on the 13th, and found their vessels from Seekonk already arrived. Capt. Mosely's company that day captured thirty-six Indians, including Indian Peter, who proved afterwards such an indispensable guide.

There were many doubtless at Smith's garrison, employed by him and gathered thither for security. Church speaks of finding "the Eldridges and some other brisk hands," and going out and taking eighteen Indians, and finding the General arrived on his return to the garrison next morning before sunrise. This would seem from his story to have been on the morning of the 12th; but the other accounts and his own reference to the General's arrival settle the day as the 13th and the time as before daybreak. This exploit of Mr. Church seems to have been unknown to Messrs. Dudley, Oliver and other contemporary writers. On Monday, 13th, no movement was made, but on the 14th the General moved his whole force, except Capt. Oliver's company, which kept garrison, out through the country to the westward, and burned the town of the Sachem "Ahmus," of whom I can find no mention except this of Mr. Dudley's, and the "Quarters" of Quaiapen, Magnus, or Matantuck, as her Indian name was understood by the English, "Old Queen" or "Sunke Squaw," as she was called by them. She was the widow of Mriksah, or Makanno, son of Canonicus first. Her dominions were in the present towns of South and North Kingston and Exeter, and near the line between the latter, upon a high rocky hill, is still to be found the remains of an old Indian fort, known from earliest times as the "Queen's Fort," and probably near the place where her deserted "Quarters" were raided. The army that day destroyed one hundred and fifty wigwams, killed seven and captured nine Indians. In the mean time Capt. Oliver had sent out "five files," i.e. thirty of his men, under Sergeant (Peter) Bennet, who, scouting abroad, killed two Indians, a man and woman, and captured four more.

Mr. Dudley, writing on the next day, Wednesday, December 15th, states that up to that time they had captured or killed, in all, fifty persons, and their prisoners in hand were forty. Capt. Oliver's account makes the number fifty-seven "young and old." Adding Mr. Church's eighteen, and we swell the number to seventy-five. From a careful survey of the matter in all its relations, I am inclined to think that Church was acting in conjunction with, and under the command of Capt. Mosely, to whom the official returns accredit the capture of the whole body, eighteen of whom Church claims to have been his own captives.

Wednesday, Dec. 15th, the army seems to have been held in parley most of the day by the pretended negotiations of "Stonewall," or "Stone-layer" John, an Indian who had lived much with the English, and had learned the trade of stone-mason, but was now hostile, and very serviceable to the Indians in many ways. Whether he was treacherous or not, the Indians were gathering and skulking about the English quarters while he was negotiating, and when he was safely away they began to pick off our men wherever they found opportunity, and later lay in ambush behind a stone wall and fired upon several companies of the English sent out to bring in Maj. Appleton's company, quartered some miles away. They were quickly repulsed with the loss of one of their leaders, and seem to have gone towards the general rendezvous at the great fort, and on the way they assaulted and burned the garrison of Jireh, or " Jerry " Bull at Pettisquamscot (Tower Hill, S. Kingston, R. I.), killing fifteen of those at the garrison, two only escaping.

Thursday, December 16th, Capt. Prentice with his troop rode out, probably following the trail to Pettisquamscot, where he found the garrison-house in ruins. This is said to have been a very strong stone house, easily defended by a small number, and its destruction, of which there is no detailed account, must have been accomplished by either surprise or treachery. The news had a very depressing effect upon the army, who had hoped that the Connecticut forces had already arrived there.

Friday, December 17th, came the news of the arrival of the Connecticut regiment at Pettisquamscot. Our army seems to have been disposing of the captives and preparing for the march. Forty-seven of the captives were sold to Capt. Davenport on this day, Saturday, Dec. 18th. The General, leaving a small garrison at Wickford, pushed his army forward to Pettisquamscot, and about 5 P.M. joined the Connecticut troops consisting of about three hundred English and one hundred and fifty Mohegan Indians. In a severe snow-storm, the whole force, about one thousand men, encamped in the open field through that bitter cold night. Sunday, Dec. 19th, before day-break (Capt. Oliver says, " at five o'clock "), the whole force marched away towards the enemy's great rendezvous.

The following, gleaned from all available sources, may be of interest at this point.

ROSTER OF THE OFFICERS OF THE ARMY OF THE UNITED COLONIES,
As organized for the Narragansett Campaign, and as mustered at Pettisquamscot, December 19, 1675.

Gen. JOSIAH WINSLOW, Governor of Plymouth Colony, Com. in Chief.

Staff. { Daniel Weld, of Salem, Chief Surgeon.
Joseph Dudley, of Boston, Chaplain.
Benjamin Church, of Little Compton, R. I., Aid.

Massachusetts Regiment.

Samuel Appleton, of Ipswich, Major, and Captain of 1st Company.

Staff. { Richard Knott, of Marblehead, Surgeon.
Samuel Nowell, of Boston, Chaplain.
John Morse, of Ipswich, Commissary.

1st Company—Jeremiah Swain, Lieut.; Ezekiel Woodward, Sergeant.
2d Company—Samuel Mosely, Captain; Perez Savage, Lieut.
3d Company—James Oliver, Captain; Ephraim Turner, Lieut.; Peter Bennett, Sergeant.

4th Company—Isaac Johnson, Captain; Phineas Upham, Lieut.; Henry Bowen, Ensign.

5th Company—Nathaniel Davenport, Captain; Edward Tyng, Lieut.; John Drury, Ensign.

6th Company—Joseph Gardiner, Captain; William Hathorne, Lieut.; Benjamin Sweet, Ensign, prom. Lieut.; Jeremiah Neal, Sergeant, prom. Ensign.

Troop.—Thomas Prentice, Captain; John Wayman, Lieut.

Plymouth Regiment.

William Bradford, of Marshfield, Major, and Captain of 1st Company.

Staff. { Matthew Fuller, of Barnstable, Surgeon.
{ Thomas Huckins, of Barnstable, Commissary.

1st Company—Robert Barker, of Duxbury, Lieut.

2d Company—John Gorham, of Barnstable, Captain; Jonathan Sparrow, of Eastham, Lieut.; William Wetherell, Sergeant.

Connecticut Regiment.

Robert Treat, of Milford, Major.

Staff. { Gershom Bulkeley, Surgeon.[107]
{ Rev. Nicholas Noyes, Chaplain.
{ Stephen Barrett, Commissary.

1st Company—John Gallop, of Stonington, Captain.
2d Company—Samuel Marshall, Windsor, Captain.
3d Company—Nathaniel Seely, of Stratford, Captain.
4th Company—Thomas Watts, of Hartford, Captain.
5th Company—John Mason, of Norwich, Captain.[108]

There were other officers and men of note doubtless who went along with the army. Two surgeons, Dr. Jacob Willard (of Newton) and Dr. John Cutler of Hingham were credited under Major Appleton for their service, and were accredited grantees of the Narragansett townships in 1733, as was also Dr. John Clark of Boston. I have no positive authority for assigning Dr. Knott to Major Appleton's staff, but the first purchase of surgical instruments on the part of the Colony was made of George Thomas, charged December 17, 1675, and were for Dr. Weld and Dr. Knott. I think that Dr. William Hawkins was afterwards sent to the wounded at Rhode Island. The roster of line officers of the Massachusetts Regiment is well attested by the accounts of the Treasurer. Of the Plymouth officers, Lieut. Robert Barker was in the spring following, March 10th, imprisoned and fined by the sentence of a council of war, for mutinous conduct in "breaking away from the army while on the march," but it is evident that this was after the battle at which he must have been present, as his heirs evidently received his claim. His defection probably occurred during "The Long March" or "Hungry March" so called, through the Nipmuck country to Marl-

---

[107] A minister, but now acting as Surgeon.

[108] From some intimations it would seem that Captain Mason was in command of a sixth company composed of Indians, but I have found no positive proof. A contemporary writer says Captain Gallop "commanded Uncas's men." Perhaps each of these had a party in his command.

borough. Of Connecticut, I have not been able to identify any
other line officers. Of the troops of Massachusetts, the quota was
527 ; the number actually impressed was 540, including troopers
75. The returns made at Dedham Plain give 465 foot, troopers 73.
See *ante*, vol. xxxviii. p. 440. The Connecticut quota was 315,
and there was also a company of Indians 150. Plymouth's quota
was 158.

THE BATTLE AT THE GREAT SWAMP FORT.

About one o'clock, P.M., the army came upon the enemy at the
edge of the swamp, in the midst of which the Indian fortress was
built, the Massachusetts regiment leading in the march, Plymouth
next, and Connecticut bringing up the rear. Of the Massachusetts
troops Capts. Mosely and Davenport led the van and came first
upon the Indians, and immediately opened fire upon them—thus at
the beginning gaining the important advantage of the first fire,
which the Indians had almost always gained and made so deadly by
deliberate volleys from ambush, as they doubtless purposed now.
The Indians returned the fire with an ineffectual volley, and then
fled into the swamp closely pursued by the foremost companies, who
did not wait for the word of command, or stand much upon the
" order of their going," until they reached the fortifications within
which the Indians hastily betook themselves. This fort was situated
upon an island of some five or six acres in the midst of a cedar
swamp, which was impassable except to the Indians by their accustomed paths, and now made passable only by the severe cold of the
previous day and night. It is probable that the Indians depended
chiefly upon the swamp to protect them, though their defences are
described as having been of considerable strength. A portion of
the high ground had been inclosed, and from a careful comparison of
the most reliable accounts, it seems that the fortifications were well
planned, probably by the Englishman Joshua Teffe, or Tift, as Mr.
Dudley calls him. Mr. Hubbard says : " The Fort was raised
upon a Kind of Island of five or six acres of rising Land in the
midst of a swamp ; the sides of it were made of Palisadoes set upright, the which was compassed about with a Hedg of almost a rod
Thickness." A contemporary writer (whose account was published
at the time in London, and is reprinted in Mr. Drake's publication
called the " Old Indian Chronicle ") says : " In the midst of the
Swamp was a Piece of firm Land, of about three or four Acres,
whereon the *Indians* had built a kind of Fort, being palisadoed
round, and within that a clay Wall, as also felled down abundance
of Trees to lay quite round the said Fort, but they had not quite
finished the said Work." It is evident from these, the only *detailed*
accounts, and from some casual references, that the works were rude
and incomplete, but would have been almost impregnable to our
troops had not the swamp been frozen. At the corners and ex-

posed portions, rude block-houses and flankers had been built, from
which a raking fire could be poured upon any attacking force.
Either by chance, or the skill of Peter, their Indian guide, the English seem to have come upon a point of the fort where the Indians
did not expect them. Mr. Church, in relating the circumstances of
Capt. Gardiner's death, says that he was shot from that side "next
the upland where the English entered the swamp." The place where
he fell was at the "east end of the fort." The tradition that the
English approached the swamp by the rising land in front of the
"Judge Marchant" house, thus seems confirmed. This "upland"
lies about north of the battlefield.

Our van pursued those of the enemy who first met them
so closely that they were led straight to the entrance used by
the Indians themselves, perhaps by their design then to attract
attention from an exposed part of their works a short distance
away. The passage left by the Indians for their own use, as before
mentioned, was by a long tree over a "place of water," across
which but one might pass at a time, "and which was so waylaid
that they would have been cut off that had ventured." Mr. Hubbard counts among the fortunate circumstances of that day that
the troops did not attempt to carry this point, and that they
discovered the only assailable point a little farther on. This
was at a corner of the fort where was a large unfinished gap,
where neither palisades nor the abbatis, or "hedge," had been
placed, but only a long tree had been laid across about five feet from
the ground, to fill the gap, and might be easily passed; only that
the block-house right opposite this gap and the flankers at the sides
were finished, from which a galling fire might sweep and enfilade
the passage. Mr. Hubbard's account is very clear about this, yet
several writers have sadly confused matters and described the first
as the point of assault.

It seems that the companies of Capts. Davenport and Johnson
came first[109] to this place, and at once charged through the gap and
over the log at the head of their companies, but Johnson fell dead
at the log, and Davenport a little within the fort, and their men
were met with so fierce a fire that they were forced to retire again
and fall upon their faces to avoid the fury of the musketry till it
should somewhat abate. Mosely and Gardiner, pressing to their
assistance, met a similar reception, losing heavily, till they too fell
back with the others, until Major Appleton coming up with his own
and Capt. Oliver's men, massed his entire force as a storming column, and it is said that the shout of one of the commanders that the
Indians were running, so inspired the soldiers that they made an
impetuous assault, carried the entrance amain, beat the enemy from
one of his flankers at the left, which afforded them a temporary shel-

[109] John Raymond claimed to have been the first soldier to enter the fort. The only
soldier of that name credited was John Rayment, under Major Appleton.

ter from the Indians still holding the block-house opposite the entrance. In the mean time, the General, holding the Plymouth forces in reserve, pushed forward the Connecticut troops, who not being aware of the extent of the danger from the block-house, suffered fearfully at their first entrance, but charged forward gallantly, though some of their brave officers and many of their comrades lay dead behind them, and unknown numbers and dangers before. The forces now joining, beat the enemy step by step, and with fierce fighting, out of their block-houses and various fortifications.[110] Many of the Indians, driven from their works, fled outside, some doubtless to the wigwams inside, of which there were said to be upward of five hundred, many of them large and rendered bullet-proof by large quantities of grain in tubs and bags, placed along the sides. In these many of their old people and their women and children had gathered for safety, and behind and within these as defences the Indians still kept up a skulking fight, picking off our men. After three hours hard fighting, with many of the officers and men wounded or dead, a treacherous enemy of unknown numbers and resources lurking in the surrounding forests, and the night coming on, word comes to fire the wigwams, and the battle becomes a fearful holocaust, great numbers of those who had taken refuge therein being burned.

The fight had now raged for nearly three hours with dreadful carnage in proportion to the numbers engaged. It is not certain at just what point the Plymouth forces were pushed forward, but most likely after the works were carried, and the foremost, exhausted, retired for a time bearing their dead and wounded to the rear; but we are assured that all took part in the engagement, coming on in turn as needed. It is doubtful if the cavalry crossed the swamp, but were rather held in reserve and as scouts to cover the rear and prevent surprises from any outside parties.

When now the fortress and all its contents were burning, and destruction assured, our soldiers hastily gathered their wounded and as many as possible of their dead, and formed their shattered column for the long and weary march back to Wickford.

Reliable details of this battle are few, and only gleaned from casual references here and there, and thus many, who have sought to write upon the matter, have quoted in full the story of Benjamin Church, who relates his own experience, and draws out his personal

---

[110] Mr. Dudley's account seems to indicate that at this point the Indians rallied and beat the English again out of the fort; but after careful weighing of the evidence, I am satisfied that in the matter of the battle itself, Mr. Hubbard's account, gathered from the officers of Massachusetts, especially Major Appleton, is most correct in details. Mr. Dudley remained outside the swamp with the General, his staff and reserve force, and the repulse, at the first onset, would naturally be magnified by those who were forced to await the issue without participation. The above account is entirely consistent. Again, when the band of volunteers headed by Church was sent forward by the General, the fort was already in full possession of our army, and when they passed the entrance many of the slain and several of our captains were lying where they fell. If there had been a retreat from the fort, these dead officers would have been removed.

reminiscences with all an old man's fondness for his deeds of "long ago." The very small part he took in this battle is evident even from his own story, and from the utter silence of other writers, especially Mr. Hubbard, who knew Church and commends him highly for his exploits in the Mount Hope campaign. No one can doubt the ability or courage of Mr. Church, but his part in this battle was simply that when the fort was carried and the fighting nearly over, he went, with some thirty others, into and through the fort and out into the swamp upon the trail of the retreating foe, discovered, ambushed and scattered a skulking party of them returning to the attack, chased a few of them into the fort amongst the huts, and was himself severely wounded by them thus brought to bay.

I wish here to record my protest against the unjust, often weak, and always inconsiderate, criticism bestowed upon our leaders in this campaign, and especially in this battle, for their lack of foresight in abandoning the shelter and provisions of the fort, their sacrifice of the lives of our wounded men through their removal and the dangers and fatigues of the long march, and their inhumanity in burning the helpless and innocent in their huts and wigwams.

It is well to remember at the start, that many of the wisest, ablest and bravest men of the three colonies were the leaders in this affair. A noble commander, wise and brave, reverend ministers, by no means backward with their opinions; the most prominent and skilful surgeons the country afforded; veteran majors and captains of Massachusetts and Connecticut, with their veteran soldiers fresh from the severe experiences in the western campaign, inured to danger and experienced in Indian wiles and deceits: against all these we have recorded only the remonstrance of Mr. Church, who up to that time, at least, had experience in Indian warfare only as a scout, and the record we have of any protest by him was made many years after the affair. And again, from the standpoint of their conditions as nearly as we can now judge, it seems that their hasty retreat was wise. They were some sixteen miles from their base of supplies (it is doubtful if they had noted the Indian supplies until the burning began). There was no way of reaching their provisions and ammunition at Wickford except by detaching a portion of their force now reduced greatly by death, wounds and exposure. The numbers of Indians that had escaped, and were still in the woods close at hand, were unknown, but supposed to be several thousand, with report of a thousand in reserve about a mile distant. These were now scattered and demoralized, but in a few hours might rally and fall upon the fort, put our troops, in their weakened condition, upon the defensive, and make their retreat from the swamp extremely difficult if not utterly impossible, encumbered as they would be by the wounded, whose swollen and stiffened wounds in a few hours would render removal doubly painful and dangerous. Added to this was the chance of an attack upon the garrison at Wickford, and the dread of the midnight ambuscade, which every hour's delay made more likely and would render more dangerous.· Thus it seems to me that from the standpoint of military strategy, the immediate retreat to Wickford was best. As to inhumanity, we must remember the harsh times in which they were living, the contempt in which the Indians were held—first, as heathen, against whom war was righteous; second, as idle and treacherous vagabonds, with no rights which honest industry was bound to respect; third, as deadly enemies, lying in wait to plunder, burn and destroy. Moreover, the very life of the colonies was threatened by this war; many thriving hamlets were already in ashes; hundreds of families were broken up and scattered up and down, with loss of all; fathers, husbands and brothers slain or in captivity, farms and homes laid waste, whole communities huddled in wretched block-houses, while the "reign of terror" swept about them. Brookfield, "Beers's Plain," and "Bloody-Brook," with their outrage and carnage, were fresh in mind, and a few days before, the destruction and massacre at Pettisquamscot; while even here at their feet were their dead and dying comrades and beloved officers. Is it strange that they were cruel, when now for the first time they came face to face with the authors of all their troubles in a fair fight? By any candid student of history I believe this must be classed as one of the most glorious victories ever achieved in our history, and considering conditions, as displaying heroism, both in stubborn patience and dashing intrepidity, never excelled in American warfare.

Of the details of the march to Wickford very little is known; through a bitter cold winter's night, in a blinding snowstorm, carrying two hundred and ten of their wounded and dead, these soldiers, who had marched from dawn till high noon, had engaged in a desperate life-and-death struggle from noon till sunset, now plodded sturdily back to their quarters of the day before, through deepening snows and over unbroken roads.[111] By the letters below, it will be seen that the General and staff, with their escort, got separated from the main column, lost their way and wandered about till 7 o'clock next morning, while the main body reached their quarters at 2 o'clock.

DEAD AND WOUNDED.

The names of those officers and soldiers of Massachusetts killed and wounded in this battle, have been given heretofore in the sketches of the companies to which they belonged.

By Capt. Oliver's letter, written a little more than a month afterwards from the seat of war, and considered official, we learn that up to that time the dead numbered about sixty-eight, and the wounded

---

[111] There is a tradition (mentioned in a note in Hon. Elisha R. Potter, Jr.'s "Early History of Narragansett ") that the English feared an ambuscade in force on the line of march by which they had come, and so marched by way of McSparran Hill on their return.

one hundred and fifty, in the whole army. Eight of the dead were left in the fort, and twelve more were dead when they started back to Wickford. Twenty-two died on the march, and before the next day, Monday, Dec. 20th, when they buried thirty-four in one grave, and six more within two days, eight died at Rhode Island, and three others, making in all but fifty-nine, if we reckon the twelve carried from the fort as a part of the thirty-four buried Dec. 20th; otherwise, seventy-one. But the first estimate of sixty-eight is satisfied if we add the twenty killed at the fort to those buried at Wickford and Rhode Island, and conclude that the twelve taken from the fort were buried somewhere on the march.[112]

Of the losses of Massachusetts we are not left in doubt, since there is still preserved in our archives a full and official return, which Mr. Hubbard gives substantially, adding to the wounded probably those whose wounds were slight and not reported at the time, and with some modifications of the list of dead, though with the same total.

The official list of those killed and wounded in the battle, including three of Capt. Gardiner's men killed previous to the battle, is dated January 6, 1675, and entitled,

A list of Major Saml Apleton souldjers y^t were slayne & wounded the 19th Decemb. '75, at the Indians fort at Narraganset.

		Killed.	Wounded.
	Major Appleton,	4	18
	Capt. Mosely,	6	9
	Capt. Oliver,	5	8
In the Company of	Capt. Davenport,	4	11
	Capt. Johnson,	4	8
	Capt. Gardiner,	7	10
	Capt. Prentice,	1	3
Mass. Archives, Vol. 68, p. 104.		—	—
		31	67

Of the officers, Capts. Davenport, Johnson and Gardiner were killed, and Lieutenants Upham, Savage, Swain, and Ting were wounded.[113]

Of the Connecticut troops, seventy-one were killed and wounded according to Hubbard; and according to the eminent historian of Connecticut, Dr. Benjamin Trumbull, seventy.

		Mr. Hubbard's Account.	
Capt. Gallop,	10		
Capt. Marshall,	14	Of New Haven Company,	20
Capt. Seely,	20	Of Capt. Siely his Company,	20
Capt. Mason,	9	Of Capt. Watt his Company,	17
Capt. Watts,	17—70	Of Capt. Marshal his Company,	14—71

[112] Ninigret, sachem of the Nianticks, sent to General Winslow word that his people had buried the dead of the English left at the Fort, and that the number was twenty-four, and he asked for a charge of powder for each. This information was given in a letter from Major Bradford to Rev. Mr. Cotton of Plymouth.

[113] The random estimates of Henry Trumbull, who published a popular History of Indian Wars in 1810, will appear absurd when compared with the above. For instance, he gives as killed and wounded of Connecticut 357, when their whole force was 300 English; and of their Indian allies, he kills 51 and wounds 82 of the 150.

Major Treat by tradition is said to have been the last man to have left the fort, commanding the rear guard of the army ; and of his captains, Gallop, Marshall and Seely were killed, and Capt. Mason mortally wounded.

Of the Plymouth forces, Major Bradford, commander, and Benjamin Church of the General's staff were severely wounded, and of the soldiers the killed and wounded in both companies were twenty, by best accounts.

The grave of the forty buried at Wickford was marked by a tree called the "grave appletree," which was blown down in the gale of September, 1815. The wounded were sent in vessels to Rhode Island, and well cared for.

Of the losses of the enemy there can be no reliable account. Capt. Oliver says, " By the best intelligence we killed 300 fighting men, and took say 350 and above 300 women and children." Mr. Dudley, two days after the fight, reckons about two hundred ; Capt. Mosely counted sixty-four in one corner of the fort; and Capt. Gorham made an estimate of at least one hundred and fifty. The desperate strait of the Indians is shown by their leaving the dead in their flight. Indian prisoners afterward reported seven hundred killed.

The conduct of the Mohegan and Pequod allies is represented by Capt. Oliver as false, they firing in the air, but securing much plunder. I have found no other notice of their part in the battle.

CORRESPONDENCE.

The following letters, written by Joseph Dudley, who was with Gen. Winslow as one of his staff or "Guard," and also served as chaplain to the army, are perhaps the most reliable official reports of the campaign that remain. The letter of the fifteenth is still preserved, as noted below. That of the twenty-first was published by Governor Hutchinson in his " History of the Colony of Massachusetts Bay," London edition (1765), page 302. I have not been able to find the original of this last. The letter of the Council to Gen. Winslow, in answer to Dudley's first, is preserved as below noted, and in two copies—the first a rough draft, the second a carefully written copy in Secretary Rawson's own hand.

Letter of Joseph Dudley.

May it please your Honn[r]   Mr Smiths 15, 10, 75

I am commanded by the Generall to give your Honn[r] account of our proceeding since our last fr[m] Pautuxet in the Sabath evening we advanced the whole body from Mr Carpenters with Intent to surprise Pomham & his Party at about 10 or 12 Miles Distance having information by our Warwick Scouts of his seat but the darkness of y[e] Night Difficulty of our passage & unskilfulness of Pilots we passed the whole Night & found ourselves at such Distance yet from y[m] y[t] we Diverted & Marched to Mr Smiths, found our Sloops from Seaconk arrived since which by y[e] help of Indian Peter by whom your Honnor had the Information formerly of y[e] Number &

resolution of ye Naragansets, we have burned two of their Towns viz: Ahmus who is this summer come down amongst them & ye old Queens quarters consisting of about 150 Many of them large wigwams & seized & slayn 50 Persons in all our prisoners being about 40 Concerning whom the generall prayes your advice concerning their transportation or Disposall all which was performed without any loss save a slight wound by an Arrow in Lieut. Wayman's face, the whole body of them we find removed into their great swamp at Canonicus his quarters where we hope with the addition of Connecticut, when arrived we hope to Coop them up, this day we Intend the removall or spoyle of y^r Corn & hope to Morrow a March toward them, our soldiers being very chearful are forward notwithstanding great Difficulty by weather & otherwise, abovs^d Peter whom we have found very faithfull will Make us believe y^t y^r are 3000 fighting Men though Many unarmed Many well fitted with lances we hope by cutting off their forage to force them to a fayr battle In ye Mean time I have only to present the Generalls humble service to your (*sic*) & to beg your Intense prayers for this so great Concern and remayn your

Honnors Humble Servant   Jos: Dudley.

Goodale[114] nor Moor arrived we fear want of shot.

My humble service to Madam Leveret Brother and ·Sister Hubbard & Dudley.

Amongst our Prison^{rs} & slayne we find 10 or 12 Wampanoags.

[Mass. Archives, Vol. 68, p. 101.]

. *Answer of the Council to Gen. Winslow.*

S^r y^r Intelligences and Advices subjected by Mr Dudley the 15 & 16 Ins^t wee received this Morning being the 18th at eight of the clock. Wee desire to blesse God y^t hee hath smiled upon you in y^r first Attempts & hath delivered some of o^r enemys into yor hands & also to Acknowledge Gods favou^r in the supporting ye hearts of yor souldiers in such a severe season & keeping up their spirits wth courage and that you have received no more losse of men: But yet also according to God's wonted manner of dealing hee hath mixed the Cup wth some bitternes; in the losse susteyned in yor soldiers especially Mr Bulls house & ye people y^{re} also y^t the forces of Conecticut are not joyned wth you nor the vessell wth supplys of Ammunition & provision then arrived; Wee hope by this time both the vessell may be arrived & the Conecticut men conjoined wth you but least that should faile wee have sent a cart wth Ammunition; and an order from Gou^{nr} Winthrop for their forces to March speedily; Concerning the disposall of ye Indian prisoners; Our Advice is if any present to buy them, they may be sould there & delivered by your Orders or if that cannot bee then to secure them at the Island or els-where at yor best discretion; Wee have no more to add at present but our hearty prayers unto the Lord of Hoasts to appear wth & for you & all wth you, in all yor enterprises, for the Lord & his people and cover all yor heads in the day of Battle, So wth our particular respects & love to y^{r}self & all ye Command^{rs} & Ministers; wee remajne

Yo^r respective friends & servants

Boston 18: December 1675   Edward Rawson Secret^y in the name
    at one of the clock.   & by ye order of the Council.

[Mass. Archives, Vol. 68, p. 102.]

[114] Richard Goodale and Thomas Moore. (See Maritime Department, p. 93.)

Second Letter of Joseph Dudley.[115]

Mr Smith's, 21, 10, 1675 (Dec. 21, 1675).

May it please your honour,

The coming in of Connecticut force to Petaquamscot, and surprisal of six and slaughter of 5 on Friday night, Saturday we marched towards Petaquamscot, though in the snow, and in conjunction about midnight or later, we advanced; Capt. Mosely led the van, after him Massachusets, and Plimouth and Connecticut in the rear; a tedious march in the snow, without intermission, brought us about two of the clock afternoon, to the entrance of the swamp, by the help of Indian Peter, who dealt faithfully with us; our men, with great courage, entered the swamp about 20 rods; within the cedar swamp we found some hundreds of wigwams, forted in with a breastwork and flankered, and many small blockhouses up and down, round about; they entertained us with a fierce fight, and many thousand shot, for about an hour, when our men valiantly scaled the fort, beat them thence, and from the blockhouses. In which action we lost Capt. Johnson, Capt Danforth, and Capt Gardiner, and their lieutenants disabled, Capt. Marshall also slain; Capt. Seely, Capt. Mason, disabled, and many other of our officers, insomuch that, by a fresh assault and recruit of powder from their store, the Indians fell on again, recarried and beat us out of, the fort, but by the great resolution and courage of the General and Major, we reinforced, and very hardly entered the fort again, and fired the wigwams, with many living and dead persons in them, great piles of meat and heaps of corn, the ground not admitting burial of their store, were consumed; the number of their dead, we generally suppose the enemy lost at least two hundred men; Capt. Mosely counted in one corner of the fort sixty four men; Capt. Goram reckoned 150 at least; But, O! Sir, mine heart bleeds to give your honor an account of our lost men, but especially our resolute Captains, as by account inclosed, and yet not so many, but we admire there remained any to return, a captive woman, well known to Mr Smith, informing that there were three thousand five hundred men engaging us and about a mile distant a thousand in reserve, to whom if God had so pleased, we had been but a morsel, after so much disablement: she informeth, that one of their sagamores was slain and their powder spent, causing their retreat, and that that they are in a distressed condition for food and houses, that one Joshua Tift, an Englishman, is their encourager and conductor. Philip was seen by one, credibly informing us, under a strong guard.

After our wounds were dressed, we drew up for a march, not able to abide the field in the storm, and weary, about two of the clock, obtained our quarters, with our dead and wounded, only the General, Ministers, and some other persons of the guard, going to head a small swamp, lost our way, and returned again to the evening's quarters, a wonder we were not a prey to them, and, after at least thirty miles marching up and down, in the morning recovered our quarters, and had it not been for the arrival of Goodale next morning, the whole camp had perished; The whole army, especially Connecticut, is much disabled and unwilling to march, with tedious storms, and no lodgings, and frozen and swollen limbs, Major Treat importunate to return at least to Stonington; Our dead and wounded are about two hundred, disabled as many; the want of officers, the considera-

---

[115] This letter is copied from the note in Hutchinson's History of Massachusetts, vol. i. page 273.

tion whereof the General commends to your honor, forbids any action at present, and we fear whether Connecticut will comply, at last, to any action. We are endeavoring, by good keeping and billetting our men at several quarters, and, if possible removal of our wounded to Rhode-Island, to recover the spirit of our soldiers, and shall be diligent to find and understand the removals on other action of the enemy, if God please to give us advantage against them.

As we compleat the account of our dead, now in doing, the Council is of the mind, without recruit of men we shall not be able to engage the main body.

I give your honour hearty thanks for your kind lines, of which I am not worthy

I am Sir, your honor's humble servant,
JOSEPH DUDLEY.

Since the writing of these lines, the General and Council have jointly concluded to abide on the place, notwithstanding the desire of Connecticut, only entreat that a supply of 200 may be sent us, with supply of commanders; and, whereas we are forced to garrison our quarters with at least one hundred, three hundred men, upon joint account of the colonies, will serve, and no less, to effect the design. This is by order of the council.

Blunderbusses, and hand grenadoes, and armour, if it may be, and at least two armourers to mend arms.

COMMISSARY DEPARTMENT.

The following accounts are inserted in this place as showing somewhat the method and material of the commissary department at that time. The accounts, as will be noticed, relate largely to the earlier part of the war, and the Mount Hope campaign under Gen. Cudworth. The preliminary accounts having been squared by Mr. Southward (Southworth), all the rest were gathered in the general settlement in January, 1675–6.—*Hull's Journal.*

27 August 1675

Plymouth Colony Dr. to Cash for severalls as followeth.
To Phillip Curtis for five men to guard powder
  and shott   00, 17, 00
To the Guard for expence at Roxbury   00, 08, 06
for ¼ bbl of biskett   00, 05, 09   02, 05, 09
for 1lb of powder besides what they brought   00, 01, 06
Expence of sd Guard at Dedham   00, 13, 00

September 14th 1675

Richard Smith for guarding Ammunition   00, 03, 00
Thomas Lawrence   ditto.   00, 03, 00
James Hosly   ditto.   00, 03, 00   00, 15, 00
James Montt   ditto.   00, 03, 00
Ebenezer Hill   ditto.   00, 03, 00

November 23d. Cr. By Received of Mr. Southward
for disbursements 03, 00, 09

January 25th 1675

Plimouth Colony Dr. to Sundry accts as hear stated in p'per p'cells, for severalls dd'. by sundry persons for the use of sd Colony at divers times from the 29th of June last to this moneth inclusive as ꝑr the acc[ts], receipts, & orders relating thereunto filed as ꝑ No. 1269 & 1270   £285, 14, 10

Armes for a muskett to Gen[l] Cudworth 00, 18, 00
Liqors for Rum to viz.
  Mr James Brown 9½ Gall.   .   .   .   2, 5, 0 ⎱ 05, 05, 00
  Their forces at Naragansett 12½ gall   .   3, 0, 0 ⎰

Apparel for severalls viz. 32, 11, 00
  To Nathaniel Gunny 1 pr shoes   .   .   0, 4, 0
  Ditto Benjamin Peirce 0, 4, 0
  To Capt Cornelius, Wastcoat, Shoes & Stokins 0, 14, 0
  To Josiah Joslin, shoes and stockins   .   .   0, 7, 0
  To Gen[l] Cudworth 6 pr. shoes and 13 p. stockins 3, 0, 0
Delivered by the Commissioners to their forces at
      Narragansett viz.
  26—shirts at   7, 16, 0 ⎫
  6—Wastcoats   2, 14, 0 ⎪
  9—ꝑ drawers   1, 4, 0 ⎪
  1—ꝑ breeches   0, 18, 0 ⎪
  2—lined coats   3, 0, 0 ⎬ 28, 2, 0
  10—ꝑ shoes ⎱   4, 15, 0 ⎪
  5—ꝑ stockins ⎰   ⎪
  6 y[ds] of canvas for neckcloaths ⎱   1, 0, 0 ⎪
  shott pouch and calicoe ⎰   ⎪
  180 y[ds] sale cloth at y[e]   6, 15, 0 ⎭

          (32, 11, 0)

Ammunition Id' viz. 103, 08, 10
To the officers a bagg with 35[lbs] powder   2, 14, 0
Ditto to Benjamin Church with 18[lbs] and 50 bullets 2, 13, 6
To the Gen[ll] 1 cask bullets qr 1[lb] or better   2, 16, 0
To Mr James Brown 5½ bbl powder at 7[lb] pr bbl. 38, 10, 0
  Ditto 9 cask & 1 chest bullets qr. 11[lb]   25, 13, 4
More dd'. by the Commissaries 480 flints   0, 10, 0
      124 bullets   2, 12, 0
8 half barrells of powder of the Mattachusetts ⎫
 detained by the Governor of Rhoad Island ⎬ 28, 0, 0
 for 4 barrells lent to Plimouth ⎭
       (103, 08, 10)

Tobacco, for 15[lb] to Nathaniel Gunny   .   .   .   0, 07, 06
Tooles, dd' to the officers viz 3 spades   0, 10, 0 ⎫
      2 Mattucks   1, 14, 0 ⎬ 02, 08, 00
      4 Axes   1, 04, 0 ⎭
Biskett dd' viz. To the Officers 150 cakes   0, 14, 0 ⎫
   To Mr James Brown 9 hhds.   31, 10, 0 ⎬ 44, 04, 00
   To Gen[all] Cudworth 3½ hhds.   12, 00, 0 ⎭
Grocery for 26[lb] Raisons solis to ditto Brown   .   .   .   01, 06, 00
Fish for 1 hhd. ditto 04, 00, 00
Porke ditto for 5 bb[l] at 4[lb] pr bb[l]   .   .   20, 00, 00 ⎱ 28, 00, 00
   2 bb[l] ditt   .   .   .   8, 00, 00 ⎰

Miscellanies, for severalls viz 24, 19, 06

To Benjamin Church 1 hh^d biscake
　　　　　2 bb^l porke　　　　} 11, 10, 00

　　　2 bsh. pease & 1 sack
　　　20^{lb} tobacoe　　　} 01, 02, 00

To Capt. Goram 1^{hhd} biskett & pease
　　　　wanting 200 cakes
　　　　1^{lb} raisons solis　　} 03, 17, 06
　　　　4 large peeces of porke

To Gen^{all} Cudworth 1 kittle 01, 10 00

To ditto Church 1 jarr oyle
　　　　2 galls wine　　　} 01, 03, 00
　　　10^{lb} raisons solis

To Lt Tanner 1^{bbl} pease
　　(4?)^{bbl} biscake　　} 04, 00, 00
　　$\frac{2}{3}$^{bbl} porke

To John Cobleigh for ditt. Ch(urch)?
　　　　1^{bbl} salt　　} 1, 16, 00

At Narragansett 2 qire p(aper)　　0, 01, 00

　　　　　　　　　　　　(24, 19, 06)

Billetings, for quartering 12 souldiers at Mr Miles hous
Alsoe Gen^{all} Cudworth's and Capt Bradfords Companies
　the 17th 18th & 19th dayes of July with bread, pease, } 10, 00, 00
　pork tobaco and liq^{ors}

Pease viz
　　To dit. Browne 3^{hhd} with Cask　　9, 00, 00 }
　　To dit. Cudworth　2^{hhd}　　　　1, 15, 00 } 10, 15, 00
Cask for 9^{hhd} to Ditto Browne 2, 01, 00
Maritim—disbursments viz 11, 00, 00
　for the frait of 4^{hhd} bisket and 2^{bbl} of tobaco } 1, 00, 00
　at guess
　Ditto to $\frac{1}{3}$ p^t of the hire of Vessells　10, 00, 00

Salt dd'. viz
　　To Ditto Browne 1^{hhd} qr. 12^{bsh} & Cask　2, 00, 00 }
　　By Ditto Commissaries 1$\frac{1}{2}$ bsh　　0, 06, 00 } 02, 06, 00

Thomas Terry for 1$\frac{1}{2}$ firkins of sope
　1^{bsh} meale, 10 wooden boules and 1 cann } 02, 05, 00

　　　　　　　　　　　　(285, 14, 10)

June 24th 1676.
Plymouth Colony Cr By Viz.
　Ammunission for powder & ball returned as } 44, 18, 04]
　p No 3185
　Biskett dit.　　　　22, 00, 00 } 69, 18, 04
　Graine for pease dit.　　03, 00, 00]

By Disbursements for Ballance as p bond 11535 fo^l 544　215, 16, 06

The account is thus carried to a later Ledger, which is lost.

MARITIME DEPARTMENT.

The following may show somewhat of the "naval" power of that day, and the methods and means of transporting supplies.

1675	Maritime Disbursements	Dr	
Nov 20	To Peter Treby for frait of the Sloope Primrose		£09, 06, 00
Dec 10	To Israel Nichols for wood for Goodall's Vessel		00, 05, 00
" "	To Stephen Hascott for dammage of the Sloope Swan		03, 10, 00
Feby 29	To Anthony Low for frait . . .		05, 00, 00
1676			
June 24	" Richard Goodall for frait . . .		22, 00, 00
"	" Nehemiah Goodall for Service . .		05, 10, 00
"	" Pilgrim Simpkin " " . .		02, 08, 00
"	" James Twisdell " " . . .		02, 08, 00
"	" Richard Earle " " . .		02, 08, 00
"	" Ezekiel Gardner " " . . .		02, 02, 00
"	" William Woodbery " " . .		05, 10, 00
"	" Anthony Haywood " " . . .		04, 00, 00
"	" Thomas Moore " " . .		10, 00, 00
"	" John Baker " " . . .		02, 08, 00

Andrew Belcher, of Cambridge, a prominent merchant, with vessels operating between Boston and Connecticut ports, was active in these affairs, but his accounts doubtless fall into a later Ledger.

In the State Archives, in some bills of Benjamin Gillam against the colony, I find the item, Jan'y 10, 1675 :

" To charges on men to cut out Andrew Belcher's Sloop to goe to Narragansett, 14s."

Mr. Church speaks of the arrival of Andrew Belcher as opportune in saving the army ; Mr. Dudley says Goodale. Mr. Hubbard's reference to the vessels "frozen in at Cape Cod," causing distress, was, I think, to a later time.

After the return of the army to Mr. Smith's Garrison, the burial of the dead and removal of their wounded to Rhode Island, they spent several weeks parleying with the enemy, watching and recruiting. Major Treat withdrew with his Connecticut forces, against the wishes, it appears, of the General and the other officers, and was later called to account for insubordination. Additional troops were sent down from Boston, and Massachusetts and Plymouth held the field for a month longer ; but their operations and the closing part of this winter campaign, and the new forces engaged, must fall into the next chapter.

Massachusetts afterwards redeemed the promise made to the soldiers at Dedham Plain, and granted to eight hundred and forty claimants, including those of Plymouth, the seven Narragansett townships. Connecticut to her volunteers in the Narragansett wars granted the town of Voluntown. (See List in Narragansett Historical Register, vol. i. p. 145, by Hon. Richard A. Wheeler.)

THE INDIAN NAMES OF BOSTON, AND THEIR MEANING.

Read before the New England Historic Genealogical Society, November 4, 1885,

By Prof. E. N. HORSFORD, A.M., of Cambridge.

THE following paper has grown out of the study of the Indian names of Eastern Long Island, New York, to which I was led in an investigation of some points of local history pertaining to the early settlement of SYLVESTER MANOR, Shelter Island. Several of these names[1] that have been kept in use there were found to be nearly related to Indian names that have been preserved in the annals of Boston; so that in the study of the one group I became, in a degree, familiar with the other. In this research light has been thrown upon some other names of New England, which were necessarily introduced into my discussion.

To illustrate my paper, I have added a tracing of Winsor's map of ancient and modern Boston; also one, somewhat modified, from Des Barres's map of Boston and its neighborhood; together with a copy of Montanus's map, showing some of the Indian names, and their substitutes proposed by Prince Charles; and, lastly, John Smith's map of 1634.

It will be seen that the region of *the Neck* to which Shawmut (Sha-um-ut) applied had its narrowest part between Haymarket Square and North Street, about on a line at right angles to the front of Oak Hall. In the time of Winthrop a canal was cut along what is now Blackstone Street, permitting small craft loaded with wood or other supplies procured on the shores of the Charles or Mystic to pass through for the needs of the dwellers on the east side of the peninsula. The Neck proper extended scarcely a hundred yards along what is now Hanover Street, and comprised with it a strip on either side, a little more than twice the width of the present street, as laid down on Winsor's map. The farthest reach of the water from the east was a point about midway between Union and Blackstone streets, and equally distant from North and Hanover streets.

The late Dr. T. W. Harris, librarian of Harvard College, as I am informed by Mr. Charles Deane, suggested that the names Boston, Hull, and Cambridge were *transferred* from the sites to which Prince Charles assigned them, and were not original selections by the first settlers, as in regard to Boston Dudley would lead us to believe. The observations presented in the following paper may throw some light on how the unanimity of assent as to the proposed change was promoted. In addition to what is stated in my paper,

[1] Agawom, Amagansett, Massapaug, Missepaug, Mashom-uk, Hashim-om-uk, Montauk, Monchonoc, Man-an-duk, Man-han-sett, Man-han-sac-kah-aquash-oo-um-uk.

I may add that Cambridge was a name assigned by Prince Charles to a point near the mouth of the Kennebec, called also Quinnebequi.[1] Kennebec and Quinnebequi differ only dialectically. Both mean *long still water*. If an Indian of the Massachusetts tribe, standing on the bank of *any* river against a stretch of "dead water," were asked what he called the stream, he would reply (that point alone being in his mind), *Quinnebequi* (*Quinne*, "long, and *bequi*, " still water"), or the same word with dialectic modification.' So he, must have replied to Winthrop and Dudley, or Saltonstall and Philips, if they stood together near Winthrop Square, Old Cambridge, or near the Saltonstall landing against the Cambridge Hospital; and when they recalled Smith's map and account, and saw Cambridge on the river called Quinnebequi, they found the Prince had already bestowed a name.

The name Anmoughcawgen, which Smith had placed higher up on the Kennebec (Quinnebequi) of Maine, qualified possibly the Charles and the Kennebec alike. It may mean *Fishing-place weir*, or perhaps *Beaver dam*. In the former case the "Fish weir" in Watertown would have borne the name associated with Cambridge; in the latter, the sources of both streams—the Charles and the Kennebec—were regions in which beaver dams and meadows abounded.

————

WHEN Winthrop came out in 1630, after a brief detention at Salem he moved around to Nantasket. Leaving the vessels there, he came up with the principal men of the Company to Charlestown, the residence of Thomas Walford, who was living within a stockaded enclosure on the slope of Breed's Hill, looking toward Copp's Hill, across the Charles River. The situation did not please Winthrop's Company mainly because of the want of good water. The spring on which Mr. Walford depended was below high-water mark, and was, of course, available only when the tide was out; and much of this time it yielded a more or less brackish water.

Mr. Winthrop, Mr. Saltonstall, Mr. Dudley and others set out to find a more desirable spot on which to erect their dwelling-houses. Saltonstall and some others established themselves at Watertown, in the neighborhood of Mount Auburn, where they found good water. Winthrop and Dudley and others began to build at Cambridge, where, also, they found water. Before Winthrop had proceeded far, Mr. William Blaxton, who had been established for some years on the westerly slope of Beacon Hill, or possibly further north, invited him to settle at *Shaumut*, as there were *good springs there*.

The substance of this interview is in a note in the early records of Charlestown.

The first utterance of the word *Shawmutt* by an Englishman, spelled precisely as if pronounced as we pronounce it *to-day*, occurred at least as early as 1630.

The inducement mentioned by Blaxton (or Blackstone) and the coinci-

---

[1] It is also printed Quinobequin and Quinibequy.

dent needs of Winthrop may have given rise to the notion that the meaning of Shawmutt was "a spring of water." For this or some other reason the notion has found wide acceptance from that day to this.[1]

In 1817 Charles Shaw, in a very interesting volume entitled " A Topographical and Historical Description of Boston," suggests that the name "Shawmut" means *Peninsula ;* and leads us to infer that it applied to the great block of land connected by the Roxbury Neck with the main-land; although he recognizes that there was the *principal* neck, and a neck *within,* known also as the "chief landing place." Mr. Shaw supported his suggestion by references to Indian names of other localities, which, however, in the light of more recent study, admit of other interpretations. The suggestion was, nevertheless, a very happy one, and came very near to rendering further research unnecessary.

In 1822 Rev. Samuel Deane, of Scituate, in a communication to the Massachusetts Historical Society, finds the origin of *Shawmut* in certain words of somewhat remote relationship, and that the word means *a fountain of living waters.* " Mishawumut " he translated *a great spring.*

Mr. Drake, the author of the "History and Antiquities of Boston," p. 457, remarks that he thinks Shawmut means " Free Country, free land, or land unclaimed." He does not give his reasons in detail.

The most recent and thoughtful of the various discussions of the meaning of Shawmut is contained in a communication from the eminent Algonquin scholar, Dr. Trumbull, of Hartford, addressed to the late Mr. Folsom, Secretary of the Massachusetts Historical Society, and published in the Proceedings of the Society some twenty years ago.

This paper derives the name from an Indian phrase, which Dr. Trumbull translates, *Where there is going by boat.*

The phrase, including Mushau-womuk as one of its stages of degradation, Mishawumut perhaps as another, and M'Shawmut as a third, became at length, in the utterance of English-speaking people, Shawmut, the meaning of which, in short, was *Ferry,* and referred to "where there was going by boat " to Charlestown.

My studies have led me to another interpretation, and its contrast with this of Dr. Trumbull illustrates the fine spirit of the intimation, in quite another connection, by this accomplished writer, that it is well to regard efforts in this direction as tentative, and our conclusions, at the best, as scarcely more than provisional.

In Wood's " New Englands' Prospect," edited by Mr. Charles Deane, there is, near the close, a short vocabulary of Indian words and a collection of Indian geographical names.

In this latter list one column gives the Indian names, and another the corresponding English names, where known.

---

[1] " Authority that can be relied upon " (Dr. Shurtleff, p. 25, " Historical Description of Boston ") " says: In the mean time, Mr. Blackstone, dwelling on the other side of Charles River, alone, at a place by the Indians called Shawmutt, where he only had a cottage—at, not far off, the place called Blackstone's Point, he came and acquainted the Governor of an excellent spring there, withal inviting him and soliciting him thither. Whereupon after the death of Mr. Johnson and divers others, the Governor with Mr. Wilson and the greater part of the church removed thither; whither also the frame of the Governor's house in preparation in this town [Winthrop's house was begun at what is now Cambridge] was (also to the discontent of some) carried, when people began to build their houses against winter, and this place was called Boston."

Prince says: (Mass. Hist. Soc. Coll., iv. p. 155) : " The want of good water and other conveniences at Charlestown made several go abroad upon discovery. Some go over to Shawmut, some go without Charlestown Neck and travel up into the main till they come to a place well watered, whither Sir Richard Saltonstall with Mr. Phillips (minister) and several others went, and settled a plantation, and called it Watertown."

Among them occur the following:—

Mishaum,	
Mishaumut,	Charlestowne.
Massachusets,	Boston.

Dr. Trumbull suggested in regard to the column of geographical names, that, through a mistake of the type-setter, the English names had been dropped a line. It will be seen that there was no error in print requiring this explanation.

In Ogilby's " America " (1671) we have, in a list of the early · settlements of New England, against Charlestown, the name *Mashawmut.*

We have, then, three forms of the Indian name of the site of Charlestown :—

Mishaumut,	Wood, 1634.
Mashawmut,	Ogilby, 1671.
Mishawumut,	Rev. Samuel Deane, 1822.

These are not different Indian words, but different results of English efforts to write what the Indian gave as the name of the site of Charlestown.

They are obviously different forms of one word. Wood was several years in the neighborhood. He prepared a vocabulary of Indian words. Neither of the other authorities had this advantage. Wood's form, Mishaumut, commends itself. He spells the name of Charles River, Mishaum.

Let us take his form, Mishaumut, as the Indian name of Charlestown.

Neither Wood nor Ogilby give Shaumut as a name for Boston. The only authority for this name is Blaxton. It differs from the name for Charlestown in that it lacks the prefix *Mi* or *Mis*.

The meaning of *Mis* we know. It occurs in *Mis*tick, a tidal river sweeping Charlestown on the north and west, and in another tidal river near Stonington in Connecticut. It occurs in *Mis*souri and in *Mis*sissippi, the great rivers ; in *Mis*tassini, the great lake south of Hudson's Bay. Its signification is well known. It means *great*. Mas is a dialectic equivalent of Mis.

Mistick River is great as compared with other tidal rivers leading up into Malden and Medford meadows.

Mis-shaumut, or Mishaumut, differs from Shaumut (whatever that may mean), in that it is something relatively *greater*.

Let us look again at Wood's column of Indian names. They are arranged thus :—

Mishaum,	
Mishaumut,	Charlestowne,

as if both names might be used for the same locality.[1] They differ from each other in that one has the terminal syllable *ut*.

Thomas Walford's residence was Mishaum*ut*.

What does this terminal syllable *ut* mean ? The answer is happily at hand. Books were printed for the use of the Indians in the two languages ; English on one page, and over against it the Indian translation.

On the English titlepage the books were printed at Boston. On the

---

[1] Dr. Palfrey, vol. i. " Hist. of New England," p. 289, says : " The visitors found at Mishawum an English palisaded and thatched house, wherein lived Thomas Walford, a smith." " Before the winter, an exploring party either began or made preparations for a settlement at Mishawam, now Charlestown. *Everett's Address at Charlestown*, June 28, 1830. Mishaum and Mishaumut were understood by the English as interchangeable or equivalent, as applied to Charlestown.

Indian titlepage they were printed Boston-*ut*. (Trumbull, Winsor's " Boston.")

When Eliot, in attempting to translate the phrase, *showing himself through the lattice* (Solomon's Song, ii. 9), for his Indian Bible, finding the nearest equivalent for *lattice* was the Indian expression for *eel-pot*, decided to transfer the English word unchanged, with the addition only of the syllable *ut*,—making " *lattessut* " do service in defining the position, when " showing himself through the lattice." (Breeches Bible, 1599, has *grates*, Solomon's Song, xi. 9, and *lattesse*, Judges v. 28.)

Ut is a syllable of location, at, near, against, on this side, on that side, etc. We cannot be mistaken as to the meaning of the terminal syllable *ut*. Thomas Walford lived *near* Mishaum, and William Blaxton lived *near* Shaum.

The peninsula of Charlestown was *near* Mishaum. The peninsula of Copp's Hill was *near* Shaum.

The unknown part of Mi-shaum-ut is reduced to two syllables. The unknown part of Shaum-ut is less by one syllable. What remains is *Shaum*.

It seems in the Massachusetts dialect that the addition of *um* to a preposition or adverb or adjective converts it into a *noun*,—na-um, wam(p)um, wong-um, shong-um, etc. That is, we may regard *um* (or *wum*, our spelling) as a terminal syllable, without meaning, *except in combination*. It is, for example, like *ness* in English, or *keit* in German. *Ness* converts *upright*, an adjective, into *uprightness*, a noun. *Keit* converts *aufrichtig*, an adverb, into *aufrichtigkeit*, a noun.

So *um* or *wum*, which we find in Shaum(ut) or Shawum(ut), and in (Mis)shaum or (Mis)shawum(ut), when taken away, leaves *Sha* as a possible adverb, or preposition, or adjective,—the remaining syllable the meaning of which is to be found.

To ascertain the meaning of this syllable, I have collected many Indian words in which it occurs, and sought, by a process of substitution, to find the word or phrase which would fit equally well in all the combinations of the syllable *sha*.

Dr. Trumbull has laid down a rule in regard to Indian geographical names, which has been found to be of almost universal appplication.[1] It is this:—

" Every name DESCRIBED the locality to which it was AFFIXED.

Of such names, in which the syllable *sha* occurs, there is Na-sha-un (Naushaun) (un for um*)*, the long, narrow island between Vineyard Sound and Buzzard's Bay; and Na-sha-we-na, another island, between the same two sheets of water.

Na-sha-wi (oue, ue) (Nashaway), a river emptying into the Merrimack, not far from Lowell.

Mi-sha-um (Mis-sha-um), the Charles River.

Mi-sha-um, Charlestown.

Sha-womet is the Indian name of a part of Warwick Neck in Rhode Island. Sha-omet and Mi-sha-womut are also found on Rhode Island maps.

Sha appears in the Indian name Chawum (Shaum) of Captain John Smith, and the same name written in the town records of Sandwich is Shaum-e (e silent. Dr. Dwight).

---

[1] The Composition of Indian Geographical Names. Coll. Conn. Hist. Soc., vol. ii. p. 4.

Sha-um, with slight modification, is the name of a neck of land not far from Dighton Rock; of another neck of land near Fall River; of another between Seconnet and New Bedford; another on the peninsula of Cape Cod.

Na-sha-quit-za describes a locality on Nantucket.

In another class of names we have Mi-sha-on.

Mi-sha-on, the trunk of a tree.

Mi-sha-on, or Misho-on, or Misho-an, or Mushau-on, the canoe made from the trunk of a tree.

Na-sha-onk, the throat.

Mi-sha-onk, the trunk of the body, distinct from the head, arms and legs.

Sha-meek is a Delaware name for eel, still used on Nantucket. The eel is also called Meek-sha, or Neek-sha.

Sha (or Schach) enters into the name of a gun-barrel, and fenced road or highway. [Delaware.]

Na-sha-wi (or ue or we) is the Indian equivalent of *between the walls*, as of a village, for example, in Eliot's Bible.

Naha-sha-wi is employed by Eliot as the Indian equivalent of *in a strait betwixt two*. *Na* is repeated for emphasis, as " out and out," or " very true."

In looking over this list, which need not be further extended, it will be readily seen that the single phrase suited to all the various uses of the syl-lable *Sha* is *parallel-sided*.

Let us apply it.

The *gun* barrel is *parallel-sided*.

The *eel* (Sha-meek) is a *parallel-sided* fish; *meek* is Delaware for *fish:*

The *sturgeon* (Keppi-sha-meek) is an *encased, parallel-sided fish*.

Na means in the middle, half way, between, divide, etc.

Onk means upright.

Na-sha-onk, the throat, is *middle-of-the-parallel-sided upright*.

Mis-sha-onk, the trunk of the human body, is *the great-parallel-sided upright*.

The trunk of the tree is *the-great-parallel-sided* Mis-sha-on (Mishaon); and the canoe made from it is Misha-on, or Misho-on, or Mushauon.

Mi-sha-um is the great *parallel-sided River* Charles.[1] (See Wood's " New Englands' Prospect.")

It is also the great *parallel-sided Neck* of Charlestown, near which was Mi-sha-um-*ut*, the residence of Walford.

Sha-um is that which is *parallel-sided*, as the *Neck* at Sandwich.

---

[1] Charles River had in its different portions different Indian names. Mi-sha-um, the *great-parallel-sided*,—the *eel* river, applied well to the portion between the Watertown Arsenal and the Cottage Farm station on the Boston and Albany Railroad. Quinobequin, given by Morse as a name of Charles River, was probably, as suggested by the late Dr. T. W. Harris, librarian of Harvard College, transferred, with Cambridge, from the region of the Kennebec, where it was placed in Smith's account, to the region of Boston. It was not the name of a river as a *proper* name. *Quinnebequi* applied to *long* stretches of *still water*, as the same name with dialectic modification applied to portions of the Kennebec. Another Indian name, *Norombégue*, is mentioned by Allefonsce, Thevet and Ogilby, which defined or described another peculiar feature or portion of the river. Captain John Smith substituted for *Massachusets*—the Indian name of the mouth of the river—the name of Prince *Charles*. On Verrazano's map (Maiollo's) of our coast, 1527, is the name *Anguileme*, which is repeated on the maps of Gastaldi and Ruscelli, and is mentioned by Thevet, and also by Buno in his comment on Cluverius (see Ogilby), as being under the forty-third degree of latitude. It has interest as a possible translation of *Mishaum*, one of the Indian names of Charles River given above.

Sha-um was the *Neck*, upon or near which was the first Indian settlement, between the cove formerly coming in from the northwest to beyond the eastern limit of Haymarket Square, and the bay extending from the east to points west of Dock Square, as shown on Winsor's map of ancient Boston.

As *Shaum* was the *neck*, Shaum-ut seems to have been applied, as already intimated, to the peninsula which was *near* it to the north as well. So Mishaum was the greater neck, and Mishaum-ut was applied to the whole peninsula of Charlestown, which was *near* it on the east, and *greater* than the peninsula north of the present Blackstone Street.

As Sha-um-ut was the residence of Blaxton, *near the* Neck, so Mi-sha-um-ut was the temporary stopping-place of Winthrop, *near the greater* Neck.

So I conceive came the name SHAWMUT.

There was another name of early Boston, of which note was taken by Dr. Trumbull:—

Mushau-womuk.

Indian books were printed at Mushau-womuk, according to the Indian title page. They were printed, as the English title page showed, at *Boston.* (Trumbull.)

The business streets or lanes of that period were in the region we now know as Blackstone and Union streets. Mushau-womuk was at the head of the cove, since filled in. It was the place where the canoes coming from Charlestown (Mishaumut) and perhaps Chelsea (Winne-sim-met) made the land. It was the *canoe-landing-place*, which is the meaning of Mushau-womuk. It *described* one side of the neck,—the *Shaum.* It was the name an Indian, *with little conception of a* PROPER *geographical name*, would give, in reply to inquiry. He would thus *describe* the spot to which he conceived his attention had been directed.

From *Mushaum*—*canoe*—the *m* was dropped for ease of utterance ; *om* was *enclosure ; uk* (ock) was *place ; w* (or *oo*) may be euphonic. The place where the canoe was kept—*the ferry landing*—was

MUSHAU-WOMUK.

Another name was recognized by Father Rasles, the Jesuit missionary among the Abnakis. It is given in his Abnaki Dictionary under the head *Noms*, p. 493.

Messatsoosec,   BASTON.

Baston was the spelling on Montanus's map; it was the same on La Hontin's map. (On Smith's map, Snodoun is spelled *Snadoun*.)

Wood, in his "New Englands'[1] Prospect," already cited, wrote the name as he understood it :—

| *Massachusets*, | BOSTON, |
| instead of *Messatsoosec*, | BASTON. |

If we analyze the name given by Father Rasles, we find familiar forms under dialectic variation.

Mess is the same as mas or mis or mus, *great.*
at-soo is adchu, wadchu, *hill.*
sec is sac, saco, or saugus, *mouth.*
The combination, according to Rasles, was *Great-Hills-Mouth*, referring

───────────

[1] Wood placed the apostrophe *after* the *s*.

to the mouth of Charles River, near Trimountain, and contrasting it with the mouths of Naponsett,[1] Weymouth, and the other lesser streams emptying into Boston Harbor.

The combination, *Massachusetts,* which is said to have been applied, and properly, to the country about the Blue Hills of Milton, was also properly employed in Massachusetts Bay.[2] It is the bay of the *Great-Hills-Mouth,* or the bay at the mouth of the Charles River.

This name was another descriptive appellation of the site, not of the *neck* or *the head of the cove,* but of the *mouth of the river* emptying into the bay near this point.

But there was still another name. It occurs in Ogilby's "America," and in some respects is the most interesting of all, from its possible immediate connection with the final adoption of the English name Boston.

Ogilby seems not to have heard of Shaumut or Shawmut, or Mushauwomuk or Messatsoosec, as Indian names of the region of Boston. He says (edition of 1671, p. 159) the name was "anciently"

Accomonticus.

It is not difficult to analyze this name. It is the same as the Abnaki name, Agamenticus.

Accom (or *Ogkome.* Eliot) means *beyond.*

Mon (or *man,* or *men,* or *min*) means *elevation,* or abrupt *rising* from water or a plain.

tuc (or *tick*) means *tidal river* or *cove.*

es (or *us*) means *little.*

Accomonticus means *Beyond-the-hill-little-cove.*

This would be the descriptive term employed by an Indian standing on the site of the Charlestown Navy Yard, and describing the head of the ancient cove reaching up to the east side of the mill-pond of earlier times and of the present Haymarket Square. To him it would be the " Beyond-the hill-little-cove."

So it would if he stood at the old Fort Washington, south of West Boston Bridge, looking across the ridge traversed by Leveret Street.

So it would be if he were at Brookline or Roxbury, looking over Beacon Hill, or if he were at South Boston or Dorchester, looking over the ancient Fort Hill.

From all these points the Sha-um or Mushau-womuk would be at or near the *Beyond-the-hill-little-cove.*

I have already intimated that this name is the most interesting of the four early Indian names of Boston, because it seems to be connected with the vote of the authorities in 1630, which determined the present English name of the locality which had at first been called *Trimountain.*

You will remember that Captain John Smith, after his return from his services at Jamestown, Virginia, sailed from England, April, 1614, on a voyage to our shores. His first land made was the Island *Monahigan,*[3] off the mouth of the Penobscot. He sent a part of his ship's company to collect fish, and with a boat's crew of eight besides himself he explored the coast as far south as Cape Cod. He obtained the various Indian names by which were known the bays, rivers, capes, etc., of the coast, and to some extent of the interior; and having placed them upon the outline chart he

---

[1] Winthrop's map of 1634 gives *Naponsett.*

[2] *Sett* means *surrounding, about, in the neighborhood of.* Wood wrote the name with one *t.* It seems here to be the equivalent of *sec.*

[3] Manheigin on J. F. W. Des Barres's map, 1776.

had prepared, solicited the young Prince Charles to substitute for them such other names as might be acceptable to his Royal Highness, that he might so remove the barbarous names, and at the same time give to the future settlers in the *New* England[1] opportunity to say that their places of residence were named by their sovereign. The Prince acquiescing, distributed familiar English and Scotch names up and down the coast. Of these, Plymouth, Cape Ann (named after his royal mother) and Charles River, became permanent.

Among these names were Boston (or Baston, on Ogilby's map, and pronounced Bawston), given to the mouth of the *Little York River* (a few miles north of Portsmouth), called by the Indians *Agamenticus* or *Acominticus* (Montanus), and *Hull*, at the mouth of the Piscataqua.

The name Accomonticus (Ogilby) described the site of the mouth of Little York River to one approaching it from *the north*, as it lay behind the hill called by the Indians Sassanows (the modern Agamenticus). Little York River, a short tidal river, was the *Beyond-the-hill-little-cove*.

For the name Piscataqua, the first river south of the Little York, the Prince wrote "Hull."

The descriptive appellation Accomonticus was encountered—that is, *must* have been, as we have seen—by Winthrop and his exploring parties at numerous points, when inquiry was made of the Indians as to the name of the *head* of the cove, *the canoe place*, and also the *neck*. (See Des Barres's map of Boston and the neighboring country, or the outline submitted herewith.)

Winthrop's Company had Smith's map. They had doubtless Champlain's and others, and recognizing how imperfect they were, and how exaggerated the distances, and how incorrect and even transposed many of the situations of localities, naturally found themselves embarrassed. To them the names were *proper* names ; not simply *descriptive appellations*, as they were to the natives, determined mainly by the *position* of the observer.

It is conceivable, therefore, that they came to think the Acominticus of Smith was the Accomonticus at the mouth of the Charles, and that *Boston* was the name *chosen happily by their King* for the settlement at the head of the bay, and was a selection of some fifteen years' standing. Dudley says it was proposed to give this name to their chief town before the company sailed from England. If this purpose governed the majority of the council, the aid afforded by the Indians must have contributed to induce the minority to acquiesce in their wish.

The recorded vote is very simple. It was taken September 7, 1630. In a long statement of what was done at that meeting appears the record : "*And that Trimountain be called Boston*" : it is not that *Shawmut*, or *Mushauwomuk*, or *Massachusets*, or *Accomonticus* be changed, but that "*Trimountain*[2] be called Boston.*"

At the same meeting it was also voted, and all recorded in one paragraph, to change *Mattapan* to Dorchester, and *Pigsgusset* (Pequusset) to Watertown. This summary statement indicates an adequate previous discussion, but what it was is not recorded.

In the history of Hull I have failed to find any note of the origin of the name. The position of the name at the mouth of the Piscataqua (Passata-

---

[1] Smith seems to have been the first to give the name *New England.*

[2] The name "Trimountain" was probably first given by Gomez, the Spanish navigator, in 1525, as identifying the archipelago which long bore his name (Dr. Kohl, Coll. Maine Hist. Soc., vol. i. 2d Ser. pp. 310–322), and which seems to have been Boston Harbor.

quack on Montanus's map) was the same, relatively, that the modern Hull holds now,—at or near the mouth of the first principal river next entering the ocean going southward,—the roadstead against Nantasket (Hull) might be regarded as the mouth of the Neponset (or Weymouth) the next to the Charles.

The name Hull seems to have been *found* where it is, by the historian of Plymouth County, but *how* it came there I have not had the fortune to find out. In reality, it seems to have been conferred by Prince Charles, when he replaced the Indian names at the request of Smith, and, like Boston, to have been transferred from the Piscataqua to the Charles.

The several Indian names of Boston and their significations are as follows:—

Sha-um-ut	(Shawmut),	*Near the Neck.*
Mushau-womuk,		*Canoe-place.*
Messatsoosec	(Massachusetts),	*Great-Hills-Mouth.*
Accomonticus,		*Beyond-the-hill-little-cove.*

NOTES AND QUERIES.

NOTES.

JOHN HARVARD AND CAMBRIDGE UNIVERSITY.—An English correspondent writes as follows:

"The two signatures of John Harvard are in the Subscription Book. Here every person, on admission to a degree, subscribed his name in token of his assent to the Royal Supremacy, the authority of Holy Scripture and the Thirty-Nine Articles of the Church of England. The declaration on these points is written, and then each person for himself acknowledges his assent to it. The order adopted is by Colleges, and Harvard's signature appears amongst those from Emmanuel on taking his B.A. degree in 1631 and his M.A. in 1635, the latter being much the better of the two. These books go back to 1613, when subscription was first required, and the originals have been preserved from that time to this day; and, as I need not say, are of the highest interest. Subscription, properly so called, has been abolished, but persons admitted to degrees still sign the book. Amongst recent signatures of interest, that of your distinguished fellow citizen, 'Robert Charles Winthrop,' caught my eye. The Register of which Mr. Shuckburgh wrote to you (REG. xxxix. 327) as having been preserved since 1544, is the Matriculation Register, but this does not contain the signatures of the persons matriculated. Signatures go back only to the period when subscription began, which, as I have said, was in 1613.

"The only original record of the period which Emmanuel College possesses is a book with the heading '*Recepta ab ingredientibus,*' which begins November 1, 1584, the year of the foundation of the College. This book I have examined. I transcribe the first two names in the list headed, 'From Oct. 25, 1627.' The payment on entrance seems to have been, for a fellow commoner, who is styled 'Mr.,' £5; for a pensioner 10 shillings, and for a sizar 2s. 6d. Thus Harvard is shown to have been a pensioner.

'from Oct. 25, 1627
Edmond Spinckes Octob. 25, Lincolneshire   0. 2. 6
John Harverd Midlsex: Decemb. 19   0. 10. 0 '

"The list has been conjectured to be a summary of previous more detailed entries, but I found no sufficient evidence to support this conjecture.

"It seems to me that, in this Harvard matter, confusion has arisen through lack of accuracy in designating things, and in particular that the word 'Register' has been, and is often, used inexactly. 'Matriculation Register of Emmanuel College' is wrong. Matriculation is an act, the record of which is kept by the University, and not by the College of the person matriculating. Each College keeps an Admission Register, but that of Emmanuel is not existing for Harvard's date. The 'Recepta ab ingredientibus' is the sole contemporary record of the kind which the College possesses. The Matriculation Register—which by the way I do not find has ever been consulted on this point—is not a book of signatures, whereas the Subscription Book, as its name implies, consists of nothing but signatures.

"I hope in due course we shall have a satisfactory volume touching John Harvard which will comprise all that is known of him, both on this side and on yours. It is a great mistake to isolate such a man. We want to know his surroundings, and to have grouped about him, for instance, his contemporaries at Emmanuel. I will give you an instance of what I mean by referring to two of those contemporaries. One is Sancroft, whose name is specially associated with Emmanuel, of which he became Master. Later still he was Archbishop of Canterbury, and was chief of the Seven who were sent to the Tower by James II. In spite of this hard usage he refused to swear allegiance to William III., was deprived and retired to a small patrimony at Fressingfield in Suffolk. Here he died. This on one side. On the other was Whichcote, he having taken his degree, and therefore having subscribed to the above described 'three articles,' was not only a good puritan, but was so good a republican that, thanks to the favor of the Cromwellites, he became the intended Provost of Kings, and thus had under his care that grandest monument of English ecclesiastical architecture in its latest development—royal not alone in its founder and in its benefactors, but in itself—King's College Chapel.

" This kind of matter would add, I think, much to the interest of any biography of Harvard. The influence of Emmanuel upon the University at large was great during the puritan sway. It furnished, if I remember, not fewer than twelve heads of Houses, most of whom, if not all, had, of course, to retire at the restoration."

The entry in the " Recepta," in which Harvard is recorded as of Middlesex, caused some to think that Col. Chester was wrong when he expressed the opinion that he was a son of Robert Harvard of Southwark in Surrey (REG. xxxvi. 319) ; but Mr. Waters's researches furnish a sufficient explanation. After Robert Harvard's death his widow married John Elletson, of London. Though John Harvard was not matriculated at Cambridge University till a year after his step-father's death, it is probable that his mother continued to reside in London till her marriage to Richard Yearwood, and that she resided there when the above entry was made.—EDITOR.

WOOD.—Rev. Abner Morse in his History of Sherborn, p. 264, says that Eleazer, son of Nicholas Wood, born 1662, died 1704, " m. Dorotha ——, perhaps Badcock, from Milton, and daughter of George Badcock." There is no Dorothy Badcock on the Milton records that this could have been. " He had Dorotha, who m. Capt. John Ware Senr. of Wrentham Dec. 21, 1709. .... Hannah, b. 1688, m. Capt. Joseph Ware 1708." The John Ware here mentioned was the father of Hannah's husband Joseph ; as he was 63 years old at this time, and as there appears to be no record of any Dorothy among Eleazer's children, it seems more probable that, like some other men of his time, John Ware married his son's mother-in-law ; that is, Eleazer Wood's widow, not his daughter. E. F. WARE.

PALMER, KENT AND PRESCOTT.—Goodwin in his work states that Elizabeth [Palmer], the second wife of Joseph Kent, of Suffield (born Feb. 26, 1709-10), was born 8 August, 1718. The Town Record, however, reads .... " Timothy Palmer 2d and Abigail Allen were joyned in marriage April ye 8th 1703 " .... and, after naming other children, ... " Elizabeth was born August ye 14th 1713." The Town Record gives also the following birth-dates of her children :

Abigail 2 Nov. 1751.
Elizabeth 20 Feb. 1752-3.
Lydia 26 Feb. 1757.

Timothy[3] Palmer, 2d, was the son of Timothy[2] Palmer, who was the son of Thomas[1] of Rowley, 1639.

In the Prescott Genealogy, p. 248 (Part II.), No. 153, 7, an error occurs, the researches of the Rev. William Churchill Reade of Candia having proved that John Prescott, born Sept. 14, 1746, married Patience Palmer (born about 1755, died " 12 Dec. 1819, aged 64 years ") and had by her

Josiah, born about 1776 (whose body was exhumed), who died 28 Sept. 1820.
Priscilla, born 1781, died single 2 Aug. 1850.
James, born 1789, died 22 Nov. 1866.

Patience was the daughter of Dea. Stephen[4] Palmer (by Priscilla his wife), he being the son of Timothy,[3] the son of Thomas,[2] the son of Thomas[1] of Rowley, 1639. From Dea. Stephen the Hon. Albert Palmer, mayor of Boston 1883, is descended —the line running Stephen,[4] Joseph,[5] Joseph,[6] Albert.[7]

Norwich, Ct. FRANK PALMER.

BRITISH STAMP FOR AMERICA, 1765.—A facsimile of the stamp for the British colonies, issued under the act of March 22, 1765, is given in the margin. It was engraved for the " Centennial of the Incorporation of Charleston, S. C.," 1883, and was loaned to Mr. Colburn of the publishing committee by the Hon. William A. Courtenay, mayor of that city. The following description of the stamps is copied from the *American Journal of Numismatics,* July, 1885, p. 20:

" They were embossed on a coarse, bluish paper, and bore the device of the English rose, crowned, surrounded by the motto of the Garter. At the left of the crown was the letter A. Above was the word America, and below, the value. On the face of the stamp at the right will be observed an oblong space, showing where a piece of lead or tin was inserted, by which the stamp was attached to the document, passing through them both, and covered behind by a counterstamp, somewhat smaller, bearing the device of a crown and the cypher G. R. This counter-stamp was printed on similar, but usually white, paper. An illustration of a smaller denomination is given in Lossing's " Field Book of the Revolution," vol. ii. ; but it lacks the word ' America,' which will be observed on this."

These stamps are rare ; but the Hon. Dr. Samuel A. Green, librarian of the Massachusetts Historical Society, has three specimens, and that society has three more.

Ten years before the famous " Stamp Act " of 1765, the Province of Massachusetts passed a somewhat similar act, which is printed entire in the REGISTER for July, 1860, vol. xiv. pp. 267-70, with descriptions of the stamps issued under it. The act was passed at the January session of the General Court, 1755, and was to continue in force two years. Holmes, in his " Annals of America," placed the act under the year 1759, an error which has been followed by later writers.

A NEW WORD (TOTALLING).—The tendency to coin new words is not confined to the makers of " slang." The latest coinage is the word " totalling," as a present participle, in the sense of " summing up." So far as appears, the London *Globe* of Nov. 16, 1885, is responsible for this illegitimate and unnecessary word.

H.

MRS. SARAH (CHAPLIN) ROCKWOOD, a native of Groton, Mass., where she was born on Nov. 8, 1785, celebrated her centennial birthday at Cortland, Cortland County, N. Y. Her father was the Rev. Dr. Daniel Chaplin (H. C. 1772), who was settled over the First Parish in Groton for half a century, and her mother was Susanna, daughter of the Hon. James Prescott, and a niece of Col. William Prescott, the commander of the American forces at the battle of Bunker Hill. Mrs. Rockwood still takes an interest in public affairs and reads the newspapers; and she can thread her needle without the aid of glasses.

S. A. G.

PLANS OF TOWNS IN MASSACHUSETTS, 1794.—On June 26, 1794, a Resolve was passed by the General Court of Massachusetts, " requiring the inhabitants of the several towns and districts in the Commonwealth, to cause to be taken by their Selectmen, or some other suitable persons, accurate plans of their respective towns, and to lodge the same in the Secretary's Office." It may be of interest for the local historians to know that this Resolve was carried out, and that the various manuscript plans are still preserved at the State House and open for inspection.

S. A. G.

BROUGHTON AND HANBURY.—In the Heralds' Visitation of Staffordshire, 1664, as lately printed for the William Salt Archæological Society, we find two settlers in New England identified as belonging to the gentry of England. Thomas Broughton, a son of Edward Broughton, of Longdon, is mentioned as " now residing in New England," the statement being made by his elder brother Edward. William Hanbury, a son of John Hanbury of Wolverhampton, is said to have " died in New England," the statement being made by his nephew Francis. From Savage's Dictionary we learn that Thomas Broughton was of Watertown and Boston, and William Hanbury was of Duxbury, Plymouth and Boston, dying in 1650, and " at P. he had the prefix of respect."　　　　　　　　　　　WILLIAM S. APPLETON.

RELATION CONCERNING NEW ENGLAND.—The number of the total population of the New England colonies given in this document, page 72, line 15, should have been printed 3000[0]. Sloane MS. No. 3448 says 3000, which is evidently an error. This is, corrected to 30000 in MSS. Nos. 2505 and 3105.

QUERIES.

BRUSH.—Among the Warrants granted by General Howe for the extraordinary Expenses of his Majesty's Forces in North America, between the 1st of October, 1775, and the 31st of December, 1775, was the following :

" 1775
Dec. 31. Drawn upon John Garnier, Esq. Deputy-paymaster, Boston, in favour of Mr. Crean Brush, £46. 0. 0. Being his pay for taking and receiving into his care all such Goods, Chattels, and Effects as may be delivered into his charge by the owners leaving the Town of Boston, from the 1st October to the 31st December, 1775, being 92 days, at 10s. per diem."

Can any reader of the REGISTER kindly inform me anything of the movements of Mr. Brush, from the adjournment of the General Assembly of New York, in which he had been one of the leading members in the spirited opposition of that legislative body to the measures of the Home Government, in April, 1775, until the following October, when he was in Boston, employed as above stated ?　　　　DELTA.
At home, Nov. 23, 1885.

FIRE IN BOSTON, 1775.—Among the extraordinary expenses of the Royal Army, paid by the Paymaster-general of his Majesty's forces, between the ninth of March, 1775, and the thirty-first of January, 1776, were the following :

" 1776.
Jan. 8. To Major Gen. Carleton, to replace sundry accoutrements and
cloathing belonging to the 47th Reg. of Foot, consumed by fire at
Boston, in North America, on 17th May, 1775　　　.　　.　£316. 19. 5.
To Messrs. Adair and Bullock, to reimburse the losses sustained by the
non-commission Officers and Private men of ditto Regiment, whose
necessaries were consumed by fire at ditto on the 17th of May, 1775,　140. 0. 0.
To Lieut. Gen. Urmston, to replace accoutrements, &c. of the 65th Reg.
of Foot, consumed by fire at Boston, in North America, on 17th May,
1775,　.　.　.　.　.　.　.　.　.　.　.　477. 4. 3."

Please state particulars of that fire and the circumstances attending the losses sustained by the two regiments above named.　　　　DELTA.
At home, Nov. 23, 1885.

WILLIAM CUNNINGHAM.—Among the Warrants drawn on John Garnier, Esq., Deputy-paymaster, at Boston, by General Howe, for the extraordinary expenses of his Majesty's Forces in North America, between the first of October, 1775, and the 31st of December, 1775, was one to Mr. William Cunningham for £50. 0. 0., " being his pay for doing the duty of Provost-martial, from the fifteenth of June to the thirty-first of December, 1775, being two hundred days, at five shillings per diem."

This was probably the same William Cunningham who, subsequently, in the same office of Provost-martial, became so conspicuously notorious in New York for

his barbarous treatment of the prisoners who were committed to the Provost-prison, now the Hall of Records, in that city. Can any of the readers of the REGISTER give any particulars of the life of that inhuman jailor, before he went to Boston, or while he was in that town?   DELTA.
At home, Nov. 23, 1885.

MEADE—LATHAM.—In his autobiography and history of the Meade family ("*Chaumiere Papers*," edited by Henry J. Peet, Esq.) Colonel David Meade says: "Andrew Meade, my paternal grandfather"—the immigrant ancestor of the family—"was an Irish Roman Catholic, born in the county of Kerry. Tradition says he left his native country and went first to London, and from thence came to New York about the latter end of the 17th century. He resided some years in New York, and there married Mary Latham, of Quaker parentage, and some time after he removed to Virginia and settled permanently at the head of navigation on "the Nansemond River." Bishop Meade adopted this statement (*The Old Churches, Ministers and Families of Virginia*, vol. i. pp. 291-2), and adds that Mary Latham was of Flushing.
Query: What was the date of this marriage, and what were the names of Mary (Latham) Meade's parents?
II. In the abstract of the will of George Fox, and of proceedings had under that will (REG. Oct. 1885, pp. 327-9), mention is made of *Sarah Meade*, a step-daughter of Fox, and of her husband *William Meade*, as of London in 1688, and, later, as of London, 30 December, 1697, when "Sarah Meade, wife of William Meade of the parish of Sᵗ Dyonis Back church, London, citizen and merchant Taylor of London, ... did declare that she is of the number of dissenters commonly called Quakers."
Query: What, if any, family relation existed between this William Meade, of London, and Andrew Meade, named above?
III. It is of record that at least as early as 1743 the aforesaid Andrew Meade was a vestryman of Nansemond Parish. He also held various public offices for the exercise of which subscription to the test-oaths was a preliminary requisite.
Query: (1) When and where did he take the oaths?
(2.) Is there any evidence that while he was in London, or in New York where he married a woman of "Quaker parentage," or after his removal to the "head quarters" of the Friends in Virginia, he became a recognized member of that religious Society?   ALBERT H. HOYT.
Boston.

HILLYER.—Nathaniel Hillyer was born at Simsbury, Conn., in 1715, and died in 1784. Can any one give the information whom and when he married, and when his wife died?
Their son Nathaniel married a daughter of David Wilcox, of Granby. What was her given name, when was she born, married and died?
Hartford, Ct.   GEORGE E. HOADLEY.

BRADSTREET, ROGERS, NICHOLL, TOWNSEND.—I desire record evidence of the birth or baptism of any children born to John Bradstreet between 1720 and 1730. He is described, Oct. 27, 1730, as "John Bradstreet of Topsfield, late of Windham, yeoman." Also any information of Lydia Rogers, who was married in Boston, 27 April, 1777, to John Nicoll. Also any information relating to James Nicoll or Eunice Townsend, who were married in Boston 24 April, 1735.
Woodford's, Me.   GEORGE C. CODMAN.

MEADE (*ante*, vol. xxxix. pp. 327, 8, 9, Genealogical Gleanings of H. F. Waters). —In the will of George Fox, the names of William, Sarah and Nathaniel Meade, residents of London, and Quakers in religious belief, appear.
It is stated by Rev. Philip Slaughter, D.D., in his admirable Memoir of Bishop Wiliam Meade of Virginia, "Memorial Biographies of the N. E. Hist. and Gen. Soc." vol. iv. p. 454, that Andrew Meade, the ancestor of the Virginia family of the name, was a Roman Catholic who "came to New York late in the seventeenth century, and married Mary Latham, a Quaker, of Flushing." Inasmuch as Andrew Meade married a Quaker and settled in a community of that belief, and in consideration of the fact that "papists" were the abhorrence of the Virginia colonists,

and were bitterly persecuted, as evidenced by legal statutes, whilst Quakers were tolerated and allowed under certain provisions to hold their meetings, there is some reason to presume that the religious belief of Andrew Meade may have been misapprehended. It may be profitable for Mr. Waters to endeavor to ascertain if the name of Andrew appears among the names of the children of William and Nathaniel Meade, as cited.

The following grants of land of record in the Virginia Registry may be of interest in connection with the investigation :

Thomas Meads [probably an error in transcription for Meade] and John Phillips, 1000 acres, "scituate or being on the south side of the ffreshes of Rappahannock river, about sixteen miles above Nanizimun Towne," Sept. 17, 1654, Book No. 3, p. 376 ; Andrew Mead, 136 acres "in the upper parish of Nansimun county, Feb. 22, 1727, Book No. 13, p. 208.   R. A. BROCK.
Richmond, Va.

STARK.—Who were the ancestors of John Stark, born March 16, 1761, died March 29, 1839 ; married (about 1785) Olive Lothrop, born July 13, 1764, died July 7, 1825 ?   C. W. BRYANT.
Granville, Licking Co., Ohio.

REV. JOHN HASLAM.—In the year 1821 the Rev. John Haslam, of Charleston, S. C., received an honorary degree of A.M. from Harvard College. Many years later he removed to the West, and then was lost sight of. Can any one tell me whether he is still living ; and if not, when and where he died ? The information is wanted for the Quinquennial Catalogue.   S. A. G.

TOWNSEND—LARMON.—Ebenezer Townsend, born in Boston, 1716, married Sept. 19, 1738, Elizabeth Larmon, who was born Sept. 6, 1718. They removed to New Haven about 1740, where they continued to reside. Can any information be given concerning her parentage?   FRANK F. STARR.
Middletown, Ct.

ROBINSON.—Information is wanted of the previous history of George Robinson, an early settler of Rehoboth, Mass. He married Joanna Ingram, April 18, 1651. At what date did he settle at Rehoboth?   CHARLES E. ROBINSON.
New York City.

WOODYEAR.—Information wanted of an American family named Woodyear, which settled, I think, in Philadelphia. They came from Rochester and Chatham, Kent, England. One of them was a customs officer in a West India island—St. Kitts or Barbadoes. The first ancestor of this family founded the present line of Crookhill, Yorkshire, but the family in America came from a younger son. Any information about them, or where to obtain this information, will be acceptable, as I am trying to trace this family back to their junction with the main stem. and hope to do so ere long.   LAMBTON YOUNG.
16 *Harcourt Terrace, Radcliffe Sq., London, S. W., Eng.*

HON. JOSHUA GRANGER WRIGHT.—He lived in Wilmington, N. C., from about 1750 to 1810, and was for several years a representative of that borough : was also at his death president of the Bank of Cape Fear. He married about 1780 Susan Bradley, and had seven children, all of whom are dead ; but grandchildren are still living. Wanted his parentage, birth-place, date of birth and early history.
                                                                              W. M. GREEN.

WALKINGAME AND WALKINHAM.—An early issue of the English "Notes and Queries" (1st Series, x. p. 66, and xi. p. 327) asks for information in a law case in which the name Walkingham is borne by the defendant, and suggests that it is probably in an American trial. Can any one throw any light upon this?

The same publication has several unanswered questions as to the history of Francis Walkingame, "the Tutor's Assistant," and others bearing a similar name. It

is remarkable that this family, though once a knightly one in Yorkshire (cir. 1300), and apparently represented as late as 1787 by a Miss Walkingame of Newington, who was married to the Rev. Ethan Evans, Vicar of New Ormsby, Lincolnshire (*alias*, Rev. Edward E. of Spilsbury, 1788), appears to be extinct in England. Are there any of the name in America? A. SIDNEY GARDNER.
Neath, South Wales.

___

SANKEY.—Is anything known of the history of this family in the United States? Besides that branch represented by the well known " Gospel Singer," Mr. Ira David Sankey, the name occurs in Philadelphia and elsewhere, I believe. It is originally an ancient house, of that ilk, in Lancashire, circa 1200 A.D.

In Hutton's " Lists of Emigrants " [and in the REGISTER] occurs the following : " Passengers which passed from the Port of London 14 Apr: 1635 in the ' Increase ' of London, Mr Robert Lea bounde for New England · · · · Robert Sankey aged 30 & others [*ante*, xiv. 309]. Theis have taken the oaths of allegiance and supremacye, & have brought certificat of their conformaty." And on 13 Oct.: on board the " Amitie," George Downes, master, bound to St Christopher, Hamblett Sankey, aged 22, is mentioned. [See also Drake's Founders of New England.] This Hamlet S. is apparently the son of a Dublin clergyman, and identical with one of the same name who compiled a " Brooke Pedigree of severall places." He signs himself " Hamlet Sanckye." He fled to Portugal ; and afterwards, apparently, emigrated on board the " Amity," landing somewhere in the States (as we would now call it).

About 1797, an Edward Sankey, son of John S. of East Langdon, Kent, by his second wife Jane Rattray, is supposed to have emigrated to America. He was heir, through his mother, to a considerable fortune ; but as nothing could be heard of him or his descendants, what remained of it went to distant relatives in England, I believe.

Thus we have a Robert, Hamlet and Edward Sankey—all descended from a common ancestor—who at different times left England for the States. Can any one help me in discovering more concerning the Sankeys in America?
Neath, South Wales. A. SIDNEY GARDNER.

___

THURSBY.—A gentleman in England wishes information concerning American families by the names of Thursby or Thoresby. Address letters to the care of the Editor of the REGISTER.

___

REPLIES.

HULEN, UNION, SAVERY (*ante*, xxxvii. 309–10).—" Heullin, chez nous, patronymique étient, est le nom de l'arraignée de mer.

" Richard Heullin, á cause de sa femme, fille de James le Roy, en son courtil de la baille des hoirs Pierre Bouillon, et en son camp de dedans le courtil James Allez, et buttant sur les Landes du Marché." (Fieu de Rossel, 1611, p. 6.) " Dans le bailliage de Caux, l'an 1470. ' Jehan Hullin se présenta en robe, et il lui fut commandé de se mettre en habit suffisant.' "

> " Les viers Haeûlíns
> N'jouent pas d'leur grins,
> Et Jacquot Guille,
> E'prîns d' la file
> D'Gersy (Colas),
> Eu aeut soulas,
> Et à Sâint-George,
> I s' mit d' bel orge,
> Ou est qui' est Liton ?
> D' Col. Colleton,
> Non n'en sait guère ;
> Un daeux, n'aguère,
> Le gros bounnuet,
> Fut barounnet."

Extract from " Nomenclature Patronymique de Guernesey," par Geo. Métivier.

The following address may be of service to Mr. Huling : " Huelin & Le Feuvre, proprietors ' Nouvelle Chronique de Jersey,' office 11 Royal Sq., Jersey, Eng."
Newton, Mass. SAMUEL P. MAY.

CUNNABELL (*ante*, xxxix. 373).—If he has not already done so, Mr. Newcomb should seek information from Bernardston, Mass., the original " Fallstown," granted to the heirs of the Falls Fight soldiers. One of those grantees was Samuel Connable. B. was my native place, and I well remember in my boyhood a descendant of S. C. (and bearing the same name) telling me an old tradition of his ancestor, as a man of energy and expedients, viz., that he brought in the maple sap, one cold spring morning, in the form of *ice*, and, in order to melt it, *heaped it up* in his kettle and confined it there by an old tub without a bottom, set into the kettle. This incident was written home to England, and it was published in the London newspapers that a man in Massachusetts " gathered sap in a basket, and boiled it in a tub "!   C. C. C.
Andover, Mass.

GREENWOOD (vol. xxxix. p. 386).—Samuel Greenwood died Dec. 10, 1711, aged 34, a few years after his deposition. His widow Phillipe (White) Carter married a third husband, James French. Samuel Phillips, the goldsmith of Salem, alluded to in the deposition, had a second wife in April, 1704, widow Sarah Mayfield, who must be the person referred to.   ISAAC J. GREENWOOD.
216 *W. 14th St., New York.*

SPRAGUE, WARREN, CORBIN.—In the REGISTER, vol. iv. p. 289, is a letter from John Corbin, dated "[Vp]way 25th March, 1651," in which the writer addresses Ralph Sprague (of Charlestown, N. E., without doubt) as his " sonne," and signs himself as Sprague's " Father-in-law." Now in Lechford's Note Book are several legal papers and letters, 1638-9, from Ralph Sprague and his wife, wherein it is expressly stated that her father had died, and that his name was Richard Warren ; so that John Corbin had probably married the widow Warren.
                                                       JOHN COFFIN JONES BROWN.

NEWGATE.—Lechford's Note-Book, as published by the American Antiquarian Society, requires us to make many corrections to the Genealogical Dictionary of New England, some of which are not mentioned by the Editor. Savage says that Theodore Atkinson " came, in the employment of John Newgate, from Bury in co. Lancaster," but Newgate's will, as drawn by Lechford, mentions his " Lands and Tenements lying in Horningerth in the County of Suffolk." This shows that John Newgate really came from Bury St. Edmunds in Suffolk, from which Horningerth or Horningsheath is only two miles distant.   W. S. APPLETON.

HISTORICAL INTELLIGENCE.

THE HUGUENOT EMIGRATION TO VIRGINIA.—The Virginia Historical Society announces that it will issue early in 1886, as its annual publication, " Documents Relating to the Huguenot Emigration to Virginia," to form Volume V. of its new series of collections (edited by R. A. Brock, Esq.), and to be uniform with the preceding volumes of the " Spotswood Letters " and the " Dinwiddie Papers." The documents to compose the prospective volume are of the highest importance and interest, a majority of them never having been printed in any form. It is desired that they shall be amply elucidated by introduction and definite foot notes to the text, historical and biographical, and, if feasible, by genealogical addenda. Among the more familiar names appearing in the documents may be mentioned the following : Amis, Apperson, Ayer, Allegre, Ammonet, Bernard, Bondurant, Brian, Cury, Chastain, Deneille, Duval, Dupre, Dupuy (or DuPuy), Esly, Edmon, Elson, Fontaine, Flournoy, Faure, Gcdse, Gore, Gillam, Guerrant, Hampton (or Hamton), Jourdan, Kempe, Leroy, LeFebre, Leverre, Lesueur, LeGrand, Landon, Loucadou,;Lacy, Mallet, Michel, Morriset, Maupain, Marye, Morrel, Martain, Orringe, Pasteur, Pero, Peronet, Parrat, Pankey, Popham, Rich, Roberd, Reno, Sumtur, Soullie, Salle, Soblet, Trabu, Taller, Trent.
The contribution of data, however meagre, towards some notice of these names, or of any others of like origin and connection, or of any document (or copy) relating to the Huguenot settlement in Virginia, is earnestly solicited from those interested. Address the editor, Richmond, Va.
The publications of the Society have been in limited editions for distribution

among its members and kindred institutions. The annual subscription to the Society is $5—no entrance fee; life-membership, $50.

COL. CHESTER'S OXFORD MATRICULATIONS AND MARRIAGE LICENCES, EDITED BY JOSEPH FOSTER.—Mr. Foster, the well-known genealogist, author of the British Peerage and Baronetage, and other works, has recently purchased, at a cost exceeding £1000, the late Col. Chester's Oxford Matriculations Registers, 7 Vols., and Marriage Licences, 5 Vols., with the intention of printing these intrinsically priceless MSS. uniformly with the publications of the Harleian Society, for the advantage of his numerous genealogical friends in America, as a memorial of the great and good work he did for them in England. He makes this preference because, so far as England is concerned, he would like to retain for himself the monopoly of these manuscripts, and because he believes the American people will appreciate the labors of their own countryman far more fully than Englishmen would, as the proposed work will enable them to place printed copies of these distant and inaccessible Old England registers on the shelves of their very own libraries ready for immediate reference. He therefore appeals to Americans to reciprocate his efforts, and hold him harmless from pecuniary loss, by subscribing for 250 copies of these works, which he desires to print only for them.

It is obvious that a work on such a scale as this can only be produced at a great cost. Including the very heavy sum paid for Col. Chester's manuscripts, and the vast amount of trained labor involved in transcribing them for publication (the annotation the editor proposes to do himself as a labor of love), the actual expense of bringing out the work is estimated as between two and three thousand pounds. It cannot be expected that so great an expense should be incurred till sufficient promises of support have been received to warrant the editor in putting it in hand without prospect of heavy loss. The Oxford Matriculations will be issued in two volumes at a subscription price of two guineas. As an inducement for Col. Chester's friends and American genealogists to coöperate with the editor, the work will be offered at nine guineas to those who subscribe for two copies, and at eight guineas to those who subscribe for three.

The Marriage Licences will be issued in five large royal octavo volumes, at £2. 12s. 6d. a volume.

This enterprise is heartily commended by the editor of the REGISTER to the patronage of the American people.

Mr. Foster's address is 21 Boundary Road, London, N. W., England.

CHURCH BELLS OF SUFFOLK, ENGLAND.—The Rev. John James Raven, D.D., who has recently been appointed to the Vicarage of Fressingfield, near Harleston, England, having now more leisure than his previous duties permitted, has resumed his labors upon the "Church Bells of Suffolk," which have long engaged his attention. The inscriptions, commemorative of donors and others, existing on the bells, doubtless preserve many old Suffolk names, and Dr. Raven's recognized qualifications for the task he has undertaken lead to the belief that his work will be a valuable contribution to the history of an English county which is of much interest to us on this side of the Atlantic.

THE BICKNELLS: THE 250th ANNIVERSARY OF THEIR SETTLEMENT IN AMERICA.—In the year 1635 a company of emigrants from the counties of Somerset and Dorset, England, under the pastoral care of Rev. Joseph Hull, sailed from Weymouth and arrived in New England. The company consisted of twenty-one families, and on application to the court sitting at New Town, July 8, they "were allowed to sit down at Wessaguscus," now Weymouth. Of this company were Zachary Bicknell, age 45, Agnes Bicknell, age 27, John Bicknell, 11, and their servant John Kitchen. Zachary died in 1636, and Agnes his wife married Richard Rockett, of Braintree. John, the son, married Mary —— as his first wife, and Mary Dyer for his second wife. The issue of the two marriages was eleven children, whose descendants now dwell in large numbers in the old home town, and others are scattered over the continent. In 1878 a family association was formed, with Hon. Thomas W. Bicknell, LL.D., of Boston, president, Alfred Bicknell, Esq., Melrose, secretary, and Robert T. Bicknell, Esq., Weymouth, treasurer. This association has, through its historian Quincy Bicknell, Esq., of Hingham, collected a large amount of genealogical matter, which will be printed in due season. The two hundred and fiftieth anniversary was celebrated with interesting proceedings in Boston, October 6 and 7, and at Weymouth October 8. The address of welcome was given by Edward Bicknell, Esq., of Boston. A paper on the Bicknell name was read by Ellery Bicknell Crane, of Worcester, in which he traced the root to De Bec or Becce, of Normandy ; the word Bicknell being a compound of Bec, a brook and knoll, a hill ; or a brook by the hill. The principal address was given by Hon. Thomas Williams Bicknell, president of the association. Poems were read from Alfred Bicknell, Esq., and Mrs. L. M. Hopkins. Rev. George W. Bicknell, of Lowell, gave an address on the Bicknells in the military service. A family dinner followed, with addresses and letters from Hon. Marshall P. Wilder, LL.D., Hon. John D. Long, Gov. George D. Robinson, and members of the family. The occasion was one of great profit. The addresses will be printed by the family, and arrangements will be made to publish a family history at an early day. The artistic programme was the work of Frank A. Bicknell, of Malden.

DESCENDANTS OF THE SIGNERS OF THE DECLARATION OE INDEPENDENCE.—I am preparing a work to be entitled : '' The Signers of the Declaration of Independence and their Descendants.'' It will be of a biographical and genealogical character, the fundamental feature, however, being a genealogy of all the descendants of the fifty-six '' Signers '' *down to the present day.* The value of such a work, from a historical point of view, must be instantly conceded.

The magnitude of the labor required in the preparation of such a volume will be recognized after a moment's reflection. So stupendous is the task that I would not presume to undertake it were it not that I confidently look for the coöperation of those descendants of the '' Signers '' who have it in their power to supply necessary data.

I therefore make this appeal, to wit: that I be furnished, at an early day, with the names and P. O. addresses of all those descendants of '' Signers '' to whose notice this statement shall come. All others interested in genealogical matters are earnestly requested to favor me with any relevant data or information in their possession.

No. 2211 *Spruce St.,*   FRANK WILLING LEACH,
Philadelphia, Pa.   Mem. Phila. Bar, Mem. Hist. Soc. of Pa., Mem.
          Numis. and Ant. Soc. of Philadelphia, etc.

UNPUBLISHED MANUSCRIPTS IN EUROPE RELATING TO AMERICA, 1772–84.—Mr. B. F. Stevens, of London, England, has been engaged for about twenty years in collecting unpublished manuscripts relating to the Revolutionary War, from the public and private archives of England, France, Holland and Spain ; and has issued a circular letter concerning this great work, and a proof specimen of the proposed form of publication. He has '' made entries of 80,000 documents within the scope of this work, the great majority of which have never been published. This collection of manuscripts is of priceless value, and the history of the Revolution can never be properly written till the papers are accessible to students.

Mr. Stevens desires that the United States government should aid him in his great undertaking. We trust that an appropriation will be made sufficient to place printed copies of these documents in the libraries of this country and in the hands of our historians.

GENEALOGIES IN PREPARATION.—Persons of the several names are advised to furnish the compilers of these genealogies with records of their own families and other information which they think will be useful. We would suggest that all facts of interest illustrating family history or character be communicated, especially service under the U. S. government, the holding of other offices, graduation from college or professional schools, occupation, with places and dates of births, marriages, residence and death. When there are more than one christian name they should all be given in full if possible. No initials should be used when the full names are known.

Ballard. By C. F. Farlow, of Newton, Mass.—Mr. Farlow has much material concerning the descendants of William and Grace Ballard, of Andover, and solicits information from parties interested.

Eliot. By Rev. John E. Elliott, of Bridgewater, Ct.—Mr. Elliott is collecting facts in regard to those who have the surname of Eliot, Elyot, Elyott, Elliot or Elliott. He will furnish circulars to applicants. Any facts concerning persons of this name in any of its various spellings, will be thankfully received.

Foster. By Paymaster Joseph Foster, U.S.N., Naval Asylum, Philadelphia, Pa. —The book which will soon be put to press will be entitled " The Grandchildren of Col. Joseph Foster; his Life and Ancestors "—it being the second edition, revised and much enlarged, of " The Grandchildren of Col. Joseph Foster, of Ipswich and Gloucester, Mass., 1730-1804," noticed in the October REGISTER. It will be for the interest of every descendant to have his or her name inserted.

Harris. By C. F. Farlow, of Newton, Mass.—A history of the descendants of John and Amy (Hills) Harris, of Charlestown, is in preparation. Persons interested are requested to furnish records of this family.

Jessup. By Rev. Henry G. Jesup, of Dartmouth College, Hanover, N. H.—This work will include a history of Edward Jessup of West Farms, Westchester County, N. Y., and a genealogical record of his descendants of all names. Information is solicited as to other families of the same name, of which there are several in this country and Canada, especially as to what is known of their English ancestry.

Kimball. By Leonard A. Morrison, A.M., of Windham, N. H., author of " History of the Morrison Family."—Mr. Morrison is preparing a History and Genealogy of the Kimball Family—descendants of Richard,[1] of Ipswich, Mass., and requests all possible information, from any source, in regard to the genealogy and history of the family.

Robinson. By Charles E. Robinson, Boulevard and 117th Street, New York City.—This book, now preparing for publication, will be devoted to the descendants of George Robinson, an early settler of Rehoboth, Mass.

SOCIETIES AND THEIR PROCEEDINGS.

NEW-ENGLAND HISTORIC GENEALOGICAL SOCIETY.

Boston, Massachusetts, Wednesday, September 2, 1885.—The first meeting after the summer recess was held at 3 o'clock this afternoon at the Society's House, 18 Somerset Street, the president, the Hon. Marshall P. Wilder, Ph.D., LL.D., in the chair.

Hon. Thomas Weston, of Newton, read a paper on " Peter Oliver, the last Provincial Chief Justice of Massachusetts." Thanks were voted to Mr. Weston for the paper.

John Ward Dean, the librarian, reported 137 volumes and 610 pamphlets as donations for the quarter ending Sept. 1.

Rev. Increase N. Tarbox, D.D., reported memorial sketches of nine deceased members, namely: Ex-President Ulysses S. Grant, William Parsons, Manning Leonard, Hon. Charles R. Train, Ebenezer B. Towne, George K. Snow, Rev. Samuel I. Prime, D.D., Franklin B. Hough, M.D., and Hon. Thomas W. Bartley.

The following nominating committee for the ensuing year was chosen, namely: Jeremiah Colburn, Rev. Dr. Increase N. Tarbox, Hon. Charles L. Flint, Henry E. Waite and George K. Clarke.

Oct. 7.—A quarterly meeting was held this afternoon, President Wilder in the chair.

Rev. Edmund F. Slafter, the corresponding secretary, announced and exhibited some of the more important donations.

Hon. Charles Crowley, of Lowell, read a paper on William Tyndall, the reformer and martyr, and the translator of the Bible into English. Thanks were voted for the paper.

The deaths of the Hon. Thomas Talbot and Henry Edwards were announced, and committees were appointed to prepare resolutions.

The corresponding secretary reported letters accepting the membership to which they had been elected, from Sir Theodore Martin, of London, as a corresponding, and Harrie C. Brownell, of Newtonville, as a resident member.

The librarian reported as donations in September, 14 volumes and 56 pamphlets.

The historiographer reported memorial sketches of two deceased members—Henry Edwards and Hon. Edward A. Rollins.

John Ward Dean, Rev. Lucius R. Paige, D.D., Rev. Edmund F. Slafter, Jeremiah Colburn, William B. Trask, Henry H. Edes, Henry E. Waite and Francis E. Blake were chosen the publishing committee.

Nov. 4.—A stated meeting was held this afternoon, President Wilder in the chair.

Rev. Henry A. Hazen reported resolutions on the death of Ex-Gov. Talbot, and Rev. Edmund F. Slafter on Henry Edwards, which resolutions were unanimously adopted.

The corresponding secretary announced donations.

Prof. E. N. Horsford, of Cambridge, read a paper on "The Indian Names of Boston," which paper is printed in this number of the REGISTER, pp. 93–103. Thanks were voted to Prof. Horsford.

The recording secretary, D. G. Haskins, Jr., read a paper prepared by Miss Frances B. James, now in England, as a supplement to her paper last June. It is entitled, "Concerning John Harvard's signature at Cambridge, England." It was printed entire in the *Boston Evening Transcript,* Nov. 11, 1885. Thanks were voted for the paper.

The librarian reported as donations in October, 33 volumes and 744 pamphlets.

The corresponding secretary reported letters accepting the membership to which they had been elected, from Capt. Asa Bird Gardner, LL.D., U.S.A., of New York, Gen. Charles W. Darling of Utica, and Francis Grigson of London, as corresponding ; and Elihu Chauncey of New York and Daniel W. Baker of Boston, as resident members.

December 2.—A stated meeting was held this afternoon. In the absence of President Wilder, the Rev. Edmund F. Slafter was chosen president pro tem.

Important donations were announced by the corresponding secretary.

Gen. James Grant Wilson, of New York, read a paper on Commodore Isaac Hull. Remarks were made by several members, and thanks were voted to Gen. Wilson.

The corresponding secretary reported letters accepting resident membership to which they had been elected, from Rev. Carlton A. Staples, of Lexington, and Benjamin C. Clarke and Major Edward B. Blasland, of Boston.

The librarian reported 18 volumes and 63 pamphlets as the donations for the month.

The historiographer reported memorial sketches of ten deceased members—Hon. Edward A. Rollins, Henry Edwards, Townsend Ward, William R. Lawrence, M.D., Hon. Edward Lawrence, Samuel T. Champney, John A. Lewis, Samuel T. Bent, Charles O. Whitmore and William W. Tucker.

On motion of Rev. William C. Winslow, a vote of congratulation was passed to Dr. Conrad Leemans of the Leyden University, the head of its Museum of Antiquities, on the intended celebration, the next day (Dec. 3), of the fiftieth anniversary of his connection with the university.

RHODE ISLAND HISTORICAL SOCIETY.

Providence, Tuesday, Oct. 6, 1885.—A quarterly meeting was held this evening at the society's Cabinet in Waterman Street, the president, Prof. William Gammell, LL.D., in the chair.

Hon. Amos Perry, the secretary, read the correspondence since the last meeting. Letters were received from Albert Jay Jones of Rome, Italy, and Samuel Briggs of Cleveland, Ohio, accepting corresponding membership to which they had been elected, and from the Northern Society of Antiquaries, Copenhagen, relative to the death of its distinguished vice-president Worsaae.

Mr. Perry, as librarian, reported that 89 volumes and 392 pamphlets had been received as donations.

Mr. Perry then read a paper entitled, A Sketch of some of the Incidents in the Dorr War.

B. B. Hammond, chairman of the committee appointed to devise plans for the celebration of the 250th anniversary of the founding of Providence, reported that it is expected that the City of Providence will celebrate this event during the month of June, and that the Burnside statue will be dedicated about the 20th of the previous month. These celebrations will be near each other, but not in conflict. The report recommended that a committee be appointed to confer with the committee of the City Council upon a plan for the celebration, and coöperate with it in regard thereto. The report was accepted, and the same committee was authorized to act in this matter for the society.

Resolutions were unanimously adopted approving of John Osborne Austin's Genealogical Dictionary of Rhode Island, now in preparation.

Nov. 3.—A stated meeting was held this evening. William Gammell, LL.D., president of the society, delivered a scholarly address on "The Huguenots and the Edict of Nantes." After remarks by Rev. J. G. Vose and Dr. C. W. Parsons, thanks were unanimously voted to Prof. Gammell. The paper is printed in full in the *Providence Evening Bulletin*, Nov. 4, 1885.

CHICAGO HISTORICAL SOCIETY.

Chicago, Ill., Oct. 20, 1885.—A quarterly meeting of this society was held in its hall, 140–42 Dearborn Avenue.

Hon. E. B. Washburne, the president, occupied the chair. The librarian, Albert D. Hager, made his quarterly report, by which it was shown that 392 bound volumes and 1058 pamphlets had been added during the quarter. These, added to the former accessions, make a total of 11,571 bound books, and 35,121 pamphlets. Of these 1108 had been purchased with the income of the "Lucretia Pond Fund."

The librarian made special mention of the generous contributions by the librarians from the duplicates of the Wisconsin, Minnesota and Massachusetts Historical Societies, the Boston Public Library, Massachusetts State Library and several eastern colleges that had obligingly furnished series of the catalogues, addresses, &c. He reported that 662 volumes had been bound during the past summer, and a large portion of them were composed of pamphlets and the publications of sister societies, scientific and literary associations and newspaper flies.

Mr. Henry H. Hurlbut was then introduced, and read an interesting paper on Samuel de Champlain, and at the conclusion he presented to the society an oil portrait of the great explorer which had been painted by his daughter, Miss Harriet P. Hurlbut. The society's thanks were tendered, and a request made that a copy of the paper be furnished for publication.

VIRGINIA HISTORICAL SOCIETY.

Richmond, Oct. 17, 1885.—A meeting of the executive committee was held this evening at the society's rooms in the Westmoreland Club House.

Valuable donations were announced.

Mr. Brock stated that the recent circular of the society announcing the preparation of "Documents relating to the Huguenot Emigration to Virginia" had elicited a number of gratifying responses.

NECROLOGY OF THE NEW-ENGLAND HISTORIC GENEALOGICAL SOCIETY.

Prepared by the Rev. INCREASE N. TARBOX, D.D., Historiographer of the Society.

THE historiographer would inform the society, that the sketches prepared for the REGISTER are necessarily brief in consequence of the limited space which can be appropriated. All the facts, however, he is able to gather, are retained in the Archives of the Society, and will aid in more extended memoirs for which the "Towne Memorial Fund," the gift of the late William B. Towne, A.M., is provided. Four volumes, printed at the charge of this fund, entitled "MEMORIAL BIOGRAPHIES," edited by the Committee on Memorials, have been issued. They contain memoirs of all the members who have died from the organization of the society to the year 1862. A fifth volume is in preparation.

GEORGE MOUNTFORT, Esq., of Boston, a resident member, died in this city, Wednesday morning, May 28, 1884, aged 86. He was a son of Joseph Mountfort, and was born in Prince Street, Boston, March 16, 1798. He was the fifth generation in descent from Edmund[1] Mountfort, who came to New England in 1656 and settled at Boston ; through John,[2] born Feb. 8, 1670 ; Joseph,[3] born April 12, 1713, and Joseph,[4] born Feb. 3, 1750. The last named, who was Mr. Mountfort's father, was one of the famous " tea party " of December 16, 1773 ; was a zealous patriot throughout the Revolution, and served under command of the gallant Commodore Manly in several severe sea engagements. It is said that he was thrice taken prisoner, and on one occasion, with sixteen others, broke from prison and in an open boat crossed the English Channel to France, whence he returned to Boston in the Deane frigate.

The early education of George Mountfort was at the school of Madame Dobel, a foreign lady, in Hanover Street, Boston. Afterwards he attended the Eliot School in Bennett Street, and Nathaniel Bridge's Academy in Salem Street. At all these schools he received tokens of commendation for good behavior and scholarship. On leaving school he served two years as a clerk in the counting-room of John Hancock, nephew of Governor Hancock, on Hancock's Wharf, Boston; and finished his mercantile education in the British commercial house of John H. Reid & Co., of Savannah, Georgia. He was afterwards corresponding clerk for Naylor, Hutchinson, Vicker & Co., New York, and next chief book-keeper for the commission and shipping house of De Peyster & Whitmarsh in that city. After leaving this firm he engaged in the commission business on his own account in New York, at No. 110 Front Street. About the year 1844 he returned to Boston. Here he carried on business first at 16 Commercial Street, and afterwards at 134 State Street. During his residence here, we are informed that he procured the charter and aided in establishing the Gas-Light Company of Lowell, and also aided in founding the Gas-Light Company of St. John, N. B. He afterwards was the agent of the Massic Falls Cotton and Batting Company of Lowell.

On the 16th of May, 1850, he was appointed, by President Taylor, United States Consul for the Island of Candia, which position he held till August, 1859. In returning to the United States he passed through a portion of Greece, visited the Ionian Islands, Trieste, Venice, Milan and Turin, crossed Mt. Cenis into Switzerland, and visited Paris and London and the principal manufacturing cities of England.

He was a frequent writer for the newspapers and magazines. Contributions by him appeared in the *Boston Gazette* when published by Beals & Homer ; in the *Boston Post*, the *Daily Bee*, and the *Evening Transcript*. Before he left Boston for the consulate in Candia he contributed articles to several newspapers in support of the Native American party. His communications to *The Signal* and *The Eagle* were under the signatures of " Justitia," " North End" and " Seventy-Six." In 1842 he wrote for "Hunt's Merchants' Magazine," a life of John Hancock, the first signer of the Declaration of Independence, which was republished in book form at New York by Saxton & Miles. Several articles by him have appeared in the REGISTER. In 1867 and 1868 he published weekly, for eight consecutive months, in the Bunker Hill Aurora, a "History of the Island of Candia." A copy of this work is in the society's library, presented by him. His official reports on the commercial resources of Candia were printed by the United States government in the volumes on the "Commercial Relations with Foreign Nations," volumes 3 to 7. In 1850 he received the first three degrees of Masonry in Massachusetts Lodge, Boston, and on the 1st of October, 1855, was admitted a corresponding member of the New England Historic Genealogical Society. This membership was changed to resident in Jan., 1862. He was a member of the New England Society of New York. In consequence of his acceptable course in promoting the commercial interests of the Island of Candia during his official and mercantile residence there, and for not compromising the neutrality of his consular flag in that region of political intrigue and bribery, the sultan Abdul Aziz conferred upon him in July, 1870, the rank and decoration of the Imperial order of Medidich or Knighthood. The decoration and the accompanying berat or diploma were bequeathed by him to this society.

By John Ward Dean, A.M., of Boston.

Hon. GEORGE PARKMAN DENNY, of Boston, a life member, admitted Dec. 8, 1870, was born in Boston, May 10, 1826, and died suddenly in the same city at Hotel Bristol, Jan. 23, 1885, aged 58.

In the early life of the deceased, his father, George Denny, Esq., removed from Boston to Westboro'. The Denny mansion was in the south-east part of the village of Westboro', and the life within it was not showy, but very solid and substantial. The tie which led the family to Westboro', and held it there for many years, is found probably in the middle name of the subject of this sketch. Ebenezer Parkman was the first minister of Westboro', having been settled there in 1724, and continuing till his death in 1782, fifty-nine years. Mrs. George Denny was a Parkman, a granddaughter of this early minister, and it was a connection which her descendants regarded as highly honorable, as it truly was.

Mr. Denny, after passing his childhood and youth at Westboro', returned to Boston when he was about twenty years of age, and became a partner in the old firm, which began as Denny & Dutton in 1830, and has passed through many changes to bring it to the firm name which it now bears of Denny, Rice & Co. Gov. Gardiner was once a member of the firm, and retired in 1856, when he was elected governor of Massachusetts. Mr. Horace McFarland, deceased, was for many years connected with the house.

During the war of the Rebellion he was for a time connected with the army. The *Boston Daily Advertiser*, of Jan. 24, 1885, has an obituary article upon Mr. Denny, from which we make the following extract: "Mr. Denny was married, when about twenty-five years old, to Miss Nancy Adams Briggs, daughter of Dr. Briggs, of Augusta, Me., by whom he had one son, Mr. Arthur B. Denny. Mrs. Denny died in August, 1882, and his son is the only survivor of his family. Mr. Denny was prominent in social as well as financial circles. At the time of his death he was president of the Art Club, to which position he had just been reëlected, after having filled the office for a number of years. He was a member of the Loyal Legion, the Commercial Club, the Board of Trade, a director in the Revere Bank and the president of the Suffolk Cattle Company of Cheyenne, Wy. He was a prominent member of the Emmanuel Church, having held the office of treasurer for many consecutive years, and at the time of his decease was one of the vestrymen. His circle of friends and acquaintances was very large, and his death will leave a vacancy that cannot be filled. He was an exceedingly genial man and a great favorite with all who knew him."

Mr. Denny's earliest American ancestor was Daniel Denny, who arrived in Boston in September, 1715. Two years later he removed to Leicester, Mass., where, it is believed, he made his home till his death in 1760.

STEPHEN BUTTRICK NOYES, A.B., of Brooklyn, N. Y., a corresponding member, admitted January 10, 1859, was born at Brookfield, Mass., August 28, 1833, and died at Deland, Florida, March 8, 1885, aged 51.

His father was the Rev. George Rapall Noyes, D.D., the distinguished professor of Hebrew and other oriental languages in Harvard Divinity School, from 1840 to 1868. In earlier life he had been pastor at Brookfield and Petersham, and it was during his pastorate at Brookfield that his son Stephen was born. The father was born in Newburyport, Mass., March 6, 1798, and died in Cambridge, June 3, 1868.

Living in his father's house at Cambridge, the subject of this sketch enjoyed every facility for early culture. He was graduated at Harvard College at the age of twenty, in 1853. He had among his classmates President Charles William Eliot, Prof. Sylvester Waterhouse, Prof. James M. Pierce and William L. Gage, D.D.

Soon after leaving college he began to reveal decided tastes and capacities as a librarian and bibliophilist. Five years after graduating he was put in charge of the Mercantile Library of Brooklyn, having then only about 3000 volumes. Such evidence did he soon give of ability in this department, that he was called away to the Congressional Library at Washington, and for some years was there employed. But the managers of the Brooklyn Library so much felt his loss that they prevailed upon him to come back. His great work as a librarian was really done in Brooklyn, though he wrought faithfully and well at Washington. The Brooklyn Library of 3000, before he left it grew to 83,000. The catalogue which he prepared of this Brooklyn Library, and which was published a short time before his death, is regarded as something new and original, and marking an era in publications of this class.

His earliest American ancestor was Rev. Nicholas[1] Noyes, colleague with Rev. Thomas Parker in the ministry at Newbury, Mass., 1635. From him the line runs through Cutting[2] Noyes, born 1649; Cutting,[3] Jr., born 1677; Jacob,[4] born 1704; Joseph,[5] born 1736; Nathaniel,[6] born 1763; George Rapall,[7] born 1798. The last named was married May 8, 1828, to Miss Eliza Wheeler Buttrick, of Framingham.

From this marriage there were seven children, of whom Stephen Buttrick[8] was the third.

Stephen B. Noyes was united in marriage, October 20, 1770, with Sophia O. Anthony, daughter of Edward Anthony, of Brooklyn. From this marriage there were two children, Annie Anthony and George Holland. The wife died in 1873, and the son about three years ago.

In 1882, June 14, he was again married to Susan W. Wylie, daughter of James Wylie, of Brooklyn. From this marriage there was a son, who, with his mother and his sister by the former marriage, survive.

Rev. SAMUEL IRENÆUS PRIME, D.D., of New York, a corresponding member, admitted June 8, 1855, was born at Ballston, N. Y., Nov. 4, 1812, and died in Manchester, Vt., where he had gone for his summer sojourn, July 11, 1885.

His earliest American ancestor was James Prime, one of the company that founded Milford, Ct., in 1640. Dr. Prime's great-grandfather was Rev. Ebenezer, who was graduated at Yale College in 1718, and was settled the year following, 1719, at Huntington, L. I., where he remained just fifty years, dying in 1779. A son of his was Benjamin Young Prime, M.D., who was graduated at Yale in 1760. He was a man of varied learning and of considerable literary ability. He was a youth of fifteen at the breaking out of the revolutionary war, and during the war was known for his patriotic songs. A son of Benjamin was Rev. Nathaniel Scudder Prime, D.D., who was educated at Princeton. He was a distinguished Presbyterian minister, and like his father and grandfather was a man of letters. He died in 1856.

Coming from such an ancestry, it was natural that the subject of this sketch should inherit a taste for books and literary studies. He had a taste for the languages in early life, and made rapid progress in them. He entered Williams College at the age of thirteen, and was graduated in 1829, at the age of seventeen. This was a common age for graduation at Harvard College in the 17th century, but in this century it is rare to find college graduates of only seventeen years of age.

Dr. Prime's early ministry was irregular because of ill health, but his life-work has been that of an editor. He is known to the world through the columns of the *New York Observer*, with which he has been for many years connected. His presence and activity there have been manifest in almost every issue of the paper. Though not a profound thinker or writer, there was a class of subjects, literary, biographical, historical, religious, which he touched with a flowing and easy pen, and his articles on such subjects were almost always found readable. They had a style that was *sui generis*, and the readers of the Observer were apt to turn at once to the IRENÆUS columns. He was also the author of several bound volumes.

The brothers of Dr. Prime, Rev. Dr. E. D. G. and William Cowper Prime, are well known for their ability.

He leaves a widow and four children, two sons and two daughters. Rev. Dr. Wendall Prime, his son, was associated with him in the conduct of the *Observer*. His eldest daughter is the wife of Rev. Dr. Charles A. Stoddard, who is also one of the editors of the *Observer*.

FRANKLIN B. HOUGH, M.D., LL.D., of Lowville, N. Y., a corresponding member, admitted Feb. 3, 1860, was born in Martinsburgh, Lewis County, N. Y., July 20, 1822, and died at Lowville, Lewis County, N. Y., June 11, 1885, aged 62.

His father, Dr. Horatio Gates Hough, was born in Meriden, Ct., Jan. 5, 1778, but went as a child, with the family, to Southwick, Mass., and in 1798 removed to the state of New York, where he married Nov. 13, 1803, Miss Martha Pitcher. His grandfather was Thomas Hough, of Meriden, Ct., who died Dec. 4, 1815, aged 66.

The subject of this sketch, after his common school days, received his education at Lowville Academy and at the Black River Literary and Religious Institute in Watertown, N. Y., whence he went to Union College, where he was graduated in 1843. He received his medical education at Cleveland, Ohio, graduating with the degree of M.D. in 1848.

He was united in marriage July 9, 1845, while pursuing medical studies, with Maria Sarah Eggleson, of Champion, N. Y. By this marriage there was one child, a daughter, born in 1846. The wife died June 2, 1848. He was again married, May 16, 1849, to Mariah Ellen Kilham, of Turin, N. Y. By this marriage there were four children, two sons and two daughters.

Dr. Hough's professional life was at first in Somerville, St. Lawrence County, N. Y., where he lived from 1848 to 1852. In May, 1854, he removed to Albany, where he remained until 1860, when he established his residence at Lowville, which was afterwards his home. As a matter of fact, Dr. Hough's life, as a physician, has been subordinate to that of a public and historical writer, in which respect he has shown a very great industry and ability.

It would be beyond the proper limits of this notice to give even the titles of all the books and important papers which he has contributed in this general department of study. A few of them we give : "History of St. Lawrence and Franklin Counties, N. Y.," 1853 ; "History of Jefferson County, N. Y.," 1854 ; "Results of a Series of Meteorological Observations made at New York Academies," 1855 ; "Census of New York," 1855, taken under his direction ; "History of Lewis County, N. Y.," 1860 ; "Munsell's Guide to the Hudson River," 1859 ; "On Military and Camp Hospitals, from the French of Bauden," 1862 ; "Northern Invasion of October, 1780," 1866. These titles will serve to give an idea of the range of his scholarship and his activities. As an illustration showing how busily he has used his pen, his daughter, Miss Elida C. Hough, in a letter written June 22, 1885, says : " I sent a list of 83 volumes [the work of his hands] to the Utica Herald this morning, and it may be published in that paper to-morrow." The daughter who writes this is a graduate (1885) of Cornell University. Another daughter has studied in Syracuse University. Still another daughter was a student at Vassar. Of the sons one studied at Union College and Albany Law School ; another was graduated at Cornell, and still another is now in his course at Cornell. There are seven children, four daughters and three sons. His wife also survives.

EBENEZER BANCROFT TOWNE, Esq., of Raynham, Mass., a resident member, admitted March 11, 1874, was born in Stoddard, Cheshire Co., N. H., Dec. 14, 1809, and died at Raynham, Ms., June 30, 1885, aged 75 years, 6 months and 16 days. His father was Gardner Towne, born in Amherst, N. H., May 1, 1765. His mother was Lucy Bancroft, born in Tyngsboro', Mass., June 7, 1773. They were married Jan. 27, 1795. His grandfather was Israel Towne, who was born in Amherst, N. H., Nov. 16, 1736, and married Lucy Hopkins, July 31, 1760. His great-grandfather, Israel, was born in Topsfield, Essex Co., Mass., March 24, 1704. This last married Grace Gardner, May 23, 1729. REGISTER xxi. 220.

In early life, the subject of this sketch, in consequence of the death of his father, lived for a little time in the family of Rev. Isaac Robinson, minister in Stoddard, N. H., and afterwards with Mr. John Farwell and his father until about sixteen years old. Before going to Tyngsboro', he was kept at the district school about four months in the year, and afterwards, till the age of sixteen, about three months yearly. From sixteen to eighteen he worked upon the farm, and from eighteen to twenty-one he was an apprentice with Samuel S. Lawrence, of Tyngsboro'.

After he was twenty-one, he became a hat, cap, and fur merchant, in company with his brother Orr N. Towne and Wm. W. Kendrick, at 34 Elm Street, Boston. In this connection he continued for thirty-four years.

He was united in marriage, August 1, 1838, with Miss Almeda Wilson, daughter of Capt Joel Wilson of Stoddard, N. H. She was born in Stoddard, Jan. 19, 1819, and died in Amherst, N. H., Oct. 21, 1845.

He was again married, Feb. 12, 1854, to Mrs. Chloe Adaline Gilman, widow of Henry T. Gilman, and daughter of Sylvanus B. Braman, of Norton, Mass. By this marriage there were three children, a son and two daughters. One of the daughters died in early life.

Mr. Towne was a man of great energy and integrity, and of very systematic business habits. He has left behind a record of honesty and uprightness.

The *Boston Journal* of July 1, 1885, speaks of him as " the wealthiest resident of Raynham," and says: " For many years he was engaged in business in Boston, where the bulk of his fortune was made. On retiring from business he went to Raynham. He was elected County Commissioner for six years, beginning in 1863, and was for a number of years Treasurer of the Bristol County Agricultural Society and held various other offices of trust."

Judge THOMAS WELLS BARTLEY, of Washington, D. C., a corresponding member, admitted Nov. 10, 1855, was born in Jefferson County, Ohio, Feb. 11, 1812, and died in Washington, D. C., June 20, 1885, aged 73.

His father was Hon. Mordecai Bartley, of Mansfield, Ohio, who was born in Fayette County, Pa., Sept. 8, 1787, and his mother was Elizabeth, daughter of Thomas

Wells, of Brownsville, Fayette County, Pa. She was born in 1789. They were united in marriage in 1806. His grandfather Elijah was born in Virginia in 1753, and married Rachel Pearshall. After marriage they removed from Loudoun County, Va., to Fayette County, Pa., where all their children were born. The earlier ancestors of this Bartley family (spelled also Barklay and Barclay) lived in Virginia from the early colonial days.

Mordecai Bartley was a prominent man in Ohio. He was a military officer in the war of 1812, was member of congress eight years, from 1823 to 1831, and was governor of the state two years, 1844–46.

The subject of this sketch, after his boyhood days were passed, was fitted for college, and was graduated at Jefferson College, Pa., in 1829, and received the degree of A.M. in 1833. After studying law one year with Hon. Jacob Parker, of Mansfield, and one year with Elijah Hayward, Esq., of Washington, D. C., he was admitted to practice in all the judicial courts of Ohio in 1833. He soon became a public man, serving in the Ohio General Assembly and in the Senate. As speaker of the Senate, he became, in 1844, ex-officio governor of the state, and in December of that year was succeeded by his own father, who had just been elected governor.

He was united in marriage, October 5, 1837, with Julia Maria, daughter of William Larwill, of Wooster, Ohio. She was born March 30, 1818, and died March 1, 1847. He married again, Nov. 7, 1848, Susan Sherman (Reg. xxiv. 160), daughter of Hon. Charles R. Sherman, Judge of the Supreme Court of Ohio. She was sister of Senator John and General William T. Sherman. By his first marriage he had four children, and by his second two.

Judge Bartley was a man eminent for his legal learning and his great power of thought. Some of his decisions occupy a high place in the estimate of his brethren of the legal profession. He was a member of the Jackson Democratic Association in Washington, and the resolutions passed by that body, after his death, are very strong in their testimony to his ability and worth of character. The last words of Judge Bartley, as reported to us by one of his friends, were these : " I have done my duty to my country, to my countrymen, to my children, to all. The world, the material world, I am going out of it. But there is a spiritual world we cannot see with our material senses." He had lifted himself upon his elbow to utter these words, when he dropped back upon his pillow and died.

BOOK NOTICES.

The Editor requests persons sending books for notice to state, for the information of readers, the price of each book, with the amount to be added for postage when sent by mail.

Families of the Wyoming Valley: Biographical, Genealogical and Historical. Sketches of the Bench and Bar of Luzerne County, Pennsylvania. By George B. Kulp, Historiographer of the Wyoming Historical and Geological Society. In two volumes. Vol. 1. Wilkes-Barre, Pa. E. B. Yordy, Printer. 1885. 8vo. pp. viii.+504. Price per volume, $7.50.

A history of the families of the Wyoming Valley of Pennsylvania is necessarily an important part of the history of Connecticut, that state having claimed, by the charter of Charles II., that portion of the present territory of Pennsylvania lying between the 41st and 43rd degrees of latitude. As early as 1753 steps were taken by Connecticut to settle this section with her own people. From 1760 to 1790 various companies of emigrants from Connecticut and the other New England states located on these lands. The claim of Connecticut was disputed by the colony of Pennsylvania, who had already granted these lands to her citizens. Out of this conflict of colonial authority, frequent and severe contests for their possession arose between the two parties, the Pennamites or Pennsylvania claimants, and the Yankees or Connecticut claimants. No one who has ever visited the historical Valley of Wyoming, and gazed upon its exquisite beauty, will wonder that the early settlers were willing to take up arms and do battle for such a prize. The struggle for its possession is narrated in the various histories of this section, and needs only to be referred to here. But from these emigrations of New England and Pennsylvania people have descended the Families of Wyoming Valley, whose history Mr. Kulp has preserved in this very interesting volume. Many of these families, repeating the history of most civil wars, have intermarried to such an extent that frequently the Pennsylvania family and name are found owning lands inherited from Connecticut ancestors, or the Connecticut family is found in possession of acres descended from some Pennsylvania ancestor. From these early settlers, who were men of bold spirit, undaunted courage, strong sense and religious principles, have come many whose names are to be found prominently placed on every page of the history of the union. To one branch of these sons of Connecticut and Pennsylvania the author of this volume has devoted his labors in efforts to rescue from oblivion the records of their personal career and that of their forefathers, i. e. the Bench and Bar of Luzerne County.

The first volume, the only one as yet issued, contains ninety-seven biographical and genealogical sketches of living members of the Luzerne Bar. The second volume will contain as many more, including those whose earthly career has already ended, many of whom were distinguished in the civil and military history of Pennsylvania. These sketches first appeared in the pages of the Luzerne Legal Register, a weekly publication by Mr. Kulp, which has reached its fourteenth volume, and is of such value that a full set commands the price of about sixty-five dollars. In this volume Mr. Kulp has given as full genealogical records as it was possible to obtain of the families from which the several subjects of his shetches descended. He has had access to old family papers, church and court records, both in Connecticut and Pennsylvania, and has gathered his mass of historical and personal reminiscences with great care and accuracy.

Among the biographical sketches will be found those of Col. Zebulon Butler, who was in the action of Wyoming, 1778, Hons. Edmund L. Dana, Henry M. Hoyt, A. T. McClintock, E. S. Osborne, Lazarus D. Shoemaker, Hendrick B. Wright; Judges Rhone, Woodward, Scott, Harding, Rice and others of the Luzerne Bar. Among the genealogies, in which a vast amount of new and unpublished material appears for the first time, will be found those of the families of Butler, Bennett, Bulkley, Bedford, Conyngham, Dixon, Dorrance, Darling, Espy, Fell, Hasley, Hand, Hunlock, Hoyt, Jameson, Johnson, Jenkins, Kulp, Lewis, Lamberton, O'Neil, Payne, Palmer, Powell, Rhone, Richardson, Richards, Scott, Smith, Sutton, Shoemaker, Strong, Welles, Wadhams, Walker, &c. &c. &c. The sketch of Edmund Griffin Butler is especially interesting, containing as it does an exhaustive account of the battle and massacre of Wyoming, in which action the ancestors of nearly all of those whose history this work sets forth participated. In his estimate of the character of living persons whom the author names, we find none of that fulsome flattery which disfigures so much modern biography. While as he says the volume makes no pretensions to literary excellence, he has given us a very readable book, and one which the genealogist will welcome as useful and valuable. Mr. Kulp promises an index of names in the second volume, the absence of which is the only defect of this volume. The typography of the book reflects great credit on the printer. The work is not stereotyped and the edition is limited.

By the Rev. Horace Edwin Hayden, Wilkes-Barre, Pa.

Emmanuel College, Cambridge. Commemoration of the Three Hundredth Anniversary of the Foundation. 1884. 8vo. pp. 99.

Laurence Chaderton, D.D. (First Master of Emmanuel). Translated from a Latin Memoir of Dr. Dillingham, with Notes and Illustrations. Richard Farmer, D.D. (Master of Emmanuel, 1775—1797). An Essay. By E. S. Shuckburgh, M.A., late Fellow of Emmanuel College, Cambridge. Cambridge: Macmillan and Bowers. 1884. 8vo. pp. 63.

We have before us two works which the Tercentenary Festal of Emmanuel College, June 18 and 19, 1884, have produced. This College, as is stated in the first book, " was founded by Sir Walter Mildmay in the year 1584. The Register gives the names of thirty persons admitted members of the college in the year 1584-5. Of the actual day of the foundation there is no record. But Queen Elizabeth's Charter empowering Sir Walter Mildmay to found a College is dated June 5, 1584. Between these two dates, therefore, the corporate life of the College must have begun."

This college has a particular interest for the people of New England, for more of the prominent men among our early settlers were educated here than at any other college. Among them were John Harvard, the founder of Harvard College ; Nathaniel Ward, author of the Massachusetts Body of Liberties, the first code of laws established in New England ; Thomas Hooker and Samuel Stone of Hartford, Thomas Shepard of Cambridge, William Blaxton or Blackstone, the first settler of Boston ; Thomas James and Zechariah Symmes, of Charlestown ; Nathaniel Rogers of Ipswich,Daniel Maude of Dover, William Leverich of Sandwich, all clergymen and men of ability.

The first work under notice contains the proceedings at the celebration in the summer of 1884, when speeches were made by our countrymen, Prof. Charles E. Norton, as a delegate from Harvard College, and the Hon. James Russell Lowell, the United States Minister to Great Britain. Speeches were made also by Dr. Phear, the master of Emmanuel ; Dr. Ferras, the vice-chancellor of the university ; Lord Powis, the high steward ; the Bishop of Winchester, Sir Henry Mildmay, descended from a brother of the founder ; Mr. Beresford Hope, Rev. W. Chawner, tutor of Emmanuel, Dr. Sebastian Evans and Dr. J. J. Raven. A sermon was preached by Dr. Edward Harold Browne, bishop of Winchester. Appended to the report of these proceedings is some valuable historical, biographical and tabular matter relative to the college. A portrait of the founder is prefixed to the book.

The bicentenary of the college was celebrated one hundred years ago, in September, 1784, by appropriate services, an account of which is preserved in this book. It is not known that the completion of the first hundred years was observed in any manner ; nor does any notice seem to have been taken in 1834 of its quarter millenary, an event now so frequently commemorated in America.

Dr. Shuckburgh's work, the second whose title we give, contains memoirs of two Masters of Emmanuel, Dr. Laurence Chaderton, the first master of the college, and Dr. Richard Farmer, the Shakspearean scholar, who was master when the bicentenary was celebrated. The memoir of Dr. Chaderton was written in Latin by one of his successors, Dr. William Dillingham, and has been translated and edited by Dr. Shuckburgh, who has written, as a companion to it, the memoir of Dr. Farmer. The two biographies are valuable contributions to the history of the college.

The Colonial Church in Virginia. Address delivered by P. SLAUGHTER, D.D., Historiographer of the Diocese of Virginia, at the Centennial Council in the City of Richmond, on the 21st of May, 1885. [Motto of the Seal of Virginia.] Boston : Printed by Rand, Avery & Company. 1885. 8vo. pp. 43.

The Rev. Dr. Slaughter has been for many years, as he now is, a zealous and indefatigable student of the history of Virginia, especially its ecclesiastical history. He has rendered most valuable service by his efforts to seek out, collect and preserve the scattered and perishing records of the ancient parishes. Among the fruits of his historical researches are the well-known histories of Bristol Parish and St. George's Parish, published respectively in 1846 and 1847, and which were subsequently incorporated by Bishop Meade in his " Old Churches, Ministers and Families of Virginia." In his excellent memoir of Bishop Meade (*Memorial Biographies* of the New England Historic Genealogical Society, vol. iv. 1885), Dr. Slaughter gives an outline sketch of the condition of the Episcopal Church in Virginia during the first half of the present century. In his Centennial Address of May last he deals more in detail, and more in the way of a discussion, with a much longer period, upwards of two hundred and fifty years of colonial history. In a survey so long as this, only the most important events could be noticed. But with this discussion we are presented with striking views of men, of society, and of ecclesiastical and political affairs, painted with the author's characteristic skill. These views represent the results of careful research, and the facts are stated frankly and clearly. This address may well serve, in the hands of the same author, or in the hands of an equally competent historian in the future, as the framework of a full history of the Episcopal Church in Virginia prior to the American Revolution.

The author throws new light upon his subject, and corrects some false and injurious statements, the coinage of ignorant or prejudiced writers. He points out the chief obstacles, whether of a local or of a foreign source, to the vigorous growth of the colonial Church. He shows how it was hampered and weakened rather than aided and stregthened, by its enforced union with the State. He shows how it endeavored to meet its obligations to the enslaved race. And he establishes the fact—

which has been ignored or denied by not a few historians—that the principal laymen in Virginia were openly among the earliest and most strenuous opposers of the arbitrary and oppressive measures of the British authorities previous to the Revolution, and that they were also amongst the most patriotic and efficient supporters of the American interests throughout the war.
By Albert H. Hoyt, A.M., of Boston.

Proceedings and Collections of the Wyoming Historical and Geological Society. Vol. II. Part I. Wilkes-Barré, Pa.: Printed for the Society. 1885. 8vo. pp. 185.

This number contains the charter, by-laws and roll of membership of the society, with the proceedings from March 2, 1883, to Feb. 11, 1884, and reports and papers. The papers on Local Shell-Beds by Sheldon Reynolds, Pittston Fort by Hon. Steuben Jenkins, Bibliography of Wyoming Valley by the Rev. Horace E. Hayden, Calvin Williams by George B. Kulp, contain much important material for the history of the Wyoming Valley. A report of a special committee, by the chairman, the late Harrison Wright, Ph.D., on the archæological remains at Tioga Point, Pa., is a valuable contribution to Indian history.

This society, which was established in 1858, is doing good service for the history and geology of that locality.

Samuel de Champlain: A Brief Sketch of the Eminent Navigator and Discoverer. Read before the Chicago Historical Society, Tuesday Evening, October 20, 1885. By HENRY H. HURLBUT. A Portrait of the Great Explorer, painted by Miss Harriet P. Hurlbut, was on this occasion presented in her name to the Society. Chicago: Fergus Printing Company. 1885. 8vo. pp. 19.

We have before us an address delivered last autumn before the Chicago Historical Society on the occasion of the presentation, in behalf of Miss Hurlbut, of a painting of Champlain. It was copied by her from an engraved portrait by Moncornet, as it appears in the works of Champlain published by the Prince Society. The frame, of which an account is given in the author's "Chicago Antiquities," p. 80, has a history, having traditionally formed a part of an old ship of some celebrity. Mr. Hurlbut is engaged on a work to be entitled " Our Inland Seas and Early Lake Navigation," and this sketch of the life of Champlain will form a part of that work. It is an interesting narrative of this early explorer of our coast.

Genealogical Gleanings in England. By HENRY F. WATERS, A.B. Vol. I. (Part First.) Boston: New England Historic Genealogical Society. 1885. 8vo. pp. 131.

John Harvard and his Ancestry. By HENRY F. WATERS, A.B. Boston: New England Historic Genealogical Society. 1885. 8vo. pp. 24.

Genealogical Gleanings in England. [No.] X. By HENRY F. WATERS, A.M. 8vo. pp. 16.

A notice in the REGISTER of Mr. Waters's " Genealogical Gleanings in England " may appear like " carrying coal to Newcastle," but a brief word will suffice. These " Gleanings " have appeared quarterly in this periodical.

The first part of Volume I., whose title heads this article, represents all the instalments published from July, 1883, to April, 1885, inclusive. The preface is by John T. Hassam, Esq., and the superb index is by Frank E. Bradish, Esq.

The second title which we give is that of a pamphlet reprint of Mr. Waters's contribution to the July number of the REGISTER, in which he dispelled the mystery which had so long enveloped the history of the founder of Harvard University.

The third title is that of the last issue of the serials which the Committee on English Research of the New England Historic Genealogical Society have reprinted from the REGISTER. Of these serials, Nos. I. to VIII. are reprinted in the work whose title we first give; No. IX. consists of the Harvard researches, and No. X. contains all of Mr. Waters's " Gleanings " which appeared in the October REGISTER with Mr. Hassam's introduction, including President Eliot's account of Mr. Waters's discoveries about Harvard.

The three works contain all of the published " Genealogical Gleanings " to the close of 1885.

Students in genealogy felt that they had a prize in the various instalments, and now when the same appear in book form, a greater prize is presented to them. The work of Mr. Waters is of highest value. To him already is due the credit of finding the Winthrop map, the Maverick MS. and the family of John Harvard. His investigations, as these "Gleanings" prove, are in no narrow way. The early families of Virginia and the other English colonies, as well as Massachusetts, are borne in mind. To many of these researches are appended notes of much value by eminent American antiquaries. The descendants of the early American families can well afford to keep Mr. Waters at this post, for which he is preëminently fitted. *By the Rev. Anson Titus, of Amesbury, Mass.*

Final Notes on Witchcraft in Massachusetts; A Summary Vindication of the Laws and Liberties concerning Attainders, with Corruption of Blood, Escheats, Forfeitures for Crime and Pardon of Offenders, in Reply to the Reasons, &c., of Hon. Albert C. Goodell, Jr., Editor of the Province Laws of Massachusetts. By GEORGE H. MOORE, LL.D., Superintendent of the Lenox Library. New York: Printed for the Author. 1885. 8vo. pp. 120. Sold by Cupples, Upham & Co., 283 Washington St., Boston, Mass. Price $1.

Prytaneum Bostoniense. Notes on the History of the Old State House, formerly known as the Town House in Boston, the Province Court House, the State House and the City Hall. By GEORGE H. MOORE, LL.D. Boston: Cupples, Upham & Co. 1885. 8vo. pp. 31. Price 50 cents.

Dr. Moore's "Final Notes" is the fifth of a series of pamphlets which have been issued by Dr. Moore and Mr. Goodell, discussing points in the history of Witchcraft in Massachusetts. On the 21st of October, 1882, Dr. Moore read a paper before the American Antiquarian Society, entitled Notes on the History of Witchcraft in Massachusetts, which was printed in the Proceedings of that society and reprinted in pamphlet form in 1883. A reply to this by Mr. Goodell, under the title of "Further Notes on the History of Witchcraft in Massachusetts," appeared in 1884. "Supplementary Notes on Witchcraft in Massachusetts" by Dr. Moore, and Reasons for concluding that the Act of 1711, Reversing the Attainder of 1692, became a Law," by Dr. Goodell, followed in the same year. Mr. Goodell's two contributions to this and Dr. Moore's "Supplementary Notes" and a part of the "Final Notes" were read as papers before the Massachusetts Historical Society, and are reprinted from its Proceedings. Various questions concerning the Witchcraft trials and the subsequent legislation of Massachusetts relative to the victims, are discussed in these pamphlets; and much curious and interesting information upon the laws and law-making of the province, which none could give but Messrs. Moore and Goodell, who have made these subjects a specialty and have spent years in investigating them and in collecting materials illustrating them.

The pamphlet before us is, as the title states, "a summary vindication of the Laws and Liberties" of Massachusetts "concerning Attainders, with Corruption of Blood, Escheats, Forfeiture for Crime and Pardon of Offenders." It displays great learning, and is a thorough investigation of these subjects. In the appendix, besides other matters of value, is a detailed history of the Records of the General Court. The originals were all destroyed with the Court House in the fire of 1747, and what we have are only copies. It is interesting to follow, as Dr. Moore enables us to do, the action of the different legislatures on the subject of copying the records for preservation, and the zealous labors of that model secretary, Josiah Willard, in the cause.

The other pamphlet, "Prytaneum Bostoniense or Notes on the History of the Old State House," is a paper read in that ancient structure, May 12, 1885, before the Bostonian Society. It is a worthy companion to Mr. Whitmore's "Old State House Memorial," issued by the city, and shows that Mr. Whitmore's volume, replete as it is with memorials of the historic halls of that building, did not exhaust his subject. Indeed, we learn that Mr. Moore has enough matter for another paper which he is to read before that society in February.

Colonel Alexander Rigby: A Sketch of his Career and Connection with Maine as Proprietor of the Plough Patent and President of the Province of Lygonia. By CHARLES EDWARD BANKS, M.D. (Dart.). 1885. Privately Printed. Sm. 4to. pp. 57. Fifty copies printed.

Though Col. Rigby never visited New England, he appears prominently in the history of the colonization of Maine; and yet but few details of his life have been known to us. Dr. Banks by patient research has supplied our want, and shown him to us as he was known to his contemporaries in England. He was an ardent supporter of the Commonwealth and was entrusted with important offices. In this pamphlet we have also an account of the Plough Patent and the abortive attempts of the Familists who obtained the patent to colonize under it ; also a history of the Province of Lygonia as administered by George Cleeves under Rigby's authority. The author treats these subjects exhaustively. A portrait of Rigby, heliotyped from a miniature in the possession of Towneley Rigby Knowles, Esq., of Pau, France, is a new attraction for us. A tabular pedigree, showing the descent from Adam Rigby of Wygan, his great-grandfather, is also given. This tract is a reprint from the *Maine Historical and Genealogical Recorder.*

Family Memorials. A Series of Genealogical and Biographical Monographs on the Families of Salisbury, Aldworth-Elbridge, Sewall, Pyldren-Dummer, Walley, Quincy, Gookin, Wendell, Breese, Chevalier-Anderson and Phillips. With Fifteen Pedigrees and an Appendix. By EDWARD ELBRIDGE SALISBURY. 1885. Privately Printed. Price in cloth, $20.00.

An accomplished scholar who has traversed many fields of learning, here presents in a superb folio volume of 696 pages (bound in boards in two half volumes), a historical and genealogical account of several distinguished families—some of them among the most distinguished in New England—whose lines of descent converge in his own family and in his own person. Professor Salisbury has given years of time and thought and labor, and has devoted a considerable amount of money, in the first place, to the collection in this and other lands, of information of every kind relating to these families, then to the classification and arrangement of the material thus accumulated, and, more recently, to the compilation and publication of a portion of it, which is thus made available for contemporaneous use, and safe for the generations which are to come. He dedicates it to the Memory of the Fathers for the Sake of the Children. For undertaking such a task the author deserves the hearty thanks of all historical students ; and for the success with which he has been able to carry out his generous and comprehensive purpose he is entitled to their congratulations. The first Mrs. Salisbury was Abigail Salisbury Phillips, of Boston, a cousin of her husband : the second, who has had an important share in the work now before us, was Evelyn McCurdy, daughter of the Hon. Charles J. McCurdy, of Lyme, Conn.

By Hamilton Andrews Hill, A.M., of Boston.

L'Intermédiaire des Chercheurs et Curieux. Fondé en 1864. LUCIEN FAUCON, Directeur Paris, 13 rue Cujas. Published on the 10th and 25th of each month, in 8vo., 32 pages each. Terms in France, 16 francs per annum : abroad, 18 francs.

Students of French history will welcome the aid of this modest and useful serial in unfolding the details of many interesting events deemed too trivial for record by the cotemporaneous chronicler, but subsequently found to be of commanding importance. It has an especial value to the searchers and gleaners amid the past manners, customs and habits of the French, in that it talks freely and without reserve concerning some matters not likely to be found elsewhere. Its independence is absolute, and the inviolability of correspondence guaranteed.

By George A. Gordon, A.M., of Somerville, Mass.

New Chapter in the History of Concord Fight ; Groton Minute Men at the North Bridge, April 19, 1775. By WILLIAM W. WHEILDON. Boston : Lee & Shepard, Publishers, No. 10 Milk Street. 1885. 8vo. pp. 32.

Mr. Wheildon has done much to preserve the local history of Boston and vicinity, and particularly the incidents in the revolutionary history of this locality. The long list of works by him on the cover of this pamphlet show how much he has published, and how long he has been engaged in such labors.

He here prints the testimony which Artemas Wright of Ayer gives on the authority of his grandfather, Nathan Corey of Groton, concerning the Concord Fight. The arrival of cannon in Groton from Concord, it is stated, raised suspicions, and Corey and nine other minute men left Groton for that place on the evening of April 18, and were in Concord early the next morning, where they took part in the defence of the North Bridge. Mr. Wheildon draws attention to the importance of Paul Revere's first Ride to Lexington, Sunday, April 16th.

An appendix contains—1, a list of towns engaged in the events of the 19th April, 1775, with the losses of each and other particulars ; 2, a description of the monuments, etc., erected to commemorate the events of that day.

A view of the " Old North Bridge " and the monument at Concord embellish the work. Mr. Wright's story was made the basis of a paper by Mr. Wheildon read before the Bostonian Society. This paper is here printed with additions.

The Attempts made to Separate the West from the American Union. A Paper read before the Missouri Historical Society, February 4, 1885. By the Rt. Rev. C. F. ROBERTSON, D.D., LL.D. St. Louis : 1885. 8vo. pp. 60.

This essay by Bishop Robertson gives a concise and interesting account of the machinations of the Spanish authorities in Louisiana Territory during the period following the American Revolution, and prior to the restoration of the territory to France, the object of the intrigues being to detach the territories now comprising the states of Mississippi, Kentucky, Tennessee and Indiana from the union, and to persuade them to seek Spanish protection. Considerable dissatisfaction prevailed in these territories from 1783–89, and even later, in consequence of the failure of congress to protect western interests, and especially the neglect or inability to secure from Spain a free navigation of the Mississippi in order that the products of the country might reach a market.

The author gives a brief history of the purchase of Louisiana from the French, and tells the story of Aaron Burr's conspiracy, in which he offers evidence of the disloyalty of Gen. Wilkinson, commander of the United States army. The pamphlet contains a map of the Mississippi valley, and portraits of Burr and Blennerhassett. The authorities for the historical statements are cited, and the paper shows extensive and thorough research.

By George K. Clarke, LL.B., of Needham, Mass.

Archæologia Americana. Transactions and Collections of the American Antiquarian Society. Vol. VII. *Note-Book kept by Thomas Lechford, Esq., Lawyer, in Massachusetts Bay, from June* 27, 1638, *to July* 29, 1641. Printed for the Society, at University Press, Cambridge. 1885. 8vo. pp. xxviii.+460.

This note-book of the first lawyer in New England is one of the most valuable and interesting publications that we have noticed. It contains copies of the legal papers drawn by Thomas Lechford, and notes on the cases concerning which he was consulted or interested. The quaint old forms are both amusing and instructive to the lawyer of to-day ; and to the historical student and the genealogist the note-book reveals the transactions and events from 1638 to 1641, in which many of the earliest settlers here were concerned. More important still, it gives the English homes of many persons, in some cases only confirming what we knew before, but in others giving facts before unknown, and perhaps vainly sought for. Copious notes are found on nearly every page, and the work is ably edited by Edward Everett Hale, Jr., who has availed to some extent of matter previously prepared by J. Hammond Trumbull, LL.D., Hon. Dwight Foster and others. Twenty-two pages are devoted to a sketch of Thomas Lechford by Dr. Trumbull, which gives some account of the difficulties into which Lechford's theological opinions led him. The birth-place and parentage of the author of " Plain Dealing " are not definitely known, but it is surmised that he may have belonged to a Lechford family in the county of Surrey. Various letters to Hugh Peters and other persons are found in the note-book, mostly on religious subjects, and it seems evident that his return to England was the result of the harshness with which he was treated here. There is also much relating to public affairs, such as addresses and " proposicons " to the Governor and General Court. It is unfortunate that a better method of indexing was not adopted. The book is attractive in appearance, and printed in the best manner.

By George K. Clarke, LL.B., of Needham, Mass.

Woburn [*Massachusetts*] : *an historical and descriptive sketch of the town, with an outline of its industrial interests.* Illustrated. Woburn : Published by the Board of Trade. 1885. The Riverside Press, Cambridge : Printed by H. O. Houghton and Company. Oblong 8vo. pp. 60. Illustrations by the Heliotype Printing Company, Boston. Price $2.

This is a beautiful book, finely gotten up, with beautiful illustrations, and issued from the press of a first class establishment. In the limits of sixty pages are a neatly writted historical sketch of the town,—which was incorporated in the year 1642, and which until within a comparatively recent period was devoted to little other than agricultural business,—and chapters on the geography, inhabitants and present business of the town, which is chiefly the manufacture of leather ; in which business, with its present number of nearly twelve thousand inhabitants, the town leads all other places in New England. The writer of the business part of the work has performed his task in a really admirable manner, giving a comprehensive and clear view of the place as it now is, and its prospective advantages. Its accuracy as a sketch can be but little questioned; and the result of the work, as a whole, is no-wise disappointing. It could be wished, however, that more of the manufacturing establishments, stores and business blocks, could have found illustration in its pages. A few slight errors, patent to the local historian, are observable. The most serious one is the statement, on page 15, that the meeting-house of the first fifty years of the town's existence was the one located on the bluff or hill east of the present common, when it is well known that this one was the second edifice for town worship, the first edifice having been erected on the common itself. Both houses, however, belonged to this early period.

The Woburn Board of Trade was organized March 25, 1885, with the object of increasing the business, population and prosperity of the town, and this work is its first publication.

Communicated by William R. Cutter, Esq., Librarian Woburn Public Library.

A Suggestion as to the Origin of the Plan of Savannah. Remarks by WM. HARDEN before the Georgia Historical Society, Monday, Sept. 7th, 1885. 8vo. pp. 4.

In this pamphlet Mr. Harden, the librarian of the Georgia Historical Society, gives good reasons for believing that "The Villas of the Ancients Illustrated," by Robert Castell, a folio published in London in 1728, suggested to Oglethorpe the plan of Savannah.

Some Observations on the Letters of Amerigo Vespucci. By M. F. FORCE. Read before the Congrés International des Américanistes at Brussels, September, 1879. Cincinnati : Robert Clarke & Co. 1885. 8vo. pp. 24.

This is an interesting criticism of the letters of Amerigo Vespucci—or rather those attributed to him. We cannot examine Mr. Force's arguments in detail, but he certainly seems to prove—if proof is necessary—that the letters in question were not written by Vespucci. Truth is sure to prevail sooner or later.

By Daniel Rollins, Esq., of Boston, Mass.

The Adventures and Discourses of Captain Iohn Smith, some time President of Virginia and Admiral of New England. Newly Ordered by IOHN ASHTON. London, Paris and New York : Cassell & Company. Limited. Post 8vo. pp. 309. Portraits and Illustrations.

This work, compiled by Mr. John Ashton, author of "Social Life in the Reign of Queen Anne, "Chap Books of the Eighteenth Century," and other works of a similar character, is an attempt to serve up for the popular taste the writings of the famous Captain John Smith. Mr. Ashton has boiled down Smith's verbosity and collated his various histories into a continued narrative, beginning with his parentage, and ending with the *post-mortem* adjudication of his estate. In a great part of the work Smith's exact language is retained, and the whole work is gotten up in the same vein as the "My Lady Pokahontas" of Mr. John Esten Cooke. For popular information it is admirably adapted, and will tend to increase the interest universally felt in this "thrice memorable adventurer." It contains, however, nothing new of historical or antiquarian interest, nor do we incline to the belief that Mr. Ashton intended it for the gratification of antiquaries. It is embellished with the well-known portraits of Smith and Pocahontas, and fac-similes of the original illustrations in his works.

By Charles E. Banks, M.D., of Chelsea, Mass.

The Works of Hubert Howe Bancroft. Vol. XIII.—*History of Mexico.* Vol. V. 1824—1861. San Francisco : A. L. Bancroft & Company, Publishers. 1885. 8vo. pp. xiii. and 812.

We have already noticed, with marked commendation, the great enterprise of Mr. Bancroft in the long series of volumes which he is publishing upon the various countries bordering upon the Pacific Coast. A literary scheme so wide and comprehensive as his, it is rare to find in any country, and readers are more and more convinced that it is not simply to cover an immense reach of time and space that these volumes are prepared, but that they hold the real history of these countries, the facts of which have been gathered with immense labor and care. The present volume of 812 pages, arranged in thirty chapters, the fifth volume of the Mexican

History, covers the period from 1824 to 1861, including, of course, the exciting period of the war between the United States and Mexico. One more volume, as we understand, will complete the Mexican History. *By the Rev. Increase N. Tarbox, D.D , of West Newton, Mass.*

A Sketch of the Life and Works of Loammi Baldwin, Civil Engineer. By GEORGE L. VOSE, Hayward Professor of Civil and Topographical Engineering in the Massachusetts Institute of Technology. Boston: Press of George H. Ellis. 1885. 8vo. pp. 28. With a heliotype portrait.

" There were," says the author of this pamphlet, " few works of internal improvement carried on during the first thirty years of the present century with which Mr. Baldwin was not connected ; and his two great works, the government dry-docks at Charlestown and at Norfolk, stand to-day unsurpassed among the engineering structures of the country." Prof. Vose considers him the " Father of Civil Engineering in America." And yet very little concerning him is known to the present generation. The author has done well to collect from scattered sources the details of his life and preserve them in these pages. Mr. Baldwin's father, who bore the same christian name, and his brother James F. (REG. xix. 97), were also distinguished as engineers.

Chairs of New England Governors. By the Rev. EDMUND F. SLAFTER, A.M. Boston: The Society's House, 18 Somerset Street. 1885. 8vo. pp. 8.

This is a " Report made at the annual meeting of the New England Historic Genealogical Society, January 7, 1885, on the acquisition of memorial chairs, which had belonged to distinguished governors of the several New England states, to occupy the dais of the public hall of the Society." It is reprinted from the annual proceedings for 1885. The governors are John Hancock of Massachusetts, Hiland Hall of Vermont, Israel Washburn of Maine, Marshall Jewell of Connecticut, Charles H. Bell of New Hampshire, and John Brown Francis of Rhode Island. Biographical sketches of each are given.

Inauguration of the Perry Statue, September 10, A.D. 1885. With the Addresses of William P. Sheffield and the Remarks on Receiving the Statue by Governor Wetmore and Mayor Franklin; with the Speeches at the Dinner, and an Appendix. Newport, R. I. : John P. Sanborn, Publisher. 1885. 8vo. pp. 60.

On September 10, 1885, a notable company assembled at the inauguration of the Perry Statue in Newport, R. I. The beloved Bishop Clark was the chaplain of the day. Our great historian, Hon. George Bancroft, was present and made an eloquent address. The oration was by Hon. W. P. Sheffield, chairman of the committee, who gave a vivid account of the battle of Lake Erie. He was followed by Governor Wetmore and Mayor Franklin, Justices Blatchford and Durfee, and Admirals Rodgers, Almy and Luce, who also made interesting addresses. The church, the civil authority and the navy were well represented on the occasion. Many distinguished men and fair women were present in the audience. They all honored themselves by gathering on the anniversary of the battle of Lake Erie to pay their respects to the memory of the departed hero.

There stands the beautiful and life-like statue opposite the house in which Perry lived. It is fitting that his own state should remember the services which he rendered. Oliver Hazard Perry has an enduring fame as the first American officer who captured a British squadron. We know how bravely he fought on his flag-ship the Lawrence, until all his cannon were dismounted and all but eight of his crew were killed or wounded. He then put off with a boat's crew for the Niagara, which was now to be his flag-ship. Signal was given to break the enemy's line, and the Niagara bore down upon the British centre, discharging broadsides into the Detroit, Queen Charlotte, Chippewa, Lady Provost and the Hunter. She was followed by the rest of the American squadron, the battle became general and lasted three hours. The British line of battle was broken, their decks were strewn with the dying and the dead, and they could hold out no longer. Perry went aboard the Lawrence and received their surrender. He then visited the wounded Barclay, the English commander, and tendered him and the wounded on both sides every service in his power. Neither did he forget the reverent burial of the dead. This brilliant victory was not easily gained, for he fought British veterans who had served under Lord Nelson at Trafalgar. Sheer hard work and bull-dog tenacity—qualities inherent in English blood wherever found—won the battle. Perry then wrote the historic lines to Gen. Harrison, " We have met the enemy and they are ours." Terse and vigorous message, showing the author to be a man of action, not of words. In his despatch to the Secretary of the Navy he mentioned the capture of all the enemy's squadron, namely : two ships, two brigs, one schooner and one sloop. This was a very important victory in our second war for Independence, as Edward Everett used to call it, for it was a turning point in our affairs in the north-west. Perry did not live long to fulfill the promise of his early manhood, for at the age of thirty-four he was attacked with yellow fever at the island of Trinidad, and died there August 23, 1819. His gallant spirit returned to Him who gave it. His mortal body found a temporary resting place at Port Spain, but was afterwards removed on a man-of-war to Newport in his native state. Like the great Napoleon he sleeps in the land he " loved so well."

> " Hark, how the sacred calm that breathes around,
> Bids every fierce, tumultuous passion cease ;
> In still small accents whispering from the ground,
> A grateful earnest of eternal peace."

By Daniel Rollins, Esq., of Boston.

History of the Goodricke Family. Edited by CHARLES ALFRED GOODRICKE. London : Printed for the Editor by Hazell, Watson and Viney. Limited. 1885. Imp. 8vo. pp. 62.

Miscellanea Marescalliana, being Genealogical Notes on the Surname Marshall. Collected by GEORGE WILLIAM MARSHALL, LL.D. Vol. II. Part I. Exeter, 1885. 8vo. pp. 142.

Genealogy of the Family of George Weekes of Dorchester, Mass., 1635–1650 : with some Information in regard to other Families of the Name. By ROBERT D. WEEKS. 1885. Press of L. J. Hardham, Newark, N. J. 8vo. pp. 468. Price $3 in cloth ; higher prices for extra binding.

Phillips Genealogies, including the Family of George Phillips, First Minister of Watertown, Mass. [and Other Families]. Compiled by ALBERT M. PHILLIPS. Auburn, Mass. 1885. 8vo. pp. 233.

Descendants of the Brothers Jeremiah and John Wood. Compiled by WILLIAM S. WOOD, Supt. City Schools, Seymour, Ind. Worcester, Mass. : Press of Charles Hamilton. 1885. 8vo. pp. 292.

Descendants of Peter Willemse Roome. 1883. 8vo. pp. 348+62.

The Bontecou Genealogy. A Record of the Descendants of Pierre Bontecou, a Huguenot Refugee from France in the Lines of his Sons. Compiled by JOHN E. MORRIS. Hartford, Conn. Press of Case, Lockwood & Brainard Company. 1885. 8vo. pp. 271.

Leighton Genealogy. An Account of the Descendants of Capt. William Leighton of Kittery, Maine. By TRISTRAM FROST JORDAN, of Metuchen, N. J. Albany, N. Y. : Press of Joel Munsell's Sons. 1885. 8vo. pp. 127. Price $1.

Genealogical Memoranda. Snively. A.D. 1659—A.D. 1882. Compiled and Arranged by (Rev.) WILLIAM ANDREW SNIVELY (S.T.D.). Brooklyn, N. Y. Printed for Private Circulation. 1883. Sm. 4to. pp. 77.

Genealogy of the Perrin Family. Compiled by GLOVER PERIN. St. Paul : Pioneer Press. 1885. 12mo. pp. 224.

The Genealogy of the Family of Gamaliel Gerould, Son of Dr. Jaques (or James) Jerauld of the Province of Lauguedoc, France. Bristol, N. H. Enterprise Power Press Co. 1885. 8vo. pp. 85. Price $1.

Sketch and Genealogy of the First Three Generations of the Connecticut Haydens. With a Map showing the Locality in which they Settled. By JABEZ H. HAYDEN, of Windsor Locks, Conn. Hartford, Conn. Press of the Case, Lockwood & Brainard Company, 1885. 8vo. pp. 20.

Genealogical Notes. 1. American Ancestry of U. S. Grant. By Dr. H. E. ROBINSON. Privately Printed. 1885. 18mo. pp. 17. Only 50 copies printed.

The Doings at the First National Gathering of Thurstons at Newburyport, Mass., June 24, 25, 1885. Portland, Me. : Brown Thurston, Publisher. 1885. 8vo. pp. 75.

Second Annual Reunion of the Hartwell Family. 1885. 8vo. pp. 15.

Hamlin. 1885. Royal 8vo. pp. 4.

Hampton Lane Family Memorial. A reprint of the Address at the Funeral of Dea. Joshua Lane of Hampton, N. H. (who was killed by lightning, June 14, 1766), by his son Dea. Jeremiah Lane of Hampton Falls, with Sketches of his Ancestry and Families to the fourth generation from William Lane of Boston, Mass., 1651. By Rev. Jas. P. Lane. Norton: Printed by Lane Brothers. 1885. 18mo. pp. 35. Price 25 cents, for sale by the Rev. J. P. Lane, Norton.

The New England Royalls. By Edward Doubleday Harris. Boston: David Clapp & Son, Printers. 1885. Royal 8vo. pp. 27.

We continue this quarter our notices of recently published genealogical works.

The Goodricke family, which heads our list, is the work announced in our January number as in preparation. Our expectations of it have been fully realized. The author, Mr. Goodricke, of London, has been very successful in collecting, from public and private records, printed books and other sources, ample materials illustrating the history of this prominent English family, which is here traced in an unbroken line to 1493. Families have been seated in the Counties of Lincoln, Suffolk, Cambridge, Norfolk and York. The book has a special interest in this country from the connection of Gov. Richard Bellingham with this family (Register, xxxvi. 381-6), from which the American Goodriches are probably an offshoot. Tabular pedigrees and full biographies of the more prominent members of the family are given. The book is handsomely printed, and illustrated by portraits of Thomas Goodricke, bishop of Ely, 1534, and the Rt. Hon. Sir Henry Goodricke, bart., ambassador to Spain, 1681-3, and other engravings. A few copies only remain in the author's hands.

Miscellanea Mariscalliana, the next book, is the first part of a second volume of the work noticed by us April, 1884, of which fifty copies were printed for presentation to institutions and friends. Dr. Marshall has for about a quarter of a century been collecting genealogical facts relative to his family name.

The Weeks genealogy is a work of much labor, and is carefully compiled. The descendants of George Weekes fill more than half the volume, and the index takes about fifty pages. The rest is devoted to other families of the name in various parts of the country. The book is well printed and bound, and is illustrated by numerous portraits and autographs.

The Phillips volume contains, besides the posterity of the Rev. George Phillips, of Watertown, among whom are many distinguished characters, descendants of Ebenezer of Southboro', Thomas of Duxbury, Thomas of Marshfield, John of Easton, James of Ipswich, and others. Till this book appeared, the fullest account of the Phillipses was in Bond's Watertown. The volume is compiled with great care, has many fine portraits, and is well indexed, well printed and well bound.

The volume on the Wood family is a very full record of the descendants of two brothers, Jeremiah Wood of Littleton, and Dea. John Wood of Framingham. The writer of this notice knows that much labor has been spent in gathering materials for this book, and the success which has crowned Mr. Wood's labors is a reward for his perseverance under the apparently hopeless prospect which met him in his investigations in the early generations. The book is well arranged and has good indexes. It is illustrated by a number of fine portraits.

The author of the book on the Roome family is P. R. Warner, Esq., who is maternally descended from it. The immigrant ancestor, Peter Willemse Roome, was married in New York, Nov. 26, 1684, to Hester Van Gelder. The author has been very successful in obtaining a full record of their descendants, which he presents to his readers in clear typography. The book is well indexed.

The Bontecou volume is devoted to the posterity of Pierre Bontecou, a merchant of Rochelle, who was driven by persecution from France, and after staying awhile in England settled in 1689 in New York. The descendants recorded in this handsomely printed volume number one thousand. There is here a history of the name, which is said to be of Dutch or Flemish origin, and appears in the form of Bonteköe. The book has a good index.

The Leighton genealogy is by Mr. Jordan, the author of the Jordan book noticed by us in October, 1882. Besides the descendants of Capt. Leighton it contains notes of the families of Frost, Hill, Bane, Wentworth, Langdon, Bragdon, Parsons, Pepperrell, Fernald and Nason; and also brief memoirs of Major Charles Frost of Kittery, and Capt. John Hill of Berwick, Me. The book is well arranged, printed and indexed. It is illustrated with portraits.

The volume on the Snively family relates to the descendants of Johann Jacob Schnebele, who was born in Switzerland in 1659, and to avoid persecution came, in

1714, to America, settling in Lancaster County, Pa. The basis of this work is a Genealogical Register by Joseph Snively, published about twenty years ago, in which some of the older data were preserved. The author of the present work, the Rev. Dr. Snivelly, has added much to it and has had it neatly printed in a volume.

The Perrin volume is compiled by Asst. Surgeon General Perin, U.S.A., of Fort Snelling, Minn. It contains the descendants of John Perryn who settled at Braintree, and afterward removed to Rehoboth, where he died Sept. 13, 1674. The work is well arranged, with an index of christian names. Blank pages with headings for additions are interspersed through the volume.

The Gerould genealogy is by the Rev. Samuel L. Gerould, of Goffstown, N. H., well known as a painstaking antiquary. Dr. Jaques or James Jerauld, the stirps of this family, was a Huguenot, who settled in Medfield, probably in the beginning of the last century. The descendants of his grandson Jabez, who reside mostly in Pennsylvania, have held several quinquenniel meetings, and this volume is the result of action at the last meeting, September, 1884. It is well arranged and printed, and has three indexes.

The next genealogy, that of the Hayden family of Connecticut, descended from William Hayden, an early settler of Hartford, gives three generations, both in narrative and in tabular form.

Dr. Robinson's pamphlet on Gen. Grant's ancestry is the first of a series of Genealogical Notes. It was first published in the *Republican*, Maryville, Nodaway Co., Mo., Aug. 13, 1885. The first person to trace Gen. Grant's ancestry to his immigrant ancestor, Matthew Grant of Windsor, was Hon. Richard A. Wheeler of Stonington, Ct. (REGISTER, xxi. 174). The present pamphlet is a reliable and interesting compilation.

The Thurston pamphlet gives the proceedings at the gathering of that family at Newburyport, June 24, 1885. The opening address was by Hon. Ariel S. Thurston, of Elmyra, N. Y., as were also the remarks at the site of the old homestead. " A history of the Thurston Genealogies," by Brown Thurston, of Portland, Me., was read by Rev. John R. Thurston.

The Hartwell pamphlet contains the exercises at the meeting of that family at Concord, Mass., Sept. 18, 1885. Remarks were made by L. W. Densmore, of Hillsboro' Centre, N. H., who is preparing a genealogy of the name, and by other prominent descendants of William Hartwell of Concord.

The leaves on the Hamlins are by the late Professor Charles E. Hamlin, of Cambridge, and were prepared as material for Mr. Daniels, of Oxford, Mass., now engaged on a history of that town, and are printed for preservation.

The Lane pamphlet is described in its title. Rev. Mr. Lane deserves the thanks of his relatives for reprinting the funeral sermon and adding the genealogical appendix.

The Royall genealogy is reprinted from the REGISTER for October last, with large and important additions. Before Mr. Harris undertook his task, the genealogy of the Royall family was very imperfectly known, and it required extensive research to reduce it into order.

DEATHS.

JOHN SALTONSTALL CLARK, of Peoria, Ill., died March 12, 1885, aged 66, and was buried in Oakland Cemetery, Geneseo. He was born at Waltham, Mass., 27 Sept., 1820, the eldest surviving son of William[7] Clark, who died at Geneseo, Ill., 16 Aug., 1869, aged 80, who was the only child of Dr. William[6] Clarke of Waltham, who died 18 Oct., 1793, aged 39. The latter was a nephew of Rev. Jonathan and Elizabeth (Clarke)[5] Mayhew. John S. Clark was of the eighth generation from Doctor John Clarke and wife Martha (Saltonstall?) of Boston.

He leaves by wife Catharine Stanley, who d. 22 March, 1877, three children: William Osgood[9] Clark, of Peoria; Clarissa P.,[9] wife of Samuel C. Dickson of Monmouth, Ill.; George R.[9] Clark of Minneapolis, Minn. There are other members of this old family still resident in Boston, descended from Samuel[3] Clarke, who died 31 Jan., 1748, aged about 75, and whose ship-yard was at the foot of Forster's Lane (or Clarke Street), North End.

I. J. GREENWOOD.

JOHN HASSAM, Esq., died in Boston, Aug. 3, 1885, aged nearly 76 years. He was born in Manchester, Mass., Sept. 4, 1809, and was the eldest son of Capt. Jonathan[4] Hassam, a retired shipmaster and a lineal descendant of William[1] Hassam, who settled in Manchester about 1684, through Jonathan,[2] William[3] and Jonathan[4] (see REGISTER for Oct., 1870, xxiv. 414). He came to Boston when a lad of fourteen and learned the trade of a book-binder, but soon after attaining his majority, began to turn his attention to real estate, and, after a brief residence in New York, finally established himself in Boston as a real estate broker. In this field, his prudence, forethought and business sagacity soon brought him well deserved success. During the later years of his life he had practically retired from active work and devoted himself principally to the care of trust property and the management of estates. He was greatly respected for his integrity and unswerving honesty, and as executor and administrator settled many valuable estates. By his wife Abby, a daughter of Capt. Amos Hilton of Manchester, Mass., he had two sons and a daughter, all born in Boston, who survive him.

WILLIAM JOHN THOMS, F.S.A., the founder and for many years the editor of *Notes and Queries*, died at his house, St. George's Square, Belgrave road, London, England, Saturday, Aug. 15, 1885, aged 81. He was buried at Brompton cemetery, on the Thursday following, Aug. 20. His son in law, the Rev. E. M. Tomlinson, vicar of Holy Trinity, Minories, read the burial service at the church which Mr. Thoms had attended (St. Mary's church, St. Vincent Square) and at the grave. His eight sons and daughters and their children were present, also many distinguished men, among them Joseph Knight, the present editor of *Notes and Queries*, and Norman McColl, the editor of the *Athenæum*. Mr. Thoms, was a son of Nathaniel and Ruth Ann Thoms, was born November 16, 1803, and baptized at St. Margaret's Church, Westminster, on the 15th of December following. His father was secretary of the first Commission of Revenue Inquiry.

Mr. Thoms commenced his active life as a clerk in the Secretary's office, Chelsea Hospital, occupying his leisure in contributing to the *Foreign Quarterly Review* and other periodicals. He was elected a Fellow of the Society of Antiquaries in 1838, and was from that year to 1873 secretary of the Camden Society. His first publication, "A Collection of Early Prose Romances," appeared in 1828. The titles of other works will be found in "Men of the Time," from which work and *Notes and Queries*, Aug. 22, 1885, this obituary has been compiled, free use being made of the language. In 1863 he was appointed deputy librarian of the House of Lords, a post he resigned in 1882 in consequence of old age. In 1849 he projected *Notes and Queries*, the first number of which appeared November 3d, in that year (REG. xxxviii. 357). He edited the work till Sept., 1872, nearly twenty-three years. This periodical is perhaps his best monument. He was able to make the work a success from the personal regard felt for him by a large circle of literary friends. His successor in the editorial chair of *Notes and Queries* gives this estimate of his character:

" A sound and an accurate scholar, the close ally during more than half a century of the best English and foreign scholars, Mr. Thoms had in an eminent degree the serviceable gift of knowing where information was to be found. This quality, invaluable in a librarian as well as in an editor, rendered him especially serviceable to the members of the House of Lords, with many of whom he was on terms of close and honorable intimacy. His genial fancy and humor and his social gifts rendered him a favorite in all companies, while such were his good nature, his kind-heartedness and tact, that he was mixed up in no archæological feud or quarrel, and preserved through his life a record of intimacies and friendships unbroken and undiversified by a single quarrel. Mr. Thoms was before all things a student. The stores of his admirably furnished mind were at the service of any one engaged in earnest work ; but he was retiring in nature, little given to promiscuous hospitality, and little addicted to the life of clubs. Few figures were less familiar than his at the Athenæum Club, of which during many years he was a member. In religion a moderate High Churchman, and in politics a strong Conservative, he held aloof from polemics, and he frequently, under a sense of official responsibility, abstained from voting when a Government opposed to his sympathies was in power."

Photo by Hovardus.

Eng.d by E.&W. Williams & Bro.

Chas. Robson. Pub Phila.

Ashbel Woodward

THE

HISTORICAL AND GENEALOGICAL REGISTER.

APRIL, 1886.

MEMOIR OF ASHBEL WOODWARD, M.D.

By P. H. WOODWARD, Esq., of Hartford, Conn.

THE death of Ashbel Woodward, M.D.,* of Franklin, Connecticut, December 20, 1885, closed a long, laborious and eminently useful career. Dr. Woodward was born June 26, 1804, in Willington, Conn., the ancestral farm lying on the border line, partly in that town and partly in Ashford. Graduating at the Medical Department of Bowdoin College in May, 1829, he settled two months later in Franklin, where he continued to reside till the end.

As a physician Dr. Woodward was noted for quickness and accuracy of perception. In the sick room nothing escaped his attention. He was especially successful in desperate cases, detecting with the rapidity of intuition the slightest change in the condition of the patient, and anticipating every emergency.

The estimation in which he was held by medical brethren is shown by the trusts confided to him, and the distinctions conferred upon him. Besides filling many other positions, he was, from 1858 to 1861, president of the Connecticut Medical Society. His annual addresses on "Life," "Medical Ethics," and "An Historical Sketch" of the Society, attracted much attention at the time, and are still remembered. He was also from its formation an active and deeply interested member of the American Medical Association, and an honorary member of several state societies.

In the early days of the Rebellion he was appointed by Gov. Buckingham one of the board to examine surgeons for the volunteer regiments of the state. Into the conflict for the preservation of the union he threw his feelings and efforts with the ardor which characterized all his undertakings. As the drain upon the resources of the country became more pronounced, he decided to go to the front himself, and as surgeon of the 26th Conn. shared in the siege and cap-

---

* Ashbel Woodward was the seventh in descent from Richard Woodward, who embarked in the ship Elizabeth at Ipswich, England, April 10, 1634, and whose name is on the earliest list of proprietors of Watertown, Mass. The Woodward genealogy is given in Dr. Henry Bond's History of Watertown.

ture of Port Hudson. He was then nearly sixty years of age, and his friends attempted to discourage the purpose on the ground that he was too old to bear the privations and hardships of life in camp. Indeed the warnings nearly proved true, for on his return home, after serving out the term of enlistment, he was long and dangerously ill with malarial fever.

Although driven with professional work, Dr. Woodward in some way found time to accomplish much with the pen. In addition to the addresses already referred to, he contributed numerous papers which are preserved in the "proceedings" annually published by the Connecticut Medical Society. At the request of the family of Gen. Nathaniel Lyon, he prepared a biography of that early martyr for the union, whose skill as a soldier was not less conspicuous than his devotion as a patriot. He had previously written a memoir of Col. Thomas Knowlton, a grand uncle of Gen. Lyon on the maternal side. Col. Knowlton commanded the continentals stationed behind the rail fence at Bunker Hill, and was killed in battle at Harlem Heights, September 16, 1776. Joel Munsell, of Albany, in 1878, published a small volume written by Dr. Woodward, upon " Wampum "—a subject to which he had given long attention. As a member of the committee of arrangements, he took an active part in the celebration of the two hundredth anniversary of the settlement of the town of Norwich, September 7th and 8th, 1859, and for the book containing the records of that event, furnished the paper on the "Early Physicians of Norwich."

October 14, 1868, the Congregational Church of Franklin celebrated the one hundred and fiftieth anniversary of its organization, when Dr. Woodward delivered the historical address. This was afterwards expanded into a "History of Franklin."

Dr. Woodward had great fondness for local historical, and especially for genealogical, investigations. His knowledge of the lineages of old New England families was extensive and at instant command. His writings on this class of subjects are to be found in the New England Historical and Genealogical Register, and in other publications.

During life he was a collector of rare books, pamphlets, coins, Indian relics and autographs. In accumulating a library he made a specialty of town and county histories, and of monographs on important events.*

In the early autumn of 1879 the neighbors of Dr. Woodward, on a sudden impulse, improvised a social gathering to celebrate the semi-centennial anniversary of his settlement among them. Infor-

---

* Dr. Woodward was one of the most thorough and reliable of our New England antiquaries. He had accumulated a vast fund of information upon family and local history, particularly of his native state, which he was always ready to communicate to those engaged in investigating these subjects. He took much interest in the New England Historic Genealogical Society, of which he was elected a corresponding member in 1853. He manifested his interest in the REGISTER by subscribing for two copies of the work and contributing many valuable papers for its pages.—EDITOR.

mal verbal invitations were passed from one to another to meet at his residence on the afternoon of September 5th. Short as was the notice, people came in throngs from near and far till the house was filled, while the overflow mingled in conversation on the lawns and beneath the trees without. Some drove fifteen miles and more. The enclosures, swarming with vehicles and animated groups, presented an appearence as picturesque as it was unusual. The day proved to be one of rare beauty, cool for the season, coming, and going in cloudless splendor. Floral testimonials decorated the tables, including several of rare flowers and of elaborate arrangement.

As the shadows from the western hills began to fall across the valley, the Rev. C. F. Jones, from the front steps, in the presence of the guests, addressed Dr. Woodward in a few sentences expressive of the esteem and affection of the community.

I have been commissioned to the pleasant duty of making the presentation address to you. You have outlived nearly all who began practice with you as your cotemporaries. To have lived long is a distinction, but to have lived well is a still greater distinction, and that distinction we regard as yours. Few occupations afford more opportunities for doing good than that of a physician. We recognize your sincerity, integrity and professional enthusiasm. In summer and winter, sunshine and storm, by night and by day, you have gone over these hills and through these valleys, seeking to relieve distress, prolonging many lives and affording much happiness. Faithful, true and self-sacrificing, you have endeared yourself to many, and it is with thanks that we gather here to-day. We desire to recognize your services in public affairs, educational, civil and religious. Through your writings, professional skill and reputation, you have honored this community. It is with sentiments of this kind that I am commissioned to present to you this testimonial of our affection, esteem and enduring friendship. May it be an emblem of the strong, unbending attachment of those gathered here.

Dr. Woodward was then presented with an elegant gold-headed ebony cane. On it was engraved:

1829.
Presented to
Ashbel Woodward, M.D.,
as a memorial
of 50 years
of professional
service.
1879.

In accepting the gift, the recipient with much feeling made a few personal remarks, substantially as follows:

I came here fifty years ago with an uncertain future before me, but I desired success only on the condition that I should be fully qualified for the practice of my profession, and should so discharge its duties as to entitle me to the favor of my employers. I posted no bills; I had no runners; I did not advertise. I procured a shingle, but did not put it out. I never sought business. The favors which came were spontaneous. But I do not stand here to boast. My career with you has been a living epistle to be read by all. And now I desire to thank you most sincerely for the gift which you have placed in my hands. Nothing could be more appropriate for an antediluvian to lean upon than a trusty staff. I shall esteem it a precious reminder of your favor.

Hon. La Fayette S. Foster, a native of Franklin and ex-United States Senator, then added a few words appropriate to the occasion, after which refreshments were served.

During the active career of Dr. Woodward, great changes were effected in the distribution of the intellectual and social energies of New England. In relative importance and prosperity the country towns steadily declined. Early in the century divines of conspicuous ability labored contentedly in rural parishes, while physicians of eminent skill found ample scope for ambition in serving the scattered population around them. Meanwhile the development of manufactures and the construction of railways have accomplished a revolution. Shadowed by growing cities, rural communities must now struggle to avoid palpable retrogression. So preponderant are the centrifugal forces, that from many the old family names, with their traditions and pride, have well nigh disappeared. Dr. Woodward preferred rural scenes. Located in a quadrangular valley of remarkable beauty, amid orchards and vines of his own planting, devoted to his profession and to his home, he could heartily quote the remark often repeated by the venerable Samuel Nott, D.D., whose residence crowned the neighboring hill, and whose pastorate in Franklin, beginning in 1782, covered a period of sixty-five years, " Our lines are cast in pleasant places."

There are solid reasons for believing that the fortunes of our country towns will ere long experience a marked and permanent revival. Indeed, at various points the improvement has already made substantial headway. The West, which has remorselessly drained us of our youth, is filling up. She no longer offers boundless areas of virgin soil to tempt immigration. At home the financial extravagance displayed in the government of cities, enhancing both directly and indirectly the cost of living, will more and more direct attention to the fair fields and limpid brooks once threatened with desertion. What is lost in the heroic virtues by the withdrawal of the hard conditions of the past, will be made up by the growing cultivation of the beautiful. Gardens will bloom, art will be pursued, homes will be made lovely, the surroundings of life will become attractive, where communities now find difficulty in keeping alive the religious and educational institutions established by the fathers.

From early manhood Dr. Woodward was a member of the Congregational Church of Franklin, and never wearied in efforts to sustain and strengthen it. He was not only a devout but also an unquestioning believer in the teachings of christianity. His last Sunday on earth found him in his accustomed place, officiating as deacon.

During his long term of active service Dr. Woodward ministered in sickness to at least six successive generations, and from the beginning to the end commanded the unqualified confidence of his clientage. Often appealed to for counsel and guidance, he was never known to discuss or even mention a matter that came to his knowledge in the sacredness of professional intercourse. Scrupulous in performing the work of each day, thorough in all undertakings, intolerant of sham and pretense, direct in aims and methods, he pursued uncompromisingly the paths marked out by his conceptions of duty. In some respects he seemed to belong more to a former age than to the present. On the maternal side inheriting from a clerical ancestry the stern theological opinions of early New England, Dr. Woodward himself in beliefs, sympathies and character, was a marked survival of the Puritans.

His wife (Emeline Bicknell), to whom he was married in May, 1832, with two sons, survive him.

A SUGGESTION AS TO HENRY JACOB.

By the Rev. EDWARD D. NEILL, of St. Paul, Min.

HENRY JACOB, the first Congregational minister in London, Wood, in *Athenæ Oxonienses* mentions, entered Saint Mary's Hall, Oxford, A.D. 1579, at the age of sixteen, took Holy Orders, was precentor of Christ Church College, and in the last years of his life pastor of the Independent Church in London, but, that while he died at about the age of sixty years, he did not know in what place.

Neal, in *History of the Puritans*, writes that Jacob, with the consent of his church, about the year 1624, went to Virginia, where he soon died. After a search of twenty-five years the writer of this article has found no trace of him in Virginia. In March, 1623, the ship Sea Flower, on its way to Virginia, while in Bermudas harbor, was blown up by the careless communication of fire to the powder magazine, and eighteen lives were lost.

In Leroy's Bermudas there is a letter from London, to the governor of the Island, in which are these words: "The poor woman, the widow Jacob, doth still follow and importune us for the restitution of those goods of hers." The first thing on her inventory was, "a black gown lined with fur." The governor replied that he could learn nothing of the gown, but he was told that the divers found a very great chest, which in attempting to put into a boat, slipped into the sea and was lost.

May not Henry Jacob have been one of the eighteen drowned by the explosion of the Sea Flower?

ADDRESS OF THE HON. MARSHALL P. WILDER.

Delivered at the Annual Meeting of the NEW ENGLAND HISTORIC GENEALOGICAL SOCIETY,
January 6, 1886.

GENTLEMEN OF THE SOCIETY :

THIS is the Nineteenth time you have called me to the presidency of this Society. Most gratefully do I appreciate the honor so repeatedly conferred, and only regret that I have not more strength and ability to discharge acceptably the duties incumbent upon me. But whether in the chair or out, I shall most cheerfully bring into service such as I may possess, while my life continues.

Men die ! One generation passeth away and another cometh, but institutions live, and those who survive must carry on their work. Thus it hath been, thus it shall be. We who live come together to-day to concert measures for the prosecution of our work.

Since our last anniversary we have to mourn the loss of thirty-nine members who have passed over to the spirit-land where life shall never cease and history never end. The average age attained by them is seventy-three years three months and twenty-seven days, still maintaining the remarkable longevity of our deceased members. Two members have passed the age of ninety, and none were less than fifty years old. Their names and characters will be recorded and reported by our historiographer, but I deem it proper to allude to some of those who have been officially connected with us, or were otherwise distinguished for their services in behalf of the public good.

Among those whom we desire to recall to mind for their eminent services in our behalf, are two vice-presidents and three directors.

The venerable Hiland Hall, LL.D., vice-president of the Society for Vermont, was the author of a history of that state, had been its governor and had represented it in Congress. He had reached the age of over ninety at the time of his death.

Mr. Edward Kidder, our honorary vice-president for North Carolina, was a warm friend of my own of long standing, a useful member of society, and a business man of the strictest integrity.

Mr. Frederic Kidder, more recently deceased, a brother of the preceding, the second treasurer of this Society, and a director of many years, did much to build it up in its early days, and labored for its prosperity as long as his health permitted.

Rear Admiral Geo. Henry Preble was a director, and, for a long course of years, one of our active members. His services to his country as a brave officer, and to literature as a voluminous writer, will long embalm his memory.

Mr. Henry Edwards was for many years chairman of our Finance

Committee and a director of the Society; a man of most estimable character in all the relations of life. He was in years one of our oldest members, an active merchant of former days, of distinguished ancestry, devoted to benevolent works, amiable in disposition, a true christian gentleman and friend of humanity.

Mr. Isaac Child, a former treasurer of the Society, who had reached the ripe age of ninety-three, was of all our members the oldest with possibly one exception.

Among my intimate friends I will name Messrs. Charles O. Whitmore, William Parsons, Joseph W. Tucker, and the Hon. Charles R. Train, with whom I have been pleasantly associated for a long course of years.

Nor should we forget the Rev. Samuel Irenæus Prime, D.D., the editor of the *New York Observer*, distinguished as an author; the Hon. Edward A. Rollins, a benefactor of Dartmouth College; Prof. Benjamin Silliman of Yale College; the Hon. Caleb Stetson, the Hon. Nathan Crosby, LL.D., the Rev. Samuel C. Damon, D.D., the devoted missionary in Honolulu; Mr. John A. Lewis, Ashbel Woodward, M.D., and Franklin B. Hough, M.D., LL.D., the last five of whom have done much work in the specialties of this Society.

And still another, greater than the rest, and for whose recent death the great heart of our nation still throbs with grief. Our Honorary Member, Gen. Ulysses S. Grant, ex-President of the United States, the great soldier, has passed on to the Final Review above, where his peaceful soul shall no more be disturbed by the storms and convulsions of earth and the revulsions of party and the crimes and criticisms of men, where war shall never lift its bloody hand, where peace eternal reigns. The whole nation mourns his death. The South and the North clasped hands over his bier, and mingled their tears in token of gratitude to the memory of him who saved our land. It was Grant who brought victory to the Union cause. A sense of justice demands for him an earthly immortality. We assign him a place among the illustrious men of our age who are entitled to the gratitude of mankind, whose worthy deeds shall bless the world long after they have passed away. He rests in the bosom of the land he loved, on the banks of the beautiful Hudson, a spot which will be forever dear to the generations of American freemen.

Thus one by one we pass away! The fell Destroyer, regardless of worth or wealth, of rank or power, consigns to the bosom of mother earth the nearest and dearest objects of our home and love, and casts a gloom over the remainder of life. But thanks to a merciful God, they still live with Him, where we shall be united with them again, where sickness, death and parting will come no more.

> Though lost to sight, they never die,
> The spirit still is ever nigh.

In my last address I made known to you that I had obtained

subscriptions to the amount of twenty-five thousand dollars for the enlargement of our House, and advised the appointment of a Building Committee for this purpose. This subject was referred to the Board of Directors with full powers, but the location of the new Court House immediately in front of our House has arrested our progress, not knowing what effect this might have on our property in the future. This money has all been collected and is now available for that purpose.

By the reports which are to be submitted to-day, it will be seen that our Society is in a very healthful and progressive state. The same spirit and personal sacrifice and enterprise still exist, which have characterized the past, and from which rich harvests of historical knowledge are continually acquired. The judicious management of our funds has given full assurance that bequests and donations will be sacredly appropriated to the object for which they have been given.

The New England Historical and Genealogical Register, the organ of the Society, has now entered the fortieth year of its publication. This series of volumes contains a vast amount of material on the history of the country and particularly of New England. I would recommend that all members of the Society and others interested in historical studies subscribe for this work, which has received the commendations of competent critics. By so doing they will enable the publishing committee to add to the interest of the work, as all moneys received for it are expended on the publication. With the issue of every volume the Register becomes more and more valuable. A complete set now commands more than one hundred and fifty dollars.

The use of the library still continues to increase, and visitors from all parts of the Union avail themselves of the opportunity that it offers them to investigate American history, biography and genealogy. Though the additions to the library have been large during the past year there are still important deficiencies, which, if more money were at our disposal, could be supplied. We need also more funds for binding books and periodicals. Would that some generous soul might endow the Society with more funds for this purpose.

I again congratulate the Society on the great success which is attending the researches now making in England under its auspices by Mr. Henry F. Waters. His discovery during the past year of the ancestry of John Harvard, a problem which antiquaries for more than forty years have in vain attempted to solve, is a most remarkable achievement, and well deserves the honorary degree which Harvard College conferred upon him at the last Commencement. These investigations are of great importance, and I trust that funds sufficient to carry them on uninterruptedly for a series of years may be speedily raised. I again commend this most worthy project to the members of this Society, and refer them to the report of Mr. Hassam, chairman of the committee in charge of the matter, for fuller details.

I have on two previous occasions referred to the publication of our early Suffolk Deeds. The third volume has now been printed by authority of the Board of Aldermen of the City of Boston acting as County Commissioners for the County of Suffolk. It brings these County records down to the year 1662. These volumes are of the greatest importance, not merely to the conveyancer, but to every investigator of local and family history. The execution of the work reflects the greatest credit on the two members of our Society to whom we are indebted for it. The antiquarian zeal, the patience and perseverance of Mr. William B. Trask in deciphering and copying these ancient records, and carrying the book through the press, we cannot too highly praise. The ingenious and thorough indexes prepared under the supervision of Mr. John T. Hassam make its contents accessible to the inquirer in every line of research. To Mr. Hassam the public cannot be too grateful. The idea of printing these volumes originated with him, and it is principally through his endeavors that the necessary appropriations have been made.

The fourth volume in the series of "Memorial Biographies" of our deceased members has been published recently. A glance merely at the table of contents shows that the volume contains not a few names of men who were eminent in their day, and who exercised a permanent influence on their fellow men. The perusal of these memoirs demonstrates the great pains that has been taken to make them full and accurate. Many of these papers may well serve as models for brief biographies; models both in their literary character and in the arrangement of the matter. The committee in charge of the "Memorial Biographies" inform me that they are making progress in securing the memoirs to be included in the fifth and the succeeding volumes.

I would earnestly call attention to this series of carefully prepared volumes, so handsomely printed and bound. The memoirs are of permanent value, and are authoritative and reliable in all respects. The price of the volumes to members is less than the cost of printing. The edition is small, and at no distant day these volumes will be scarce.

These are precious volumes, and should be possessed by all our members, not only by those who are connected by ties of kindred and blood with the men whose memoirs are here preserved, but by students of biography, as they embrace many of the most distinguished men of our day. And I desire to remind you of the great obligations we are under to the Memorial Committee for the patient, critical, and able manner in which they have brought forth these elegant volumes.

In my last address I referred to the gratifying progress of the exploration going on under the Egyptian Fund, and I am now informed by its treasurer, Rev. William C. Winslow, that the progress since is equally flattering in its good results. He informs me that the second book of exploration has arrived in this country, and will soon be ready for distribution. In our own Society are many contributors to that fund, who will be glad to learn this and also that a second collection of antiquities is now on the ocean and will soon reach Boston. It is from Naucratis, the Greek Emporium in Egypt before Alexandria was built. Mr. Petrie discovered the site last winter, and the collection is of great value. I again commend this subject to the patronage of our members.

Celebrations to perpetuate the settlement and history of the older towns of New England have now become of frequent occurrence and great interest. Among those of the last year we may mention Concord, the home of Emerson, Thoreau, Shattuck, the Hoars, and Alcott, the spot where British rule received its fatal repulse, and freedom's gun spoke "round the world"; Newbury and its offshoots, the home of Caleb Cushing the statesman, of Joshua Coffin the historian of the town, Leonard Withington the able divine, Adolphus W. Greely the intrepid arctic explorer, and Ben Perley Poore the time-honored journalist; Hingham, the home of Gen. Benjamin Lincoln, who received the surrender of Cornwallis and the British army at Yorktown; of our old associate Solomon Lincoln, its historian; Gov. Andrew, a president of this Society; Albert Fearing, and of John D. Long, now living, and the first home of the Wilders in America, through whom I trace our branch of lineage to an English ancestry. Among other town celebrations we record those of Salisbury, East Hampton and others, all of which will be preserved in the archives of this and kindred institutions.

But the most imposing ceremony of the year, if we except the funeral obsequies of Gen. Grant, was the dedication of the Washington Monument, the tallest structure of which we have any record in history, successfully completed under the supervision of Col. Thomas Lincoln Casey, of the United States Army, a member of this Society. A vast concourse of people from all parts of the Union assembled at Washington to do honor to the memory of the man whom this monument commemorates. But the crowning incident of the occasion was the oration of our associate member the Hon. Robert Charles Winthrop, who, thirty-seven years before, delivered the address on the laying of its corner-stone; thus he was the orator and historian, from the corner-stone to the capstone, symbolic in its towering height of the character it represents. As Mr. Winthrop said, "The Father of his country, and the foremost figure in all human history, whose example for all nations, for all ages, is never to be forgotten or overlooked. Our matchless obelisk stands proudly before us to-day in all its consummate purity and splendor, and will more and more command the homage of succeeding ages in all regions of the earth." The names of Washington and Winthrop will be happily associated in the history of this monument until it shall have crumbled into dust.

It is gratifying to the student of history to see the increasing interest now manifested by societies and individuals in local celebrations and in the prosecution of historical and genealogical researches, from which we are constantly reaping rich harvests of knowledge. I desire to express our gratitude to the Massachusetts Historical Society, for her noble example in the good work, and especially are our thanks due to Mr. Winthrop its late president, for his able and meritorious labors during a term of thirty years in which he has occupied the chair of that Society.

We do not overlook the eminent services which have been rendered by his associates, and we rejoice that his chair has been filled by our friend the Rev. Dr. George E. Ellis, who will discharge its responsible duties with honor to himself and to the venerable Society over which he presides.

I have frequently spoken to you of the importance and influence of history, and now I wish for a few moments to call your attention to the relations which exist between Biography and History, with which it is so intimately connected. Biography is the record of human genius, power and principle, affording examples which live to bless the world long after the actors have passed away. It is therefore our duty to gather up and preserve not only the record of events, but of the words and deeds of the men whose examples have energized mankind and controlled the moral sentiment of the world. History, without the story of the men and women which have moulded and made society what it is, would indeed be a barren, leafless tree. Biography is the soul of history, and is like a tree whose branches yield perpetual harvests, and on whose leaves are imprinted the wisdom of all ages. It is an old maxim that history repeats itself. So it does. Plutarch says, "Availing myself of history as a mirror from which I learn to adjust and regulate my own conduct, by attention to history and biography, I fill my mind with the sublime images of the best and greatest men. When Zeno consulted the oracle as to what manner he should live, the answer came, ' inquire of the dead.' " Biography is the schoolmaster of all time, the past, present and future. We are pupils of the past and teachers of the future, so the examples and principles which have influenced the world for good will be handed down from generation to generation.

> They speak in reason's ear
> And in example live.

If any one will examine the thirty-nine volumes of our REGISTER and the four substantial volumes of the memoirs of our deceased members, he will find that biography has been a prominent feature in our work. Every person has some influence over the men with whom he associates. By preserving the events of his life in print, this influence is extended beyond his immediate neighborhood and beyond his own life for years after he is slumbering in his grave. It is desirable, therefore, and it is also the design of this Society, to perpetuate the events of the lives of those who have benefited their race, whether on a large or a small scale, and to embalm their virtues in enduring words, so that their trials, industry, perseverance and success may strengthen the characters and cheer and encourage those who come after them.

The lives of the great have always had a fascination for youth, and the biography of those who have been eminent in any walk of life, as military chieftains, as civilians or as writers, has been read with avidity, and has had an influence, more or less strong, upon the characters of the readers of this class of literature.

Every nation takes pride in its great men, and points to them as examples for the guidance of the young. It is not surprising to find the youth of our own country tracing the careers of her heroes and benefactors. The Scotchman is proud of the daring deeds of Wallace and Bruce, and of the writings of Burns and Scott. Ireland honors Emmett, Curran and O'Connell; and England, our mother country, teaches her young men to revere Shakspeare and Milton, Pitt and Nelson. American Biography presents her Washington and Franklin, Lincoln and Grant, Webster and Everett, Edwards and Channing, Emerson and Longfellow, Garrison and Phillips, Fulton and Morse, Morton and Jackson, Hannah Adams and Harriet Beecher Stowe.

The importance and usefulness of biography has been sufficiently and satisfactorily settled as a matter of fact, independently of any theory or reasoning. An examination of any well selected library, either public or private, would show that a great and increasing interest is felt for this kind of reading, beginning with the old classic authors of Greece and Rome, and coming down to our own times, when the biographies not only of the dead but of the living are eagerly sought for and read.

Whenever we are reading the history of any time, or incidents of a revolution or civil war, or a single campaign, of the formation of a government, or of the peaceful development of a community, or wonderful discovery in art or science, we always find ourselves looking for information in regard to the originators and leading actors, their characters, traits and talents, their aims and influence. To be informed merely about events is wholly unsatisfactory unless we know something about the human forces which have directed them, whether by wise or stupid, good or wicked, mean or noble, men. In all that concerns the inner and private life of a community it is the career of men and women, born, trained, educated, and filling private spheres, that we need most to know, by careful, discriminating and impartial biographies. History would indeed be useless if it gave us only a narrative of events. This fact has long been recognized by the most eminent and popular historians, that History needs the illuminating element of Biography to illustrate and enforce examples worthy of imitation.

It is enough to mention Chancellor Clarendon's History of the Great English Rebellion, and Bishop Burnet's History of his Own Times. Both of these great and important works owe much of their charm to the keenly drawn sketches of the lives and characters of all the men and some of the women, who appeared prominently on the stage of action. The writers have shown a marvellous skill in delineating characters correctly, sharply and impartially. Their biographical sketches of character stand out on the page like portraits around our walls, so that we may feel acquainted with them and talk with them.

Macaulay, as a historian, owes more to the brilliant portraitures of character and biography which he introduces into his sketches than to his narrative of events. Carlyle thought the best History of the English Civil War would be a life of Cromwell, its chief actor, drawn from his own letters and speeches; and so we may find in the lives of Lincoln and Grant the best history of our own civil war.

But the most striking illustration of this subject is found in the collection of forty-four biographies which goes by the familiar name of "Plutarch's Lives," written about seventeen hundred years ago, those charming volumes of the character and career of eminent men. We have in our literature now the biographies of many so-called "self-made men," men who have risen to the highest rank as statesmen, inventors and benefactors, who in their youth had the most slender opportunities of education, and who in toil and poverty seized every spare moment, under the impulse of latent talents and capacities, to improve their minds. A long list might be made of such men, who have ascribed the most stimulating effect on them to "Plutarch's Lives." Says Oliver Wendell Holmes, "Montaigne, Franklin and Emerson all showed a fondness for Plutarch." They, as well as Webster, Everett, Choate and Hillard, were all indebted to "Plutarch's Lives," and made that author a familiar companion. Thus the old and new in biography are ever furnishing instruction; Emerson says, "old and new make the warp and woof of every moment. There is not a thread that is not a twist of these two strands."

And now, in conclusion, let me again impress on you the duty of prosecuting our researches in history and genealogy, and more especially in biography, with which they are so intimately associated. It is a sacred duty to preserve and hand down to future generations, not only the lineage and history of our families, but to record the names and virtues of those men and women who have been benefactors to our race. Archdeacon Farrar, who has so lately honored our city with his presence, has said, "Next to the scriptures, there could hardly be found any reading more satisfactory and more exalting to the human heart than the contemplation of the lives of the saints." So say we, not only of the great and good men and women who have made the world what it is, but of all who have in any way promoted the welfare of mankind, of our race.

Next to training the spirit for the life eternal, there can be no more noble employment than that of treasuring up and perpetuating a record of the lives, principles and virtues of those who have been benefactors and blessings to mankind. Such were many of those of whom I have spoken, and whose names will gild the pages of American biography with a lustre, which will shine brighter and brighter while gratitude shall have a place in the heart of mankind. Of these we have striking examples of patriotism, discoveries in science, and startling enterprise which has set elements in motion that are fast revolutionizing the character and business of mankind. Of such was Washington and his associates, who achieved the liberty which still lives and marches on in triumph and glory through the earth. Of such was Lincoln, who, heaven-inspired, engraved on the pillars of our Constitution, Eternal Freedom for the Slave ! Of such was Grant, who conquered the rebellion and brought again peace and union to our states. Of such was Garrison, who stormed the battlements of American Slavery, and saw them prostrate at his feet. Of such was Franklin, whose miraculous hand drew from the clouds the spark which now electrifies the globe. Of such was Morse, who taught the mystic wire to speak with tongues of fire all the languages of the earth. Of such was Fulton, who woke the spirit of the waters, and gave a new impulse to the commerce of the world. And last, not least, of such were those messengers of mercy who brought a sovereign balm to blot from the memory conscious suffering in the human frame. These and others of immortal fame have trod the paths of human glory, and stand out like golden stars in the constellation of American genius, to light the road to honor, to virtue and to renown.

Their mission on earth is ended, but the principles they established and the blessings they conferred are still moving on to a more full and perfect development; and as they advance toward their glorious consummation, grateful millions shall honor and perpetuate their names. They shall live forever in grateful hearts, until the last star shall have fallen from the sky, and earth itself and man shall have passed away !

DESCENDANTS OF JOSIAH AND CATHERINE (HARTWELL) UPTON.

By WILLIAM H. UPTON, B.A., LL.M., of Walla Walla, W. T.

1. JOSIAH[4] UPTON* (*Ebenezer,*[3] *Joseph,*[2] *John*[1]) was born in North Reading, Mass., August 24, 1735. He married 1st, Dec. 28, 1756, Susannah Emerson, of Reading, by whom he had five sons and three daughters. Their descendants will be found in "The Upton Memorial." He lived in North Reading until about 1770, about which date he lost his wife. He then removed to Bedford, whence he went to Charlemont in 1778. He married 2d, Catherine Hartwell. Attempts to ascertain the date and place of this marriage and the parentage of Catherine Hartwell have been unsuccessful. The date must have been about 1774, and the place near Bedford, Mass.

Josiah Upton died in Charlemont, Dec. 10, 1791. His widow was taken to Victor, Ontario Co., N. Y., by her children in 1799, and died there. Their children were:

- **2.** i. SARAH,[5] b. June 18, 1776; m. Israel Blood.
- **3.** ii. JAMES, b. Feb. 2, 1779; m. Olive Boughton.
- **4.** iii. JOANNA, b. June 13, 1781; m. Norman Brace.
- **5.** iv. DAVID, b. July 2, 1783; m. Mary Marsh.

2. SARAH[3] UPTON (*Josiah,*[4] *Ebenezer,*[3] *Joseph,*[2] *John*[1]) was born at Charlemont, Mass., June 18, 1776. She married Israel Blood, evidently at Charlemont, and shortly afterwards removed with her husband to that part of Bloomfield, which is now Victor, N. Y. She was in Charlemont in June, 1797, and in Bloomfield in April, 1799. Her husband was one of the first settlers in Bloomfield, now Victor, where we find him as early as 1797. He acquired large tracts of land, including what is now the Upton homestead in Victor, and died there highly respected, at the age of 83. His wife died aged about 70. They had:

- i. ANNA,[6] b. Charlemont, Mass., June 7, 1797; m. E. Calkins, and had : 1. *Sylvester ;*[7] 2. *Lucy Ann ;*[7] 3. *Elisha Avery ;*[7] 4. *Kingsby.*[7]
- ii. LUCY UPTON, b. Bloomfield, N. Y., April 2, 1799; m. James Manwaren, and had : 1. *Philo ;*[7] 2. *Norman ;*[7] 3. *James ;*[7] 4. *Caroline ;*[7] 5. *Bradley ;*[7] 6. *Joanna.*[7]
- iii. ROSEL L., b. Bloomfield, Nov. 14, 1800; m. Clarissa Phillips, and had 1. *Hartwell ;*[7] 2. *Norman ;*[7] 3. *Laura ;*[7] 4. *Lucy.*[7]
- iv. NORMAN B., b. Bloomfield, Feb. 4, 1802; d. Albany, N. Y., aged about 30, unm.
- v. NATHANIEL UPTON, b. Bloomfield, Feb. 2, 1804; m. Hannah Shoots, and had : 1. *Mary ;*[7] 2. *Thomas ;*[7] 3. *Lucy.*[7]
- vi. STEPHEN HARTWELL, b. Bloomfield, Feb. 26, 1806; m. Louisa Knapp. He was living in Victor, N. Y., 1880, having had : 1. *William ;*[7] 2. *Emma.*[7]

---

* J. A. Vinton's "Upton Memorial," published in 1874, gives a fairly satisfactory account of the Uptons of America, but the value of the book is diminished by some errors and many omissions. Vinton's account of the descendants of this Josiah[4] Upton by his second wife is so incomplete that the supplemental account given in the text seems to be demanded. No attempt is made to give an outline of the life of Josiah[4] Upton himself, but it may be said that he was very prominent in the affairs of western Massachusetts during the last twelve years of his life, and was well known as a mathematician and student of the physical sciences.

vii. JAMES MITCHELL, b. Bloomfield, Feb. 14, 1808 ; m. Lydia Ann Nelson ;
     removed to Victor, Mich., about 1838. Ch.: 1. *Norman* ;[7] 2. *Ardella.*[7]
viii. DANIEL HARTWELL, b. Bloomfield, Jan. 7, 1810 ; m. Susan Turner ; re-
     moved to Victor, Mich., Jan. 1838, and took up a farm upon which
     he still resided in 1881, P. O. Laingsburgh. Children : 1. *Achsah* ;[7]
     2. *Samuel* ;[7] 3. *Adyarn* (?) ;[7] 4. *Susan* ;[7] 5. *Sarah* ;[7] 6. *Eliza* ;[7] 7.
     Charles ;[7] 8. *Amanda* ;[7] 9. *Daniel* ;[7] 10. *Lucy* ;[7] 11. *Ernest* ;[7] 12.
     Carrie.[7]
ix. HANNAH, b. Bloomfield, Jan. 19, 1812.

3. JAMES[5] UPTON (*Josiah,*[4] *Ebenezer,*[3] *Joseph,*[2] *John*[1]) was born at Charlemont Feb. 2 (one record says 19), 1779. He was fourteen years
of age when the death of his father made him the main-stay of the
family. In 1797 he went to Victor, N. Y., and worked a year for
his brother-in-law, Israel Blood (see No. 2, *ante*). He then returned to Charlemont, and in the winter of 1799 (probably of 1798–9)
" took his mother, brother, two sisters and a swarm of bees " to Victor in an ox sledge. He bought the land where the Upton homestead now stands from Israel Blood for seven dollars per acre, and
built upon it a log house. This was burned by his brother David
in drying flax. They then built another log house and afterwards
a frame one. The latter was afterwards moved back, and forms the
wood-shed of the present homestead, which was built in the winter
of 1817–18. He resided all his life in Victor, where he became
wealthy and one of the most influential men in his county. He
married April 21, 1808, Olive, daughter of Samuel and Lucy
(Tracy*) Boughton, and died in 1857. His wife died April 24,
1824. Their children† were :

   i. ACHSAH,[6] b. March 21, 1809 ; m. July 5, 1830, Dr. Hiram Thompson,
     and died leaving one child, *Mariette Emeline,*[7] who d. unm. in 1864.
   ii. SAMUEL BOUGHTON, b. July 23, 1810 ; d. unm. April 6, 1832.
   iii. JOSIAH W., b. Sept. 19, 1812 ; m. Sophia Roe.
   iv. JAMES, b. April 19, 1815 ; m. Elvira E. Hawkins.
6. v. WILLIAM W., b. July 11, 1817 ; m. Maria Amanda Hollister.
   vi. UNICE, b. Dec. 25, 1818 ; d. unm.
   vii. EDWARD, b. March 30, 1820 : m. Achsah Thayer, who survived him and
     remarried. He d. April 19, 1863, leaving twin daughters : 1. *Ara-*
     bella,[7] who is living unmarried with her uncle William W. Upton, in
     Washington, D. C. ; 2. *Isabella,*[7] m. —— Hitchcock, of Oramel,
     N. Y., and d. July, 1876, leaving one daughter, born June, 1876.
     These twins never lived in W. T., as stated in the " Memorial."
   viii. OLIVE, b. Sept. or Oct. 19, 1823 ; d. Aug. 6, 1843, unm.
   ix. CAROLINE HART, b. May 13, 1826 ; m. Floyd D. Torrance ; d. *s. p.* Feb.
     9, 1853.
   x. MARY EMELINE, b. April 19, 1829 ; m. William C. Moore ; d. Oct. 1,
     1879. She was one of the noblest of her sex, and was like an angel of
     mercy to hundreds of the poor and suffering living around Victor.
   xi. MARIA, b. Aug. 21, 1831 ; d. June 29, 1832.
   xii. CHARLES E., b. July 4, 1833 ; m. Louise Racket.
   xiii. ELVIRA EMELINE, b. May 24, 1838 ; m. her brother-in-law Floyd D.
     Torrance.

* She was descended from Lieut. Thomas Tracy, one of the founders of Norwich, Conn.
Most of the early Boughtons of Victor came from Stockbridge, Mass., and there is evidence
tending to connect them with John Bouton, of Norwalk, Conn., 1655. But it is claimed
that Mrs. Upton's father, though related to the Stockbridge Boughtons, was born in Connecticut.
† It is not deemed necessary to give any further account of their descendants than may
be necessary to correct the " Upton Memorial," as Vinton gives a tolerably full account of
them.

4. Joanna[3] Upton (*Josiah,[4] Ebenezer,[3] Joseph,[2] John[1]*) was born at Charlemont, June 13, 1781. As stated above, she went to Victor, N. Y., with her brothers in 1799, and she resided there all her life. She married 1st, Norman Brace; 2d, Isaac Marsh, but had no children. She, however, adopted, reared and educated twenty-one children, including her brother David's daughter Lucy and all the children of her husband Marsh, and dying, left her fortune to charitable uses, and a name for goodness and charity which will long be cherished among the descendants of those to whom she was more than a mother.

5. David[5] Upton (*Josiah,[4] Ebenezer,[3] Joseph,[2] John[1]*) was born at Charlemont, July 2, 1783. When about sixteen years of age he removed to Victor, N. Y., with his brother James, with whom he resided for several years. He married, Sept. 12, 1805, Mary Marsh. She was born at Danbury, Vt., Nov. 9, 1786, and died on their farm in Rollin, Mich., Dec. 31, 1870. They removed from Victor to Ontario, Wayne Co., N. Y., about May, 1817. He seems to have lived in Walworth also, and may have resided in other parts of New York state, as his youngest child was born at Palmyra in October, 1826, but he was still in Ontario in March, 1825. In 1846 he removed to Wheatland, Hillsdale Co., Mich., and about three years later to Rollin, Lenawee Co., where he died. Vinton says, " He had a large family, but their names are unknown." His children were :

  7. i.   Olive,[6] b. Oct. 29, 1806 ; m. Levi Wilson.
  8. ii.   Abiathar, b. Oct. 14, 1808 ; m. Jane Hazlett.
     iii. Joanna, b. Aug. 10, 1810.
     iv. Mary, b. Aug. 6, 1812.
  9. v.   David, b. March 2, 1814 ; m. Barbara Buckley.
10. vi.   Lucy, b. Oct. 28, 1816 ; m. Henry H. Taber.
    vii. Baby, b. June 14, 1818.
11. viii. Catherine, b. Jan. 29, 1821 ; m. Girdon Patch.
12. ix.   James M., b. March 24. 1823 ; m. Martha Hatfield.
13. x.   Mary Ann, b. March 27, 1825 ; m. Nelson Wood.
14. xi.   Cordelia, b. Oct. 30, 1826 ; m. William Eldridge.

6. William W.[6] Upton (*James,[5] Josiah,[4] Ebenezer,[3] Joseph,[2] John[1]*) was born in Victor, N. Y., July 11, 1817. Our space will not permit an adequate biography of Judge Upton, nor could a complete account of his active life be written without a discussion of burning political questions which would be out of place in these pages. The son of a wealthy farmer in a newly settled part of the state, he received somewhat more than a common school education, and early acquired that love of learning and faculty for hard study which has always been one of his most marked characteristics. Yet his love was for learning, not for show, and in later life, when he was familiar with the most advanced branches of mathematics, and could read Latin and French as readily as English, he declined the degree of LL.D., tendered him by one of our leading colleges, on the ground that " he thought such distinctions should be conferred sparingly, and only upon those who have received a thorough classical education."

Mr. Upton went to Victor, Mich., in the winter of 1837–8, but returned to his native town the following September, where he remained about a year and was married. He then, in 1840, returned to Victor, Mich., and was admitted to the bar. He rapidly gained a leading position at the bar of his adopted state, and was frequently elected to office by his fellow citizens. He was a supervisor of Victor, 1840–5; surveyor of Clinton Co., 1841–5; treasurer of Clinton Co., 1845–7; and was a member of the legislature which made Lansing the capital. He removed to De Witt in 1845, and to Lansing in 1847, in which place he built the first house that was not of logs. He was appointed district-attorney for Ingham Co. in 1848, and was elected to the same office for two terms of two years each in 1849 and 1851. Resigning this office, he left Michigan with his family, April 1, 1852, for California by the overland route. There he settled, at first at Weaverville, but in 1855 removed to Sacramento. He was a member of the legislature in 1856, and in the fall of 1861, when there were three political parties in California, he was elected prosecuting attorney of Sacramento Co., which office he held till 1864. In the presidential contest of 1860 he was a Douglas democrat, but on breaking out of the war he became a firm supporter of President Lincoln, and he has ever since been a republican. In 1864 he was urged to become a candidate for congress, but the ill health of his family compelled him to remove from a climate which had proved fatal to his wife and three of his children. He accordingly removed to Portland, Oregon, in the spring of 1865. He was almost immediately elected to the legislature of Oregon. In 1867 he was appointed a Justice of the Supreme Court of Oregon, and in 1868 was elected to that position for a term of six years. He became Chief Justice in 1872. So satisfactorily did he fill these offices. and so high was his reputation as a lawyer, that in 1872 the legislature ordered more than eighty of his *nisi prius* decisions to be printed and bound up with the decisions of the Supreme Court.

At the expiration of his term of office, financial reverses compelled him to decline a renomination and to resume the practice of his profession. In the presidential controversy of 1876, the vote of Oregon being in doubt, the republicans practically rested their case before the Electoral Commission upon a decision rendered by Judge Upton at *nisi prius* upon the question of the power of the governor of Oregon to exercise judicial functions. A majority of the state Supreme Court had differed with Judge Upton, but the Electoral Commission by a unanimous vote sustained his view, thus giving the state and the presidency to the republicans. In 1877 Judge Upton, unexpectedly to himself, was appointed Second Comptroller of the Treasury of the United States, an office, according to Alexander Hamilton, "next to the secretary of the treasury." As this was practically a judicial office and a court of last resort (the comptroller's decisions being reversible by act of congress only), Judge Upton accepted the appointment with pleasure, removed with his family to Washington city and entered upon the discharge of his duties, Oct. 1, 1877. He filled the office with great credit to himself through three administrations, passing upon about 160,000 accounts and claims, involving about $600,000,000.00. Soon after the inauguration of President Cleveland Judge Upton tendered his resignation, and on its acceptance, June 1, 1885, at the age of 68, resumed the practice of his profession in Washington city. Early in 1885 he published a " Digest of Decisions of the Second Comptroller of the Treasury, 1869 to 1884," which a jurist of national reputation has said, "contains more law than a hundred textbooks."

Judge Upton married, 1st at Victor, N. Y., Feb. 8, 1840, Maria Amanda Hollister, eldest daughter of Hon. Joseph and Amanda (Adams) Hollister.* She was born at Danby, N. Y., August 13, 1818, and died at Sacramento in December, 1858. He married 2d, at East Avon, N. Y., March 29, 1860, Marietta, daughter of Amasa and Alida Ann (Ketcham) Bryan.

Judge Upton's children have been as follows. By wife Maria Amanda:

    i. A Son,[7] b. and d. at Victor, Mich., March, 1843.
15. ii. James Boughton, b. Victor, Mich., March. 19, 1844; m. Anne Amanda Shaw.
    iii. Charles Backus, b. De Witt, Mich., Dec. 18, 1845. He went to California with his parents in 1852, graduated at the Sacramento High School in 1865, removed to Portland, Oregon, where he was admitted to the bar, and was successively deputy sheriff, deputy prosecuting attorney and deputy U. S. attorney. He practised his profession with marked success, both in Portland and at Walla Walla, W. T., to which place he removed about 1878. He has travelled and read much, and is a man of liberal ideas, a large land owner, and unmarried.
    iv. Marietta, born at Lansing, Mich., March 4, 1848. She lived with her father in Michigan, California, Oregon and Washington, and died in the latter city, Oct, 1, 1880, unm. In this young lady, whose life was devoted to the happiness of those around her, all the strongest and noblest qualities of her family seem to have united and reached their highest development. With all the intellectual power of her father, she inherited from her mother all those gentler graces of mind and heart which are the crowning ornament of her sex. With mental training which enabled her to fit one brother for Yale College and another for West Point, and social accomplishments which made her a favorite in the best society in the land and charmed all who knew her, she found her favorite occupation in relieving the sufferings of the poor and the afflicted. Short as was her life, who can measure the good she accomplished, or the effects of her life and example upon those who were brought within their influence!
    v. Charlotte, b. Lansing, Mich., March 18, 1850; d. there the same year.
16. vi. William Henry, b. Weaverville, Cal., June 19, 1854; m. Georgia L. Bradley.
17. vii. George Whitman, b. Sacramento, June 1, 1857; m. Harriet Taylor.
    viii. Daughter, b. and d. in Sacramento, Dec. 1858.

By wife Marietta:

    ix. Alida Bryan, b. Sacramento, May 21, 1861; d. there July 12, 1862.
    x. Victor Bryan, b. Sacramento, Oct. 12, 1864; d. there Feb. 27, 1865.
    xi. Ralph Richard, b. Portland, Oregon, June 12, 1869; resides with his parents at Washington, D. C.

7. Olive[6] Upton (*David,[5] Josiah,[4] Ebenezer,[3] Joseph,[2] John[1]*) was born at Victor, N. Y., Oct. 29, 1806, and there married Levi Wilson,

* Mrs. Upton's line of descent was: Maria Amanda,[9] Joseph,[7] Joseph,[6] Joseph,[5] Joseph,[4] Joseph,[3] John,[2] John.[1] The wife of her grandfather Joseph[6] Hollister was Patience[6] Hollister (Nathaniel,[5] Gideon,[4] Thomas,[3] John,[2] John[1]). Mrs. Upton also descended from Richard Treat, Wethersfield, 1637; William Goodrich, a first settler at Wethersfield; Matthew Marvin, one of the proprietors of Hartford; William Hills, Roxbury, 1632; Richard Lyman, Roxbury, 1631; John White, Boston, 1632; Hugh Mould, New London, 1660; John Coyte, Salem, 1638; Nathan Disbrow, of Fairfield; John Talcott, Boston, 1632; Edward Holyoke, Lynn, 1630; and William Pynchon, Roxbury, 1630. Her mother was of an Adams family which settled at Redding, Conn.

Feb. 14, 1827. After a short residence at Victor they removed to Ferrington, N. Y., whence they went to Lyons, Mich., in the autumn of 1832. A few years later they removed to Ovid or Coldwater, Mich., where they were still residing in 1880. Their children have been:

i.   CAROLINE,[7] b. Victor, N. Y., June 2, 1828; d. aged 1 year 4 mos.
ii. EMELINE, b. Ferrington, N. Y., Jan. 25, 1831; m. Sept. 27, 1849, Heman A. Russel. They were living at Ovid, Mich., in 1880. Children: 1. *Charles,*[8] b. March 20, 1853, m. Aug. 1874, Calista L. Fenner, and had Fenner E.,[9] b. Oct. 1875; 2. *Nelson C.,*[8] b. Ovid, Jan. 11, 1858; 3. *Jessie,*[8] b. Ovid, April 7, 1866.
iii. MARY, b. Ferrington, Aug. 26, 1832; m. Sept. 27, 1857, Wilsey Quimby. They lived at Ovid, Mich., in 1869, where their children seem to have been born, viz.: 1. *Mary,*[8] b. Aug. 21, 1858, m. Loren E. Coffman, had one daughter; 2. *Adah,*[8] b, March 29, 1859; 3. *Wilsey E.,*[8] b. Aug. 24, 1863; 4. *Wilson R.,*[8] b. July 6, 1865: 5. *Dora,*[8] b. June 24, 1870; 6. *John E.,*[8] b. Jan. 23, 1873, d. Jan. 19, 1875.
iv. CHARLES, b. Lyons, Mich., Aug. 11, 1835; m. July 4, 1868, Ann Armstrong, at Ovid, Mich., where he lived 1880, having one child: *Norman E.,*[8] b. Sept. 1873.
v.   CATHERINE, b. Ovid, Mich., April 1, 1839; d. Sept. 1847.
vi. GEORGE HOMER, b. Ovid, Nov. 25, 1844: d. aged 3 years 3 mos.
vii. DAVID UPTON, b. Oct. 26, 1851; m. at Coldwater, Mich., Aug. 24, 1874, Annette Reed. They seem to have lived at Ovid. He d. Jan. 2, 1880, leaving one child: *Bernice,*[8] b. Ovid, —— 2, 1875.

8. ABIATHAR[6] UPTON (*David,*[5] *Josiah,*[4] *Ebenezer,*[3] *Joseph,*[2] *John*[1]) was born in Ontario Co., N. Y., October 14, 1808. He received a good education and was a farmer, at least until his 33d year. He married, about 1840, Jane Hazlett, who was born in Scotland and came to this country with her parents when a child. He seems to have settled in Michigan. His children, "born during the first years of his married life," were:

i.   MARGARET.[7]
ii. MARY, evidently b. in Ontario Co., N. Y., about 1844; m. Sept. 1861, Lyman Hodges, who lived in Bath, Mich., 1881. Children: 1. *Luella,*[8] b. June 28, 1862; 2. *Ethie,*[8] b. July 5, 1864; 3. *Archie,*[8] b. May 18, 1866; 4. *Alice,*[8] b. May 8, 1874.
iii. JANE, b. Ontario Co., N. Y., May 20, 1846; m. at Rome, Mich., Dec. 22, 1870, Rodolphus Lagore, a painter and furniture finisher of Adrian, Mich., in which town they resided in 1881, with one child, *William,*[8] b. Sept. 16, 1871.
iv. ESTHER.
v.   JOANNA, m. Nov. 29, 1868, Fred. A. Maltman. Children: 1. *Edna,*[8] b. Nov. 13, 1869; 2. *Jennie,*[8] b. Feb. 15, 1871; 3. *Mark H.,*[8] b. May 6, 1873; 4. *Irving,*[8] b. Oct. 18, 1875; 5. *Rodolph,*[8] b. Nov. 2, 1879.
vi. WILLIAM.
vii. THOMAS A.

9. DAVID[6] UPTON (*David,*[5] *Josiah,*[4] *Ebenezer,*[3] *Joseph,*[2] *John*[1]) was born in New York state, probably in Victor, March 2, 1814. He married Oct. 16, 1844, Barbara Buckley, of Walworth, N. Y., and in 1846 removed to Michigan. The following year he located on the farm in Rome, Mich., where he still resided in 1880. In January, 1880, he had a partial stroke of paralysis, but it left his mind unimpaired. His children have been:

i.   CAROLINE,[7] b. in Michigan, Oct. 5, 1847; m. Jan. 1, 1867, William A. Griffin. They live in Rollin, Mich. Children: 1. *Ida May,*[8] b. Oct. 5, 1867; 2. *Nellie S.,*[8] b. Feb. 10, 1879.
ii. OLIVE, b. Dec. 30, 1848; m. July 4, 1870, Joshua W. Linsner, of Rol-

lin, Mich. Children : 1. *Laverna*,[8] b. Oct. 7, 1872; 2. *La Monte*,[8] b. April 29, 1879.

18. iii. CHARLES MARSH, b. Dec. 30, 1850 ; m. Hattie L. Maxon.

10. LUCY[6] UPTON (*David*,[5] *Josiah*,[4] *Ebenezer*,[3] *Joseph*,[2] *John*[1]) was born at Victor, N. Y., October 28, 1816. At the age of six months she was taken by her parents to Ontario, N. Y., but when seven years old returned to Victor, where she was one of the children reared and educated by her aunt Joanna[8] (Upton) Marsh (No. 4, *ante*). She remained there eleven years. She taught district school four years, keeping a select school during vacation. She married Henry H. Taber, April 25, 1839. They removed to Wheatland, Mich., in May, 1842. About 1865, in order to be where they could educate their children, they exchanged their 160 acres of land in Wheatland for 206 acres adjoining the city of Adrian, Mich., and they were living upon the latter farm in 1880. They have had :

i. NORMAN B.,[7] b. in Ontario Co., N. Y., May 31, 1840. He went with his parents to Michigan, m. 1st, July 4, 1861, at Wheatland, Myra Hurley or Hawley, and settled in Pittsford, Mich. They had one child : *Lillian M.*,[8] b. Feb. 1, 1863. In 1880 she was a student in Adrian. He m. 2d, Hattie Darriel, of Wawconda, Ill.

ii. MARY E., b. Wheatland, Oct. 9, 1844 ; d. April 9, 1846.

iii. ADELBERT, b. Wheatland, Sept. 9, 1850 ; removed with his parents to Adrian ; was educated at Adrian College ; m. Dec. 31, 187–, Ellen M. Gunsolas, daughter of the proprietor of the Adrian Mills, and in 1880 had one child : *Lena M.*,[8] b. April 20, 1876.

iv. HENRY H., b. Dec. 13, 1851 ; was educated at Adrian College ; m. Dec. 25, 187–, Hettie, daughter of Edwin Lammoreaux, of Rome, Mich. In 1880 they lived in Adrian and had one child : *Bertha*,[8] b. Oct. 20, 1874.

v. SIONE, b. Wheatland, June, 1855 ; d. Aug. 19, 1856.

11. CATHERINE[6] UPTON (*David*,[5] *Josiah*,[4] *Ebenezer*,[3] *Joseph*,[2] *John*[1]) was born at Walworth, N. Y., Jan. 29, 1821 or 1822. She lived there with her parents until 1844, when she went to Michigan, where she married, Jan. 1, 1846, Girdon Patch, of Bethel, Mich. They have had :

i. FREEMAN D.,[7] b. Oct. 11, 1846 ; m. Oct. 23, 1865, Angeline Elliott, and had : *Flora*,[8] b. July 15, 1871.

ii. EUGENE, b. June 3, 1852 ; m. July 2, 1871, Melissa Piatt. Children : 1. *Emera*[8] (a son), b. Feb. 10, 1873 ; 2. *June*,[8] b. Dec. 15, 1876.

iii. DOLLY B., b. April 1, 1862.

12. JAMES M.[6] UPTON (*David*,[5] *Josiah*,[4] *Ebenezer*,[3] *Joseph*,[2] *John*[1]) was born March 24, 1823, probably in Ontario, Wayne Co., N. Y. He removed to Michigan and married, Dec. 17, 1852, Martha Hatfield, of Wheatland, in which town he died, April 27, 1873. His widow and daughter were living in Wheatland in 1880, P. O. Hudson. James M. Upton's children were :

i. ADELBERT,[7] b. Rollin, Mich., June 22, 1858 ; d. Sept. 14, 1859.

ii. JUNIE, b. June 27, 1864.

iii. JAMES, b. Wheatland, May 3, 1872 ; d. Oct. 27, 1874.

13. MARY ANN[6] UPTON (*David*,[5] *Josiah*,[4] *Ebenezer*,[3] *Joseph*,[2] *John*[1]) was born in Ontario, N. Y., March 27, 1825. She was educated at Walworth Corners, N. Y., and went to Michigan with her parents in 1846. Here she married 1st, in September, 1847, Nelson Wood, a merchant, formerly of Wayne Co., N. Y. He died Sept. 16, 1849.

She married 2d, March 27, 1853, Shepherd Weter, of Palmyra, Mich. Her children were, by Nelson Wood:

i.   NELSON Z.,[7] b. Nov. 16, 1848 ; d. Feb. 1850.

By Shepherd Weter:

ii. SHEPHERD, b. Jan. 4, 1854; educated at Adrian College.
iii. ARABELL, b. July 16, 1855 ; m. Harross Freeman, of San Francisco, afterwards a merchant at Richmond, Mich. They have : *Maggie*,[8] b. Dec. 15, 1876.
iv. JAMES E., b. April 9, 1857 : was educated at Adrian College, and in 1880 was a farmer at Palmyra, Mich.
v.   NELSON C., b. April 1, 1859 ; received a classical education at Adrian College, graduated 1880 and began the study of law in Adrian. P. O. Lenawee Junction.
vi. DAVID E., b. Nov. 16, 1862.
vii. CORA M., b. March 4, 1865.

14. CORDELIA[6] UPTON (*David*,[5] *Josiah*,[4] *Ebenezer*,[3] *Joseph*,[2] *John*[1]) was born at Palmyra, N. Y., Oct. 30, 1826. She went to Michigan with her parents in 1846, and there taught school from 1846 to 1855, when she married William Eldridge, of Branch Co., farmer. They removed in 1859 to Boon Co., Ill., in 1869 to Franklin Co., Ia., in 1879 to Logan, Kansas. They have three children:

i.   CATHERINE P.,[7] b. Aug. 28, 1859.
ii. NELLIE, b. Feb. 22, 1861.
iii. CHARLES, b. Sept. 12, 1863.

15. JAMES BOUGHTON[7] UPTON (*William W.*,[6] *James*,[5] *Josiah*,[4] *Ebenezer*,[3] *Joseph*,[2] *John*[1]) was born in Victor, Mich., March 19, 1844. He lived in Michigan and California with his father. He graduated at the High School in Sacramento and was admitted to the bar there. He removed to Portland, Oregon, soon after his father did, and went from there to Oregon City. In 1869 he returned to Portland, and was for four years in the real estate business in connection with his profession, devoting much time and money to the promotion of emigration from the eastern states and Europe to Oregon. In 1873 he removed to Washington County, but returned again to Oregon City. In 1876 he retired from practice and took up his residence at Oretown, Oregon, which has since been his home except during about two years when large business interests required his presence in Colfax, W. T. He married Nov. 9, 1869, Anne Amanda Shaw, of Oregon City, by whom he has five children:

i.   CHARLES SAMUEL,[8] b. at Portland, Aug. 9, 1870.
ii. WILLIAM WESLEY, b. at East Portland, May 31, 1872.
iii. ANNA MAUD, b. in Washington Co., Oregon, Feb. 3, 1874.
iv. JAY HOLLISTER, b. at Colfax, W. T., April 28, 1879.
v.   MARY ETTA, b. at Oretown, Oregon, Jan. 7, 1882.

16. WILLIAM HENRY[7] UPTON (*William W.*,[6] *James*,[5] *Josiah*,[4] *Ebenezer*,[3] *Joseph*,[2] *John*[1]) was born in Weaverville, Cal., June 19, 1854. Having pursued his preliminary studies in Portland, Oregon, he received a classical education at Yale College, where he graduated in 1877. He then entered the office of Hon. R. W. Thompson, Secretary of the Navy, where he remained nearly three years. Entering the Law School of Columbian University, he graduated LL.B. in 1879, and LL.M. in 1880. In the latter year, having previously been admitted to the bar, he resigned his position, formed a professional

partnership with his brother Charles B., and removed to Walla Walla, W. T., where he has since been in active practice.

Several large collections of MSS. relating to the genealogy, English and American, of the Uptons and allied families,* having come into Mr. Upton's possession, he has become, little by little, a kind of registrar or universal secretary for many of these families. He is always glad to receive or furnish data relating to any of them.

He married at Washington, D. C., June 23, 1881, Georgia Louise, youngest daughter of the late Samuel William Bradley, of Olean, N. Y., by his wife Aditha (Barr) Bradley, and has two children :

i. WILLIAM HOLLISTER,[8] b. Sept. 21, 1882.
ii. GEORGE BRADLEY, b. June 20, 1885.

17. GEORGE WHITMAM[7] UPTON (*William W.,[6] James,[5] Josiah,[4] Ebenezer,[3] Joseph,[2] John[1]*), who was known as George Washington Whitman Upton till 1876, was born at Sacramento, Cal., June 1, 1857, and lived with his father in California and Oregon. In 1876 he was appointed by President Grant a cadet at large to West Point. He remained at the Academy nearly four years, but on the death of his sister in 1880, resigned and went to live with his father in Washington city. There, having declined a lieutenancy in the army, he received an appointment in the War Department, which he held until, having graduated at Columbian University, he was admitted to the bar. In 1884 he married Harriet, only daughter of Hon. E. B. Taylor, M.C., and, having formed a professional partnership with his father-in-law, settled in Warren, Ohio, where he now resides.

18. CHARLES MARSH[7] UPTON (*David,[6] David,[5] Josiah,[4] Ebenezer,[3] Joseph,[2] John[1]*) was born in Rome, Mich., Dec. 30, 1850. He married, July 14, 1872, Hattie L. Maxon. To this intelligent and accomplished lady the writer is indebted for invaluable assistance in compiling this account of the descendants of David[5] Upton.

Mr. and Mrs. Upton reside near Geneva P. O. in Rome township, Mich., and in 1880 had two children :

i. PAULINE,[8] b. July 7, 1873.
ii. OLIVE, b. Sept. 19, 1877.

CHURCH RECORDS OF FARMINGTON, CONN.

Communicated by JULIUS GAY, A.M., of Farmington, Conn.

[Continued from page 33.]

Deaths.

Septr. 15, 1776	Departed life Huldah Andruss.
Septr. 17, 1776	Departed life a Child of Hannah Davis.
Septr. 19, 1776	Departed life Sarah Daugh[r] of James Root.
Septr. 22, 1776	Departed life Moses Whiting Bull—young Lad.
Septr. 24, 1776	Departed life Will[m] son of Will[m] Wadsworth.
Septr. 26, 1776	Departed this life Abigail, Daug[r] of Jon[th] Bull Jun[r].

* Viz.: Adams, Boughton, Bouton, Bradley, Goodell, Goodrich, Hale, Hartwell, Hill, Hollister, Stewart, Talcott, Tracy, White, Williams and other families.

Septr. 27, 1776	Departed this life Noadiah son of Joseph Bird.
Octr. 5, 1776	Departed this life Wid° Sarah Gridley.
Octr. 15, 1776	Departed this life Maj^r Simeon Strong.
Octr. 15, 1776	Departed life Widow Ruth Lewis.
Octr. 17, 1776	Departed life Elizabeth Wadsworth.
Octr. 23, 1776	Departed this life the Wife of Samuel Bird.
Octr. 29, 1776	Departed this life a Child of John Hamlin.
Octr. 30, 1776	Departed life a Child of John Hamlin.
Novr. 3, 1776	Departed life Samuel Scott.
Novr. 11, 1776	Departed this life Daniel Woodruff.
Novr. 14, 1776	Carried to ye grave a Babe of Joshua Woodruff.
Novr. 24, 1776	Departed life a Child of Lieut. John Hamlin.
Novr. 1776	Departed this life Aaron North.
Jany. 11, 1777	Departed life Jon^th Ingham—young man.
Jany. 19, 1777	Departed this life Charles Curtiss.
Jany. 20, 1777	Departed this life Solomon North.
Jany. 21, 1777	Departed this life Jemima Stedman.
Jany. 1777	Departed life at N. York, Lot Portter.
February 2, 1777	Departed this life Colo. John Strong.
February 3, 1777	Departed this life Abijah Woodruff.
February 7, 1777	Departed this life the Wife of Capt. Hotchkiss.
Febry. 10, 1777	Departed this life Asahel Woodruff.
Feby. 15, 1777	Departed this life Widow Chestina Woodruff.
Feby. 17, 1777	Departed this life Susana Dagr. of Wid. Abigail Wadsworth.
Feby. 18, 1777	Departed this life W^m son of Bethuel Norton.
Feby. 21, 1777	Departed this life Captn John Newell.
March 1, 1777	Departed this life the Wife of Dea^n Noah Porter.
March 3, 1777	Departed life Susanna a Babe of Asahel Wadsworth.
March 1777	Departed this life a child of Doct^r Tim° Hosmer.
March 10, 1777	Departed this life Eliasaph Dorchester.
March 15, 1777	Departed this life James Hart.
March 29, 1777	Departed life Mary Daughter of John Portter.
April 10, 1777	Departed this life Samuel Woodruff.
April 13, 1777	Departed this life the Wife of Salmon Root.
April 14, 1777	Departed this life Oliver Stevens.
April 16, 1777	Departed life Samuel son of Lieut. Elnathan Gridley.
April 16, 1777	Departed this life the Wife of Wise Barns.
April 18, 1777	Departed this life Ezekiel Woodruff.
May 2, 1777	Departed this life Daniel Hart.
May 1777	Departed this life Doct^r Josiah Hurlbutt.
May 13, 1777	Departed this life Martha Woodruff.
May 19, 1777	Departed this life Sybil Warner—young woman.
July 22, 1777	Departed life a Babe of Solomon Welton.
August 24, 1777	Departed this life Abel Andruss.
August 26, 1777	Departed this life Erastus son of Roswell Stevens.
August 27, 1777	Departed this life a Child of Mr. Kenedy.
August 28, 1777	Departed this life George Welton.
Septr. 1, 1777	Departed this life a Child of Elijah Goodrich.
Septr. 7, 1777	Departed life the Wife of Ens^n James Luske.

Septr. 18, 1777	Departed life the Wife of Solomon Whitman, Esq.
Septr. 19, 1777	Departed this life a Child of Joseph Root.
Septr. 19, 1777	Departed this life Eunice Newell.
Octr. 13, 1777	Departed this life Josiah North.
Octr. 22, 1777	Departed life a Child of Israel Freeman.
Novr. 13, 1777	Departed this life a Babe of Joshua Parsons.
Novr. 24, 1777	Departed this life a Child of Jesse Curtiss.
December 3, 1777	Departed this life wid: Lewis, of Da¹ Lewis.
Januy. 12, 1778	Departed life John Livy son of Mr. John Lewis.
Feby. 25, 1778	Departed life Israel a young mulatto man.
March 21, 1778	Departed this life Benjamin Andruss.
———— 1778	Departed this life Asa Brownson in yᵉ Army.
March 21, 1778	Departed life the Wife of Ezekiel Hosford.
April 5, 1778	Departed this life a Babe of Oliver Woodruff.
May 5, 1778	Departed this life a Babe of John Woods.
May 31, 1778	Departed this life a Babe of Joshua Woodruff.
Novr. 16, 1778	Departed this life Jonathan Gridley.
December 21, 1778	Departed this life John Root.
March 26, 1779	Departed this life Wid° Mary Newell.
March 29, 1779	Departed life a Babe of Doctʳ Asa Johnson.
May 28, 1779	Departed life a Babe of Solomon Cowles.
June 9, 1779	Departed life a Babe of Elisha Woodruff.
July 13, 1779	Departed this life Widow Anne Porter.
August 1, 1779	Departed life the Wife of John Porter.
August 4, 1779	Departed life Wid° Elizabeth Newell.
August 8, 1779	Departed this life Joseph Hawley.
Sept. 15, 1779	Departed this life Tabitha Rose.
Septr. 27, 1779	Departed this life a Child of Simeon Hamlin.
Novr. 20, 1779	Departed life Widow Anna Woodruff.
December 6, 1779	Departed this life Wid° Eunice Lee.
Decbr. 9, 1779	Departed this life the Wife of James Gridley.
Decbr. 15, 1779	Departed this life Huldah Wadsworth.
Decbr. 30, 1779	Departed this life Wᵐ son of Wᵐ Wadsworth.
Jany. 12, 1780	Departed this life a Child of Benjamin Welton.
Jany. 19, 1780	Departed this life Samuel Bird.
Jany. 30, 1780	Departed life Wᵐ a Babe of Asahel Wadsworth.
Febr. 1780	Departed life a Child of Isaac Ingham.
Febry. 12, 1780	Departed life Lucy Keyes.
April 2, 1780	Departed this life Mercy Smith.
April 6, 1780	Departed life a Babe of Joshua Woodruff.
May 29, 1780	Departed this life Mr. Noah Andruss.
May & June 27 & 7, 1780	Departed life two Babes of Eleazer Curtiss.
June 14, 1780	Departed this life the Wid: Mary Portter.
June 23, 1780	Departed this life the Wife of Daniel North.
July 16, 1780	Departed this life Deacon Timothy Porter.
July 15, 1780	Departed this life James Bishop.
August 13, 1780	Departed this life the Wife of Wᵐ Hooker.
August 13, 1780	Departed this life the Wid: Elizᵗʰ Sedgwick.
Decbr. 17, 1780	Departed this life Abraᵐ son of Joshua Parsons.
Decbr. 18, 1780	Departed life Sarah Woodruff Dr. of Joshua Parsons.

[To be continued.]

GENEALOGICAL GLEANINGS IN ENGLAND.

Communicated by HENRY F. WATERS, A.M., now residing in London, England.

[Continued from p. 49.]

DOROTHY LANE of London, widow, 17 January, 1605. My body to be buried in the parish church or churchyard of St Dunstans in the East, London, where I am a parishioner. To Susan Harrys, daughter of my late son in law William Harrys, late of Wapping in the County of Middlesex, mariner deceased, and of Dorothie my daughter, late his wife, ten pounds. To George Stake, son of my late sister Elizabeth, thirty shillings. To my cousin Jeffery Thorowgood twenty shillings. To my cousin Bennet Burton twenty shillings. To my cousins Elizabeth and Sara Quaitmore, daughters of Rowland Quaytmore and of my said daughter Dorothie, his now wife, five pounds apiece. To the said Rowland Quaytmore, my son in law, thirty shillings to make him a ring. To Helen Averell, late wife of William Averell, Schoolmaster, deceased, my small joyned chair with a back. To the said Dorothie Quaytmore,* my daughter, and William Harrys, her son, and to the heirs of the said William Harrys, the son, lawfully begotten, all those my two tenements and two acres in Saffron Walden in the County of Essex, which late were Symon Burton's, my late brother's deceased, the said Dorothie Quaytmore & William Harrys her son to pay out to Samuel Harrys, son of my said daughter Dorothie Quaytmore, ten pounds upon reasonable request, within two months next after such day or time as the said Samuel Harrys shall attain and come to the lawful age of twenty-one years, and unto Jane and Joane Burton, daughters of my said late brother Symon Burton of Saffron Walden aforesaid, five pounds apiece within four years next after such day or time as my said daughter Dorothie & William her son or her heirs or assigns shall first enter and enjoy the said two tenements, &c. To Susan & Dorothie Harrys, daughters of my said daughter Dorothie Quaytmore (certain bequests). To Mary Quaitmore five pounds. To my cousin Elizabeth Quaytmore (certain table linen) and to Sara Quaytmore her sister (a similar bequest). To Mary & Sara Thorowgood, daughters of my cousin Jeffery Thorowgood, twenty shillings. To Richard Weech of London, merchant, twenty shillings. The residue to my daughter Dorothie and she and the above named William Harrys the son appointed full & sole executors. The said Jeffery Thorowgood & Richard Weech appointed overseers. To my cousin Walter Gray five shillings, and to his wife my stuff gown lined with furr.

The witnesses were William Jones, Scr., Jeffery Thorowgood, signum Roberti Powell, shoemaker, and me Richard Perne.

Commission was issued 4 March 1608 to Dorothie Quaytmore, with power reserved for William Harrys, the other executor, &c.

Dorsett, 23.

THOMAS RAINBOROWE of East Greenwich in the County of Kent, mariner, 4 December 1622, proved 23 February 1623. My body to be buried in the church yard of East Greenwich with such solemnity as my executors in their discretion shall think fit. My wife Martha and eldest son Wil-

---

* Rowland Coitmore and Dorothy Harris (widow) married at Whitechapel, co. Mid. 28 March, 1594–5. Elizabeth, their daughter, bapt. 25 Feb. 1595–6.—I. J. GREENWOOD.

liam Rainborowe to be executors. Ten pounds to be given for the putting forth of poor children of the parish of Greenwich aforesaid, &c. To said Martha my wife all my plate and household stuff and the furniture of my house and also my one sixteenth part of the good ship called the Barbara Constance of London and my one sixteenth of the tackle, apparel, munition, furniture, freight, &c. of the said ship. To my said son William two hundred pounds within one year next after my decease, and one sixteenth of the good ship Rainbowe of London & one sixteenth of her tackle, &c., one sixteenth of the ship Lilley of London (and of her tackle, &c.), one forty eighth part of the ship Royal Exchange of London (and of her tackle, &c.). To my son Thomas Rainborowe two hundred pounds within one year, &c. To my daughter Barbara Lee two hundred pounds within one year, &c. To my daughter Martha Wood two hundred pounds within one year, &c. To my daughter Sara Porte two hundred pounds within one year, &c.

Whereas I have taken of the Right Honorable Edward Lord Dennie, Baron of Waltham Holy Cross in the County of Essex, by Indenture of Lease bearing date the eight and twentieth day of September Anno Domini 1619, a capital messuage called by the name of Claver Hambury and certain lands, with their appurtenances, situate, lying & being in the said County of Essex, for the term of two and twenty years, &c. and for and under the yearly rent of a peppercorn, &c.; for which said lease I have paid to the said Lord Denny the sum of two thousand three hundred pounds of currant English money; and the said messuage and lands, &c. are worth yearly in rent (*de claro*) two hundred and twenty pounds or thereabouts, &c. &c. it is my will that there shall be paid out of the rents, profits, &c. to Martha my wife one annuity or annual rent of one hundred pounds, to my son William an annuity, &c. of twenty pounds, to my son Thomas an annuity, &c. of twenty pounds, to my daughter Barbara Lee an annuity, &c. of twenty pounds, to my daughter Martha Wood an annuity, &c. of twenty pounds, to my daughter Sara Port an annuity, &c. of twenty pounds.

The residue of my personal property to my two executors to be divided equally, part and part alike. My dwelling house and lands in East Greenwich shall be sold by my executors for the most profit they can & within as short time after my death as conveniently may be, and of the money arising therefrom one third shall go to my wife Martha, one third to my son William and the other third to my said four other children, Thomas, Barbara, Martha & Sara.

The witnesses were J. W. the mark of John Wotton, of the precinct of St Katherine's, mariner, John Woodward, Not. Pub., and John Brooke his servant. Byrde, 8.

ANTHONY WOOD of Redrith in the county of Surrey, mariner, 13 August 1625, proved at London 3 January 1625 by the oath of Martha Wood his relict and executrix. To wife Martha all my lease &c. in my now dwelling house in Redrith & my part of the good ship Exchange of London & of the Charity of London. To son Richard all my portion of the good ship Rainbow of London & my adventure in her &c. To my sons Richard, Thomas & Anthony five hundred pounds apiece, & to my daughter Sara five hundred pounds, at one & twenty. To my brother John Wood five pounds a year for eighteen years. To my mother Raynborrowe three pounds for a ring. To my brother William Raynborowe five pounds for a cloak. To my brother Francis Port three pounds for a ring. To my brother Thomas Lee three pounds. To my brother Thomas Raynborowe three pounds. To my uncle William Wood & his wife four pounds, for & in remembrance of tokens of my love unto them. I give to my said wife all my lease of certain lands at Waltham which I have & hold from the Lord Denny, &c. My said wife & my said son Richard to be full & sole executors &c., and I name & appoint overseers of this my will my loving friends the wor[ll] Henry Garway & William Garwaye of London merchants.

A codicil made Tuesday the 23[d] of August A.D. 1625 revokes the bequest of his portion of the ship Rainbow to son Richard & bequeaths it to Martha Wood his wife.	Hele, 4.

ROWLAND COYTEMORE of Wapping in the County of Middlesex, mariner, 5 June, 1626, proved 24 November 1626 by Katherine Coytemore, relict and executrix. To son Thomas Coytemore and his heirs, &c. the messuage or tenement, lands, hereditaments and appurtenances in the manor of Milton in the parish of Prittlewell *als*. Pricklewell, in the County of Essex, now in the tenure and occupation of John Greene, &c. and my farm and copyhold land of forty four acres or thereabouts, in the parish of Great Bursted in the County of Essex; wife Katherine to have the use and rents until my son Thomas shall accomplish his age of one and twenty years. To my daughter Elizabeth Coytemore three score pounds at her age of one and twenty years or day of marriage, also the tenement or messuage known by the sign of the Blewboare in the town or parish of Retchford, in the County of Essex, now in the tenure of William Ashwell *als*. Hare. To my son in law Thomas Gray* and his heirs my two copyhold tenements, &c. in Rederith *als*. Rederiff, in the County of Surrey, now in the several occupations of Francis Welby and John Moore. If my children and children's children die before they accomplish their several ages of one and twenty or be married, then my aforesaid lands shall remain, come and be unto my kinsman Hugh Hughs *als*. Gwyn, my sister Elizabeth's son. To my grandson William Ball, son of William Ball, forty shillings. To my daughter in law daughter Dorothy Lamberton forty shillings. To the poor of Wapping three pounds and to the poor of the Upper Hamlet of Whitechapel forty shillings. To the masters of Trinity House, for their poor, ten pounds within one year, &c.

My wife Katherine to be executrix and sons in law Thomas Gray and William Rainsborough of Wapping aforesaid, mariners, to be overseers. The witnesses were Raphe Bower pub. scr. and John Wheatley serv[t] to the said scr.	Hele, 125.

MARTHA RAINBOROWE of the parish of S[t] Bridget *als*. Brides, near Fleet St. London, widow, late wife of Thomas Rainborowe, late of East Greenwich in the county of Kent, mariner, deceased, made her will 29 November 1626, proved 23 September 1631. In it she referred to her husband's will & the lease of the messuage called Claverhambury and the disposition of its rents, bequeathed her own annuity among her five children, devised to her daughter Barbara Lee her sixteenth part of the good ship called Barbara Constance and gave the residue of her goods, chattels, &c. to her said daughter Barbara, wife of Thomas Lee, citizen & armorer of London, whom also she appointed sole executrix.

The witnesses were Robert Woodford, Thomas Turner and Tho: Eastwood.	S[t] John, 102.

* See Gray and Coytmore Families, REG. xxxiv. 253.—ED.

WILLIAM RAINBOROW of London Esq. 16 July 1638, with codicil of 1 February 1642, proved 8 April 1642. To the Hamlet of Wapping as a stock for their poor fifty pounds ; to the Hamlet of Whitechapel ten pounds, &c. To the Trinity House fifty pounds, with the condition that they give to poor seamen or their widows of the Hamlet of Wapping, every St. Thomas Day, forty shillings. To my eldest son Thomas Rainborowe all those my houses in Southwark purchased of Mr William Gambell and some of them lately built. To my son William Rainborowe those my houses in Gun Alley in Wapping purchased of my father in law Renold Hoxton and also one thousand pounds. To my son Edward twelve hundred pounds. Item I give and bequeath to my daughter Martha Coytmore, the wife of Thomas Coytmore now in New England, the sum of seven hundred pounds, if she be alive at the time of my death. To my daughter Judith Rainborowe one thousand pounds & to my daughter Joane Rainborowe one thousand pounds. All this to be paid to them, by my executors, at their several days of marriage or at their age of one and twenty years, and those that be of age at six months after my decease. To the four sons and one daughter of my deceased sister Sara Port, namely Robert, John, Thomas, William and Martha Porte, two hundred and fifty pounds, that is to each fifty pounds, at twenty one. To my brother Mr Thomas Rainborowe fifty pounds. To my sister Buckridge fifty pounds. To my sister Wood fifty pounds. To my father in law Renold Hoxton and to my mother in law Joane Hoxton ten pounds apiece to buy them each a ring. My executors to be my loving sons Thomas and William Rainborowe and I appoint them to bring up my younger children to their age of twenty one years or day of marriage and to have the tuition of them and be at the charges of meat & drink & clothes & learning. For overseers I desire my loving brothers in law Mr Robert Wood and Mr John Hoxton to have a care that this my will be fulfilled and do give them twenty pounds apiece for their pains. Witnesses Robert Wood and William Ashley.

To my mother in law Jone Hoxton my house at Wapping now in the occupation of Mr Sander Bence, during her natural life, toward her maintenance. To my grand child William Rainborowe one hundred pounds.

Codicil. Whereas the said William Rainborowe hath by his will given to Martha Port fifty pounds the said William Rainborow did about a year since and at other times afterwards declare his mind and will to be that the said Martha should not have or expect the said legacy because he had given her the sum of ten pounds and all her wedding clothes in marriage with William Ashley. Subscribed by witnesses 1 February 1641.

Witnesses to the codicil, John Hoxton, Thomas Hoxton & Mary Bennfes.

Campbell, 51.

STEVEN WINTHROP of James Street, Westminster, Esq., 3 May 1658, proved 19 August, 1658. To wife Judith the house wherein I now dwell, with the house adjoining, lately erected, for her life, and then to all my children. All the rest to my daughters Margaret, Joanna and Judith and such child or children as my said wife shall now be great withall. To my nephew Adam Winthrop, son of my brother Adam Winthrop deceased ; to the children of my brother Deane Winthrop; to my brother Samuel Winthrop's children ; to my half brother John Winthrop's children ; to my cousin Mary Rainborowe daughter of my brother in law William Rainborowe Esq.; to my cousin Judith Chamberlaine, daughter of my brother in law John Chamberlaine Esq.—sundry bequests. " To the poor of Boston in New

England one hundred pounds of lawfull money of England upon Condition that the Inhabitants of Boston aforesaid doe build and erect a Tombe or Monument, Tombes or Monuments, for my deceased ffather and Mother upon their graue or graues of ffifftie pounds value att the least, whoe now lyeth buried att Boston aforesaid, according to the Loue and honour they bore to him and her in theire life time." The executors to be my wife Judith Winthropp, my brother in law John Chamberlaine Esq. and Thomas Plampyon, gentleman.

The witnesses were Leo: Chamberlaine, Elizabeth Baldrey and Clement Ragg (by mark). Wootton, 418.

[In Suffolk Registry of Deeds (Book 8, p. 193) may be found record of conveyance made by Judith Winthrop and John Chamberlain, executors of Stephen Winthrop, 20 April, 1671, to Edward Rainborow of London, of all the said Winthrop's land in New England, consisting of one half of Prudence Island and fifteen hundred acres in Lynn or Salem, &c. This latter property included the well known Pond Farm (Lynnfield), originally granted to Colonel John Humfrey.—H. F. W.

In addition to the ten letters of Stephen W., printed in Part IV. of the Winthrop Papers (5 Mass. Hist. Coll., viii. pp. 199–218) we have found several others, but they are of no importance. Before his final return to England he was Recorder of Boston and a Representative; and, but for the failure of his health caused by sleeping on the damp ground, there is reason to believe Cromwell would have made him one of his generals, as Roger Williams, writing to John Winthrop, Jr., in 1656, says, "Your brother Stephen succeeds Major-General Harrison." By his own desire he was buried with his ancestors at Groton in Suffolk, where were also interred a number of his children, most of whom died young. Only two daughters are known with certainty to have survived him : *Margaret*, who married 1st, Henry Ward, and 2d, Edmund Willey, R. N., and had issue ; and *Joanna*, who married Richard Hancock, of London, and died s. p. During his military service his wife resided partly at Groton and afterwards at Marylebone Park near London, a portion of which estate he had purchased. This gave rise to an absurd tradition, perpetuated in some pedigrees of the last century, that the Winthrops were " of Marylebone Park *before* they settled in Suffolk." Besides his house in James Street, Westminster, he owned, at the time of his death, his father's house in Boston, on the southerly portion of which estate the Old South Church now stands ; this was subsequently sold by his widow, but whether she ever returned to New England I do not know. My kinsman Robert Winthrop, of New York, has a portrait (of which I have a copy) of a young officer of the Stuart period, which has been in our family for generations, and is called " Colonel Stephen Winthrop, M.P." If authentic, it must have either been sent by him as a present to his father before his death, or subsequently procured by his brother John, or his nephew Fitz-John, during their residence in England.—R. C. Winthrop, Jr.]

Thomas Rainborowe of East Greenwich in the County of Kent, gentleman, 24 November, 1668, proved 2 January 1671 by Mary Rainborowe, his widow & executrix. To wife Mary, for life, an annuity bought of Ralph Buskin of Oltham in the County of Kent Esq. one bought of Edward Turner of East Greenwich, gentleman, and all my other goods, moneys, &c. She to be executrix and to pay two hundred pounds (on a bond which testator made to his mother*). I give to my brother's son Edward Rainborowe twenty pounds, to my brother's daughter Judith Winthrop twenty pounds and to my said brother's daughter Joane Chamberlaine fifty pounds. To the poor of East Greenwich ten pounds. The witnesses were William Richardson & John Fuller. Eure, 7.

[The following notes on the Rainsborough family, collected some years ago, will throw light on Mr. Waters's abstracts :

1537.—Reynold Ravynsbye, freeman of the Co. of Cloth Workers, London.

1598.—Roger Rainseburye of Stawley, co. Somerset. Will dated July 24, prov-

---

* His mother had been dead many years.

ed Aug. 23, 1598. Bequeaths to the poor of Kettleford 3-4. To the poor of Ashbrittle 3-4. To his goddaughter Agnes Gover 20s. To each of his other godchildren, not named, 4d. To Edward Blackaller his wife's godson 20s. Residue to wife Honor, whom he appoints executrix, and her friends John Gover and William Golde overseers.—*Book Lewyn*, fo. 68.

1603.—Nicholas Rainbury of Stawley. Will dated April 19, 1603; proved May 4, 1611. To the poor of Stawley the interest of £10,—to be used in keeping them at work. To each of his godchildren, not named, 6s. To Mary, dau. of Richard Wyne 20s. To each of the children of John Grover 12d. To the poor of Ashbrittle 10s. To the poor of Kettleford 5s. To each of the ringers 12d. To Parson John Blackealler 10s. Residue to his sister-in-law Honour Rainsbury, whom he appoints executrix, and William Golde and John Gover, overseers.—*Book Wood*, fo. 46.

Stanleigh or Stowley, Kittesford and Ashbuttel, all in Milverton Hundred.

1615.—Henry Raygnesburye of Culmstock, co. Devon, husbandman. Will dated Feb. 8, 1615; proved March 9, 1615. To his son Henry £60. To daughter Alice R. £80, to be paid to her uncle Christopher Baker, clothier, for her use. To George, son of Andrew Bowreman 10s. To each of his godchildren, not named, 12d. To the poor 20s. Residue to wife Susan whom he appoints executrix.—*Book Cope*, fo. 29.

During the Protectorate the Baker family held the Manor of Columbstock, Hemyoke Hundred, co. Devon.

1636.—Henry Raynsbury, of the parish of St. Austin (Augustine) in London, factor. Will dated March 15, 1636, proved May 8, 1637. To Mr. Stephen Denison, Doctor and Lecturer, of Great All Hallows, 10s, to preach a sermon at his burial, and to the minister of the parish, where he shall be buried, for giving him way to preach the sermon £5. To each poor man and woman of the parish as the church wardens may select 10s. To the parish of Cullumstock, co. Devon, where he was born £100—for the use of the poor forever, the interest to be divided once a year among eight poor men and women. To the poor of Samford Arundel (Milverton Hund.) co. Somerset, £10—for the use of the poor forever. To his sister Alice Wood, widow, of Henryoke, co. Devon, all his inheritage lands in the county of Lincoln, during her life, then to be divided among her five children. To Mrs. Susan Fleming, wife of Mr. John Fleming of St. Austin's, London £100. To their three children, Roland, Mary and Susan, each £10. To each of his godchildren, not named, 20s. To ten poor laboring porters of Blackwall Hall (market for selling woolen cloths), each 10s. To cousin Edward, son of cousin Edward Baker of Henryoke £20. To ten poor servant-maids of Cullumstock, each 20s. Residue to his godson Henry Baker, son of cousin John Baker the elder, of Cullumstock, clothier, when 21 years of age. Appoints the said John Baker executor, and his uncle Christopher Baker, cousin Henry Holwaye, and gossip John Rew, overseers, and gives each of them £5.—*Book Goare*, fo. 59.

The Hundreds of Milverton, co. Somers and Henryoke, co. Devon adjoin.

The parish registers of Whitechapel, co. Mid., which begin in 1558, record the marriage of

THOMAS[1] RAINEBOROW and Martha Moole, Nov. 11, 1582.

In Chancery Proceedings, temp. Elizabeth, P.p. No. 23, occurs a bill, filed 1641; Thomas Raynsbury and others, to vacate an annuity charged by George Peirce *plaintiff* on a freehold messuage in Gate Lane, parish of St. Mary Staynings, London, for use of plaintiff's daughter Eliz. Peirce.

Thomas Rainborowe of East Greenwich, mariner, had a lease of certain lands, 28 Sept. 1619, at Claverhambury, co. Essex, from Lord Edward Denny, which manor, with Hallyfield Hall, &c., had been granted by Henry VIII., 1542, to his lordship's grandfather Sir Anthony Dennye.

His children, baptized at Whitechapel, were:

1. 1583, April 28. Barbara,[2] m. Thomas Lee, armorer, of London, and after Mr. —— Burbridge, or Buckridge.
2. 1584-5, Feb. 21. Elizabeth,[2] d. unm. before 1619.
3. 1587, June 11. William.[2]
4. 1589, Sept. 23. Martha,[2] m. Anthony Wood.
5. 1591-2, Feb. 20. Thomas,[2] d. young.
6. 1594, Oct. 15. Thomas.[2]
7. 1597, June 19. Sarah,[2] m. Francis Porte.

The name is spelled variously on the registers, as Rain(e)borow(e), Rain(e)sborow(e), Raynsborow, Raineburrow(e), Rainsberry, and, though possibly it is synonymous with Ramesbury or Remmesbury [of co. Wilts, &c.), the armorial bearings of the two families do not coincide, the Rainsborowe arms being similar to those of the Raynes, Reynes, or Reymes.

The will of Thomas[1] Rainborowe, mariner of East Greenwich, co. Kent, dated 4 Dec. 1622, and proved 23 Feb. 1623, is given in this article by Mr. Waters, as also that of the widow, Martha Rainborowe, who afterwards resided in the parish of St. Bridget's, London, where she died in 1631.

Before considering the elder son William,[2] it may be briefly stated that the second son—

THOMAS[2] RAINBOROW, bapt. at Whitechapel 15 Oct. 1594, in his will of 24 Nov. 1668, proved 2 Jan. 1671 (as given by Mr. Waters), is styled " of East Greenwich, gent." He evidently died without issue surviving him, though he had a son Thomas,[3] bapt. at Whitechapel, 18 Sept. 1614. The will of his widow is as follows : Mary Rainborow of Greenwich, co. Kent, widow ; dated 11 Feb. 1677, proved 9 Apr. 1678. Whereas she has heretofore expressed her kindness to her brother and sister, not named, to the utmost of her ability, she now gives them but twelve pence. Appoints her niece Sarah Trott, who now lives with her, executrix, and makes her residuary legatee.—*Book Reeve*, fol. 37.

WILLIAM[2] RAINBOROW (eldest son of Thomas[1]), bapt. at Whitechapel, 11 June, 1587. In Nov. 1625, we find him a part owner and in command of the Sampson of London, 500 tons, built at Limehouse, and now granted the privilege of carrying great guns. His name occurs frequently in the Cal. Dom. State Papers. Secretary Lord Edward Conway writes him, 20 March, 1626, relative to taking aboard the trunks, &c. of Sir Thomas Phillips, Ambassador for Constantinople. Letters of Marque were granted 24 Oct. 1627, and finally, when the reconstruction of the navy was paramount with King Charles, the merchantman Sampson, well fortified with iron ordnance, was one of the vessels presented, in Dec. 1634, by the City of London, for his Majesty's service. William Raynisborowe, as one of the inhabitants in the vicinity of the Tower, complained, in the summer of 1627, of the nuisance of an alum-factory erected at the west end of Wapping. Five years later we find his knowledge and experience of maritime matters duly recognized by the Lords of the Admiralty, who in their order of 21 April, 1632, appoint Capt. Rainsborough one of the gentlemen to attend a meeting of the Board on the 26th, to give their opinion concerning the complements and numbers of men to be allowed for manning each of his Majesty's ships.

Jan. 2, 1634–5. the King in Council had expressed his desire that the Merhonour, the Swiftsure, the City of London and other vessels should be presently put forth to sea. The order was confirmed March 10, and the first named vessel was ordered to be fitted out and victualled by April 24 for six months' service, the charge to be defrayed with moneys paid by the several ports and maritime places. To the Merhonour, at Chatham, the Lords of the Admiralty appoint Capt. William Rainborough, March 30, with Capt. William Cooke as Master. This 44 gun vessel (800 tons), sometimes called the May Honora, had been rebuilt and launched, 25 April, 1614, at Woolwich, by Phineas Pett. Other vessels commissioned at the time were the Constant Reformation, Capt. Thomas Ketelby ; the Swallow, Capt. Henry Stradling ; the Mary Rose, Capt. George Carteret ; the Sampson, Capt. Thomas Kirke, &c. &c. ; and these were under the command of Sir William Monson, Vice Adm. in the James, and Sir John Pennington, Rear Adm. in the Swiftsure. Since the death of the Duke of Buckingham in 1628, the office of Lord Admiral had remained in commission, but on May 14, 1635, one of the Navy Commissioners, Robert Bertie, Lord Willoughby de Eresby and Earl of Lindsey, was appointed Admiral, Custos Maris, General and Governor of His Majesty's Fleet, for the guard of the Narrow Seas. He was to defend the King and the Kingdom's honor, which had been lately called in question by a fleet of French and Dutch off Portland, and to exact " the due homage of the sea " from passing ships, and so restore to England her ancient sovereignty of the Narrow Seas ; he was also to clear the neighboring waters of pirates and Turks ; to convoy merchants and others desiring it ; to guard against any infringement of the custom on the part of returning vessels, &c. About the middle of April the Merhonour repaired to Tilbury Hope to receive the remainder of her stores ; and on May 16 the Admiral came on board, the ships meeting twelve days later in the Downs. Rainsborough's vessel, though a good sailer, proved somewhat leaky, and the Admiral was desirous at first of changing to the Triumph ; however, the leaks having been found and her foremast repaired, he concluded she would do well for her present employment, and continued cruizing in her until he brought the fleet into the Downs once more on Oct. 4. Most of the ships were now ordered to Chatham and Deptford, though a few continued out under Sir John Pennington. The Earl despatched his journal of the expedition to the King, and hoped he might, with his Majesty's favor, return home. The Hollanders, who in pursuit of the Dunkirk frigates, had been accustomed to land on the English coast, committing depredations upon the inhabitants, had been checked; one of their armed bands had been arrested at Whitby, and a vessel of 21 guns had been taken and sent into Hull; moreover, Capt. Stradling, in the Swallow of 30 guns, being off the Lizard alone, had met the French Admiral Manti with two vessels, who after receiving an admonitory shot apiece, had each struck their flags and topsails, and saluted with three pieces of ordnance.

Writs were now sent to the sheriffs of the various counties of England, to levy money to defray the charge of a fleet for next year of double the strength of that which had just been employed, and attention was paid to the improvement of the vessels in the removal of the cumbersome galleries, as suggested by Capt. Rainsborough. This gentleman, together with one of the commissioners, Sir John Wostenholm and others, was appointed Dec. 9 to inquire into the institution, state, order and government of the Chest at Chatham, as established in 1588 by Queen Elizabeth, with Adms. Drake and Hawkins, for the relief of wounded and decayed seamen, and to certify their doings to the Co. of Chancery.

Towards the close of Feb. 1635–6, a list of Naval Captains, twenty-five in number, was handed in for the year, with Algernon, Earl of Northumberland, as Adm., Sir John Pennington as V. Adm., and Sir Henry Mervyn as Rear Adm. The Earl, in the Triumph, had chose Rainborow as his Captain, with William Cooke as Master, and during the next month he desired the Lords of the Admiralty that his Captain's pay might be made equal to theirs, and that he might have a Lieut., as he had more business to do than any other captain of the fleet. April 9, the ships at Portsmouth were awaiting the arrival of Capt. R. to take them out to sea, the Admiral having promised to send him down for that purpose.

At this time, and for a long series of years previous, England was and had been suffering from a grievous scourge, viz.: the pirates from the north of Africa. So bold and venturesome had they become during the summer of 1636, as to land within twelve miles of Bristol and successfully carry off men, women and children. Their chief place of refuge was the port of Cardiff and its vicinity, whence they carried on their depredations along either coast of the St. George's Channel. No relief, save an occasional collection for the redemption of captives, had heretofore been devised, and numerous were the petitions and statements now being presented to the King and the H. of Lords. The Court was moved to proclaim a general fast, and a sermon was preached in October by the Rev. Charles Fitz-Geffry, of St. Dominick, in Plymouth, from Heb. 13, 3; this was printed at Oxford, and entitled, "Compassion towards Captives, chiefly towards our Brethren & Countrymen who are in such miserable bondage in Barberie." A cotemporaneous document reads: "It is certainly known that there are five Turks in the Severne, wher they weekly take either English or Irish; and that there are a great number of their ships in the Channell, upon the coast of France and Biscay. Whereby it is come to passe that our mareners will noe longer goe to sea, nor from port to port; yea, the fishermen dare not putt to sea, to take fish for the country. If timely prevention be not used, the Newfoundland fleet must of necessity suffer by them in an extraordinary manner." The greater part of the captives, reported to be some 2000 in number, had been taken within the last two years, and the sea-rovers, most to be dreaded, were the pirates of New Sallee, who had revolted from the Emperor of Morocco, headed by a rebel who was called the Saint. The matter coming to be more seriously discussed, three plans were suggested—peace, war, or suppression of trade. Finally it was proposed that Capt. Rainsborough should be employed in an expedition against Sallee, and he and Mr. Giles Penn (father of the future Adm. William Penn) were called upon by the King, Dec. 28, to give their opinion concerning the particulars. In a letter, some three weeks earlier, Capt. R., then an invalid at Southwold, on the Suffolk coast, states his great willingness to attend the Lords and further their project, as soon as he can set out for London. The plan, which he subsequently submitted, states that to redeem the captives would require over 100,000*l.*, the payment of which would but encourage the pirates to continue their present course. Whereas to besiege them by sea would not only effect the purpose, but give security for the future, or a fleet might be kept on their coast for two or three years, until their ships were worm-eaten. That "the maintenance of the suggested fleet would be very much to the King's honor in all the maritime ports in Christendom,

&c." He recommends himself to go as Admiral in the Leopard, Capt. George Carteret as V. Adm. in the Antelope, Capt. Brian Harrison in the Hercules, Capt. George Hatch in the Gt. Neptune, Capt. Th. White in the largest pinnace, and Capt. Edmund Scamon in the lesser. The plan was adopted, and, Feb. 20, 1636-7, Sec. Coke writes from Whitehall to the Lord Dep. Strafford : " This day Capt. Rainsborough, an experienced & worthy seaman, took his leave of his Majesty, and goeth instantly to sea with four good ships and two pinnaces to the coast of Barbary, with instructions & resolution to take all Turkish frygates he can meet, & to block up the port of Sally, & to free the sea from these rovers, which he is confident to perform."

March 4 the little squadron was in the Downs and on the eve of departure. The port of Sallee was reached in good season, and the enemy's cruisers, about to start for England and Ireland, were hemmed in and twenty-eight of their number destroyed. A close siege was now maintained, assisted on the land side by the old Governor of the town, and the place was delivered up to the English, July 28th.

The Emperor now agreed to join in a league with King Charles, promising never again to infest the English coasts, and forthwith delivered up some 300 captives, with whom Capt. Carteret immediately returned homeward. Rainsborough, however, on Aug. 21, proceeded to Saffee to treat for about 1000 English captives who had been sold to Tunis and Algiers. Here he remained till Sept. 19, when the Emperor's Ambassador came aboard, accompanied by Mr. Robert Blake, a merchant trading to Morocco, for whom the Emperor had formed a friendship, and who had obtained the position of Farmer of all his Ports and Customs. On the 21st they left the coast, and arriving fifteen days later in the Downs, landed, Oct. 8, at Deal Castle. Detained at Gravesend through sickness, it was not until the 19th that the Ambassador was conducted to London by the Master of Ceremonies, and, landing at the Tower, was taken to his lodgings " with much display & trumpeting." In the procession were the principal citizens and Barbary merchants mounted, all richly apparelled, and every man having a chain of gold about him, with the Sheriffs and Aldermen in their scarlet gowns, and a large body of the delivered captives, some of whom had been over thirty years in servitude, arrayed in white, and though it was night, yet the streets " were almost as light as day." Sunday, Nov. 5, the Ambassador was received by the King, to whom he brought, as a present from his imperial master, some hunting hawks and four steeds, " the choicest & best in all Barbary, & valued at a great rate, for one Horse was prized at 1500 pound." These, led by four black Moors in red liveries, were caparisoned with rich saddles embroidered with gold, and the stirrups of two of them were of massive gold, and the bosses of their bridles of the same metal. An account of the proceedings was printed towards the close of the month, entitled, " The Arrival & Entertainment of the Morocco Ambassador Alkaid (or Lord) Jaurar Ben Abdella, from the High & Mighty Prince Mully Mahamed Sheque, Emperor of Morocco, King of Fesse & Susse, &c."

Great was the enthusiasm created by the successful issue of the expedition, and even Waller was prompted to eulogize the event in the following rather ponderous lines :

> " Salle that scorn'd all pow'r and laws of men,
> Goods with their owners hurrying to their den ;
> *   *   *   *   *   *
> This pest of mankind gives our Hero fame,
> And thus th' obliged world dilates his name.
> ◆   *   *   *   *   *
> With ships they made the spoiled merchant moan ;
> With ships, their city and themselves are torn.
> One squadron of our winged castles sent
> O'erthrew their Fort, and all their Navy rent :
> *   *   *   *   *   *
> Safely they might on other nations prey ;
> Fools to provoke the Sov'reign of the Sea !
> *   *   *   *   *   *
> Morocco's Monarch, wondering at this fact,
> Save that his presence his affairs exact,
> Had come in person, to have seen and known
> The injur'd world's revenger, and his own.
> Hither he sends the chief among his Peers,
> Who in his bark proportion'd presents bears,
> To the renown'd for piety and force,
> Poor captives manumis'd and matchless horse."

Even grumbling Master Andrew Burrell, who, in a pamphlet of 1646 condemns the entire Navy, its officers, &c., though he had himself built for them the Marie Rose, " the most sluggish ship " they had afloat, confesseth that Rainsborough's Fleet " performed better service than England's Navie did in 44 years before." The King was very willing and forward to have knighted the gallant Admiral, but he declined the honor, and order was given that he should have a gold chain and medal of the value of 300*l.*; a memorial of loyal service perhaps still extant, " should not very opposite family feelings have melted it down in the days of the Rump," observes Disraeli in his Life of Charles I. An augmentation to the family arms was undoubtedly conferred at the time in the shape of " a Saracen's head couped ppr. in the fesse point."

Meanwhile the raising of funds and supplies for the equipment of the fleet for the following year had again become necessary, and Strafford, writing to the Abp. of Canterbury from Dublin, 27 Nov., says in connection, " this action of Sallee, I assure you, is so full of honor, that it will bring great content to the subject, and should, methinks, help much towards the ready, cheerful payment of the shipping monies." Early in Feb. 1637-8, the list of ships, which were to keep the seas during the following summer, was published, headed by the Sovereign of the Seas. This vessel, launched at Woolwich the preceding year, had been in progress since May, 1635, and surpassed in size, tonnage and force anything heretofore constructed for the English Navy. Thomas Heywood published an account of it, with a view of this " his Majesty's royal Ship, the Great Glory of the English Nation, and not to be paralleled in the whole Christian World," while Marmaduke Rawdon, of York, mentions in his Life,[*] a visit, in 1638, to the Royal Sovereign, Capt. Rainsberry, then newly finished and riding at Erith, below Woolwich.

Burrell, in his pamphlet before alluded to, condemns the vessel as " an admirable ship for costly Buildings, & cost in keeping ; and, which adds to the miracle, the Royall Ship is never to be used for the Kingdom's good," &c. The Commissioners of the Navy answered in reply : " Capt. Rainsborough, whom Master Burrell confesseth, in his time, was the most eminent Commander in this Kingdom, had the trial of her in the Channel of England, and at his return reported to his Majestie that he never set his foot in a better conditioned Ship in all his life. And as for her Forces, she is not inferior to the greatest Ship in Christendom."[†]

On Sunday, March 18th, Algernon, Earl of Northumberland, obtained the position of General at Sea, or Lord High Admiral, during his Majesty's pleasure, the King designing to eventually bestow that office upon his younger son, the Duke of York. That Capt. Rainsborough was ever in active naval service after his cruise in the Sovereign does not appear. He and others, owners of the 200 ton ship Confidence of London, were allowed Feb. 19, by the Lords of the Admiralty, to mount her with 20 pieces of cast-iron ordnance, and, during the fall of the year, together with some 155 other sea-faring men, he signed his consent to a proposition made by the Lord High Admiral and the Att. General, that an amount be deducted from their wages for the establishment of the Poor Seamen's Fund, to be administered by the officers of the Trinity House. The following year, as appears by a paper among the Duke of Northumberland's MSS., he submitted a proposition, in the form of articles, suggesting that 10,000 pieces of ordnance, with carriages, &c., be kept in readiness to arm 100 collier-ships, which may fight with a great army ; stating their superiority for such service. Commission was given, Oct. 20, 1639, to Sir Edward Littleton, Solic. General, Sir Paul Pindar and Capt. William Rainsborough, to inquire into the truth of the statements made in the petition to the Privy Council, by Edward Deacon, who with his goods had been seized and detained in Sallee for debts there contracted by Mr. Robert Blake, as factor for some London merchants ; petitioner having come to England, after leaving his son in Barbary as a pledge, in pursuit of said Blake, who, at the time, or immediately subsequent, was one of the gentlemen of the Council.

As William Rainsborough, Esq., he, with Squire Bence, merchant, were members from Aldborough, a seaport of co. Suffolk, in the Fourth Parl. of Charles I., held at Westminster from 13 April to 5 May, 1640 ; as also in the Parliament which convened 3 Nov. following ; that most notable of English Parliaments, before which, a week later, Thomas, Earl of Strafford, was accused of high treason. May 27, 1641, he with others took the oath of Protestation, for the defence of the religion

[*] Camden Soc. Pub.

[†] She subsequently did such good service that the Dutch nicknamed her " the Golden Devil."

established, of the King's person, and the liberty of the subject; the same having been assented to by both houses on the 3d and 4th of the same month. Aug. 25th Capt. R. was at the head of the committee for taking the whole state of the navy into consideration, and providing ships for transporting the ordnance and ammunition from Hull and other parts of the north. Five days later the merchants' petition for erecting a Company for America and Africa, &c., was referred to Sir John Colpeper and Mr. Pymm especially, assisted by twenty-three other members, among whom was Capt. Rainsborough. The same day he was included in a committee to whom had been referred the Act for making Wapping Chapel parochial. He was also appointed, Sept. 9, a member of the Recess Committee, during the adjournment of Parliament till Oct. 20th ; and on Nov. 19, was on a committee for naval affairs, with some other members, including Sir Henry Vane. Three days later it was ordered " that citizens that serve for the City of London and Capt. Rainsborough do inform themselves what shipping are now in the River that are fit to transport the Magazine at Hull to the Tower, and to give an account of it to-morrow morning " ; this was in pursuance of a resolution of the 3d.

And so ends his life and public services, for no more is heard of him till Feb. 14, 1641–2, when the Speaker of the House was ordered to issue a warrant to the Clerk of the Crown in Chancery for a new writ to be issued forth for the election of a new Burgess to serve for the town of Alborough in co. Suffolk, in the room and stead of Capt. Rainsborough deceased, and Alex. Bence, Esq., was accordingly elected. On the 17th his body was interred in St. Catherine's (Tower), London. At the time of his decease the Captain was a widower, his wife Judith, a daughter of Renold and Joane Hoxton, having been buried at Wapping, 3 March, 1637–8. The will of William Rainsborow of London Esq., dated 16 July, 1638, with codicil of 1 Feb. 1641, proved 8 April, 1642, has been already given.

1. THOMAS[3] RAINSBOROWE, Esq., of Whitechapel, co. Midd. (William,[2] Thomas[1]), commonly known in history as Col. Rainsborough. A naval captain at first under the L. H. Adm. Warwick ; then a colonel of infantry under the Parliament, and finally V. Adm. of their Fleet. A member of the Long Parliament. A more detailed account of this prominent and distinguished individual may be given hereafter. Suffice it to say that the Rev. Hugh Peters, alluding to the services of this officer at the taking of Worcester, that last stronghold for the King (in July, 1646), observes, " and truly I wish Colonell Rainborow a suitable employment by Sea or Land, for both which God hath especially fitted him ; foraine States would be proud of such a Servant."[*]   Resisting a seizure of his person on the part of the royalists, he was killed at Doncaster, 29 Oct. 1648, and buried at Wapping, 14 Nov. Administration on his estate was granted, 24 Nov., to his widow Margaret, maiden name probably Jenney.

1. *William,*[4] eldest son ; mentioned in wills of his grandfather 1638, and his uncle Edward 1677. He was a Captain in the army, it would appear, during the Protectorate, and judging from the Winthrop Letters (Mass. Hist. Soc. Col. 5, viii.) was in Boston, N. E., 1673 ; living 1687.

2. WILLIAM[3] RAINSBOROW (William,[2] Thomas[1]) ; mentioned in Savage's Geneal. Dic. as being of Charlestown, Mass. Col., 1639 ; Artillery Co. same year ; purchased 17 Dec. 1640, of Th. Bright, house and land in Watertown, which had been the homestall of Lt. Robt. Feake. Budington mentions his purchase of the old meeting-house. He was evidently a trader or sea-captain. March 7, 1643–4, the treasurer of the Colony was ordered to attend to the discharge of Mr. Rainsborow's debt, with allowance of £20 forbearance for the time past, and the loan of two sachars for two great pieces for one voyage. He had been in England in 1642, when in April his name, and that of his brother Thomas, are found on the list of the proposed Adventurers by Sea, against Ireland. This was the expedition against Galway, &c., whereof, under Lord Forbes, his brother Thomas was commander, and the Rev. Hugh Peters chaplain.

Judging from the discharge of his debt and the loan of cannon, Capt. R. again returned to the old country in 1643–4, and though there are subsequent entries as to the debt, the moneys are always to be paid to parties abroad on R.'s account. He immediately espoused the people's cause and joined that division of the army which was in the west under Lord Essex. Finding himself in a critical position, the Lord General despatched Stapleton, his General of Horse, to Parliament, calling for aid, and on the night of Aug. 30th, Sir William Balfour, his Lieut. General, passed safely through the King's Quarters with 2300 horse, and reached London. Two nights thereafter Essex himself and Lord Roberts fled in a cock-boat to Plymouth, and the following day, Sept. 2, 1644, the commanding officer, Serj. Major General Skippon, surrendered with all the infantry and a few horse. According to a return* found in the quarters of Sir Edward Dodsworth, Com. Gen. of the Horse, we find that the cavalry had previously mustered at Tiverton, co. Devon, 39 troops, 420 officers and 2785 men. The first division of 8 troops, 639 men, under Sir Philip Stapleton, Major Gen. Philip Skippon and Maj. Hamilton; the six troops of the second division (62 officers, 432 men), being commanded by Sir William Balfour, 14 officers, 100 men; Major Balfour, 9 officers, 77 men; Sir Samuel Luke (Gov. of Newport Paganel, co. Bucks), 10 officers, 72 men; Capt. Rainsborow, 9 officers, 57 men; Capt. Sample, 10 officers, 61 men; Capt. Boswell, 10 officers, 65 men.

Prestwich's "Republica" describes the cornet of Capt. Rainsborough's troop as follows: "Azure; from the sinister base point all over the base, and up to the middle of the dexter side, clouds Argent, shaded with black and crimson; near the middle or base, a book in pale closed and clasped and covered Or, on the front or side thus: $\frac{\text{VERBUM}}{\text{DEI}}$; between this book and the dexter side, and a little above the base, an armed arm and hand uplifted, as issuant from the clouds, and as in pale, holding in his hand a Hussar's sword as barrways, and waved on both sides, and the point burning and inflamed with fire proper, hilted Or; in chief a scroll, its end turned or doubled in, and then bent out and split, and fashioned double like two hooks, endorsed Argent, lined Or, and ends shaded with crimson and Argent, and in Roman capital letters Sable, VINCIT VERITAS. Arms.—Chequered Or and Azure, and in fess a Moor's head in profile, bearded and proper, his head banded with a wreath Argent."

In the list of officers for the New Model of the army, which was sent up from the House of Commons to the House of Lords, 3 March, 1644-5, and approved on the 18th, Col. Sheffield's squadron of horse consisted of his own troop and those of Major Sheffield and Captains Eveling, Rainsborow, Martin and Robotham. He subsequently obtained the rank of Major, and Whitelock informs us of letters received, July 2, 1647, from the Commissioners in the Army, certifying "that the General had appointed Lt. Gen. Cromwell, Cols. Ireton, Fleetwood, Rainsborough, Harrison, Sir Har. Waller, Richard Lambert and Hammond, and Major Rainsborough, or any five of them, to treat with the Parliament's Commissioners upon the papers sent from the Army to the Parliament, and their Votes."

From the Journals of the House of Commons, under date of 27 Sept. 1650, we read that "Mr. Weaver reports from the committee for suppressing lycentious and impious practices, under pretence of religious liberty, &c., the confession of Lawrence Clackson (or Claxton), touching the making and publishing of the impious and blasphemous booke called the 'Single Eye,' and also Major Rainsborrow's carriage" in countenancing the same. Claxton, departing from the established church, appears to have joined all the prominent sectaries of the day, and from a tract of his published in 1660, entitled "the Lost Sheep Found," we gather that much of his trouble and imprisonment resulted from his own licentious behavior, he maintaining that "to the pure all things are pure." He was sent to the house of correction for one month and then banished, and his book was burned by the common hangman. Major Rainsborough, residing at the time at Fulham, was one of his disciples, "and seems to have been an apt scholar in improving his relations with the female part of the flock."† It was resolved by the House that he be discharged and disabled of and from being and executing the office of Justice of Peace in co. Middlesex, or any other county within England or Wales.

For almost nine years we hear nothing of him, but on Tuesday, 19 July, 1659, he presented a petition to the House on behalf of the Sheriffs, Justices of the Peace and Gentry of the co. of Northampton, and on the same day was made a Commissioner for the Militia for the same county. In accordance with a report from said commissioners, he was appointed by Parliament, Aug. 9, Colonel of a Regiment of Horse in co. Northants.‡ After the Restoration, a warrant was issued, 17 Dec. 1660, to Lieut. Ward for the apprehension of Col. William Rainsborough at his residence, Mile End Green, Stepney (near London), or elsewhere, for treasonable designs, and to bring him before Secretary Sir Edward Nichols. He was accord-

---

* Symond's Diary of Marches, Camden Soc. Pub.
† Notes and Queries, 4th Series, xi. 487.
‡ In the limits of Charleton, parish of Newbottle, co. Northants, is a camp and hill commonly called "Rainsborough Hill," supposed to be of Danish origin.

ingly arrested and confined in the Gatehouse. On his examination next day he declared he was a Major of horse, but dismissed by Cromwell in 1649; that the Rump Parliament made him a Colonel of Militia-horse, 1659, but nothing was done; that he had bought 40 cases of pistols for militia, and had since tried to dispose of them. He gave bond for 500*l.*, Feb. 7, 1661, with Dr. Richard Barker of the Barbican as security for his good behavior.

His wife's name was Margery, and, as we have seen before, the will of Capt. Rowland Coytmore of Wapping, in 1626, mentions a son-in-law William Rainsborough, mariner, of Wapping; while the will of Stephen Winthrop, 1658, leaves a legacy to " cousin Mary Rainsborowe, daughter of my brother-in-law William Rainsborowe, Esq." From the Winthrop Letters (Mass. Hist. Soc. Coll. 5, viii.) he appears to have been in Boston, N. E., in 1673, with his nephew William.

3.   MARTHA,[3] bapt. at Whitechapel, 20 April, 1617; married at Wapping, 14 June, 1635, Thomas Coytmore,* son of Capt. Rowland Coytmore, an East India trader. He came to N. England next year and was wrecked, 27 Dec. 1644, on the coast of Spain, leaving issue. Her second husband, whom she married 4 Dec. 1647, was Gov. John Winthrop, to whom she was fourth wife; he died 26 March, 1649, aged 61. She married thirdly, 10 March, 1652, John Coggan of Boston, as his third wife; he died 27 April, 1658, leaving issue. Disappointed of a fourth marriage, we are given to understand that she committed suicide in 1660.

4.   JUDITH,[3] bapt. at Wapping, 14 Sept. 1624; married about 1644, Stephen Winthrop, son of Gov. John W., born 24 March, 1619. He returned to England 1645, became a Colonel of Horse under Parliament, receiving 474*l.* 10*s.* per annum, and in 1656 was M.P. for Banff and Aberdeen. Resided at time of decease in James Street, Westminster. His will of 3 May, proved 19 Aug. 1658, mentions three daughters, Margaret, Joanna and Judith, as before given. She is mentioned 1668, in her uncle Thomas's will.

5.   SAMUEL,[3] b.   ob. infs.; buried at Wapping, 24 Nov. 1628.

6.   JOANE,[3] b.   ; m. John Chamberlain, a captain under Parliament; living in May, 1687, a brewer at Deptford, co. Kent. She is mentioned 1668 in her uncle Thomas's will. The will of S. Winthrop, 1658, mentions their daughter Judith.

7.   REYNOLD,[3] bapt. at Whitechapel, 1 June, 1632.

8.   EDWARD,[3] bapt. at Whitechapel, 8 Oct. 1633. Richard Wharton, writing from Boston, N. E., Sept. 24, 1673, to a kinsman of rank and influence in England, suggests that his Majesty should send out two or three frigates, by the ensuing February or March, with some 300 soldiers, for the recapture of New York from the Dutch. That the expedition should be assisted by a colonial force, the whole to be under the command of some native leader, such as Maj. Gen. Daniel Dennison. He continues: " for a more certain knowledge of the constitutions of o[r] government & complexions of the people I refer you to M[r] Edw[d] Rainsborough an intellig[t] Gentleman who went home three months since. I have requested him to wait on you & communicate w[t] I have advised him. .... M[r] Rainsborough dwells at Knights bridge & is to be heard of at M[r] Whiting's shop upon the old Exchange."† He appears to be the same party whose will runs as follows: Edward Rainborow of Cranford, co. Middlesex, gentleman; Sept. 14, 1677 (proved May 4, 1682), being in good health, but going beyond the seas, do make this my last will, &c. Bequeaths to his wife Christian one fourth of all his real and personal estate during her life. To his dear friend Mary Alcock, widow, for and in consideration of a very considerable sum of money for which he stands indebted to her, one fourth part of his real and personal estate either in England or N. England, during her life; one eighth part to be at her absolute disposal. To son Mytton Rainborow one fourth of all his real and personal estate when twenty-one years of age. To daughter Judith Rainborow one fourth of his real and personal estate until her brother Mytton shall enjoy that part which is given to his mother and also the

---

* Katherine, daughter of Thomas and Martha Quoitmore, bapt. at Wapping, 13 April, and buried 19 April, 1636.

† Hist. Mag., 1867, p. 299.

eighth part given to Mary Alcock. To his nephew William Rainsborow five pounds to buy him a ring. Appoints his wife's sister, Mrs. Sarah Mackworth of Shrewsbury, and Mrs. Mary Alcock of Cranford, executors.—*Book Cottle,* folio 62.

Concerning the New England estate referred to by Edward Rainsborowe in his will of 1677, as above, we have evidence on file in the Registry of Deeds, Salem, of which the following is a summary : Whereas Judith Winthrop and John Chamberlain, two of the Executors of Stephen Winthrop deceased, had by certain deeds of Indenture, Bargain & Sale conveyed to Edward Rainsburrowe of London, merchant, all those parcells of lands lying & being in N. England in America, viz : one moiety of Prudence Island, lying in or near yᵉ bay of Narragansett, in Rhode Island Colony, and all that Farm at Lynn or Salem, containing by estimation 1500 acres more or less, now, considering the great hazard of transmitting ye conveyances beyond sea, the said Executors do acknowledge before a notary public the said deeds of bargain and sale, 21 April, 1671. The document was signed in presence of Nich. Hayward, Not. Pub., Symon Amory, Timᵒ Prout senʳ, and his son Wᵐ Prout. Timothy Prout, shipwright of Boston, testified to the same before Dep. Gov. John Leverett, 5 Mar. 1672-3, and the instrument was recorded and compared 5 July following. As late as 21 March, 1695-6, the above was compared with the original and found an exactly true copy of ye record in ye booke of Deeds Lib: 8ᵒ Page 195.

Meanwhile John Chamberlain, the sole surviving executor of Stephen Winthrop deceased, having been shown a copy of the instrument above referred to, as being on file in some court in N. England, made oath 31 May, 1687, that he had never signed nor executed any such writing or instrument, nor did he believe that Judith Winthrop, widow & executrix, had made any such conveyance to the late Edward Rainsburrow. This testimony of Mr. Chamberlain appears to have been given at the request of his nephew William[4] Rainsburrowe, son of Vice Adm. Thomas[3] Rainsburrowe, being, we may infer, at the time the only, or at least the eldest, male representative of the family, and acting in the interest of his cousins the children of Stephen Winthrop deceased. Robert Wildey, of the parish of St. Paules Peters, co. Middlesex, cook, and "Thomasine Jenney, of the same place spinster, aunt of ye said William Rainsburrowe," swore to their knowledge of and acquaintance with John Chamberlayn for thirty years and upwards last past ; that he and Stephen Winthrop, Esq., whom they had also known, had married two sisters, "both these deponent William Rainsburrow's Aunts, and sisters of Edward Rainsburrow in ye above written affidavit named, &c. &c." Nicholas Hayward, the Notary Public, mentioned in the first instrument, swore that he had never drawn up such a paper, and the whole denial was witnessed by four parties on the point of departure from London for New England, and was also compared with the original about nine years later, viz : 21 March, 1695-6.   I. J. GREENWOOD.]

EDMUND SPINCKES of Warmington in the County of Northampton, clerk, 2 October 1669, proved 11 August 1671. I give out of that seven hundred & fifty pounds which will be due to me or mine from the heirs or executors or administrators of Thomas Elmes of Lilford Esq. (after the decease of himself the said Thomas Elmes and the Lady Jane Compton), to my eldest son Nathaniel Spinckes one hundred pounds, to Seth, my second son, one hundred and fifty pounds, to William, my third son, one hundred & fifty pounds, to Elmes, my fourth son, one hundred & fifty pounds, and to Martha, my only daughter, two hundred pounds. To Nathaniel Spinckes, my eldest son & heir, all that land in Ireland, in King's County, which is now in the possession of the heirs or assigns of Thomas Vincent sometimes alderman of London, which is due to me according to a writing signed by him to that purpose 6 March 1642. Item I give to the said Nathaniel Spinckes all that fifty pounds, more or less, with the profit of it, that is now in the Iron works in New England, acknowledged received by John Pocock then Steward of the Company and living then in London, his Acquittance bearing date March 19ᵗʰ 1645. Item, I give to the said my son Nathaniel all that estate whatsoever it be that falleth to me or shall fall in New England, as joint heir with John Nayler of Boston in Lincolnshire, clerk, to Boniface Burton, now or late of Boston in New England, my uncle and mother's brother and only brother; also my library of books, only such excepted as his mother shall choose out for her own use. To Seth Spinckes, my second son, five pounds at the age of twenty-four years, to William five pounds at twenty-four, to Elmes five pounds at twenty-four and to Martha, my only daughter, five pounds at twenty-four. All the rest to my wife Martha, whom I appoint sole executrix. My loving friend Mr. Saml Morton, clerk & rector of the parish church of Haddon, in the County of Huntingdon, and my much respected cousin Mr Richard Conyer, clerk and rector of Long Orton and Butolph-Bridge in the County of Huntingdon, to be overseers. A schedule to be annexed to the said will &c. that Seth shall have paid him out of the estate that my father Elmes left my wife &c. &c. (So of all the other children.)

18 May 1693   Emanavit commissio Nathanieli Spinckes, clerico, filio et administratori Marthæ Spinckes defunctæ &c. &c.   Duke, 107.

[I presume that this is the "Edmond Spinckes" whose name immediately precedes that of John Harvard in the *Recepta ab ingredientibus* of Emmanuel College (REGISTER, xxxix. 103).

Boniface Burton, whom Mr. Spinckes calls his mother's only brother, died June 13, 1669, "aged 113 years," according to Judge Sewall, who calls him "Old Father Boniface Burton" (REG. vii. 206). Hull in his Diary (Trans. Am. Antiq. Society, iii. 279) gives his age as "a hundred and fifteen years." Both ages are probably too high. Burton's will was dated Feb. 21, 1666-7, and proved June 24, 1669. An abstract of the will is printed in the REGISTER, xx. 241, and on page 242 are some facts in his history. He left nothing to the family of Mr. Spinckes nor to John Nayler. After bequests to Increase Mather, to his niece Mrs. Bennet, her husband Samuel Bennet and their children, Burton leaves the rest of his property to his wife Frances Burton.

For an account of the Iron Works in which Mr. Spinckes had an interest, see "Vinton Memorial," pp. 463-74. John Pococke is named among the undertakers. —EDITOR.]

NOTES AND DOCUMENTS CONCERNING HUGH PETERS.

Communicated by G. D. SCULL, Esq., of London, England.

[Continued from page 31.]

NOTES.

AT the meeting held 22nd of *April*, 1644, attention was called to the despoiling of his Majesty's palace of Holderby in Northamptonshire, and summons were directed to five or six persons to appear and answer. Robert Eyre Innholder, especially in Holderby was to render account for "certain bookes, papers, writings, records or copies that are in his custody."

10th *June*, 1664—"a charge made against ye persons undernamed—Mr Benjamin morley in partnership with one Smyth and Hall a spiny grove—six acres—60£—a length of buildings 25£—a myle and a halfe of ye parke pailing—20£, John Wills for stone and tymber of Holderby house used about his owne house—4£—John Jay for divers materialls valued at 6£—John Stanley for divers materials 6£—John Hill for severall materialls 12£ 10s. 0—in all 133£ 10s. 0 for which ye Committee demand ye full value."

20 *July*, 1664. The several persons undermentioned having possessed

themselves of divers parcels of tymber belonging to his Majesty's parkes of Clarendon and Bowood in Co. Wilts—the several persons named are summoned to make satisfaction and appear at Denmark house (London) ye 5 *day October* 1664. To Jaspar Townesend—To " Sellers—Wm Ball—Richd King—Hugh Webb—Jon Wills—Jo^n Preter—Jo^n Norman."

Tho° Barnard—M^r Th° Nipp—and Widdow Chapman of Petsworth Sussex are summoned (1. Augt 1664) for having possession of some plate. Mr Boardman at Drury Lane has a marble head, he is ord^d to deliver it to Geo. Sherley, Messenger (11 *Nov^r* 1664). Also 16 *Nov^r* 1664. It is ordered by the said Com^tee that Elias Ashmole be desired to re-deliver ye picture of the late King on horseback now in his custody unto Mr Rhemy unles the s^d Mr Rhemy doe agree to pay for divers pictures belonging to his maj^y in his Custody ye summe of 200£ in money or ye like value in pictures but wth this proviso that before ye said picture be re-delivered he is to appeare & to give good & sufficient baile to answer to such accts as shall be brought against him in his maj^ties name for ye recovery of sattisfaction according to law."   Signed JOAN SINGLETON, Clerk.

Some time before his execution Hugh Peters issued a little pamphlet, " the case of Hugh Peters &c." * in which he corrects various evil reports about himself " as basely and Scandalously suggested by black mouths." It thus commences: " They which think to Vindicate themselves to the World by writing Apologies, rarely reach their ends, because their Game is an after game; prejudice is strong and the Plaister can hardly be made broad enough, nor apologies put into all hands who have pre-judged and received the first tincture." .... " I shall briefly give an account of my coming into England, my behaviour since I Came, and my present condition in this Juncture. A colony going to settle in New England by his Majesties Patent, I went thither; who by my birth in Cornwel was not a meer stranger in that place, and fishing trade; and thither invited often, I say, went, and was with another sent into England by the Majistrates there, for ease and Excise in Custom, and some supplies for Learning &c., because I had been witness to the Indians receiving the Gospel there in Faith and Practice; they having the Bible translated by us into their Language, and part thereof printed and hundreds of them professing the Gospel and teaching each other the Knowledge of the true God, and the rather, from the example of the English there, when in seven years among thousands there dwelling, I never saw any drunk, nor heard an Oath, nor any begging, nor Sabbath broken; all which invited me over to England; but Coming, found the Nation imbroyled in troubles and War; the Preaching was, Curse ye Meroz, from Scotland to England; the best ministers going into the field; in which (not without urging) I was imbarqued in time; and by force upon me here, failed of my promise of returning home; which was and is my sad affliction. My first work was, with the first to go for Ireland; which I did with many hazards, then was at Sea with my old Patron the Earl of Warwick, to whom I ow'd my life; then was imploy'd by the City; then by the Earl of Essex, my Lord Say, and others; and my return stopt by the Power that was; and so was in the last army in several places, but never in the North: In all which affairs I did labour to perswade the Army to their duty. My Principles in Religion guided me to those Orthodox truths exprest in the Confession of Faith in England; and am known to joyn

* The Case of Mr Hugh Peters, Impartially Communicated to the Vievv and Censure of the Whole World, written by his own hand. London. Printed for Sam. Speed, and are to to be sold at his shop, at the Signe of the Printing-Press in St Pauls Church-yard. (8 pp.)

with the Protestants who are found in the Faith, in Germany upper and lower, France &c. I have and do hereby witness against all Errours of all kinds. For the War, I thought the Undertakers their Work; I was inconsiderable, yea, heartily sorry for mistakes about me. For my Carriage, I challenge all the Kings party to speak if I were uncivil; nay, many of them had my Purse, Hand Help every way, and are ready to witness it; yea, his present Majesties servants preserved by me through hazards. I. was never privy to the Armies transactions about the late King at Holmby or elsewhere, or of any Juncto, Council or Cabal. But when his majesty sent for me, I went to him, with whom I dealt about my New England business, &c. was three or four times with him, and had his special acceptance, and served him to my utmost, and used all my little skill for his and the Nations good more than twice; for which I have witness; though it be hard to cut my   through so many Rocks. But God is good. It is true, I was of a Party, when I acted zealously, but not with malice or mischief: it hath been accounted honourable, Et Cæsare in hoste probat, to keep to principles of honour and honesty. I never quarrelled others for their judgement in Conscience. It is received, that Religio docenda est, non coercenda. I saw Reformation growing, Laws made, and some against debauchery and evil (which I was glad to read in his Majesties late Proclamation). I saw a very learned, godly, able Ministry as any the world, well provided for; I saw the Universities reformed and flourishing; and such things much encouraged me in my Endeavours. I studied the 13 of the Rom and was tender; but found the best of Scotland and England of the ministry engaged and so satisfied me, that I understand the first undertaking is still maintained good. By the War, I never enriched myself ; I have often offered my personal Estate for 200£ and for Lands, I never had any but that part of a noblemans, which I never laid up penny of; nor never urged the Lord Grey, or others, to buy, nor knew not of the sale till done, nor justifie any unworthy thing in it. I never plundered nor cheated, never made penny over the Sea, nor hoarded or hid any in England. I never was guilty of Secluding the Members in 48, nor knew it, till done, and sent by my Lord Fairfax to fetch off two of them, and to know who they were that were secluded. I never had Jewels, nor anything of Court or State, more then before, directly nor indirectly. Never had any Ecclesiastical Promotion in my life in the Nation to enrich me; but lived on my own when I had anything; nor have been a lover of money. The many scandals upon me for uncleanness &c., I abhor as vile and false, being kept from that and those aspersions cast, and such I make my protest against as before. I know how low my name runs, how Titleless, how contemned. *David* knew why *Shemei* curst him. For the Laws of England, I know no place hath better; onely having lived where things are more expedite and cheap, I have shewed my folly so to say : and having no evil intention, a very worthy Lawyer took exception at something of mine or my friends; which was never intended in his sense by either, and crave his excuse; I can charge myself with evil enough, as any excentrick notion of mine from my own Calling, want of a solemn spirit in slight times, with unbelief, if I have gone about to reach Religious ends by trampling upon Civil duties, breaking of any Covenants, or slighting them; and do fear Gospel, and the Spirit also may be undervalued by mine and others unworthy dealing with them. Much to these I might add, who have seen many vanities under the Sun ; and the World hung with Nets and Snares: Alas, there is nothing to Christ.

" And lastly, I understand what exception is upon me for Life and Estate in the House of Commons. I have taken hold of the Kings Majesties gracious Pardon, as others did ; and know not truly where this exception lies grounded. I wish I had been with their Honours to have clear'd it. I hope a Vagrant report or Airy noise takes no place with them: for I challenge all the World for my innocence for these suggestions; and appeal to their Honours, and the noble Lords for a review of the Charge or Information ; and crave no favour if any sober man can charge me; otherwise I most heartily beg just favour, unless my evil be only for acting with such a party, I must have it ; For I know before whom my Cause is, and may not despair.

" I must again profess were I not a Christian, I am a Gentleman by birth, and from that extract do scorn to engage in the vile things suggested, and that by one creditless witness, that only supposeth, but asserts nothing.

" I wish from my heart that our present Prince may be, and the Nation by him more happy then any ; and that the true ends of *Government* may be had and communicated fully ; that every honest heart may have cause to rejoyce in God, the King, and their Laws. And for my self (through Grace) I resolve to be quiet in a corner (if I may) to let God alone with ruling the World, to whose Wisdom and Power we ought to submit ; yea to mind mine own work, though never so small ; to be passive under Authority, rather than impatient ; to procure the quiet and peace of the Nation to my utmost ; to mind things invisible, and Of a better consistence then these below ; and to pray, when I can do no more.   HUGH PETERS."

Hugh Peters to Capt. Allen.

Capt. Allen. I have received yʳˢ and I have advis'd your friends what were best viz to come home upon sight hereof because the act of oblivion takes place till ffeb. 3ᵈ, and come directly to me to Whitehall and I shall further advise you. wishing the Lord may doe you good at the heart,
   24 Jan: | 52.   Yʳ loving friend   HUGH PETERS.

Endorsed—ffor my loving friend Capᵗ Thoˢ: allen.

[To be continued.]

PAPERS IN EGERTON MS. 2395.

Communicated by HENRY F. WATERS, A.M., now residing in London, Eng.

THE following is an account of some of the papers contained in a volume of Egerton MSS. (No. 2395) British Museum. This volume was purchased at Sotheby's, 16 Feb. 1875, being No. 1149 of sale catalogue and entered as follows : WEST INDIES (STATE PAPERS RELATING TO).—A VOLUME CONTAINING SEVERAL HUNDREDS OF ORIGINAL PAPERS, PETITIONS, PATENTS, MEMORIALS, DESCRIPTIONS, LETTERS AND OTHER DOCUMENTS TRANSMITTED TO THE LORDS OF THE COUNCIL OF STATE AND PRIVY COUNCIL, DURING THE REIGNS OF THE COMMONWEALTH AUTHORITIES AND KING CHARLES THE SECOND, RELATIVE TO THE PLANTATIONS AND SET-

TLEMENTS IN THE WEST INDIES, JAMAICA, CARIBBEE ISLANDS, NEW ENGLAND, VIRGINIA, NEWFOUNDLAND, AND NOVA SCOTIA, large folio, *rough calf*, 25*l.* Then follows a summary of the contents. In the following list I undertake to give a somewhat fuller account of the papers relating especially to Nova Scotia, New England and Virginia, taking them in the order in which I find them in the volume. The numbers affixed to each paper indicate the folios, as marked by the Museum authorities.*

17.—Oct: 16th 1629.—Articles d'accord entre le Chevalier Guillaume Alexandre Seignr de Menstrie Lieutnt de la Nouvelle Escoss en Amerique par sa Matie de la Grande Bretagne, et le Chevalr Claude de St Estienne Seignr de la Tour, et Charles de St Estienne son filz, et le Chevlr Guillaume Alexandre filz audt Seignr Alexandre by dessus nome.

18.—Copy of a Lre from the Councill of Scotland concerning His Matys Title and Right to New Scotland.—Dated at Halyrudhouse 9th Sept 1630.

19.—Report made to His Maty of the Commodities of the Plantation of Canada. Novr 24th 1630.

20-21.—His Maties Right & Title to Port Royall.

22.—Propositions and Considerations for the busines of Canada.

23.—Sr William Alexanders Information touching his Plantation at Cape Breton & Port Reall.

24.—An Extract of the Patent granted to Sr Wm Alexander &c. concerning Canada.—5 March 1630.

25-25*.—Remembrances concerning the patent graunted to Sr William Alexander, George Kirk Esqr., Capt: Kirke, William Barkley and Company, for the sole trade into the Gulfe and River of Canada, and for a plantacon there: wch is opposed by my Lord Starling and his Sonne the said Sr William Alexander.

26.—Treatie concern' Kebeck, &c.

27-29.—Quo Warranto against the Massachusetts 1635. [Printed in the REGISTER, xxxviii. 210-16.]

36.—Letter from his Maty concerning Lady Hopkins, Dated Newport Novembr 11th 1648: ; addressed to Sr David Kirke; beginning—" Yor sister my Lady Hopkins wth her family having occasion to visit you in Newfoundland— "; and signed (in his own handwriting) " Your frend Charles R."

199-201.—Queries and Objections agst the Massachusetts encroaching power upon several other propriaties.

258.—Letter of the Lady (Sara) Kirke to His Majesty.

259-261.—A Narrative made by the latt Sr Dauid Kirke Knight and Governor concerning Newfoundland.

262.—The Peticon of John Treworgey Comander of the Colony of this Nation in Newfound land.

263-4.—Report concerning Newfoundland upon Lady Hopkins Information,—by Thos Povey, May 11th 1660.

* This list was prepared by Mr. Waters and sent to the Committee in the year 1884. It is thought that the cause of historical research will be advanced by printing it in the REGISTER. Some of the documents have already appeared in these pages from transcripts made by Mr. Waters and Mr. Scull. The volumes and pages where these documents are printed are given in brackets. Other documents in this list, of which copies are found in other collections of manuscripts, have been printed elsewhere, particularly in the New York Colonial Documents and Hutchinson's Collection of Papers. Mr. Waters has transcribed other papers from Egerton MS. No. 2395, which are now in the hands of the Committee, and will in due time appear in the REGISTER.—EDITOR.

265.—Record of " Councell of State at Whitehall" (concerning New-foundland) "Thursday the xvii[th] of May 1660."

266. 1660.—The infformation and relation of the Lady Hopkings who came porposely ffrom Newfoundland to macke knowne to his Royall Maj[ty].

296.—Letter from M[r] Povey concerning the naturall products of Virginia in behalf of the Royall Society; March 4, 1660.

297–8.—Enquiryes concerning those severall kind of things which are reported to be in Virginia & ye Bermudas, not found in England.

299–300.—Report of the Councill for forreigne Plantations, concerning the Encroachm[ts] of the Massachusetts Colony. [1661.]

308.—Letter to M[r] John Kirke from Charles Hill, Ferryland, 12 Sept. 1661, " concerning L[d] Baltemores interest in Newfoundland."

309.—Testimony of W[m] Wrixon & others concerning the same.

310.—The Lord Baltemore's Case, concerning the Province of Avalon in New-Found-Land, an Island in America (a printed broadside).

311–323.—Copies of certain Papers relating to Nova Scotia; comprising

(1) Indenture, made before Josue Mainet Royal Notary living in London, 30 April 1630, between Sir William Alexandre Knight Lord of Menstrie & Principal Secretary of State of the Kingdome of Scotland for his s[d] Ma[ty] of Great Britain & Counsellor of His Council of State, & Lieutenant for His Ma[ty] in New Scotland in America on the one part (referring to a royal grant to him of the country of Lacadie, bearing date of the 10th of the month of September, in the year one thousand six hundred & twenty one) and Sir Claude de Saint Estienne Knight Lord of la Tour & of Vuarre, & Charles de Saint Estienne Esq[r] Lord of S[t] Denicourt his son on the other part. (Translated into English 1 Feb. 1655.)

(2) Indenture, made 20 Sept. 1656, between Sr Charles St Stephen Lord of La Tour Barronet of Scotland of the one part, and Thomas Temple and William Crowne esq[res] of the other part. (Entered and recorded in the book of Records for the County of Suffolk in N. E.)

(3) Test. of Robert Howard Not: publ: Massachusitt: Coloniæ novæ Angliæ:, Boston 1 August 1678.

(4) Historical account of the " Restitution of Acadie," by the Ambassador of France.

(5) An Answer to the French Ambassadours Claime to the Forts and Country in America Exhibited in the behalfe of the Lord La Tour, Temple and Crowne, Proprietors.

324–5.—Extract from severall pieces relateing to the Title to Nova Scotia (ranging from 1606 to 1656).

326–7.—An Account of Nova Scotia or Acadia.

328.—Memoriall of the French Amb[r] about the restitution of part of Acade to Mon[sr] le Borgne.—Read in Councill 27 Nov[r] 1661.

335–6.—The Draught of a Letter to Virginia from the Council of Trade and Plantations.

340–1.—Minutes from the Records of the Privy Council at Whitehall relating to Nova Scotia, dated 26 Feb. & 7 March 1661 and 23 April 1662, referring to petitions of S[r] Lewis Kirke K[nt] John Kirke Esq[r] and others of the one part, and of Coll: Thomas Temple in his own behalf. The business of the last meeting was a grant of the Government of Nova Scotia &c. to Col. Thomas Temple during life.

354–9.—A " Treatise of S[r] W[m] Berkley," said to be " in Print," entitled a Discourse and View of Virginia.

360–1.—(Copy of) Letter of 28 March 1663 from William Berkley, Francis Morryson, Tho: Ludwell, Secr:, Richard Lee, Nathaniel Bacon, Ab: Wood, John Carter, Edward Carter, Theodo: Blande, Thomas Stegge and Henry Corbyn, referring to a royal grant made " Sep^t the 18th in the first year of his Reigne," to the Lord Hopton and others of a tract of land " between the two Rivers of Petomake and Rappahanoke," &c.

362–4.—(Copy of) Letter of Sr Wm Berkley, 30 March 1663, in which the following is found : " let mee therefore only begg this, that your Lordship would desire the King to send over one or two Gentlemen, that he can trust, that may truly report to his Maj^ty what a growing Empire he has here, in which all the Plantations in the West Indies beginn to center, for hither from all p̃ts they come : Two hundred ffamilies from new England wee hear are seated a little to the South of us : Continuall Letters from the Barbadoes tell us of ffamilies that if they can gett leave to depart thence will settle here : "—Reference is made to " My cozen Norwood."

365.—(Copy of) A letter from the same, dated 18 April 1663, ending as follows : " My Lord I have sent by one Captain Willy forty-nine pieces of black Walnut Trees ; they will wainscott 5 or 6 Roomes ; wch I beseech your Lordshipp may be called the Virginia Chambers. I hope this next year to send your Lordshipp a Hogshead of Virginia wine, for the last year, I drank as good of my own planting as ever came out of Italy : My Dear Lord, for ever I am Your Lo^pps most humble obedient servant," &c.

366–7.—(Copy of) Letter from Anthony Langston relating to the condition and needs of Virginia and especially the need of Iron Works. This bears no date.

368–9.—Computation of an Iron Work in Virginia.

387–92.—Instructions to the Royal Commissioners appointed to visit the Colony of the Massachusetts, 23 April 1664.

393–5.—Similar Instructions to the same for the Visitation of the Colony of Connecticut.

396.—Mem. of Import^t Points for the Settlem^t of New England.

397–411.—A Briefe discription of New England, &c. [Printed in the REGISTER, xxxix. 33–48.]

412–13.—The Names of the Rivers and the names of ye cheife Sagamores y^t inhabit upon them from the River of Quibequissue to the River of Wenesquawam.

414–24.—Certain Notes and Informations concerning New England.

425.—Proposalls for New England (signed by James Bollen).

426–34.—Reports of the Royal Commissioners, in 1665.

435.—A list of certain magistrates and prisoners.

436–41.—" 30 May 1665. A letter from the Governour of New England with affidavits," &c. (concerning the Northern Limits of the Massachusetts Colony).

442.—Royal Letter to the King's Commissioners, of 10 April 1666.

447.—(Copy of) Petition of De Belleville and others, householders & Inhabitants of ye Province of Avilonie & other harbours adjacent to ye same Continent,"—" March ye 18, 1666 "—addressed " To the Honorable George Kirke Esquier—& one of the Lords Propriators of Newfoundland."

448.—Original Order of the Privy Council, 30 August 1667, " to the Com^tee concern^g the rendition of places in America."

449–50.—Original Order of the Privy Council, 2 Oct. 1667, appointing " ffriday next the 4th instant," for a meeting of the Comittee for the Affayres of New-England, with a rough list of the said Committee attached.

451–53.—Directions for the boundinge of l'Acadie. In order to the Restitution thereoff to the French.—With Notes evidently made at the meeting of the Committee, 4 Oct. 1667.

454.—An Acompt of the Bound[e] of Acada Noua Scosia and Penobscott. Delivered by M[r] Newdigate 18 7[br] 67.

471.—M[r] Matthews testificacon concerning Newfound Land given in y[e] 28th of Jan: (70).

496.—S[r] W[m] Berkeley's copy of proceedings " At a General Court held at James Citty the 21th day of November 1674, in the matter of a complaint made by Tho: Ludwell Secretary of State against M[r] Giles Bland, by whom the complaint avers that he was " abused, and called pittifull fellow, Puppy, and son of a whore." " contrary to the Laws of Hospitality and Human Society;"—and the further complaint " that the said Bland taking one of his gloves, without his knowledge or consent, did ignominiously, presumtuously and unworthily nayl the same up at the State House doore with a most false and scandalous Libel, which contained these words, That the Owner of that glove was a son of a whore, mechanic fellow, puppy, and a coward," &c.

497–8.—" Draught of a Lett[r] frō his Ma[tie] to the Corporatiō of Boston in New Engl[d] ab[t] New Hamp & Maine, Deb[r] 18: 1674." Also " A Draught of his Ma[ties] pleasure to be signified upon the Petition of Ferdinando Gorge and Robert Mason."

511–14.—Letter from M[r] Bland to y[e] Gov: of Virginia concerning ye execution of his Office as Collector of the Customs in Virginia. Dated at Bartlett Sept[r] 16th 75.

515–16.—Lrē from M[r] Bland concerning the suspention of his Office, Bonds & Certificate of Ships.

517.—M[r] Blands Case as Collector of the Customs of Virginia.

518–19.—Extract of a letter from New England concern[g] y[e] Indian Warr. 1675. [Printed in the REGISTER, xxxviii. 381–2.]

520–1.—Pages 9 to 12 inclusive of a printed work giving an account of " the Battel with the Indians on the 19th of *November*, 1675, with a List of the English slain & wounded. The last paragraph is as follows:—" Time, the consumer of all things, we hope will once more subject this Adversary. *Amen*."

522.—This Account of New-England—1675. [Printed in the REGISTER, xxxviii. 379–80.]

539.—Proclamation by the Governor and Captain General of Virginia, 10 May 1676, referring to the Indian War in New England. Endorsed " Virginia News," " S[r] W[m] Berkeley's Declaration, 1676."

540.—Another Proclamation (1676) dissolving the present Assembly and ordering a grand assembly to be held at James city in June next.

541.—The Copy of M[r] Bacon's Letter sent by mee May the 25th 1676. (Signed Nath: Bacon.)

542–3.—A copy of a Description of the Fight in Virginia May 1676.

544.—A copy of " The humble appeale of y[e] Volunteers to all well minded and charitable men."

445–6.—The Virginians Plea for opposing the Indians without the Governor's Order, &c.

547–9.—A copy of " The Declaration of y[e] People ag[t] S[r] W[m] Berkeley, and present Govern[r] of Virginia. (Signed by Nathaniell Bacon, Generall by the Consent of the People.)

550–1.—(1) A copy of M[rs] Bacon's letter, the wife of Nathaniell Bacon in

Virginia, June ye 29th 76, sent to her sister & received the 26th of Septemb^r 1676 concerning a murder committed by the Indians.

(2) Mr Birds relation, who lived nigh to Mr Bacon in Virginia, and came from thence in July last, for feare of the Indians.

(3) Mr Bacon's Acc^t of their troubles in Virginia by ye Indians, June ye 18th 1676.

552–3.—A copy of the Declaration of the chief psons in Virginia, touching their Adherency to Bacon. Aug: 76. (With the list of names of the signers.)

555.—A copy of Mr Giles Blands Letter to Mr Povey. Received Aug: 28. 76.—Concerning grievances at Virginia, written 8th July.

560–3.—(Copy of) A Breif Narrative concerning New-found-land, by John Downing. Recd 24th 9^ber 1676.

564.—Other notes on the same, 14th Dec. 1676, signed J^o Downing.

565–6.—A description, by the same, of " The maner of Catching and makeing drie fishe " there.

573.—A List of all Books (in the Plantation Office) Treating of New England. [Printed in the REGISTER, xxxviii. 261–2.]

593–4.—Lett^r to Mr Lewen at New York concern^g Mr Pen's Patent.

595–6.—Copy of Mr Randolph's Queries and R. Sawyer's opinion thereon.

601.—A rough account of the History of New York & affairs there.

661–5.—Proposals in order to the Improvement of the County of Albemarle in Carolina in point of Towns, Trade & Coyne. By George Milner.

666–7.—(1) Proposalls concerning building of Towns in Virginia.

(2) Proposals concerning the Custome of Tobacco.

670.—An account of all the trading Townes and Ports lying upon the Sea & navigable riuers, wth number of Houses in euery Towne. (New England.) [Printed in the REGISTER, xxxviii. 380–1.]

671.—Petition of Lyonell Copley & others, concerning the Iron Works. [Printed in the REGISTER, xxxviii. 378–9.]

672–6.—(1) Proposition de Louis Le Page.

(2) Description des Lacs nouvellement descouverts à la Source du Fleuve de St Laurent. (Evidently addressed to the King of France.)

JOHN HARVARD.

Communicated by JOHN T. HASSAM, A.M., of Boston.

THE interest excited by Mr. Waters's researches in England is not confined to those who speak the English language. The following editorial from the Paris journal " La Renaissance " of September 4th, 1885, shows that some of the results of these researches are becoming known on the other side of the English Channel. The ignorance of French writers about everything that takes place outside of the limits of their own country is proverbial, and this ignorance is never more conspicuously displayed than when they undertake to treat of American or English matters. Of course there are exceptions to this rule. This editorial, however, barring some inaccuracies, is otherwise remarkably free from errors, and shows an appreciation and knowledge of the subject which is most unusual in a Frenchman.

Harvard did not give to the College " toute sa fortune," nor has his " acte de mariage" as yet been found, and " Elève d'Oxford" he certainly was not. But these mistakes serve to give the true Gallic stamp to the article which is here reprinted verbatim.

HARVARD.—Le nom que nous venons d'écrire, aussi connu en Amérique que ceux de Washington, de Franklin ou de La Fayette, n'est probablement pas inconnu de nos lecteurs. Ils savent sans doute que le plus ancien et plus célèbre des établissements d'instruction des Etats-Unis, s'appelle *Harvard collège* et que le mot collège ne doit pas être pris ici dans le sens qu'il a en français. Harvard n'est aucunement un lycée, un établissement d'instruction secondaire, c'est une université que les américains comparent, à bon droit, bien quelle soit de création plus récente, aux vieilles universités d'Oxford et de Cambridge.

D'où vient ce nom de Harvard? C'est celui d'un pasteur puritain, John de son prénom, qui en mourant, en 1638, légua à un collège, dont la création avait été décrétée deux ans auparavant, toute sa fortune, y compris une bibliothèque de 300 volumes, ce qui représentait une somme deux fois supérieure à la subvention votée par la colonie du Massachusetts pour la création projetée. Ces ressources imprévues amenèrent l'ouverture immédiate de cet établissement, Harvard College, le Collège de Harvard, situé à New Cambridge, près de Boston, qui bientôt devint célèbre et a fourni à la République américaine bon nombre de ses hommes les plus éminents, dans toutes les branches de l'activité humaine.

Le nom de John Harvard, lié pour toujours à l'université la plus célèbre du Nouveau Monde, est depuis plus de deux siècles dans toutes les bouches, mais le nom seul était connu, l'homme ne l'était nullement; on ne savait à peu près rien de son origine, ni de sa carrière, et quand on avait dit de lui: c'était un pasteur, puritain d'opinions, qui mourut en 1638, on avait tout dit. Cet inconnu vient de trouver son Christophe Colomb, un laborieux et sagace investigateur, M. Henry F. Watters, vient de publier dans le *New England Historical et Genealogical Register*, numéro de juillet, un article intitulé " John Harvard et ses ancêtres" qui a fait sensation. M. Waters a été assez heureux pour pouvoir mettre la main sur des actes de baptême, de mariage, de décès, ainsi que sur dix testaments qui permettent de suivre dans sa rapide carrière, brusquement terminée par la maladie à l'âge de trente-un ans, son jeune et sympathique héros. Il ressort de ces différentes pièces que John Harvard naquit à Southwarck, Londres, où il fut baptisé le 29 novembre 1607, qu'il était fils d'un boucher dont le nom, à une époque où l'on était très indifférent aux questions d'orthographe, s'écrivait tantôt Harvye, tantôt Harverd, tantôt et plus souvent Harverde, qu'il avait étudié et pris ses degrés à Cambridge (Angleterre), qu'il s'y était marié; après quoi nous le trouvons en 1637, un an avant sa mort, établi à Charlestown, Massachusetts, comme pasteur dissident.

La lumière est donc aujourd'hui pleinement faite sur la vie de J. Harvard. Né dans *l'Eglise établie*, dont les membres seuls étaient admis alors dans les Universités anglaises, il a rompu avec elle pour embrasser les idées des puritains, bien plus protestants que les anglicans. Comme beaucoup d'autres puritains, il a été chercher dans le Nouveau Monde la liberté que l'Angleterre lui marchandait. Elève d'Oxford, il avait compris l'immense influence qu'une grande université peut exercer sur les destinées d'une nation, et il a voulu en assurer les bienfaits à sa nouvelle patrie. L'événement lui a donné pleinement raison et il a aujourd'hui cette rare fortune qu'étant mieux connu, il n'en est que plus estimé.

HARVARD'S EXAMPLE.—And well does the example of Harvard teach us that what is thus given away is in reality the portion best saved and longest kept. In the public trusts to which it is confided, it is safe, as far as anything human is safe, from the vicissitudes to which all else is subject. . . . . Here it will not perish with the poor clay to whose natural wants it would else have been appropriated. Here unconsumed itself, it will feed the hunger of the mind,—the only thing on earth that never dies,—and endure and do good for ages after the donor himself has ceased to live, in aught but his benefactions.—EDWARD EVERETT.

SOLDIERS IN KING PHILIP'S WAR.

Communicated by the Rev. GEORGE M. BODGE, A.M., of East Boston, Mass.

[Continued from page 93.]

No. XIV.

CLOSE OF THE NARRAGANSETT CAMPAIGN; THE "HUNGRY MARCH;" CAPT. SAMUEL BROCKLEBANK AND HIS MEN.

AFTER the battle at the Narragansett Fort, several weeks of partial inactivity ensued, while both the English and the Indians were seeking to recover somèwhat from the severe blow each had received. The forces of Massachusetts and Plymouth remained at Smith's garrison at Narragansett, while Major Treat with the Connecticut regiment returned to Stonington about December 28th.[116]

From various sources, the accounts of the most reliable historians of the time, from contemporary letters and notices, we are able to glean some few items indicating the situation of affairs at the seat of war.

The Indians were greatly demoralized and evidently very solicitous as to the immediate future action of our army, as they sent in a delegation to the General on Thursday, December 23d, four days after the fight, ostensibly to negotiate in regard to peace, but in reality, doubtless, to ascertain the strength and intentions of the English. Some of the Indians had returned to their fort upon the retreat of the troops, and it is likely were able to rescue a part of their provisions from the flames, but the main body was gathered into a swamp some three miles distant, while those who had joined the Narragansetts from neighboring tribes returned home. Mr. Dudley wrote that Philip was seen by one of ours with a strong body-guard during or after the battle. If so he must have made a rapid march between that and January 6th, upon which date Governor Andros, of the New York Colony, writes to the Connecticut Governor:

" This is to acquaint you that late last night I had intelligence that Philip & 4 or 500 North Indians fighting men, were come within 40 or 50 miles of Albany northerly, where they talk of continuing this winter; that Phi: is sick, and one Sahamoshuha the Comander in chief. Whereupon I have despatched orders theither."

I have found no reliable proof that Philip or his Wampanoag warriors, as a body, had any part in the Narragansett fight, while there

---

[116] In the treasurer's account with Connecticut colony there is a charge " For billiting 40 wounded men 7 days," and as there is no other occasion on which so many were wounded, it is fair to assume that the Connecticut forces did not retire before the 28th.

is some direct testimony that they did not. Indian captives refer the command of the Indians to other chiefs, and a cotemporary writer in the series of letters published in London under the title, " Present State of New England, with respect to the Indian War," says positively, " King Philip hath not yet been at Narraganset, as we feared, but is retired with his Men near Albany where he hath kept his Winter Quarters." This place is since known as Scattacook, and is situated in Rensselaer County, about twenty miles north of Albany.

The great snow-storm that began at the time of the battle and lasted for several days, rendered any movement of the infantry impossible, even if they had been in condition, and then suddenly there came a great mid-winter thaw, which further prevented their motion. Capt. Prentice's troop kept scouting and watching to guard against surprise, and to gather in whatever was possible of their enemy's supplies of corn, of which they obtained quantities, but the provisioning of this large body of men had to be done chiefly by vessels sent from Boston, and by some, at this time, gathering corn along the port towns of Connecticut, as we learn from their archives and from other sources.

On the 27th of December Capt. Prentice with his troop made a march into Pomham's country (now Warwick) and destroyed near a hundred wigwams. December 28th, a squaw captured at the fort was sent to the Indians with an offer of peace, if they would agree to the terms of the former treaty, and such other conditions as the English might impose, and give up all "Philip's Indians." The squaw did not return, but on December 30th a message came from the sachems proffering their thanks for the offer, but complained that the English made war upon them without notice. This Indian owned, as did the squaw, that the Indians lost three hundred of their best fighting men. January 4th, two prisoners were taken, of whom one, being a Wampanoag, was put to death. January 5th, the Indians sent in a captive child, three or four years of age, belonging at Warwick. On the 7th, messengers came from them laying the blame upon Canonchet, who when he had visited Boston and made his treaty with the English, had returned and deceived his people as to the terms ; but all these overtures were evidently practised to gain time and take the attention of the English from the real movements of the Indians while they were making ready for their flight to the north-west. On the 8th these were sent back with positive instructions as to terms of peace. On the same day old Ninigret, sachem of the Niantics, sent in declaration and evidence of the reality of his friendship and of the dire straits to which the hostile Indians were reduced. In the mean time the Commissioners of the United Colonies were making every exertion to put a fresh army into the field. As early as December 25th it had been voted to raise one thousand men to recruit the army in the field, and the first of these were sent out about Jan. 6th[117] under Capt. Samuel Brocklebank of Rowley (I think). The weather was extremely cold, and they suffered severely on the march, part of the way through a fierce snow-storm "that bit some of them by the heels with the frost," according to Mr. Hubbard. The writer of " The Present State of New England," the letters above mentioned, says that eleven of the men were " frozen to death, and many others were sick and disheartened." January 10th these recruits arrived at head quarters and were joyfully received.

An order of the Council of Massachusetts, given January 14th, directs Major Gookin " to order the Eastern Souldiers with Horse and Foot, as soon as they come to Cambridge, to march to the army and to put them under such conduct as he sees right, until they get to Narraganset to Major Appleton, sending away with them the Armorer that is there already." On Jan. 17th the Council ordered the Committee of the Army to " forthwith furnish James Foord of Ipswich, a Souldjer under Capt. Brocklebank, now going up under Leut. Swett to Narraganset, with one pr. of good shoos and on good Coate and place it to his acco^t." Ephraim Sawyer and Walter Davis, also, " now going forth to ye Narraganset," were furnished with apparel. These referred to in the above orders were a second body of recruits that were sent by the Massachusetts Council ; the Commissioners having voted on January 6th, that the colonies should have their recruits at head quarters at Smith's Garrison on or before January 20th.

January 12th, a proposition came from the sachems for a cessation of hostilities for a month, which so stirred General Winslow's indignation and convinced him of their treachery, that he determined on a forward move at once, but still felt his force to be too weak in the absence of the promised troops of Connecticut. He fears the foe is escaping, and sends frequent messages to the Commissioners and to Major Treat and the Connecticut Council, to hurry up their preparations.

The Connecticut Colony meanwhile was making every endeavor, the while however being somewhat impatient of the urgency of the General, feeling that their own borders were threatened by the Indians quite as much as the other colonies. Their archives afford ample proof of the thorough and energetic manner of their preparation. Major Treat's reorganized army rendezvoused at New London. From all the settlements recruits and arms and supplies were gathered as speedily as possible, and yet it was not until the 26th of January that their troops started for the field. The following

---

[117] Capt. Brocklebank and the main part of his company probably entered the service January 1st, but did not march to the seat of war until other recruits were ready. January 18th, Capt. Daniel Fisher, of Dedham, has an order from the Council to send all " Horse and foote " that come into Dedham under Lieut. Benja. Swett, " away to ye Enemy ;" and the order shows Dedham to be the common rendezvous of the four counties.

extract relating to the occasion is from a "Letter of Major Palmer of New London to the Governor and Council of Connecticut."

New London ye 26th Janua: 1675–6

I having this oportunity by Mr Plom, could not omitt acquainting you of Maj^r Treat's departure this day, with all his forces, who is accompanied with Mr. Fitch, Mr Buckley & Mr Wise. They expected to reach Badcock's this night and so get to Mr Smith's tomorrow: For Major Treate hath had two late ord^rs from the Generall one rece^d on Lord's day, the other this morning, to hasten his coming; the Indyans being seated 8 or 10 miles northwest of Providence, and about 25 miles from Mr Smith's. The information was gayned by two Indyans taken by a party of Capt Prentis' troope, which killed nyne more one escaped there being 12 in that party.

The Barke with the Provitions went out last night and hath had a fayre wind to cary her in today. They have added tenn barrels of meate to the twenty you ordered from Milford: which doth afflict our people more than the trouble of quartering both well and wounded men, which have so impoverished them that sundry will much suffer, without ye speedy supply of corne for their releife......

In the margin of this letter is added the item,

" Unkas has gone forth in person."

It will be seen by the letter that the march from headquarters was begun on the 26th of January. James Babcock's place was in what is now Westerly, R. I. By good marching they could have reached Smith's Garrison and joined the main army on the evening of the 27th; and thus January 28th must be the earliest date at which we can place the general forward movement of the whole army. The Council orders and references and letters in the Connecticut Colonial Records serve to confirm the account of Mr. Hubbard, although derived from independent sources, and as they give very few items besides, it seems evident that we have all of importance that happened. On January 23d Major Treat wrote to the Connecticut Council, quoting a letter from General Winslow, which he says he has lost, but which contained nothing of importance except to hasten their coming and "grateing on our disorderly retreat," and the good news of the taking of Joshua Tift[118] by Capt. Fenner, of Providence. From some Indian prisoners which the Connecticut scouts had taken, it was found that the Narragansetts were lying in small parties along the way leading into the Nipmuck country, and with scouting parties so posted that our army could not surprise their main body.

From a letter of Roger Williams to Governor Leverett, dated Providence, 14 January, 1675, and published in the " Winthrop Papers," vol. 36, p. 307, Coll. Mass. Hist. Society, we learn much about this Joshua Tift, different from the accounts of contemporary

---

[118] Capt. Oliver's letter previously given, as to its facts, was " attested " by this Joshua " Teffe."

historians.   Mr. Williams was called upon to take down the examination of Joshua Tift, and afterwards reports the answers to
the Governor.

Being questioned by Capt. Fenner, who had captured him, Tift
answered that he had been with the Narragansetts about twenty-
seven days ; that he was captured by Canonchet and his property
destroyed, but his life saved on condition that he would become the
slave of Canonchet ; he accepted the conditions, and was taken to
their fort and there compelled to work for the Indians.   He testifies that the Mohegans and Pequots with our troops made terms with
the Narragansetts at the beginning, and shot over their heads.
After the English entered the fort, Canonchet and other sachems
fled and halted beside a spruce swamp after crossing a plain.   When
night came the word was brought to the chiefs, of the English retreat, and they sent back to the fort to ascertain their losses, and
found ninety-seven dead and forty-eight wounded, and five or six
bodies of the English.   He said that the Narragansetts' powder was
mostly gone, but that Philip had sent word that he will furnish them
enough from the French, who have sent Philip a present, " a brass
gun and bandaliers sutable."   The sachems are now about ten miles
northwest from Mr. Smith's ; speaks of the squaw that was sent by
the English, but that the sachems believed that the proposals of the
English were merely a trap to catch them.   Canonicus was for
peace, and would not consent to lie to the English ; but his nephew,
the young sachem Canonchet (or Nanunteno) was fierce for war,
and the young warriors were with him, so that it was impossible to
curb them.   He speaks of Quaquackis as Canonchet's chief captain,
" a midling thick-set man of a very stout fierce countenance."   " He
saith that Philip is about Quawpaug, amongst a great many rocks
by a swamepside ; that the Nahigonsiks have bene these 3 days on
their march & flight to Philip, that he knows not what number
Philip hath with him, & that this day the last and rear of the company departed, that they heard that Gen: was pursueing after them,
& therefore several parties, to the number of 400 were ordered to
lie in ambuscadoes, that several parties were left behind to get and
drive cattell."   He also testified that Ninigret's men fought the
English in the fort, and that some of the Mohegans have joined the
Narragansetts.

This letter throws some light inferentially upon the motions of
Philip, whom the Narragansett sachems evidently believed to be at
Quabaog.   As no mention of him is made by Tift in referring to
the fort fight, we have thus strong inferential proof that he was not
there.

At last, then, the army being in readiness, began the pursuit of
the Indians towards the Nipmuck country, in the somewhat famous
march known to the succeeding generations as the " Long March, "
or the " Hungry March," but of the details of which we have very
meagre accounts.

Mr. Hubbard relates that on January 21st Capt. Prentice surprised a party of the Indians, killed nine and captured two, and within two or three days, the weather changing, our forces were very anxious to take the field, hearing, as they did, that the Indians were in full flight. " But so many difficulties were cast in the way that they could not be ready in time to prevent the mischief the Indians did at Warwick. For January 27 they despoiled Mr. Carpenter of two hundred sheep, fifty head of neat cattle and fifteen horses, drove them all away safely and escaped before our forces set out." They wounded two of Mr. Carpenter's people, and one of theirs was slain.

The account of the writer of " The Present State," &c., mentioned above, says :

" The winter being now broken up, the Snow and Ice all gone, our Army, consisting in all of 1600 Men began their March to the Rocks, where the Indians were fled for protection; but in their Way they had Intelligence that 300 Indians had been at Patuxit, an English Plantation on the Narraganset Bay, where they burnt Mr. Carpenter's Corn and Hay and all his houses except his Dwelling-house, which likewise they had set on fire, but it was again quenched by some English that were in it. They likewise drove away with them 180 Sheep, 50 Head of large Cattle and 15 Horses; besides, they took much Cattel from young Mr. Harris, and killed a Negro Servant of his ; and having done this Mischief, returned Home with their Booty."

The haste and unreliability of this writer's account is seen in his mixing up of different events, because he goes on from this point to relate the burning of Pomham's town, where they had " a small Reincounter," and " wounded his chief Captain *Quaqualh* on the knee, and killed five of his men, and had four of our Connecticut men wounded ;" and then goes on to tell the story of the taking of Joshua Tift, who as we know was taken on January the 14th. This writer says of Tift that he was tried by a " Counsel of War," while he pretended that he was taken prisoner by the Indians and compelled to bear arms in their service, but this was proved to be false (his musket when he was taken was heavily charged with slugs) and " he was condemned to be hanged and Quartered, which was accordingly done." And then the story goes on :

" Our Army beat the Indians from the foresaid Rocks, and pursued them almost as far as Quabog, in which Pursuit we killed about 60 or 70 of them, and found many of the Matts scattered in the Way with which they cover their Houses, which we suppose they could not carry with them by Reason of our close pursuit. Some Prisoners taken from them inform us, that their Body consists of 4000, whereof 1800 were fighting Men, half of which wanted Arms, that they were in great Want of Powder, and greater want of Provisions."

" Provision growing scarce in the Army, and the Enemy having cleansed the Country of Things that might tend to our Relief, our General resolved to pursue them no farther, but to hasten homeward, which accordingly was done with what speed we could, but the Scarcity of Victuals daily increasing we were forced to kill several of our Horses for Sustenance. Our General dismist the Connecticut Men, and sent them Home the nearest Way, and old Unkus and his Indians along with them. They proved very faithful in our Service, and were well treated by us."

This writer says that a garrison of sixty men was left at Smith's House in Wickford, and that many of our men, including General Winslow, were troubled with the "Flux," and that they marched home by way of Marlborough.

In Mr. Church's account there is a very palpable error in the matter of time, because it gives three months (instead of weeks) as the time of his stay at Rhode Island, thus:

" Mr. Church was moved with other wounded men over to Rhodeisland, where in about three months' time he was in some good measure recovered of his wounds and the fever that attended them ; and then went over to the General to take his leave of him with a design to return home. But the General's great importunity again persuaded him to accompany him in a long march into the Nipmuck country, though he had then tents in his wounds, and so lame as not able to mount his horse without two Men's assistance."

Mr. Church says that the first thing remarkable in this march was their coming to an Indian town of many wigwams, but an icy swamp was between our army and this village, and it was only after much firing on each side that they were able to pass over, whereupon the Indians made good their retreat, the Mohegans in full pursuit. One of these caught a wounded Indian and brought him before the General, where being condemned to die, he managed to escape the blow of the executioner, and Mr. Church then branches off into a long account of an exploit of his own in recapturing him, closing his account of the march which to us now is of such interest, in a simple sentence, saying that in this march they killed many of the enemy, until at length, their provisions failing, they returned home.

Now taking these accounts, with what we are able to glean elsewhere, and it appears that the Indians very skilfully eluded our army, and succeeded in pushing forward all their wounded and helpless to places of safety in the northern tribes, and then when all was ready made a raid upon Patuxit and Providence and the neighboring settlements, and succeeded in carrying off large supplies, without a blow struck against them, except that of Capt. Fenner's party from Providence.

It seems to have been the popular idea that the army of the united colonies, after the junction of the Connecticut troops, numbered about sixteen hundred, horse and foot. I have not been able to find any definite official statement, but as nearly as can be determined from available data, Massachusetts sent out about three hundred fresh troops in January ; Connecticut, including her veterans and Indian allies, about five hundred; and Plymouth probably about one hundred. With allowance for the dead, wounded and disabled of Massachusetts and Plymouth, about two hundred; sixty left in garrison at Wickford, and there would be, at a rough estimate, fourteen hundred serviceable men at Narragansett on January 28th.

From accounts above given it is impossible to determine the locality of the "Rocks" referred to by the writer of the letters to London above quoted, and by him probably quoted from the testimony of Tift, which seems to have been, at that time, the chief information the English had concerning the Indians. It will be noticed that Tift's evidence is that Philip is "about Quawpaug amongst a great many rocks by a Swampeside," and this may be taken as the supposed objective point or rendezvous of the Indians. The rear guard of the Indians were, at the date of his trial, or when he was captured, prowling about the settlements at Patuxit and Providence for an opportunity to drive off cattle, which purpose they succeeded in carrying out, some days later, when the witness, who in this matter at least had given true testimony, had been " hung and quartered." The route of the main body of the Indians was in a northwest direction towards Quaboag. Rev. J. H. Temple suggests the "Old Narragansett Trail," or "Greenwich Path," through the Wabbequasset country (now Woodstock) to the old Quabaog fort. Capt. Henchman, in the Mount Hope campaign, August, 1675, had marched into the Nipmuck country as far as the " second fort," at a place called " Wapososhequish" (probably Wabbaquasset), and then turned aside and marched to Mendon. In a direct line Woodstock is about forty miles from Wickford; by the regular trail it was doubtless much farther. In midwinter, with their scant knowledge of the country, with swollen streams to cross, an alert foe forever vanishing into the great wilderness, and eluding attack or luring to ambuscade, with provisions which the long waiting for Connecticut had served to reduce, their march was a hazardous undertaking, and probably was inspired by the hope of striking a final blow against their enemies, already reduced to great straits for provisions, arms and ammunition. They found " more than sixty horses' heads " at one place, probably at the late rendezvous of the Indians, " 25 miles north of Mr. Smith's and 10 miles north of Providence." There seems to have been but one battle worthy of mention, and that is described by Mr. Church as at an icy swamp, and here sixty or seventy were killed; and it seems that the Mohegans and Pequots did most of the fighting and execution here. The capture of the " Matts" referred to, is thought to indicate a Wabbequasset settlement, as these mats were a peculiar covering used by that tribe. I think it possible that the battle was at the old fort of the Indians at Memenimisset.

Finding his provisions growing short, and his men worn with their long march and severe exposure, and seeing no prospect of bringing the enemy to a battle, General Winslow determined to abandon the pursuit, when the Indians betook themselves to the wilderness beyond Quaboag. I think the march commenced from Wickford on January 28th, and it was probably on February 2d or 3d that the skirmish took place. It would seem that the Connecticut and Indian forces were dismissed as early as February 3d, as they arrived home on the 5th, while the cavalry of Massachusetts and Plymouth got to Boston on the same day, the infantry remaining over at Marlborough, but a part of them marching down to Boston the next day. They were reduced to such straits that they killed and ate many of their horses, and the march was thence called by the people "the Hungry March." I find on the treasurer's books, February 29th, "Edward Cowell Cr for horsmeat £03. 06. 00," as were others. Those that took part in this march were included in the "Narragansett Grantees."

CAPT. BROCKLEBANK'S COMPANY.

Samuel Brocklebank, of Rowley, is said to have been born in England about 1630, and to have come to this country with his mother Jane, a widow, and his brother John. Samuel Brocklebank and his wife Hannah had children—Samuel, born 1653; Francis, born 1655; Hannah, Mary, Elizabeth, Sarah, and Joseph who was born 1674. He was appointed deacon of the first church in Rowley in 1665. Elected captain of the Foot Company of Rowley in 1673. Was active in recruiting for the Narragansett campaign, and after the fort fight, on the second call for recruits, went out with a company about January 1st, as I judge from his credits and those corresponding credits of his men, which according to my best estimates were for five weeks, up to February 5th, when they returned to Boston, and reckoned from the time they left Rowley. These are only inferences, however, drawn from the Journal and various casual references, and I have yet found no direct statement as to the officers or men who went out to Narragansett at the second call, and I have not found any mention of Capt. Brocklebank or other officers whom I shall hereafter credit with such service. After the return to Boston, Capt. Brocklebank with his company, within one week, was called to Marlborough, where he was placed in command of the garrisons and military operations, and remained until April 21st (not as some think the 18th), when he marched to Sudbury, where Capt. Wadsworth with his company having joined him, they were ambushed by the Indians, and both captains, with most of their men, were slain. This battle, however, and the affairs at Marlborough, properly fall into the next chapters, in which Capt. Wadsworth and his men are to be given.

After the death of Capt. Brocklebank his widow married Richard Dole, of Newbury. His descendants of the name are quite numerous by his son Samuel and Elizabeth Platts his wife; by his daughters Mary and Sarah, who married William and Henry, sons of Richard Dole; and by his daughter Hannah, who married John Stickney.

Soldiers credited under Capt. Samuel Brocklebank:

February 29th 1675-6					Francis Gefford	03 18 00
Samuel Mower	01 08 04				Nath. Pease	05 08 00
Joseph Parker	01 10 00				Samuel Hills	02 16 00
Rowland Ravensbee	01 07 04				Simon Groe	03 09 04
John Abbott	01 10 00				Nicholas Richardson	03 09 04
March 24th 1675-6					Robert Rand	01 10 00
Thomas Stamford	01 10 00				Richard Haven	01 10 00
John Wilson	01 10 00				James Day	01 17 08
Philip Butler	02 01 00				Daniel Hutchins	03 10 00
John Linsy	01 10 00				Samuel Brocklebank Capt.	14 11 00
John Humkins	02 02 00				July 24th 1676	
Samuel Brocklebank Capt.	07 10 00				John Brown	02 08 00
John Hobson	01 10 00				Nathaniel Stephens	02 09 06
John Woodin	01 16 00				Zechariah Ayres	01 10 00
Benjamin Peirson	01 10 08				Richard Bryan	08 11 00
Daniel Tenny	01 10 00				Thomas Kemball	02 08 00
John Jackson	01 10 00				Philip Kertland	01 12 06
John Wood	01 10 00				John Stanwood	01 02 00
April 24th 1676					Philip Stanwood	03 08 06
James Ford	01 15 00				Robert Pease	03 12 00
John Giddings	03 00 00				Thomas Baker	05 09 06
Peter Jennings	01 15 00				Benjamin Jones	01 16 00
John Pollard	01 10 10				Joseph Fellows	01 17 00
June 24, 1676					John Lynd	05 09 06
Richard Potter	02 02 00				Joshuah Boynton	05 10 04
Peter Jennings	04 16 00				August 24th 1676.	
John Lovejoy	01 10 00				Jonathan Fantom	05 10 12
Jonathan Emery	03 12 00				Peter Chever	03 04 00
Josiah Clark	06 06 00				Samuel Perkins	03 18 00
Henry Cooke	00 10 00				Richard Jacob	14 15 10
Samuel Ireson	04 04 00				Sept 23d 1676	
Simon Adams	04 11 08				Richard Prince	02 11 04
Moses Bennett	03 18 10				Samuel Peirce	00 18 00
John Burrell	03 06 00				James Chafe	01 12 06
Thomas Brown	04 03 00				Edward Sewery	02 02 00
John Wood	03 19 08				Michael Derick	10 00 00

Capt. Brocklebank wrote from Marlborough to Gen. Denison, March 26, 1676, asking that he and his company may be relieved to go home, giving his reason that they had been in the country's service " since the first of January at Narraganset, and within one week after their returne were sent out again, having neither time nor money (save a fortnight's pay upon the march) to recruite themselves." Fortunately the Journal contains the credits of these men, seven of whom were paid by Capt. Brocklebank, £00 12 00, showing that six shillings per week was the wages of a private in the service of Massachusetts Colony at this time; and there is not, that I am aware, any other direct proof of this, or any statement, except that given below, showing the wages of soldiers at that time. My own calculations agree with those of Mr. Sheldon, of Deerfield, that this was the price. This will show the time of their service up to February 5th to be five weeks, and £01 10 00 will represent the wages of those who were discharged at that time, and by this reckoning they entered the service Saturday, January 1st. I think thirty shillings was captains' pay, and Capt. Brocklebank's credit of £7 10 00 covers the same time.

I have found one other confirmation of my own calculations that this was the rate, viz., a bill presented by Serg't Ezekiel Woodward[119] of Maj. Appleton's company, in which his pay was for nine weeks as a common soldier, £2 14 00, and he petitions for sergeant's pay. This shows the term of service in the Narragansett campaign to begin Saturday, Dec. 4th, as it closed, we know, on Feb. 5th.

NEWBURY AND THE BARTLETT FAMILY.

By JOHN COFFIN JONES BROWN, Esq., of Boston.

NO colony in the Province of Massachusetts had so definite a purpose in its settlement as Newbury, and none furnished men of more exceptionally sterling character than this old town, whose 250th anniversary was celebrated during the past year. The capitalists who organized this settlement for the *first* stock-raising town in the province, had selected the site as the only place left in its domains which was well suited for stock-raising and distribution, at a time when the prices obtained for domestic animals was the highest, and the earlier settlements were arranging to secure the broader meadows of Connecticut.

Sir Richard Saltonstall, Henry Sewall, Richard and Stephen Dummer, with others in England and here, were the projectors of this movement. After having offered sufficient inducement to the Wiltshire colonists, who came with Rev. Thomas Parker in the Mary and John, to become the nucleus of the settlement,* they completed their plans by the purchase of Flemish stock to add to their own domestic herds, and largely increased the number of ori-

---

[119] Serg't Woodward had been under Maj. Appleton in the Fall Campaign, but in the Narragansett Campaign served in Capt. Gardner's company, and was there credited. Many of the veterans were thus transferred and acted as officers to the newly raised companies, without their rank and pay being officially credited by the Council, as the promotions were made in the field, and the stress of events precluded formalities and details in discipline.

* "Mr. Parker was at first called to Ipswich to join with Mr. Ward; but he choosing rather to accompany some of his countrymen (who came out of Wiltshire in England) to that new place, than to be engaged with such as he had not been acquainted withal before, removed *with them* and settled at Newbury."—*Hubbard's Hist. of N. E.*, p. 192.

ginal settlers by contracting with the Wiltshire people, accustomed to the care of cattle and to the handicrafts growing out of the developments of such a community, to join their Old-England neighbors in this new settlement.

Gov. Winthrop, in his History of New England, under date of June 3, 1635, records the arrival of the new colonists and of the Dutch cattle : "Here arrived two Dutch ships who brought 27 Flanders' Mares at £34 a mare, and 3 horses ; 63 heifers, at £12 the beast ; and 88 sheep at 50 shillings the sheep. They came from the Tressell in 5 weeks and 3 days, and lost not one beast or sheep. Here arrived also, the same day, the James, a ship of 300 tons, with cattle and passengers, which came all safe from Southampton, within the same time. Mr. Graves was Master, who had come every year for these seven years."

In the Massachusetts Records, July 8, 1635, is the following order : " It is ordered, that there shalbe a convenient quantity of land sett out by Mr. Dumer and Mr. Bartholemewe within the bounds of Newebery, for the keepeing of the sheepe and cattell that came over in the Dutch shipps this yeare, and to belong to the owners of said cattell."

The simultaneous arrival of these different vessels from different countries, in precisely the same length of passage, and that a very rapid one, must have created considerable excitement in Boston, and have been looked upon as providential.

The ship James had upon its passenger list the names of John Pike (representing his family also) and Thomas Coleman. Robert Pike, the son of John, was the moral and fearless hero of New England. His name stands to-day as the first and strongest representative of the right of petition—as the potential power which squelched the witchcraft delusion—and as a man who proved to the church and the state that a man's position in the state could not be governed by the theological opinion of its legislators and rulers.

Thomas Coleman, who had based a contract with the projectors of this new colony for the care of its cattle, upon their glowing account of the temptation of the climate and the small expense for housing, found that he had been deluded by the proprietors, and notwithstanding the importance and esteem which would come from their wealth, he boldly threw the responsibility upon them for the proper care of their cattle, and the General Court ordered a division of the provender so that each owner should take care of his own cattle.

The same disregard of position by those who imposed upon the rights of others, has been a noticeable quality in his descendants, who were among the earliest and most persistent to show the wrongs of slavery and the rights of man.

Judge Sewall, "the Diarist," was impressed with the truth of the opinions of Robert Pike and the Colemans, and the regret of the

Judge for his share of the witchcraft delusion came from the impressions forced upon him by the townsmen of the Merrimac valley. Whenever referring to the Judge, it is always pleasant to think of the general kindness of his nature in such direct opposition to the character of his grandfather, who was one of the capitalists to found Newbury, and who was in quarrelsome condition with church and man from his landing here until his death—the probable cause of which will be referred to in a note to his mother's will in the Genealogical Gleanings in England in the next number of the REGISTER.

Of the projectors of Newbury, Sir Richard Saltonstall was represented by Dr. John Clarke, the patentee of a stove a century before Franklin's invention. He was the owner of the Flemish mares and horses, and he, as well as the Sewalls, transferred that part of their stock-raising to Plymouth and the Cape. Many descendants of the doctor were famous in Boston as physicians and surgeons, and his live stock was noted and valuable through scores of years.

The names of Dummer and Sewall require no special note, as the generosity of the Dummers is proverbial, and the Sewalls have maintained until now the qualities of mind and of heart which become judges and rulers, but was unfortunately beclouded in the original settler from personal and financial troubles of his own, caused by losses at sea, when insurance companies did not exist.

On the last day of Feb. 1633–4, nine ships were lying in the river Thames, bound for New England, when orders were issued that the vessels be detained until new articles in relation to passengers should be promulgated. These required the masters to furnish bonds of £100 each, to cause to be observed and "putt in Execucion these Articles" among others:

" 2nd. That they cause the Prayers contained in the Book of Common Prayers established in the Church of England to be said daily at the usual hours of Morning and Evening Prayers, and that they cause all Persons on board said Ships to be present at the same."

" 3d. That they do not receive aboard or transport any Person that hath not a certificate from the officers of the Port where he is to embark that he hath taken both the Oathes of Alleigeance and Supremacy."

Among these vessels were the ships Mary and John, and the Hercules, in which Rev. Thomas Parker and his Wiltshire friends and neighbors embarked. The principal number of passengers came over in the Mary and John, while those most interested in the cattle accompanied them in the Hercules. Changes of passengers were made in these vessels after they had first embarked.

The Elizabeth and Dorcas, which had a cargo of cattle and goods belonging principally to Henry Sewall, was also one of this fleet. This property was in charge of Henry Sewall, Jr. Bad luck struck this vessel from her start—striking upon the rocks off Scilly Isles near England, then making an extremely long passage, losing sixty of her passengers by death on the way over, and many more in

Boston who landed sick but soon died. In consideration of the great loss of human life the lives of the cattle were too trivial to notice; that the loss was large there is no doubt. When the goods of Henry Sewall were being shipped later on from Boston to Ipswich in an open pinnace, the pinnace was sunk in a storm off Cape Ann and all the goods were lost.

Lists of passengers were made up without much detail, some giving the names of men only in representing the family; others giving an accompanying list of the names of women and children, and other lists combined the two.

Upon the list of the Mary and John is the name of Rev. Thomas Parker, the religious leader of this moving colony. He had been driven away from Oxford, shortly after entering, on account of the nonconformity of his father with the forms and ceremonies required. After studying awhile in Ireland he went over to Leyden and finished his education in the University at Holland. Like most of the Pilgrims he found solace in singing the tunes of his own home, while surrounded by those who spoke in a different language. He had a very sweet voice, and was a remarkably good singer. We can appreciate the zest with which he led the music at the devotional exercises on the passage over. Winslow wrote: "We refreshed ourselves with singing of psalms, making joyful melody in our hearts as with our voice, there being many of our congregation very expert in music; and indeed it was the sweetest music that mine ears ever heard."

Rev. Thomas Parker could have repeated this with truth. The love of music went with him to Ipswich and to Newbury. To both of these towns he introduced the music printed with Sternhold and Hopkins's metrical version of the psalms; and besides, he had no disrespect for the service of the Episcopal Church, if shorn of its genuflexions and peculiar dress. Evidently the daily services on board the vessel were looked back to with pleasure, and Mr. Parker was stigmatized by one of the Boston ministers as being like "a colt who kicked its dam," because he was not now averse to Bishops, after they had persecuted his father in previous years. However, the Mathers wrote very complimentary lines regarding the bishops of their time, and said that if the established church had been as kindly in the earlier days, there would have been no New England.

Among this moving Wiltshire colony was Richard Bartlett* and family. It is most likely that they were on the same ship with Parker, as we find the name of his son, John Bartlett, representing the family.

Richard[1] Bartlett was probably married in 1610, as his first child was born in 1611, according to modern ways of dating. In 1612 he purchased a Bible, which Mr. John Ward Dean, the editor of

* The name of Bartlet is found in Wiltshire. See pedigrees on page 201.

the REGISTER, has minutely described on p. 203. This book, which
for more than twenty years had been the full source of their religious
instruction, at home and in the parish church, was now to be used with
joy and reverence twice each day while they were crossing the broad
Atlantic. It contained also the Book of Common Prayer, together
with Sternhold and Hopkins's metrical version of the Psalms and the
music to them; prefixed to which was instruction in music, and the
spiritual songs of Veni Creator, Te Deum, Benedictus, Magnificat,
Audi Israel, Pater Noster, the X. commandments, and many others.
The Rev. George E. Ellis stated at the 250th anniversary of the
first church in Boston, that "The very rarest volume—so rare, that
I know not of a single copy—in all our treasured repositories, shelves
and cabinets of relics, books and papers, gathered from the homes
of our first generation here, is the Book of Common Prayer of previous or cotemporary editions."

When this richly prized and sacred memento of the Bartlett family was displayed at the Newbury celebration, it brought up to the
minds of those familiar with its daily use on ship-board and in the
churches at Ipswich and Newbury, the potent power of a single volume used as this had been. After the prescribed services of the
morning and afternoon were concluded, we can see the groups of
passengers enjoying a regular praise meeting of song, and particularly noticeable is that of the Bartlett family; perhaps now the
children are singing "The song of the three children praising God,
provoking all creatures to doe the same," the boys Richard and
Christopher joining with no uncertain tones, as the diamond-shaped
notes are scanned, with the hideously crowded old black-letters beneath them, giving the music and words to the quaint old song;
now, the whole company will close in singing "The Lord's Prayer
or *Pater Noster*," and the rich voices of the father and elder son,
with the flute-like voice of Joan, combined with those of the child-
den, give us an idea of the home-concerts of this music-loving
family.

It has been considered doubtful whether Richard[1] Bartlett the father had ever come to New England; but in the Salem Probate
papers, in the will of Richard[2] the son, born in 1621, he mentions
his honored father, late of Newbury. Joshua Coffin only found
one piece of evidence of his life: "Richard Bartlett petitioned the
general court and was granted twenty pounds according to his petition." But Coffin did not copy the record correctly. It was Richard Brackett, the gaoler of the province, who had petitioned. The
record is in June, 1639.

In Coffin's list of grantees, dated 1642, the names Richard, John
and Christopher appear, and there was no known reason why John
and Christopher should each have a right in commons and their brother Richard have none, but it is now supposed that the senior Richard's right was arranged to be given to his son Richard, Jr.

On page 295 of Coffin's History of Newbury, was given the genealogy of the Bartlett family, to the best of his ability, with the imperfect records* for assistance. He supposed Richard and John were brothers, instead of being father and son, and he misplaced some of the children of the next generation. The venerable Levi Bartlett, of Warner, N. H., has adopted some of Coffin's errors. The record in the family Bible, as given at the end of this article, transcribed by Mr. Dean, gives an authentic base to start upon.

RICHARD[1] BARTLETT, above mentioned, died May 25, 1647 ; his daughter Joane,[2] born Jan. 29, 1610–11, married William Titcomb, who is stated by Savage to have come in the Hercules. If so, the name of William Latcome (REG. x. p. 266) is probably intended for William Titcomb. Probably Thomas[2] and Anne[2] died in England.

JOHN[2] BARTLETT (*Richard*[1]), born in England, Nov. 9, 1613. His name is upon the list of passengers of the Mary and John, 24 March, 1633–4 (REG. vol. ix. p. 267), and upon the list of 91 proprietors of Newbury, dated Dec. 7, 1642, "having proportionable right in all waste lands, commons, &c." (Coffin's Hist., p. 292.) Jan. 11, 1643–4, new town laid out. His lot is No. 27. He was elected Way-warden, April 27, 1648, constable 1649, and was selectman twenty years afterward. There are no church records of Newbury before 1674. At this date, according to a printed church manual, John[2] and his wife Joan were members. He died, as appears upon a list of deaths furnished by William Little (president of the Newbury Hist. Soc.), Feb. 5, 1678. Children :

i. JANE, b. ——. (The first book of Births, Marriages and Deaths is in bad condition, and many entries are destroyed. The first date of an entry of the Bartlett family which is preserved, is in 1645.) She m. William Bolton, Jan. 16, 1664–5.

ii. JOHN, b. 1639. He took the anti-papal oath required by the King (and ordered by the General Court) of all his subjects within this colony, who were of years to take an oath. (REG. vol. vii. 349) He had an only son Gideon ; the daughter Mary (mentioned by Coffin and Bartlet) was the child of John and Mary (Rust).

CHRISTOPHER[2] BARTLETT (*Richard*[1]), born in England, Feb. 25, 1623–4. He died March 15, 1669–70. His daughter Mary died Dec. 24, 1660. The records as printed by Coffin and Bartlet are correct. The only son of this line, Christopher,[3] lived in Haverhill, who, besides daughters, left an only son Christopher,[4] whose property was situated in that part of Haverhill which was in New Hampshire after the boundary line of 1741 was settled. (See History of Haverhill by Chase.)

RICHARD[2] BARTLET (*Richard*[1]), born in England, Oct. 31, 1621. The records of his marriage, his wife Abigail's maiden name, and the details of his early history, can only be known when the lost papers

* The church records of Newbury prior to 1674 have either been lost or destroyed. It has been said that they were destroyed " to bury in oblivion the old quarrel." The town records from 1635 to 1685 were combined with the proprietary records, and the volume has been subject to hard usage ; for year after year the records are entirely lost. What remains of this book was copied very carefully by Lothrop Withington, at the expense of Robert N. Toppan, now of Cambridge, and this copy was presented to the Historical Society of Newbury. The land grants had been copied in 1680 into another volume, but the dates were omitted,—only the names being given.

and records of Newbury come to light—if ever they do. He probably died in Amesbury, as there is no record of his death at Newbury; the date given by Coffin is 1698.

Richard[2] Bartlet was prominent in church affairs, after Rev. Thomas Parker had changed his attitude in relation to church government and discipline. From the beginning Mr. Parker felt the necessity of a head of authority in the church, but allowed the voice of the brethren in church affairs while he had confidence in the judgment of the majority. At the settlement of Newbury, the brethren acted in the admission of members by vote, and all the affairs were conducted in a congregational way ; but in 1669 Parker had determined that the pastor represented the government of the church, and members in opposition to the pastor could only " express themselves by their silence ;" in matters approving his own course, " he no ways approved a *governing vote* in the *fraternity*, but took their consent in a *silential way.*" Either way, he appeared to be a petty-pope in his own parish. Finally, in 1671, Mr. Parker had a majority to act with him, and succeeded in obtaining a judgment of the court at Ipswich ; in consequence of which, Richard Bartlet and his brother-in-law William Titcomb were fined four nobles each,—26 shillings 8 pence ; and John Bartlet, Sr. and John Bartlet, Jr.—the brother and nephew of Richard—were each fined 13 shillings and 4 pence.

We can judge of the respect felt towards him in Newbury by the fact that he was its delegate to the General Court for many years, beginning with 1679 ; this was shared by the neighboring towns. Haverhill had been greatly troubled for want of proper accommodation from those to whom its mill-privileges had been granted, but who had not fulfilled their agreements to the town's people ; to remedy the evil, in 1678, " the town unanimously ' voted, that Richard Bartlett of Almsbury be granted the privilege to set a saw-mill in Haverhill, on the north meadow river.' " Bartlett lived near the Haverhill line, and we presume that his mill was built on the site of what are now known as *Peaslee's Mills* (Chase's History of Haverhill, p. 132). He agreed, among other conditions, that he should pay the regular rates (that is, taxes) at Haverhill.

It appears by his will, a summary of which is given hereafter, that he had, while living, given liberally of his real estate to each of his sons ; the writer does not know to which of them he gave the house in Amesbury, mentioned by Chase; " thre parsells of upland and meddow in Amesbury bounds," consisting of 300 acres, valued at £80., remained in his possession, as appears by the inventory of his estate, and were distributed in accordance with his will.

When in 1688 taxes were levied under Gov. Andros, Richard Bartlett's taxable property in Newbury was given, and the law required that all males above 14 years of age should also be registered upon the lists ; yet it was noticed that no " head," meaning person, was indicated as represented with his property. This fact tends to recognize the idea that he was *personally* rated at Haverhill, in fulfilment of his contract. The thrift of the family can be judged of by perusal of the Newbury tax lists in the REGISTER, vol. xxxii. pp. 156–164. A copy of his will, and of the inventory of his estate, I have deposited in the vault of the N. E. Historic Genealogical Society, for reference. The following items are upon the inventory, the spelling modernized:—

Wearing apparel, woolen and linen and *books*   £8.   0s. 0d.

A carpet, flax, wool, a piece of cloth, yarn, *a cutlass* £3. 10s. 0d.

These two lines were selected because each line mentioned a power in the family; without doubt the Bible bought in 1612 by his father was one of the *books ;* and I have no doubt but that identical cutlass was girt by Richard himself around the loins of his son Samuel as he mounted his horse to hasten to Boston and join in the overthrow of Andros; this was in April, 1689. This Samuel Bartlett was the great-grandfather of Bailey Bartlett of Haverhill, who accompanied John and Samuel Adams to Philadelphia in 1776, when the Declaration of Independence was proclaimed; and Bailey Bartlet was grandfather of that intrepid hero, Gen. William F. Bartlet, who left his studies at Harvard College in April, 1861, to join in suppressing the Rebellion; he was the youngest General in our army,—twenty-two years of age,—to which position he was appointed for his gallantry. The details of his valor are fresh in the minds of the whole people, north and south, and his generous fraternal feeling towards the foe who tried his mettle, has been one of the many noble examples of the brave soldiers who have found the enemy worthy of their steel.

When Richard[2] made his will he committed his soul, body and spirit " into the everlasting arms of God, all sufficient, my Heavenly Father," and had " hope of a happy and glorious resurrection in the great day of the Man Christ Jesus." There was no cant in these expressions ; their idea of religion has been expressed by a west-of-England poet,

> .... as designed
> To warm and cheer the human mind
> And make men happy, good and wise,
> To point where sits in love arrayed
> Attendant to each suppliant call,
> The God of universal aid—
> The God, the father of us all.

The family was remarkable for its united fraternal feeling, embracing their marriage connections with the cordiality of consanguinity. They held together in the troubles of the first church on the broad ground of equal brotherhood in heart and voice. After a second church had been formed in the vicinity of their homes, which a larger neighborhood threatened to draw away, they offered to maintain the church in their own vicinity, and bear their portion of expense of the distant church until dismissed;* but a mob came from the larger neighborhood and ruthlessly tore down and carried away the meeting-house near the Bartlet homes. This aroused their righteous indignation, and resulted in their felling trees and hauling them towards the desecrated site of their worship, and expressing their determination to erect a new church in a fortnight. This the people and the Court tried to prevent, but were unsuccessful, except in delays. Finally, after it was completed, the only way in which it was found possible to use it, was to announce that they considered the Church of England, with whose services they were familiar, as orthodox, and had appealed to the Bishop of London and to the governor of the colony (Dudley) for protection and encourage-

---

* Eleven men of this family signed the petition in February, 1709, against the removal of the meeting-house to Pipe-stave Hill, viz.: Richard, Sr., Jr., and Tertius ; John, Sr., Jr., and Tertius ; Samuel, Sr. and Jr. ; Thomas, Daniel and Nathaniel. Six used one *t* terminal, five used *tt.* Variation in spelling Sawyer occurred in the same paper ; Samuel, Benjamin, John and Josiah wrote their names Sawyer ; Jonathan omitted the w. Of the men who " cut and halled timber " for the new church, Stephen Bartlet was one, not Stephen Brown as printed in Coffin's History of Newbury. The name of the carpenter who assisted, is written Ischipher Lunt, not *Skipper* Lunt, as Coffin gave it, which was doubted by Savage. How is his name recorded at his birth, 29 Nov., 1679 ? It appears like a " bad spell " intended for Ichabod.

ment. As their old church building had been destroyed, they would no longer consent to pay towards the expenses of "the dissenters." The governor promptly replied, favoring the views of the petitioners; and the Bishop was happy to pray, "God prosper your pious endeavors." This was early in 1712.

The influence of Parker in favor of home services and music was carried by his pupils to their homes. Judge Sewall had the Psalms read in his family in regular course; at home and in the meeting-house he liked to lead the singing, but frequently found that when he had intended to start with one tune, he had led off with another. The Bartletts had no trouble of this kind; fortunately this family possessed a violin, and after prayers and collect, the instrumental music was a correct guide for the voices, in time and tune, and without doubt they too went through the Psalms in order, following the music in their family Prayer-book. Samuel[3] Bartlett, the son of Richard,[2] was widely known as a fine fiddler in his time. These Wiltshire men had high hopes of the restoration of the Stuarts, and many of the first settlers, like Parker, lived long enough to see it, and to be disgusted with Charles II. The Prayer-book of the Bartletts contained a prayer for Queen Anne of Denmark, wife of James I. (the first of the Stuarts); when her great-granddaughter Queen Anne, wife of George of Denmark, was upon the throne, this first Episcopal Church at Newbury was named in her honor—Queen Anne's Chapel. Rev. Matthias Plant, its third Rector, married the youngest daughter of Samuel[3] Bartlett, and he had the pleasure of recording among his memoranda of natural phenomena in the church records, under date of October 9, 1727, in his full description of the earthquake, " The very first shock opened a new spring by my father Samuel Bartlet's house in the meadow."

Under the auspices of this Chapel, St. Paul's Church of Newburyport was developed,—a monument to the power of the use of a Book of Common Prayer brought over by a first settler.*

WILL OF RICHARD BARTLETT, SENIOR.

In the Name of God and by His Assistance, I Richard Bartlet Sen[r], of Newbury in the County of Essex in the Province of the Massachusetts Bay in New England do humbly comitt my soule body & spiritt both in life & death into the everlasting arms of God all sufficient my Heavenly Father & unto Jesus Christ my allone Saviour & Blessed Redeemer thru the power & presents of His eternal Spirit my body to ye earth whence its originall was taken in hope of a happy & glorious resurrection in ye great day of the Man Christ Jesus to Him be Glory both now and ever, Amen:

And for such good things of this world as it hath pleased God to comitt to my stuard ship I as much as in me is do dispose as is hereafter expressed.

Imprimis I give to my son Samuel Bartlet one third p[t] of my lott of upland & meadow in Almsbury called the Pond Lott by the plaine. Also one third part of my Sawmill Lott in Almsbury. Also, one third part of that lott of upland w[ch] I bought of James George in the towneship of Almsbury wth all the priviledges to the said parcells of land belonging to be

* William Little, president of the Newbury Historical Society, kindly aided the writer by examining Newbury records from its settlement in 1635 to 1700, for details regarding this family.
J. C. J. B.

the lawful inheritance of my said son Samuel Bartlet his heirs and assignes forever. As also all the lands & meadow wch I have formerly given to my said son as by deeds maye appear. As also one third p^t of a freehold or priviledge in the comons or undivided lands in the towne of Newbury origenaly belonging to my *honored father* Richard Bartlet *late of Newbury, deceased* wth all the priviledges that may or shall arise thereby in time to come.

[The same item repeated to sons Richard and John—the words in Italics not having been written in the item to son Samuel.]

Item   I give to my granddaughter Tirza Bartlet the daughter of my son Thomas Bartlet (late of Newbury deceased) three acres of upland adjoining to his house, &c.—but if she die, &c. then to my three daughters Abigail, Hannah & Rebecca Bartlet.

Item, to my three daughters (above named) I give my dwelling house and barn and orchard and land adjoining about 12 acres; also one freehold in the comons of Newbury, purchysed of Mr. Henry Sewall of Newbury, &c.—also several lots of land, specified.

Ite   My will is & I do hereby appoint my three daughters, namely, Abigael Bartlet, Hanah Bartlet & Rebecca Bartlet to be the executors of this mye last will & testament, giving and bequeathing to them besids what I have formerly given them, all the rest of my estate not mentioned in this my will, whither debts dew to me bye bill bond booke or other wise or what ever may heer after appeer to be mine my debts & funerall charges being by them discharged.

Lastly   I do apoynt Tristram Coffin Esqr & my cosen* John Bartlet and my three sons aforenamed as overseers to advise my execut^r in the management of the trust committed to them in this my last will & testament.   Heerby renouncing all former wills of mine.

Dated 19 April, 1695.   Proved July 18, 1698.

WILTSHIRE BARTLETS.

From Visitation of Wiltshire, 1623. By G. W. Marshall, LL.D.

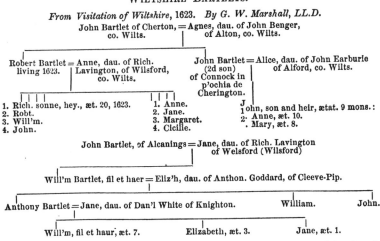

Cherington (called Cherton) is about four miles south-east of Devises; All-Cannings is the same distance, a little north of east. These towns contained the landed property of the wealthier families of the Bartlets. Alton is about three miles east from All-Cannings, while

* Indicating a brother's child.

Wilsford is two miles east of Cherington. Clyffe-Pypard (called Cleeve-Pip) is nine miles as the bird flies north of All-Cannings. This area contained the homes of the younger sons of these families. The name of the heir only is given in the second pedigree—William may have had a brother Richard (unrecorded here), named for his grandfather Richard Laving-ton. Anthony Goddard had a nephew Thomas; was this the Thomas Goddard who came in the James and probably returned to England ?

The Catalogue of Cambridge graduates (Eng.), from 1760 to 1866, contains the names of thirteen Bartletts, and one Barttelot, viz., George Smythe Barttelot, A.D. 1775—1778 A.M.; the Barttelot pedigree states that he died unmarried, October, 1773 !

From Oxford, between 1673 and 1882, twenty Bartletts graduated. (No Barttelots.) The name of Bartlett is common in Wiltshire, Devonshire, Somersetshire, &c.

NOTE.

It has been claimed, within the last quarter of a century, that Richard and John Bartlett of Newbury, and Thomas Bartlett of Watertown, were three brothers,—sons of Edmund Barttelot of Ernley, who died in 1591, who was a son of Richard Barttelot of Stopham ; and that they "sold back" their portion of the land in 1634 to make a fair start in New England. This fabrication has been built up on the mere resemblance of name, and is disproved by every known fact. John of Newbury was the *son* of Richard of Newbury ; while Thomas of Watertown, who was born in 1594, was a poor servant in the employ of Pelham in 1631, and sold his master's tools to raise money enough to bridge over some of his expenses ; and not one of them ever signed his name as Barttelot, although the home chapel of the latter family is full of memorials of family pride, with its surname distinct and un-variable from A.D. 1428 until the most recent times.

The surnames Batt, Bartlett and Barttelott, are all mere pet diminutives of the baptismal name of Bartholomew ; the two latter merely indicating little-Bart, and shows that the family names, like those of John-son, Jack-son and Williamson, came out of the personal name of a landless father.

W. S. Smith, a distinguished English writer on heraldry, says " it is the ambi-tion of every family in England, which seeks to display genealogical and heraldic honors, to claim descent from some ' Norman knight ' who came over with the Conqueror."

The Barttelot family may be classed among them. They claim descent from Adam[1] Bartelot, who is stated on the family pedigree to have come over with Wil-liam the Conqueror, and to have died in A.D. 1100. From him in direct descent are given William,[2] John,[3] Robert,[4] Thomas,[5] John,[6] who married Joan de Stop-ham, and died A.D. 1428. Six generations, covering 328 years, or nearly 55 years to a generation.

If the pedigree is examined from A.D. 1428 towards our time, which covers a period with corroborative record, 11 generations average less than 25 years each.

It is almost needless to say that every thing given of a previous date to John[6] was fabulous. The indenture by which he acquired possession of the Stopham lands is dated 7th year of Richard II. (A.D. 1384), and his father may have been a man without a surname—simply known as Bartholomew.

I have not known an instance where a New Englander of intelligence, descended from our early settlers through lines of increasing wealth or reputation, had not been handsomely received and entertained by the present representatives of the " County Family " from which he supposed that his New England progenitor was derived.

Many members of the Bartlett family have visited Stopham, and while appreciat-ing the courtesy of the host, listened to stories of chivalrous knights, and questioned about the broad acres of the family. Prof. S. C. Bartlett, of Chicago, wrote after visiting Stopham in 1874, that " an accurate pedigree of the line has been kept from 1069 down to Ada Mary, the youngest daughter of Col. Walter B(arttelot), who cel-ebrated her 12th birthday in August, 1874," and Col. Bartlett himself wrote that " the records in the church are complete from John Barttelot, who was born early in 1300 ! down to the present day." I have before mentioned that this John Bar-tellot acquired the estate in 1344 and died in 1428. In the same letter Prof. Bart-lett wrote that " the estate is a large one, some 7000 or 8000 acres," but the gov-ernment record gives it as 3633 acres, with a gross income of £4793.

It is necessary in writing of genealogical matters to show the diversity of printed statements, so that the present reader, after hearing both sides of the story, may judge of its truth.

THE BARTLETT BIBLE AND ITS RECORD.

We have before us the copy of the Breeches Bible, which was exhibited at the Newbury Quarter Millenary Celebration, June 10, 1885 (REG. xxxix. 389). It belongs to Miss Elizabeth G. Hoyt, of Chelsea, Mass. It is a black-letter Bible, quarto post, very much trimmed down. Prefixed to the Bible, which includes the Apocrypha, is the Book of Common Prayer, and appended are a Concordance, with Sternhold and Hopkins's version of the Psalms. The latter has printed notes for singing the tunes. The title-page and several pages of the Prayer Book are wanting, and this is also the case with the Old Testament. A portion of the title-page of the New Testament is gone, including the date. The title-pages of the Concordance and the Psalms are preserved, the first dated 1611 and the latter 1610. Some pages at the end of the Psalms are wanting. The title of Concordance states that it was "Collected by R. F. H.," and the preface is dated 1578, and signed "Robert F. Herrey."

On the front margin of the page on which the 4th Chapter of 1st Esdras is commenced, is the following writing, of which a fac-simile is given in the margin:

Richard Bartlett Bought this booke Anno Domyni 1612.

At the end of the Prayer Book is a blank page on which is written in the same handwriting the following record:

I Richard Bartlett writ this for
the age of my children

Joane Bartlett borne in
Januarey 29. 1610 wensday 8– of the
cloke at nyght

[–]eaues   John Bart borne . the . 9 . of
day   november . 1613 . a. 11. of the clok
       in the day

Thomas Bart borne Januarey . 22
1615

Rich Bart was borne october
           day
the 31 . 1621 wens ⌄ mor 3 clok

Cris B the . 25 . of febru'
being yᵗ yeare S. mathias 1623
betwen . 12 . & . 1 . in the morn

[All above this is written in one shade of ink and apparently at the same time, except the marginal entry and the interlined word *day*, which are in the same ink as the following entry :]

> Anne Bart was borne the . 26. of
> februarye being sonday about . 12 .
> of the clocke in the day in the
> yeare 1625　　　　　Editor.

☞ Miss Hoyt gives this history of the Bible: " This Bible came to my father's mother, who was Sally Kennison, the daughter of Dolly Bartlett and Moses(?) Kennison. Dolly Bartlett, my great-grandmother, was the sister of Joseph Bartlett who lived, in my father's boyhood, at Bartlett's Corner, about half way between Amesbury Ferry and ' The Mills.' Joseph lived exactly on the corner, and Dolly, my father's grandmother, lived three houses beyond. They were descended from the Bartletts who settled originally, in 1635, at Bartlett's Cove, near Chain Bridge. The Bible was brought over by the original settlers. My father, Mr. William Hoyt, son of Aaron Hoyt and Sally Kennison, was born in Amesbury, June 14, 1803. He is now living at 16 Suffolk Street, Chelsea, Mass."

BRIEF NOTICES OF THE EARLY AMERICAN ENGRAVERS.

By Mr. Richard C. Lichtenstein, of Boston.

MR. LICHTENSTEIN, who has the largest collection of book-plates in New England, has furnished us with the following list of engravers who did work in that line for New England families. We shall give reproductions in future numbers, showing the style of the work of each, with lists of their productions. So little was known in relation to descent from definite English ancestry of many of the owners of the plates, that the heraldic claims indicated by the engravings require proof of consanguinity before their right to the use of the armorial bearings can be admitted.—Ed.

A. Anderson, born 1775, died 1870. Engraved on copper before 1812, after that only on wood. Have seen no book plate engraved on wood.

Callender's name first appears in Boston Directory for 1789, and from that time until 1805, and not after.

Dawkins came over from England ; first settled in Philadelphia ; engraved music in 1761. Plate in American Magazine, 1767, etc. Was in New York about 1774. Anderson remembers seeing coats of arms done by him before 1775.

T. M. Furnass, Hurd's nephew, about 1775.

S. Hill. Name appears in Boston Directory for 1803. Engraved portrait of Dr. John Clarke, 1799.

N. Hurd, born 1729, died 1777. Earliest dated plate of his 1749 ; very rude.

Benjamin Hurd, about 1750.

Thomas Johnson, born 1706, died 1767. Engraved music, Boston, 1755.

P. R. Maverick, born 1755 ; in 1787 had a shop in New York. Dunlap the painter was a pupil of his.

P. Maverick, son of the above, born 1780, died 1831. Was superior as an engraver to his father.

P. Revere, born December 1734 O. S., January 1735 N. S. ; died May, 1818. All the book plates I have seen have the evidence of having been done before the Revolution.

Turner. Engraved music, Boston, 1744 ; portrait of Dr. Watts, 1746. Book plates evidently done about this period.

NOTE.—In the Boston Evening Post for 1745, there appears an advertisement of Francis Garden, lately from London, who engraves book plates on copper. Have come across no signed work of this engraver in this country ; have several specimens of his London work.

NOTES AND QUERIES.

NOTES.

THE RECORDS KNOWN AS " BISHOPS' CERTIFICATES."—The Public Records of England cover so much ground and extend through so long a series of years, that there are few Englishmen who have ever been, or are likely ever to become, the subject of historical or biographical research, about whom something may not be gleaned from them. It was a wise and judicious course, amply justifying the great outlay, to bring together into one building, from their scattered repositories, a collection of records which no other country in the world possesses in nearly so ample a measure. All honor to the late Lord Romilly, whose bust so fittingly finds place in the Literary Search Room of the great national building in Fetter Lane, which his wisdom and forethought not only called into existence, but made to promote, in so striking a manner, the interests of historical truth. In having recourse to its treasures, the only difficulty is to know just where to look, what class of documents to consult, a point on which it is of course necessary to be definite and precise, and this difficulty is due to the extent, variety and multifarious character of the stores which it contains. Books are accessible in it which throw light upon its innumerable contents, but the time which persons can spend within its precincts is too precious to be consumed in details which might be mastered at home. I therefore counsel those who contemplate availing themselves, either personally or by an intermediary, of the facilities which the Record Office affords, to prepare themselves by some adequate knowledge of its contents. I am usually able to visit the office myself, and thus have no need to employ those professional agents, most of them respectable, intelligent and competent, who make a business of Record work. Speaking for myself, I have often been astonished how new sources of information seem to open up when fresh subjects engage the attention.

I desire now to notice the documents known as " Bishops' Certificates," which give particulars of the Institutions to ecclesiastical dignities and parochial cures, a subject of very general interest which comes before almost all writers of biography.

Until the new order of things with respect to the Public Records came into effect, the only practicable way of obtaining information of this nature was by application at the Registry of the jurisdiction within which the benefice was situate, a step which might be, and often was, attended with considerable expense. The officials, with gradually increasing exceptions, naturally required payment of the fees to which they were rightfully entitled, making no distinction between inquirers for literary purposes and professional inquirers for purposes of legal business. This afforded no ground of complaint, for the Registrars could not be expected to place their time and the time of their clerks at the service of strangers gratuitously. Now this is changed, so far at least as respects a period commencing in the reign of Henry VIII., and particulars which could heretofore be obtained only from episcopal officials scattered throughout the country, can now be readily procured in one metropolitan office.

How it comes to pass that what has been done for that period cannot be extended to an earlier, may be explained in a word : the means do not exist. The government has no control over episcopal registers, and the documents which, having found their way from one of the courts of law to the Public Record Office, have made that possible which has been accomplished, only begin in Henry's reign, and originate from an enactment which was then made. Henry, who was so fond of meddling with the Church for purposes of his own pecuniary gain, took care that First Fruits, which before his time had gone to the Pope, should thenceforth be paid to the Sovereign. With a view to their being duly collected, the Archbishops, Bishops, and any other bodies (of whom there were some few) exercising episcopal jurisdiction, were required to send in half-yearly, to the Barons of the Exchequer, a return of the names of all the persons whom they had collated, instituted or admitted in the previous six months to any ecclesiastical preferment liable to the payment of First Fruits. The returns, which were regularly made, and have been well preserved, extend to all cathedral and collegiate dignities, as well as to all rectories and vicarages, with the exception only of benefices of a value so small as to have been discharged in the King's Books from the payment of First Fruits. They are entered on parchment rolls, which are kept in bundles, each bundle comprising a period of five years. The following will give an idea of the particulars recorded :

" Octavo die mensis Februarii, anno supradicto, Reginaldus Courtenay, clericus, in artibus magister, institutus est ad vicariam ecclesiæ parochialis de Leighton Beaudesert, in comitatu Bedfordiensi [ad præsentationem Decani et Canonicorum Liberæ Capellæ Regis infra Castellum suum de Windsor] per mortem [Joannis Buckeridge, clerici], ultimi incumbentis ibidem, tunc vacantem."

But so complete a form, not being necessary for the purposes of the return, did not commonly obtain, and the usual entry does not comprise the details which I have placed within brackets. Institution, as I need scarcely say, is a function specially appertaining to the episcopal order, but in some instances other bodies have acquired the right to institute, or to admit to benefices. Thus, the Dean and Chapter of St. Paul's, as to various parishes in Essex, and as to some in the city of London, exercise episcopal or quasi-episcopal rights, and the returns of such bodies are included under the general head of Bishops' Certificates. Sometimes, as in the case of the numerous dignities in St. Paul's Cathedral, all of which were in the gift of the Bishop of London, we get a two-fold return, because the practice was for the Bishop to " collate " his nominee, and for the Dean and Chapter to " admit " him. During the vacancy of a see,—and Queen Elizabeth kept the see of Ely vacant for many years,—the Archbishop gave institution, so that when what is required is not found in its natural place, the Archbishop's certificates should always be searched. Care should be taken to ascertain to what jurisdiction in matters ecclesiastical the benefice was subject. In the City, for example, where the parishes are very numerous and very small, so small that the site of the Bank of England occupies the entire parish of St. Christopher le-Stocks, church included, great diversity prevailed in this respect. In the olden time a man liked to see the parish in which he was born, or his college, become a peculiar, exempt from the ordinary ecclesiastical authority of the district, and acknowledging that of some dignitary of his own choosing. Curious examples might be mentioned, but I will content myself with specifying one. Cambridge is, locally, within the diocese of Ely, but King's College, with its precincts, which once comprised some few houses, is part of the diocese of Lincoln, whilst the Provost, as the head of the college is termed, formerly had the right of granting probate of the wills of all persons dying within the college or its precincts. Within his jurisdiction he was paramount, both in civil matters and in matters ecclesiastical, subject only to the Visitor appointed by the Royal Founder. So with respect to the small London parishes, one might be in the peculiar jurisdiction of the Archbishop of Canterbury, its neighbor in that of the Dean and Chapter of St. Paul's, and another adjoining parish might be subject to the Bishop of Rochester, all three being entirely independent of any authority of the local ordinary, the Bishop of London. Newcourt's *Repertorium*, in two volumes, is the most complete authority upon all ecclesiastical matters relating to the old diocese of London, which comprised the counties of Middlesex and Essex, with some parishes in adjoining counties. And here I may congratulate this Society upon the thoughtful action of the librarian in purchasing a copy of this work, which he was able to secure at a price not exceeding, I imagine, one fourth of that at which any former copy had been sold. Newcourt was Registrar of the diocese of London, and derived his materials from the records in his official custody, so that he is silent with respect to those parishes which, though locally within the diocese, were not subject to the diocesan. In such cases as these, the series of Bishops'-Certificates is most useful, and by its aid I have myself supplied various omissions in Newcourt.

There is another mode in which the approximate date of Institution may be arrived at, when the actual date cannot be ascertained. An incumbent was allowed time for payment of the composition for First Fruits, which was secured by his bond, with sureties. I forget at this moment whether the bonds themselves are preserved in the Public Record Office, or whether the particulars only of them are to be seen there. The date of the bond is a clew to the date of Institution, and may serve in its place, whilst the names of the sureties are often a guide to further researches respecting the incumbent. In my own investigations I have frequently been able to rest content with an examination of the Index to the Composition Records. This most useful compilation is arranged either in dioceses or in counties (my memory does not enable me to say which), and the Compositions, with date of each, are arranged in chronological order, so that it is easy to single out and collect the succession of the incumbents of any particular benefice. It was probably an aid in the transaction of his duties which was prepared by some former official of the First Fruits office, and was afterwards purchased by the nation. B.

JOHN HARVARD AND CAMBRIDGE UNIVERSITY.—In the article with this heading in the January number, after " John Harvard Midlsex: Decem. 19, 0.10.0," the following lines were accidentally omitted :

" On the same page, in a list of names is this :
'Hawered 0. 10. 0.' "

It is to this list in which the name " Hawered" occurs that the next paragraph refers:
" The list has been conjectured to be a summary of previous more detailed entries, but I find no sufficient evidence to support this conjecture."

I find that I was wrong in supposing that the entry " Midlsex " against Harvard's name in the " *Recepta* " indicates the residence of his mother. The following article in the New York *Nation*, February 18, 1886, states the matter correctly.

John Harvard: A Difficulty Solved.—To the Editor of the Nation: Sir: It appears to be clear that John Harvard was born in Surrey, at Southwark, and it is certain that when he went up to Cambridge in 1627 he was described at Emmanuel College as of Middlesex. This is the matter upon which I propose to offer some observations, with the view of removing an apparent discrepancy, for which some would account by the statement that in 1627 he was probably living in London with his mother and her husband. How far this is satisfactory will appear from what follows.

The first point of inquiry is in what manner in Harvard's time the questions addressed to a young man on entering college were put, and I think we are not without a guide which will lead us in a certain direction. When St. John's College published the first part of its Admission Register, which begins in 1629-30, it was an object of interest with me to identify, for my own information, some of the places which appear in it in a form truly grotesque. For reasons into which I need not here enter, I was led to rely mainly upon sound, and, having thus succeeded in overcoming difficulties which appeared almost insuperable, I arrived, upon independent grounds, at the same conclusion as the editor of the Register [of St. John's College], namely, that the entries were made from statements taken down from the lips of the persons admitted ; and there was no doubt uniformity of practice among the different colleges of the University.

The next point is, What was the nature of the questions ? and this renders it necessary to speak of the object which they had in view. That object was not, as the man of to-day might suppose, the mere collection of useful statistics, but was to indicate for what scholarships and other advantages, restricted to those born in a certain district, the person admitted was eligible. It is ignorance of this leading fact which has led into error those who hitherto have attempted to explain the matter. The place at which the person was residing when he went up to the University, was foreign to the scope of inquiry : the place of birth being alone material.

The chief question, then, which was put to John Harvard at Emmanuel College was, where he was born, and the entry of Middlesex leaves no doubt that his reply was "in London." It is stated that the precise locality of his birth was the High Street of Southwark, and the statement derives corroboration from that which proceeded from his own lips. The High Street of Southwark, which extended southward from London Bridge to the spot where stood St. Margaret's Hall, formed part of the City of London, being included in the City Ward of Bridge Without, so that a person born in that street properly described himself as born in London. Z.

Cambridge, England, Feb. 12, 1886.

PROCLAMATION, 1814.—The REGISTER has been furnished by N. J. Herrick, Esq., with the following interesting document from the original in the possession of Mrs. Charles A. Milliken, of Malden, Mass.

A Proclamation.

Whereas, Sir John Sherbroke did by proclamation capture all that part of the District of Maine lying betwixt the Penobscot & St. Croix Rivers for and in behalf of His Majesty the King of Great Britain, I do by all the power in me vested declare it recaptured excepting Castine & Eastport for and in behalf of the United States of America, and the subjects thereof having again become citizens are hereby ordered to conduct themselves accordingly.

And whereas, it has been customary for British officers to declare large extent of sea coasts in a state of blockade without a sufficient force to enforce such blockade ; I do by my power as aforesaid declare all the Ports, Harbors, Rivers, Bays, and Inlets from the River Penobscot to the River St. Croix that remain in actual Possession of the En'y in a state of vigorous blockade, having under my command a sufficient force to enforce the same, and the officers under my command are hereby ordered to govern themselves accordingly.

Done on board the Schooner Faun in Machias River this 17th day of November 1814 and nailed to the Flagstaff of the Fort at Machias.

ALEXANDER MILLIKEN,

Commander of the private armed Schooner Faun.

FACTS GATHERED FROM THE TOWN RECORDS OF NORWICH, CT., BY FRANK PALMER.—

Mr. Isaac Lawrence Sen. d. 19 Apr. 1731, aged 73 years. His wife, Abigail, d. 13 Sept. 1726, in the 64th year of her age.

Isaac Lawrence (son of the above) mar. Susannah Read 15 Apr. 1708. Their children were

Samuel, b. 27 May 1710:
Hannah, b. 18 Mar. 1711–12:
Deborah, b. 6 May 1714 : and their son Jonathan, who d. 20 May 1733.
Isaac mar. 2d, Oct. 9, 1755, Mary Jackson, he being then styled " Deacon."

The children of Samuel Lawrence* (above) by his wife Mary were

Josiah, b. 18 Aug. 1734:
Jonathan, b. 15 Apr. 1736:
Samuel, b. 5 Jan'y 1738–9:
Mary, b. 8 Apr. 1741:
Hannah, b. 23 July 1743:
John, b. 19 Feb. 1745–6.
Deborah, b. 23 Jan'y 1747–8:
Anne, b. 21 Dec. 1754:
Susannah, b. 8 Feb. 1757.

Hannah Lawrence (dau. of Isaac Jr. above) mar. 28 Feb. 1740 David Palmer (son of Thomas), and had by him

Diah, b. 31 Jan'y 1740–1:
John Davis, b. 1 Apr. 1743:
Hannah, b. 15 Apr. 1744.
Deborah, b. 12 Jan'y 1745–46 (who mar. Darius Webb ; see *Giles Memorial*, p. 522):
David, b. 3 Aug. 1747:
Lydia, b. 14 July, 1749:
Susannah, b. 11 Mar. 1752.

Josiah Lawrence (son of Samuel above) mar. 18 Mar. 1761 Mary Branch, and had

Mary, b. 19 Dec. 1761:
Josiah, b. 29 Nov. 1763:
Lucy, b. 23 Apr. 1765.

Jonathan Lawrence (above) mar. Zeruiah Orsmby 29 Aug. 1759, and had
Reuben, b. 23 June 1760:
Lydia, b. 15 Jan'y 1762:
Joanna, b. 31 May 1765.

* Samuel Lawrence's inventory was taken 25 July, 1759.

Samuel Lawrence (son of Samuel above) mar. 27 Nov. 1766 Thankfull Cady and had
  Solomon, b. 14 Sept. 1767.

Hannah Lawrence (dau. of Samuel above) mar. 12 Sept. 1765 Samuel Palmer (son of Samuel, and gr'd-son of Thomas), and had
  Desire, b. 3 June 1766:
  Molly, b. 2 Apr. 1769.

Note.—Mr. Isaac Lawrence, Sen., was the son of John Lawrence, originally of Watertown, but afterwards of Groton, Mass. He " Publickly owned ye Covenant of Grace " at the First Church of Norwich, Conn., in 1700; and was " Received into Full Communion " in 1702. He was, as was his son Isaac Lawrence, Jr., one of the seven members—" the seven pillars on which the church rested "—forming 10 Dec. 1723, the Newent or Third Ecclesiastical Society of Norwich, Conn. The Rev. Daniel Kirtland (the father of the Rev. Samuel Kirtland, the famous missionary to the Oneida Indians, and the grandfather of John Thornton Kirkland, president of Harvard College, 1810–1828) was another of the seven and their first pastor. Our town records spell the name " Lawrance," though in every case it is spelled " Lawrence " by the family and in the church records. The earliest town records exist only in a copy.

Guilford Genealogies.—Alvan Talcott, M.D., of Guilford, Conn., will furnish in MS. for a moderate consideration, extended genealogical notes of the descendants of any of the early fathers of Guilford. The records will be arranged in families in a regular order, giving dates of birth, marriage and death, and bringing the line down to the present time, covering about two hundred and fifty years. The families bearing the following names have their records nearly completed : Bartlett, Benton, Bishop, Blatchly, Bradley, Bristol, Burges, Chittenden, Coan, Collins, Crampton, Cruttenden, Dowd, Dudley, Evarts, Field, Fowler, Graves, Griswold, Hall, Hand, Hart, Hill, Hotchkiss, Hubbard, Johnson, Kimberly, Landon, Lee, Leete, Meigs, Munger, Murray, Norton, Parmelee, Pierson, Robinson, Rossiter, Ruggles, Russell, Scranton, Seward, Shelley, Starr, Stowe, Weld, Willard.

Extensive notes can also be given of the following : Baldwin, Coe, Conklin, Davis, Foster, French, Hopton, Hoyt, Jones, Kirkham, Soper, Spencer, Stevens, Talman, Vaill, Walkley, Ward, Wilcox.

Scotch Record Examinations.—The Government has made provision for examinations which are purely antiquarian or genealogical, without office fees, it being distinctly understood that such examinations have no legal bearing.

In order to obtain permission, the person for whom the work is to be done must apply by letter to Thomas Dickson, Esq., Curator of the Historical Department of H. M. General Register House at Edinburgh.

As the Government must be well satisfied as regards the antiquarian or genealogical character of the work, it would be well to state, in asking permission, that the examinations will be conducted by some one well known at Edinburgh. No better name could be suggested than the Rev. Walter MacLeod, for he is considered the man there for such work, his charges are reasonable, and he acts there for the leading libraries and antiquarian societies.   A. D. W. French.

Washington, &c. *Extracts from the Parish Register of Hurst, co. Berks, communicated by the Rev. Francis J. Poynton, rector of Kelston, Somersetshire, England.*—
  Marriages. 1587 Aug. 3, John Washington & Alice Nashe, Widow.
  Burials. 1600 Aug. 30 John Washington.
  Marr: 1601 April 21 Thomas Newbeire [*sic*, I consider for Newberie, f. j. p.] & Alice Washington.
  Marr: 1656 July 21 Mr Humphrey Newberry & Mrs. Katherine Hestar.
  Marr: 1646 Mr. John Deane & Mrs. Mary Blagrave.

QUERIES.

FOUNDERS OF IPSWICH, MASS.—What are all the names of the persons who settled at Ipswich in 1633?

Felt gives the names of John Winthrop, Jr., William Clerk, Robert Coles, Thomas Howlett, John Biggs, John Gage, Thomas Hardy, William Perkins, John Thorndike and William Serjeant, and states there are three wanting to make up the list. A. D. W. F.

GURTLEY.—Can any one give me information concerning William Gurtley, " of Boston," Matross in Col. Lamb's N. Y. Reg't of Artillery, Continental army, during revolution, and " served through war " ? F. E. HURLEY.
Ithaca, N. Y.

THOMAS THACHER, JR., merchant, oldest son of Rev. Thomas Thacher of the Old South, married Mary, daughter of Major Thomas Savage. Are there any descendants of any child or children of this marriage surviving? Peter, the minister of the New North Church, died without children. So also, so far as is known, did Thomas, a mariner, though twice married. John married Mary Mould, August 4, 1709. The Boston records show no children, nor the death of either husband or wife. If they removed from Boston, whither? The daughter Elizabeth died at the age of seven, as appears from the journal of her uncle, Rev. Peter, of Milton. The only other child, Mary, appears to have married George Kilcup, May 15, 1712. The birth of two children of this marriage is recorded, George and Samuel, but no further notice of this family is found in the Boston records.

Information on the subject of this inquiry would be gratefully received.
85 *Milk Street, Boston.* P. THACHER.

CLARKE.—Who was Elizabeth, wife of William Clarke, of Ipswich, Mass., about 1650?

John Winthrop, Jr., William Clarke and several others, were the founders of Ipswich, Mass., in 1639. Address G. ALBERT LEWIS.
1834 *De Lancey Place, Philadelphia, Pa.*

ATWELL.—In Boltwood's "Hadley Families" appears the following: " Oliver Atwell married June 8, 1781, Jerusha Smith." Said Oliver was born in 1755, and was a soldier of the Revolution. Can any one give his ancestry, parentage and birth-place? Was he a descendant of Benjamin Atwell mentioned in Savage's Genealogical Dictionary? GEO. W. ATWELL, JR.
Lima, N. Y.

SEARS.—Jacob Sears, of Lancaster, Mass., *circa* 1790, had sons Jacob, Jr., Artemas and David ; perhaps other children.

Any information relative to him, his birth-place, parents and wife, will be thankfully received by SAMUEL P. MAY.
Newton, Mass.

DRIVER.—Information is wanted of the previous or past history of Richard Driver, who married Nov. 16, 1758, Ann Wilson Robinson, who was born in 1740, and died in Boston, Nov. 11, 1779, as found on Trinity Church record, where the baptisms of their seven children are given. Their names were : Rosanna, m. James Holbrook ; Mary, m. John Berry ; Ann Wilson, m. Richard Motley ; Richard ; Richard Thomas ; Victor John ; Sarah. He married second, May 3, 1781, Mary Christopher, as found recorded in Trinity Church records, Boston. His will was probated in Suffolk County, August 14, 1792. Anything concerning the aforesaid will be gladly received by MATTHEW A. STICKNEY.
119 *Boston Street, Salem, Mass.*

THACHER.—In the London Guardian of Feb. 17, 1886, we find the following notices, which we insert as being of interest to many readers of the REGISTER :

" One pound reward will be paid for the discovery of the record of the marriage of Peter Thacher and Anne ——, in 1614, probably in the County of Somerset. Mr. Thacher was Vicar of Milton Clevedon, Somerset, from 1616 to 1622, and Rector of St. Edmund's in Salisbury, from 1622 to 1640."

"One pound reward will be paid for the discovery of the record of the birth of Thomas, son of Peter and Anne ——— Thacher, believed to be May 1, 1620, probably in the County of Somerset. Address, in each case, Rev. F. W. Weaver, Milton Vicarage, Evercreech, Bath."

REPLIES.

BRUSH (*ante*, p. 106).—Observing in the REGISTER for the current year, page 106, the inquiry of "Delta" regarding Crean Brush, and thinking that whatever I may contribute, if it do no good can do no harm, I will remark that I find in Hall's Eastern Vermont, page 609, in a biographical notice of Crean Brush, the following : "With the adjournment of the Assembly on the 3d of April, ended Mr. Brush's career as a legislator." .... "During the summer which followed the commencement of hostilities in the colonies, Mr. Brush probably remained in the city of New York, working as best he might for the good of the King. In the fall he repaired to Boston."

The address of the author referred to is B. H. Hall, Esq., Troy, N.Y.

 Bennington, Vt.   G. W. HARMAN.

FIRE IN BOSTON, 1775 (*ante*, p. 106).—" 1775, May 17. On the evening of this day, a store on the south side of the Town Dock, occupied as a barrack by British Troops, took fire by the bursting of some cartridges, imprudently handled by the soldiers. About thirty warehouses and buildings were destroyed, with great part of the effects, contained in them, some of which were donations to the town, for re-relief of the inhabitants suffering under the oppressive Port Bill."—*Mass. Hist. Soc. Coll.*, 1st *Series*, 3, 271.

HISTORICAL INTELLIGENCE.

COL. CHESTER'S OXFORD MATRICULATIONS AND MARRIAGE LICENCES, EDITED BY JOSEPH FOSTER.—Mr. Foster, the well-known genealogist, author of the British Peerage and Baronetage, and other works, has recently purchased, at a cost exceeding £1000, the late Col. Chester's Oxford Matriculations Registers, 7 Vols., and Marriage Licences, 5 Vols., with the intention of printing these intrinsically priceless MSS. uniformly with the publications of the Harleian Society, for the advantage of his numerous genealogical friends in America, as a memorial of the great and good work he did for them in England. He makes this preference because, so far as England is concerned, he would like to retain for himself the monopoly of these manuscripts, and because he believes the American people will appreciate the labors of their own countryman far more fully than Englishmen would, as the proposed work will enable them to place printed copies of these distant and inaccessible Old England registers on the shelves of their very own libraries ready for immediate reference. He therefore appeals to Americans to reciprocate his efforts, and hold him harmless from pecuniary loss, by subscribing for 250 copies of these works, which he desires to print only for them.

It is obvious that a work on such a scale as this can only be produced at a great cost. Including the very heavy sum paid for Col. Chester's manuscripts, and the vast amount of trained labor involved in transcribing them for publication (the annotation the editor proposes to do himself as a labor of love), the actual expense of bringing out the work is estimated as between two and three thousand pounds. It cannot be expected that so great an expense should be incurred till sufficient promises of support have been received to warrant the editor in putting it in hand without prospect of heavy loss. The Oxford Matriculations will be issued in two volumes at a subscription price of ten guineas (not *two* guineas as printed in the January REGISTER). As an inducement for Col. Chester's friends and American genealogists to coöperate with the editor, the work will be offered at nine guineas to those who subscribe for two copies, and at eight guineas to those who subscribe for three.

The Marriage Licences will be issued in five large royal octavo volumes, at £2. 12s. 6d. a volume.

This enterprise is heartily commended by the editor of the REGISTER to the patronage of the American people.

Mr. Foster's address is 21 Boundary Road, London, N. W., England.

PARISH REGISTER OF WILTON, ENGLAND.—The oldest register of the parish of Wilton, Somersetshire, entitled, " A Boocke of Register whearin are conteyned the names of those wch have beene Christnied, Wedded, and Buried w'thin the P'ish of Wilton ffrom the yeare of our Lorde God 1558 untill the yere 1714," has been transcribed by Mr. Houghton Spencer, and will be published by subscription. The work will consist of 80 pages, corresponding with the number in the original. The price will be 5s. post free. Any profit arising from the publication will be devoted to the funds of the voluntarily supported Parish School of Wilton. Address Houghton Spencer, Corse, Taunton, England.

FLETCHER FAMILY UNION.—This association, instituted at Lowell, Aug. 30, 1876, and consisting of descendants of Robert Fletcher of Concord, Mass., will hold its fourth meeting at Lowell, Mass., August 25 and 26, 1886.

LEIGHTON GENEALOGY.—This book, noticed in the January number, was published by subscription at \$3 instead of the price there named. It is an octavo of 127 pages, and copies can be furnished at the subscription price by the author, Mr. T. F. Jordan, Metuchen, N. J.

TOWN HISTORIES IN PREPARATION.—Persons having facts or documents relating to any of these towns are advised to send them at once to the person engaged in writing the history of that town.

Durham, N. H.—At a town meeting in March last $900 was appropriated for publishing a history of the town. An additional sum is to be raised by subscription. The work is placed in the hands of a committee consisting of Lucien Thompson, W. S. Meserve, Joshua B. Smith, E. Jenkins and J. W. Coe. It is proposed that the price of the book shall be between three and five dollars a copy.

GENEALOGIES IN PREPARATION.—Persons of the several names are advised to furnish the compilers of these genealogies with records of their own families and other information which they think may be useful. We would suggest that all facts of interest illustrating family history or character be communicated, especially service under the U. S. government, the holding of other offices, graduation from colleges or professional schools, occupation, with places and dates of births, marriages, residence and death. When there are more than one christian name they should all be given in full if possible. No initials should be used when the full names are known.

Conant. By Frederick Odell Conant, A.M., 229 Commercial Street, Portland, Me.—Mr. Conant has spent much time and money in collecting materials for this work, and has now enough matter to fill a substantial octavo volume. The records include the Connet, Connett and Connit families. It will be embellished with a view of All Saints Church, East Budleigh, England, where Roger Conant was baptized, and other engravings, such as portraits, autographs, etc. Circulars and blanks for genealogical returns will be furnished on application. A limited number of copies will be printed. Price $5, with the right to advance the price after the subscription is closed. Correspondence in regard to family portraits and residences is solicited.

Gile and Guile. By Charles Burleigh, Portland, Me.

Ginn, Genn, or Ghen. By Thomas Smyth, 3 Cordis St., Charlestown, Mass.—Mr. Smyth has a large collection of materials relating to this family, which was early in Northumberland County, Va., and later of Dorchester and Caroline Counties, Maryland ; Barnstable County, Mass., and the eastern part of Maine.

Goodrich.—The Goodrich Association, which has issued two parts of the " Goodrich Family Memorial," having obtained new and important matter, have abandoned their design to issue a third part of this work, and announce that Parts I. and II. will, if sufficient subscription be obtained, be enlarged and thoroughly revised, and with the matter intended for Part III. published in one volume of not less than 275 pages. Price to subscribers $2.50. Money already received for Part III. will be returned or applied towards the new work. Address H. C. Goodrich, secretary and treasurer of the Association, 70 Ogden Place, Chicago, Ill.

Hayward and Howard.—By Marcus T. Janes, No. 8 Mathewson Street, Providence, R. I.—Mr. Janes is preparing a genealogy and brief history of the descendants of William Hayward, of Swansea, Mass., now generally bearing the name of Howard.

Kidder.—Miss S. B. Kidder is collecting materials for a full genealogy of the Kidders in the United States. All communications will be thankfully received from persons possessed of any facts concerning them. The coöperation of those of the name is respectfully requested. Address Miss S. B. KIDDER, 39 Court St., Boston.

Kidder. By F. E. Kidder, Allston, Mass.—The work which will be put to press this spring will be a history of the family in England, and a genealogical record of the descendants of James Kidder, of Billerica, Mass., through his son John, who married, in 1684, Lydia Parker of Chelmsford.

Leach. By Josiah Granville Leach, 733 Walnut Street, Philadelphia, Pa.—Having been engaged for more than a year past in gathering material for a genealogy of the family descended from Lawrence Leach, one of the planters that came in the "fleet" with Rev. Francis Higginson, 1629, and settled at Salem, Mass., where he continued to live until his death, 1662. The compiler solicits correspondence with all who have information to give, or who desire information, with reference to persons bearing the name of Leach, or that have intermarried with the family.

L'Hommedien.—By Frederick L'Hommedien, of Deep River, Conn.

Philbrick. By Rev. Jacob Chapman, Exeter, N. H.—The book, which has before been announced in the REGISTER, will be put to press as soon as the author receives orders for a sufficient number of volumes to pay for printing and binding the book. Price $2 a copy.

Sears, Sare, Sayer, Sayre. By Samuel P. May, Newton, Mass.—Mr. May is preparing a genealogical record of the descendants of Richard Sares, who settled in Yarmouth, Mass., *circ.* 1640, and requests all possible information from any source in regard to the genealogy and history of this family. Information is solicited as to other families of the same name, of which there are several in this country and Canada, and of those by name of Sayre, Sayer, etc., especially as to what is known of their English ancestry. Blanks for family record will be mailed on application.

Smith. By H. Allen Smith, 13 Fulton Street, Brooklyn, N. Y.—This genealogy will be devoted to the descendants of Rev. Nehemiah Smith, who came to this country in 1637, and died at Norwich, Ct., in 1686. It covers a period of ten generations, and includes one generation after the change of name by marriage. It now numbers 400 families. Any information will be gratefully received. Something in a biographical way is desired, if convenient—education, occupation, professional or military life. Photographs from life or from portraits or profiles are desired; also of plate, arms, furniture and other antiquities. Gravestone inscriptions and obituary notices will be of use. It is intended to publish the work at a price just sufficient to cover the cost. Circulars will be furnished to those who apply.

SOCIETIES AND THEIR PROCEEDINGS.

NEW-ENGLAND HISTORIC GENEALOGICAL SOCIETY.

Boston, Mass., January 6, 1886.—The annual meeting was held at the Society's House, 18 Somerset Street, this afternoon at three o'clock, the president, the Hon. Marshall P. Wilder, in the chair.

The recording secretary, David Green Haskins, Jr., read the record of the proceedings at the December meeting.

George K. Clarke, LL.B., in behalf of the nominating committee, reported a list of officers for the current year, and the persons nominated were unanimously elected. The officers for 1886 are:

President.—Hon. Marshall P. Wilder, Ph.D., LL.D., of Boston, Massachusetts.

Vice-Presidents.—Hon. Joseph Williamson, A.M., of Belfast, Maine; Hon. Joseph B. Walker, A.B., of Concord, New Hampshire; Hon. Horace Fairbanks, of St. Johnsbury, Vermont; Hon. George C. Richardson, of Boston, Massachusetts; Hon. John R. Bartlett, A.M., of Providence, Rhode Island; Hon. Edwin H. Bugbee, of Killingly, Connecticut.

Honorary Vice-Presidents.—George William Curtis, LL.D., of West New Brighton, N. Y.; Hon. Rutherford B. Hayes, LL.D., of Fremont, Ohio; Hon. John Wentworth, LL.D., of Chicago, Ill.; Hon. William A. Richardson, LL.D., of Washington, D. C.; Rev. Joseph F. Tuttle, D.D., of Crawfordsville, Ind.; Lyman C. Draper, LL.D., of Madison, Wis.; Rt. Rev. William S. Perry, D.D., LL.D., of Davenport, Iowa; Rev. William G. Eliot, D.D., of St. Louis. Mo.; Rt. Rev. William I. Kip, D.D., LL.D., of San Francisco, Cal.; Rev. Charles Breck, D.D., of Wellsboro', Pa.; Rev. Edward D. Neill, A.B., of St. Paul, Minn.; Hon. Hovey K. Clarke, of Detroit, Mich.; Charles C. Jones, LL.D., of Savannah, Ga.; Rev. Willard F. Mallalieu, D.D., of New Orleans, La.

Corresponding Secretary.—Rev. Edmund F. Slafter, A.M., of Boston, Mass.

Recording Secretary.—David Greene Haskins, Jr., A.M., of Cambridge, Mass.

Treasurer.—Benjamin Barstow Torrey, of Boston, Mass.

Historiographer.—Rev. Increase N. Tarbox, D.D., of Newton, Mass.

Librarian.—John Ward Dean, A.M., of Boston, Mass.

Directors.—Hon Nathaniel Foster Safford, A.B., Milton; Hon. William Claflin, LL.D., Newton, Mass.; William G. Means, Boston; Charles L. Flint, A.M., Boston; Hon. John F. Andrew, A.M., Boston.

Committee on Finance.—Hon. Alvah A. Burrage, Boston; Cyrus Woodman, A.M., Cambridge; Hon. Samuel C. Cobb, Boston; Hamilton A. Hill, A.M., Boston; J. Montgomery Sears, A.B., Boston; William Wilkins Warren, Esq., Boston.

Committee on Publication.—John Ward Dean, A.M., Boston; Rev. Lucius R. Paige, D.D., Cambridge; Rev. Edmund F. Slafter, A.M., Boston; Jeremiah Colburn, A.M., Boston; William B. Trask, Boston; Henry II. Edes, Boston; Henry E. Waite, West Newton; Francis E. Blake, Boston.

Committee on Memorials.—John Ward Dean, A.M., Boston; Albert H. Hoyt, A.M., Boston; Rev. Henry A. Hazen, A.M., Auburndale; J. Gardner White, A.M., Cambridge; William B. Trask, Boston; Daniel T. V. Huntoon, Canton; Arthur M. Alger, LL.B., Taunton.

Committee on Heraldry.—Abner C. Goodell, Jr., A.M., Salem: Hon. Thomas C. Amory, A.M., Boston; Augustus T. Perkins, A.M., Boston; George B. Chase, A.M., Boston; John C. J. Brown, Boston; George K. Clarke, LL.B., Needham.

Committee on the Library.—John T. Hassam, A.M., Boston; Willard S. Allen, A.M., Boston; Jeremiah Colburn, A.M., Boston; William B. Trask, Boston; Deloraine P. Corey, Malden; Edmund T. Eastman, M.D., Boston; Walter Adams, A.M., Framingham.

Committee on Papers and Essays.—Rev. Henry A. Hazen, A.M., Auburndale; Rev. Increase N. Tarbox, D.D., Newton; Rev. David G. Haskins, S.T.D., Cambridge; William C. Bates, Newton; Charles C. Coffin, Boston; Rev. Artemas B. Muzzey, A.M., Cambridge; Rev. Waldo Burnett, A.M., Southboro'; Alexander Williams, Boston.

Col. Wilder, having for the eighteenth time been elected president of the society, proceeded to deliver his annual address, which is printed in full in this number of the REGISTER (*ante*, pp. 138–146).

After the address Mr. Wilder called the Hon. George C. Richardson, vice-president for Massachusetts, to the chair, and withdrew, the members rising as he passed from the hall.

Hon. Nathaniel F. Safford offered a preamble and resolution which was unanimously passed, that whereas our venerable president has secured to this society for building purposes a sum exceeding $25,000, collected personally by himself, the profound thanks of the society be tendered to him for his earnest and successful efforts in its behalf, and that thanks be also extended to the noble and generous benefactors who have contributed this munificent endowment.

The following annual reports were then presented :

Rev. Edmund F Slafter, the corresponding secretary, reported that fifty-eight resident and ten corresponding members had been added to the society during the year. He also reported the usual correspondence relating to historical subjects.

Rev. Increase N. Tarbox, D.D., the historiographer, reported the number of members who have died during the year, as far as known, to be thirty-nine, and that the average age was 73 years, 4 months, 27 days. Memorial sketches have been prepared and printed as promptly as the space at command will allow.

Benjamin B. Torrey, the treasurer, reported the total income of the year to be $3,637.92, and the current expenses $3,510.61, leaving a balance on hand of

$127.31. The amount of the Librarian's Fund is $12,763.13; of the Life Membership Fund, $10,947.74; of the Bradbury Fund, $2,500; of the Towne Memorial Fund, $3,654.90; of the Barstow Fund, $939.30; of the Bond Fund, $859.46; of the Cushman Fund, $97.51; of the Sever Fund, $5,000; of the Alden Fund, $1,000; of the Russell Fund, $3,000; and of the Building Fund, $25,028.19; making a total of the several funds in the hands of the treasurer of $65,790.23.

John W. Dean, the librarian, reported that 522 volumes and 1878 pamphlets had been added to the library during the year. The library now contains 20,778 volumes, and 64,604 pamphlets.

John T. Hassam, chairman of the committee on English Research, reported gratifying results, particularly in relation to the ancestry and birth of the founder of Harvard College (REG. xxxix. 265, 325).

Rev. Henry A. Hazen, chairman of the committee on papers, reported that nine papers had been read before the society during the year.

Col. Albert H. Hoyt, secretary of the committee on memorials, reported that the fourth volume of "Memorial Biographies" had been completed and issued.

John T. Hassam, chairman of the library committee, John W. Dean, chairman of the publishing committee, and Abner C. Goodell, Jr., chairman of the committee on heraldry, submitted the reports of these several committees.

MAINE GENEALOGICAL SOCIETY.

Portland, Wednesday, January 27, 1886.—The annual meeting, adjourned to this evening, was held in Reception Hall, F. M. Ray, Vice-President, in the chair.

The nominating committee reported the following list of officers, the first president of the society, John F. Anderson, having declined a reëlection. The candidates were elected, namely:

President.—William H. Smith.
Vice-President.—F. M. Ray.
Treasurer.—Frederick O. Conant.
Secretary.—Charles Burleigh.
Librarian.—Stephen M. Watson.

F. O. Conant, the treasurer, reported that the receipts for the last year were $85.35, expenses $67.50, balance in the treasury $17.75.

F. M. Ray read a paper, entitled "A Batch of Old Papers and Books."

L. D. Chapman read a paper on the "Ancient Military of Stroudwater."

John T. Hull read a paper, entitled "A Stranger's Grave: James Bannatyne." Abstracts of these papers were printed in the *Eastern Argus*, Jan. 28, 1886.

VIRGINIA HISTORICAL SOCIETY.

Richmond, Saturday, January 23, 1886.—A meeting of the executive committee was held this evening, William Wirt Henry, chairman, and Robert A. Brock, secretary.

A long list of donations of books, relics and manuscripts, was reported, among them a highly interesting document from George Fortunatus Judah, Searcher of Records, Spanish Town, Jamaica, W. I., namely, a handsomely engrossed copy of the Royal Charter granted by Charles II., Sept. 27, 1668, to the Royal African Society, the head of which was James, Duke of York, brother to the king. A description of this document and a history of the company is printed in a report of this meeting, in the *Richmond Dispatch*. Jan. 24, 1886.

Letters from several gentlemen were read, among them one from B. F. Stevens of London, in relation to his proposition to furnish the United States government with copies of unpublished documents relating to the American Revolution, in the public and private depositories of Europe; another from George H. Moore, LL.D., of New York, in relation to the record, Feb. 21, 1682, given in Hening's Statutes at Large of Virginia, in which John Buckner is stated to have been called before Lord Culpeper and his Council for printing the laws of 1680 without his excellency's license, and ordered to give bonds in £100 "not to print anything thereafter until his Majesty's pleasure be known." Dr. Moore inquires whether this record has "ever been further fortified or discredited." The Secretary replies, that the records quoted by Hening were destroyed April 3, 1865, when the Court of Appeals building was burnt, but there is no reason to doubt that the entry was in the records.

February 27.—A meeting was held at 8 o'clock this evening, Mr. Henry chairman, and Mr. Brock secretary.

Gifts of books, relics and manuscripts were reported. Mr. Brock, the corresponding secretary, reported that the next volume of the Society's collections, relating to the Huguenot Emigration to America (*ante*, pages 110–11), has been committed to the printer.

RHODE ISLAND HISTORICAL SOCIETY.

Providence, Tuesday, Nov. 17, 1885.—The regular fortnightly meeting was held last evening, the president, William Gammell, LL.D., in the chair.

A paper on "The Huguenot Influence in Rhode Island," by Miss Esther Bernon Carpenter, of South Kingston, was read by Prof. Lincoln. The paper is printed in full in the *Providence Journal*, Nov. 18, 1885.

December 1.—A stated meeting was held this evening, President Gammell in the chair.

Amasa Eaton, of Providence, read a paper on "French Spoliation Claims and Rhode Island Claimants." An abstract of this paper is printed in the *Evening Bulletin*, Providence, Dec. 2, 1885.

December 15.—A stated meeting was held this evening, President Gammell presiding.

Carl W. Ernst of Boston, editor of *The Beacon*, formerly a resident of Providence, read a paper on "International Law: its Theory and Practice as Defined by Henry Wheaton." He was followed by Hon. Abraham Payne with a "Biographical Sketch of Henry Wheaton," who was born in Providence Nov. 27, 1785. Abstracts are printed in the *Evening Bulletin*, Dec. 16, 1885.

December 29.—A stated meeting was held this evening, President Gammell in the chair.

George C. Mason, Jr., of Newport, read a paper on "Apprenticeship and the Manual Training System." The paper is printed in full in the *Evening Bulletin*, Dec. 30, 1885.

CHICAGO HISTORICAL SOCIETY.

Chicago, Ill., Wednesday, Nov. 17, 1885.—The annual meeting was held this day, Hon. E. B. Washburne in the chair.

The librarian, Albert D. Hager, submitted his annual report, which showed that the accessions of books to the Library were 2709 bound volumes and 4532 pamphlets, which added to former collections made 12,024 bound books, and 35,388 pamphlets, a total of 47,412 books. Of these, 1308 were purchased with the income from the "Lucretia Pond Fund."

During the year 795 volumes have been bound at an expense of $760.15, of which 314 were newspaper files, and a large proportion of the other were serials and the publications of sister societies.

The entire expenses for the year, including bills for book-binding, salaries, taxes, &c., were $1869.86. A balance of $725.30 was in the Society's treasury.

Hon. Thomas Drummond, in behalf of the family of the late I. N. Arnold, presented an oil portrait of Mr. Arnold, late President of the Society, which Mr. Washburne received for the Society with appropriate remarks.

Mr. E. G. Mason, for the Executive Committee, made a report of the two trust funds of the late Jonathan Burr and Miss Lucretia Pond. The Burr Fund of $2000 is safely invested in 6% interest bearing bonds, and $120 accumulated interest is in the treasury.

The "Lucretia Pond Fund" amounts to $13,500, which is also safely invested. The accumulated interest, at last annual meeting, was $971.96. The amount received since is $810, making $1781.96. Of this amount $1400.53 have been expended in the purchase of books.

Hon. A. H. Burley, for Trustees of the "Gilpin Fund," made report showing that the total of that fund was $71,279.67. Rev. M. Woolsey Stryker, Hempstead Washburne and John Moses were elected members.

An election of officers for the ensuing year was then held, and the following was the result of the election:

President.—Hon. E. B. Washburne.
Vice-Presidents.—First, Edward G. Mason; second, Alexander C. McClurg.
Treasurer.—Henry H. Nash.
Secretary and Librarian.—Albert D. Hager.
Executive Committee.—Hon. Mark Skinner, Hon. D. K. Pearsons.

NECROLOGY OF THE NEW-ENGLAND HISTORIC GENEALOGICAL SOCIETY.

Prepared by the Rev. INCREASE N. TARBOX, D.D., Historiographer of the Society.

THE historiographer would inform the society, that the sketches prepared for the REGISTER are necessarily brief in consequence of the limited space which can be appropriated. All the facts, however, he is able to gather, are retained in the Archives of the Society, and will aid in more extended memoirs for which the "Towne Memorial Fund," the gift of the late William B. Towne, A.M., is provided. Four volumes, printed at the charge of this fund, entitled "MEMORIAL BIOGRAPHIES," edited by the Committee on Memorials, have been issued. They contain memoirs of all the members who have died from the organization of the society to the year 1862. A fifth volume is in preparation.

WILLIAM PARSONS, Esq., a benefactor and life member, admitted June 2, 1847, was born is Gloucester, Mass., August 30, 1804, and died in Newton, Mass., July 1, 1885, aged 80 years and 10 months.

His earliest American ancestor was Jeffrey Parsons, of Gloucester, and we are indebted chiefly to Hon. John J. Babson, of Gloucester, for the following details of his family line. Jeffrey[1] Parsons and Sarah Vinson married Nov. 11, 1657. He died Aug. 19, 1687. She died Jan. 12, 1708. Jeffrey,[2] born Jan. 31, 1666, married Abigail Younglove, of Ipswich, May 5, 1686. The date of his death is not known. She died in 1734. Jonathan,[3] born Feb. 8, 1687, married Lydia Stanwood, Feb. 1, 1711. Among their children were twin sons. James,[4] one of these twins, born Feb. 15, 1722, married Nov. 8, 1744, Abigail Tarr. They settled in Sandy Bay, now Rockport, Mass. He died in January, 1789. James,[5] born Oct. 25, 1746, married Deborah Lane in 1767, and died August 20, 1796. William,[6] married Martha Post, and died Nov. 3, 1823, leaving an only son, the subject of this sketch.

William[7] Parsons was married to Georgiana B. Messer, of Stratford, N. H., Dec. 10, 1834. She was born in that town, March 14, 1816. From this marriage there were seven children, four sons and three daughters. Of these one son died in 1858, and one daughter in 1883. Three sons and two daughters, with their mother, survive.

Mr. Parsons having lost his father, who died when the son was nineteen years old, was called naturally to take charge of the business and shipping interests in which his father had been engaged. He received, therefore, an early practical business education. He remained as a merchant in Gloucester until he was more than forty years old, removing to Boston in 1845.

Since coming to Boston, in the various business relations which he has sustained, he so conducted himself as to secure prosperity and success, and leave behind a record of honor in the wide circle of his associates and friends.

JOSEPH WARREN TUCKER, Esq., of Roxbury, a resident member, admitted Dec. 26, 1871, was born in Dorchester, Dec. 1, 1800, and died in Boston Highlands, April 21, 1885. His father, Elijah Tucker, was born in Milton, Mass., Feb. 24, 1765; and his mother, Rebecca Weatherby, was born in Dedham, Mass., May 7, 1769. His earliest American ancestor was *Robert* Tucker of Weymouth, 1635. Of his eight children *James*[2] was born in 1640. He was married, but the name of his wife is not given. Of his three children, *James*[3] was born in 1680, and married Sarah Baker, of Dedham, in 1707. Of their eight children, *Joseph*[4] was born in 1725, and married, 1754, Mary Dana. Of their eleven children, *Elijah*[5] was born as above, Feb. 24, 1765. Joseph Warren[6] was therefore of the sixth American generation. He married Nov. 12, 1856, Mary Porter, daughter of Mr. Samuel Porter, of Portland, Me. From this marriage there were no children, and his wife died before him.

The subject of this sketch, until the age of twenty-one, labored hard upon his father's farm in Roxbury, and having no advantages for education, except such as were afforded by the district schools of that period, which were of an inferior grade. However, by special studies after he had come of age, he prepared himself for school-teaching, and for some years taught district-schools in the winter. Then he began to serve as clerk in stores, until in 1827, when he went into the grocery business for himself.

From 1837 to 1843, he represented the town of Roxbury in the Legislature. He was also upon the board of assessors, overseers of the poor, and surveyors of highways. In 1840, he was elected selectman, serving till Roxbury was made a city, in 1846, when he was elected city clerk, and held the office during the whole period that Roxbury remained a separate city.

Few men have had so many offices of trust. He was clerk of the First Religious Society (which was the John Eliot Church), he was justice of the peace, notary public, one of the directors of the People's National Bank, trustee of the Eliot Savings Institution, &c. In short he lived a long, laborious, honorable and useful life, and passed away quietly and peacefully in a good old age. His funeral was attended in the meeting-house of the First Religious Society of Roxbury, Friday afternoon, April 24.

Dea. JOTHAM GOULD CHASE, of Springfield, Mass., a life member, was born in Anson, Me., March 30, 1816, and died of pneumonia in Springfield, Mass., Dec. 5, 1884, aged 68 years, 8 mos. 5 days.

He was the eldest son of Col. Jotham Sewall Chase and Mary Gould, daughter of Dea. Moriah Gould, of Norridgewock, Me., who were married in the year 1814. Jotham Gould Chase was the seventh in direct succession from Aquilla[1] Chase, through Thomas,[2] Thomas,[3] Josiah,[4] Josiah,[5] and Jotham S.[6] to Jotham G.[7]

Jotham Gould Chase was twice married—first, to Sarah C. S. G., daughter of James Brown Thornton, Esq., of Saco, Me., born July 22, 1820 ; married April 29, 1816 ; died in Springfield, Mass., March 10, 1847, leaving one son, James Brown Thornton Chase, born in Springfield, Mass., Feb. 22, 1847, and who is now living in Dakota Ter. He married second, Cornelia S., daughter of Jesse Savage, Esq., of Hartford, Conn., May 28, 1850, who with two adopted daughters, Cora J. and Ada G. Chase, survive him, residing in Springfield, Mass. Two grandchildren, Sarah Thornton and Jessie, daughters of James B. T. and Annie Chase, are now residing with their mother in Newport, R. I.

Dea. Chase in early youth joined the Baptist church in South Berwick, Me. In 1839 he removed to Boston, uniting by letter with the old Federal Street (now Clarendon Street) Baptist Church ; but he remained in Boston less than a year, removing to Springfield, Mass., in the spring of 1840, where he united by letters with the first Baptist Church in August of that year. For a long period he had entire charge of its choir and music, and for more than forty-four years has been one of its most active, earnest, reliable and spiritual members. Though voted for many times, it was not till January 1, 1880, that he would consent to accept the office of deacon of the church, to which he was elected unanimously, and which he held until his death.

In public life he was honored by his fellow citizens several times with offices of trust in the city government, unsought by himself. Never a political partisan, he was a true, decided republican, heartily sustaining the general government in its struggle with rebellion, and rejoicing in the stability, freedom and emancipation which crowned its success.

Dea. Chase entered the dry-goods business with Mr. Edward C. Wilson in Springfield, in 1840, the firm being at first Wilson & Chase, and afterwards Wilson, Chase & Co. He continued in the dry-goods trade some six or seven years, when he left it to enter the lumber and building business with Messrs. Decrete, Bayington & Co., with whom he remained until his partners removed to Chicago. He continued in the lumber trade, sometimes with partners and sometimes alone, until the close of his life.

As a business man his character and integrity were ever beyond suspicion. He was cautious, industrious and persevering, giving his whole energies to his business enterprises, but winning success only by fair, upright and honorable dealing. The writer of this sketch has been personally and intimately associated with Bro. Chase in business, social and religious life, for nearly forty-five years, from our first meeting in the choir and Sabbath School of old Federal Street Baptist Church in Boston to the last thirty-two years of almost constant intercourse in Springfield. As a christian he was humble, trustful and joyous. He delighted to contemplate " the house of many mansions," and looked with sure hope to be received to "his own prepared." As a friend he was true, tender and faithful. As an associate, lively, warm-hearted and cheerful. His eminent social qualities, his large information and easy conversational powers, his knowledge and enthusiastic love of music, made him a most welcome addition to every social circle which he entered.

Dea. Chase had been a great sufferer, during his later years, from a painful chronic disease, which he bore with patient fortitude and resignation; but his last illness was pneumonia, resulting from a cold taken only a week before his death. Sweet peace and joy, and faith without a cloud, sustained his last moments, and his mortal eyes caught a glimpse of the glories beyond the River ere yet he had passed over, which left upon his countenance the radiant stamp of the signet ring of Heaven.

By George P. Geer, Esq., of Springfield, Mass.

Hon. WILLIAM WARREN TUCKER, a benefactor and life member, admitted March 19, 1869, was born in Boston, March 18, 1817, and died at Paris, France, Nov. 26, 1885. His father was Alanson Tucker, born in Middleborough, Mass., Jan. 25, 1777, and his mother was Eliza Thom, born in Londonderry, N. H., April 19, 1790. His father and mother were united in marriage May 9, 1809, and the father died June 1, 1863. His grandfather, Nathaniel Tucker, was born in Middleborough, Mass., Oct. 15, 1744, and his great-grandfather, Benjamin Tucker, was born in the same town in the year 1705 or 1706.

After being fitted for college he entered Dartmouth and was graduated there in 1835. He received the degree of A.M. from Dartmouth in 1838, and from Harvard College in 1861. His class in Dartmouth College consisted of fifty members, among whom were numbered Hon. Amos Tuck, member of congress, Hon. John P. Healy, late City Solicitor of Boston, and Hon. Nathaniel Foster Safford of this city.

He was united in marriage, March 30, 1843, with Susan Elizabeth, daughter of William and Susan (Ruggles) Lawrence, of Boston. From this marriage there were two children, William Lawrence, born Nov. 4, 1844, and Allan, born April 20, 1848.

He was a trustee of the Lawrence Academy of Groton, an institution endowed in part by his father in law, from 1844 to 1852, and in 1878 was a member of the Executive Council under Gov. Rice.

At some time before 1851 he had entered into business arrangements under the firm name of Upham, Appleton & Co. This continued for a few years, when it was changed into Upham, Tucker & Co., commission merchants, No. 4 Milk Street.

Mr. Tucker was the translator or compiler of the following works:

His Imperial Highness the Grand Duke Alexis in the United States of America during the Winter of 1871–72. .... For private distribution. [Compiled by W. W. Tucker.] 8vo. pp. 221. (1). Cambridge, 1872.

His Royal Highness Prince Oscar at the National Celebration of the Centennial Anniversary of American Independence, held in Philadelphia, U. S. A., July 4, 1876. [Compiled by W. W. Tucker.] 8vo. pp. +119. Boston, 1876.

The Republic of San Marino. Translated from the French. Printed for private distribution. 12mo. pp. xiv. 170. Cambridge, 1880.

The Neutral Territory of Moresnet. Printed for private distribution. [Translated from the French.] 12mo. pp. 18. Cambridge, 1882.

The Valley of Andorra. Translated from the French, and printed for private distribution. 12mo. pp. 66. Cambridge, 1882.

ISAAC CHILD, Esq., a life member, admitted June 9, 1846, was born in Newton, Mass. (now West Roxbury), May 1, 1792, and died in Boston, Dec. 23, 1885. His father was Daniel Child, born in Brookline, Mass., Feb. 19, 1754. His mother was Rebecca Richards (daughter of Capt. Jeremiah Richards), born in Roxbury, Dec. 18, 1760. His earliest American ancestor was Benjamin[1] Child, born near Bury St. Edmunds, England, about 1615. From him the line ran through Joshua,[2] born 1658; Isaac,[3] born 1688; Isaac,[4] born 1722, and Daniel,[5] as above given, born in 1754.

From a record left by himself we copy the following quaint and suggestive sentences:

"My education, in common parlance, has been very limited, but that obtained in commerce with men and things through life, somewhat more extensive. .... My good mother, being a past school teacher of Roxbury, singled me from my four older brothers as fit for a higher range of education, should the pecuniary circumstances of my father seem to warrant, but that time did not arrive, and I did not attain even an academical education. But while she sat and treadled her little linen wheel, being ' apt to teach,' she prepared me for a three months term under female tuition, in summer, and a similar term with male teachers in the winter."

Mr. Child was three times married. His first wife was Eliza, daughter of Benjamin Billings, of Roxbury, to whom he was married Nov. 22, 1821. His second wife was Maria, daughter of Phineas Eastman of Franklin, N. H., and his marriage with her took place July 4, 1848. She died April 2, 1853. His third wife, to whom he was married May 31, 1854, was Abby, daughter of Ely Forbes Baker, of Steuben, Me. This third wife survives him. There was one child, a daughter, by the first marriage, and two daughters by the third marriage. All these children are dead.

Mr. Child was variously employed during his active life, and held several important trusts and responsibilities, as treasurer of the Williams Market, treasurer of our own society for three years, from Jan. 1857 to Jan. 1860 ; town clerk of Argyle, Me., selectman, assessor, &c.

All the initiatory work of the Child Genealogy, a solid volume of 842 pages, was performed by him. His kinsman, Elias Child, who completed and published the work, says in his preface: " Correspondence was opened with Mr. Child, of Boston, who had hitherto been unknown to me, which led to an arrangement with him for placing in my hands the material which he had, to be incorporated in the proposed genealogy. His matter forms the *nucleus* of this work ; not that it constitutes the larger amount, nor that it was arranged as incorporated in this work. The filling up of many branches partially traced by Mr. Isaac Child, and the discovery of many new lines, will swell the volume to threefold or more beyond his material. Yet had it not been for his industry and perseverance, it is probable the present work would not have been undertaken."

Capt. PEARCE WENTWORTH PENHALLOW, a resident member, admitted May 9, 1878, was born in Portsmouth, N. H., Feb. 27, 1817, and died in Boston, Mass., Dec. 9, 1885. His father was Hunking Penhallow, born in Portsmouth, N. H., October, 1766, and died Sept. 24, 1826. His mother was Harriet Pearce, daughter of David and Bethiah (Ingersoll) Pearce, born in Gloucester, Mass., March 28, 1780. His earliest American ancestor was Samuel Penhallow, born July 2, 1665, at St. Mabon, County of Cornwall, England, who came to New England in 1686, living first at Charlestown, Mass., and then at Portsmouth, N. H., where he married Mary Cutt, and by her had thirteen children. John,[2] born January 13, 1693, married Elizabeth, widow of John Watts, and had four children. Of these, John[3] married Sarah, daughter of Hunking Wentworth, and had eleven children. Of these, Hunking[4] (whose record is given above) was the sixth son.

The subject of this sketch, being of the fifth American generation, was united in marriage, Oct. 16, 1845, with Elizabeth Warner Pitts Sherburne, daughter of John Nathaniel Sherburne. By this marriage there were four sons, two of whom are dead. The others are Thomas Wibird and Charles Sherburne, the latter a graduate of Harvard College in the class of 1874. Their mother also survives.

Captain Penhallow had an eventful and eminently successful life on the sea, following in this the occupation of his father. At the age of twenty-three, in 1840, he was put in command of the ship Margaret Scott, of Portsmouth, trading between New England and the southern states. In 1844 he was transferred to the ship Rockingham, engaged in the same general line of trade. In 1850 Glidden & Williams gave him the command of the ship George Raynes, one of the vessels of the San Francisco line. This was in the very height of the great movement to California, and the ships of this line were loaded down with passengers and merchandise. In 1854 Glidden & Williams gave him the command of the ship Sierra Nevada, of nearly 2000 tons, in the guano trade. With a full load of guano, this ship, under the command of Capt. Penhallow, was ordered to sail for Liverpool. In entering the dock the ship caught on the dock sill and was broken and the cargo lost. After long and vexatious suits, under the charge of Capt. Penhallow, the sum of $150,000 was recovered from the dock company. He continued to follow the sea, having those large and important trusts on his hands, until his retirement, only a few years ago.

He was a man greatly beloved in the wide circle of his acquaintance. Of winning address, with the law of christian kindness and simplicity in his whole look and manner, he strongly attracted men of all conditions to himself, and has left behind a bright and shining name.

He contributed an article on the Penhallow family to the REGISTER for January, 1878, which was re-printed in an 8vo. pamphlet of 22 pages. In 1885, he revised and enlarged this work, and it was published in an octavo volume of 47 pages.

JOHN ALLEN LEWIS, Esq., a resident member, admitted Oct. 11, 1873, was born in Barnstable, Mass., Nov. 19, 1819, and died in Boston, Nov. 2, 1885.

His father was Josiah Lewis, of Barnstable. His earliest paternal ancestor was George Lewis (Lewice, Lewes), who as a clothier came from East Greenwich, Kent, England, in 1632 or 33, settling first at Plymouth, Mass., and living also for a time at Scituate before removing to Barnstable in 1639.

Mr. Lewis's mother was Sally Gorham, a direct descendant from Capt. John Gorham, who was born in England in January, 1620-1, and married Desire Howland, daughter of John Howland, of Plymouth, one of the original Mayflower company.

Gustavus A. Hinckley, Esq., of Barnstable (to whom we are indebted for much valuable information touching the Lewis, Gorham and allied families), says: "Mr. Lewis was an excellent representative of the inherited Lewis and Gorham elements of character that were often exhibited in the generations back to the early colonial period ; more particularly the love of education and of culture characteristic of his Lewis ancestry." We regret that, in the limited space allotted to this obituary notice, we can make use of only a small portion of the material which Mr. Hinckley has furnished. But the whole will be carefully preserved, and will come into larger use by and by in the preparation of a more extended biography for our Memorial Volumes.

S. B. Phinney, Esq., president of the First National Bank of Hyannis and formerly publisher of the *Barnstable Patriot*, says: "Mr. Lewis entered my office in Barnstable at the early age of 11 years, and learned the setting of type under my own instruction in 1831. .... When the California gold fever was at its height, more than thirty-six years ago, he had still his fondness for printing, and took with him to San Francisco a small printing establishment, and while detained some weeks in crossing the Isthmus of Panama, edited and printed a small daily newspaper, to the edification of the large number who were detained with him *en route.*"

He remained some years in California and was employed upon the *Alta California*, and afterward, in company with his relative, William H. Rand, Esq., established a paper in Los Angelos, which was issued half in English and half in Spanish.

Soon after returning from California he was united in marriage, Nov. 12, 1856, with Miss Elizabeth Ritchie, daughter of Mr. John Ritchie, of Boston. They made their home for a time in Chicago, and Mr. Lewis was employed by the Illinois Central Railroad, in what might be called the literary department of the road, a range of miscellaneous writing made necessary in every large enterprise of this kind.

While in Chicago their only child, Richard Lewis, was born, Oct. 19, 1858. As it was thought the health of this child suffered in Chicago, Mr. and Mrs. Lewis returned to Boston. But the child died at the age of five years. Mr. Lewis still continued in the employ of the Illinois Central Railroad for such writing as could be done in Boston. In his later years his eye-sight was seriously impaired, but he continued to use his pen in various ways as long as he was able, being for years a contributor to *The Nation*, in such matters as were to him specialties. This labor he performed by request of the managers of the paper, but would take no pay for it. For many years he was slowly gathering a choice library, very rich and rare in Mather publications. Mr. Lewis was a man of most kind and companionable nature, and was greatly beloved by those well acquainted with him.

HENRY EDWARDS, Esq., a resident member, admitted Feb. 17, 1866, was born in Northampton, Mass., Oct. 22, 1798, and died in Boston, Sept. 24, 1885. His father was William[6] Edwards, born in Elizabeth, New Jersey, Nov. 10, 1770, and his mother was Rebecca Tappan, born in Northampton, Mass., July 14, 1775. These two were united in marriage Nov. 11, 1793, and had eleven children, eight of whom lived beyond December, 1868.

His earliest American ancestor was William[1] Edwards, of Hartford, Ct., who was resident in that town about 1640, and in 1645 married Mrs. Agnes Spencer, widow of Mr. William Spencer, she having three children by her first marriage. By her Mr. Edwards had only one child. Richard[2] Edwards, born May, 1647, first married 1667, Elizabeth Tuthill (Tuttle), of New Haven, and by her had six children, the eldest of whom was Timothy[3] Edwards, born May 14, 1669. He married 1694, Esther Stoddard, of Northampton. By this marriage there were eleven children, ten daughters and one son. Jonathan[4] Edwards, born Oct. 5, 1703, in East Windsor, Ct., was the great theological and metaphysical writer of his age. He married, July 28, 1727, Sarah Pierrepont, of New Haven. From this marriage there were three sons and nine daughters. The eldest son was Timothy[5] Edwards, born in Northampton, July 25, 1738, and married Rhoda Ogden, of Elizabeth, N. J. He was a merchant in Elizabeth, but in 1771 removed to Stockbridge, Mass.

William[6] Edwards's record is given above. Henry Edwards, therefore, was of the *seventh* generation from William, of Hartford. The family of Tappans, from whom his mother was chosen, had a very honorable line of descent.

In the year 1828, Sept. 4, Mr. Edwards was united in marriage with Miss Martha Ann Dorr, daughter of Hon. Samuel Dorr, of Boston. By this marriage there were four children, two of whom died in infancy and two in youth, one whilst a member of college.

Mr. Edwards began his mercantile training in 1821, in the store of his uncle, Arthur Tappan, in the city of New York. In 1823 he associated himself with Charles Stoddard, of Boston, and under the firm name of Edwards & Stoddard they carried on a large business in French dry-goods. Mr. Edwards lived much in France as purchaser of these goods, and there he enjoyed the friendship of Lafayette, and visited by invitation at his chateau at La Grange. This business relation with Dea. Stoddard continued from 1823 to 1845, and was very successful.

Mr. Edwards was a man in whom his fellow-men safely trusted. Many large public interests, city, state and national, have been placed in his keeping, where they always received faithful attention. He was a man exceedingly polite and affable, with a winning address. He has passed the later years of his life in quiet and retirement, but it was a pleasure to his friends when they chanced to meet him on the street or in social gatherings.

Rev. WILLIAM BARRY, A.M., of Chicago, Ill., a corresponding member, admitted June 3, 1847, was born in Boston, January 10, 1805, and died in Chicago, Jan. 17, 1885, aged 80 years and seven days. His father was William Barry, a somewhat public man of Boston, and member of the legislature. His mother was Esther Stetson. His brother, Rev. John Stetson Barry, was the author of a History of Massachusetts, in three volumes.

Mr. Barry entered Brown University in 1818, graduating in 1822, having among his classmates Alexis Caswell, D.D., afterwards president of the college, Isaac Davis, LL.D., and Benjamin Clarke Cutler, D.D. After graduating, he first studied law in the office of Chief Justice Shaw. Changing his plan of life, he entered the Divinity School in Cambridge in 1826, and after two years went to Germany and pursued his studies two years more in that country. He was licensed in 1830, and was first settled in Lowell, Mass., where he remained five years.

In 1835 he accepted a call to the First Unitarian Church in Framingham, where he remained as pastor nine years, but continuing his residence at Framingham for some years longer, while he was engaged in literary labors, including a History of the Town of Framingham, with genealogies of the Framingham families, a work of 456 pages. From 1844 and onward, so long as Mr. Barry remained in Framingham, the writer of this notice was his near neighbor, and familiar with his busy literary labors. He was a most kind, polite and companionable man. About the time of his coming to Framingham, he was united in marriage with Miss Elizabeth Willard. He found in her a rich and choice treasure. She was of a modest, lady-like deportment, gentle in all her ways, but of refined mind and great literary culture. The hymn which she wrote for the dedication of the Edgehill Grove Cemetery in Framingham, was rare for its beauty and fitness.

But the great work of Mr. Barry has really been in the West, in the building up of the Historical Society of Chicago. At this work he wrought for long years, until in 1868 he resigned his position as president of the society. In this connection his literary labors have been very great.

Such has been his state of health through all the labors of his life, that he has been compelled often to diversify work with travel. His European travel and study, however, have been of the greatest assistance in his peculiar enterprises. His wife died about a year and a half ago, and soon after her death her hymn was read on a beautiful October day in the Framingham Cemetery—a day like that gentle October day thirty-seven years before, when it was first sung on that spot, Mr. Barry leaves two married daughters. Other children and grandchildren passed away in earlier life.

HON. JOHN DAGGETT, a corresponding member, admitted Feb. 3, 1881, was born in Attleborough, Mass., Feb. 10, 1805, and died in same place, Dec. 13, 1885. He was the son of Ebenezer Daggett, who was born in Attleborough, Apr. 16, 1763, and died March 4, 1832. His mother was Sally Maxcy, born in Attleborough, Nov. 20, 1778. His earliest American ancestor was *John*[1] Daggett, who came over in Winthrop's Company in 1630, and went with Thomas Mayhew to Martha's Vineyard. From him the line runs through *Thomas*[2] who married Hannah Mayhew, *John*[3] who removed from Martha's Vineyard to Attleborough, *Ebenezer*[4] who married Mary Blackintor, *John*[5] who married Mercy Shepard, and *Ebenezer*[6] above given. He was therefore of the seventh American generation.

He was fitted for college at Wrentham Academy, and entered Brown University in 1822, graduating in course in 1826. His law studies occupied three years, one year with Joseph L. Tillinghast of Providence, R. I., one year with J. J. Fiske of Wrentham, and one with Judge Theron Metcalf of Dedham. He was admitted to the bar in Dedham in Dec. 1829, and immediately commenced the practice of law in Attleborough, where he remained till his death.

He was united in marriage, June 18, 1840, with Miss Nancy McClellan Boomer, of Sutton, Mass. From this marriage there were seven children, of whom five died in infancy, and two, a son and daughter, Mrs. Sheffield of New Haven, Ct., and John M. Daggett of Arkansas, with their mother, survive.

Mr. Daggett was a member of the Massachusetts House of Representatives for four years, 1836–1839 inclusive, and was again a member in 1866. He was a member of the Senate in 1850.

He has been, for a long course of years, the President of the Old Colony Historical Society at Taunton, and has devoted much time to antiquarian and historical pursuits. He was the author of the History of Attleborough, published in 1834, and had a second and much enlarged edition ready for the press. He has written many articles for the different periodicals of the day.

The Bristol County Republican, under date of Dec. 18, 1885, says of him: "On the 10th of February last, there was a large gathering of relatives and friends to greet him on the advent of his octogenarian birthday—a day of gratulation to him and his esteemed wife. His genial kindliness, courtesy and integrity of character as a counsellor and friend—always to say a kind word, never a hard one—secured for him the title of honest John Daggett, which he wore with modest grace and merit from his college days, during these sixty years, to the time when death claimed him as a shining mark. He has passed away, but his life-long deeds of kindness will live after him, and his memory as the Christian gentleman will ever be cherished."

Hon. NATHAN CROSBY, LL. D., of Lowell, a resident member, admitted Nov. 3, 1866, was born at Sandwich, N. H., Feb. 12, 1798, and died in Lowell, Feb. 11, 1885. One day more would have made him exactly eighty-seven years old. His earliest American ancestor was Simon[1] Crosby, who with his wife Ann, then twenty-five years old, and one son Thomas, came to Cambridge, Mass., in 1635, and was made a freeman in the following year.

From Simon,[1] the line runs through Simon,[2] born in 1637, who settled in Billerica and married Rachel Brackett; Josiah[3] of Billerica, who married, Nov. 2, 1703, Mary Manning; Josiah,[4] born in 1704, who in 1729 married Elizabeth French; Josiah,[5] born 1730, who married Aug. 23, 1750, Sarah Fitch; Asa,[6] born July 15, 1765; to Nathan[7] the subject of this sketch. His mother was Betsey Hoit, daughter of Col. Nathan Hoit, and was born in 1770. Judge Crosby's father Asa was a physician of decided ability and large practice, who died in Hanover, N. H., Apr. 12, 1836, aged 70.

The family of Judge Crosby was a very notable one. It consisted of seventeen children by two mothers. Of these children six died in childhood or early youth. Of the eleven who lived to manhood and womanhood, five received either the Bachelor's degree or the degree of M.D., from Dartmouth College, and two of the daughters married professional men. Judge Crosby was the last of this large family. Two of them died between 70 and 80 years of age, and four between 80 and 90.

Three of his brothers were Professors at Dartmouth College. In the plans of his father and mother young Crosby was destined to the farm. But other influences wrought upon him, and his parents were easily made to consent to a public education. He was fitted for college under good instructors for those days, and was graduated from Dartmouth in 1820 at the age of twenty-two.

Judge Crosby was twice married. His first wife was Rebecca M. Moody, daughter of Stephen Moody, Esq., a graduate of Harvard, 1790, and a lawyer at Gilmantown, N. H. With him Judge Crosby studied law at first, and afterwards with Hon. Asa

Freeman of Dover. Judge Crosby and his brother Dixie both married daughters of Lawyer Moody. His first wife died Jan. 30, 1867. Judge Crosby's second wife was Mrs. Matilda (Pickens) Fearing, daughter of James and Charity (Mackie) Pickens of Boston, and widow of Dr. Joseph W. Fearing of Providence, R. I. They were married, May 19, 1870.

He leaves five children, his son, Stephen Moody Crosby, a graduate of Dartmouth College and Harvard Law School, and four married daughters.

There was about Judge Nathan Crosby a sturdy Saxon honesty and strength, and he will be greatly missed in the circles where he has so long moved as a leader in the cause of truth and righteousness. In this notice, necessarily brief, we have no space to enter upon the details of a life which has been very busy. These particulars will doubtless be kept in store, for that fuller biography which in due time will find its place in our Memorial Volumes.

BOOK NOTICES.

THE EDITOR requests persons sending books for notice to state, for the information of readers, the price of each book, with the amount to be added for postage when sent by mail.

The Civil, Political, Professional and Ecclesiastical History and Commercial and Industrial Record of the County of Kings and the City of Brooklyn, N. Y., from 1683 to 1884. By HENRY R. STILES, A.M., M.D., Editor-in-chief. Assisted by L. B. PROCTOR, Esq., and L. P. BROCKETT, A.M., M.D. With Portraits, Biographies and Illustrations. New York : W. W. Munsell & Co., Publishers. Imp. 4to. pp. 1408.

This bulky volume contains a vast amount of matter, illustrating the history of Brooklyn and Kings County, in its various phases ; " civil, political, professional, ecclesiastical, and industrial." The editor-in-chief, Henry R. Stiles, M.D., has had much experience in historical writing, and the publishers of this work were very fortunate in obtaining his services to prepare and supervise the great work which they have given to the public. Dr. Stiles's first historical book, the " History of Ancient Windsor," published more than a quarter of a century ago, gave him a reputation which his subsequent works have increased. His " History of Brooklyn," in three thick octavo volumes, one of the most thorough and satisfactory local histories that have yet appeared, had particularly fitted him for the present undertaking. The following extract from his preface will show why he undertook the work, and the spirit in which he has performed the labor on which he has been engaged for the last three years :

" In presenting to the public this ' History of Kings County and the City of Brooklyn,' a few words of explanation and acknowledgment are due. The preparation of so large a mass of historical, biographical and statistical information as is contained in these pages (equivalent to nearly 4,000 pages octavo) was undertaken by the publisher in a spirit of enterprise and liberality before unequalled in works of this character. By myself, the charge of its editing was accepted in a spirit of loyalty to the best interests of a city in which, for many years, I was a resident, and of which I had formerly been the historian. My long familiarity with the ground, and my acquaintance with its leading citizens, encouraged me to believe that such a work would be most acceptable to them, and would secure their general interest and personal co-operation. The result has more than justified my anticipations. From the moment of my entrance upon the work I have been cheered by a renewal of the same generous response to my requests for information, and by the same personal encouragement from all classes of citizens, which attended my former efforts in behalf of the ' History of Brooklyn.' "

Dr. Stiles's assistants, Mr. Proctor and Dr. Brockett, are both well known by their writings, the former being the author of " The Bench and Bar of the State of New York," " Lives of Eminent American Statesmen " and other works ; while the latter was the statistical editor of the " New American " and " Johnson's Cyclopædia," and is the author of " Our Western Empire," and kindred books.

Separate histories of the several towns in the county are furnished, prepared by able authors who have given particular attention to the history of the different localities. Special topics are also treated exhaustively by writers of ability. Besides having a general superintendence of the work, Dr. Stiles has contributed a large portion of the separate articles. Mrs. Lamb, in a notice of the work in the *Magazine of American History*, pronounces it, " the best county history that has yet been issued from the American press," in which opinion we fully concur. She adds : " Dr. Stiles seems to have borne constantly in mind, the general scope of the whole, and the relations of its several parts to the other, and thus has been able to secure a nearer approach to harmony of detail than is usually found in similar publications."

The work is printed in the best manner on white heavy paper, and is handsomely bound. It is profusely illustrated by portraits, of which there are not less than two hundred ; and by buildings, views, maps, etc.

The Siege and Capture of Fort Loyall; Destruction of Falmouth, May 20, 1690 (*O.S.*). *A paper read before the Maine Genealogical Society, June* 2, 1885. By JOHN T. HULL. Printed by order of City Council of Portland. Owen, Strout & Co., printers. 1885. 8vo. pp. 116.

The printing of the above interesting monograph by the authorities of the City of Portland as " a valuable contribution to our local history, treating as it does of the earliest settlements within the present city limits, the preservation and perpetuation of which properly belongs to the city as a part of its records, of which relating to this matter, there is at present in its archives not a single fragment," evinced a very proper appreciation by them of the labors of Mr. Hull in collating all the obtainable material relative to a thrilling episode of the early history of Falmouth (now Portland).

Concentrating his efforts upon one epoch, he has not only brought together extracts from some fifty recognized authorities, quoting therefrom two hundred and seventy-five passages, but has also dug out and brought to light thirty-three original documents bearing upon this subject, many of which were found among the Massachusetts Archives. These forgotten or overlooked bits of evidence supply many a missing link, the digging out and forging of which into a chain of binding and irrefragable history has been a task heretofore exceeding the patience of our earlier historic writers, and is therefore the more creditable to Mr. Hull.

The pamphlet is ornamented as well as explained by a beautiful map of ancient Falmouth, that is invaluable alike to the historical student, the investigator of ancient titles and the present owners and occupants of those historic sites. A very thorough index, carefully prepared, affords desirable access to particular passages and every proper name.

The paper, taken as a whole, exceeded the reasonable expectations of the members of the Society, at whose request its elaboration was undertaken ; and so far as it deals with the narration of events is graphically and forcibly written, and will prove a source of gratification to the descendants of the worthy sires who experienced such noble sacrifices, privations and sufferings, the alternations of defeat and ultimate success, that finally wrested from savage foes the goodly heritage of such fair fields. As to the conclusions and deductions of the author, he is open to the criticism of writing from a partisan stand-point ; and his strictures upon the course of Massachusetts and her alleged neglect of her annexed District of Maine will not only fail of carrying conviction to the ardent supporters of her cause, but are apparently irreconcilable to certain passages and authorities he has cited ; indeed the weight of evidence as adduced and printed seems against the author on certain material points. But Mr. Hull is entitled to the just praise of suppressing nothing that bears on either side of this argument ; and as these conclusions are avowed to be only his own, they do not preclude the formation of other and quite divergent ones by his readers.

His foot notes contain so much reliable information of our early settlers ; so many facts that if known were too widely scattered to be found without wearisome research, and add so generally to a full and fair understanding of events concurrent with the text, that they justify the very considerable space they occupy, doubling at least the length of the original paper.

The fertility of resources developed by this systematic research into a single chapter of our history, indicates but a part of the historic gems in store for a thorough investigator of our general history ; and with the encouragement of such

grateful recognition as this effort has already received may serve to stimulate others to bring together a set of jewels that will brighten and adorn our civic crown.
By William M. Sargent, A.M., of Portland, Maine.

The Glasse of Time, in the First Age. Divinely handled. By THOMAS PEYTON, of Lincolnes Inn, Gent. Seene and Allowed. London : Printed by Bernard Alsop, for Lawrence Chapman, and are to be sold at his shop over against Staple Inne. 1620. *The Glasse of Time, in the Second Age. Divinely handled.* By THOMAS PEYTON, of Lincolnes Inne, Gent. Seene and Allowed. London : Printed by Bernard Alsop, for Lawrence Chapman, and are to be sold at his shop over against Staple Inne. 1623. New York : John B. Alden. 1886. 8vo. pp. 177.

I may say, by way of preface, that it is difficult to do justice to this poem in the necessarily limited space alloted me. Perhaps a few words concerning the history of its author may not be out of place. The brief notice of his life by the editor is so interesting that only lack of space prevents my transcribing it.

Thomas Peyton came of good British stock, and was born in Royston, Cambridge County, England, A.D. 1595. He studied at the schools in his native town, and afterwards finished his education at the University of Cambridge. He then went to London and was admitted to the Society of Lincoln's Inn, and there entered upon the study of the law in the year 1613. He was only eighteen years old at the time. It is probable that he did not wait to be called to the Bar, for he decided shortly afterwards to give up his law studies for an even more ennobling pursuit, that of theology. He entered upon the work of his short but well spent life, at a peculiarly fitting time, for the fair field of English literature was not then overgrown with the ephemeral tares which are the bane of scholarship to-day. The Bible was substantially the only book in England at the time. But what a book it was and is. It was read and studied by all sorts and conditions of men. It was the classic, the source of inspiration for the English speaking race, from the sovereign down. Grotius, the great Jurist, who was the Dutch Envoy to England ten years after the death of Elizabeth, said : "Theology rules there, all point their studies in that direction."

It is safe to say that the author was a Churchman and a Royalist judging from his thrusts at the Romanists on the one side, and the Puritans (Puritents he called them) on the other. He was a representative country gentleman of his time and believed in his Church and King. He died at the early age of thirty-one, and thus had no opportunity to take a hand in the struggle which was impending. Although his grave is unknown, his poem constitutes a more enduring monument than any that the hand of man could raise ; it is a link connecting him—with all reverence be it said—with his Creator.

The first volume of "The Glasse of Time" commences with the beginning of existence, and treats mainly of the fall of man ; the second follows the descendants of Adam to the time of Noah. He promised to continue the story, but death called him away. For upwards of a century and a half no knowledge existed of the poem, which turned up about eighty years ago. The account of its finding reads like a fairy tale. The editor in his introduction says : " A copy of this book, elaborately bound in vellum, ornamented with gold, with coat of arms and regal device, illustrated with curious cuts, and quaintly printed, had been kept in the possession of some English family, and was buried in the chest of an illiterate descendant until his recent death created a train of circumstances, which in the end placed the treasure before our eyes." Meanwhile Milton's " Paradise Lost," with its harmonious and sonorous numbers, had appeared.

A thoughtful article by L. E. Dubois, entitled " An ' Inglorious Milton,' " came out in the North American Review for October, 1860. The writer concludes that Milton used it in the preparation of the Paradise Lost, in short that his great work was not entirely original with him. Space will not allow to adduce parallel passages from Peyton and Milton. After a careful reading of this remarkable poem, I can safely say it contains many points of similarity with Milton. That the theology of the two writers should be alike is not surprising, for Calvinism was deeply rooted in English theology at the time. But it is surprising that the scope and trend of the two poems should be the same, for I do not know that there was any other epic at the time to compare with either. There seem to be two ways of explaining the dilemma. 1. That both writers used a common original. 2. That Milton used Peyton's work to a greater or less extent. It does not seem probable that the first hypothesis is a true one, for had they used a common original is it not very strange that no mention of it even has survived? To account for it on this ground would seem to be to introduce another difficulty. I draw my main argument for the second hypothesis from internal evidence, and I submit that it is a very strong one. It may have been made over by Milton in much the same way that Bunyan made over the reveries of a pious mediæval monk into the Pilgrim's Progress; as Shakspeare did some of the dramas that came to his hand; as Scott did the old romances that he found. It seems as if Milton must have drawn from the earlier poem to a greater or less extent.

This poem is written in the quaint language and spelling of the period, and many of the words are obsolete. The style is terse and vigorous. If criticism of such a work is pardonable, I should say that it contains occasional passages which doubtless conformed to the canons of good taste in the seventeenth century, but would hardly do so in the nineteenth. The verse is not as polished as Milton's, but it contains thoughts worthy of an Ossian. I give a short extract below :

> " O heavenly God ! why should we here below
> Trouble ourselves thy secrets past to know :
> When thy dread word which Thou from heaven hath sent,
> The world and all can give us scarce content,
> But still we strive and at thy secrets aim,
> Till Thou our reason in our Sense doth maime,
> Here is the glory of the eternal crowne,
> Mans earthly wisdom utterly throws downe."

By Daniel Rollins, Esq., of Boston.

Costume in England. A History of Dress to the End of the Eighteenth Century. By the late F. W. FAIRHOLT, F.S.A. Third Edition. Enlarged and thoroughly revised by the Hon. H. A. DILLON, F.S.A. Two Volumes. Vol. I.—History ; II.—Glossary. London :George Bell and Sons, York St., Covent Garden. 1885.

In 1846 the first edition of Mr. Fairholt's famous work on English Costume made its appearance, and in 1860 the distinguished author brought out the second edition filled with the garnerings of the fourteen years that had passsd. For a quarter of a century this edition has been the hand book of historical students until its scarcity, and the continual supply of new and important material, brought to light by various writers, and the many reprints of scarce tracts by the societies, have furnished sufficient reasons for a revised edition. Mr. Fairholt being deceased, the task of editing the new work was entrusted to Mr. H. A. Dillon, F.S.A., who brings to his labor the zeal and intelligence of the true antiquary. It is indeed a monument of extensive research into the nooks and crannies of early literature, and is a worthy companion of those works it so much resembles in minuteness of description and reference—Brand's " Popular Antiquities " and Strutt's " Sports and Pastimes." The work is admirably arranged for intelligent understanding of the subjects discussed, by a division into periods, Britons, Danes, Saxons, Normans, Plantagenets, Tudors, Stuarts, etc., so that the development of dress is seen in chronological sequence as a whole, rather than by an examination of the component parts of dress through various gradations. The Stuart period is of especial interest to the New England antiquaries, as it furnishes a ground for comparison with the dress of the emigrants to this country during that time, and will be an excellent guide to that future student in our midst who shall write for us, what we all hope to see, a view of the social life in the colonies. Seven hundred engravings amply illustrate the text, and the Glossary, occupying an entire volume, is at once a dictionary and an index to the work. The hand of Mr. Dillon is seen through the whole in the addition of text, elaboration of notes and the collation of thousands of valuable references.

By Charles E. Banks, M.D., of Chelsea, Mass.

Report of the Commissioner of Education for the year 1883–'84. Washington : Government Printing Office. 1885. 8vo. pp. cclxxi.+943.

A very well arranged classification of the condition and methods of the schools of the cities and towns of the United States of 7,500 inhabitants and over, is presented in this volume. The report proper, which is the fourteenth annual one, of the present commissioner, Gen. John Eaton, embraces nearly one fourth of the contents. To this is appended abstracts of the official reports of the School Officers of states, territories and cities, which form another quarter of the work. The remaining half is devoted to statistics comprised in twenty-five tables, the whole terminating with an index. In the statistical portion, not only the ordinary school institutions of the several states are tabulated, but those for the deaf, dumb and blind, asylums for feeble-minded children, universities and colleges, kindergarten, reform schools, schools of law, science, theology, industry and commerce, and other systems of education are represented. The work has been prepared on a systematic and comprehensive basis, and is a valuable authority for those proposing to write on educational subjects.

By Oliver B. Stebbins, Esq., of South Boston, Mass.

Mémoires de L'Académie des Sciences Inscriptions et Belles-Lettres de Toulouse. Huitième Série. Tome VII. Deuxième semestre. 8vo. pp. 436. Toulouse: Imprimerie Douladoure=Privat.

This valuable half-yearly volume of the learned Academy of Toulouse presents the text of a series of papers, within the scope of the different classes of its members, which are of especial interest to scholars and students in such departments. The mathematician finds two deep and abstruse papers, on " Canonical Equations " and " Surfaces of Revolution " ; the botanist, an article on the " Flora of the Pyrenees," and another on the " Partition of the Axes " ; the naturalist, a disquisition on " the Equality of Intelligence between the Sexes of the Human Race " ; the meteorologist, studies of the " Storms of 1883 in the Haute Garonne " ; the historian and the philologist, critical essays upon " Roger Ascham," " Catullus," and eight unedited letters of " Madame Maintenon " ; and the chemist, " Researches on the Persulphide of Hydrogen." Add to these a series of eulogies upon the deceased members of the preceding year, and one recognizes the activity of this prominent society among the learned bodies of Europe, its wealth of illustrious savants, and the contribution it is constantly making to science and learning in scholarly and exhaustive essays.

By George A. Gordon, A.M., of Somerville, Mass.

Address before the Essex Bar Association, December 8, 1885. By WILLIAM D. NORTHEND. From the Historical Collections of the Essex Institute. Vol. XXII. Salem, 1885. 8vo. pp. 59.

This address is of much historical value and interest, containing as it does a carefully prepared summary of the history of the courts of Massachusetts from the days of Winthrop and Dudley to the commencement of the last century. The various changes from the original Court of Assistants to the courts under the charter of 1692, and finally to the present system, are here presented in a clear and comprehensive form, and some insight is given us into the methods of procedure in the time of the witchcraft trials. There are brief notices of many noted men who have practised at the bar of Essex County, and at the close of the pamphlet is appended a list of the members of that bar to the present time. The historical notes add much to the value of the address, which is worthy a more extended notice than space will permit us to give.

By George K. Clarke, LL.B., of Needham, Mass.

Inauguration of the Statue of Lafayette.—Presentation and Reception of Bartholdi's Statue of Liberty Enlightening the World, Paris, July 4, 1884. Paris: Printed by Waterlow & Sons. 1884. Sm. 8vo. pp. 22.

Mr. Morton in France.—The Inauguration at Paris of the Original Model of " Liberty Enlightening the World," May 13th, 1885.—*The Farewell Dinner given by the Americans in Paris, May 14th,* 1885. Paris: The Galignani Library. 1885. 8vo. pp. 52.

The first of these two pamphlets is devoted to the proceedings at two important ceremonies in France,—the unveiling of a bronze statue of Gen. Lafayette at Le Puy in Haute Loire, Sept. 6, 1883, and the presentation by the Count de Lesseps, and the reception by the Hon. Levi P. Morton, the United States Minister to France at Paris, July 4, 1884, of Bartholdi's colossal statue of " Liberty Enlightening the World." Addresses on the former occasion were made by Mr. Morton, M. Waldeck-Rousseau, as the representative of President Grévy, and Senator Edmond de Lafayette, grandson of Gen. Lafayette ; and on the latter by M. de Lesseps and Mr. Morton.

In the second pamphlet the proceedings on two other interesting occasions are given, namely, at the inauguration at Paris, May 13, 1885, of a reproduction in bronze of the original Model of Bartholdi's famous statue, which had been cast for American citizens for presentation to the people of France ; and at a Farewell Dinner the following day, May 14, 1885, given by his countrymen in Paris, to Mr. Morton, then about to leave France to return home after ably representing his government for four years at that court. On the former occasion, Mr. Morton made the presentation speech, and was replied to by M. Brisson, president of the Council of Ministers, M. Boué, president of the Municipal Council, M. de Lesseps and Senator Lafayette. On the latter occasion speeches were made by Mr. John Munroe, who presided at the banquet, Mr. Edmond Kelly of the Paris and New York bar, Mr. Morton, M. Floquet, president of the Chamber of Deputies, Hon. Robert M. McLane, Mr. Morton's successor as minister of France, M. René Goblet, minister of public Instruction, Consul General George Walker, Senator Lafayette and the Marquis de Rochambeau. A brilliant assembly of celebrities was present on these several occasions. The addresses showed how acceptable Mr. Morton had made himself not only to his own countrymen, but also to the government and people of France.

Some Account of the Worshipful Company of Painters, otherwise Painter-Stainers. Imprinted at the Chiswick Press, London. 1880. 8vo. pp. 22.

"The Company of Painter-Stainers," we are told in this pamphlet "is of considerable antiquity. According to Horace Walpole, their first Charter, in which they are styled Peyntours, was granted in the sixth of King Edward IV., but they existed as a fraternity in the time of King Edward III. They were called Paynter-Stayners because a picture on canvass was formerly called a stained cloth, as one on panel was called a table, probably from the French ' tableau.' " Their present charter was granted by Queen Elizabeth, and bears date July 19, 1581. The present Painters' Hall, which was finished about 1669, "stands on the site of old Painters' Hall, once the residence of Sir John Browne, Sergeant Paynter to King Henry VIII.," which building was burnt in the Great Fire of London in 1666. Extracts from the records of the Company relating to this and other matters are here printed.

Two signs used in the last century in Boston, bearing the arms of the London Painter-Stainers Company, and called the "Painters' Arms," are preserved. The arms of this company are thus blazoned in Burke's General Armory : " Quarterly, 1st and 4th, az., three escutcheons ar. ; 2d and 3d, az. a chev. betw. three phœnix heads erased or. *Crest*—A phœnix close or, in flames ppr. *Supporters*—Two leopards ar. spotted with various colors, ducally crowned, collared and chained or. *Motto*— Amor et obedientia." The earliest of these signs is now let into the wall of the Hanover street front of the building at the corner of Hanover and Marshall streets. The motto on the sign is " Amor queat [*sic*] obedediencia." Above the arms is " 17 $_{T K}^{C}$ 01." Whose initials these are is unknown to me, as is also the history of the sign. The other sign, which bears the date 1755, is now at the rooms of the Bostonian Society, but is said to have been hung on a building in the vicinity of the present Scollay square. It has neither supporters, crest nor motto. The tradition is that it was brought to this country by Christopher Gore, afterwards governor of Massachusetts ; but as he was a lawyer, and was not born till three years after the date on this sign, it is more probable that it was brought here by his father, John Gore, who was a painter of mature age at that date. The latter is supposed to have been the owner of the " Gore Roll of Arms." printed by Mr. Whitmore in his " Elements of Heraldry," pages 80 to 94, from a copy of the original roll made by the late Isaac Child, Esq., which copy now belongs to the Historic Genealogical Society.

Genealogical Record of Condit Family, Descendants of John Condit, who settled in Newark, N. J., 1678—1885. *Also an Appendix containing a Brief Record of the Harrison, Williams, Pierson, Smith, Lindsley, Munn and Whitehead Families.* By JOTHAM H. CONDIT [Brick Church, New Jersey], and Eben Condit, Jersey [Licking Co., Ohio]. Newark, N. J. : Printed and published by Ward & Tichenor. 1885. pp. 410. Limited Edition. $4.00.

Two members of the Condit family have rendered royal service in preserving the genealogy and history of their tribe. They descend from John Cunditt, who came in 1678 and settled in Newark, New Jersey. He is the ancestor of nearly all of the name in the country to-day. He died in 1713. He had one son who grew to manhood, Peter, by first wife, and born in England. Peter married, 1695, Mary, daughter of Samuel[3] Harrison [Richard,[2] Richard[1]], by whom he had seven children, six of whom were sons, namely, Samuel, Peter, John, Nathaniel, Philip and Isaac. Peter died in 1714, the year following his father. From these six sons descends the family of to-day.

By the Rev. Anson Titus, of Amesbury, Mass.

The Antiquary: A Magazine devoted to the Study of the Past. London : Elliot Stock, 62 Paternostor Row. New York : David G. Francis, 17 Astor Place. Published Monthly. Medium 4to. 44 pages to a number. Price one shilling each. Mr. Francis will furnish the work to American subscribers at $3.50 a year, or 30 cts. a number including postage.

The numbers of this magazine for January, February and March are before us, and show that it is a valuable aid not only to the antiquary but to the genealogist also. American readers will find much in its pages in which they have a common interest with those of England. Besides articles on antiquarian subjects, the result of great research, there are here reports of the meetings of English Antiquarian Societies, reviews of antiquarian books, antiquarian news, obituaries and other matters of interest. Some of the best antiquarian writers contribute to the magazine.

The History of Farmington, Franklin Co., Maine, from the Earliest Explorations to the Present Time. 1776—1885. By FRANCIS GOULD BUTLER, Member of the Maine Historical Society. Farmington : Knowlton, McLeary & Co., Printers. 1885. 8vo. pp. 683. Price $3.25. Illustrated with Portraits and Views.

The author, the Hon. Mr. Butler, is a native of Farmington, and has always resided there. From early manhood to the present time he has been identified with all its leading interests. No person could have been better situated to collect the material for this work than himself. He tells us, however, in the preface, that it was not until he was approaching his seventy-first birthday in 1883, that he seriously undertook the preparation of this history. That he must have been diligent and indefatigable in his efforts to accomplish his purpose, during the two years he has devoted to this work, these 348 pages of General History and nearly the same number of pages of Genealogy, plainly indicate.

This is literally a Farmington book. It has not only been written there by a native-born citizen, but the printing has also been done there, and does great credit to the firm from whose press the volume has been issued. The senior partner of this firm is also a native of the town, whose ancestors have been long and favorably known there.

The Introductory Chapter of this history informs its readers what so many town histories fail to do, where the place is located concerning which the book has been written. The account of early explorations, the difficulty experienced by the pioneers in obtaining titles to their lands, because of the disputed boundaries of the territory claimed by the Kennebec or Plymouth Company, with a full account of the Colburn Association, make the next few pages deeply interesting. The conclusion of the author relative to the time of the final departure from the vicinity of Sandy River, and the destination, of the Indian (Pierpole or Pealpole), is probably incorrect. The copy of an original document bearing his signature and addressed to the General Court of Massachusetts, brought before the house of representatives in February, 1801, was published in the "Wilton Record" some time since. In this document it is plainly told that Pealpole's relatives live in Canada, that he desires to go there in order to live near them, and also to be able to attend on the observances of his own religion.

The permanent settlements were begun at Farmington in 1781, and increased quite rapidly after the close of the Revolutionary War. The early settlers were principally from Dunstable, Mass., Damariscotta, Me., and vicinity. About 1790, 1792 and later, a number of families from Martha's Vineyard settled in the place. The township never had a plantation organization, but was incorporated as a town in 1794. In 1800 the number of inhabitants had increased to 942. In 1810 every lot within the limits of the town had been taken up. The pioneers very early took an interest in the subject of education, and the author asserts that it is not known there was an illiterate person among the first settlers ; and considers it doubtful if there has ever been an adult native-born citizen unable to write his own name or read a clause in the constitution.

Much care has been taken to record the military history of the town in entire completeness. Farmington may well be proud of her war record.

A chronological table of incidents has been arranged, which occupies twenty pages. As Farmington is the shire town of Franklin County, a history of the former necessarily includes more or less of the latter. In the appendix is a complete list of the county officers, with dates of terms of office since the incorporation of the county in 1838.

Parker's History of Farmington, published in 1846, contains facts that could not now be found, and Mr. Butler acknowledges his indebtedness to that work. It is presumed, however, that he did not have access to the valuable historical material concerning Farmington collected by the late Rev. Josiah S. Swift, as no mention is made of any such authority having been consulted. This is to be regretted, as it is probable no person in Franklin County is in the possession of so much historical data concerning this town as was Mr. Swift. His decease, which occurred at Wilton, Me., March 26, 1883, prevented the further publication of the Franklin Historical Magazine, of which only two numbers had been issued. Mr. Swift was publishing this magazine as an appendix to Parker's History. It is hoped the memoranda left by him concerning the towns in Franklin County, Me., will at some time, in the not far distant future, be arranged and printed.

Great care has been devoted by Mr. Butler to the genealogical portion of his book. It is arranged after the method adopted in the History of Rindge, N. H. The author has endeavored to give the ancestry of each family mentioned, of which there are eighty-one. This has required extensive research, but has met with marked success. In addition a biographical sketch is given of each head of a family who was an early settler in the town, and of many of their descendants. The Genealogy occupies 325 pages. The book is faithfully indexed, but the proof-reading in this department was somewhat neglected.

By Mrs. A. C. Pratt, of Chelsea, Mass.

Truro Baptisms 1711–1800. By JOHN HARVEY TREAT. Lawrence: James Ward, Jr. 1886. 8vo. pp. 66. Price $1, post free. Address J. H. Treat, Lawrence, Mass.

"The records of the ancient church of Eastham, Cape Cod," Mr. Treat informs us in his preface, "are entirely lost, and the church itself has become extinct. The records of the churches at Wellfleet and Orleans, formerly precincts of Eastham, are also lost." The adjoining town of Truro, which was settled mostly by emigrants from Eastham, is more fortunate. Its church records "are in a perfect state of preservation, except that, in a few instances, the ink has faded somewhat, so that the writing is rendered obscure."

Mr. Treat is deserving of much credit for his labor of love in copying these valuable records, and having them printed in so acceptable a style. Only a small edition is printed, and the price asked for the work will hardly pay the expenses of publication.

The Narragansett Fort Fight, December 19, 1675. By Rev. GEORGE M. BODGE, A.M. Boston : Privately printed. 1886. 8vo. pp. 21. With Map. A few copies for sale by G. E. Littlefield, 67 Cornhill, Boston. Price 50 cts.

The series of articles on the Soldiers of King Philip's War, which Mr. Bodge is contributing to the REGISTER, are acknowledged to be a positive contribution to the history of what has been called "one of the most thrilling periods in the early history of New England." Perhaps the most interesting of these valuable articles is that giving a history of Narragansett Fort Fight, which appeared in the January number. A small edition of this article has been printed for distribution to his friends by the author, the Rev. George M. Bodge, of East Boston.

The Public Records of the Colony of Connecticut from May, 1768, *to May,* 1772, *inclusive.* Transcribed and edited in accordance with a Resolution of the General Assembly, by CHARLES J. HOADLY, State Librarian. Hartford : Press of the Case, Lockwood & Brainard Company. 1885. 8vo. pp. 689.

This is volume thirteen of the Connecticut Colonial Records, the last number having been published four years since, and the first of the series thirty-five years ago. It is not known that the journals of either House are in existence for the years 1768–72, but the journal of the Council, from May, 1770, to May, 1772, is here contained. These records are of great value to the historian and the genealogist, containing as they do a large number of petitions and memorials relating to the settlement of estates and the private affairs of individuals, matters which do not now commonly receive the attention of the legislature. Comparatively few general laws are found in this volume, but there is a large amount of matter relating to the appointment of military and other officers, together with complete lists of the executive and legislative officers of the period. In May, 1771, a resolve was passed requesting Gov. Trumbull to collect the public letters and papers relating to the colony, and to have them bound together. The note on page 424 gives some account of these papers, a large number of which were presented in 1794 by David Trumbull, son of the governor, to the Massachusetts Historical Society, and form the Trumbull Collection.

The volume is ably edited, well indexed and handsomely printed. *By George K. Clarke, LL.B., of Needham, Mass.*

Letters of John, Lord Cutts to Colonel Joseph Dudley, then Lieutenant Governor of the Isle of Wight, afterwards Governor of Massachusetts, 1693–1700. Cambridge: John Wilson & Son, University Press. 1886. 8vo. pp. 31.

This is a reprint from the Proceedings of the Massachusetts Historical Society, of remarks made before that Society Jan. 14, 1886, by Robert C. Winthrop, Jr., A.M., with the letters in full to which they relate and of which extracts were read by Mr. Winthrop at the meeting. They throw light upon a period of Gov. Joseph Dudley's life of which little has heretofore been known, and show the intimate relation between Dudley and Lord Cutts. Dudley was probably the first native of America who sat in the British House of Commons. This distinction has been claimed for Henry Cruger, a native of New York, who was chosen a member in 1774, but Dudley was a member about three quarters of a century earlier. Mr. Winthrop deserves credit for the manner in which he has brought out these letters, and the careful editing he has given them. A heliotype copy of a portrait of Gov. Dudley belonging to Mr. Winthrop's father, the Hon. Robert C. Winthrop, LL.D., and which gives a truer idea of the man than the usual engravings from the Gilbert portrait, embellishes the pamphlet.

Notes on St. Botolph, without Aldergate, London. By JOHN STAPLES, F.S.A. Printed for Private Circulation. 1881. 8vo. pp. 52.

The occasion which caused Alderman Staples to prepare this account of the Church of St. Botolph and the ancient fraternities established in it, is stated to have been the opening, on the 28th of October, 1880, of the garden formerly reserved as the burial place of the Church, for the recreation of the public. In these proceedings the author took part and delivered an historical address, which is the foundation of this book. The church is first mentioned by name in 1279 in a writ of Edward I., but is much older. There were three Fraternities, or Brotherhoods, or Gilds, founded in this church, namely, those of the Holy Trinity, of St. Katherine, and of St. Fabian and St. Sebastian, and they all date back to the fourteenth century. Many facts of historical and antiquarian interest concerning the church and the several fraternities have been collected by Alderman Staples and preserved in these pages.

Appended is an account of St. Botolph and Botolph's town or Boston, whence our Massachusetts city of Boston derives its name. Concerning the history of St. Botolph and the time in which he lived, authorities differ, one placing him in the second and another in the eighth century. Few English saints have been more honored. Four parishes in London, and many churches throughout the country are called after him.

An Historical Sketch, Guide Book and Prospectus of Cushing's Island. By WILLIAM M. SARGENT, A.M. New York: American Photo-Eng. Co. 1886. Small 8vo. pp. 96. Price 25 cts.

We take pleasure in transferring to our pages from the *Portland Transcript* the following notice of this work, prepared from advance sheets :

" The author has shown indefatigable research in compiling an authentic history of our city and vicinity, and his data in relation to the original settlement on Casco Bay, which he locates on what is now known as Cushing's Island, instead of upon the main land, will sustain critical examination. The book is very attractively printed and arranged, and freely embellished by cuts, by the American Photo-Engraving Company, of high merit. Many of these are from sketches by Mr. John Calvin Stevens, whose success as an artist is bringing him into prominence, and others are designed from faithful photographs of the natural scenery. Besides contributing greatly to the attractiveness of the book, they will accurately represent to the distant reader the charming environs of the Island, which, to be appreciated, need but to be seen. Mr. Sargent has been happy in his descriptions, and while omitting to mention none of the marked features of scenic beauty, directs attention to many a lesser charm that might have easily escaped the notice of a writer less enamored of his subject. A particularly graceful feature of the arrangement is the appropriate lines of verse accompanying each illustration, which have not been taken haphazard, but evidence, in their employment, a fine discrimination. One part of the book sets forth the steady advance in building on the Island, which has proceeded on an unalterable plan for permanency, and freedom from objectionable features such as have given to less wisely conducted settlements a short-lived prosperity, and justly portrays Cushing's Island as the most desirable site possessed by any summer colony."

Education. A Monthly Magazine. Devoted to the Science, Art, Philosophy and Literature of Education. WILLIAM A. MOWRY, Editor. Boston: William A. Mowry, Publisher, No. 3 Somerset Street. Published Monthly. 8vo. pp. 108 each number. Price $3 a year. Single numbers 35 cts.

This periodical was commenced as a bi-monthly in September, 1880, by the New England Publishing Company, under the editorship of the Hon. Thomas W. Bicknell, LL.D. It was noticed by us in January, 1882. It has proved an efficient aid in advancing the cause of education in this country, and a valuable addition to the higher order of educational literature. In January last, William A. Mowry, Ph.D., became both editor and publisher of the magazine, and the numbers, for January, February and March, which have been issued by him, prove his scholarship and ability to meet the needs of his readers.

Walford's Antiquarian; a Magazine and Biographical Review. Edited by EDWARD WALFORD, M.A. London: George Redway, 15 York Street, Covent Garden. J. W. Bouton, Agent for America, 706 Broadway, New York. Published monthly. 8vo. 48 pages to a number. Price one shilling each.

This periodical, which has before been favorably noticed by us, still maintains its interest for the antiquarian student, not only in the English dominions, but in the United States also. The several numbers, of which the latest received is that for March, contain carefully prepared articles by distinguished antiquarian writers on antiquities, archæology, bibliography and kindred subjects. Here the doings of the learned societies of Great Britain are reported, recent antiquarian books reviewed, obituaries of prominent personages preserved, and the latest antiquarian news furnished.

Records of the Descendants of Nathaniel Ely the Emigrant, who Settled first in Newtown, now Cambridge, Mass., was one of the First Settlers of Hartford, also Norwalk, Conn., and a Resident of Springfield, Mass., from 1659 until his Death in 1675. Compiled by HEMAN ELY. Including material collected by Mrs. Amanda (Ely) Terry. Cleveland, Ohio: Short and Forman, Printers. 1885. Imp. 4to. pp. 515. Edition, 520 copies. Price in cloth, $7; in half morocco, $8. If sent by mail, 55 cts. extra.

The Marshall Family, or a Genealogical Chart of the Descendants of John Marshall and Elizabeth Markham his Wife. Sketches of Individuals and Notices of Families connected with them. By W. M. PAXTON, Platte City, Mo. Cincinnati: Robert Clarke & Co. 1885. 8vo. pp. 415. With a folding Genealogical Chart.

Genealogical Memoir of the Cunnabell, Conable or Connable Family. John Cunnabell of London, England, and Boston, Massachusetts, and his Descendants, 1650–1886. By EDWARDS J. CONNABLE, of Jackson, Mich., and JOHN B. NEWCOMB, of Elgin, Ill. Jackson, Mich.: Daily Citizen Book Printing House. 1886. 8vo. pp. 183 +4. Price $2.60, delivered free.

The Joseph Kimball Family: a Genealogical Memoir of the Ascendants and Descendants of Joseph Kimball of Canterbury, N. H. Ten Generations. 1634–1885. Compiled by JOHN KIMBALL, A.M., Member of the N. H. Historical Society. Concord, N. H.: Printed by the Republican Press Association. 1885. 8vo. pp. 103.

Lee Family. Quarter Millenial Gathering of the Descendants and Kinsmen of John Lee, one of the Early Settlers of Farmington, Conn., held in Hartford, Conn.,

Tuesday and Wednesday, Aug. 5th and 6th, 1884. Meriden : Republican Steam Print. 1885. 8vo. pp. 116.

Genealogical Sketch of the Nova Scotia Eatons. Compiled by Rev. ARTHUR WENTWORTH EATON. Halifax, N. S. : Printed at the Morning Herald Office. 1885. Roy. 8vo. pp. 128.

A Private Proof printed in Order to Preserve certain matters connected with the Boston branch of the Perkins Family. Intended only as an Indication of the Best Points of Future Investigation. Boston : T. R. Marvin & Son, Printers. 1885. 8vo. pp. 29.

The Surnames and Coats of Arms of the Williamses, with an Account of Robert Williams of Roxbury and Some of his Descendants. Compiled by A. D. WELD FRENCH. Privately Printed. 1886. 8vo. pp. 26+2.

A Sketch of the Life and Character of Dea. Joshua Upham of Salem, Mass. To which are appended a Sketch of his First Wife, his Ancestral History and a Genealogical List of his Descendants. By Prof. JAMES UPHAM, D.D. Boston, Mass. 1885. 12mo. pp. 80.

Genealogical Notes, showing the Paternal Line of Descent from William Torrey of Combe St. Nicholas, Somerset County, England, A.D. 1557, to Jason Torrey of Bethany, Penn'a, with the Descendants of Jason Torrey and his Brother and Sister to A.D. 1884. Compiled by JOHN TORREY. Scranton, Pa. : James S. Horton, Printer and Publisher. 1885. 8vo. pp. 50+2.

Hutchins Genealogy. Compiled by CHARLES HUTCHINS. Boston : 1885. 8vo. pp. 16.

Genealogy of the Ancestors and Descendants of Joseph Chase who died in Swanzey. His will proved March, 1725. Fall River : Printed by William S. Robertson. 1874. 8vo. pp. 86.

Genealogy of the Andrews Family. By Lieut. GEORGE ANDREWS, U.S.A., of Fort Snelling, Min. 1886. 8vo. pp. 8.

The Wiswall Family of America. Four Generations. By the Rev. ANSON TITUS, of Amesbury, Mass. 1886. 8vo. pp. 4.

We continue in this number our notices of genealogical works recently issued.

The Ely genealogy which heads our list, is by the Hon. Heman Ely, of Elyria, Ohio. It seems to have been compiled with the utmost thoroughness, and has been brought out in a costly and highly satisfactory manner. The emigrant ancestor of this family was Nathaniel Ely, who died at Springfield, Dec. 25, 1675. He probably came to this country in 1634. On the 6th of May, 1635, he was admitted by the General Court a freeman of Massachusetts. At that time he probably resided at Cambridge. The Rev. Thomas Hooker and about one hundred of his parishioners it is well known removed from Cambridge to Hartford, Ct., and Mr. Ely is supposed to have gone with them, as he is subsequently found in that town. He afterwards removed to Norwalk, Ct., and in 1659 to Springfield, Mass., where the rest of his life was spent. The English ancestry of this family has not been positively traced ; but the late Col. Chester made a thorough investigation of the subject, and gives strong reasons for believing that Nathaniel of Springfield was a son of Rev. Nathaniel Ely, and grandson of the Rev. George Ely, vicar of Tenterden in Kent from 1571 to 1615, the date of his death. Col. Chester's letter to the author, dated Nov. 19, 1881, only six months before his death, fills more than three of the large pages of this volume, and gives an interesting account of the result of his investigations into the history of the Ely family in England. The families of both Rev. George Ely and his son Nathaniel are given in detail. Nathaniel, son of the latter, was probably born as early as 1602. After giving his reasons, Col. Chester proceeds : " I cannot in my own mind resist the conviction that he was identical with the Nathaniel Ely who appeared in New England about 1634. Of course, there is no absolute proof, but this group of facts is strongly suggestive." The book before us is arranged in a clear style, and is handsomely printed and bound. It is illustrated with numerous portraits, some elegant steel engravings, and many fine phototypes ; besides autographs and other engravings. The volume is an honor to a family which can boast of many distinguished personages, and is a credit to its author.

The Marshall genealogy is devoted to families who trace their ancestry to Virginia, Maryland and Kentucky. The author says : " This work is intended for a book of reference. To this end it is furnished with an ample index. I have dealt in facts rather than panegyric, I have flattered no one, and have written nothing in malice. It has been a labor of love, and my expenses have been freely contributed.

Though pecuniary assistance has been proffered, I have accepted nothing." The book contains a large collection of facts relating to the Marshalls, and must have cost the author a great deal of labor. The chart the author thinks " combines more advantages than any form heretofore used." Besides the full index to the book there is a separate index to the Chart.

The Cunnabell genealogy contains a genealogy of the descendants of John Cunnabel of Boston, Mass., and much other matter of interest to persons of the name and blood. The origin of the work is this. " About twenty-five years ago, Rev. Joseph Conable Thomas, then a student at Evanston, Ill., and John B. Newcomb of Elgin, Ill., commenced collecting genealogy and other data " concerning this family. Mr. Newcomb, who has since become known as an indefatigable worker in the field of genealogy, continued to collect matter as opportunity offered. In 1883, Edwards J. Connable of Jackson, Mich., became interested in the history of his ancestors, and the two having combined their labors, the result is the present very satisfactory book. It is chiefly through the instrumentality of Mr. Connable of Jackson that the facts in this volume have been placed beyond the reach of destruction. He has done a large amount of gratuitous work, besides contributing liberally in the expenditure. " Mr. Newcomb collected the data relating to the earlier generations and history of the family, and all respecting the Nova Scotia branch ; also prepared the maps for the engraver and the manuscript for the printer." The work bears evidence of faithful research, and is well arranged and handsomely printed. A view of the residence of Samuel Connable of Bernardston, Mass., erected 1739, and standing till 1770, faces the title. A plan showing the residences of John, the emigrant, and a son and a grandson in Boston, and a map showing the residences of a number of his descendants in Bernardston and Berlin, with numerous autographs, illustrate the book. It has a folding tabular pedigree ; and excellent indexes are furnished.

The Kimball genealogy is devoted to the ancestry and descendants of Joseph Kimball, who was born at Exeter, N. H., May 23, 1772, settled at Canterbury and died in Gilmanton, June 19, 1863, aged 91. He was a descendant of Richard[1] Kimball, who came to New England in 1634, and settled first at Watertown and afterwards at Ipswich, where he died June 22, 1675, aged 80 ; through Richard,[2] Caleb,[3] John[4] and Joseph[5] his father. The book is compiled with care, is handsomely printed, is illustrated with portraits on steel of the Hon. John Kimball (the author) and Benjamin A. Kimball, both of Concord, N. H., and William S. Kimball of Rochester, N. Y. ; and has full indexes.

The Lee book gives the proceedings at the quarter millenial gathering at Hartford in August, 1884. A great deal of historical and biographical matter is here preserved. The volume is well printed and embellished with a map of Hartford in 1640, and numerous portraits on stone. The early generations of this family were printed in the REGISTER for October, 1874, and a full genealogy by Sarah M. Lee, which appeared in 1878, was noticed by us in July, 1879.

The Eaton genealogy is by the Rev. Mr. Eaton of New York city. The ancestor of the Nova Scotia Eatons, to whom this book is devoted, was David Eaton, born at Haverhill, Mass., April 1, 1729, and died in Cornwallis, N. S., July, 17, 1803. He was the fifth generation in descent from John Eaton the emigrant, who settled at Salisbury, Mass., as early as 1640 ; through Thomas,[2] Jonathan[3] and his father James.[4] An introductory sketch by the Rev. William H. Eaton, D.D., of Keene, N. H., gives the genealogy previous to David,[5] who settled in Nova Scotia. The descendants of David are here fully carried out. Appended is an account of the Eaton Association, with a list of its officers for 1884-5. The volume is well printed and has a good index.

The Perkins book is fully described in its title page. It is by Augustus T. Perkins of Boston, who says in his preface : " After much reflection, I have determined to give an account of such traditions of our family as I have heard, and of such as I have had investigated for me, although I know them to be far from complete and in some ways inaccurate." Mr. Perkins has acted wisely in preserving in print these traditions of his family. With them he has combined the result of some of his researches on the same subject. The work is handsomely printed.

Mr. French's book on the Williamses is a useful compilation for those of the name. It gives the origin of the name, descriptions of the various coats of arms borne by Williamses, arranged under their principal charges, and brief accounts of Robert Williams of Roxbury, and some others of the name in New England. The volume is well printed.

The Upham book is by the Rev. James Upham, D.D., of Chelsea, Mass., formerly President of the New Hampshire Literary and Theological Institute. It contains a memoir of his father, Dea. Joshua Upham, with a brief history of the family and a record of the descendants of Dea. Joshua. The book is embellished by portraits, and a folding tabular pedigree is appended.

The Torrey book is sufficiently described in the title page. The researches of the Hon. Alphonso Taft of Cincinnati, and H. A. Newton of Weymouth, have traced the ancestry of this family for several generations in England. Four brothers, the sons of Philip and Alicie Torrey of Combe St. Nicholas, came to this country. This Philip was a son of William, who was a son of Philip, who was a son of William Torrey, of Combe St. Nicholas, who died in June, 1577. A deposition dated 1674, of Philip Torrey of Roxbury, one of the emigrants, is printed in the REGISTER, xl. 62. The present work is neatly printed and seems to be carefully compiled.

The Hutchins pamphlet gives descendants of David Hutchins, born in 1694 in Yorkshire, who settled in Attleboro', Mass., and died there in 1790. The author is Dea. Charles Hutchins, who for some twenty years has been the General Business Agent of the American Board of Commissioners for Foreign Missions in Boston. These few pages give much genealogical information relative to this family.

The Chase book is by the Hon. Oliver Chace of Fall River, who died May 6, 1874, aged 61 (REGISTER, xxix. 222). Joseph Chase, whose descendants are given in this work, was a grandson of William Chase, the emigrant, who settled in Barnstable, Mass., and died in 1659. The book is well compiled.

The Andrews and Wiswall pamphlets are reprints from the REGISTER for January last.

RECENT PUBLICATIONS,

PRESENTED TO THE NEW ENGLAND HISTORIC GENEALOGICAL SOCIETY, TO DEC. 1, 1886.

I. *Publications written or edited by Members of the Society.*

Thoughts on the American College; an Address delivered in the Macalester College Chapel, Snelling Avenue, Saint Paul, Minn., September 16, 1885. By Rev. Edward D. Neill. Also A Brief History of the College. St. Paul: The Pioneer Press Company. 1885. 8vo. pp. 21.

The Narragansett Fort Fight, December 19, 1675. By Rev. George M. Bodge, A.M., Boston. 1886. 8vo. pp. 21. With a map.

Rutland and the Indian troubles of 1723–30. By Francis E. Blake, Worcester, Mass. Published by Franklin P. Rice. 1886. 8vo. pp. 53.

Prytaneum Bostoniense. Notes on the history of the Old State House, formerly known as the Town House in Boston, the Court House in Boston, the Province Court House, the State House, and the City Hall. By George H. Moore, LL.D. Read before the Bostonian Society, May 12, 1885. Boston: Cupples, Upham & Co. The Old Corner Book-store. 1885. 8vo. pp. 31.

Memorial Exercises held in Castleton, Vermont, in the year 1885, including the addresses, biographical sketches, reminiscences, list of graves decorated, roster of the veterans in line —giving company and regiment—history of previous memorial days in Castleton and an account of the relics exhibited. Compiled by John M. Currier, M.D., Secretary of the Memorial Organization. Albany, N. Y.: Joel Munsell's Sons. 1885. 8vo. pp. 66.

The life, literary labors and neglected grave of Richard Henry Wilde. By Charles C. Jones, Jr., LL.D. 8vo. pp. 21.

An analysis of the population of the City of Boston, as shown in the State census of May, 1885. By Carroll D. Wright, chief of Bureau of Statistics of Labor. Boston: Wright and Potter Printing Co., State Printers, 18 Post Office Square. 1885. 8vo. pp. 17.

Proceedings at the third annual session of the National Convention of Chiefs and Commissioners of the various Bureaus of Statistics of Labor in the United States, held at Boston, Massachusetts, June 29, June 30, and July 1, 1885. Boston: Wright and Potter Printing Co., State Printers, 18 Post Office Square. 1885. 8vo. pp. 143.

Sepulture of Major General Nathanael Greene, and of Brig. Gen. Count Casimir Pulaski. By Charles C. Jones, Jr., LL.D.

New chapter in the history of the Concord fight: Groton minute-men at the North Bridge, April 19, 1775, and appendix. By Wm. W. Wheildon. Boston: Lee and Shepherd, Publishers, No. 10 Milk Street. 1885. 8vo. pp. 32.

American Constitutions: the relations of the three departments as adjusted by a century. Read before the Chit-Chat Club of San Francisco. By Horace Davis. San Francisco: 1884. 8vo. pp. 76.

Some Worcester matters, 1689-1743. By Francis E. Blake. Worcester, Mass.: Franklin P. Rice, Publisher. 1885. 8vo. pp. 17.

The dedication of the Washington National Monument, with the orations by Hon. Robert C. Winthrop and Hon. John W. Daniel, February 21, 1885. Published by order of Congress. Washington: Government Printing Office. 1885. 8vo. pp. 122.

Reminiscences of the last year of President Lincoln's life. By Chaplain Edward D. Neill. Read at a meeting of the Minnesota Commandery of the Military Order of the Loyal Legion, St. Paul, Minn., Nov. 4, 1885. St. Paul, Minn.: The Pioneer Press Company. 1885. 8vo.

Public Records of the Colony of Connecticut from May, 1768, to May, 1772, inclusive, transcribed and edited in accordance with a resolution of the General Assembly. By Charles J. Hoadly, State Librarian. Hartford: Press of the Case, Lockwood and Brainard Company. 1885. 8vo. pp. 689.

Sermon by Rev. Carlton A. Staples, commemorative of Mrs. Susan E. Huston, founder of the Taft Public Library, delivered in Mendon, Mass., August, 1884. Printed by vote of the Trustees. Uxbridge, Mass.: L. H. Balcom Stearns, Printer, Compendium Office. 1885. 8vo. pp. 15.

Roll of the Officers of the York and Lancaster Regiment, containing a complete record of their services, including dates of commission, etc. By Major G. A. Raikes, F.S.A. The First Battalion, formerly 65th (2d Yorkshire North Riding) Regiment, from 1756 to 1884. The Second Battalion, formerly the Royal Highland Emigrants (1775-1783), late 84th (York and Lancaster) Regiment, from 1758-1884. London: Richard Bentley and Son, New Burlington Street, Publishers in Ordinary to Her Majesty the Queen. 1885. 8vo.

The Indian Names of Boston and their meaning, by Eben Norton Horsford. Read before the New England Historic Genealogical Society, November 4, 1885. Cambridge: John Wilson & Son, University Press. 1886. Large 4to. pp. 26. [This paper was printed in the present volume of the REGISTER, pp. 94-103.]

John Cabot's Land fall in 1497, and the site of Norumbega. A letter to Chief Justice Daly, President of the American Geographical Society, by Eben Norton Horsford. Cambridge: John Wilson and Son, University Press. 1886. Large 4to. pp. 42.

The Huguenots and the Edict of Nantes. A paper read before the Rhode Island Historical Society, November 3, 1885. By William Gammell. Providence. 1886. 8vo. pp. 25.

Noah Emery of Exeter, Member of the Provincial Congress, and Clerk of the Assembly in New Hampshire, in the Revolution. By his great-grandson, Charles Emery Stevens. Privately printed. 1886. 8vo. pp. 39.

Groton Historical Series, No. IX. Groton District Schools. Groton, Mass. 1886. 8vo. pp. 26. [By Samuel A. Green, M.D.]

Women under the law of Massachusetts, their rights, privileges, and disabilities, by Henry H. Sprague. Boston: W. B. Clarke and Carruth. 1884. 8vo. pp. 70.

A brief catalogue of books; illustrated with engravings, by Dr. Alexander Anderson. [Collected by Evert A. Duyckinck.] With a biographical sketch of the artist [by Benson J. Lossing]. 1885. 8vo. pp. 35.

A report of the Record Commissioners of the City of Boston, containing the Boston Town Records, 1742 to 1757. Boston: Rockwell and Churchill, City Printers, No. 39 Arch Street. 1885. 8vo. pp. 349.

Catalogue of the library of the State Historical Society of Wisconsin. Vol. VI. Fourth supplement prepared by Daniel S. Durrie, librarian, and Isabel Durrie, assistant. Madison, Wisconsin: Democrat Printing Company, State Printers. 1885. 8vo. pp. 820.

II. *Other Publications.*

John Harvard. St. Saviour's, Southwark and Harvard University, U. S. A. By William Rendle, F.S.C.S., author of "Old Southwark and its People." 1885. 8vo. pp. 24.

The U. S. Veteran Signal Corps Association, including a partial roster of the corps during the war, with a brief résumé of its operations from Aug. 14, 1861, to March 14, 1862. 1884. Copyright 1884 by J. Willard Brown, West Medford, Mass. 12mo. pp. 52.

Two brief papers, being the Abandoned Boston, the Extent of the Continental Line of the Revolutionary Army misconceived. By Justin Winsor. Cambridge: John Wilson and Son, University Press. 1886. 8vo. pp. 10.

Reminiscences of seven years of early life. By Richard S. Smith. Wilmington, Del.: Ferris Bros., Printers. 1884. 8vo. pp. 122.

Archæologia or miscellaneous tracts relating to antiquity. Published by the Society of Antiquaries of London. Volume XLVIII. London: Printed by Nichols and Sons, 25 Parliament Street. Sold at the Society's apartments in Burlington House.

One hundred and fifty-fourth annual report of the directors of the Redwood Library and Atheneum, Newport, R. I., to the Proprietors, submitted Wednesday, August 20, 1884. 8vo. pp. 30.

Fifth annual report of the State Board of Health, Lunacy and Charity of Massachusetts. Supplement containing the report and papers on public health. Boston: Wright and Potter Printing Co., State Printers, 18 Post Office Square. 1884. 8vo. pp. 283.

Papers relating to the foreign relations of the United States, transmitted to Congress, with the annual message of the President. December 4, 1882 and 1883. Washington: Government Printing Office. 1883-1884. 8vo.

History of the Eighteenth Regiment, Connecticut Volunteers, in the war of the Union. By Chaplain Wm. C. Walker, Norwich, Conn. Published by the Committee. 1885. 8vo. pp. 444.

Unveiling of the Pilgrim Statue by the New England Society in the City of New York at Central Park, June 6, 1885. 8vo. pp. 33.

Collections of the Nova Scotia Historical Society for the year 1884. Volume IV. Halifax, N. S.: Wm. Macnab, Printer, 12 Prince Street. 1885. 8vo. pp. 258.

Bradford Academy. Historical sketch of Harriette Briggs Stoddard. By Mrs. J. D. Kingsbury. Lawrence, Mass.: American Printing House. 1885. 8vo. pp. 14.

Proceedings of the Bunker Hill Monument Association at the annual meeting, June 17, 1885, with the annual address by the Hon. Frederic W. Lincoln, and remarks by Hon. Charles Devens, President of the Association. Boston: Bunker Hill Monument Association. 1885. 8vo. pp. 47.

Proceedings of the American Antiquarian Society at the semi-annual meeting held at Boston, April 29, 1885. Volume III. New series, Part IV. Worcester: Press of Charles Hamilton, 311 Main Street. 1885. 8vo. pp. 339-513.

Record of the semi-centennial anniversary of St. Nicholas Society of the City of New York. February 18, 1885. 8vo. pp. 43.

Proceedings at the public celebration of the One Hundredth Anniversary of the Institution of the Academy of the Protestant Episcopal Church in the City of Philadelphia, held in Association, April 16, 1885. Philadelphia: Collins, Printer, 705 Jayne Street. 1885. 8vo. pp. 62.

Transactions of the Massachusetts Horticultural Society for the year 1885. Part I. Boston: Printed for the Society. 1885. 8vo. pp. 219.

A sketch of the life and works of Loammi Baldwin, civil engineer. Read before the Boston Society of Civil Engineers, Sept. 16, 1885. By George L. Vose. Boston: Press of Geo. H. Ellis, 141 Franklin Street. 1885. 8vo. pp. 28.

Sketch of the life and times of Col. Israel Ludlow, one of the original proprietors of Cincinnati. By Henry Benton Teetor, A.M. Cincinnati: Printed by Cranston and Stowe. 1885. 8vo. pp. 52.

Harvard College. Class of 1878. Secretary's report. No. II. 1884. Printed for the use of the class. Cambridge: John Wilson and Son, University Press. 1885. 8vo. pp. 152.

Annual report of the City Auditor of the receipts and expenditures of the City of Boston and the County of Suffolk, State of Massachusetts, for the financial year 1884-85. Boston: Rockwell and Churchill, City Printers, 39 Arch Street. 1885. 8vo. pp. 345.

One hundred and fifty-fifth annual report of the directors of the Redwood Library and Atheneum, Newport, R. I., to the proprietors, submitted Wednesday, August 19, 1885. Newport, R. I.: John P. Sanborn, Printer. 1885. 8vo. pp. 16.

Sacred memorial services in memory of the late Sir Moses Montefiore, baronet, held in Boston at the Church Street Synagogue, Zion's Holy Prophets, on Saturday, Ab. 20, A.M., 5645. New York: "Hebrew Journal" Print, 177-179 Grand Street. 5645. 8vo. pp. 26.

Some observations on the letters of Amerigo Vespucci. By M. F. Force. Read before the Congrès International des Americanistes at Brussels, September, 1879. Cincinnati: Robert Clarke & Co. 1885. 8vo. pp. 24.

Essex Institute Historical Collections. January, February and March, 1885. Vol. XXII. Salem, Mass.: Printed for the Essex Institute. 1885. 8vo. pp. 80.

Society of the Army of the Cumberland. Sixteenth re-union, Rochester, New York, 1884. Published by order of the Society. Cincinnati: Robert Clarke & Co. 1885. 8vo. pp. 282.

The life and character of Mrs. Sarah Byram Dean. A monograph by Rev. Enoch Sanford, D.D. Raynham, Mass.: October, 1885. 8vo. pp. 30.

Woburn. An historical and descriptive sketch of the town, with an outline of its industrial interests. Illustrated. Woburn: Published by the Board of Trade. 1885. 8vo. pp. 60.

Inauguration of the Perry Statue, September 10, A.D. 1885, with the addresses of William P. Sheffield, and the remarks on receiving the statue by Governor Wetmore and Major Franklin, and the speeches at the dinner. Newport, R. I.: John P. Sanborn, Publisher. 1885. 8vo. pp. 60.

A memorial of Stephen Salisbury, of Worcester, Mass. Worcester: Press of Charles Hamilton. 1885. 8vo. pp. 158.

Services at the dedication of a mural Monument to James Walker, D.D., LL.D., in the Harvard Church in Charlestown, in the City of Boston, January 14, 1883. Cambridge: John Wilson and Son, University Press. 1884. 8vo. pp. 64.

The State of New Hampshire. Rolls of the Soldiers in the Revolutionary War, 1775 to May, 1777, with an appendix embracing diaries of Lieut. Jonathan Burton. Compiled and edited by Isaac W. Hammond, A.M. Concord, N. H.: Parsons B. Cogswell, State Printer. 1885. 8vo. pp. 799.

Proceedings of the Tennessee Historical Society at Murfreesboro', Tenn., December 8, 1885. Nashville, Tenn.: James T. Camp, Printer and Binder. 1886. 8vo. pp. 26.

The Peace Negotiations of 1782 and 1783. An address delivered before the New York Historical Society, on its seventy-ninth anniversary, Tuesday, November 27, 1883, by John J. Jay. New York: Printed for the Society. 1884. 8vo. pp. 237.

Collections of the New York Historical Society, for the year 1880. New York: Printed for the Society. 1881. 8vo. pp. 489.

Documents relating to the Colonial history of the State of New Jersey. Edited by Frederick W. Record and Wm. Nelson. Vol. IX. 1757–1767. Newark, N. J.: Daily Advertiser Printing House. 1885. 8vo. pp. 656.

The Parish Register of St. Anne's Church, Lowell, Mass. Rev. Theodore Edson, S.T.D., the first and only rector from March 7, 1824, to June 25, 1883. Lowell, Mass.: Morning Mail Print. 1885. 8vo. pp. 155.

Re-Dedication of the Old State House, Boston, July 11, 1882. Third Edition. Boston: Printed by order of the City Council. 1885. 8vo. pp. 216.

Vol. IV. New Series, Part I. Proceedings of the American Antiquarian Society, at the annual meeting held in Worcester, October 21, 1885. Worcester: Press of Charles Hamilton, 311 Main St. 1886. 8vo. pp. 59.

Our Third Re-union. An address delivered at the third re-union of the Old Hawes School Boys, March 2, 1886. By R. J. Monks. Boston: David Clapp and Son, Printers. 1886. 8vo. pp. 11.

Sketch of the Musical Fund Society of Philadelphia. Read before the Society, January 29, 1885, by William L. Mactier. Philadelphia: Press of Henry R. Ashmead, 1102 and 1104 Sansom Street. 1885. 12mo. pp. 54.

Manual with rules and orders for the use of the General Assembly of the State of Rhode Island 1885–86. Prepared by Joshua M. Addeman, Secretary of State. Providence, R.I.: E. L. Freeman and Son, printers to the State. 1885. 8vo. pp. 298.

Papers of the Historical Society of Delaware. V. History of the First Regiment Delaware Volunteers, from the commencement of the "three months service" to the final muster-out at the close of the rebellion. By William P. Seville. The Historical Society of Delaware, Wilmington. 1884.

Dedication of the Wallace Library and Art Building, July 1, 1885. Fitchburg, Mass. 8vo. pp. 72.

Random Recollections. By Henry B. Stanton. Second Edition. Macgowan and Slipper, Printers, New York. 1886. 8vo. pp. 134.

Celebration of the Thirty-fifth anniversary of the Society of California Pioneers, held at Pioneer Hall, September 9, 1885. San Francisco. 1885. 8vo. pp. 42.

A discourse delivered at Blandford, Mass., Tuesday, March 20, 1821, giving some account of the early settlement of the town and the history of the Church, by Rev. John Keep. Printed from a recently discovered manuscript copy, by Charles W. Eddy, Ware, Mass. 1886. 8vo. pp. 23.

DEATHS.

Mrs. RELIEF MOULTON, widow of Joseph Moulton, of Lynn, a member of the Historic Genealogical Society, whose necrology appears in the REGISTER, xxviii. 338, died at Lynn, October 19, 1885, aged 87. She was the last survivor of twelve children of Thomas Todd, one of the early settlers of

Poultney, Vt., and was born March 11, 1798. She was married June 7, 1821, to Mr. Moulton, and resided with him in Poultney, Gouverneur (since Watertown), N.Y., Schenectady, N.Y., and Lynn, Mass., to which place they removed in 1835. For fifty years her home has been in Lynn. It was her good fortune to enjoy more than fifty years of wedded life with the husband of her youth, their golden wedding having been observed in 1871, with an unbroken family circle. Naturally she possessed a strong and hardy constitution, and enjoyed vigorous health. She was a useful and respected member of the Methodist church. See obituary in the *Lynn Transcript*, Oct. 30, 1885.

Hon. JAMES MURRAY ROBBINS, of Milton, Mass., died at his residence in that town, Nov. 2, 1885, aged 89. He was a son of Lieut. Gov. Edward Hutchinson and Mrs. Elizabeth (Murray) Robbins, and was born in Milton, June 30, 1796. He was the sixth in descent from Nathaniel[1] Robbins, who came from Scotland about 1670 and settled in Cambridge, through Nathaniel,[2] Thomas,[3] Rev. Nathaniel[4] and Edward H.,[5] above named. He was educated at Milton Academy. Early in life he established himself in business as a commission merchant, from which many years ago he retired, and has resided at his beautiful seat in Milton.

He represented Milton in the Massachusetts legislature in 1837 and in 1860, and was president of the trustees of Milton Public Library from the year 1871, when it was opened, till his death. In 1862 he delivered the address at the Bi-Centenary of Milton, which was printed. He was also the author of the early chapters of the History of Dorchester, prepared by the Dorchester Antiquarian Society. He married Oct. 7, 1835, Frances Mary Harris, who died Feb. 20, 1870. See a biographical sketch of Mr. Robbins by the Rev. A. K. Teele, D.D., in the *Milton News*, Nov. 7, 1885.

JOHN LANGDON SIBLEY, A.M., Librarian Emeritus of Harvard University, died at his residence in Cambridge, Wednesday, December 9, 1885, aged nearly 81. He was a son of Jonathan[5] and Persis (Morse) Sibley, and was born at Union, Me., Dec. 29, 1804. He was the 6th generation in descent from Richard[1] Sibley of Salem, Mass., through Sam-

uel,[2] Jonathan,[3] Jacob[4] and Jonathan[5] his father. He was fitted for college at Phillips Exeter Academy, graduated at Harvard College in 1825, was assistant librarian at that college 1825-6, was graduated at the Divinity School there in 1828, ordained May 14, 1829, over the Congregational church at Stow, of which he continued the pastor till March 31, 1833, when he again took up his residence at Cambridge. For about eight years he devoted himself to literary work. During a part of the year 1837, he was editor and became proprietor of the *American Magazine of Useful and Entertaining Knowledge*, a monthly periodical commenced by the Bewick Company of Boston. On the removal of the Harvard College Library to Gore Hall in 1841, Mr. Sibley was appointed assistant librarian, and on the death of the librarian Thaddeus William Harris, M.D., in 1856, he was chosen librarian. He held this office till 1877, when he was succeeded by Justin Winsor, A.M., and he became librarian emeritus. From 1841 to 1880, he edited the Harvard Triennial, now Quinquennial Catalogue. He also edited the Annual Catalogue, from 1850 to 1870.

He was the author of History of Union, Me., 12mo, 1851; Biographical Sketches of the Graduates of Harvard University, 8vo. 3 vols. 1873, 1881 and 1885. These three volumes are model biographies for fulness and minute accuracy of detail. For more than forty years he conducted an exhaustive research for materials for the biography of all the graduates of Harvard. His collections on this subject have been left to the Massachusetts Historical Society, and the bulk of his property, amounting to about one hundred and fifty thousand dollars, will ultimately be available for continuing the series he has begun in so excellent a style. Soon after the issue of the first volume of Sketches of Harvard Graduates, Mr. Sibley became blind from cataract; but, after an operation, his sight was sufficiently restored to enable him to use his eyes a portion of each day, and to complete and publish two more volumes.

Mr. Sibley was a liberal benefactor to Phillips Exeter Academy, and his portrait adorns the chapel walls. He married, May 30, 1866, Miss Charlotte Augusta Langdon Cook, daughter of Samuel Cook, a Boston merchant, who survives him.

NOTMAN PHOTO. CO. BOSTON, MASS.   COPLEY, PINX.

PETER OLIVER,
CHIEF JUSTICE OF MASSACHUSETTS.

THE

HISTORICAL AND GENEALOGICAL REGISTER.

JULY, 1886.

PETER OLIVER,

THE LAST CHIEF JUSTICE OF THE SUPERIOR COURT OF JUDICATURE OF THE PROVINCE
OF MASSACHUSETTS BAY,

By THOMAS WESTON, Jr., Esq., A.M.

Read before the New England Historic Genealogical Society, September, 1885, and before the
Bostonian Society, November, 1885.

THE judiciary of Massachusetts has always been distinguished for its ability and its high personal character. These character-istics have come down as a part of our heritage of the past. The judges of the colonial period were rarely men of other than un-questioned integrity, and often combined eminent legal ability with the most liberal culture the times could produce. Their reputation, however, seems never long to have survived them. They have left scarce any traces of their learning, of their legal attainments or of their influence, even in shaping the laws which so effectually secured, during the formative period of our history, the amplest protection of life, property and reputation to the humblest citizen. But a single volume of reported decisions* has come down to us,

NOTE.—Although frequent mention is made of Judge Oliver in the books and papers re-lating to the period in which he lived, no detailed account of his life has come down to us. Gov. Hutchinson, in his History of Massachusetts, gives a full account of his impeachment, and Gov. Washburn, in his Judicial History of Massachusetts, devotes a few pages to his life; and this is about all that has been published concerning him.

I have been enabled to supply, from what I deem authentic local tradition, much con-cerning his life and character. He lived in Middleboro', Mass., some thirty years. Soon after the sale of his estate by the commissioners appointed to sell confiscated property of royalists, my grandfather came into possession of a portion of his real estate and the iron works he formerly owned in Middleboro'. The housekeeper of Judge Oliver, a very intelligent woman, lived to an advanced age. She spent some time in the latter part of her life in the family of my grandfather. My father remembers many of the stories and anecdotes she was always fond of relating concerning Judge Oliver and the life at Oliver Hall. Several years ago some of these stories were published in the Middleboro' Gazette, by Dr. Granville Sproat, as they were related to him by this lady. From these sources I have gathered much for this article.

I have also been especially interested in whatever relates to his life and character, from the fact that Oliver Hall stood near my father's house, who for many years owned the estate upon which Judge Oliver had lived; and I early became familiar with the many local traditions, concerning him and his home, which then lingered about the place.

The accompanying heliotype of Judge Oliver is from Copley, painted in England, in 1772.

* Quincy's Mass. Reports.

and the cases there reported are so fragmentary and meagre as to be of no value, except as legal curiosities, and give us no proper estimate of the learning and ability of the court at that period.

Among these judges, no one was more distinguished than Peter Oliver, the last of the chief justices of the Superior Court of Judicature of the Province of Massachusetts Bay, the highest court in the Province, under the Crown. The course he conscientiously took during the turbulent times which followed his appointment as Chief Justice, and which culminated upon the breaking out of the war for Independence, his intimate personal connection with the leading officers of the Crown, his warm espousal of the cause of his King, provoked the bitter hostility of the patriots, and he left with Gov. Gage, upon the evacuation of Boston, in disfavor, never to return. Had his life gone out in any other period of our history, his name and character would doubtless have stood among the highest in the long line of illustrious men who had adorned the Bench of Massachusetts. The little that can be gathered from the scanty records of his time, and the local traditions which have survived concerning him, represent a life and character that ought not to be forgotten.

The Oliver family was one of the oldest and most respectable in the Massachusetts Colony. His ancestor, Thomas Oliver, came from London in the William and Francis, in the year 1632, and settled in Boston. He was a surgeon by profession, one of the ruling elders in the First Church, and a man much esteemed in the colony.* Upon his death, which occurred January 1, 1656, he was spoken of in Hull's Diary as "living to a great age, and in his former years as very serviceable." One of his sons, James Oliver, was a captain in King Philip's war, and reputed a brave man ; another son, Peter, was an eminent merchant in the town of Boston, one of whose sons married a granddaughter of Gov. Bradstreet. Daniel Oliver, a son of the last named and the father of Judge Oliver, was a wealthy merchant of Boston, and for several years a mandamus councillor. His two sons, Andrew and Peter, were destined to fill very conspicuous places in the later times of the Province. Andrew was for many years Provincial Secretary and afterwards Lieutenant Governor, and did much towards hastening the progress of events which finally precipitated the colonies into open hostility with the mother country. His second wife was a sister of the wife of Gov. Hutchinson, and the relation was made still more intimate by intermarriages between the children of both the Olivers with those of Gov. Hutchinson.† Peter Oliver was also connected by marriage with Copley the distinguished portrait painter of the period. The family were thus closely related to some of the most prominent supporters of the Crown, and early espoused the cause of royalty.

* New Eng. Hist. and Gen. Reg., April, 1865.
† Mem. Hist. of Boston, vol. ii. p. 539.

George III. had no more able or zealous friends in America than the Olivers.

Peter Oliver was born in Boston, March 17, 1713. But little is known of his early boyhood. He used to say that his father spared no pains in the education of his two boys. They both showed a taste for books, and at an early age Peter had attained considerable proficiency in the literature of the times.

He entered Harvard College in 1726, at the age of 16 years. In his class were John Cotton, Joseph Mayhew, Stephen Minot, Samuel Parsons, Peter Prescott, and others who afterwards occupied prominent positions in the Province.

It seemed to be the wish of the father that young Peter should be bred a gentleman and follow no business or profession. While in college he was interested in history, political science and general literature, and showed great fondness for the law as a science. His father took pains early to introduce his sons into the best society of the Province, and before he came to manhood he had formed an intimate acquaintance with many of the prominent men of the times.* This early acquaintance, which seems to have continued, contributed not a little in giving him the position and the great influence he afterwards exerted in the events which were to transpire in his maturer years. At his graduation he was undoubtedly as well fitted for the bar as any of his classmates who afterwards commenced practice before the courts. He was one of the best scholars of his class, and his close habits of study followed him all through his life. His proficiency and reputation as a scholar gained for him in after years the honorary degree of Doctor of Laws from Oxford University.

On July 5, 1733, Mr. Oliver married Mary, the daughter of William Clark, of Boston, who was a prominent man in the town, a member of the General Court for the years 1731, 1732, 1733, 1734, and a man of influence throughout the province. Mrs. Oliver was an accomplished lady, well fitted for the social position she was called to fill. The charm of her conversation, her courtly manners, her generous hospitality at Oliver Hall, aided not a little in making this famous place so memorable in the social history of the times. After her removal to Middleboro', she was a constant attendant at the church in the town, and her many deeds of kindness and christian charity have come down with the traditions of the place as memorials of her goodness.

For a few years after his marriage Mr. Oliver seems to have spent his time in rendering his father such assistance as his business required. He had become interested in the early history of the colonies, and had given much thought to developing their agricultural and manufacturing resources. He had already collected something of a library and had transcribed several MS. local histories.

---

* Among these early friends was the celebrated lawyer, Jeremiah Gridley, and this friendship continued during his life.

Among them was a MS. copy of Rev. Mr. Hubbard's history of New England.* He was also a close student of the stirring events which were transpiring in the Old World, and kept an extensive correspondence with friends in London. He probably spent some time in the old country at about this period. He early showed a fondness for royalty and a great love for the customs and institutions of Old England, which seemed to increase with his years. Although interested in everything that in his judgment could tend to develop the prosperity of the provinces, he never allowed anything to come between him and the cause of his King.

In 1744, Mr. Oliver purchased about three hundred acres of land in Middleboro', in what had been known as the Indian village of Muttock, on the Nemasket River, where he soon after removed from Boston.

The estate he purchased in Middleboro' had been recently occupied by the Nemasket Indians. In 1737, they had petitioned the General Court for leave to sell their lands at this place, "alleging that by long cultivation they had become worn out, and that there were no fish in the river, nor game in the forests for their sustenance, and prayed for leave to remove to another part of the town where the land was better adapted for their cultivation, and game more abundant." While the subject-matter of this petition was being discussed in the General Court, Mr. Oliver's attention was directed to this locality as one of unusual beauty, and affording rare facilities for business. At the foot of the hill adjacent to the old settlement of the Indians, the town had previously authorized a dam to be built across the river. A saw mill and grist mill had been built there, and the water privilege was one of the best in the county. The lands and great ponds in the vicinity abounded in the richest iron ore ; timber was abundant, and, notwithstanding the allegation in the petition of the former inhabitants, the soil was more than ordinarily fertile. His purchase included the site of the first settlers of the town, whose houses were burned in King Philip's war, and who had been consequently obliged to return to Plymouth. It bordered upon the oldest burial place of the settlers, and upon the other side was the spot where the Indian braves, for generations, had been laid to rest. Upon the summit of the high hill bordering upon the pond were the remains of the wigwam of the old Indian chieftain from whom the place had taken its name.

Immediately after coming to Middleboro', Mr. Oliver repaired the mills on his estate, and made preparations for a large manufacturing business. Just before his purchase, there had been built a blast furnace, which with many others in Plymouth county did a prosperous business for those early times. His keen business eye foresaw that iron manufacture was to be the prominent industry for the Province,

---

* Pres. Stiles's Literary Diary, 2d series, Mass. Hist. Col., vol. ii. p. 200.

and the branch of it next to that done by the blast furnaces was to be that of making the hammered nails which were the only ones in use at that time. For that business a forge was necessary, and the mechanics of the county could readily construct one. There were one or two in the country, one at Raynham and one or two near Boston. But the necessary mill for this business was a rolling or slitting mill, which would take the iron hammered into bars from the forge and split them into nail rods, out of which the nails were to be hammered. These rods were then to be taken home by the farmers and hammered into nails of any required length and size. There was but one such mill in the country, and that was in Milton, near what is now Milton Mills. Its owner was reaping a large profit from it. All admittance to this wonderful mill was forbidden. Its mysteries were kept a profound secret; its entrance was carefully guarded, and the workmen were under heavy bonds never to reveal the mysterious process by which nail rods were there produced.

At this time a young man by the name of Hushai Thomas lived in Middleboro'. Mr. Oliver had put him in charge of his works. He had superintended their repair, and was of bright parts, a natural mechanic, of accurate eye and keen perceptions in everything that related to his craft. Tradition has it that Judge Oliver offered him a large sum of money if he would build him a slitting mill that would do the work done at Milton. The offer was too tempting to be rejected without trial. Early in the week, one bright summer day, young Thomas was missing from his home. His wife knew nothing of his whereabouts, although she did not seem to share the anxiety of the neighbors as to his fate. The next morning a shabby, ill-kempt, idiotic person came to the quiet town of Milton, and was seen sauntering about the place, begging for something to eat. At first the villagers were frightened at his appearance and were shy of him. He remained there for some weeks, and the honest people regarding him as a poor, simple-minded unfortunate, allowed him to sleep in their barns. He was playful with the children, and they became gradually attached to the foolish fellow. He seemed to prefer to play about the mill, and the workmen, as they went out and in, became accustomed to his idiotic ways. One day at noon, while playing with some small children, the workmen as they left for dinner neglected to close the door of the mill. The simple-minded man, to hide from the children, ran into it. He was there but a short time and then ran out. The next day he disappeared, but, alas, the mystery of the wonderful mill went with him. In a few days it was told that young Thomas had returned, and that foundations were being laid for a new mill at Oliver's works. The mill when completed produced as good work as that done by the mill at Milton, and the neighbors began to see that in some way the fortunes of young Thomas had wonderfully improved.

During the French and Indian war Mr. Oliver was also largely engaged at his works in Middleboro' in making ordnance, shot and shell, for the colonies.* His prudent management, his extensive acquaintance and warm personal friends, made his business very lucrative, and enabled him to maintain a style of living far superior to the average citizen.

Soon after coming to Middleboro' he erected, for his country residence, Oliver Hall. It stood on a level tract of land about half way up what is now known as Muttock Hill, on the Southeasterly side of the road leading from Middleboro' to Bridgewater. It commanded an extensive view of the adjacent country. The borders of the land upon which the house stood sloped to the banks of the Nemasket River and the large winding pond formed thereby. The grounds were very extensive, laid out after the manner of English parks, with broad avenues bordered with ornamental trees, shaded walks, with flower and fruit gardens, and a lawn in front of the house overlooking the pond and river.

The Hall was approached from the road through an avenue lined with ornamental trees, which wound from the top of the hill passing the Hall, and descended by gradual descent to the margin of the banks of the pond and river.† About the grounds were many shaded walks and groves, beautified by the choicest shrubs and flowers. As this avenue wound about the grounds down the sloping hill it passed a summer house on the borders of the pond, pleasantly situated under the shade of the original oaks of the forest. It was beautifully designed, and had accommodation for a large number of guests. Just back of it was a flowing spring of water, with an ingenious device for cooling wine kept in an adjoining apartment. The Hall itself was patterned after the Manor House of the old country, stately and spacious. Its frame was shipped from England. Its internal decorations, its carving, its wainscotting, its hangings were all made expressly for it in London. It had its grand staircase, its spacious parlor, its high ceilings. The Library formed an L of the Hall, and was entered through an elaborate carved lattice work. It was a large room, high studded, and upon its shelves were to be found the best books the times could produce. It was one of the best libraries in the province. The Hall had elegant guest chambers and extensive servants' apartments. The parlor, library and dining hall were richly wainscotted, their walls covered with elaborate hangings, and the floors laid in polished English oak. Gov. Hutchinson remarked at one time after visiting Oliver Hall, that it was the finest residence in his Majesty's dominions in New England.‡

The spacious and elegant apartments, the generous hospitality of

---

* Hist. of Plymouth County, p. 1023.
† Traces of this avenue and the site of the summer house are still to be seen on these grounds.
‡ Middleboro' Gazette.

the host and the elegance and extent of the grounds, made Oliver Hall a favorite resort of the wealth and fashion of the time. Governor Bowdoin, considered one of the wealthiest men of the colony, was often there, Governor Hutchinson and family spent many summers there. Andrew Oliver, then Lieut. Governor, and Sir John and Sir Grenville Temple, were among the frequent guests. Distinguished gentlemen from the old country visiting the province were considered as not completing their tour through the colonies without a visit to the famous country seat of the Chief Justice.*

A description of the social parties there given, and the prominent men and elegant women in attendance, would form an interesting chapter in the social history of the times. One of these famous occasions, the old housekeeper of the Hall was ever fond of narrating. A special messenger came riding all the way from Boston bearing the news of the birth of an heir to His Majesty, King George the Third. He approached the Hall on a gallop, swinging his hat and shouting "Long live the King! a prince has been born to the royal family of England." She took great pleasure in describing the grand company assembled that night in the Hall, how the tables were loaded and toasts given in honor of the occasion. Governor Hutchinson was there, and Governor Oliver came with some ladies from Boston. He wore a suit of scarlet silk velvet, with gold buttons and lace ruffles for the sleeves and bosom; short breeches, white silk long stockings with gold shoe and knee buckles made up his suit. Governor Hutchinson was dressed nearly in the same way, only his suit was trimmed with gold lace. Many other illustrious men with their wives and daughters were there, dressed with all of the taste and elegance of the times. There was dancing and music and wine in abundance, and the assembly did not disperse until late at night.†

During the early years of his residence in Middleboro', Mr. Oliver found time to attend to many public duties, representing the town in the General Court during these years. He was specially interested in agriculture, horticulture and floriculture,‡ taking great pains to introduce the choicest kinds of fruit and flowers adapted to the locality. John Adams in his diary speaks of seeing some rare flower, the seed of which came from Judge Oliver's garden.§ He imported some new breeds of stock, which he supposed would be better than those found on the farms of his neighbors. He seemed always anxious to improve the condition of the farming interest in the county, and gave it an impetus which was not lost during his generation.

His chief delight seemed to be in gathering about him men and women of the culture and refinement of the times, and discussing in

---

* Middleboro' Gazette.   † Ibid.
‡ 2d Series Mass. His. Col. Vol. 3, p. 169.
§ John Adams's (Diary) Works, Vol. 2, p. 137.

his spacious and well-filled library the questions of literature and politics of the day.* Scholars from all parts of the colony came to consult his books and manuscripts, and for such information as he only could give them in matters of history, literature and art.

Nor were his tastes confined merely to literary and political subjects. He was considered as an authority in matters of architecture and music. After his appointment to the Court of Common Pleas he planned, in 1749, and superintended the erection of the Court House in Plymouth,† which stood as late as 1815, a structure much admired for its architectural beauty. He had a cultivated ear and a good voice for singing, and so desirous was he to improve the musical tastes of the people of the town, that he took an active part in the singing in the church near his domains. One of the venerable dames of the parish, disgusted with the innovation of the times and the new-fangled music in the meeting-house, in writing to one of her friends, expressed her contempt and disgust by saying, " even the Judge of the land was bawling in the gallery with the boys."

Notwithstanding his wealth, official position and style of living, he mingled freely with the people, was always considerate towards them and did much towards furnishing them with remunerative employment at his works or on his estate. No poor man ever went from his door without his necessary wants being supplied. The people of the town looked up to him for advice upon all matters of business, or whenever they needed counsel, and always found in him a warm and sympathetic friend. His strong common sense, his extensive reading, his knowledge of law and men were of great service to them, and his advice much sought after and usually heeded. His kindness of heart, his generosity and the interest he seemed to take in their welfare, gave him great influence in the place of his home. At one time he complained to a friend that there was only one man in town who would express an opinion contrary to his if he had previously stated his views on the subject; with his townsmen his word was regarded as law.

Mr. Oliver was appointed a Justice of the Court of Common Pleas for Plymouth County during Governor Shirley's administration, in December, 1747, and continued to hold that office until his promotion to the bench of the Superior Court. At the time of his appointment the Court of Common Pleas had been in existence since 1702.‡ It was originally known in the Old Colony as the Associates' Court,§ but during the administration of Andros it assumed the name of Court of Common Pleas, and so continued until the Revolution. Upon the adoption of the Constitution the Court was continued with substan-

---

* He left a very full Diary of the prominent events of his life, with an account of the public men of his time with whom he was associated, which is about being published in London.
† Thatcher's Hist. Plymouth, p. 174.
‡ Washburn's Jud. His. Mass. 354.
§ Baylies.

tially the same jurisdiction and powers. Under the Charter the Justices of this Court did not go beyond the County for which they were commissioned. Their salary was small and not uniform, and but a small portion of their time was occupied in the discharge of their official duties. His acceptance of the position did not seem to interfere with his business or his habits of study which he had continued from his early years. At this time his business was large and lucrative, and enabled him to live in the princely style we have already indicated. The grounds about Oliver Hall were carefully cultivated and improved, and he continually added such adornments as his taste suggested.

With him, on the bench of this Court, were Isaac Lothrop, Elijah Cushing and Thomas Clapp. These men, though not educated for the bar, were all of them men of mark and ability, and enjoyed the confidence of the bar and of those who came before the Court. Upon the dedication of the new Court House which Judge Oliver had planned, and whose construction he had superintended, his first duty was to pronounce an eulogy upon the death of his associate Judge Cushing, which was published at the time, one copy of which has come down to us and is in the Library of the Athenæum. This Court, however, although composed of men of high character, was not surrounded with the pomp and display of the Superior Court, and its justices did not assume the rank and dignity accorded to the latter Court. The barristers of the province, whose talents and legal abilities would well compare with the practitioners of the time before the highest Courts in Westminster, were often before this Court. It was the fashion for them often to speak disparagingly of it, and they professed to have a contempt for any ruling on matters of law or opinion, which this Court might give, which happened to be against their particular client.

One of the ablest lawyers who practised in this time in the Courts of Plymouth County was Timothy Ruggles. He was a barrister of large practice, his only rival being James Otis. He was generally known as Brigadier Ruggles, from his conspicuous service in the French and Indian wars. The late venerable Abraham Holmes, in an address before the Bristol bar in 1834, gives this anecdote of Brigadier Ruggles, in a case before this Court at this time. While he was engaged in the trial of a cause, a very old woman who was a witness, told him that she could stand no longer and asked him where she might sit; Ruggles looking about and seeing no vacant seat except on the bench, told her inadvertently to go and sit there. The old woman hobbled to the bench, crept up the stairs, got within the enclosure occupied by the Judges before they noticed her, and was sitting down, when one of them asked her what she was there for. She replied that Mr. Ruggles had told her to go up there and sit down. The Court with offended dignity asked him if he had so told her. Ruggles could not evade the question and answered that he had. The Court asked, how came you to do this, Sir? He could not retreat, and must make the best of it, and looking with a dignified smile, hesitatingly said, I—I—really thought that place was made for old women. The Court regarded this answer as an insult, but, after consultation, concluded the easiest way out of it was to let the matter drop, and the trial proceeded, and the old lady kept her place. Mr. Ruggles, however, did not hesitate a few years after to accept the same position as a Justice of that Court for Worcester County.*

Upon the death of Judge Saltonstall in 1756, Judge Oliver was appointed his successor on the bench of the Superior Court.† The importance of the various matters over which it had jurisdiction, it being the appellate Court of the Colonies, the high character of the men who were on its bench, the pomp and dignity which attended its deliberations, all served to impress upon the people the importance of this, the highest judicial tribunal of the land. The court then consisted of Stephen Sewell as Chief Justice, and Benjamin Lynde, John Cushing and Chambers Russell as associate justices.

This was the happiest period of his life. He was known and honored throughout the Province. His judicial ability was recognized by the entire bar, and his accession to the bench of this Court was cordially welcomed by his associates. His income from his business was large. Oliver Hall had become celebrated in both countries, not only for its generous hospitality, the beauty and extent of its grounds, but for the men of rank and culture that were there entertained. A writer of the times says of this place, that it was " Where the native grove under his forming hand had become such an one as Thomson found in the shades of Hagley." ‡ The troubles between the Colonies and the Mother Country, which ere long were to undermine his influence and render him an exile, had not assumed such form and magnitude as to indicate the results which were to follow.

The duties of his office now absorbed much of his time, and he discharged them conscientiously and fearlessly. His business was entrusted to the care and management of others. He nevertheless always found time to continue his studies in literature and in the politics and history of the times.

His salary at this time was but 160 pounds per annum,§ a sum wholly inadequate to meet his personal expenses. The Judges of this Court were obliged to maintain the same pomp of style and display as the English judges of the period. They wore the same style of robes, wigs and swords‖ when on the bench, and wherever they were great deference was paid to them. Judge Oliver always made his journey to and from Boston with his coach and four, his

---

* Washburn, p. 226.   † Dr. Eliot says, " It was a very popular appointment."
‡ 2d Series Mass. His. Col., Vol. 3, p. 169.
§ Washburn, p. 162.   ‖ 2 Loyalists of Am. Rev., p. 128.

coat of arms emblazoned on the panels of the doors, with attending outriders and postillion. Wherever these courts were to be held, the High Sheriff of the County, the prominent men of the place and the barristers were in the habit of going out to meet them as they approached the town, and escorting them with great pomp and display to the public inn where they were to remain during the term of Court. None of the English Courts of the times were more dignified than that of the Superior Court of the Province of Massachusetts Bay.

No better idea of its dignity while in session in 1761 can be given than by transcribing President Adams's description of it in a letter to Mr. Tudor.* It was at the hearing upon the matter of granting the celebrated writs of assistance. It was in the Council Chamber of the old State House in Boston, where the courts were held for Suffolk. All the members of the Court were present. The most prominent counsel of the province were engaged on the one side or the other; there was Gridley for the petitioner, and Thatcher and James Otis for the remonstrants. He says, " In this chamber near the fire were seated the five Judges, with Lieut. Governor Hutchinson at their head as chief justice ; all in their fresh robes of scarlet English cloth with their broad bands and enormous judicial wigs. In this chamber were seated at a long table all the barristers of Boston and its neighboring County of Middlesex, in their gowns and bands and tye wigs. They were not seated on Ivory chairs, but their dress was more solemn and more pompous than that of the Roman Senate when the Gauls broke in upon them." Mr. Adams adds, " then and there was the first scene of the first act of opposition to the arbitrary claim of Great Britain."

It is worthy of note in the light of events which soon after followed, that Judge Oliver, although known to be an intense royalist, honestly supporting every measure of the Crown, as a matter of course, before and long after the trial of this great question of the power of this Court to grant writs of assistance, was regarded by the bar and the entire community not only as a polished gentleman,† but as an able and fearless Judge, who would under all circumstances do exact justice in all matters that came before him.

Perhaps the most memorable trial before this Court in which Judge Oliver sat as an associate Judge was that of Capt. Preston and his soldiers in 1770, for manslaughter in what is familiarly known as the Boston Massacre. His charge to the jury‡ in this case,

---

* Letter written in 1817. John Adams's Works, Vol. X., page 245.

† John Adams in his diary, under date of November 9, 1771, thus alluded to the subject of this sketch. " Dined this day, spent the afternoon and drank tea at Judge Ropes's with Judges Lynde, Oliver, and Hutchinson, Sewall, Putnam and Winthrop. Mrs. Ropes is a fine woman, very pretty and genteel. Our Judge Oliver is the best bred gentleman of all the judges by far; there is something in every one of the others indecent and disagreeable at times in company—affected witticisms, unpolished fleers, coarse jests, and sometimes rough, rude attacks—but these you don't see escape Judge Oliver."—(*John Adams's Works and Diary, Vol. 2, p. 291*) A writer in the Mass. Hist. Col. 2d Series, Vol. 3, p. 169, thus alludes to him. " Judge Oliver was one of the Corinthian ornaments of the County of Plymouth while he resided in it."

‡ Trial of British Soldiers, Boston, 1807, p. 114.

is the only one that has come down to us, of the many he gave
during his administration of justice.   It is a model of its kind and
fully justifies the high estimate given him, as an able and impartial
judge.*

The excitement over this affair was intense.   The court met a
week after the tragedy in King Street.   Indictments were immediately found against Capt. Preston and his men.   On account of the
high state of feeling the court had continued the case until the next
term.   But the desire of the people was so intense for their immediate trial, that a considerable number of prominent men of Boston,
with Mr. Adams at their head, went in a body to the Superior Court
and were so earnest for a speedy trial that the Court thought it
advisable to annul their order for a continuance, and appointed a
special term for the trial.†   Attempts were made to prejudice the
minds of the people against the prisoners.   Popular feeling was so
strong that an appeal was even made through the newspapers to
prejudice the Court against them.   Judge Oliver in his charge to the
jury alluded to this as an insult to him personally and his associates.
So intense was the feeling and so great was the pressure brought to
bear upon some of the judges that they through fear of personal
harm hesitated to sit at the trial.   Governor Hutchinson, in a private
letter at that time, says, he "found it difficult to prevail upon three
of the judges to sit at the trial for fear of losing their popularity."
In this letter he refers to the firmness of Judge Oliver in his charge
to the jury, and his exposition of the law in opposition to the false
principles of government lately set up.

As further illustrating the excitement of the times and the weakness of some of the members of the Court, he says, under date of
Aug. 28, 1770 :   "I have persuaded Judge Lynde, who came to
town with his resignation in his pocket, to hold his position a little
longer.   Timid as he is, I think Trowbridge more so.   The only
difference is that little matters, as well as great, frighten Lynde.
Judge Oliver appears to be firm, though threatened in yesterday's
paper, and I hope Cushing will be so likewise."

Notwithstanding the timidity of some of the Court, at the trial
they all showed great firmness and presided with strict impartiality.
The prisoners were fearlessly and ably defended by John Adams
and Josiah Quincy.   The trial lasted eight days, and resulted in the
acquittal of Capt. Preston and six of his soldiers, and the conviction of two of them for manslaughter.   Although the popular clamor
was strong for the conviction of Capt. Preston and his men, and the
prejudice against them most bitter, these verdicts were soon after regarded as just, and the trial a triumph of justice.

[To be continued.]

* The trial was before the full bench, and in accordance with the practice of the court at
this time each judge gave a charge to the jury.
† Hutchinson's Hist., Vol. 3, p. 286.

EARLY MATTERS RELATING TO THE TOWN AND FIRST CHURCH OF DORCHESTER.

Communicated by WILLIAM BLAKE TRASK, Esq., of Dorchester.

———

DEED OF WILLIAM HANNUM TO JONAS HUMFREY, DORCHESTER, 1637.

THE following memorandum of a deed is the earliest unrecorded conveyance that we have seen.* It is of the house, home lot, &c., of William Hannum, then of Dorchester, Jonas Humfrey, grantee, the original of which is in possession of the venerable Deacon Henry Humphreys, of Dorchester, who is a descendant of Jonas in the seventh generation. Mr. H. is living on the same plat deeded to his first ancestor, the property having been owned and the land occupied by the family to the present time.

Constable Jonas Humfrey came from Wendover, co. Bucks, England. The family tradition is that he arrived in Dorchester on the 9th of September, 1637, and the next day bought the premises hereafter mentioned. (See REG. xxxvi. 274.) It appears by record that, on the 10th of September, 1637, the town granted " William Hannam " that part of the swamp lying over against his house, so far as Richard Wade's pale, on condition that said Hannam pay his part of the charge with the rest of the neighbors, maintaining a bridge over the water. The next paragraph reads thus :— " The howse of Willm̄ Hannam with the sayd p'te of his swamp, his hoame lott and great lot, and one aker of meddow hee hath made sales of vnto Jonas Humphries with his Interest in the Com̄ons." (See Dorchester Town Records, page 29; Fourth Report of Record Commissioners, Boston, page 24.)

William Hannum had a son John, born in Dorchester. The father removed to Windsor, Conn., Savage thinks as late as 1639; afterwards he went to Northampton, Mass., where he died June 1, 1677. His widow, Honor Hannum (whom Dorothy Upshall, widow of Nicholas, calls sister in her will), died at Westfield in 1680.

Jonas Humfrey died March 19, 1661–2. (See abstract of his will, REGISTER, xi. 37, 38.) His son James, a witness to this deed, was a Ruling Elder in the Dorchester church. He died May 12, 1686.

———

* On the 2d of September, 1637, John Branker, a schoolmaster, who removed to Windsor, sold Ambrose Martin, afterwards of Weymouth, his dwelling house, and about thirty-six acres of land in Dorchester. This was a few days, only, before the grant made by the town to William Hannum.

William Pynchon, also, in 1634, or earlier, sold his land with the house in Dorchester he had built and doubtless occupied, to Thomas Newberry, a great real estate owner of his time.—See Dorchester Town Records, Vol. I. pages 11 and 28. Also, Fourth Report of the Record Commissioners, pages 7 and 24.

Oliver Purchase sold land in Dorchester to Thomas Swift, Sept. 21, 1640 ; removed to Taunton, subsequently to Lynn, thence to Concord, where he died, Nov. 20, 1701. He was a representative to the General Court in 1660, and after that, at the last, says Savage, in 1689.

It will be noticed that the following deed is called a "Memorandum." One definition of this word, according to Webster, is "an instrument drawn up in a brief and compendious form." The date is not given, but circumstances, stated above, settle it satisfactorily to be about the 10th of September, 1637.

The names of the grantor and of the witnesses were placed at the top instead of the bottom of the conveyance, but it is thought more appropriate to print them in the usual form.

Memorandum

That I William Hammon of Dorchester; Together with the consent of my wife do sell vnto the saide Jonas Humfrey of Dorchester my house and whom lott of 3 Acres belonging therevnto: with the corne and all other fruite vpon together with the Swamp before the doore; and alsoe wth plott of land that is my right & pper due and is to be taken at the West end of my whome lott: next vnto Roxberry: My Medow ground pmised at the fresh marsh the ualue of one Acre or thereabouts with my greate lott and all other Rights in commons or alotments that shall heereafter be allotted : for the sum of fiue and Therty Pounds to be paide vnto the saide William Hammon; or his assignes by the saide Jonas Humfrey or his assignes. For payment whereof it is thus agreed; that he ye saide William Ham̄ shall haue 20 pounds at the present sealing heereof and 8 pounds at the present tyme when the saide William Hammon shall haue cleared the house of all goods and annoyances, and the other seauen pounds Remayning the saide william Hammon is to haue of the saide Jonas Humfrey a hogshead of meale of the value of 9 Bushels at the price of 3 pounds 12 shillings. and the other sum of the payment remaining to be thus. 40 shillings in money yf that it canbe conveniently pvided, or otherwise the whole to be paide in such sufficient goods as the saide Jonas Humfrey hath to pay : In witnesse whereof: I haue set to my hand & seale in the presence of these aboue written

the marke of William Hammon   X

Witnesses.
    James Humfrey   (Seal)
    Oliuer Purchis

On the back of this Memorandum is written the following covenant, witnessed probably by the same parties, but names not repeated.

       [th]ese presents I william [Ham]mon of Dorch[ester] [   ] do: couenant & pmise [   ] [sai]de Jonas [Hum]frey that In case either the Swamp before this my house or lots in my pp̄ry righ[t] These which I haue sold to the saide Jonas Humfrey the parcell of that land that is to be taken in behind the saide swampe lott belonging to the saide house: shalbe in after tyme demaunded or required of the saide Jonas

Humfrey or his ayres or assignes I the saide william Hammon aforesaide Doe couenant & ꝑmise to the saide Jonas Humfrey [afore] saide or his ayres or assignes to yᵉ said Jonas Humfrey or his assignes to be fully satisfyed either in possession [or pai]ment for the saide [   ] land of either side: and heereunto I haue my hand [in] pres[ence] of these witnesses heere vndernamed:

DEED OF JOHN MINOT TO JONAS AND JAMES HUMPHREY, OF DORCHESTER, 1656.

This early unrecorded deed of land in Dorchester was made, probably, to the father and son bearing the above names, though strangely enough, through the whole instrument, it is nine times written "Jonah" and James.   It will be noticed that they are called glovers, the manufacture of gloves probably being their occupation when in England.   They early turned their attention, according to tradition, to the tanning of hides, "whose pits were employed," says Mr. Savage in his mention of Jonas the father, "by six generations of most worthy descendants."

John Minot, the grantor, was a son of Elder George Minot, of Dorchester, who came from Saffron-Walden, Essex, England, and settled at Neponset.   The son was born April 2, 1626, in England; married Lydia Butler, of Dorchester, May 19, 1647.   He died August 12, 1669.   He was styled "Captain," and is first mentioned by name, we think, on the Town Records in 1652 (page 71).   See Minot Genealogy, REG. i. 172.

We take great pleasure in furnishing in fac-simile the autographs of the two witnesses to this deed, Henry Conliffe and John Gingill, as their names have been so variously written.   We are not aware of their signatures being extant elsewhere.

Henry Conliffe, of Dorchester, was made freeman May 29, 1644. (See REG. iii. 190, where the name reads "Gunlithe.")   He had wife Susan or Susanna.   She was admitted to Dorchester church "1 mo decimo 43."   They had a daughter Susanna born in Dorchester, 15. 1. 1641.   (REG. v. 98.)   Mr. Conliffe removed to Northampton with the early settlers, and with others from Dorchester aided in forming the church there.   The following paragraphs, copied from the Dorchester Church Records, show the action taken by the church in relation to these matters.   "28 (2) 61.   Mr. Eliazer Mather, William Clarke, Henery Cunlife & Henery Woodward dismissed to Joyne wᵗʰ some others for yᵉ gathering of a Church at Northampton."

"9 (4) 61 was deakon Edward Clapp & Mʳ Peletiah Glouer now at Springfeild & Tho Tilstone chosen as messengers of yᵉ Church to goe to Northampton to yᵉ gathering of yᵉ Church ther wᶜʰ is to be don vpon yᵉ 18ᵗʰ of this instant."

"23 (4) 61 the messengers of yᵉ Church wᶜʰ weer sent vnto

Northampton made report of what work ther done namly that vpon yᵉ day appointed ther was a Church gathered in that place & yᵗ Mʳ Eliazer Mather was then ordained pastor to that Church the same day." Mr. Mather was a son of the Rev. Richard Mather, of Dorchester.

"1 (7) 61 Sarah, wife of William Clarke, Elizabeth, wife of Henry Woodward, and Susan, wife of Henery Cunlife dismissed vnto yᵉ Church at Northampton."

Mr. Conliffe died at Northampton, Sept. 14, 1673; the widow departed this life, Nov. 19, 1675. (Reg. iii. 176.) "His only child Susanna," says Savage, "had been betrothed to Eldad Pomeroy, who died in 1662; she married in 1663, Matthew Cole, and Dec. 12, 1665, John Webb, Jr."

John Gingill, according to Baylies, was among the first purchasers at Taunton, his name being the thirty-sixth in order. (Baylies' Plymouth, i. 286.) In 1643 there were 54 males in Taunton, between 16 and 20, subject to military duty, John Gingill among the number. On the 6th of May, 1646, he was made freeman. As early as the 2d of the 12th month, 1646, he was an inhabitant of Dorchester, for at that date we find his name, with other proprietors of lands in Dorchester, namely, Richard Mather, John Glover, Edward Breck, William Blake, Roger Clap, Christopher Gibson, William Sumner, &c., who, in regard to the fencing of their lots, referred the subject to the arbitration of Isaac Heath, John Johnson and William Parke, of Roxbury. This committee made their report, 23. 12. 1646, as on record in the Dorchester Town Book, pages 100 and 101. (See Fourth Report of Record Commissioners, 76–78.)

Bray Wilkins, husbandman, and John Gingill, tailor, both of Dorchester, went afterwards to Lynn. They purchased of Richard Bellingham 700 acres of land, Mr. Bellingham's farm, called "Will Hill," situated "on the head of Salem, to the north west from said Towne, there being within the said place, a hill, where an Indian plantation sometime had been, & a pond, and about a hundred or a hundred & fifty acres of meadow." The territory was granted to Mr. Bellingham by the General Court, Sept. 6, 1638. To secure the payment of 225 pounds sterling, interest at 8 per cent., this land was mortgaged to said Bellingham, who with his wife Penelope, on the 9th of March, 1659, reconveyed the farm to Wilkins and Gingill. In 1661 the latter parties petitioned the General Court to be put under the jurisdiction of Salem, which was allowed.

March 31, 1673, Wilkins and Gingill mortgaged two third parts of the 700 acres, as security for 50 pounds, "with interest, after 6 pound pᶜcent," unto John Oxenbridge, Anthony Stoddard and James Allen, of Boston, executors of the will of Richard Bellingham. In 1723 the inhabitants of this territory were released from their ecclesiastical obligations to Salem village, on condition of having a minister settled over them.   In 1728 these lands, with parts of Andover, Boxford and Topsfield, were incorporated into a town by the name of Middleton.   (See Felt's Annals of Salem, i. 210.)

The will of John Gingill, of Salem, was made April 10, 1685, he being at that time, as he states, 70 years old, so that he was born about the year 1615.   This instrument was proved, March 24, 1686–7, by Aaron Way and " Thomas bayle," two of the three witnesses, the other being Mary Way.   He gave to John Wilkins his lot of upland on the south side of the pond, next Thomas Fuller's, with meadow at the end of the hill, between the pond and the " flous." To his three sisters 10 pounds, " Elizabeth baile " 40 shillings, Mary Wilkins 3 pounds, Abigail Wilkins 5 pounds.   To Bray Wilkins four sons, children to Samuel Child, Thomas Wilkins, Henry Wilkins, Benjamin Wilkins, " leadday knickels," " margaret knit " [to each family 40 shillings].   To the church of Dorchester, 5 pounds ; to m^r Lawson, then minister of Salem village, if he continue there till a church be gathered, five pounds.   Richard Hall Senr, of Dorchester, William Ireland Senr & John Wilkins, executors.

Inventory of the estate taken by Thomas Fuller and Aaron Way, Dec. 20, 1686.   Mentions 2 Cows, 2 Heifers, 5 Swine.   House and Land, £150.   Total, £174.16.9.

A John Gingden took the oath of fidelity, July 23, 1674, at a court at Pemaquid.   (REG. iii. 243.)

Besides his own signature, we have seen his name spelled at least fourteen different ways, namely—Gengel, Gengell, Gengels, Gengen, Gengill, Gingden, Gingell, Gingen, Gingin, Gingine, Gingion, Gingle, Gingley, Ginjion.

Thi[s] Deede made the Twentie fourth Day off Decemb^r in the yeare off o^r Lord one Thousand six hundred fiftie & six Betweene John Minott off Dorchester in New England yeoman off the one ptie and Jonah & James Humphrey of Dorchester aforesayde Glouers off the other ptie Witnesseth That the sayd John minott ffo^r good & valuable Consideration in hand payed haue Giuen granted Bargayned & sold Enfeoffed & Confirmed and by Thesse p^rsents Doe Giue grant Bargayne & sell & Enfeoffe and Confirme vnto the sayd Jonah & James humphrie a pcle off land in Dorchester lyinge in the first Deuision Beinge eight acres more or lesse with all the apurtenances Theroff lyinge within The feild Commonly Called ye eight acre lotts Beinge Bounded with the land off Jonah & James Humphrey on the north pte & the land of Richard Ha[wes ?] on the south pte off the same & the fence off the eight acre lotts on the east pte as alsoe the fence off the eight acre lotts on the west pte To Haue Hold occupie posses and injoy the sayd p^rmises & Euery pte Theroff with the ffence Therto belonginge with all other the appurtenances Theroff vnto the sayd Jonah & James humphrie Ther heires & assignes ffo^r Euer and the sayd John Minott his heires executo^rs & administrato^rs Couenanteth & Granteth to and with the sayd Jonah & James humphrie ther heires executo^rs Administrato^rs and assignes by thesse p^rsents That the sayd p^rmises shallbee and Continue to bee the pper right & inheritance off the sayd Jonah & James humphreye There heires executors & assignes for Euer without any the lett mollestation Trouble or expullsion off him the sayd John Minott his heires executors or assignes or any Clayminge any title clayme or interest to the same or any pte or pcle theroff ffrom or vnder him or any off Them Alsoe the sayd John Minott Doe for himselfe his heires executors & Administrators Warrent & Defend the sayd prmises & every pte theroff with the appurtenances theroff vnto the said Jonah & James humphrie ther heires & assignes for euer by thesse prsents against the lawfull Clayme off any other pson or psons whattsoeuer. And shall & will pforme & doe or Cause to bee pformed & donn any such further act or acts as hee the sayd John Minott shalbee thervnto Advised or Required by the sayd Jonah & James humphrie or Ther assignes for a more full & pfect Conveighinge or assuringe the sayd prmises vnto the sayd Jonah & James humphrie Ther heires or assignes accordinge to the lawes off This Jurisdiction   In witnes the sayd John Minott haue hearvnto put his hand & seale The Day & yeare abouesayd

JOHN MINOTT (Seal)

Signed sealed & Delivered
  in the prsence of us. viz

[signatures]

COMMUNION CUPS.

It will be noticed that John Gingill, in his will, gave 5 pounds to the church of Dorchester. A silver cup bearing the name of " John Gengen, 1685," is still in possession of the First Church in Dorchester, of which the Rev. C. R. Eliot is now pastor.

It may be interesting in this connection to give the following extracts from the old Church Records : " April 6, 1709. The Church hath Nine Pieces of Plate for ye sacramt (2 Given by sd mr Stoughton, 2 by mr Thomas Lake, one by mrs Thacher, one by mr Isaac Jones, one by mrs Patten, one by mr John Gingen, one by Anothr hand, all of Silver. In pewter the Chh hath 4 flaggons, 4 pewter Dishes, one Basin & Tankard, & one pewter Cup. Agreed that a Strong Chest be bought to Lock up ye Churches Plate in."

In a report made to the Church, May 11th, 1709, it mentions " a Certain Legacy of Three Pounds bequeathed by mrs Burgesse alias Gurnet to be laid out in a Piece of Plate for the said Church."

This person was doubtless Mrs. Jane Burge, widow of John Burge, and formerly the wife of John Gornell, a man well known in Dorchester history.

In referring to the original will of Jane Burge, at the Probate office in Boston, made March 2, 1677–8, proved May 9, 1678, we find that she gave " to the church of Dorchester three pounds in money for to purchase A siluer cup for the vse of the church;" her land was to go to John Mason and his heirs forever; in case of their death, to the poor of the town. In the old cemetery at Dorchester, facing Stoughton Street, may be seen, side by side, two prominent brown gravestones, one bearing the name of John Gornel, who died July 31, 1675, the other, "Jeane Wife to John Gornel, Aged 78 Years Dyed 4 Apryl 1678." See Reg. iv. 166. Why her gravestone bears the name of Gornel, rather than Burge, we know not. John Burge is mentioned in her will as "my husband John Burge," who is to have the use of house, land, &c. during life.

The Dorchester Church Record continues :

"May 22, 1721, Elder Preston gave account of a New Piece of plate given to ye Church for ye Lord's Supper, by m^r Eben. Withington."

"At a meeting of the first Church in Dorch. N. E. Lawfully warned by ye Deacons & Convened in the Publick Meeting House May 18, 1724. It is called the First Church to distinguish it from ye New Church at Punkapog." Article seventh—"That of ye Churches revenues the deacons adde so much to ye 40sh. bequeathed by an Aged Brother old m^r Williams deceased, as may produce a midling new silver Cup for ye Lords Table. Voted in ye Affirmative."

Earlier in this ancient volume we read—" 6 of January 1679, Henery Leadbetter Executor to ye Estate of Tho. Lake deliuered two siluer Cups or small beakers wch was giuen by Tho. Lake vnto ye Church.

" Also Mrs Thecher of Boston gaue ye Church formerly a Siluer Cup with two ears.

" Also ye Widdow Clements of Boston gaue another siluer Cup to ye Church ye 17 Nouem 1678."

It is a singular coincidence that the First Church in Dorchester voted Dec. 17, 1877, to give to the Second Church in that town, now the Rev. E. N. Packard's, then the Rev. J. H. Means, pastor, two silver cups, as a token of good fellowship. The cups presented were, one, the gift to the First Church of "M. T.," doubtless Mrs. Margaret Thacher, wife of the Rev. Thomas Thacher, first minister of the Old South Church in Boston, who died in October, 1678, the other that of Mrs. Elizabeth Clement, widow of Augustine Clement, of Dorchester and Boston.

Mrs. Thacher was the only child of Henry Webb, a wealthy merchant of Boston. She was born in Salisbury, Wilts, and baptized there, Sept. 25, 1625. She married, in 1642, Jacob Sheafe, who " seems," says Savage, " to have had the largest estate of any that had hitherto died at Boston." Widow Margaret Sheafe became subsequently, as before stated, the second wife of the Rev. Thomas Thacher. The name of Margaret Thacher, with that of twenty-five other females, members of the First Church in Boston, desirous of joining the Third or Old South Church, may be found appended to an earnest appeal in behalf of their religious rights, dated August 27, 1674. The council decided in favor of the petitioners. See a fac-simile of the names in " *An Historical Catalogue of the Old South Church, Boston,*" facing page 246.

On the 4th of January, 1882, the Dorchester First Church voted one cup each to other societies in the town, namely, to the Third Church, Rev. George M. Bodge, pastor; Harrison Square Church, Rev. Caleb Davis Bradlee; Neponset, Rev. Charles B. Elder. The original donors of these cups to the First Church were in the following order. Mrs. Justin Patten, widow of Nathaniel Patten, will made Jan. 2, 1673, proved Feb. 3, 1675, gives " To the Church of Dorchester, five pounds to be Layd out in a peece of plate for the service of the Lord's table " (Third Church). Ebenezer Mawdsley, 1744, will made March 8, 1739–40, proved Sept. 27, 1740, gives "to the Church in Dorchester Twenty pounds, to the Revd Pastor [Rev. Jonathan Bowman] five pounds, to the Church in Stoughton, Twenty pounds " (Harrison Square). Ebenezer Withington, probably the donor of 1721, before mentioned (Neponset).

JOHN BURGE.

We give a few more items relating to his family. The second wife of John Burge was the widow of Isaac Learned, who was the son of William of Charlestown, according to Savage. Mr. Learned married Mary Stearns, of Watertown. He settled first in Woburn. In 1652, he sold his house and lands to Bartholomew Pierson, of Watertown, and moved to Chelmsford, where he was a selectman. He died Nov. 27, 1657. Mary, his widow, married, says Dr. Bond, June 9, 1662, John Burge, late of Weymouth. She died Jan. 8, 1663. It would appear that Mr. Burge next married widow Grisell Gurney, he being her fourth husband, she having been previously wedded to Thomas Jewell and Humphrey Griggs, both of Braintree, and a Mr. Gurney, whose christian name and residence we have not ascertained. "Grisol wife of Jn° Burge died July 9, 1669," in Chelmsford. In June, 1676, Burge married Jane, widow of John Gornell, of Dorchester. She died, as before mentioned, April 4, 1678, and he died on the 22d of October following. (REGISTER, xvi. 79.) The will of John Burge, of Chelmsford, on file at the Suffolk Probate office, but not on record, bears date, June 1, 1671. He bequeaths twenty shillings apiece to the six children of Isaac Lerned, namely, Mary Barron [wife of Moses Barron], Hannah Farwell [wife of Joseph Farwell], William Lerned, Sarah Lerned, Isaac Lerned, Benony Lerned, on condition that he be acquitted from the four [*sic*] pounds that was claimed in their behalf by the grandmother of the children, probably widow Mary Stearns. Upon further consideration and at the grandmother's request, Mr. Burge, in a codicil, gives the six pounds to four of the children of Isaac, bearing the name of Lerned, viz. William, Sarah, Isaac and

Benony, "becaus that Mary & hanna," who were married, the latter Dec. 25, 1666, "had somthing given before." The rest of his estate John Burge gives to his "too suns," Samuel Burge and John Burge. To Samuel, the eldest, a double portion, being land at Stony brook, with all the accommodations, and his horse. To his "youngist sun John," his house and land in the town of Chelmsford, with the accommodations thereunto belonging. The residue of his stock, after the debts and legacies are paid, to be divided between sons Samuel and John; the former to be his executor. This will was proved in court, at Boston, Nov. 4, 1679, the two witnesses, Hannah Thacher and Samuel Sternes, testifying. It would seem that John, senior, had four wives, the first one being the mother of his sons Samuel and John.

John Burge was one of the proprietors of land in Chelmsford; had six acres in possession, 12. 1st month, 1666. Allen's Chelmsford, page 169. May 4, 1674, he conveyed to Thomas Hinchman, a house and upwards of 22 acres of land in Chelmsford, situated partly upon Beaver brook. His son, John Burge, who married Triall Thayer, of Braintree, left two sons, John and Samuel. Inventory of his estate rendered March 8, 1705-6. John, the third, had wife Sarah. Will proved, Oct. 26, 1761, mentions sons Josiah and David, and daughters Sarah Blanchard, Lydia Taylor, Esther Burge, Elizabeth Burge, Lucy Burge. In 1718, John Burge contributed ten shillings towards building the first school-house in Chelmsford, says Allen. Among the children of Josiah Burge, above, who settled in Westford, was a daughter Susanna, who married Reuben Kidder in 1754. They were the grandparents of the late Frederic Kidder, of Melrose, author of various historical works.

Dr. John G. Metcalf, of Mendon, Mass., in 1868, contributed an article to the REGISTER, xxiii. 43–46, entitled "Grisell Gurney," in which is noted the connection of Grisell with John Burge and others.

SOME DOUBTS CONCERNING THE SEARS PEDIGREE.

By SAMUEL PEARCE MAY, Esq., of Newton, Mass.

SOME years since, at the earnest solicitation of members of the family, I undertook the task of revising the "Sears Genealogy" and bringing it down to date. I did so in the belief, common to the family and public generally, that the English ancestry of Richard Sares, of Yarmouth, as published, was entirely reliable, and that little more was to be learned on that head.

Soon after commencing my labors, my attention was drawn to discrepancies in the pedigree, seemingly irreconcilable, and an investigation was found necessary. The result of my researches proves beyond question that not one step of the pedigree can be substantiated by records, and on the contrary some portions are impossible, and others in conflict with known authorities.

I have been desired to give the facts publicity, *in order that the pedigree may no longer be copied, and quoted as authority*, as has been done in numerous local histories and family genealogies, *and in the hope that, attention being drawn to the subject, renewed searches may discover the true origin of Richard Sares of Yarmouth.* Want of space forbids my alluding to many errors, and I will therefore only refer to those most vital to the pedigree, as printed in " Pictures of the Olden Time," etc., ed. 1857, Crosby, Nichols & Co., Boston.

PART II.

P. 10.   " JOHN SAYER of Colchester, Alderman, etc. d. 1509, leaving by Elizabeth his wife, three sons, viz. JOHN, Robert and George.

" The eldest of these, JOHN, d. in 1562, leaving two sons, viz. RICHARD and George.

" The eldest of these, RICHARD, is the subject of the first of the sketches in ' Pictures of the Olden Time.' He was born in Colchester in 1508, married Anne Bourchier, dau. of Edm^d Knyvet of Ashwellthorpe, co. Norf., second son of Sir Edwd Knyvet, ... Richard became a fugitive to Holland in 1537, and d. Amsterdam, 1540.   . . . .   His wife, the Lady Anne, clung faithfully to her husband in his adversity, and incurred the lasting displeasure of the Knyvets.

:   " It is inferred that her father became so bitterly estranged from her, as to erase her name from all his family records, that she might be forgotten for ever, for he gave to a younger daughter the name of Anne, while she was yet living, ...

" George Sayer, in consequence of Richard's flight, secured for himself possession of the patrimonial inheritance.

" This George d. 1577.   . . . .   His descendant and eventual heiress married Sir John Marsham."

NOTE. The Registers of St. Peter's Church, of which John Sayer and his descendants in Colchester were parishioners, commence in 1653, more than one hundred years after the alleged flight of Richard Sayer to Holland ; and of course contain no reference to the family previous to that date. The brass to John Sayer, Ald. represents him kneeling with his wife, four sons and a daughter, and gives the name of his wife, but not those of his children. The Heralds' Visitations of Essex do not mention the Sayer family previous to that of 1612, which gives, " George Sayer, of Col. in co. Ess., gentle, sonne & heire, & John Sayer of Col. 2^d sonne," as children of "—— Sayer of Col. in Essex, Gent."

George and John married sisters, co-heiresses of Wesden ; and their children quartered their mother's arms, which perhaps led Morant to err in his History of Colchester, where he makes George the father to John's children.

If we may believe the Heralds, George Sayer was the eldest son and rightful heir ;—that his brother John was a *second* son, is confirmed by his brass in St. Peters, which is differenced with a crescent. A special, but not exhaustive, search in London, by Mr. H. F. Waters, resulted in finding many Sayer wills, but none certainly identified with the Colchester family, except that of the above-named George Sayer, ob. 1577. He mentions his children and grandchildren, brother Robert's children, and nephew Richard Sayer. The latter, son of John Sayer, died 1610, æt. 80, leaving an heiress.

It will be observed that the parentage of George Sayer is not given in the Visitation, and John was his brother, not his father.

There was perhaps one generation between them and John Sayer, Ald.

The middle names of Bourchier, given to Anne Bourchier Knyvet, and later to John Bourchier Sayer, father and son, are clearly anachronisms, as is also that of Ann Knyvet Sayer, and tend to discredit the pedigree. Rev. Aug. Jessop, D.D., of East Dereham, Norfolk, has for years made the history and genealogy of the Knyvet family an especial study. I am informed by him that Edmund Knyvet had four married daughters, but none named Anne, much less two of that name ; that he died *insolvent*, and in his will mentions *none* of his children by name. If there was an Anne, she does not seem to have been treated differently from her sisters.

P. 12. "JOHN BOURCHIER SAYER was born, say the family papers, in 1528.

"I suspect, however, that this is a mistake, and that the date is too early, for it would make his father but little more than 19 years of age at his marriage.....

"Another date has it in 1535.....

"He m^d Eliz^h, dau. of Sir John Hawkins, ..., and d. Holland, leaving by Eliz^h, his wife, four sons, viz : JOHN BOURCHIER, Henry, William and Richard. Of the last three we have no facts, except that they were born in Plymouth, Eng^d, and that they settled in Kent. Plymouth was probably the temporary residence of their mother, while their father was with Hawkins as a navigator. Of John Bourchier I have given some account in the ' Pictures.' The date of his birth is given in the family papers as 1561.

"I have put it a little later for several reasons. He m^d Marie L. dau. of Philip Lamoral van Egmond, and acquired with her a large fortune, principally in money."

NOTE. Mr. Sears's ideas in regard to dates, so important in a genealogy, are very elastic. The biographies generally state that Sir John Hawkins was born 1520, but they are in error. He died Nov. 12, 1595, and his widow erected a monument to his memory in St. Dunstans-in-the-East, London (of which he was parishioner some thirty years), with a Latin inscription, setting forth his *forty-three years* of service by sea and land ; and a wooden mural tablet with English verses, printed in Stow's London, ed. Strype, 1720, Vol. I. Book ii. pp. 44, 5. It ends thus :

"Ending his life with his experience,
By deep decree of God's high Providence,
His years to six times ten, & three amounting,
The ninth, the seventh climacterick by counting.
Dame Katherine, his first religious wife,
Saw years, thrice ten, & two of mortal life." ....

We see, therefore, that he was but 63 years of age in 1595, and so born about 1532, and this is confirmed by reckoning his " 43 years of service " back from 1595, which brings us to 1552, when he would have been about 21, also by the fact that he was admitted freeman of Plymouth in 1555-6, a step altogether necessary at that period to a man in his position, and one that would not have been unnecessarily delayed after he attained his majority.

He removed to London in 1573, and succeeded his father-in-law, Gunson, as Treasurer of the Navy. His wife was then living, and as she died at the age of 32, she could not have been born earlier than 1541.

John Bourchier Sayer, Jr., is said to have been born in 1561. At that time John Hawkins was 29, and his wife 20 years of age. Neither could have had a daughter of marriageable age at that date.

These dates are confirmed by R. N. Worth, F.G.S., author of " History of Plymouth " and " History of Devon," and of an address on " Sir John Hawkins, Sailor, Statesman and Hero," reprinted from Trans. Devon Ass'n, 1883.

The Registers of St. Andrews Church, Plymouth, to which parish the Hawkinses belonged, commence in 1573, in which year John Hawkins removed to London, and no record of him or the Sayers is to be found there.

As to the marriage with Marie L. van Egmond. —— The late Mr. S. Alofsen, of Jersey City (a well-known and esteemed antiquarian), addressed to the late S. G. Drake, then Editor of the REGISTER, a letter which is on file. In it he states that the Egmond family never had a residence in Amsterdam, and that the family genealogy has been brought down to the latter part of the last century and printed;—that it contains the name of but one Philip v. Egmond, viz., the son of Count Egmond, and that if John Bourchier Sayer did marry one of the family, his wife must have been of an obscure and unknown branch;—a fact somewhat inconsistent with the "large fortune," even in money, which she is said to have brought her husband.

P. 13. "JOHN BOURCHIER SAYER, m^d Marie L. van Egmond, Amsterdam, 1585, and had Marie L. b. 1587, RICHARD 1590, John 1592, and Jane Knyvet 1596.

" These dates are copied from the family papers of the Searses of Chatham, and I think they are correct. Such a series depending upon each other would not be all wrong. John Bourchier Sayer purchased with his wife's fortune, property in England, adjoining the lands which he hoped soon to recover.

" Among the estates thus bought were Bourchier and Little Fordham Manors, both of which had in former times belonged to his ancestors."

NOTE. In the parlor of Richard Sears, of Chatham, there formerly hung a chart pedigree of the family, now in possession of a descendant.

This chart states that Richard Sares was born Amsterdam, 1613, twenty-three years later than the printed account, and much more likely to be the correct date.

Morant and Wright, in their histories of Essex, state that Bourchier Hall, *or* Little Fordham, derives its name from its ancient owners, the Earls of Essex. Sir Robert Bourchier died possessed of Bourchier's Hall in 1328, and it remained in the family until confiscated.—Queen Elizabeth regranted it to William, Marquis of Northampton, who sold it to George Sayer in 1574. It continued in his descendants, finally passing to the Marsham family by marriage, fell into decay, was divided and sold. A part is now used as a farmhouse. I find no record that it ever before belonged to the Sayers.

P. 14. Here Mr. Sears prints his only piece of documentary evidence, viz., a letter from J. Hawes, Yarmouth, June 20, 1798, to Daniel Sears, of Chatham, in which he signs himself,

" Your affectionate relative, and friend J. Hawes."

In it Mr. Hawes refers to sundry "curious and important documents,"
. . . . " I have heard from your brother Richard, that Knyvet Sares, or Sears, before he went to London, and some years before his death, collected and arranged these valuable papers with the intention of using them. They had long remained neglected and uncared for.

" Among them was a list of marriages, births and deaths, similar to that which I now send, and many original deeds and letters, with a long correspondence between the Sayres, the Knyvets, and others in England.

" It seemed to be closed by a letter from John Bourchier Sares, dated Leyden, 1614.

" Your brother always speaks highly of this letter. . . . . A highly interesting manuscript was compiled from these papers, and came into possession of Daniel Sears, your father.

" The original letters were taken to England, by Knyvet, and are possibly still there in the hands of some of the family. The manuscript was last seen and read so late as 1760,—but neither the one nor the other are now to be found. It may be the originals are not lost, but the copy, your brother thinks, was either burnt, or carried away when the family mansion was nearly destroyed in 1763. . . . . I send such facts as I have been able to collect, assisted by Richard and Mr Colman."

NOTE. I have been unable to identify the writer of this letter, or ascertain his relationship to the family.

The signature attracts attention by its variance from the universal custom of the period, of writing the name in full. The only marriage recorded between the Sears and Hawes families is that of Jonathan Sears and Elizabeth, daughter of Dea. Joseph Hawes, of Yarmouth, in 1721. This Jonathan was second cousin, once removed, to Daniel Sears.

I am aware that the Sears Genealogy says that Daniel Sears, of Chatham, married 1708, Sarah Hawes, daughter of J. Hawes, of Yarmouth (another mysterious J.), and this error, for such it is, has been perpetuated on the Sears monuments in Chatham, Yarmouth and Colchester. On Yarmouth town records the name is clearly written *Howes*, and the will of Samuel Howes, of Yarmouth, recorded Barnstable Prob. Rec. iv. 90, mentions "daus. Sarah Sears, & Hope Sears," who married the brothers Daniel and Richard Sears, and "Mercy Sears," who married their cousin, Josiah Sears. "J. Hawes" the letter writer may stand for Dea. Joseph Hawes, the schoolmaster, who flourished in 1798, and long after.

There is no record, or tradition, in Chatham, of the family mansion having been "nearly destroyed in 1763." Benjamin Bangs, of Harwich, who chronicled in his diary more trivial events happening in Chatham at that time, makes no mention of the occurrence, and when the old building was taken down in 1863, the original timbers were in place, with the bark still on, and there was no trace of its ever passing through the fiery ordeal.

A tradition that Deborah Sears broke through the floor of "the long chamber," while dancing on her wedding night in 1742, was confirmed by a patch in the floor boards. And, we may ask, why should J. Hawes relate to Daniel Sears particulars with which he should have been conversant from childhood, and when his brother Richard, living in the same town, could have given the information at first hands?

We admire the vivid recollection, after the lapse of thirty-eight years, of Richard Sears, of the letters, etc., read last, when he was scarce eleven years of age.

P. 16. "JOHN BOURCHIER SAYER, d. 1629. By Marie L. Egmond, his wife, he left two sons, and two daughters, viz.: RICHARD, John, Marie and Jane. The three latter went to England and settled in Kent. ....

" RICHARD SAYER or Sears. .... His birth is variously given, but 1590, we think, is the true date. He m^d Dorothy Thacher, at Plymouth, in 1632. The likeness of him was taken from a painting in Holland, in possession of the Egmont family, and is supposed to be correct. .... He d. 1676, and his wife in 1680. By her he had the following children, viz.: Knyvet, Paul, Silas and Deborah. .... Knyvet Sears was b. 1635, m^d Eliz^h Dymoke, ... went to England on a second voyage, and d. 1686, at the residence of his relative, Catherine (subsequently Baroness Berners), dau. of Sir John Knyvet, and wife of John Harris, Esq.

"The evidences he carried with him were never recovered. He left two children, Daniel and Richard."

NOTE. I have already alluded to the doubtful date assigned for Richard Sares's birth. The statement that he married Dorothy Thacher at Plymouth in 1632, needs confirmation. His name first appears there in the tax list of 25 March, 1633. There is no known record of the marriage, and no Dorothy is known to the Thacher genealogists. It is claimed that she was sister to Antony Thacher, and Richard Sares in his will calls him " bro. Thacher," and Antony's son John, in an affidavit, calls him " Uncle Sares."

Thomas Thacher, of Beckington, co. Somerset, in his will proved 1611, mentions " bro. Antony," and Clement Thacher of Marston Bigot, in his will dated 1629, and proved 1639, names " bro. Antony " and others. Rev. Peter Thacher of Sarum made his will in 1640, and mentions " bro. Antony " and " sister Ann, wife of Chris. Batts, and other relatives, among them his " wife's sister Dorothy " (of whom I would much like to learn further; she is supposed to have been an Allwood). It would seem, if they had a sister Dorothy, one or the other would have remembered her. But it is more probable that Richard Sares (so he wrote his name) married Dorothy Batts, a sister of the above-named Christopher, who came over with her brother and his family, in " Bevis " from Southampton to Lynn, in 1638, she then being aged 20.

The precise date of their arrival is not known, but it appears by an endorsement on Lord Treas. Warrant, that the vessel sailed before May 2, and they probably arrived in June, or even earlier.

Richard Sares was then in Marblehead, as we learn from Salem tax list, 1 Jan. 1637-8, and on 14 Oct. 1638, he was granted three acres of land " where he had formerly planted." The connection of Dorothy Batts and Antony Thacher fully justified the terms of relationship quoted,—see a parallel case cited by the late Col. J. L. Chester, in REGISTER, xxi. 365. The same cause perhaps influenced Richard Sares to remove to Yarmouth in 1639, with the party led by Antony Thacher. In a note to first edition of the " Pictures," the portrait of Richard " The Pilgrim," is said to be from the Egmont gallery in *Amsterdam*, which more definitely locates it.

There formerly hung in the west parlor of Squire Richard Sears of Chatham, a painting which Mrs. Sears was wont to call " Sir Richard," supposed by some persons to have been the original. This is an error. It was given after the Squire's death to his widow, by his nephew, and is a copy. It doubtless originally represented one of the family, judging from the resemblance to some of them, but who, and when, and where painted, is a mystery.

It is evident Rev. E. H. Sears did not know of Richard Sares's will recorded in Plymouth, or he would not have written that he had an eldest son Knyvet, born 1635, died 1686. In his will dated 10. 3 mo. 1667, Richard Sares names "my elder son Paule Sares," and in the codicil dated 3 Feb. 1676, he again mentions " my eldest son Paule Sares." Paul made oath to the inventory, 15 Nov. 1676, before John Freeman, Assistant. who calls him " Paule Sares eldest son of Richard Sares deceased." John Freeman lived near by, and must have known the whole family.

There is no allusion to Knyvet in the will, although he is said to have been alive twenty years after the will, and ten years after the codicil were written ; nor is there any reference to estates in England. Neither the name of Knyvet Sares, or Elizabeth Dymoke his wife, is to be found in colony, town, court or church records, nor is there any gravestone to either ;—no record of administration upon the estate of either, or appointment of guardian to their infant children.

Richard Sares never had a son Knyvet. The name was unknown on the Cape until the publication of the " Pictures," and has never been adopted as a family name, except by the Chatham branch in one instance, and then for a tenth child.

Although " the papers taken to England by Knyvet were never recovered," and the copies in Chatham were " lost, or destroyed," a tablet was erected in 1858 to his memory in Colchester, which states that it was " Inscribed by Catherine Harris in 1687 " !

P. 19. "PAUL SEARS, b. 1637. He inherited most of his father's property. . . . .

" He adopted the children of his bro. Knyvet after the death of their father in England, and they were brought up in his family.

" His will is on Old Colony records, in which his brother's children are named as his own sons. . . . . The names of his sons were, Samuel, Paul and John."

NOTE. Paul Sears died Feb. 20, 1707. 8, in his 70th year, according to his gr. stone in Yarmouth Cemetery, and was therefore born not earlier than 1638. His will is recorded in Barnstable, not in Old Colony records. The names of his children on Yarmouth records have been obliterated, but the dates of birth of seven remain. From other sources we have been enabled to learn the names of five sons and four daughters, leaving one daughter unnamed. His last two children were his sons, Richard, born 1680, and Daniel, born 1682. In the Sears Genealogy these names are reversed, Richard being said to be the youngest, and born 1684. Their grave-stones in Chatham prove the contrary. In his will Paul Sears gives his real estate to his sons Samuel, Paul and John, charged with a payment to their " brothers," Richard and Daniel, towards their purchase of land in Monamoy. We may feel sure that they were the sons, and not adopted sons merely of Paul.

To sum up briefly : the " English pedigree " cannot be proved ;—it is doubtful if Richard Sares was ever in Holland, or that his wife was a Thacher ;—he never had a son Knyvet,—and Richard and Daniel Sears, of Chatham, were *younger* sons of Paul, and not " *Head of the American Family*."

The claim to estates in England is purely mythical. The "family papers," if still in existence, are not now accessible to inquirers.

For the benefit of future investigators, I will note the genesis of the Pedigree, etc., so far as seems desirable.

About the year 1845, the late Mr. H. G. Somerby was employed to collect data regarding the Sears family in England, and a pamphlet was issued, entitled "Notices of the Sears Family, from Sir Bernard Burke's Works, and Somerby's Collections in England, etc." The manuscript of his collection is in the library of the Mass. Hist. Society, Boston. It consists of a mass of extracts from local histories, &c., showing no connection with the American family, and of "Extracts from parish registers, and family papers in possession of Hon. David Sears, Boston."

It is evident Mr. Somerby found nothing to connect the English and American families, or he would have given the data in full, with authorities, as he has done in other genealogies. In conversation with a well-known Boston gentleman, he gave him clearly to understand that he did not assume responsibility for many of the statements in the pedigree. In 1852, Sir Bernard Burke published the first volume of "Visitations of Seats and Arms," which contains at p. 52 of Part II. an amplified account of the family, claiming that by right of primogeniture the Chatham branch is the "*Head of the American* Sears Family." This was followed in 1863, in third series of "Vicissitudes of Families," by a sketch entitled "A Pilgrim Father." Burke now repudiates the articles, and they are left out of later editions.

In 1884, he wrote me that he received the material from Mr. Somerby, but had since made investigation and found "that the details were not only not proven, but also incapable of proof, if not altogether wrong, and opposed to fact."

In 1857, Rev. E. H. Sears published "Pictures of the Olden Time," to which was added in a later edition a Genealogy of the family. In his preface he states that he derived his facts mainly from Burke's "Visitations of Seats and Arms," and from "family papers." But few copies were distributed.

In the letter of J. Hawes, before quoted, he says he has been "assisted in his collections by Mr Colman and Richard." This is confirmed by a manuscript in handwriting of Hon. David Sears, of Boston, dated Feb. 10, 1845, in possession of Gen. C. W. Sears, of Oxford, Miss., entitled "Memoranda of the Sears, from Minutes collected by J. Hawes and William Colman to 1800,—and continued by Richard Sears of Chatham to 1840," "Copied from the original in possession of Mrs Richard Sears of Chatham." It is full of important errors, and varies from the records and from the published genealogy.

We cannot fix the share of either of the trio in the production of these "minutes," but one fact will show how little "Squire Richard" could have known of them.   In this document his mother, Fear Freeman, is said to have been the daughter of John Freeman, of Sandwich, and the printed genealogy makes a similar statement. She was in fact the daughter of Benjamin Freeman of Harwich, by his wife Temperance Dimmick, as shown by his will recorded in Barnstable.

Richard Sears was 9 years old when his gr.-father died, and 24 when his gr.-mother died.   They lived in adjoining towns, and it is absurd to suppose that he did not know his grandparents' names and residence, or that such a gross error could have escaped his notice.

Mr. Colman was his brother-in-law, and resided in Boston; his part in the matter is not evident.   Of J. Hawes I have already written.   If we accept his letter as evidence, then the story is apparently traced back to Daniel Sears who died Chatham, 1761, a. 49.

It appears by records of Probate Court in Barnstable, Feb. 10, 1758, that "upon inquisition of the Selectmen of Chatham," Daniel Sears was adjudged *non compos*, and his wife Fear was appointed his guardian.

Swift's "History of Old Yarmouth," published 1885, states that "the marriage of Richard Sears and Dorothy Thacher, and the birth of Knyvet Sears, are recorded in a bible left by Richard Sears of Chatham, kept in the family for several generations."   I have been unable to hear of any person who has seen this bible.   An inquiry addressed three years since to a descendant of Squire Richard, was the cause of letters to all her "Uncles, Aunts and Cousins," who one and all replied, "they had never seen or before heard of such a bible."   They would be grateful for any hint of its whereabouts.

In conclusion :—it is possible there may have been some ancient alliances of the Sayer, Knyvet and Hawkins families, and the family genealogist may have erred in placing "the flesh on the wrong bones."

About 1500, one Edmund Knyvet died at Stanway, the next parish to Colchester, leaving his second sister, Lady Thomasine Clopton, his heir; and about the same time a family of Hawkinses were settled at Braintree, some twenty miles distant, of which one John Hawkins, a wealthy clothier, bought estates in Colchester, and settled at Alresford Hall, hard by, *circa* 1600.

There was more than one family of Hawkins in Plymouth, and another John was made a freeman there the same year as the famous Admiral.   Somerby does not notice these families, and they were apparently *unknown to him.*

" *Magna est veritas, et prevalebit.*"

NEW ENGLAND GLEANINGS.

[Continued from page 66.]

XIV.

THE following summary of the genealogical matter in Lechford's Note Book, which identifies the English homes of early settlers in this country, is taken from the *Nation* (New York, March 4, 1886); and with a few additional items found in the Note-Book and inserted by the writer, is offered as appropriate for publication among the "New England Gleanings" of the REGISTER. The dates of the entries are omitted, but they are all between the years 1638 and 1641.

GEORGE K. CLARKE.

1. Augustin Clement of Dorchester, N. E., leased land in Wockingham, co. Berks, to John Tinker of Boston. Mentions sisters Margaret Mathew and Anne Clement, the latter of Shenfield, also brother John deceased.

2. John Hood of Cambridge, N. E., leases land in Halsted, co. Essex, to William Dineley of Boston. Mentions father-in-law, Thomas Beard. Mother Anne.

3. Samson Shotton of Mt. Wollaston, N. E., son of Thomas S. of Cropston, co. Leicester, mentions brother Anthony S.

4. The will of John Newgate of Boston, N. E., mentions land in Horningerth, co. Suffolk.

5. William Wilson of Boston, N. E., sells land in Dunnington, co. Lincoln. Brother Thomas Wilson, father William.

6. Katherine Coytmore of Charlestown, N. E., states that her husband was Thomas Grey of Harwich, co. Essex, and her daughters were Parnell, wife of Increase Nowell of Charlestown; Katherine, wife of Thomas Graves of Wapping; and Susanna, widow of —— Eaglesfield. She was daughter of Robert Myles of Sutton, co. Suffolk.

7. Rev. John Cotton of Boston, N. E., makes Robert Brown of Poynton or Horbling, co. Lincoln, his attorney.

8. Ralph Sprague of Charlestown, N. E., some time of Fordington, co. Dorset, and wife Joan, daughter of Richard Warren of said F., make William Derby of Dorchester, co. Dorset, their attorney. Sister Alice Eames.

9. John Graves of Roxbury, N. E., makes Robert Wood of Harlow and Nicholas Campe of Nasing, co. Essex, attorneys to receive rents from his sister, the widow Lydia Ford of Nasing.

10. Elizabeth and Mary Woolcott, daughters of John W. of Glaston, co. Somerset, and late of Watertown, in N. E., appoint their uncles, Richard Vayle and Christopher Atkins of said G., attorneys. [Note in margin, write to Henry Woolcott of Windsor in N. E., and Edward W. of Axbridge, co. Somerset.]

11. James Cade of Northam, co. Devon, now of Boston in N. E., had father Christopher C., brother John, and sister Thomasine, wife of John Roe of Abbotsham, co. Devon.

12. Henry Grey of Boston had a brother who was a citizen of London.

13. Matthew Allyn of Connecticut sold land to Thomas Allyn of Barnstable, co. Devon.

14. Osmond Douch of Bridport, co. Dorset, had wife Grace and son Robert. He was afterwards of Gloucester in N. E.

15. Thomas Purches of Pagiscott in N. E. makes Daniel Adams, roper and citizen of Bristol, his attorney.

16. Edmund Brown and wife Anna, late widow of John Loverun of Watertown in N. E., appoint attorneys to collect her dower in lands in Ardley, co. Essex, or Aldham, co. Suffolk, in possession of William or George Loverun.

17. William Cole, late of Sutton in Chewmagna, co. Somerset, and Elizabeth his wife, a daughter of Francis Doughty of the city of Bristol, make brother John Cole of Farrington, co. Somerset, their attorney.

18. Thomas Foster of Boston, cannonier at the Castle, makes Richard Foster of Ipswich, his brother and others, attorneys to receive his legacy under will of father Thomas Foster, minister. His wife was Abigail, daughter of Matthew Wimes of Ipswich, co. Suffolk.

19. John Iles of Dorchester in N. E. owed £28 to Adam Hurden of Barnstable, co. Devon.

20. Joseph Hills of Charlestown states that he came in the *Susan and Ellen,* and that in that vessel were goods of Joseph Loomis, late of Brayntree, co. Essex.

21. Thomas Rucke of Charlestown makes Thomas Rucke of London and Thomas Plum of Malden, co. Essex, his attorneys to collect debts.

22. Edmund Hubbard of Hingham in N. E. married Sarah, widow of Rev. John Lyford, who had children Rev. Obadiah and Mordecai L. The last-named made Hubbard his guardian, who appointed William Bladen, Alderman of Dublin, and John Fisher of the same place, attorneys to sell a lease at Leballeglish, co. Ardmagh. Elsewhere Lyford is called the minister at Levelegkish near Laughgaid, co. Ardmagh. Mentions land in co. Tyrone.

22¹. Gabriel Fish of Exeter in N. E., appoints an attorney to receive money due him from James Carrington of Thorsthorp, co. Lincolne.

23. John Cogan of Boston in N. E. makes Isaac Northcot of Hunniton, co. Devon, his attorney to receive any legacy under the will of his mother, Elianor Cogan of Tiverton, co. Devon, widow, deceased.

24. John Cogan appoints his friend John Stoning, citizen and haberdasher of London, to sue one John Harrison, late of Boston in N. E., for £26 he owes said Cogan.

25. John Faber of London, cooper, sells to Christopher Stanley of Boston in N. E. his house there.

26. John Cogan of Boston appoints Nicholas Carwithye, citizen and grocer of Exeter, his attorney to collect of the executors of Ignatius Jordan, of said Exeter, £66 due him by bond, and also all legacies from I. J. to C. or his wife or children.

27. Anne Coleman of Watertown in N. E., spinster, aged 16, and Samuel Hosier of the same, her guardian, appoint Jeffrey Coleman of Colchester, co. Essex, and James Wade of the same, attorneys to receive a legacy for her under the will of her father, William Coleman of said Colchester.

28. Francis Godsome of Lynn in N. E. is to sell his house to John Fuller of Boston, if Edward Fuller of Olney, co. Bucks, pays £60 unto said F. G.

29. John Crabtree of Boston, joyner, takes as apprentice Solomon, son of John Greene of Hadley, co. Suffolk. Mary Greene, sister of Solomon, was to be taken by William Hudson, the younger, fisherman. Elizabeth Leger, mother of Solomon Greene, was to pay Crabtree annually £5.10, and the boy was to get £20 at the end of his apprenticeship.

30. Edward Wood assigns his apprentice Thomas, son of Henry Cooper of Little Bowden, co. Northampton, to Leonard Buttolpe, of Boston in N. E.

31. Thomas Mayhew of Watertown in N. E. and Jane his wife, widow of Thomas Payne of London, as guardian of Thomas Payne, aged seven years, appoint Richard Payne of Abingdon, co. Berks, and others, attorneys to lease lands in Whittlebury, co. Northampton, descending to said child.

32. David Offley of Boston and wife Elizabeth appoint Edward and Henry Woolcott, Richard Payne, and Christopher Atkins attorneys to sell their lands in Glaston. (See No. 10, *ante*.)

32¹. Elizabeth Glover of Cambridge in N. E. receives money from executors of late husband Josse Glover of London.

33. Katherine Earwing, widow, of Dorchester, makes Anthony E. of London her attorney.

34. Josiah Stanborough of Lynn in N. E. and wife Frances, one of seven daughters of Henry Gransden of Tunbridge, co. Kent, appoint Richard Young of London their attorney to obtain their part of his lands.

35. Michael Williamson and wife Anne make Anthony Stapley of Patcham, co. Sussex, their attorney to receive of Elizabeth Geere, widow, of Lewes, co. Sussex, executrix of Dennis Geere, late of Saugus, a legacy of £50 given to said Anne by the name of Anne Panckhurst. (See will of Dennis Geere, REG.)

36. Thomas Nichols of Hingham had a brother who was the executor of Walter Nichols of Coggshall, co. Essex.

37. Joseph Cooke of Cambridge in N. E., son of Thomas Cooke of Great Yeldham, co. Essex, makes his brother Thomas C. of Wormingfold in Essex his attorney.

38. William Sergeant of Charlestown in N. E. was formerly of Northampton, hatter, and his wife Sarah was the widow of William Minshall of Whitchurch, co. Salop.

39. Lt. Robert Feke of Watertown in N. E., gent., and William Palmer of Yarmouth and Judith his wife, and Tobias Feke, aged 17, son and daughter of James Feke, late of London, goldsmith, deceased, make Tobias Dixon of London their attorney.

40. Agreement between Edward Heale of Bristol and William Pester of Salem in N. E.

41. Thomas Scudamore of Cambridge in N. E. was from Westerley, co. Gloucester.

42. Edward Hall of Duxbury in N. E. was son of Francis Hall of Henborough, co. Gloucester.

43. Samuel Freeman of Watertown in N. E. was from Mawlyn, co. Kent.

44. Thomas Matson of Braintree in N. E. and wife Anne draw for £20 in favor of George Hussey of London, on his sister-in-law Mrs. Chambers of London, widow of Thomas C., citizen and clothworker of London, for part of their legacy.

45. John Coltman of Wethersfield in N. E. was son of Thomas C. of Newton Harcoate in Weston, co. Leicester.

46. Richard Betscombe of Hingham in N. E., late of Bridport, co. Dorset, in behalf of daughters Mary and Martha, appoints his brothers Andrew, Robert, and Christopher to receive two legacies given said daughters by Philip Strong of the Devizes, co. Wilts.

47. Isaac Sterne of Watertown in N. E., late of Stoke Nayland, co. Suffolk, and wife Mary, daughter of John Barker of the same, appoint Thomas Gilson of Sudbury, co. Suff., to collect £5 of one Munnings of Gaynes Colne, co. Essex, due on a bond given by M. before his marriage with Margaret Barker, mother of said Mary.

48. John Bent of Sudbury in N. E. was from Wayhill, co. Southampton, and his brother-in-law was William Baker of New Sarum, co. Wilts.

49. William Talmage of Boston in N. E. had brothers Robert and Thomas, and sister Jane, wife of Richard Walker; they were children of Thomas T., who was the brother of John Talmage of Newton Stacey, co. Southampton.

50. William Longley of Lynn in N. E., son of John L. of Frisby, co. Lincoln, makes Thomas Meeke of Waynflete St. Mary, co. Linc., his attorney.

51. John Mayo of Towne Marroling, co. Kent, deceased, had by wife Rebecca, son Thomas (who had died leaving a son John and a widow Elizbeth remarried to Robert Gamlyn of Roxbury in N. E.), daughters Mary of Dorchester, N. E., and Frances, wife of Steven England of Sandwich, co. Kent.

52. John and Daniel Prior of Scituate in N. E. were sons of John P. late of Watford, co. Hertford.

53. Abraham Harding of Boston in N. E. was son of John H., late of Boram, co. Essex, whose widow was Agnes Greene of Tarling, co. Essex.

54. John Floyd of London and wife Anne had put their son Thomas in charge of Arthur Howland of Duxbury in N. E.

55. Thomas Odingsell of Salem draws a bill on his father, John O., of Epperston, co. Notts., or brother John O. at Mr. Mansfield's on Ludgate Hill.

56. William Pester of Salem draws a bill on his uncle William P. in Thames St., London.

57. Ralph Sprague of Charlestown N. E., and wife Joan, appoint John Holland of Tinnckleton, co. Dorset, to receive of John and Elizabeth Cox of Bowlington a legacy from Richard Warren to said Joan and her six children.

58. William Rix of Boston, N. E., was one of the sons of Robert R. of Kenninghall, co. Norfolk. His sister was Elizabeth Waters of K., and he mentions also Henry Rix of Pagrave, co. Suffolk.

59. Thomas Grubb of Boston, N. E., was son-in-law of Jeffrey Salter of King's Lynn, co. Norfolk.

60. Benjamin and Nathaniel Bosworth draw bills on Joseph B. of Coventry, co. Warwick.

61. John Clerk of Newbury in N. E., late citizen and chirurgeon of London, was one of the executors of widow Anne Ward, of Stratford, co. Suff.

62. Owen Williams, son of Mark W. of St. John's parish, co. Cardiff, apprentices himself to William Withington of Portsmouth in N. E.

63. Edward Bridges was second son of E. B., late of Raynham, co. Somerset, Esquire.

64. Nathaniel Patten was late of Crewkerne, co. Somerset.

65. Edward Howell of Lynn, in N. E., gent, was late of Marsh Gibbon, co. Bucks. He had lands in Wotton Underwood, co. Bucks, and £100 in the hands of Richard Francis, of Marsh Gibbon.

66. Henry Russell of Weymouth in N. E., deceased, left widow Jane and daughter Elizabeth. He was the son of Thomas R. of Chalfont, St. Giles, co. Bucks.

67. Thomas Nichols of Hingham, N. E., makes John Cockerell of Cockshall his attorney to receive, of Geo. N., a legacy given him by his father Walter N.

68. William James of Boston in N. E. was son of Albon James, citizen and mercer of London. He had an uncle George Strange, gent.

69. John Bibble had a wife Sibyl at Shadwell in Stepney parish.

70. Elizabeth Freestone of Boston in N. E., spinster, was late of Alford, co. Linc. She was daughter of Richard F. of Horncastle, co. Linc. Mary F. of Thimbleby, co. Linc., was widow of her uncle Robert F., who was executor of her grandfather Robert F. Her father and sister Mary were dead. Her grandmother was Mary Cuthbert, whose executor was Nathaniel C. of Warmington, co. Northampton.

71. Samuel Haskell seems to be the grandson of George Cooke, inkeeper at the White Horse in Algate, who died 13 years since.

72. Abraham Shaw of Dedham in N. E., deceased, was from Halifax, co. York, and left his eldest son Joseph S. and son-in-law Nicholas Biram, his executors.

73. Anne Stratton of Salem, N. E., was widow of John S. of Shotley, co. Suff., gent, whose brother Joseph S. was of Harwich, co. Essex, and now of James City in Virginia. She had a son William S. of Ardley, co. Essex, deceased, son John S. of Dedham, co. Essex, and daughters Elizabeth, wife of John Thorndike of Salem, and Dorothy. Her own mother was Mary Dearhaugh of Barringham, co. Suff.

74. John Pollard was late of Belcham, co. Essex.

75. Robert Hempenstall of Boston in N. E. was son of Thomas H. of Southold, co. Suff.

76. George Crispe of Plymouth in N. E. had a brother Robert C. of Southwark, co. Surrey, an uncle George C. of Blackwall in Stibenheath, co. Mid., and land in the parish of Word, near Sandwich, co. Kent.

77. George Denison of Roxbury in N. E. had wife Bridget, who was daughter of John Thompson late of Preston, co. Northamp., gent, and Mrs. Alice T. now of Roxbury. They claimed their legacy from Spencer Clarke, parson of Scaldwell parish, co. Northampton.

78. Thomas Allen of Barnstable in N. E., had a brother, Richard A. of Branton, co. Essex, and father-in-law, John Marke of the same place.

79. Samuel Nash of Weymouth in N. E. was from Burrough Green, co. Cambridge.

80. John Bartoll of Marblehead, N. E., was son of John B. of Crewkerne, co. Somerset.

81. Robert Wing of Boston, N. E.. had a cousin Wing of Lomford, dwelling in the Lady's place, by Dedham.

We have thus gleaned the major part of the items, omitting such as relate to the Winthrops, Hutchinsons, Saltonstalls, and other well-known colonists. The book will be for years a source of information to genealogists, because in many cases these references will lead to a knowledge of other colonists. Our only regret is, that the record is so brief, and we wish that Lechford had stayed for a decade at least.

EXTRACTS FROM THE PARISH REGISTER OF ARDELEY, CO. HERTFORD, ENGLAND.

Communicated by GEORGE W. MARSHALL, LL.D., F.S.A., of London, Eng.

THE following extracts from the first Register of Ardeley (originally spelt Yardley) were made with the object of taking out every entry relating to the family of Sir Henry Chauncy, the Hertfordshire historian, who resided in that parish. At the same time I noted every other entry relating to persons whose rank appeared to me above that of the common people, of the families of the incumbents of the parish, and of some persons non-resident whose record might not be sought for in an out-of-the-way country parish. The Chauncy entries will I know be of interest to many readers of THE REGISTER, and amongst the others, names will be found which are not unknown or uncared for by its readers. This is I think the first time that the pages of THE REGISTER will contain extracts of a general character, from an English Parish Register. Such gleanings can hardly fail to be of use to some workers in the genealogical field in New England, and if one of them should perchance supply a missing link in the pedigree of any descendant of the persons recorded, my trouble will not have been in vain, and my labor will be amply rewarded.

"Yardley Church booke of Christenings Weddings and burialls Collected & Written out by me Robert Tattersall* who was instituted Vicar ther the xxiij^ti daie of Julye 1576, made and Written into Parchment accordinge to the provinciall Constitutiones houlden at London the fyue and twenty daie of October 1597."

Contains. Baptisms   1546—1701.
           Marriages   1546—1701.
           Burials.   1546—1701.

BAPTISMS.

1546. Elizabeth Gailer dau. of George Gailer, 25 July.
1547. Jone Clynton dau. to Thomas, 11 June.
1548. Margaret Shotbolte dau. of James, 29 April.
1551. John Shotboulte, 7 June.
1552. Symon Shotboulte, 25 Sept.
1553. James Shotbolts daughter, 2 July.
1562. Elizabeth Cheeke dau. of John Cheeke vicar of Yardley, 3 Feb.
1563. (1562 in margin) Thomas Shotboulte filius Thomæ Armig'ri, 17 May.
1564–5. Marye Shotboulte dau. of Thomas Shotboulte, Esquier, 24 March.
1570. Helen Downes al's Stafford filia Gulielmi, 26 Dec^r.
1571. John Shotbolte sonn of John, 15 Oct.
1572. Thomas Shotbolt sonn of James, 29 April.
1573. Margaret Gurnay dau. of Will'm, gent., 5 April.
1574. Frauncis Gurnay dau. of Will'm gent., 9 May.
"   John Shotbolte sonn of James, 7 Nov^r.
1575–6. Thomas Gurnay son of Will'm gent, 4 March.
1576. Mary Tattersall dau. of Robert Tattersall,† vicar of Yardley, born 17 & bapt 24 June.

* It appears from a note below that he was chaplain to the Earl of Essex, K. G.

† John,   son of same, born 25 and bapt. 28 June, 1579.
  Phillip, "   "   " 15 and "   17 Sept. 1581.
  Robert,   "   "   " 23 Sept.   1584.
  Leonard, "   "   " 22 and bapt. 24 Oct. 1585.
  Thomas,   "   "   " 18 and bapt. 20 June, 1590.

1577. Jane Chauncye dau. of George, gent. 19 Sept^r. (Written in margin in a
 later hand " 1st Wife Jone Cornwell.")
1578. George Gurnay sonn of Will'm gent, xi Sept^r.
 "   Will'm Shotbolte sonn of James 15 Feb.
1579. Marye Chauncye dau. of George, gent. 12 April.
1580. Francis Chauncy dau. of George, gent. 24 July.
 "   Marye Shotbolte, dau. of James Shotbolte of Shefford, gent, 23 Oct^r.
 "   Elizabeth Shotbolte, dau. of Thomas of Mooregrene, 3 Nov^r.
 "   Thomas Downes al's Stafford, 15 Jan'y.
1581-2. Elizabeth Shotbolt dau. of Tho. of Woodend, 7 Jan'y.
 "   Barbara Chauncy dau. of George, gent, 18 March.
 "   Marye Shotbolte, dau. of James, 25 March. (born 20 March.)
1582-3. Tunney Shotbolte sonn of John, gent, 17 March. born 11 March.
 ("Heres Job'nis " in margin.)
1583-4. Helen Shotbolte dau: of Tho: of Woodend, 17 Feb.
1584. Marian Shotbolte dau. of Thomas of Moregrene, 20 April.
 "   ₁George Chauncye sonne of George, gent, 22 Dec^r. [in margin—by a 2^d wife
 Humberstone, widow.]
 "   Edward Gurnaye sonn of Will'm, gent, 21 March.
1585. Phillip Shotbolte sonn of John, gent, 16 May.
 "   John Humerston sonn of John, 11 July.
 "   Elizabeth Chauncye dau. of George, 30 Jan'y.
 "   William Shotbolte sonne of Tho. of Woodend, 6 March.
1586. Marmaduke Gurnay sonn of Will'm, gent. 24 July.
1587. Edward Chauncy sonn of George, 3 Sept^r.
1587. Mathias Shotbolte dau. of James of Munnes, 10 Dec^r.
1588. Raffe Shotbolte sonn of John, gent., borne the 20 March 1587 and baptized
 the 29 March, 1588.
 "   Judith Chauncye dan. of George, 3 Nov^r.
 "   Thomas Shotbolte sonn of Thomas of Woodend, 15 Nov^r.
1589. Thomas Shotbolte, son of John gent, (born 18) 22 June.
 "   Mercye Sterne dau. of Will'm, gent. 8 Sept^r.
 "   Helen & Elizabeth Humm'ston dau's of John 11 Jan'y.
 "   Luce Chauncye dau. of George, 15 Feby.
1590. Marye Gurnay, dau. of Will'm, gent., 10 May.
1591. William Sterne sonn of William, gent., 17 Oct^r. (born 10th)
1592. Luce Shotbolt dau. of Tho. of Woodend, 26 March (Easter daye and born
 21 same month.)
 "   Gryssell Bawtrye dau. of Leonard Bawtrye of Leake in the Countye of
 Lyncolne Esquire borne upon Wednesday in the fornoone, about seaven
 of the Clocke beinge 12 Aprill and baptized 16 Ap'ill. ("Heres" written in margin.)
 "   William Humm'ston sonn of John, 17 Sept.
 "   Charles Chauncye sonn of George, gent. 5 Nov^r.
1593. Leonard Shotbolte sonn of James, born 25 April, bapt 29 April.
 "   Ann Chauncye dau. of George gent, 25 Nov^r.
1594. Jane Shotbolte dau. of James, 12 Jan'y.
1595-6. Henry Shotbolte sonn of Thomas, 15 Feb'y.
1596. Marye Sterne dau. of Will'm, gent., 31 May.
1596-7. Frauncis Shotbolte dau. of John Shotbolte gent, 6 Feb'y. (born 1st)
 "   Marye Shotbolte dau. of James, 25 March.
1598. Esdras Blande sonn of John Bland, clerke, 21 May.
1598-9. Frauncis Sterne dau. of Willia' Sterne, gent., born 25 Feb'y. bapt 4 March.
1599. Joh'nnes Parsons, filius Nicholai cleri', 9 Sept.
1599-1600. Jana Shotbolte filia Jacobi, 17 Feb'y.
1600. Johnnes Chauncy filius Henrici generosi natus 17 Nov. bapt 25.
1601. Alexander Walker filius Thomæ Ciuis piscatoris London, 22 June.
 "   Robertus Sterne filius Gulielmi, 19 July.
 "   Barbara Lauson filia Tho: Lauson generosi, 22 Nov.
1602-3. Elizabeth Shotbolte filia Jacobi iunior', 12 Feb.
1605. Tho: Chauncie filius Henrici gener', 26 May.
 "   Franciscus Shotbolte filius Jacobi iunioris, 1 Nov^r.
1607. Anna   do   filia   do   do 10 May.
1607-8. Rodulphus Audley filius Eduardi, 17 Jan'y.

1607–8. Gulielmus Shotbolte filius Joh'nis de Munnes, 22 March.
1608. Gulielmus Tailor filius Thome Tailor generosus, born 14 June & bapt 26th.
1609. Thoma Shotbolte filius Phillippi Shotbolte gen', 14 Decr. (born 4th.)
1610. Thoma Tailor filius Thomæ Tailor gener', 29 Apl. (born 23rd)
" Maria Audeley filia Eduerdi, 5 Augt.
" Maria Shotbolte filia Phillipi gen', (born 27 Oct,) 1 Novr.
1611. Maria Tailor filia Thomæ gen', nata fuit 7° die Aprilis, bapt 14 Apl.
" Joh'nes Shotbolte filius Jacobi, 4 Aug't.
" Joh'nes Shotbolte filius Phi' gener', 8 Dec'r. (born 27 Novr.)
1612. Katherina Boteler filia Philipi Boteler Armigeri, 29 Decr (born 19th)
1613. Maria Shotbolt filia Philippi Shotbolt generosi, 18 April. (born 15th)
" Elizabetha Tattersall filia Thomæ Tattersall, 23 Jan'y.
1614. Francisca Boteler filia Philippi Boteler Gencr', 1 Septr.
" Anna Shotbolt filia Philippi Shotbolt, Gener', 1 Septr.
1615. Elizabeth Tailor dau. of Thomas Tailor, gent., 18 Septr.
" John Boteler son of Phillip Boteler esqr 8 Octr.
" • Thomas Tattersall son of Thomas Tattersall, 5 Novr.
" John Shotbolt son of Phillip Shotbolt, gen., 12 Decr.
1616–17. Will'm Shotbolt son of Phillip Shotbolt, gent., 23 March.
1618. An Tattersall dau. of Thomas T., 25 Octr.
" Henry Tailor son of Thomas Tailor, gent., 27 Decr.
1619. Constance Gaddesden dau. of John Gaddesden gent, 23 May.
" Lettice Boteler dau. of Phillip Boteler, Gent., 25 May.
1619–20. Elizabeth Sikes dau. of Robt. Sikes Vicar of Yardley, 12 March.
1620. Ellenor Shotbolt dau. of Philip Shotbolt gent, 27 August.
1621. Robert Tattersall son of Thomas T. 21 May (Henry son of same bapt 21 Jan'y 1623–4).
1622. John Sikes son of Robt. Sikes vicar of Yardley, 19 May (born 8th)
1624. Mary do dau. do do do do 30 May.
" Phillip Shotbolt son of Phillip Shotbolt, Gent., 26 Septr.
1627. John Tattersall son of Thomas Tattersall, 27 May. (Wm son of same bapt. 29 Augt 1630.)
1627–8. Anne Sikes dau. of Robart Sikes vicar of Yardley, 10 Feb'y.
1630. Henry do son do do do do 3 Oct.
1632. Henry Chauncy son of Henry Chauncy, gent., 24 April.
1633. John Chauncy son of do do do 30 Decr. Bur. 1704.
1635. Anne do dau'r do do do 31 Decr.
1637. Elizabeth do do do do gent, and Anne 26 Octr.
1640. Mary Chauncy dau. Henry Chauncy gent., and Anne 25 March. (1st entry in this year.)
" John Butler son of John Butler Citizen and Grocer of London & of Alice his wife, 13 May.
1641. Edward son of same, 5 Septr.
1643. George Chauncy son of Henry Chauncy Gent & An his wife, 7 Septr.
1644. Jone Watson dau. of Thomas Watson, Clarke, & Elizabeth his wife, 15 Decr.
1648. Peter Chauncy son of Henry Chauncy Esqr. 3 Octr.
1651. John Sykes son of John Sykes Vicar of Yardley & Frances his wife, 10 July. Buried 1726.
1652–3. Henry son of same .... March.
1654. Elizabeth dau. of same. born 27 March, bapt 3 April.
1655. Frances dau. of same. born 28 Septr, bapt 23 Octr.*
1656. Anne Marshall dau. of Jonathan Marshall, 25 March.
1659. John Mitchell son of Mr Richard Mitchell, 1 Aug't.
1661. Mary Milton dau. of John Milton and Hanna his wife, 26 May.
1663. Joyce Chauncy dau. of Mr John Chauncy gent., and Joyce his wife, 10 Aug't.

* 1657. Anne   dau. of same, born 7 March, bapt 20th (1656–7)
  1659. James   son of same, born 19 Apl., bapt 24th.
  1660. James   son of same, 3 May.
  1661. Arthur   son of same, 26 Septr.
  1663. Edward   son of same, 5 Augt.
  1664. Jane   dau. of same, 31 Decr.
  1666. Nathaniel   son of same, 18 April.
  1669. William   son of same, 14 May.

1666. Henry Chauncy son of Henry Chauncy Esq and Jane his wife, 26 April. Bur. 26 Nov. 1703.
1667. John Chauncy son of Henry Chauncy the younger of Yardley Bury Esqr and Jane his wife, 14 May. Buried 9 July 1704.
1668. Hellen Willett dau. of Thomas Willett, gent., and Elizabeth his wife, 21 June.
1675. John Maynard son of George and Joane his wife, 5 Decr.
1680-1. Mary Beamont dau. of Simion Beamont of Shingy in the County of Cambridge and Magdalen his wife, 16 Jan'y.
1683. Arthur ye son of Sr Henrey Chauncey Knight & the Lady Elizabeth Chauncey his Wife was born April 29, & Bapt. May 6. (Over is written in a later hand A.D. 1752 Obijt Arthur ye (etc?) vafer idem idemque nefastus apud Hoxon juxta Eye in Com Suffolc : ἀνὴρ ἔι τις ἄλλος γοῦν.
1684. Thomas ye son of Tho. Rycorn of Congerton in Cheshire and Margaret his W. 8 May.
1688. Margaret ye Daughter of James Forrester of Cottered Esq and Martha his wife, 28 Oct. Added in later hand—James dyed 1696. Martha his Widow dyed Sept. 1745.
1689. Humphrey ye son of Mr Humphrey Forster & Mary his wife (the fourth Daughter of Sir Henry Chauncey) was born Dec 16 and baptized Decr 28.
1701. John Bray of Hitchin (aged about 30 years) 27 April.

MARRIAGES.

1546. William Olyuer and Jane Abdall wid' were Mariede the 6 November. [First Entry.]
1546. Richard Hoye of Auberye and Ellen Halfhide of Woodend 16 Januarye.
" John Halfehide and Ellen Myles both of Yardley, 23 Jany.
1547. William Fann of Cople in the Countye of Bedd and Helen Bardalfe of Yardley, 25 October.
1552. Phillip Bardalfe and Jane Gayler, 19 June.
1552. John Cornewell gentleman and Jone Varney, 19 June.
1557. George Bruster gent and Jone his wife, 30 Novr.
1559. Edmunde Halfehide and Dorothye his wiffe, 8 Aprill.
" John Mylles and Alice Shotboulte, 26 Novr.
1560. Edmunde Halfehide and Elizabeth Austyn, 16 Septr.
1562. John Clysbee and Elizabeth Shotboulte, 7 May.
1570. John Shotboulte and Jone Mylles, 29 Oct.
1571. Thomas Halfehide and Helen Austyne, 15 July.
1572. William Norton gent and Margaret Hamond widdowe, 6 Oct.
1573. Thomas Blowes and Alice Shotbolte, 8 Novr.
" Edward Crofte and Jone Shotbolte, 22 June.
1577. William Halfhide and Margaret Lawrence, 20 Jany (1577-8).
1578. Jacobus Shepherd et Jona Halfhid, 27 Decr.
1579. Wylliam Shotbolte and Margaret Halfehide, 6 Decr.
" James Shotbolte gentleman and Agnis Pabda, 28 Decr.
1580. Thomas Smyth of Rushden and Helen Halfehid dau. of Will'm Halfehide, 17 Aprill.
" Edmund Bardalfe and Helen Halfhide, 10 July.
1585. Leonard Bawtrey of Leake in the Countye of Lincolne, gent, and Mary Shotbolte daughter of Thomas Shotbolte Esquier, 27 Aprill.
1588. William Sterne gent and Mary Halfhide, 17 Decr.
1589. Thomas Waite and Lettice Halfhid, 3 Augt.
1590. Thomas Cole and Jone Lane, 14 Sept.
" John Rowley and Marye Bardolfe, 4 Octr.
1593. William Halfehid and Susana Walbye, 30 Septr.
1598. George Bardalfe and Marye Kettle, 20 June.
" John Halfehide and Agnis Halfehide, 15 Oct.
1600. Symon Thruckston and Prudence Bardolph, 2 Oct.
1604. Henricus Edwards & Helena Halfhid, 5 June.
1606. Michael Bardalfe & Maria Halfehide, 20 Novr.
1607. Thomas Tailor generosus & Maria Shotbolte filia Joh'nis Shotbolte Armigeri, 6 July.
1608-9. Thoma Halfehide & Miriana Walbie, 2 Feb.
" Henricus Walbie & Gratia Halfhid, 2 Feb.

1609-10. Gulielmus Skegg et Maria Graue, 5 Feb. Lic.
1611. Richardus Bardalfe & francisca Halfehide, 24 Oct.
1612. Joh'nes Haruie & Helena Halfehide, 7 May.
1621. Edward Northe & Alice Cole, 19 Aug^t.
"   John Browne & Mary Shotbolt, 18 Oct^r.
1622. James Bardolfe son of Edmund Bardolfe & Elizabeth Edwards dau. of Henry
       Edwards, 1 May.
1623. John Peacocke & Elizabeth Shotbolt, 16 Oct^r.
1624. Mr Robart Greene of Bobbin in the County of Kent, Esqr & M^ris Frances
       Shotbolt the daughter of Mr John Shotbolt of Yardley Esqr 26 Sept^r.
1625. Mr Angell Gray of Kingston in the County of Dorset esq^r & M^ris Katherine
       Stowell of Yardley in the County of Hertford gent., 28 March.
1626. Leonard Cole of Benington & Alice Hill of Aston widow, 7 Augt. Lic.
"   Theophilus Lynche Cittizen & Girdler of London & M^ris Rickson of London,
       spinster, 26 Dec^r.
1630. Robart Sewell of Stevenage & Joane Shotbolt, 18 Oct^r.
1632. Richard Wright & Elizabeth Shotbolt, 1 Nov^r.
1635. Henry Budder weaver & Elizabeth Bardolf spinster, 13 Aug^t.
"   John Halfhid & Rebecca Bardolfe, 8 Oct.
1636. Henry Wallis & Mary Bardolfe, 13 Oct.
1641. Will'm Peirson Cittize' & Goldsmith of London & Frances Sikes dau'r of
       Robt. Sikes vicar of Yardly, 2 Dec^r.
1643. Will'm Clarke of Purton widower & Anne Tattersal widow, 1 Dec^r.
1645. John Austine* wierdrawer & Citizen of London & Mary Sykes dau'r of Rob't
       Sykes late vicar of Yardley, 18 Sept.
1647. Richard Hall and Alice Lincolne, 28 Sept^r.
1651. Wm Rayment of Cotterid single man and Matthew (sic) Jordan of Yardley,
       30 Sept^r.
1652. Henry Sykes of Hypolets in ye County of Hertford Clerke and Mrs Mary
       Raynsford of Tewin in ye said County widdow, 5 Sept^r.
1653. Timothie Bristow of Richden Clerke and Abigaill Stratton of Yardley wid-
       dow, 2 May.
1659. Mr Robert Harrington of Aspeden in ye Countye of Hertfort.... and M^rs
       Sarah Wellingham of the same Spinster were marr.... 23 June.
"   Mr Henry Hall of Popler in the county of Middlesex gentl' and Mrs Anne
       Chauncy of Yardley in ye county of Hertf. spinster, 27 Oct^r.
1665. John Peacocke of Much Munden and Anne Shotbolt of Weston, 1 May.
1669. Litton Faireclough of S^t. Giles Cripplegate, London, singleman and Francis
       Gorsuch of Weston in this County, 7 April.
1677. James Cater widdower and Elizabeth Rainsford widdow both of Little Mun-
       den, 29 Nov^r.
1678. William Linsey of Hengham in the Mount in Com. Essex widdower & Su-
       san Walby of Cottered, widdow, 8 June.
1684. Edward Palmer of Sandon Singleman & Elizabeth Hall of this Parish single-
       woman, 9 Oct^r.
1686. Mr Francis Bragg of East Greenwich in Kent and Madam Jane Chauncey
       of Yardley Bury, 29 Sept^r.
1688. John Kent of Little Munden singleman & Mary Godfrey of this Parish Maid-
       en, 20 Sept^r.
1691. John Daniel Cittizen & Grocer of London and Mary Sell of this Parish
       Maiden, 13 April.
1692. Mr Edward Lane of Walkern, Widower, & M^s Mary Lane of ye same Maiden,
       24 May.
1695. John Clarke of this Parish B & Jane Hilliard of ye same M, 14 Oct^r.
1697. George Shelford of Hormead Mag: Wid: & Mary Marshal wid., 26 Jan'y.

Burials.

1546. Thomas Austyne son of John Austyne of Luffenhall,† 25 Aug^t.
1547. Roger Halfehide of Garners ende, 12 June.
1548. George Halfehide, 9 Oct.
"   Joseph Halfeside, 20 Jan^y.

* Many Austins in regr. before this date.
† First entry in Register and only one in this year.

1552. Edward Halfehide, 18 Sept.
1558. James Halfehide son of Thomas, 2 Aug^t.
" Phillip Bardalfe, 18 Sept^r.
1559. Mother Shotboulte, 20 March.
1561. John Cornewell, gent., 12 April.
" Thomas Halfchide, 5 Aug^t.
" John Bardalfe, 7 Oct.
" Mother Annis Halfehide, 20 Oct.
" John Halfehide, 6 Dec^r.
1563. Edmund Halfehide, 7 May.
1568. Jone Brewster wiffe of George Brewster, gent., 5 June.
" Thomas Shotbolte, 6 July.
1570. Edward Halfehid sonn of Richard, 28 Nov^r.
1575. Jane Shotbolte wife of Thomas of Moorgrene, 22 Dec^r.
1577. Margaret Halfehide wiffe of Will'm, 2 July.
1578. Robt. Shotbolte sonn of John of Standon, 19 Feby.
1579. Helen Bardalfe, 25 June.
" John Halfehide son of Thomas, 2 Feb^y.
1581. Richard Halfhid of Woodend, 30 Dec^r.
1582. Jane Chauncye wife of George } buried 25 Julye.
     Charles Chauncy sonn of George }
1583. James Shotbolte senio^r, 3 April.
1584. John Halfhid the Cooke, 9 Oct.
" Robt Tattersall sonn of Robt., Clark vicar of Yardley, 23 Oct.
1585. Alice Shotbolte of Luffenhall, widd., 21 May.
1587. Marmaduke Gurnay sonn of Will'm gent, 3 May.
1589. Thomas Shotbolte sonn of John, gent, 18 July.
" Susana Bowles dau'r of Thomas, gent, late of Enfeilde, 2 Sept^r.
1590. Thomas Cole, sonn of Thomas, 25 Dec^r. (Eliz. d of same, 7 Nov. 1596.)
1592. Will'm Shotbolte sonn of Tho. of Woodend, 12 Jan^y.
1597. Thomas Cole, 21 Sept^r.
" Robt Clarke sonn of George, 22 Jan^y.
1598. Daniell Bennion sonn of Thomas Cytizen of London, 10 June.
" Roger Walpoole sonn of Cæsar Walpoole p'son of Wormeley, 25 Jan^y.
1599. Thomas Shotbolte sonne of James, 15 April.
" Thomas Shotbolt Armiger cum 70 annos In Deum pie: in proximū iuste in seipsū sobriè vixerat: tandem anima' expirauit 9° die mensis Junij: sepultusq'. 10° die eiusdē mensis: euisq' exequiæ solemnizabantur 2° die Julij Anno vt supra. Viuit post funera virtus.
" Jane Shotbolte Widd, 17 Feb.
1605–6. Elizabeth Hunter filia Tho: Hunter Ciuis London, 12 March.
1606. Anna Chauncie vxor Henrici generosi, 28 Sept^r.
1607. Gulielmus Shotbolte filius Jacobi de Munnes, 17 Dec^r.
1607–8. Georgius Cook filias Joh'nis Ciuis London, 19 Feb.
1609. Eliz. Wilkes filia Randulphi Wilkes, Ciuis London, 21 Dec^r.
1612. Maria Shotboulte filia Philipi gener', 19 April.
" Joh'nes Garret al's Bacon, 23 Oct^r.
1613. Robertus Tattersall quondam Vicarius istius Ecclesiæ quum 37 Annos, 4 Menses, et Vnam Hebdomadam verbum dei sincerè fideliterq' huic populo prædicasset, tandem animam expirauit suam 19° die Mensis Nouembris Anno Domini 1613 ac sepultus 21° eiusdem Mensis. Anno Ætatis suæ 74°.
1613–14. ....naell Tattersall 23 March.
1614. Elizab. Shotboult daught^r of Thom., 10 July.
" Katherine Boteler dau'r of Phillip Boteler esquier, 31 Aug^t.
1616–17. John Shotbolt sonn of Phillip Shotbolt, gent., 28 Jan^y.
1620. Mrs Alice Boteler wife of Phillip Boteler, gent., 27 April.
1621. Ould James Shotbolt of Luffenhall, 19 May.
" Mr John Shotbolt sonn of John Shotbolt esq^r, 13 Sept^r.
1622. Mrs Mary Tailor wife of Mr Thomas Tailor esq^r., 29 June.
1623. Ould Thomas Shotbolt, 3 June.
1625. Henry Tattersel son of Thomas Tattersall, 11 Nov^r.
1627. Ould Mrs Mary Shotbolt widow, April ....
" Margaret Shotbolt widow, April ....
" Mr Thomas Shotbolt, Gent, April 22.

1628. Anne Tattersell dau'r of Thomas T., 9 July.
1631. An Sikes dau'r of Robt. Sikes, Vicar of Yardley, 29 March.
"   Mr Henry Chauncy, Gent. in the chauncell, 19 April.
"   Mary Shotbolt wife of James Shotbolt, 21 Jan^y.
1632. Phillip Shotbolt a child, son of Phillip Shotbolt, Gent, 10 May.
"   James Shotbolt of Luffenhall, 29 Nov^r.
1638. Thomas Tattersall of Churchend, 22 Jany.
1639. Will'm Shotbolt son of John S. 3 July.
1640. Elizabeth Tattersall dau'r of widow T. 13 July.
1644-5. Mr Robert Sykes late Vicar of Yardly. 3 Jan^y.
1652. John Parker of Yardley Bury, 23 Aug^t.
1655-6. Mrs Mary Chauncy wife to Mr Henry Chauncy late of Yardley bury was buried in the Chauncell, 5 Feb.
1656-7. John Shotbolt of Luffenhall, 3 Jan'y.
1657-8. Mrs Judith Chauncy of Yardley Bury, 13 Jan^y.
1658. Grace Marshall wife of Jonathan Marshall, 9 Sept^r.
"   Jonathan Marshall of Luffenhall, 31 Dec^r.   [April.
1663. Mrs Elizabeth Sykes wid. the relict of Robert Sykes late Vicar of Yardley, 11
"   Mrs Elizabeth Chauncy daughter of Henry Chauncy of Yardley Bury, Esq., 11 Aug^t.   [Dec^r.
"   Henry Chauncy an infant son and heire of Henry Chauncy jun^r, Esqr. 7
1664-5. John Chauncy son of John Chauncy gent, second son of Henry Chauncy of Yardley Bury Esq, 3 March.
1665. Mr Benjamin Harmer gent, 1 May.
1667. Willia Willett, gent, 29 Sept.
1669. Mr John Nevill, gent, 25 Oct.
"   Jane Sykes dau'r of John Sykes vicar of Yardley ....
"   George Chauncy citizen & Drugster of London third son of Henry Chauncy of Yardley Bury, Esq was buried in the Chauncell at Yardley, 21 Feb^y.
1672-3. Mrs Jane Chauncy wife of Henry Chauncy jun' of Yardley Bury Esqr, 2 Jan^y.
1673-4. Mrs Mary Markham wife of Robert Markham, Esq, 19 Feby.
1681. Henry Chauncey Esq, The Father of Sir Henry Chauncey of Yardley-Bury K^t., 6 May.
1682. Jane ye dau'r of Michæl Seymour, 14 Aug^t.
1686. Mr Christopher Yeadon of Yardley-Bury, 29 Dec^r.
1687. M^s Grace Beaumont, widow, 19 Dec^r.
1691. Frances the wife of John Exton of London, 1 Oct^r.
"   M^s Frances Peerson, 6 Oct^r.
1696. M^s Catharine Tower, 25 Aug^t.

The following names are of frequent occurrence in this Register, but are apparently those of common people.

Green, Olyver, Thorogood (Thurgood), Austyn, Crane, Hall, Hummerston (? for Humberston), Archer, Watson, Wright, Lane, Christie, Bond, Chessam, Myles, Cooke, Chapman, Shepherd, Kympton, Lodge, King, Skegg, Cave, Overall, Pallat, Cantrell, Parker, Semer *vel* Seymour, Forster, North.

Register of Papworth Everard 1565-1692.   Add MS. 31,854, British Museum.

1600. Susanna filia Henrici Chauncey baptizata vicesimo nono die Augusti.

THE WRIGHTS OF NORTHAMPTON, MASS.

By WILLIAM K. WRIGHT, Esq., of Northampton, Mass.

I HAVE gathered from old records the names of many of the descendants of Dea. Samuel Wright, who was one of the first settlers of Northampton. A few of these names in the line of Judah Wright, the youngest son of Dea. Samuel, I send to you for publication in the REGISTER.

In the REGISTER, vol. iv. pp. 355–358, is an article written by Mr. Joseph W. Wright containing a partial genealogy of Dea. Samuel Wright.

In the article referred to it is said that Judah Wright went to Deerfield. It was Judah,[3] son of Judah,[2] and grandson of Dea. Samuel,[1] who settled in Deerfield, and was ancestor of most of the Deerfield Wrights. The will of Dea. Samuel Wright contains the following:

" Forasmuch as my two sons have jointly carried on the work about a new house, my will is yᵗ James doe still help to finish yᵉ house till it be made comfortable to live in. Likewise my will is yᵗ in consideration my son James hath yᵉ house and home lot, yᵗ he pay to his brother Judah fifteen pounds—the manner of paying this fifteen pounds to my son Judah to be five pounds a year in work till all be paid."

The homestead of Judah[2] Wright, situated on Bridge Street in Northampton, continued in his line five successive generations.

The homestead of James, first granted to his father about 1657, situated a few rods northeasterly from meeting-house hill, continued in the line of James until 1799.

The homestead of Samuel Wright, Jr., who came to Northampton with his father, has continued in that line from 1657 till the present time.

1. Dea. SAMUEL[1] WRIGHT, by wife Margaret, had children:

   i. SAMUEL,[2] m. Elizabeth Burt, Nov. 24, 1653. For their descendants, see REG. iv. 355-6.
   ii. JAMES, m. Abigail Jess, Jan. 18, 1664.
   iii. MARY.
   iv. MARGARET, m. Thomas Bancroft, Dec. 8, 1653.
   v. HESTER, m. Samuel Marshfield, Feb. 18, 1651-2.
   vi. LYDIA, d. Feb. 13, 1699; m. first, Lawrence Bliss, Oct. 25, 1654; m. second, John Norton, Oct. 3, 1678; m. third, John Lamb, 1688; m. fourth, George Colton, 1692.
2. vii. JUDAH, b. May 10, 1642.
   viii. HELPED, b. 7 mo. (i. e. September) 15, 1644, probably died young.

2. JUDAH[2] WRIGHT (*Samuel¹*) was born at Springfield May 10, 1642; died at Northampton, 1725. Was twice married—first to Mercy Burt, Jan. 8, 1666; married second, to widow Sarah Burke, July 11, 1706, being her third marriage. She was daughter of Thomas and Mary Woodford, was born Sept. 2, 1649, married first, Nehemiah Allen, Sept. 4, 1664, when but two days more than fifteen years of age. She married second, Richard Burke, 1687; married third as above. Judah Wright and wife Mercy were admitted to the church 1672, and in 1675 personally took the covenant and admitted to full communion.

The date of the death of the first wife not known. The second wife Sarah died March 31, 1712. Children of Judah and Mercy:

   i. SAMUEL,[3] b. Nov. 6, 1667; d. 1668.
   ii. MERCY, b. March 4, 1668-9; m. Dec. 15, 1692, Samuel Allen* of Deerfield; was his second wife. Samuel Allen m. first, Mary Baldwin, July 14, 1687 (daughter of Joseph Baldwin, Jr., of Hadley). Samuel Allen had two children by his first wife, viz.: Samuel, b. May 29, 1688, and Mary, b. Feb. 6, 1690—died. The children of Samuel Allen and Mercy: 1. *Nehemiah*,[4] b. Sept. 21, 1693—died; 2. *Mercy*,[4] b. June 29, 1695; 3. *Nehemiah*,[4] b. Sept. 19, 1697; 4. *Mary*,[4] b. Oct. 22, 1699, m. Benjamin Smalley of Lebanon; 5. *Daniel*,[4] b. Nov. 1, 1701; 6. *Hester*,[4] b. Feb. 26, 1704, d. Dec. 18, 1707; 7. *Lydia*,[4] b. May 15, 1706, m. Selah Murray of Guilford; 8. *Joseph*,[4] b. Oct. 14, 1708, in Deerfield. This Joseph was father of Col. Ethan[5] Allen, the celebrated warrior. 9. *Ebenezer*,[4] b. April 26, 1711.

---

* Samuel Allen was a son of Nehemiah and grandson of Samuel Allen of Windsor, Ct. See Allen Genealogy, REG. xxx. 444.

 iii. HESTER, b. Aug. 18, 1671 ; d. 1674.
 iv. JUDAH, b. Nov. 4, 1673 ; d. young.
3. v. JUDAH, b. May, 1677 ; m. Mercy Hoyt, of Deerfield.
4. vi. EBENEZER, b. 1679 ; m. Mary Judd.
 vii. THOMAS, b. April 8, 1682 ; was a weaver ; d. unmar. 1744.
 viii. PATIENCE, b. April 18, 1684 ; m. John Stebbins, 1710.
 ix. NATHANIEL, b. May 5, 1688 ; d. at Deerfield, 1711.

3. JUDAH[3] WRIGHT (*Judah,*[2] *Samuel*[1]) married Mercy Hoyt of Deerfield, April 4, 1707. He died Aug. 3, 1747. Children:

 i. JUDAH,[4] b. Jan. 28, 1708.
 ii. MARY, b. 1709 ; m. Noah Chapin, May 23, 1733.
 iii. DAVID, b. June 12, 1711 ; m. Elizabeth Hitchcock, 1745. Elizabeth Wright appointed guardian of Submit, heir and only daughter of David Wright of Deerfield, 1747.
 iv. SARAH, b. Oct. 23, 1713 ; m. Samuel Childs, 1739.
5. v. NOAH, b. March 27, 1716 ; m. Jan. 20, 1746, Esther Scott.
6. vi. ASAHEL, b. Oct. 8, 1721 ; m. Lucy Wait.

4. EBENEZER[3] WRIGHT (*Judah,*[2] *Samuel*[1]) married Mary Judd, July, 1709. He died Feb. 22, 1767. She died April 15, 1748, aged 65. Children:

 i. MARY,[4] b. May 8, 1710 ; m. Waitstill Strong of Southampton, Feb. 23, 1752 ; second wife. She d. 1770.
 ii. MERCY, b. June 9, 1713 ; m. Joseph Clark, May 2, 1734. She d. Feb. 13, 1735, in her 22d year. Said to be the first person that died in south precinct (Southampton). She left one daughter, b. Feb. 12, 1735, who married Noah Bridgman.
 iii. EUNICE, b. Aug. 17, 1715 ; m. Selah Clark, Sept. 22, 1737. She died Nov. 15, 1806. Their children : 1. *Eunice,*[5] b. Sept. 13, 1738 ; m. Aaron Pomeroy, 1764 ; 2. *Anne,*[5] b. June 17, 1740 ; 3. *Mary,*[5] b. September 28, 1742 ; 4. *Hannah* ——,[5] ; 5. *Selah,*[5] b. Sept. 30, 1747 ; 6. *Rhoda,*[5] b. Nov. 9, 1749 ; 7. *Amasa,*[5] bapt. April 6, 1755 ; 8. *Isabel,*[5] m. Joseph Pomeroy, 1778.
 iv. EBENEZER, b. July 23, 1717 ; d. Sept. 22, 1802.
 v. NATHANIEL, b. Oct. 18, 1720 ; d. Jan. 22, 1796.
 vi. RACHEL, b. Oct. 6, 1723 ; m. Gideon Clark. She died Sept. 7, 1748 ; left two children, viz., Rachel, b. Sept. 12, 1746, and Gideon, b. 1748.
7. vii. BILDAD, b. about 1726 ; m. first, Elizabeth Oakes, Dec. 19, 1753. She died Jan. 30, 1771. He m. second, Sarah, widow of Elijah Moody, 1778. He d. July 8, 1799, aged 72. She d. Dec. 29, 1821.

5. NOAH[4] WRIGHT (*Judah,*[3] *Judah,*[2] *Samuel*[1]) married Jan. 20, 1746, Esther Scott of Sunderland. He died Nov. 7, 1797. She died Oct. 24, 1806, aged 91. They had two children, viz.:

 i. NOAH,[5] who d. young.
 ii. EUNICE, who m. Sept. 22, 1768, Samuel Childs, of Deerfield.

6. ASAHEL[4] WRIGHT (*Judah,*[3] *Judah,*[2] *Samuel*[1]) married Lucy Wait. He died 1816.

 In his will, recorded at Greenfield, 1817, are mentioned—daughters LUCY,[5] wife of Thomas Sanderson ; MARY, wife of Solomon Field ; LOIS, wife of Isaac Baker ; MERCY, widow of the late Joshua Hawks ; and sons JUDAH and ASAHEL.

7. BILDAD[4] WRIGHT (*Ebenezer,*[3] *Judah,*[2] *Samuel*[1]) married first, Elizabeth Oakes, Dec. 19, 1753. Children:

8. i. ENOS,[5] b. Jan. 15, 1755 ; m. Elizabeth Wright, 1776.
 ii. ELIZABETH, m. Thomas Bridgman, April, 28, 1791. She d. May 25, 1806. Their children : 1. *George,*[6] b. Feb. 12, 1792 ; 2. *Laura,*[6] b. June 19, 1793 ; m. first, Ralph Stebbins, Oct. 12, 1813 ; m. second, Amanda

Wood, 1827 ; 3. *Thomas,*[6] b. July 14, 1795 ; 4. *Betsey,*[6] b. March 11, 1797, d. Feb. 20, 1798 ; 5. *a dau.*,[6] died in 3 1-2 hours, July 8, 1798 ; 6. *William,*[6] b. October, 1799, d. Sept. 28, 1802.

   iii.   JERUSHA, m. William Clark, Jr., July 19, 1787 ; she d. Feb. 17, 1816, aged 51. Their children : 1. *Lucius,*[6] bap. Feb. 1, 1789 ; 2. *Sarah,*[6] b. Oct. 24, 1790, d. Sept. 16, 1823 ; 3. *Jerusha,*[6] b. Feb. 3, 1793, m. —— Ogden ; 4. *William,*[6] b. April 5, 1795 ; 5. *Rufus,*[6] b. May 27, 1797, d. April 5, 1811; 6. *Miranda,*[6] b. Jan. 5, 1800, d. Nov. 6, 1825 ; 7. *Betsey,*[6] b. June 30, 1802, d. Sept. 21, 1803 ; 8. *Elizabeth,*[6] b. July 7, 1805, d. Oct. 16, 1806.

   iv.   BILDAD, bap. Feb. 10, 1760 ; was in the revolutionary army.

   v.   PEREZ, bap. April 4, 1762, d. 1816, at Cincinnati, Ohio.

Bildad Wright's wife Elizabeth died Jan. 30, 1771. He married, second, Sarah, widow of Elijah Moody, 1778. Children :

   vi.   ELIHU, bap. Aug. 15, 1780 ; d. 1781.

   vii.   SARAH, bap. July 24, 1782 ; m. John King.

8. ENOS[5] WRIGHT (*Bildad,*[4] *Ebenezer,*[3] *Judah,*[2] *Samuel*[1]) married Elizabeth Wright, daughter of Timothy, July 18, 1776. He died May 30, 1834. She died Dec. 15, 1854, aged 98 years and six months. He was deacon of the first church from 1791 to his death. Children :

   i.   MARY,[6] b. April 27, 1777 ; m. Thaddeus Russell, June 23, 1796 ; she d. Nov. 30, 1836. Their children : 1. *Charles,*[7] b. May 26, 1797 ; settled in Colerain, has a family ; 2. *James,*[7] b. July 15, 1799, d. May 21, 1836 ; 3. *Mary,*[7] b. July 23, 1802, m. Jacob Parsons ; 4. *Sylvester,*[7] b. April 27, 1805, d. May 25. 1805 ; 5. *Sylvester*[7] 2d, b. May 5, 1807 ; 6. *Elizabeth,*[7] b. Aug. 28, 1810, d. Aug. 29, 1810 ; 7. *Elizabeth*[7] 2d, b. March 1, 1812 ; 8. *Edward*[7] and *Sarah,*[7] b. March 24, 1817, both d. same year.

9.   ii.   EBENEZER, b. Feb. 22, 1779 ; d. June 2, 1814 ; m. Betsey Pomeroy, Nov. 30, 1807 ; she d. June 15, 1874, æt. 90.

   iii.   FLIZABETH, b. July 22, 1781 ; d. Oct. 1, 1787.

10.   iv.   ENOS, b. Jan. 18, 1784 ; m. Aurora Searle.

   v.   ELEANOR, b. March 1, 1786 ; d. 1787.

   vi.   ELIZABETH 2d, b. June 25, 1788 ; m. Melzer Warner, of Williamsburg, Nov. 17, 1816, second wife. Their children : 1. *Eunice,*[7] b. Sept. 15, 1817 ; 2. *Francis S.*,[7] b. April 21, 1819 ; 3. *Edwin W.*,[7] b. Jan. 31, 1821.

   vii.   ELEANOR 2d, b. July, 1790 ; m. Nov. 24, 1813, Calvin Wilder. He d. Oct. 28, 1838, æt. 48. She d. Aug. 15, 1838. No children.

11.   viii.   LEVI, b. Jan. 7, 1793 ; m. first, Phimela Smith ; m. second, Sophia Wilder, Feb. 9, 1832.

   ix.   SYLVESTER, b. Aug. 17, 1795 ; d. 1803.

   x.   MIRIAM, b. July 12, 1799 ; d. June 30, 1801.

   xi.   MIRIAM 2d, b. June 28, 1802 ; m. April 11, 1832, Moses Bryant.

9. EBENEZER[6] WRIGHT (*Enos,*[5] *Bildad,*[4] *Ebenezer,*[3] *Judah,*[2] *Samuel*[1]) was a graduate of Williams College, 1805 ; studied for the ministry ; employed by the Hampshire Missionary Society in St. Lawrence County, N. Y., from 1809–14 ; died at Russell, N. Y. Married Betsey Pomeroy, Nov. 30, 1807. She was daughter of Gaius Pomeroy, a descendant of Eltwed Pomeroy. Children :

   i.   ELIZABETH POMEROY,[7] b. Sept. 24, 1808 ; d. at Yarmouth, N. S., Feb. 19, 1823.

12.   ii.   WILLIAM KING, b. Dec. 26. 1811 ; m. April 26, 1836, Phebe Phelps.

   iii.   SARAH CLARK, b. Aug. 4, 1814.

☞ Widow Betsey Wright married second, Rev. Abel Cutler, Nov. 26, 1815. Their children :

   i.   EMILY PAMELIA, b. Nov. 17, 1817 ; d. at Yarmouth, N. S., 1822.

   ii.   MARY NIXON, b. Nov. 24, 1820 ; m. May 18, 1842, William N. Bryant.

   iii.   EMILY, b. July 24, 1824 ; m. May 23, 1850, Ransom L. Crowell, now a merchant of Bernardston, Mass.

10. Enos[6] Wright (*Enos,[5] Bildad,[4] Ebenezer,[3] Judah,[2] Samuel[1]*) married
    Aug. 7, 1809, Aurora Searle. She was born Jan. 31, 1788. Ch.:
    i. Samuel,[7] b. April 10, 1812; m. Sarah Pulver.
    ii. Enos, b. July 25, 1814; d. July 26, 1815.
    iii. A daughter, b. Sept. 14, 1816; d.
    iv. Julia, b. March 18, 1820.
    v. Nancy, b. Nov. 20, 1823.
    13. vi. Enos, b. June 8, 1826; m. Oct. 23, 1849, Anna Maria Phelps.
    vii. Eleanor, b. Aug. 28, 1829.

11. Levi[6] Wright (*Enos,[5] Bildad,[4] Ebenezer,[3] Judah,[2] Samuel[1]*) married
    first, Phimela Smith. She died Jan. 16, 1831, aged 37. He mar-
    ried second, Feb. 9, 1832, Sophia Wilder. She died April 27,
    1862. Children of Levi and Phimela:
    i. Sylvester,[7] b. 1813; m. first, Harriet Clark; second, widow Amanda
       Smith (formerly Moody).
    ii. Elizabeth, bap. 1815; m. Frank Cook, of Hadley, Mass.
    iii. Levi, bap. 1817; m. Harriet Graves. She d. Nov. 1846; he d. Aug.
       19, 1846.
    iv. Ebenezer, bap. 1819; d. unmarried, July 26, 1860.
    v. Phimela, bap. 1822.
    vi. Mary, bap. 1825.
    vii. Amelia, bap. 1827; m. —— Charters.

12. William King[7] Wright (*Ebenezer,[6] Enos,[5] Bildad,[4] Ebenezer, Ju-
    dah,[2] Samuel[1]*) married first, April 26, 1836, Phebe Phelps. She
    died Oct. 25, 1878. He married second, March 24, 1881, widow
    Keziah M. Williams (formerly Phelps). Children:
    i. William Henry,[8] b. March 4, 1841; d. Jan. 26, 1851.
    ii. Elizabeth Pomeroy, b. Jan. 18, 1847; m. Edward S. Niles, April 15,
       1880. Their children: 1. *Eliot Wright,[9]* b. March 19, 1881; 2. *Helen
       Adora,[9]* b. June 18, 1883. They now reside in Boston.
    iii. Mary Phelps, b. Oct. 5, 1849; d. Aug. 3, 1853.
    iv. Caroline Ellen, b. March 28, 1854; d. July 22, 1856.

13. Enos[7] Wright (*Enos,[6] Enos,[5] Bildad,[4] Ebenezer,[3] Judah,[2] Samuel[1]*)
    married Oct. 23, 1849, Anna Maria Phelps. Children:
    i. Annette Maria,[8] b. Oct. 19, 1851.
    ii. Edward Enos, b. April 29, 1854; d. July 30, 1856.
    iii. Henry Lewis, b. Nov. 20, 1857; d. Dec. 8, 1857.
    iv. Ellen Aurora, b. July 23, 1859; d. Aug. 28, 1861.
    v. Charles Samuel, b. Aug. 31, 1861.
    vi. Martha Anna, b. June 4, 1868.

NOTES AND DOCUMENTS CONCERNING HUGH PETERS.

Communicated by G. D. Scull, Esq., of London, England.

[Continued from page 175.]

Excerpted out of the Inventory Book of his Maj[tie]
Goods in Whitehall, St. James's, Somerset
House, the Tower, Windsor, &c. &c.

Plate & Jewells in the upp' Jewell house in the Tower in charge of S[r]
Hen: Myldmaye Appraised the 13: 14: & 15 dayes of August
1649

Fol: 36.

<table>
<tr><td>delivᵈ to the Mint to be Coyned.</td><td>The Imp'iall Crowne of Massy Gold weighᵍ 7ˡᵇ: 6ᵒᶻ: enriched &c: at 40 £: pʳ lb.</td><td></td><td></td></tr>
</table>

		valued	£	s.	d.
	one blew Saphir		50.	00.	00.
	one Saphir		15.	00.	00.
	Two Saphirs		30.	00.	00.
	One Saphir		3.	00.	00.
These 19: Saphirs	One Saphir		3.	00.	00.
	One Saphir		10.	00.	00.
sold to Roger Humfries	Two Saphirs		15.	00.	00.
30 April 1650	Two Saphirs		8.	00.	00.
	One Saphir		8.	00.	00.
for 198£.	One Saphir		3.	00.	00.
	1 Saphir		20.	00.	00.
	1 Saphir		15.	00.	00.
	1 Saphir		3.	00.	00.
	1 Saphir		5.	00.	00.
	2 Saphirs		10.	00.	00.

198. 00. 00.

			£	s.	d.
Sold to Mʳ John Crooke 3ᵈ Jan: 1649 for 320£	Ruby Ballasis				
	232 pearles at —15ˢ apeece		174.	00.	00
	Four Rubies in the Flower de luce		20.	00.	00
the sᵈ 56 Rubies	4: in the Cross		6.	00.	00
	2: in the de Luce		12.	00.	00
sold Mʳ Leigh:	4: in the Cross		6.	00.	00
7 Jan: 1649	2: in the de luce		3.	00.	00
for 200£	5: in the Cross		12.	00.	00
	4: in the de Luce		30.	00.	00
2 Rubies sold Derrick	4: in the Cross		20.	00.	00
	4: in the de luce		20.	00.	00
	4: in the de Luce		20.	00.	00

			£	s.	d.
	37 valued at 149£		149.	00.	00
	2i Rubies at		16.	00.	00
Sold Mʳ Murrey as appraised.	2 Emeralds at		5.	00.	00
Sold Robᵗ Mallary, 3 Jan'y 1649 for 191£ 10ˢ 6ᵈ	28 Diamonds at		168.	00.	00

189. 00. 00.

			£	s.	d.
the Gold d'd to the Mint to be Coyned.	The Queenes Crowne weighing 3ˡᵇ:10ᵒᶻ½ vallued at 40£ pʳ lb: | 5 oz being abated for the weight of the stone		136.	13.	04
all sold 3: Jan. 1649, for 210£ to Mʳ Crooke.	20 Saphirs { 4 at		70.	00.	00
	16 at		50.	00.	00
all but 81 pearles sold.	22 Rubies		40.	00.	00
the 2 pearles sold Derrick.	83 Pearles		41.	10.	00

201. 10. 00

		£	s.	d.
2^{oz} of the Gold sold Mr. dumarsque for 6 : 13 : 4. 21 Jany 1649	A small Crowne found in an Iron Chest formerly in the custody of the Lord Cottington, weighing 2^{lb} : 1^{oz} whereof 3^{oz} to			
the rest of the Gold d'd to the Mint to be coyned	be allowed for the weight of the stones and valued at 3[£] : 6^s : 8^d per oz . .	73.	06.	08
sold to James Guinon 3 Jan. 1649 for 65£	8 Saphirs	60.	00.	00
Sold Mr Mosey as appraised 23 Oct. 1651.	i Diamond	200.	00.	00
Sold Mr dumaresq. 21 Jany. 1649 for 13£	i Emerald	12.	00.	00
	i rock ruby	15.	00.	00
The 10 rubies, 13 diamonds & 70 Pearls sold	8 Rubies	20.	00.	00
	i oriental Ruby	8.	00.	00
Mr. Crooke for 130£ : 2^s	8 Diamonds	24.	00.	00
7^d the 3 Jan. 1649.	5 Diamonds	8.	00.	00
	70 Pearls at 2^s 6^d each	8.	15.	00
		355.	15.	00

fol: 37 :

d'd to the Mint to be coyned.	The Globe weighing 1^{lb} 5^{oz}$\frac{1}{4}$ at 3[£] 6^s 8^d per ounce, vallued at . . .	£57.	10.	00
d'd to the Mint, y^e Gold valued at 20£	Two Coronaçon Bracelets weighing 7^{oz}$\frac{1}{4}$ (whereof one ounce to be deducted for the weight of the stones & pearles) at 3[£] 6^s 8^d per oz is	20.	00.	00
The stones & pearles of these 3 peeces sold Mr Crooke 3 Jany 1649, with some other broken stones for 25£	3 Rubies Ballass set in each of the Bracelets vall : at	6.	00.	00
	12 Pearles vall : at	10.	00.	00
		16.	00.	00
d'd to y^e Mint.	Two Septers weighing 18oz$\frac{1}{4}$ at 3£ : 6^s : 8^d per oz	60.	00.	00
d'd to the Mint.	A long rod of Silver gilt weighing 1^{lb} : 5^{oz}. at 5^s : 4^d per oz . . .	4.	10.	08
Mint.	One gold Porringer & cover weighing 15oz$\frac{1}{2}$ valued at 3£ : 6^s : 8^d per oz .	51.	13.	04
Mint.	One gold Cup set wth 2 : Saphirs & 2 Ballas Rubies weighing 15^{oz}$\frac{1}{2}$ at 3£ : 6^s 8^d per oz	51.	13.	04
Mint.	Two gold Trencher plates enamelled, weighing 25^{oz}.$\frac{1}{2}$ at 3£ : 6^s : 8^d per oz vallued at	85.	00.	00
Mint.	Two gold Spoones wth flat heads weighing 5oz$\frac{1}{4}$ at 3£ : 6^s : 8^d per oz valued at .	17.	10.	00
Mint.	One Toster of gold enamelled wth a phœnix weighing 5oz$\frac{1}{4}$ at 3£ : 6^s : 8^d per oz .	6.	13.	04

fol°. 37b.

d'd to y^e Mint.	A George on Horseback of Gold wth a pearle in his Helmet & a dragon enamelled oz 33 at 3£ per ounce . .	99.	00.	00
sold to Mr. Mallary the 31 Decr 1649 for 14£. 14^s. 4^d.	Brass & Copp' medalls of sevrall sorts found in an Iron Chest in y^e Lower Jewell house formerly in the Lord Cottington's charge in number 139 & valled at .	13.	10.	00

d'd to the Mint.	Two Offring peeces & a Set of Gold weighing 10oz$\frac{1}{4}$ at 3£: 12ˢ per oz . .	37. 00. 00

fol: 40.

Part of the Regalia Removed from Westmʳ to the Tower Jewell house.

One oz sold Mʳ dammaresque 21 Jan. for 5ˢ 4ᵈ which is advanced. Mint.	Queen Ediths Crowne formerly thought to be of Massy gold, but upon tryall found to be of silver gilt, enricht wᵗʰ Garnets foule pearles, Saphyrs & some odd Stones weighed 50 ozˢ vallued at .	16. 00. 00
d'd to yᵉ Mint.	King Elfrids Crowne of gold wyre worke set wᵗʰ slight stones & two litle Bells weighing 79oz$\frac{1}{2}$ at 3£ per oz. alias 80oz$\frac{3}{4}$	248. 10. 00
Mint. The Stones sold Mʳ damaresque 21 Jan. for 9£ which is advanced.	A Gold plate dish enameled set wᵗʰ slight stones—23oz$\frac{1}{2}$ at 3£: 6ˢ: 8ᵈ per oz. vallued at	77. 11. 00
Sold Mʳ Milner 30 of Dec 1649 for 110. 15. 00	One large Glass cup wrought in figures & set in Gold wᵗʰ some stones & pearles weighing 68oz$\frac{1}{2}$ vallᵈ at 30ˢ per oz .	102. 15. 00
d'd to yᵉ Mint.	A dove of gold set wᵗʰ stones & pearles 8oz$\frac{1}{2}$ set wᵗʰ studds of silver gilt in a box vallued together	26. 00. 00
d'd to yᵉ Mint.	The Gould & Stones belonging to a Collar of Crimson Taffety wrought with Gold and Stones set in plates of silver enameled weighing 27oz$\frac{1}{2}$ at 50ˢ per oz. . .	18. 15. 00

fol 40.b.

Sold Mʳ Lavender 31 Decʳ 1649 for 5£. 10ˢ. 0	One Staffe of black & white Ivory wᵗʰ a dove on the Top wᵗʰ binding and feete of Gold vallued at	4. 10. 00
d'd to yᵉ Mint.	A large staff wᵗʰ a dove on the topp formerly thought to be all gold but upon triall found to be, the lower pte wood wᵗʰin & silver gilt wᵗʰout, the upp p̃ᵗ. wood wᵗʰin & gold wᵗʰout weighing vi oz & vallued at	35. 00. 00
to yᵉ Mint.	One small staff wᵗʰ a Flower de Luce on the top formerly thought to be all of gold, but upon tryall found to be Iron wᵗʰin & silver gilt wᵗʰout, vallued at .	2. 10. 00
to yᵉ Mint.	Two Septers one set wᵗʰ pearles & stones the upp end gold, the lower end silver the gold weighing 23ᵒᶻ at 55ˢ per ounce, the lower end horne & litle silver gilt, valued at 12ˢ. The other silver gilt wᵗʰ a dove formerly thought gold weighing 7ᵒᶻ$\frac{3}{4}$ at 5ˢ: 6ᵈ per ounce . .	65. 19. 7$\frac{1}{2}$
Sold Mʳ Kinnersly 27 of Decʳ 1649, for 16ˢ.	A silver spoone gilt weighing 3oz at 5ˢ: 4ᵈ per ounce	00. 16. 00
4. The Coate Roabe & pearles sold Mʳ dammaresque, 21ˢᵗ Jany for 6£ the gold to yᵉ Mint at 8£.	The gold of yᵉ Tassels of yᵉ Livʳ colour'd Robbe weighing . . . . oz: vallued at 2£ per oz= 8£: and the C̃oate wᵗʰ the neck	

button of gold vall^d at 2£. The Roabe having some pearles vall^d at 3£ : in all vall^d at 13. 00. 00

According to order of Parli^t : all these are broken and defaced.

d'd to y^e Mint. One pair of silver gilt spurrs wth Buckles set wth 12 Stones & crimson silk strapps po^r 6oz¾ at 5^s : 4^d p^r ounce . . 1. 13. 04

fol. 41.

An Inventory of the Regalia in an Iron Chest formerly kept in Westm^r Abbey.

	£	s.	d.
One Crimson Taffatie Roabe val^d .	00.	10.	00
One Roabe trim'd wth Gold lace . .	00.	10.	00
One Liver-colour'd silk Robe worth nothing	00.	00.	00
One Robe of Crimson Taffate sarsenet .	00.	05.	00

All sould
Mr Humfryes
the 28 of Novr 1649
for 5£

One p^r of Buskins of Cloth of Silver & Silv stocking at 00. 02. 06
One p^r of Shoes of Cloth of Gold . 00. 02. 00
One p^r of imbrodered Gloves val^d at . 00. 01. 00
Three swords wth scabards of Cloth of gold valued at 03. 00. 00
One horne Combe worth nothing.

Sevrall things rec^d from some Gent : & (a° 1649) remain^g in Somerset house Closet.

This the King had on
when he was beheaded.
Sould Mr Ireton the 3^d
of Jany 1649 for 2^c5£.

A Garter of Blew velvet set wth 412 : small diamands formerly in the Custody of Captaine Preston & now in the Closet, val^d at 160. 00. 00

fol° : 41. b.

to ye Mint.
One Collar of Esses of Gold formerly in Co^{ll} Harisons custody, weigh^g 35oz½ at 3£ per oz 106. 10. 00

Rec^d fro Mr Hunt a
Clarke belongg to y^e
parliament.
to ye mint.

A silver seale called the dutchy seale weighing 32 : oz at 5^s per ounce . . 8. 00. 00

to ye mint.
The Gold & silver belonging to an old Cross, being all wood underneath & set wth counterfeit stones, the Gold weighing 13oz¼ at 3£ per oz., the silver weighing 31oz & 5^s per ounce, valued . . . 48. 05. 00

Excerptfd out of a Booke Intituled Denmarke house Wardrobe, A p'ticular of such Goods as were viewed the 12th : of Feb^r : 1648.

fol : 21.

Queene Annes parliament & Coronation Robes.

Sold to
Elianor Thomas
30 Oct 1649
for 22£

A kirtle of Crimson velvet lyned wth white Taffety bordered about wth Ermynes wth a Traine joyned to the same lined quite through wth Ermynes, wth an Hood & Bodyes of the same. A surcoate to the same wth a long Traine lined wth Ermynes wth Gold Tassells to the same and strings suteable.

fol. 21 b.

A Kirtle of purple velvet lyned wth white Tafety bordered about wth Ermynes wth a Trayne to the same lyned quite through wth Ermynes & Hood & Bodies. of the same.

Sold to
Elia: Thomas
30 Oct. 1649
for 22£

A Surcoate to the same wth a long trayne lined wth Ermynes wth gold Tassells to the same & strings suteable.

fol° ibid.

Robes of King Hen: the 8

Sold Mr Noell
24 Oct 1649 for 80£

(69)

Two Robes of white cloth of silver of the Order of St Michaell val^d at   .   .   20. 00. 00

A Skreene cloth of white Satyn embrodered all on wth needleworke of gold & silver wth the colours of England & Scotland joyn'd together & wrought in the same in a circle of fine needleworke wth the Armes. of the Kn^ts of the Garter wrought in the s^d cloth lyned with changeable Taffity frindged at the ends & sides wth narrow frindge of gold & Silver & cõnt in

2yds¼ length
1 yd in a breadth

fol: 43.

Hampton Cort Wardrobe.

One peece of Arras of the coming into England of King Hen: the 7th wth one hand taking the Crowne from Richard the 3^d & wth the other hand hold^g a Rose Crowned, lyned wth blew Canvas, cont^s Length 4yds¾ Breadth 4yds½—⅛

6.

One peece of the History of St George lyned wth blew Buckrome con^t 1 yd¾. 3 na | 1yd¾

fo: 74.

One Garter of Stoole worke embrodered wth Gold wth out Buckle or pendant.

fol. 99.

Wyndsor wardrobe.

Three (altered into 6) peeces of purple velvet embrodered wth the Garter, wch were heretofore a Ceeler Tester & Counterpoint, but now cometed into Hangings & lyned wth Canvas cont^s   Length 1. = 4 yds ¾ depth 3 yds ½.   1 = 4 yds depth 4 yds ½.   length. 1 = 5 yds ¼ depth 6 yds ½—⅛.

Six single vallences of the like velvet embrodered wth a Garter frindged wth purple silke & gold cont^g 25 yds ¼ of a y^d or thereabout, made into Hangings wth the former 3 peeces.

fol. 102

A Unicornes Horne con^t — 2 yds i na = 9^lb 2oz weight.

P — A peece of Arras of St George & the dragon.

103.

In the Garter Roome in the Custody of Colonell Whichcote.

A large Bible in folio cover^d wth purple velvet wth Brass at the Corners.
A pulpet cloth of purple Satin lay^d all over wth Crownes & Portcullesses

of Gold.   A great cloth carpet.   Nyne longe Cushions.   6 Banners.   The Roome hanged round wth woolen hangings checked wth red, white and greene.   A large sword.   A picture of Ed. ye 3^d at length wth a greene Curtaine before it.   Two Tables of the Order of the Garter.

fol. 103. b.

One Bell & Clock on y^e Gate by the Wine Celler dore wch is said to cost 200£.   A. 1111

HENRY JOSSELYN, THE FIRST AND ONLY ROYAL CHIEF MAGISTRATE OF MAINE.

By WILLIAM M. SARGENT, A.M., of Portland, Me.

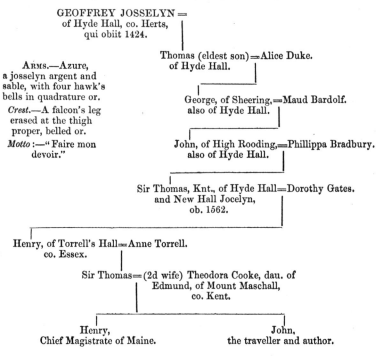

HENRY JOSSELYN, whose pedigree is traced above, arrived in New England in the ship "Pide-Cow," at Piscataqua, in 1634,* as chief agent for Capt. John Mason, the Patentee.   He continued to act in that capacity until the death of Mason in 1635; undertaking the discovery of Erocoise [i. e. Champlain] Lake in the Laco-

* See Mason's letter of 5 May, 1634, to Gibbons, endorsed, "received July 10th," two days after the arrival of the ship.

nia Patent. He intended to settle himself at Newichewannock [Berwick, Maine], but because of his patron's death and the subsequent confusion of his affairs, he removed to Black Point (Scarborough) in 1635.*

There was probably some agreement between him and Sir Ferdinando Gorges, the Patentee of that region, relating to private grants of land; and such lands as he became possessed of this way added to Capt. Thomas Cammock's Patent,—part of which was devised to him, and the remainder of which he became seized of by marrying the widow Margaret Cammock in 1643,—made him the owner of a considerable portion of that township, and he thus became the most extensive proprietor who has ever lived in Scarborough.

He resided with Captain Cammock until the latter's death, and afterwards in the same house, near the "Ferry Rocks," which is supposed to have stood over the old cellar near "Garrison Cove" on the neck, and which was at the time of the Indian troubles in 1675 converted into a garrison, to which many of the inhabitants resorted with their families. The situation of this garrison rendered it one of the strongest in the Province—and it might easily have been defended against any number of Indians.

In 1635 Josselyn was a Commissioner under William Gorges; and again under the Patent of 1639 under Thomas Gorges. In 1645 chosen vice-Deputy Governor under Richard Vines as Deputy Governor; at Vines's departure from the country, he became acting Deputy-Governor, and held the last General Court under the authority of Gorges, at Wells, July, 1646.

He was heartily attached to Gorges and his cause, but he preferred to obey Rigby rather than to disturb the promised peace of the Province by unavailing contention. He was appointed among the Judges of Lygonia, with Cleeves and Jordan. Strongly opposed to the authority of Massachusetts, he held out for five years; was arrested and obliged to give bond to appear before the General Court, which he did, as did Jordan, in 1657; submitted to Massachusetts July 3, 1658, and, with Henry Watts, was appointed a Commissioner for the Town; was Associate and Town Commissioner in 1661; but in 1662 Josselyn and Shapleigh refused to take the oath of office as Associates for the Province, and in the contest which followed was backed up by his fellow-townsmen; but being again elected Commissioner by his townsmen in 1664, was then accepted by the Massachusetts authorities.

Soon after young Gorges's application to the King, he appointed Josselyn one of twelve Magistrates under his authority. In 1664 he was appointed a Royal Justice by the four Commissioners sent over by the King, and there being eleven of them, the Commission-

---

* Mason did not die till late in 1635. His will was made Nov. 26, 1635, and proved Dec. 22.—EDITOR.

ers directed that in case the Justices were equally divided Josselyn should have the casting vote; thus constituting him the Chief Justice of the Province. He was its first, and only Chief Magistrate ever appointed by Royal authority. With the establishment of the royal government in the Province, the jurisdiction of Gorges ceased and was never resumed. This royal government, with Josselyn at its head, continued till 1668.

Long and bitterly partisan accounts of the particulars of the usurpation of authority by the Commissioners of Massachusetts and their deposition of the subject of this sketch in that year have been written. Suffice it here to say that this terminated his public services in this region.

Living the retired life of a gentleman planter till August, 1676, he was, with numbers of his neighbors, then surprised and besieged by the Indians in his garrison-house. Accepting the invitation of Mogg Hegone, their chief, to a parley, he found on his return that all the garrison, except his own family, had rowed away in boats. Surrendering, he was treated with a kindness and consideration by the savages that evinced their appreciation of his undeviating justice and many kindly acts shown them in the past, and was allowed to depart to the eastward.

Exhausted at his age by the protracted civil contests; disgusted with their results; viewing the destruction by savage hands of the accumulated industries of a lifetime, and considering the impracticability of immediate resettlement, he cast in his lot with the more favored maritime settlement at Pemaquid, appearing there immediately upon the establishment of the Duke of York's government in 1677—in which it is inferable he was an active participant, as he appears continuously acting as a Justice, considering, doubtless, his old commission valid anywhere in his Majesty's domain. He was reinvested, or newly commissioned, however, by the Governor of New York in 1680; and subsequently received other distinguishing marks of consideration and confidence.

He was as distinguished for uprightness and probity amidst his new surroundings as of yore; *Cœlum non animum mutant qui trans mare currunt;* and while perhaps not as conspicuous a figure thereafter as in the previous annals, his honorable reputation made new friends, and he seems never to have alienated old ones—while a letter of Governor Andros to Ensign Sharp in command at Pemaquid, September, 1680, shows that official appreciation but confirmed the estimation of his neighbors, and extended the fostering aid of judicious patronage to a tried and proven public servant, alleviating his necessities as a merited mark of royal recognition of the gentleman and scholar, the Magistrate and Governor, than whom we have never had one more worthy and seldom one so pure. He writes :

As to Mr. Jocylne whom I would have you use with all fitting respect Considering what he hath been and his age. And if he Desire and shall build a house for himself to lett him choose any lott and pay him ten pounds towards it or if he shall Desire to hyre soe to live by himself then to Engage and pay the rent either of which shall be allowed you in yor account as alsoe sufficient provision for himself and wife as he shall desire out of the stores.

In the scarcity of records that have survived the chances and changes of those troubled times, the nearest approximation to the time of his death is that it was shortly before May 10th, 1683, for Captain Brockholls, writing that day to Lawrence Dennis, speaks of him as deceased.

" No storied urn nor animated bust," no epitaph even, marks his unknown resting place, but in the hearts and memories of his successors is he ever justly famed.

Note.—I have to express my very great obligation to Lt. Col. John Henry Josselyn, of Ipswich, England—a practising lawyer and Town Councillor there—for the construction of the above used pedigree, from his own printed pedigree of this family, by which it appears that the subject of the above sketch and Col. Josselyn are " second and eighth " cousins ; also for many valuable citations from his MS. collections; from these I quote his opinion : " I have a note that Henry Josselyn, of the County of Kent, was admitted to Corpus Christi College, Cambridge, 1623. This might very well have been your Henry before he went to America, and his being described as of the County of Kent is consistent with his being the son of Sir Thomas, whose second wife (Henry's mother) came from that County." " For genealogy of the elder branch of our family, refer to title ' Earl of Roden ' in ' Burke's Peerage ' of 1883 and subsequent years. The genealogy given in editions prior to 1883 is incorrect. Sir Bernard corrected the 1883 edition after a correspondence I had with him about it." " The proper arms of the family are those borne by the Earl of Roden and by ourselves, viz." [description as at the head of this article]. " It would seem to be probable that Thomas Josselyn, fourth son of Ralph of Roxwell, co. Essex, whose will (dated 4 Aug. 1626, and proved 4 May, 1632) is identical with the Thomas Josselyn who embarked for America in ship ' Increase,' 17th April, 1635. I base this theory on the coincidence that the family names Dorothy, Mary, Nathaniel and Elizabeth, are repeated in the issue of the last named Thomas. As regards the name ' Abraham,' given by said Thomas to his eldest son, it may have been the name of his (Thomas's) father-in-law, for what more likely than that a woman bearing the Scriptural name ' Rebecca ' should have had an ' Abraham ' for her father? Roxwell is adjoining parish to Willingale Doe in which is Torrel's Hall. But I cannot trace the origin of this branch of the Josselyn family, nor its connection, if any, with the Torrel's Hall branch. Search of registers might do it." *Vide passim* Register, xiv. 15 ; " Tuckerman's Introduction to John Josselyn's ' New England Rarities.' "

This last citation erroneously states that " Sir Thomas Josselyn . . . . did not come to this country "—a mistake previously made by Mr. Southgate in his " History of Scarborough " ; while Sir Ferdinando Gorges, by implication, states the contrary in this extract: " Whereas Sir Thomas Josselyn Knt was named chief in the said Commission and Ordinances [dated Mch. 10: 1640] Now for that I am informed he is returned into England he is left out of the Commission and my Cousin Thomas Gorges put in his place and the same power given unto him as to the said Sir Thomas Josselyn." (From the files of the Maine Historical Society—MS. copy of State Papers, 40: e.)—W. M. S.

NATHANIEL EATON, THE FIRST PRINCIPAL OF HARVARD.

By the Rev. EDWARD D. NEILL, of St. Paul, Min.

NATHANIEL EATON, the first Principal of the school which has expanded into Harvard University, disappointed the friends of learning and mortified his most estimable relatives by his irregular course, violent temper, and lack of integrity. He was born in 1609, and in 1638 came to Massachusetts. His father had been a clergyman in England, and his brother was the respected and the first Governor of New Haven Colony.

A recent examination of the records of Northampton County, Virginia, has thrown some additional light upon Eaton's erratic career.

Until the year 1635, when William Cotton, whose mother resided at Bunbury, in Cheshire, England, was the minister, there had been no formal organization of a church vestry, on the eastern shore of Chespeake Bay. Cotton was a brother-in-law of William Stone, of Accomack, who subsequently was the first protestant Governor of the Province of Maryland, and on the 20th of August, 1640, he made his will, and soon died.

His successor was John Rozier, who appears to have been an estimable person. One of the colonists, in his will, calls him his " dear and respected friend," and John Holloway, a physician, bequeaths to him a folio Greek Testament. Rozier seems to have employed Nathaniel Eaton an assistant, and owing to a difference between them, Nathaniel Littleton, Obedience Robins, John Neale and John Gookin, probably a brother or uncle of Daniel, whose dust is in the grave-yard of Cambridge, Mass., were appointed arbitrators, and they, on March 23, 1642–3, decided that Rozier should pay six hundred pounds of tobacco to Eaton; and that the next year, the vestry of Northampton would pay him that amount, showing that he was engaged in ministerial duties.

In January, 1646–7, there is a suit brought by John Cougan or Cogan, against the estate of Nathaniel Eaton, clerk. Cougan was probably from Boston.

Another brother-in-law of Governor William Stone was Francis Doughty, who had been minister to the English speaking people at Manhattan, but who had become a resident of the eastern shore of the Chesapeake Bay, in Virginia. Ann, the widow of Nathaniel Littleton, in her will, of 1656, speaks of Doughty " of this County, Minister, and Preacher of ye word, in this parish." At this time he was a widower; but in June, 1658, he gives notice of an intended marriage " between me Francis Doughty of Northampton County in Virginia, Minister, and Ann Eaton of the same County," and that he does not wish to have any interest in her estate.

Winthrop in his Journal mentions that Eaton, after he went to Virginia, was a drunken preacher, and that he sent for his wife and children, who embarked in a vessel that was lost. Subsequently he married the only surviving child of Thomas Graves, of Virginia, formerly of Dorchester, Mass. Ann Eaton was possibly his widow, although he deserted his wife about 1646; and Mather, in the *Magnalia*, writes, that he went from Virginia " to England, where he lived privately, until the restoration of King Charles II. Conforming to the ceremonies of the Church of England, he was fixed at Biddefield, where he became a bitter persecutor of the Dissenters, and died in prison for debt."

EARLY NEW ENGLAND AND NEW YORK HERALDIC BOOK PLATES.

By Mr. RICHARD C. LICHTENSTEIN of Boston, Mass.

THE following list comprises, as far as has come under the observation of the compiler, the names of those persons and families in New England and New York who used armorial engraved book plates prior to 1830. In all cases where a date was printed or an engraver's name signed, it has been noted. Though the compiler has reasons for believing that many of the unsigned plates can be credited to the various engravers named in the list, he has refrained from giving them the credit unless the plate was actually signed.

The plates of Courtenay, Loring, Will. Smith, Wilson, Simpson, Price and others, all bear the marked characteristics of Hurd's design and engraving, while those of Gray, Emersons, Hallowell, Vaughan, &c., bear the same evidence of being Callender's. Of the two hundred and four plates on the list, more than two thirds were engraved in America, the remainder being ordered by their owners from English engravers; while of plates belonging to families south of New York, owing to the few engravers there, just the reverse is the case.

A noticeable difference between the New England and New York plates and those of the more southern colonies, is the rarity of dated and addressed plates in the former section of this country, the southern field being far more prolific in this respect. The earliest dated plate is that of Robert Elliston, 1725, recently reproduced in the Book Buyer; but the plates of John Allen and Isaac Royall, although not dated, bear evidence of being somewhat earlier. The plate of Joseph Dudley, 1754, has the appearance of having been used by some of the earlier members of the family, possibly by the Governor, as the general design of the plate is one that was in use at the beginning of the eighteenth century.

In general design, the American engravers followed very nearly in the line of their English brethren, and few show any marked originality or differences. The work of Hurd is well known, and stands at the head of the list, both in execution and fertility of design. His earlier work is of extremely rude and conventional character. It is shown in the reproduction of Dr. E. A. Holyoke's book plate given herewith ; and his improvement is noticeable in the Wentworth, which is of exactly the same design. In his later work his talents as an engraver show to a greater advantage, and his work equals that of the best book plate engraving done in England in his day. Dawkins's neat although not always original attempts make one regret that his plates are not more numerous. The few pieces that are known are all interesting from the melancholy interest attached to the engraver. Callender was at first inclined to a distinct style of his own, but he seems to have soon left it for the conventional shield with a slight ornamentation. Most of Maverick's work is well done, the shield in most cases being decorated with light sprays of leaves and flowers, falling around in graceful profusion. Anderson's, Revere's, Turner's and Johnson's work, although examples are not so numerous, bears evidence of careful workmanship in design and engraving. Their plates are interesting specimens of early American engraving.

The names of two early American book plate engravers do not appear on the list—those of Amos Doolittle, 1754–1832, and E. Gallaudet, of New York. The compiler has seen no heraldic specimens of their work, but the former engraved several very curious allegorical plates for different societies connected with Yale College, while the latter has an extremely crude plate of the New York Society Library, which was improved upon later by the Mavericks.

Phillips Academy of Exeter, N. H., has a curiously engraved book plate, done about 1785, with a representation of the Phillips arms; and the plate of the Boylston Medical Library of Cambridge, Mass., engraved by Callender, has an engraving of the Boylston arms.

This list makes no claim to completeness. Undoubtedly a large number of other families used heraldic plates, but owing to the many changes and vicissitudes to which the volumes have been subjected they have failed to reach the eyes of those interested in heraldry. The books have been scattered, and the plates in many cases lost to public view by being hid in public and private libraries. It is hoped that this beginning may induce any person who meets with an early American book plate, to note the fact and communicate it to the compiler, so that in the near future a more complete list may be issued.

The following plates are of interest as showing the addresses of their owners :—John Burnet, Attorney at Law, New York—Myles Cooper, LL.D., Coll. Regis. Nov. Ebor in Amer. Præses et Coll. Regina de Oxon. Socius, &c.—Robert Elliston, Gent., Comptrol. of his Majesty's Customs of New York in Amer. 1725—Col. John Skey Eustace, State of N. York —John Franklin, Boston, New England—Robert Hale of Beverly—Jared Ingersoll of New Haven, Conn.—Robert R. Livingston of Clermont— Isaac Royall of Antigua.

A list of plates belonging to families south of N. York is in preparation.

Name	State	Engraver
Adams, John Quincy,	Mass.	
ditto, (crest only)		
Agnew, James,	N. Y.	
Allen, John	Mass.	
Alsop, Richard	Conn.	
Anderson, Alexander	N. Y.	A. Anderson.
Apthorp	Mass.	
Atkinson, Theodore	N. H.	Hurd.
" Wm. King	"	Callender.
Baldwin, Jonathan	Mass.	"
" Luke	"	"
Ball, Flamen	N. Y.	P. R.Maverick.
Bancker, A.	"	Maverick.
" Charles N.	"	Jones.
" Gerard	"	Dawkins.
Belcher, Jonathan	Mass.	
" " son of above	"	
Blackley, Absalom	N. Y.	Maverick.
Bowdoin, James	Mass.	
Brasher, Philip	N. Y.	Maverick.
Bridge, Charles	"	Child.
Brown, Thomas	Mass.	Hurd.
Burnet, John	"	
" " 1754	N. Y.	Dawkins.
Cabot, William	Mass.	
Callender, John	"	Callender.
Carrol, Charles	"	Hurd.
Cary, A.	"	H. Morse.
" Thomas	"	Callender.
Chandler, Gardiner	"	Revere.
" Rufus	"	Hurd.
Child, Francis	N. Y.	Dawkins.
" Thomas	Mass.	Hurd.
Clinton, DeWitt	N. Y.	Maverick.
Cock, William	"	"
Coffin, John, 1771	Mass.	
Colden, Cadwallader D.	N. Y.	
Cooper, Myles	"	
Courtenay, Henry	Mass.	
Curwen	"	
Cutting, James S.	N. Y.	Maverick.
Dana, Francis	Mass.	Hurd.
" Richard H.	"	
Danforth	"	Hurd.
DeBlois, Lewis	"	"
Dering, Thomas, 1749	"	"
Duane, James	N. Y.	Dawkins.
Dudley, Joseph, 1754	Mass.	
Dumeresque, Philip	"	Hurd.
DuPeyster, Ferd	N. Y.	Maverick.
Elam, Samuel	R. I.	
Ellery, Benjamin	"	
Elliston, Robert, 1725	N. Y.	
" Robert	"	
Emerson, William	Mass.	
Erving, William	"	Callender.
" "	"	
Eustace, Col. John S.	N. Y.	
Foot, Eben.	"	Maverick.
Foster	Mass.	Furnass.
" Isaac	"	Hurd.
Fowler, C.	R. I.	
Foxcroft, John	"	
Franklin, John	Mass.	Turner.
French, Jonathan	"	
Gardiner, John	Maine	
Gibs, James	N. Y.	P. Maverick.
Giles, James	"	Maverick.
Gœlet, John	"	"
Gray	Mass.	
Green, Francis	"	Hurd.
Greene, Benjamin	"	"
" " 1757	"	"
" David	"	Revere.
" Thomas, Jr.	"	Hurd.
Greenleaf, W.	"	Revere.
Hale, Robert	"	Hurd.
Hallowell, Robert	Maine	
Harrison, Richard	N. Y.	
Hay, Barrack	"	I. Hutt.
Herbert, W.	"	
Hicks, Elias	"	P. Maverick.
Hoffman, Philip C.	"	Maverick.
Holyoke, Edward Aug.	Mass.	
Hurd, Isaac	"	

Name	State	Engraver
Ingersoll, Jared	Conn.	
Inglis	N. Y.	
Jackson	Mass.	Hurd.
Jackson, James	"	
Jarvis, Sam. Farmer	"	
Jeffries, Dr. John	"	
Jenkins, Robert	"	Hurd.
Johnson, John S.	N. Y.	Maverick.
" Thomas	Mass.	
" W. S., LL.D.	N. Y.	
Johnston, J.	"	Maverick.
" Thomas	"	"
Jones, Samuel	"	Dawkins.
Judah, Benjamin P.	"	Maverick.
" " S.	"	"
Keese, John	"	Maverick.
King. Rufus	"	"
Kip, Isaac L.	"	
Kissam, Benjamin	"	Dawkins.
Ladd	N. H.	S. Felwell.
Lewis, Morgan	N. Y.	
Livingston, William, of the Middle Temple	"	
Livingstone	"	Maverick.
" Peter R.	"	Hurd.
" Robert R.	"	
" Walter	"	Maverick.
" Wm. S.	"	"
Lloyd, John Nelson	"	
Loring	Mass.	
Low, Cornelius	N. Y.	
Lowell, John	Mass.	Hurd.
" " Jr.	"	Annin & Smith
Ludlow, Gab.	N. Y.	Dawkins.
Mann, John Preston	R. I.	
Merchant, Henry,	"	Hurd.
Masterton, Peter	N. Y.	Maverick.
McComb, John	"	
McCoun, William T.	"	Rollinson.
McLean, Hugh	"	Maverick.
Meredith	"	"
Minot	Mass.	
Moore, Lambert	N. Y.	
" Nathaniel F.	"	P. Maverick.
Morris, James	"	
" Roger	"	
" Wm. Lewis	"	
Murray, Joseph	"	Maverick.
Oliver, Andrew	Mass.	
Osborne, Samuel	"	Hurd.
Otis, Harrison Gray	"	
Pace, Henry	"	Hurd.
Panton, Francis	N. Y.	
" " Jr.	"	Maverick.
Parker, Samuel	N. H.	
Pasley, William	N. Y.	Maverick.
Paulding, W.	"	"
Pepperell. Sir William	Maine	
Perkins, Thomas H.	Mass.	
Pickering Henry	"	
" John, Jr.	"	
Pierce, W. L.	N. Y.	Maverick.
Pintard, John	"	"
Popham, W.	"	"
Prescott, William	Mass.	
" William H.	"	Annin & Smith
Price, Ezekiel	"	
Pride, H. B.	N. Y.	Maverick.
Provost, Samuel	"	"
" John	"	
Quincy, Josiah	Mass.	
Revere, Paul	"	Hurd.
Robinson, Beverly	N. Y.	
Royall, Isaac	Mass.	
Russell, Joshua	N. Y.	Anderson.
" Thomas	Mass.	Callender.
Rutgers, Hendrick	N. Y.	
Sargent, Daniel	Mass.	Callender.
Schuyler, Philip	N. Y.	
Sears	Mass.	
Sears, David	"	
Seton, William	N. Y.	Maverick.
Sewall	Mass.	
Silvester, Peter	N. Y.	Maverick.
Simpson, Jonathan	Mass.	

Smith, Hezekiah	Mass.		Vaughan, Benjamin	Maine	
" James Scott	N. Y.	Maverick.	" Samuel	"	
" Thomas J.	"	"	" " Jr.	"	
" William	Mass.		Warren, John C.	Mass.	
" " A.M.	N. Y.		Wentworth	N. H.	Hurd.
" Wm. P., A.M.	"		Wetmore, Prosper	N. Y.	Maverick.
Spooner, Joshua	Mass.	Hurd.	" W.	Mass.	Revere.
Spry, William	N. Y.	W. Smith.	Wheelwright, Nath.	"	
Stearns	Mass.		Whitebread, W.	N. Y.	Dawkins.
Stephens, William	N. Y.	Maverick.	Wilkes, Charles	"	Rollinson.
Sullivan, John	N. H.	Callender.	Williams	Mass.	
Swan, James	Mass.	"	"	"	Harris.
Taylor, William	N. Y.	Maverick.	" John C.	"	Hurd.
Thomas, Isaiah	Mass.		Wilson, David	"	
Tillotson, John	N. Y.	Maverick.	" James	"	S. Hill.
Tracy, Nathaniel	Mass.	Hurd.	Winthrop, W.	"	
Tripp, Lott	N. Y.	Anderson.	Wisner, Polydore	N. Y.	Maverick.
Tyler, Andrew	Mass.	Hurd.	Wolcott, Oliver	Conn.	
" Joseph	"	Johnson.	Wynkoop, C. C.	N. Y.	
Tyng, Dudley A.	"	Callender.	" Peter	"	
Van Berchell	N. Y.	Maverick.	Yates, Christopher C.	"	
Van Rensselaer, H. K.	"	"	" Peter W.	"	Dawkins.
" " S. K.	"	"			

BYTHEWOOD FAMILY OF SOUTH CAROLINA,

From a Stray Bible Record.

Communicated by Isaac J. Greenwood, Esq., of New York City.

Children of Daniel[1] and Elizabeth Bythewood, of Weymouth, Dorsetshire, England:

2. i.   Daniel,[2] b. 30 Oct. 1764.
  ii. John Hinkston, b. 20 Oct. 1767; d. at Beaufort, S. C., April, 1815.
  iii. Ann, b. 8 Dec. 1769.
  iv. Thomas, b. 18 Aug. 1771 ; d. at B., Oct. 1809.
  v.   Miriam, b. 12 May, 1774.
  vi. Harriet, b. 10 Jan. 1777; d. at B., 181–.
  vii. Mary, b. 14 Nov. 1780 ; d. young.
  viii. Mary, b. 30 June, 1785 ; d. at B., 18—.
  ix. Richard Turner, b. 2 Dec. 1789.

2. Daniel[2] Bythewood and Elizabeth Taylor were married at Charleston, S. C., 17 April, 1792. She was born in New York, 5 April, 1770, the second daughter of William and Elizabeth Taylor. Her widowed mother married a second husband named Russell, and died at Beaufort, S. C., in 1822, aged 94. Mrs. Bythewood died at B., 25 September, 1828, " 40 minutes past midnight, aged 58 years, 5 months, 20 days." Her elder sister, Mrs. Isabella (Taylor) Stone, died at Charleston in 1824, aged 59, leaving a daughter Martha Stone who died at Beaufort, 4 October, 1842, aged 53 years, 7 mos.

  i.   Benjamin Russel,[3] b. at Charleston, S. C., 18 Oct. 1793 ; m. Sarah Johnson Fickling, at Beaufort, 14 Jan. 1813.
  ii. John William, b. at C., 27 Sept. 1795 ; lost at sea on a passage from Boston, Mass., the vessel foundering about 1 Sept. 1815.
  iii. Thomas Stone, b. at C., 23 Aug. 1798 ; d. 23 Oct. 1799.
  iv. Thomas Stone, ⎰ b. at C., 20 Oct. 1800 ; d. at Beaufort 23 Oct. 1813.
  v.   Eliza Taylor, ⎱ twin.
  vi. Rachel Ann, b. at C., 29 Sept. 1804 ; d. 3 Oct. 1804.   [1817.
  vii. Daniel Hinkston, b. at Beaufort, S. C., 9 Sept. 1805 ; d. at B., 30 Sept.
  viii. Mary Isabella, b. at B., 18 Oct. 1807 ; d. at B., 27 Aug. 1812.
  ix. Joseph Cook, b. at B., 26 Sept. 1809 ; d. at B., 2 Oct., 1817.
  x.   James Graham, b. at B., 12 Aug. 1811 ; m. Sarah McConnico, at Allenton, Wilcox Co., Al., 20 Dec. 1835.

Among the New York Marriage Licenses we have William Taylor and Elizabeth Hunter, 13 November, 1760. Query.—Is there any connection between the names of Bythewood and Bathurst ?

GENEALOGICAL GLEANINGS IN ENGLAND.

Communicated by Henry F. Waters, A.M., now residing in London, England.

[Continued from p. 172.]

George Ludlowe[1] of the County and Parish of Yorke in Virginia Esq. 8 September 1655. To my nephew Thomas Ludlow, eldest son to my brother Gabriel Ludlowe Esq. deceased, all my whole estate of lands and servants, &c. that I have now in possession in Virginia, to him and his lawful heirs forever; also my sixteenth part of the ship Mayflower, whereof Capt. William White is commander, which part I bought of Mr Samuel Harwar of London, merchant, only this year's "fraught" excepted, which I have reserved for my tobacco &c. My executor, yearly and every year during the natural life of my now wife Elizabeth Ludlowe, to pay unto her fifty pounds sterling in London. My crop wholly this year to be consigned to Mr William Allen of London, merchant, and one Mr John Cray that lives at the Green man on Ludgate Hill, whom I make my overseers of my estate in England. Moneys due from Mr Samuel Harwar at the Sun and Harp, in Milk Street, London. To my brother Gabriel all his children, now in England, one hundred pounds apiece, and the remainder of the money (in England) to my brother Roger Ludlowe's[2] children equally; and Mr Thomas Bushrode[3] to be paid seventy five pounds.

Whereas my brother Roger Ludlowe hath consigned divers goods to me as per my book appears, as debts in New England and in Virginia as by his letters and other writings appear &c. To my said brother the hundred pounds I lent him. To my cousin Samuel Langrish three thousand pounds of tobacco &c. To George Bernard,[4] son to Col. William Bernard, my great silver tankard with my arms on it &c. To George Webster,[5] son to Capt. Richard Webster of Jamestown the silver tankard that Mr Bowler brought in the year 1655. To Col. William Bernard, Major William Gooch[6] and Capt. Augustine Warner[7] ten pounds apiece, and I desire and nominate them to be overseers here in Virginia. To Doctor Henry Waldron all the debt he owes me on book, and the physic I have sent for for him. To Mr Bushrode five pounds. To my man Archyball a cloth suit &c. To Jane Greeham my servant one year of her time. To Mrs Rebecca Hurst all the clothes that I have sent for her in full of her time being with me in my house.

Wit: Nicholas Trott, Augustine Hodges.

Codicil:—I Colonel George Ludlowe &c. My nephew Thomas Ludlowe intends to intermarry with one Rebecca Hurst that is at this present living in my house. In that case my will is and my desire that my overseers here in Virginia take into their custody all my whole estate and dispose of the same until they can send into Ireland to my nephew Jonathan Ludlowe, eldest son to my brother Roger, who lives in Ireland at Dublin. Now in case my aforesaid nephew Thomas shall marry with the said Rebecca then it is my will that I give and bequeath unto my said nephew Jonathan all the estate that I did formerly give unto my nephew Thomas Ludlowe and make and constitute the said Jonathan my full and sole executor. Otherwise my former bequest to stand valid and the said Thomas shall enjoy what I have formerly given him to his use and heirs as my executor and heir. 23 October 1655. Witness:—James Biddlecombe.

On the first day of August, in the year of Our Lord God 1656, there issued forth Letters of administration to Roger Ludlow Esq., the father of and curator lawfully assigned to Jonathan, Joseph, Roger, Anne, Mary and Sarah Ludlowe, minors, the nephews and nieces and residuary legataries in this will, during the minority of the said minors; —— —— for that no executor is therein named as touching the said deceased's estate in England.

Berkeley, 256.

Administration on the goods &c. of John Ludlow, late of Virginia bachelor, deceased, granted to his brother Francis Ludlow 15 September 1664.

Admon Act Book p. c. c.

[1 George Ludlow (or Ludlowe), of the text, was a prominent and influential colonist. Grants of land to him, aggregating some 17,000 acres, are of record in the Virginia Land Registry; the first, of 500 acres, " in the upper county of New Norfolk," being dated August 21, 1638. He was long County Lieutenant of York county, and thus by title " Collonell "; Member of the Council 1642–55. There is a tradition that his brother Roger Ludlow was a fugitive in Virginia from Connecticut near the close of the 17th century.—R. A. BROCK, of Richmond, Va.

The testator was probably the Mr. George Ludlow whose name appears on the list of those who desired Oct. 19, 1630, to be made Freemen of Massachusetts. He must have returned soon after to the old world, as a petition received from him in England was acted upon by the General Court of Massachusetts, March 1, 1630–31. —EDITOR.

2 Roger Ludlow was an assistant of the Massachusetts colony, 1630–4, and was deputy governor in 1634. In 1635 he removed to Windsor, Ct., and was the first deputy governor of Connecticut colony. In 1639 he removed to Fairfield. He was a commissioner of the United Colonies in 1651, 2 and 3. He removed to Virginia subsequent to April 13, 1654, but probably about that time. A full memoir of him by Hon. Thomas Day, LL.D., is printed in Stiles's History of Ancient Windsor, pp. 687–8. Mr. Day styles him the " Father of Connecticut Jurisprudence." We have in this will, for the first time, the names of his children. His daughter Sarah, who is said to have been " distinguished for her literary acquirements and domestic virtues," married Rev. Nathaniel Brewster, of Brookhaven, Long Island, whose memoir will be found in Sibley's Harvard Graduates, i. 73.—EDITOR.

3 Thomas Bushrod was a Burgess from York county, March, 1658–9. Richard Bushrod was granted 2000 acres in Westmoreland county, Oct. 15, 1660 (Land Registry, Book No. 4, p. 450). There were probably marriages of members of the Washington family with that of Bushrod, and hence the transmission of Bushrod as a Christian name, instanced in Bushrod Washington, nephew of George Washington, and Justice of the United States Supreme Court.—R. A. BROCK.

4 The name Bernard is of early mention in the records of Virginia. Thomas Bernard was granted 189 acres of land in James City county, January 20, 1641, No. 1, p. 762; William Bernard, 1050 acres in Warwick county, December 16, 1641, No. 1, p. 761; " Collonell " William Bernard, 800 acres in Lancaster county, October 8, 1659, No. 4, p. 372. William Bernard, with title of Captain, was a Member of the Council in 1647, and with that of " Collonell," 1655–58. Captain Thomas Bernard, Burgess from Warwick county in 1644.—R. A. BROCK.

5 Major Richard Webster was a Burgess from James City county, March, 1657–8. Thomas Webster was granted 251 acres in Henrico county, October 20, 1665 (No. 5, p. 519, Land Registry). Lucy, daughter and heir of Roger Webster, dec'd, was granted 250 acres in Hampton parish, Nov 19, 1642. Head rights: Edward Spark, Stephen ——, Thomas Webster, Susan Webster, Book No. p. 857. Lucy, Judith and Jane Webster were granted 500 acres in James City county, July 20, 1646, No. 2, p. 52.—R. A. BROCK.

6 William Gooch, " Gent.," was granted 1050 acres on the south side of the Potomac river, Oct. 18, 1650 (No. 2, p. 251, Land Registry). Captain William Gooch was a Burgess from York county in 1654. Major William Gooch died October 29, 1655, aged 29 years. His tomb in the burying ground at " Temple Farm," York county (where Gov. Alexander Spotswood was also buried) bears the arms of Gooch of Norfolk county, England (of which family was Sir William Gooch, Lieutenant Governor of Virginia, 1727–40), as follows: Paly of eight, ar. and sa. a chevron of the first, between three dogs of the second, spotted of the field. *Crest.*—A greyhound passant ar. spotted sa. and collared of the last.

Jeffery Gooch was granted 500 acres in Northumberland county, January 30, 1650 (No. 2, p. 279, Land Registry). The Gooch family, descended probably from Major William Gooch or Jeffery Gooch, as above, has been most estimably represented in Virginia.—R. A. BROCK.

[7] Colonel Augustine Warner (son, it is presumed of Augustine Warner, granted 250 acres " called Pine Neck, on New Pocoson," October 12th, 1635 (No. 1, p. 298, Land Registry), born June 3, 1642; died June 19, 1681; Burgess from Gloucester county, 1658, and Member of the Council during the administration of Governor Sir William Berkeley, is buried at " Warner Hall," Gloucester county. The Lewis, Washington and other prominent families have intermarried with that of Warner, which is a favored Christian name in Virginia.

John Lewis, second son of Robert Lewis, from Brecon, Wales, of Abington, Ware parish, Gloucester county, Virginia, married Isabella Warner, "daughter of a wealthy and retired India merchant;" called his seat " Warner Hall," a spacious mansion of 26 rooms, in which was long illustrated the refined hospitality typical of the Old Dominion. This Isabella Warner was probably a daughter of the Augustine Warner, the first grantee as above.—See article, " Descendants of Robert Lewis from Wales," *Richmond Standard*, Feb. 5, 1881.—R. A. BROCK.]

JOHN CUTLER of Ipswich in the County of Suffolk, merchant, 10 November 1645, with codicil dated 6 January 1645, proved 29 January 1645. To Robert Cutler, my cousin, youngest son of my deceased uncle Samuel Cutler, one half of my manor of Blofields als Burnivalls and of all lands, tenements, hereditaments, rights, members and appurtenances thereunto belonging &c. in Trimly St Mary and Walton in the said County of Suffolk. If the said Robert die without heirs of his body lawfully begotten or, having such heirs, if the same shall die before they come to the age of one & twenty, then the said half to my cousin Martha Noore, the wife of Raphe Noore of Ipswich, merchant, sister of the said Robert (on certain conditions). The other half to the said Martha Noore. John Smithier of Ipswich, to be assistant to my executor in & about the getting in of my estate beyond the seas and elsewhere. To Elizabeth Smithier his daughter and all the rest of his daughters and to his three sons John, William and Henry and to Nicholas Kerrington, the said Mr John Smithier's wife's brother's son. The said Mr John Smithier and his wife and the longer liver of them shall dwell in my messuage or tenement wherein they now dwell in St Nicholas' Parish, Ipswich, rent free for three years. To Mr Samuel Snelling, son in law to my cousin Mr Ralph Noore, and to my cousin Martha Snelling his wife, and Mary Noore and Alice Noore her sisters and Richard Noore her brother. To my cousin Thomas Cutler Secretary to the Company of Eastland merchants, resident at Ipswich. To Elizabeth Hubbard and Mary Ward, maidservants to my cousin Mr Raphe Noore. To Mrs Ward, widow, late the wife of Mr Samuel Ward, late town Preacher of Ipswich, and to Samuel & to Mr Joseph Ward her sons. To the poor of St Nicholas, Ipswich, to the poor of the parish of Whatfield, near Hadley in Suffolk. To Mr Lawrence, common preacher or lecturer of the said town of Ipswich. Mr John Revett, merchant, to assist my executor in getting in of my estate beyond the seas. To John Cressall, to Johan Nowell. To my cousin Margaret Skinner, wife of Jonathan Skinner, clerk, and all her children now alive. Others named. George Raymond one of the witnesses. Twisse, 3.

[There were several early emigrants to New England by the name of Cutler :—1. John Cutler, who came from Sprowston in Norfolk, with his wife, seven children and one servant, and settled in Hingham, Mass., in 1637 (REG. xv. 27) ; 2. James Cutler, who settled at Watertown as early as 1634 ; 3. Dea. Robert Cutler, who was here as early as 1636. See Genealogical Record of the Cutler Families, by Rev. Abner Morse, Boston, 1867.

Mr. Samuel Ward named in the will was the author of The Life of Faith. He was a brother of Nathaniel Ward, the compiler of the Massachusetts Body of Liberties. A sketch of his life is appended to the Memoir of Rev. Nathaniel Ward by the editor of the Register. His son Joseph, also named in the will, was rector of Badingham in Suffolk.—Editor.]

Mariane Sevier of Yenstone, in the parish & peculiar of Henstridge in the County of Somerset, widow, 9 May 1607, proved 26 June 1607. To be buried in the churchyard of Henstridge. To the parish church of Henstridge ten shillings. To the poor folk of Henstridge parish ten shillings. To Deane Haskett, the daughter of Ellis Haskitt forty shillings. To Ellis Haskett's three other daughters and William Haskett his son four pounds, provided if any of them die before they come to the age of one & twenty years or be married then the money to remain to the survivors. To Margaret Sevier, daughter of Richard Sevier, a gown cloth and ten pounds; to Alce Sevier, another daughter, a gown and ten pounds. To Marie Royall of Henstridge, widow, one featherbed and three pounds. To Annis Harte twenty shillings. To Cicely Royall, daughter of Marie Royall, three pounds; to Richard & to Dorothie Royall, son & daughter of Marie Royall, twenty shillings apiece. To brother in law Reynold Sevier three pounds & to John Sevier, his son, forty shillings. To Dorothie Pennie a gown. To Marrian Harris, wife to Richard Harris, five sheep. To John Moores nine sheep. To the children of John Wollfres nine sheep. To Thomas Seavier the younger nine sheep. To the children of Gregorie Royall four pounds eight shillings and four pence, which money is in the hands of the said Gregorie, the father of the said children. To John & Dorothy Penny, my servants, ten shillings apiece. To Rose Collis, wife of John Collis, three pounds. To Marie Haskett, wife of Ellis Haskett, twenty shillings. To every of my godchildren twelve pence apiece. All the rest of my goods to Gregory Royall, whom I ordain & constitute sole executor &c. The overseers to be Ellis Haskett & Richard Chippman and I bequeath to them three shillings four pence apiece.

The witnesses were John Bryne, William Pittman, Richard Chippman, Ellis Haskett & John Royall.   Huddleston, 62.

Katherine Sampson, of the parish and peculiar jurisdiction of Hengstridge, in the Diocese of Bath & Wells, maiden, 30 April 1627, proved 14 June, 1627. To be buried in the parish church of Hengstridge. To the said church, in money, twenty shillings. To the poor of the said parish ten shillings. For the love I bear to my cousin Nicholas Locke I do forgive him all the debts that he to me doth owe &c. To my mother my best band of linen and my best apron. I forgive my cousin John Sampson, out of the bond of forty shillings which he oweth unto me, twenty shillings thereof, and the other twenty shillings of the said Bond I do give unto my cousin Susan Sampson. To my sister Joane Sampson one silver spoon. To cousin Mary Sampson, my brother William's daughter, my best gown, my best petticoat, my best hat and sixteen pounds ten shillings which is due to me upon bond from Ellis Hasket and William Haskett, his son &c. To my two sisters Jane & Edith Sampson the residue, and they to be executrices. The overseers to be Richard Sampson the younger & Thomas Morris the younger. Brother Henry Sampson oweth me twenty six pounds. Richard Eburne, vicar, was one of the witnesses.   Skinner, 63.

JOHN CARTER of the parish of St Mary Matfellon, alias Whitechapel, in the county of Middlesex, gentleman, 14 February 1691, proved 16 June 1692. To my two attorneys in Barbadoes, Mr Peter Fluellin and Capt. George Paine, twenty pounds each to buy them mourning. To my executors Mr Samuel Shepheard and Mr Samuel Perry twenty pounds each (for mourning). " Item I doe give, devise & bequeath unto my brother RoBert Skelton of New Yorke in America the full summe of five hundred pounds soe soone as Assetts shall come into my Executors hands to that value" &c. on condition that he pay to Samuel Shepheard seventy pounds that he owes to the said Shepheard. To Mr William Shawe, Mr Edwarde Shawe and Mr Francis Shawe, to each six pounds to buy mourning and to each of their wives twenty shillings to buy rings to wear for my sake. The residue to my sister Sarah Slaymaker, wife of Thomas Slaymaker, of the city of Oxford, cook. (By a codicil made the same day bequests to Mr Mark Bedford Whiteing, and his wife and two daughters, Angellick & Annett, to Alexander Staples Esq and his wife, and son Alexander and his wife, and son John and daughter Dorothy. To John Hickman, Elizabeth Hickman, Hannah Hickman and Mary Staples (gold rings). To cousin Elizabeth Carter of Barbadoes, widow and her children Thomazine Gibbs, James Carter, and her other children James, Anne, William, Richard, Jane, Dam.. aris, John & Agnes (gold rings). To cousin John How, of Barbadoes his wife Elizabeth and daughter Mary, to every of them a gold ring of the' value of ten shillings. Fane, 103.

Mem. that on or about the first day of March 1691 John Lee, heretofore of Charlestown in New England, carpenter, lying sick on board the ship Swallow &c. I desire the captain, meaning and speaking of and to Gyles Fifield, Captain of the said ship, to take care of all my concerns and get in what is due me in England or elsewhere. I give two parts of my whole estate to my two children. The other part I give to the captain and desire he would bestow something of the ship's company. Witness Geo. Robeson, Samuel Boyes. 2 June 1692 the witnesses were sworn.

11 June 1692 Emanavit Commissio Egidio Fifield fidei commissario et legatario nominat in Test Nuncupativo Johannis Lee aliquandiu de Charlestowne in Nova Anglia sed in nave Le Swallow super alto mari deceden &c.
Fane, 112.

I, William Read of New England in the parts beyond the seas, mariner, have constituted John Harlock of Ratcliff, Stepney, in the county of Middlesex, gentleman, and Elizabeth his wife my attorneys &c. On board the good ship Granado, Capt. Loader commander, on a voyage for Jamaica. 2 October 1691.

Witness Fred. Johnson, Ja^s Travers. Proved 12 September 1692.
Fane, 173.

JOHN SYMONDS of Yeldham Magna in the County of Essex, Esq. 20 March, 1691, with codicil dated 16 February 1692, proved the last of May 1693. I do confirm the jointure made to my wife (Jane) and give her my mansion house called the Poole, &c. Manors of Panfield Hall & Nichols in Panfield & Shalford, in the County of Essex, to my kinsman Mr Martin Carter and his heirs (& other lands). To my niece Elizabeth Pepys all moneys due to her by bond or otherwise by Martin Carter dec^d, father of the said Martin Carter. To my nephew Mr John Pepys, of Cambridge ; to my 'sister Thomasin Pepys; to my nephew Thomas Pepys; to my nieces Anne Whaples and Elizabeth Pepys, to my niece Ellen Bacon. To each of the children of Martin Carter decd. (except the two eldest sons) fifty pounds. To my sister Mrs Judith Burgoyne, to my nephew and godson Mark Guyon, to my niece Jane Guyon, to my nephews Roger and Lucy Burgoyne, sons of Sir John Burgoyne, Baronet. To Mr John Brooke our worthy minister. To the Society of Lincoln's Inn of which I am a member. My wife and sister Thomasine Pepys and nephew John Pepys to be executors.

(In the codicil) to my cousin Mr William Simonds of Ipswich in New England one hundred pounds. To Mr Fisk forty shillings. To my cousin John Carter and his heirs (certain lands). My nephew Thomas Pepys of Felsted. Mr Fisk my chaplain.

Sworn to &c. die Lunæ vizt Decimo die mensis Aprilis A.D. 1693.

Coker, 86.

The testimony of the witnesses shows that Mr. Symonds had been cursitor for Lincolnshire and Somersetshire.

[John Symonds was the 2d son of John and Ann (Elyott) Symonds, and was born in Yeldham Magna, Sept. 4, 1618. He was a nephew of Samuel Symonds of Ipswich, deputy governor of Massachusetts. See Appleton's Ancestry of Priscilla Baker, pp. 19–102.—EDITOR.]

JANE COAKER of Kingsbridge in the County of Devon, widow, 6 June 1651, proved 1 August 1651. To the poor of Kingsbridge twenty shillings at the day of the funeral. To son Robert Coaker forty pounds within one month after my decease, and I release him of all debts owing unto me, and ten shillings a year to be paid him by my executor so long as they shall live together. To grandson James Coaker, son of William Coaker, my son, all my right &c. in the messuage wherein I live. To grandchild Jane Ball ten pounds within two years after my decease. To son Richard Coaker five shillings, to be paid him at his return into England. To daughter-in-law Agnis Coaker thirty shillings. To daughter Agnis Bound, wife of Thomas Bound, ten pounds within a quarter of a year, and to Jane Kingston five shillings. To daughter Johane Borton (wife of Henry Borton) twenty pounds within one month after my decease and ten bushels of barley malt. To Agnes Risdon, wife of Thomas Risdon, to godchild Thomas Phillipps, to Francis Hingston & to Johane Heyman, my godchildren. To grandchild Jane Coaker forty shillings. To grandchildren Anne Davie and Elizabeth Coaker ten shillings apiece. To grand children Leonard & Francis Kent fifty shillings apiece. To grand children Richard, Henry, Robert, William, Flower and John Coaker ten shillings apiece. To grand child Henry Borton six silver spoons. To grand child Jane Coaker three pounds besides the forty shillings before bequeathed. Residue to son-in-law John Hardie, who is made sole executor. The will was proved by John Hardye.

Grey, 157.

[The foregoing will may refer to Richard Coaker who was of New England in 1640.—H. F. W.

It may not be relevant, but I offer that the following grants are of record in the Virginia Land Registry:—John Corker, 6 acres in James Island, Feb. 10, 1637, Book No. 1, p. 521 ; John Cocker, 1150 acres in Surry county, March 20, 1677, Book No. 4, p. 301.—R. A. BROCK.]

SARAH ELMES, of the parish of St. Saviour's, Southwark, in the County of Surrey, widow 25 August 1653, proved 20 April 1654. To son Anthony Elmes five pounds. To son Radolphus Elmes (now in parts beyond the seas) the sum of ten pounds if he shall be living at the time of my decease. To son Jonathan Elmes ten pounds within one month after my decease. To grand child Jonathan Elmes, son of the said Jonathan, ten pounds, and to such child as Mary, the wife of the said son Jonathan, now goeth withall ten pounds. To sonᵉ Henry Elmes ten pounds within one month. To my two grand children Curtis and Henry Elmes (minors) sons of my said son Henry, ten pounds apiece. To my two grand children John and Sarah Maries, children of my daughter Margaret Maries, of the parish of St. Saviour's, Southwark, widow, twenty pounds apiece at the age of one & twenty years or day of marriage. To my loving cousin Sarah Best twenty shillings (for a ring) and to sister Elizabeth Sturmey, twenty shillings and good friend Mʳˢ Hamond of Pudding Lane twenty shillings (for rings). Daughter Margaret Maries to be sole executrix and Mʳ John Chelsham and loving cousin Mʳ Ralph Collins overseers.

Alchin, 83.

[The testatrix of the above will was undoubtedly the mother of Rhodolphus Ellmes (see Savage), of Scituate, who came in the Planter, 1635, aged 15, and married, 1644, Catharine, daughter of John Whitcomb.

See deed of Rodolphus Emes of Scituate to John Floyd, Oct. 2, 1656, for money lent and paid for passage in Suffolk Deeds, vol. ii. p. 294.—H. F. W.]

EDWARD WINSLOW, of London, Esq., being now bound in a "Viage" to sea in the service of the Common Wealth, 18 December 1654, proved 16 October 1655 by Josias Winslow, son and executor. All my lands and stock in New England and all my possibilities and portions in future allotments and divisions I give & bequeath to Josia, my only son, and his heirs, he allowing to my wife a full third part thereof for her life. To the poor of the church of "Plimouth" in New England ten pounds. To the poor of Marshfield, where the chiefest of my estate lies, ten pounds. I give my linen which I carry with me to sea to my daughter Elizabeth; and the rest of my goods which I carry with me to sea to my son Josias, he giving to each of my brothers a suit of apparell. Son Josias to be executor and Col. Venables my overseer of my goods in the voyage and my four friends, Doctor Edmond Wilson, Master John Arthur, Master James Shirley and Master Richard Floyd, to be overseers for the rest of my personal estate in England.

The witnesses were Joⁿ Hooper, Gerard Usher servant to Hen: Colbron.

Aylett, 377.

[Edward Winslow, the third governor of Plymouth Colony, was the son of Edward and Magdalen Winslow, of Droitwich in Gloucester, England, and was born Oct. 18, 1595. (See REGISTER, xxi. 209-10, where his pedigree is given.) He was one of the Mayflower passengers. He was appointed by Cromwell one of three commissioners to superintend the expedition against the Spaniards in the West Indies, and died May 8, 1655, on the passage between Hispaniola and Jamaica. An article on his life, by G. D. Scull, Esq., was printed in the REGISTER, xxxviii. 21-6. See also REGISTER, iv. 297; xvii. 159; and xxxvii. 392.—EDITOR.]

JOHN STOUGHTON Doctor "in devinitie" & curate of the parish of Sᵗ Mary Aldermanbury, London, beginning "Laus Deo the fowerth daie of May 1639" [on which day he died], proved 20 May 1639. To my poor kindred twenty pounds to be disposed of according to the discretion of my wife Jane Stoughton, one of my executors. To the parishioners of the parish of Sᵗ Mary, Aldermanbury aforesaid five pounds, to be bestowed unto the poor of the said parish.

To my two daughters Jane & Marie five "hundreth" pounds, to say, to my eldest daughter Jane "fower hundreth marks which twoe hundred three score and six poundes thirteene shillings and fower pence, and the remainder beinge twoe C. hundreth thirtie three poundes six shillings and eight pence to my youngest daughter Marie Stoughton, to be paied them att theire age of one & twenty yeares or the day of theire marriage, which shall first happen " &c.   If both depart this life before they attain the age specified or day of marriage that then " two hundreth and fieftie poundes thereof shall come unto my wife and two hundred pounds thereof to my nexte of kynn, and twentie fiue poundes thereof to Emanuell Colledge in Cambridge and the other five and twentie poundes to Master Hartlipp a Dutchman."

To four or five persons such as my loving wife & one of my executors shall think fit twenty shillings apiece for a ring, provided Mr Janeway be one of them.   The executors to be my dear and loving wife Jane Stoughton and my loving father in law and her father John Browne of Frampton in Dorsetshire Esq. and for overseers Robert Edwards and Edmond Foord of London merchants.

The remainder to my wife Jane Stoughton.

Wit: Robert Edwards   Thomas Davies.   Harvey, 69.

[May 4, 1639, " Dr. Stoughton of Aldermanbury died." See Smyth's Obituary. —H. F. W.

The Rev. John Stoughton was a brother of Israel and Thomas Stoughton, early settlers of Dorchester, Mass. Israel was the father of Lieut.-Gov. William Stoughton. Thomas removed from Dorchester to Windsor, Conn. Rev. John Stoughton, the testator, was also the stepfather of Gen. James Cudworth, of Scituate, New England, and of the Rev. Ralph Cudworth, author of The Intellectual System of the Universe. See articles on Stoughton and Cudworth in the REGISTER, xiv. 101 ; xxi. 249.—EDITOR.]

EXCERPTS FROM THE HITCHCOCK GENEALOGY.

Compiled for the REGISTER by H. G. CLEVELAND, Esq., of Cleveland, Ohio.

LUKE[1] HITCHCOCK (brother probably to *Matthias Hitchcock*, New Haven, 1639), place and time of birth unknown, took freeman's oath in New Haven, Ct., 1644, and soon after removed to Wethersfield, Ct.; in 1659 signed an agreement to remove to Hadley, Mass. He died Nov. 1, 1659, leaving a wife Elizabeth, probably sister of William Gibbons, of Hartford, Ct., and three children, as follows :

   i.   JOHN,[2] b. ——; m. Sept. 27, 1666, Hannah Chapin (daughter of Dea. Samuel Chapin), and d. Feb. 9, 1712.

   ii. HANNAH, b. 1645; m. Oct. 2, 1661, Chiliab Smith, of Hadley, Mass.

   iii. LUKE, b. June 5, 1655; m. Feb. 14, 1676–7, Mrs. Sarah Dorchester, widow of Benjamin Dorchester and daughter of Jonathan Burt, and d. Jan. 24, 1727.

JOHN[2] HITCHCOCK, by wife Hannah Chapin, had :

   i.   HANNAH,[3] b. Sept. 10, 1668 ; m. Samuel Parsons.

   ii.   JOHN, b. April 13, 1670 ; m. Mary Ball.

   iii. SAMUEL, b. Aug. 21, 1672 ; m. Sarah Weller.

   iv.   LUKE, b. March 23, 1674–5 ; m. Elizabeth Walker.

   v.   NATHANIEL, b. Aug. 28, 1677 ; m. Abigail Lombard.

   vi.   DAVID, b. Feb. 7, 1678–9 ; m. Elizabeth Ball.

   vii. JONATHAN, b. Nov. 26, 1682 ; d. Feb. 26, 1683.

   viii. SARAH, b. Jan. 11, 1686–7 ; d. April 17, 1690.

Ensign JOHN[3] HITCHCOCK, by wife Mary Ball, daughter of Samuel and Mary Ball, of Springfield, Mass., had :

i. John,[4] b. Dec. 14, 1692 ; m. Abigail Stebbins.
ii. Mary, b. March 20, 1694–5 ; d. young.
iii. Sarah, b. Dec. 20, 1697 ; m. Samuel Gunn, Jr.
iv. Mary, b. March 20, 1699 ; m. —— Ames.
v. Abigail, b. May 4, 1703 ; m. Samuel King.
vi. Nathaniel, b. Sept. 23, 1705 ; m. Hannah Taylor.
vii. Thankful, b. Oct. 1, 1707 ; m. Jonathan Scott.
viii. Jerusha, b. Feb. 23, 1709 ; m. Daniel Warner.
ix. Margaret, b. Oct. 25, 1712 ; m. —— Cooley.
x. Samuel, b. June 9, 1717 ; m. Ruth Stebbins.
xi. Mercy, b. June 9, 1717 ; m. —— Sikes.

Samuel[4] Hitchcock, by wife Ruth Stebbins, had:

i. Ruth,[5] b. Oct. 5, 1739 ; m. —— Bush.
ii. Margaret, b. May 25, 1741 ; m. Richard Falley, of Westfield, Mass., Dec. 24, 1761. She d. Feb. 18, 1820.
iii. Lois, b. March 1, 1742–3 ; m. Oliver Chapin.
iv. Samuel, b. Dec. 16, 1744 ; m. Thankful Hawks.
v. Eunice, b. Dec. 8, 1746 ; m. —— Alexander.
vi. Naomi, b. Oct. 29, 1749 ; m. —— Parsons.
vii. Arthur, b. Sept. 15, 1751 ; m. Lucy Cooley.
viii. Editiha, b. Sept. 27, 1754 ; m. —— Flagg.
ix. Elias, b. April 19, 1757 ; m. —— Ferry.
x. Oliver, b. Feb. 18, 1760 ; m. Elizabeth Hitchcock.
xi. Heman, b. Feb. 17, 1762 ; m. —— Tolman.
xii. Gaius, b. April 30, 1765 ; m. Sarah Wells.

Margaret[5] Hitchcock (*Samuel,*[4] *John,*[3] *John,*[2] *Luke*[1]), b. Westfield, Mass., May 25, 1741 ; died in Volney (now Fulton), N. Y., Feb. 11 or 18, 1820. She married in Westfield, Mass., Dec. 24, 1761 or 1762, *Richard Falley,* Jr., who was born in the District of Maine, at George's River, Jan. 31, 1740, and died in Westfield, Mass., Sept. 3, 1808, a son of Richard and Anna (Lamb) Falley. He commanded a company at the battle of Bunker Hill, and his eldest son Frederick[6] (afterward a Major), then fourteen years old, was his drummer, and drummed all through the fight. Previously, at the age of sixteen, he became a soldier in the French and Indian war, and at the capture of Fort Edward, on the Hudson, was made prisoner by the Indians, adopted by an Indian chief, taken to Montreal, and was finally bought by a lady for sixteen gallons of rum, and by her was sent home to Westfield, Mass. He was for many years superintendent of the Armory at Springfield, Mass., and noted as a man of powerful physique and great strength. Children, all born in Westfield and Springfield, Mass., were:

i. Lovisa[6] Falley, b. Dec. 3, 1763 ; m. Medad Fowler ; d. May 20, 1807.
ii. Frederick[6] Falley, b. Jan. 2, 1765 ; d. unm. July 5, 1828, in Ohio.
iii. Margaret[6] Falley, b. Nov. 15, 1766 ; m. William Cleveland ; d. Aug. 10, 1850, at Black Rock, near Buffalo, N. Y.
iv. Richard[6] Falley, b. Sept. 15, 1768 ; m. Amanda Stanley ; d. Feb. 28, 1835, in Ohio.
v. Russell[6] Falley, b. Oct. 5, 1770 ; m. Pamelia Chapman, of Blandford, Mass. ; d. March 29, 1842, in Perrysburg, Wood Co., Ohio.
vi. Daniel[6] Falley, b. Dec. 3, 1772 ; d. young.
vii. Daniel[6] Falley (again), b. Nov. 15, 1773 ; m. Elizabeth Holland, of Chester, Mass. ; d. Fulton, N. Y., at 80.
viii. Ruth[6] Falley, b. Dec. 7, 1775 ; m. Samuel Allen ; d. 1827, in New York city.
ix. Lewis[6] Falley, b. Jan. 15, 1778 ; d. unm. 1810, Charleston, S. C.
x. Samuel[6] Falley, b. Oct. 9, 1780 ; m. Ruth Root of Montgomery, Mass. ; d. 1873, Granville, O.

xi. ALEXANDER[6] FALLEY, b. April 4, 1783. Lost—not heard from after age of 35 years.

Dea. WILLIAM[6] CLEVELAND (*Aaron,*[5] *Aaron,*[4] *Aaron,*[3] *Aaron,*[2] *Moses*[1]) was born in Norwich, Conn., Dec. 20, 1770, and died at Black Rock, near Buffalo, N. Y., August 18, 1837, at the residence of his son-in-law, Hon. Lewis Falley Allen. He learned the trade of silversmith and watchmaker, and lived some time in Salem, Mass., but finally settled in Norwich, his native place. He married in ———, Mass., 1795-6, Miss *Margaret Falley,* a granddaughter of Richard Falley, who was a native of the Isle of Guernsey, France, but kidnapped when a lad at school and brought to Nova Scotia. She was born in Westfield, Mass., Nov. 15, 1776, and died at Black Rock, near Buffalo, August 10, 1850. Children were as follows :

 i. FRANCIS,[7] b. Dec. 28, 1796, in Worthington, Mass. ; m. Harriet Stuart, a native of Winchester, Va.
 ii. WILLIAM FALLEY, b. Sept. 10, 1798, in Salem, Mass. ; d. Feb. 13, 1801.
 iii. MARGARET, b. Jan. 19, 1801, in Salem ; m. her cousin, Hon. Lewis Falley Allen, now of Buffalo.
 iv. SUSAN, b. Jan. 6, 1803, in Salem ; d. in Norwich, Conn., Feb. 6, 1805.
 v. RICHARD FALLEY (Rev.), b. June 19, 1804, in Norwich, Conn. ; m. Anne Neale, of Baltimore, Md.
 vi. SUSAN SOPHIA, b. May 7, 1809, in Norwich, Conn. ; m. George D. Fuller. She d. May 30, 1838, leaving a son and a daughter.

Rev. RICHARD FALLEY[7] CLEVELAND (*William,*[6] *Aaron,*[5] *Aaron,*[4] *Aaron,*[3] *Aaron,*[2] *Moses*[1]), and in the HITCHCOCK line (*Margaret*[6] *Falley, Margaret,*[5] *Samuel,*[4] *John,*[3] *John,*[2] *Luke*[1]), was born in Norwich, Conn., June 19, 1804; graduated at Yale and at Princeton, N. J. He married at Baltimore, Md., Sept. 10, 1829, Miss Anne Neale, daughter of Abner and Barbara (Real) Neale, and became the pastor of a church in Windham, Conn., subsequently in Caldwell, Essex Co., N. Y., Fayetteville, Onondaga Co., N. Y., and Holland Patent, Oneida Co., N. Y., in which latter place he died, Oct. 1, 1853. She survived her husband many years, and passed away July 19, 1882, aged 78, at the old home there. Children were nine, as follows:

 i. ANNE NEALE,[8] b. Baltimore, Md., July 9, 1830; m. Rev. Eurotas P. Hastings.
 ii. WILLIAM NEALE (Rev.), b. Windham, Conn., April 7, 1832; m. Mrs. Anne Thomas.
 iii. MARY ALLEN, b. Portsmouth, Va., Nov. 16, 1833 ; m. William E. Hoyt.
 iv. RICHARD CECIL, b. Caldwell, N. J., July 31, 1835 ; lost at sea Oct. 22, 1872.
 v. STEPHEN GROVER (Hon.), b. Caldwell, N. J., March 18, 1837 ; elected governor of New York, 1882, and president of the United States, 1884 ; m. at the Executive mansion in Washington, D. C., June 2, 1886, Frances, dau. of the late Oscar Folsom, Esq.,* of Buffalo, N. Y.
 vi. MARGARET LOUISA, b. Caldwell, N. J., Oct. 28, 1838 ; m. Norval B. Bacon.
 vii. LEWIS FREDERICK, b. Fayetteville, N. Y., May 2, 1841 ; lost at sea, Oct. 22, 1872.
 viii. SUSAN SOPHIA, b. Fayetteville, N. Y., Sept. 2, 1843 ; m. Hon. Lucien T. Yeomans.
 ix. ROSE ELIZABETH, b. Fayetteville, N. Y., June 13, 1846.

---

* Oscar Folsom, Esq., was a descendant in the eighth generation from John[1] Folsom (a native of Hingham, in Norfolk, England, who came to New England and settled at Hingham and afterwards removed to Exeter) ; through John,[2] Abraham,[3] Daniel,[4] Abraham,[5] Asa,[6] and John B.[7] his father.—See *Folsom Genealogy,* REGISTER, xxx. 207-31.

THE NAME " COLUMBIA."

By ALBERT H. HOYT, A.M., of Boston.

IN a learned and instructive paper by George H. Moore, LL.D., recently read before the Massachusetts Historical Society, he gives the history of the origin of this poetical name for America, and makes the following inquiry: " When and where did the name *Columbia* first appear in the land to which it justly belongs?" In his answer to this question, Dr. Moore remarks as follows: " Until an earlier date is found for it, I am disposed to claim the honor of its introduction for . . . , a negro woman, a native of Africa, and a slave at the time, the property of a citizen of Boston." Phillis, a servant of Mr. John Wheatley, of whom mention is here made, while temporarily staying in Providence, R. I., and under date of October 26, 1775, addressed a very creditable tribute in verse to General Washington, which he acknowledged in a note dated from Cambridge, February 2, 1776, and which was first published in the Pennsylvania Magazine for April, of the same year. Her poem contains the following lines :—

> " One century scarce perform'd its destined round,
> When Gallic powers Columbia's fury found ;
> And so may you, whoever dares disgrace
> The land of freedom's heaven-defended race !
> Fix'd are the eyes of nations on the scales,
> For in their hopes Columbia's arm prevails."

As Dr. Moore anticipates that a date earlier than 1775 may be found, and invites further contributions, the following notes, made by the present writer while pursuing investigations on another subject, are submitted. They give instances of the use of *Columbia,* as a poetical equivalent for America, at dates prior to the date of Phillis's poem. The first instance noted occurs in the volume of elegiac and complimentary poems,[*] in English, Latin and Greek, composed mostly by graduates of Harvard College in 1761, at the suggestion of Governor Bernard, in commemoration of George II. (whose death occurred in the preceding year), and in congratulation of George III. on his accession, and nuptials with the Princess Charlotte. This elegantly printed volume—perhaps the most meritorious literary work produced in America in the eighteenth century—contains thirty-one poetical compositions, of which the one numbered xxix. has the following lines :

> " Hence, jarring discord, tumults, carnage, wars ;
> Embattl'd nations ! cease a while to deal
> Destruction ; Peace ! on balmy wings, descend ;
> Let Hymen and the Paphian Goddess hold
> Imperial sway, soft'ning each heart to love.
> Behold, Britannia ! in thy favour'd Isle ;
> At distance, thou, Columbia ! view thy Prince,
> For ancestors renown'd, for virtues more ;
> At whose sole nod, grim tyranny aghast,
> With grudging strides, hies swift from British climes ;
> While liberty undaunted rears her head."

* **Pietas et Gratulatio Collegii Cantabrigiensis apud Novanglos. Bostoni-Massachusett-ensium. 1761. Typis J. Green & J. Russell. 4to. pp. 106. For the history of this volume, see Duyckinck's Cyclop. Am. Lit., vol. i. pp. 11—14; and Winsor's Bibliographical Contributions, No. 4.**

The names of the writers are not given in the volume, nor have they in every case been definitely ascertained, but the weight of the evidence now at hand seems to indicate that the author of the poem from which the above quotation is made, was Thomas Oliver (H. C. 1753), Lieutenant Governor of Massachusetts in 1774, and subsequently a loyalist refugee.

The next noticed instance of the use of the name *Columbia* occurs in a poem published in the Massachusetts Gazette of April 26, 1764, and which was inspired by the destruction by fire of Harvard Hall and the college library, on January 24, of that year. This poem is here given at length, in the hope that some reader may be able to supply the name of the author.

THE LAMENTATION OF HARVARD.

Alas! how am I chang'd! Revolving Suns
Through many a Period joyfully have smil'd,
On my once happy Seat; where uncontroll'd
I sat, the Mistress of this western World,
And sent my learned Youth throughout the Land,
To guide with happy Skill, both Church and State.
Around my sacred, venerable *Elm*
My frequent Buildings rose; whose ample Domes
Inclos'd my fav'rite Sons, an happy Tribe
On either Side th' *Atlantic* far renown'd.
My Fame throughout the LAND of LIBERTY
Was circulated wide: Nor did I want
Instructors of my own, to lead the Youth
Their younger Brethren, through the lovely Fields
Of *Science*, humane and divine; whose Paths
Delightsome, Hand in Hand they trod apace
With eager Steps, till at the sacred Shrine
Of fair *Philosophy* arriv'd, they paid
Their humblest Adoration at her Feet.
  But now, how chang'd the Scene! Behold the Walls,
Not long ago the fam'd Repository
Of solid Learning, levell'd to the Dust.
Ye Flames, more merciless than the fell Hand
Of all-devouring Time; more savage far
Than Earthquake's horrid Shocks; why did ye not
Recoil with Shame, when near the sacred Volumes,
Arrang'd with Care, your pointed Spires approach'd?
Why could ye not, the fam'd *Museum* spare,
Unrivall'd in *Columbia*, where my Sons
Beheld, unveil'd by WINTHROP's artful Hand,
The Face of Nature, beautiful and fair?
Ah fatal Night! Why didst thou not remain
Perpetual, and with dusky Pinions, veil
These awful Ruins, Beauty laid in Dust?
  Where are my Comforters? Where the whole Band
Of laurell'd Bards, once nourish'd at my Breast,
Who not long since condol'd BRITANNIA's Loss,
When GEORGE the great resign'd his earthly Crown?
Where is my *Ch—ch*,[*] my *L—w—l*,[†] *H—p—r*,[‡] *D—n*,[§]
The *Popes* and *Priors* of our western World?
Alas their Harps are on the Willows hung!
Sated with Fame, and all the World's Applause,
Their tuneful Pens be dumb; not one of all
Can " pay the grateful Tribute of a Song."[‖]
But should our Land again (which Heav'n forbid)
Be call'd to mourn our happy Sov'reign's *Death*,

---

[*] Benjamin Church (H. C. 1754).   [†] John Lowell (H. C. 1760).
[‡] William Hooper (H. C. 1760).   [§] Samuel Deane (H. C. 1760).
[‖] See *Pietas et Gratulatio*, No. VII.

Should *golden Prizes*, once more be propos'd ;
How would *their* Fancies take poetic Fire ;
How would *they* mount the *Pegasæan* Steed,
And soar aloft, to gain immortal Fame !
AVRI SACRA FAMES ! — — — —
  What base Ingratitude then, to neglect
Their *Alma Mater* in her mourning Weeds !
  Ye sleeping Bards light up your wonted Fires,
Let not the schoolBoy's *Hexametric* toil *
Remain the only lasting Monument
Of my sad Overthrow : But come my Bards
Approach my awful Ruins, stand around
Your once lov'd Nursery, behold my Woe,
Gather my Ashes, and let that reward
Your *pious* Care to mitigate my Grief,
And to perpetuate in elegiac Verse
The sad Remembrance of that fatal Night,
When Science fell a Victim to the Flames.

In the Boston Gazette of February 13, 1775, there is a poem from the pen of the ablest female writer in America of that time—Mrs. Mercy Warren. As it appears in the *Gazette*, the poem is prefaced with this statement : " The following Piece was wrote more than twelve Months past ; and is now published as a Prophecy hastening fast to a Completion." This poem, with many alterations, is included in Mrs. Warren's collected Poems, where it is entitled a " Poetical Reverie." Referring to the westward course of *Empire* the author says :

" She, o'er the vast Atlantic surges rides,
Visits *Columbia's* distant fertile Plains,
Where LIBERTY, a happy Goddess, reigns ;
Where no proud Despot rules with lawless sway,
Nor Orphan's spoils become the Minion's prey."

Colonel David Humphreys, one of the distinguished wits and poets of Connecticut in the Revolutionary era, like Trumbull, Dwight, Hopkins, Barlow and Alsop, wrote many inspiring and patriotic verses. Humphreys entered the military service at the outbreak of the war, and in his " Sonnet to my Friends at Yale College on my leaving them to join the Army," gave the key-note of his devotion to the " cause of liberty."

" While dear Columbia calls no danger awes,
Though certain death to threaten'd chains be join'd."

On December 19, 1776, the Independent Chronicle contained a song by the gifted New Hampshire poet, Jonathan M. Sewall, Esq., in which we find these lines :

" Michael ! go forth ! (the Godhead cry'd,)
Wave thy dread Ensign o'er the Tide,
And edge *Columbia's* Sword ! "

In conclusion, it may be added that the newspapers of Massachusetts and New Hampshire, from 1772 to 1778, and other publications of that period, show that the writers of verse frequently used the term " Columba " instead of *Columbia*. Perhaps the first instance will be found in the " Retrospect " by James Allen, a Boston poet and friend of General Warren. This was evidently a composition of no little merit, and extended to several " Books," but it was never published as a whole. It would be interesting to know what has become of it. Extracts from the " Retrospect " were

---

* See Mass. Gazette, Feb. 2, 1764.

published by Allen's friends in 1772, with his poem on the Boston Massacre, and a defensive "commentary" thereon. The poem on the Massacre was prepared at the request of General Warren to accompany his commemorative oration; but although the poem had been accepted at first, it was finally suppressed by the committee, of which Samuel Adams was chairman, on the suspicion that Allen was not really in sympathy with the popular party.

SOLDIERS IN KING PHILIP'S WAR.

Communicated by the Rev. GEORGE M. BODGE, A.M., of East Boston, Mass.

[Continued from page 192.]

No. XV.

THE GARRISON AT MARLBOROUGH.

OKKOKONIMESIT was what Major Daniel Gookin called, and Ognonikongquamesit was the name by which Mr. Eliot knew, the "Praying Indian Village," situated within the limits of what became the town of Marlborough. The first English settlers went from the parent plantation of Sudbury. The Court's grant to the Indians through Mr. Eliot, in 1654, being prior to that made to the English, the latter found to their disappointment that this Indian reserve, right in the midst of their own grant, must be respected by them if they wished to retain their own rights; for it is to the credit of the Massachusetts Council, that its members were, almost without exception, in favor of upright and humane dealing with the friendly Indians. These Indians above were a branch of the Wamesit tribe, it is said, and had submitted to the Massachusetts Colony as early as 1643, and had received assurance of its protection of their rights. In 1674 this Indian town contained ten families, and about fifty souls. They were self-supporting, peaceable, and were becoming industrious and thrifty, but were evidently regarded with contempt and distrust by many of the neighboring English, who grudged them the possession of their grant of six thousand acres, including some of the best land in the township.

The Indian name of the locality was something like Whipsuppenick, but this became corrupted with the English settlers to "Whipsufferage."

The town was incorporated as Marlborough in 1660. The first actual English settler was John Howe, who settled in 1657–8; and at the division of land in 1660, there were thirty-eight who were then, or soon after, residents.

Rev. Wm. Brimsmead was settled as their minister, and the new plantation flourished fairly until the breaking out of Philip's War. At this time, being a frontier town, it was exposed to attacks from all directions, and being situated upon the road to Connecticut, it had been regarded by the General Court as a point of military advantage and a fort had been built, and a small garrison was kept there. Upon the outbreak of Philip's War, the retreat of Philip and his followers to the Nipmucks, and the consequent disturbance of the neighboring tribes, the people of Marlborough, under the lead of their minister, met early in October, and adopted measures of defence in addition to that afforded by the garrison which was under the command of Lieut. John Ruddock, of whose conduct of their military affairs, his townsmen, it seems, were jealous; and the people, as was the case generally, were averse to the presence of the soldiers in their houses. After hostilities began, the Praying Indians, who had lived so long beside the settlers, became objects of suspicion and, in many instances, of unreasoning persecutions, in spite of the constant remonstrances of their friends Rev. John Eliot, Major Gookin and the magistrates and leading men generally. Philip used all his powers of persuasion and intimidation to draw these Praying or Christian Indians to his side; but in spite of his arts, and the bitter popular prejudices of the English, and although forced to suffer great injustice and hardships, they were nearly all faithful to their engagements with the Colonists. The "new praying villages," which under Mr. Eliot's efforts were established, in the way of missionary stations, in the vicinity of several neighboring tribes, were broken up by the "rumors of war," and the real converts came with their families into the older villages under the protection of the Colony. The Indian village at Marlborough was increased to about forty men besides women and children, and under the direction of the English they built a fort of considerable strength for themselves, and were furnished with ammunition and some with arms by the government, and others had suitable arms of their own. There is no doubt that these Indians were well disposed and faithful with very few exceptions, and might have been of very great help in all the subsequent movements of the war, if the headstrong prejudices of the people had not frightened and antagonized them in manifold ways. The hostile Indians sought to fix the stigma of their own depredations, often committed for that very purpose, upon the Christian Indians; and the attack upon Lancaster, Aug. 22, 1675, in which seven persons were killed, was attributed to them by "Indian David," who was tied up to a tree and forced to implicate somebody, himself having fallen under suspicion of shooting the Irish shepherd boy at Marlborough just before this. Those whom David particularly accused were the Hassanemesit Indians, now gathered into the Indian fort at Marlborough; and the popular clamor was so loud against them that Lieut. John Ruddock, in command of the garrison at Marlborough, demanded the arms and ammunition of the whole body of Indians to be given up. This demand was quietly acceded to, although there was no evidence against the Indians, and the act was entirely without the sanction of the Court; but the prejudices of the people were so strong and their clamors so persistent, that Capt. Mosely, then in the vicinity with his company of sixty men, was appealed to, and nothing loth, under cover of his authority, gave the Indian fort up to the plunder and abuse of his soldiery. Fifteen of the Indians were arrested and sent down to Boston, tied neck to neck like galley-slaves, and the integrity of the Council was sorely taxed to keep the rage of the populace from executing these poor creatures without trial; but the law did prevail, and after a long trial and imprisonment at Boston of the eleven (out of the fifteen) who were accused, all were fully acquitted except their first accuser, David, who was condemned for the suspicion as to the shepherd boy and also for his false accusations, and also the Indian Joseph Spoonant, tried by another jury; these two were condemned to be sold out of the country as slaves. This persecution seems to have broken up the Indian settlement at Marlborough.

In the meantime the garrison at Marlborough became a rendezvous for the troops going and coming to and from the western towns, and while it was occupied by soldiers the people felt some degree of security in their homes; but when the companies were drawn off they felt the danger of their exposed condition, and after the disasters of Captains Beers and Lothrop, and the experiences of Springfield, Deerfield, &c., they resolved upon measures for better security. Upon October 1st they were called together, and took action as shown in the following paper preserved in the Massachusetts Archives, Vol. 67, p. 277.

Marlborough the : 1 : of October : 1675.

At a meeting of the inhabetants in order to take care for the safty of our town these following proposals were Agreed upon And volentaryly chosen unto that in case of asalt these places heare After mentioned should be defended by the persons that are expressed by name that is in

William Kerly's hous. of the town soulders : 2 : or soulders allowed to the town

John How senior	John ffay	Thomas Marten
Thomas How	Joseph Wait	Thomas King
John Wetherbe	John Mainard	John Brigham

In Serjant Woods his hous of the town Souldears–2—6 of the Newtons, or solders Allowed to the town

John Woods Junior	Isack How
James Woods	John Bellows
Isack Woods	Samuel Bellows

At Joseph Rices

Samuel Stow	John Barret	Samuel Rice

In John Johnson's hous : 9 : and of the town Souldears 3 :

In Deacon Wards hous of the town soulders–3—or soulders allowed the towne his own family 3

Abraham How	Gershom Yeams
William Taylor	Samuel Ware.

In Abraham Williams his hous of the town soulders–3—or soulders allowed the towne

Richard Barnes   John Rediat Junior
John Rideat Senior   Samuel Brigham
               John Rooks.

In Thomas Rices hous of the town soulders—2—or soulders allowed to the town

John Brown   John Bowser   Peter Rice
Increas Ward Thomas Rice Junior And three men of Peter Bents

To the Leftenant him self and the magazeen : 13 : of the soulders that weare allowed to the town

to John Johnson: 3 :   to Deacon Ward 3
to Serjant Woods }   to Abraham Williams 3
And William Kerly } 4   to Thomas Rice 3

All these men to be maintained in their respective percels by the familyes In the several fortifications wheare they are placed.

Also that the Ammunition of the town should be proportioned to the soulders of the town in these fortifications; this Above written is that which Acted and Assented unto by the persons whos names are subscribed.

Mr Brensmead   Thomas Rice   Josias How
Deacon Ward   John Johnson   John Mainard
Thomas King   Samuel Rice   John Rediat
Solomon Johnson   John Bellows   John ffay
Abraham How   Nathaniel Johnson Moses Newton
John How senior   John Woods Junior Richard Barnes
John Woods senior Joseph Newton   James Taylor
Richard Newton   Thomas Barnes   William Kerly
Abraham Williams

This Above writen was the Act of the town Agreeing with the Act of the Comettee of melecti as Attest   William Kerly—clarke

That this action was somewhat in opposition to the wishes of the military officer of the garrison, Lieut. John Rudduck, is proved by his letter below, from Vol. 68, p. 4 :

Letter of Lieut. John Rudduck to the Council.

For the honored Councell

Honored Sirs.   After my humble Duty p^rsented these are to informe the honored Councill that Capt. Pool have sent to me four times for things spesefied in the note inclosed which I had none of but bread and liquors wch he have had but the other things I have none of and now the Rum is all gon he have had seven gallons of Rum all Redy and the souldirs and posts passinge to and agen and the army have had the Rest allsoe our men at the garison want shoos and stockins and shurts very much they complaine to me dayly to goe home and suply themselves but I dare not let them goe becaus sum have gon on that acount and Com not againe namly John Boudage of Roxbury and John Orres a smeth of Boston and on Samuell Castin is Run away I sent to Mr Davison to aquaint athority with it but I heare noe more of it heare is but littell of anythinge Left in the Magaseen and if it please the hono^rd Councell to give me order to remove what is left to my hous it would be less trouble to me and if anything be sent I may have it heare at my own hous I have set the garison soulders to fortify about my hous now they have fortified the Magaseen all Ready by my order and soe I intend to imply them for the defense of the Town   I humbly pray this honored Councell to send a suply for the soulders heare and at quo-

boag or derection how they shall be suplyed.   Capt. Wayt comanded me
to returne James Cheavers for absenting himself after he had prest him
whom I have sent to make his own defence.   Your humble Servant,
Marlborough Octob: y[e] 1st, 1675.   JOHN RUDDUCK.

Sum of the gareson souldirs Informed me when I was geting to seale
my letter that the Constable had been this morning and warned the soulders to com to me for theire vectls for the Town would diet them no longer
I desire derection in this case and allsoe that he had warnd them that did
quarter them to quarter them no more   JOHN RUDDUCK.

I am of Nesessity constrained to provid victles for them till I heare
from the Councell how they will order it.

Capt. Poole's requisition, enclosed in the above letter.

To the Comisary at Malbery   Sur we want drawers and wastcots and I
am forsed to let men goe home to fetch clothing becas they want and have
no supply   Sur I pray send sum soft tobacow and bred by thos persons
I pray send me the runlit of lickours for the army will drene us doutles
not els but rest yours
date 30 : 7[th] : '75   JONATHAN POOLE Capt.

Another letter from him is in Mass. Archives, Vol. 67, p. 279 :

Second Letter of Lieut. John Rudduck to the Council.

For the honoured Governor & Council.

Honored Sir   After my humble Duty p[r]sented these are to signify to
this honored Councel that upon hearinge the Councell was Informed the
Constable had forbed the men that were quartered in the town and sent
them to me for quarter sum cam to me this morninge and threatened me
if the men were taken away I should Answer it and many threateninge
words and many were gathered together about it   I understand great
Complaints are like to be made against me to the Councell but I hope the
honoured Councell will have Charity for me till I can com to Answer for
myself : in Regard to the charge of the town and of the Country.   I cannot with convenience come down the charge of the mageseen beinge committed to me troubles me very much   they are offended that I bringe the
souldiers to meetinge with me and say I must have soe many men to gard
me   it well known to many that it have bene my practise ever since I
have had a family I use to have them to meetinge with me   I thinke it my
duty having a garison of Souldiers to have them to meeting with mee
allsoe I seet sum of them the on half to gard the Town in the forenoon and
the other in the Afternoon and them that do not ward I have to meeting
with me : when we met together to apoynt houses to be ffortified I would
have had houses apoynted and men apoynted to these houses but the In-
sign would not yeald to that but would have the town caled together to see
what houses they were willinge to goe to and to fortify soe the designe was
that my house should not be ffortified nor have any gard if danger be they
themselves will have the Inhabitants to gard theire houses but if I have
any I must have of the soulders and be at Charges to maintaine them myself   I have propounded to them that the Inhabitants be equally devided
to the houses that are to be garded and the garison soulders divided likewise but they would not yeld to that soe unless the honoured Councell be
plesed to determin this thinge it will not be determined   sum have man-
edged theire maters soe that I have Leetle or noe comand of the Inhabitants of the town   the sum of all is there are that cannot swolow that pill

that I should have so much trust and pour commeted to me soe I desire to leve myself with God and this honored Councell   The pore leve themselves with God   Your humble Seruant
   Marlborough this 4 Octo 1675   JOHN RUDDUCK.

When the army returned from the Narraganset campaign, and most of the troops were discharged at Boston, Feb. 5, 1675–6, we learn from Gen. Gookin's "History of the Christian Indians" that Capt. Wadsworth with his company was left at Marlborough "to strengthen that frontier." He remained there until early in March, when the newly levied army was gathered there under the command of Major Thomas Savage, and was organized under the immediate personal inspection of Maj. Gen. Daniel Denison.   It was at this time that Capt. Mosely's haughty and unrebuked insubordination, backed up by the lawless, Indian-hating element of the army, occurred and gave the commanders so much difficulty; for when Job Kattenanit, a friendly Indian, whose fidelity had been proved by successful and faithful report of the condition of the hostile Indians, to whom he with James Quannapohit had been sent as a spy, and in order to keep faith with the English, had left his wife and children in the hands of the hostiles and returned to our army, bringing information which, if it had been heeded, would have saved great destruction and suffering,—when this man had been given a permit to go and bring in his family, who were to meet him on a certain day, Capt. Mosely raised such a hue and cry, that the commanders were obliged to submit, and sent after him at once.

The course of events in the town, including the attack, is shown in the following letters :

Capt. Brocklebank's Letter to the Council.

Much Honnored sirs.   Malborough 28 of : 1 : 1676
   After the duty I owe unto your Honnor this may let you understand that the assault the enemy made upon the towne of Malborough upon sabbath day did much dammage as the inhabbitants say, to the burning of 16 dwelling houses besides about 13 barnes and seemingly did indeaver to draw out the men out of the garisons but we not knowing ther numbers and our charge of the Countries ammunition and provission durst not goe out then on Sabbath day night there came about 20 men from Sudbury and we out of the severall garison drew out about twenty more and in the night they went out to see if they could discover the enemy and give theme some checke in ther proceeding who found them laid by ther fires and fired on them and they run away at present but the number being few and not knowing the number of the enemie but aprehending by ther noyse and fireing at them they indeavored to compass them in the returne home without any losse of any man or wound from the enemie only one of my men by the breaking of his gun his hand is sorely shattered which for want of helpe here I have sent to Charlestowne or elsewhere in the bay where your honnors may thinke best for his helpe: we have great cause to acknowledge the goodnesse of God toward us for his gracious preservation of us the enemye is gone at the p'sent as we aprehend by the scouts that went

out yesterday the which we may expect eare long will fall on us with greater strength and rage by reason of the breakfast that they had on Monday morning   the scouts found only one indian dead   thus in briefe your honnors will understand how it is with us: from him who is your honnors servant   SAMUELL BROCKLEBANKE Capt

Mass. Archives, Vol. 68, p. 180.

General Daniel Denison's Letter.

Sʳ.

Yesterday I received a letter from Capt. Brocklebanck at Marlborough signifying his desire of being dismissed with his company the reasons he alleadges are   1. their necessities & wants having beene in the countryes service ever since the first of January at Narriganset & within one weeke after their return were sent out againe having neither time nor money (save a fortnights paye upon their march) to recruite themselves   2. he saith they doe little where they are: & he understands the are called off by the Council.   I shall make bould to request the like favor in the behalfe of those (at least) some of those troopers & dragoons of Essex that went out last, intended for Hadley but by reason of the disaster at Groton diverted to Concord &c. to beate of & prosecute the enemy in those parts and I directed orders to Major Willard, that with those he first tooke up wᵗʰ him & then sent, together with the garrisons at Marlborough Lancaster & Chelmsford (if need more) in all above 200 men he might not only defend the townes but might prosecute the enemy to his being with 2 dayes march, but I heare of no such attempt nor indeed of any considerable improvement of them that hath beene, or is like to be.   I am therefore sollicitous for many of them that out of a respect to myself went willingly, hoping of a speedy returne to their families and occasions some of them more than ordinary great and urgent   I intreate therefore they may be pʳsently considered & eased to attend the seed time &c. and if there be necessity that others may be sent in their roomes, who may with far less detriment be spared.   The stockade from Watertowne to Wamesit, might better be from Watertowne to Sudbury river 9 miles taking in more country, & that river being as good a stop as the stockade the greatest objection is Merrimack river though broad yet I understand is fordable in 20 places betweene Wamesit & Haveril, & cannot be safe without guards wᶜʰ must be kept upon it, for hast I Jumble many things, wᶜʰ be pleased to pardon   The Lord Look in mercy upon his poore distressed people upon your selves in particular so prayes   your humble Servant
Ips.   March 27: 1676   DANIEL DENISON.

The inclosed are certificates of delinquents on the last press in Norfolk & of the troopers that should have gone with Capt Whipple to Hadley

Mass. Archives, Vol. 68, p. 179.

Left Jacob.   The Council having lately received Information of Gods further frowne upon us in taking in depriving the Country both of yʳ Captaine and Capt Wadsworth wᵗʰ severall others by permitting the enemy to destroy them yesterday so yᵗ yʳ Capt. Brocklebanke's chardge is devolved on yʳself   The Councel judge meet to leave the souldiers under his charge to yoʳ care and chardge, and doe order you to take the care and chardge of the sayd Company that you be vigilant & diligent in that place & as seasonably & speedily as you cann to give Information to yᵉ Councel of the state, numbers & condition of y^r souldiers in that Garrison under y^r command desiring God's Gracious & blessing to be wth you.　Remayne

yor loving freinds

EDW. RAWSON, *Secretary*

Boston 22 Aprill 1676　　　　　　　　　　by Order of the Council

Postscript.　you are alike ordered to take care & command of the place (ie) Marlborrow to preserve it what in you lyes.

EDW. RAWSON, *Secretary*

Mass. Archives, Vol. 68, p. 222.　　　　　　　　like order

Soldiers Credited with Military Service at the Garrison at Marlborough

September 21st 1675				
Darby Morris	01 13 04	John Nash	00 18 00
John Dunster	02 00 00	Jonathan Jackson	01 05 08
William Turner	01 19 04	Obadiah Searle	06 08 00
Thomas Owen	04 13 04	Daniel Davison,	
Joseph Barber	02 14 00	Commissary,	05 14 00
October 19th 1675		Jonathan Orris	03 12 00
James Cheevers	02 14 00	Richard Roberts	02 16 06
Thomas Turner	02 12 00	William Turner	04 16 00
William Blackwell	03 02 06	**February 29, 1675–6**	
Henry Gibbs	03 07 00	Robert Rownden	07 04 00
Richard Roberts	04 04 00	Thomas Owen	02 18 02
November 20 1675		William Farman	03 17 00
Timothy Laskin	04 13 04	Gustin John	01 19 04
William Ferman	02 08 00	**March 24^{tb} 1675–6**	
Samuel French	03 00 00	Richard Young	00 13 00
Richard Young	03 12 00	**April 24th 1676**	
Daniel Roff	03 02 00	Thomas Hopkins	00 09 00
Jacob Adams	04 13 04	Benjamin Parmater	02 03 08
Jonathan Jackson	04 13 04	**June 24th 1676**	
Daniel Weight	04 13 04	Daniel Weight	02 09 08
John Figg	01 10 00	Thomas Dennis	01 05 06
John Broughton	02 12 02	**July 24th 1676**	
January 25th 1675–6		Timothy Laskin	02 09 08
John Baker	03 08 06	John Burges	03 00 10
Richard Young	03 06 00	**September 23^d 1676**	
Henry Gibbs	02 19 00	Morgan Jones	08 02 00
		Joseph Davis	06 00 00

Most of the inhabitants deserted their farms after the destruction of the town on March 26th, 1676, and with the exception of a few families who remained for a time in the garrisoned houses, the families came to the towns nearer Boston, and returned only after the war was over.　Further correspondence of Lieut. Richard Jacob and others, relating to the Sudbury fight and the disposal of the garrison, will be given in the next chapter.

NOTES AND QUERIES.

NOTES.

HARVARD.—We have received from William Rendle, F.R.C.S., of London, Eng., a communication, in which he takes substantially the ground which the editor of this periodical did in the January number, that Harvard was probably residing in London with his mother, the widow Elletson, when he was admitted to Emmanuel College, in 1627, and that the entry "Midlsex" in the *Recepta* may have been intended for his residence at the time. In our April number we quoted an English correspondent of the New York *Nation*, who asserts that this is not the correct explanation of the entry in the *Recepta*, as such entries always denote the birth place and not the residence. The same correspondent of the *Nation*, in the issue of May 20, furnishes examples to prove his position, and till instances are produced in which the residence was entered in such cases, we shall rely on his authority.

Mr. Rendle calls our attention to his own discovery of the home and birth place of John Harvard. We take pleasure in bringing this subject to the attention of our readers. Mr. Rendle, in his pamphlet on John Harvard, referred to in the REGISTER for January, 1886, page 36, describes certain "Token-books" preserved in the Vestry of St. Savior's, which contain lists of streets, courts and alleys, with the names of the inhabitants in whose families were individuals over 16 years old, to whom leaden token had been distributed implying that such persons would at their peril neglect to receive the sacrament. From these books Mr. Rendle obtains facts that convince him that the house of Robert Harvard, the father of John Harvard, was opposite the Boar's Head Tavern and Alley in Southwark. A map, showing the locality of Robert Harvard's house and other places of interest in the vicinity, is given in the pamphlet, also facsimiles of entries in the Token-books.

SMOKES.—*Taxing Fire-places.*—While consulting the public records of Washington, Conn., in April, I opened a package of tax-lists, extending from 1790 to 1812. (A few are missing.) A curious item in all the lists was "Smokes." And these articles were of four grades, first rate, second rate, third and fourth. It was common for men to have more than one. Thus, in 1797, John Munson had three fourth rate smokes. What might this thing be? Chimneys? There was objection. Antiquaries and local historians of western Connecticut had no knowledge of the matter. One suggested smoke-houses for treating hams; another, coal-pits; another, tar-kilns; and so on.

The 13th of May I was examining the records of Simsbury. The ancient tax-rolls of that place cleared up the mystery. "Smokes" were *fire-places.* The tax on a house was determined by the number and the quality of its fire-places. One might almost think that the list of 1795 was made expressly to interpret this obscure term to future centuries; for pages 2—10 have "fireplaces" at 15s. 0d.; fire-places at 11s. 3d.; fireplaces at 7s. 6d.; fireplaces at 3s. 9d.; while pages 1 and 11 have, instead, "Smoaks," 15s.; do. 11s. 3d.; do. 7s. 6d.; do. 3s. 9d.

A few lists define the several qualities. Thus, that of West Simsbury (now Canton) for 1797, has—"Houses, Fire-places at 2 Dolls 50 cts pr fire-place; Houses, Fire-places depreciated 1 Qr. at 1 Doll. 88 cts pr do.; Houses, Fire-places depreciated 1 half at 1 Doll 25 cts. do.; Houses, Fire-places depr'd 3 Qr. at 63 cts. pr. do."

The "smokes" of the first class, according to the records of the assessors, were scarce. The last-named list enumerates of the first rate, none; second rate, 21; third rate, 188; fourth rate, 145.

This disinclination to find fire-places which were unimpaired probably led to the reduction of the number of grades to three. Thus the Simsbury list for 1808 has but three classes,—fire-places at $3.75, at $2.50, and at $1.25.

The list of 1801, on some pages, specifies 'houses with fire-places' of the first, second, third and fourth rates; and on others, as page 7, "houses" of the first, second, third and fourth rates; but of course the *rate* in either case was determined by grade of the "smoke."   MYRON A. MUNSON.
New Haven, Ct.

CUSHING. (*Com. by Gen. Lewis Merrill, U.S.A., Philadelphia, Pa.*)—The following records concerning a well-known Massachusetts family are found here. As of possible present, at least of prospective value, I have copied them for the REGISTER. The " Old Swedes " Church (Gloria Dei) is one of the oldest churches in America.

Inscriptions on tombstones in the church yard of " Old Swedes," Church, Philadelphia, Pa.

" In memory of | Captain Caleb Cushing, | who departed this life | fourth day of December 1820 | aged 47 years 6 months & 9 days | also | In memory of | the following children of | Caleb and Margaret Cushing. | Eliza Cushing who departed this life | on the 31st day of July 1795 | aged 6 months and 9 days. | Mary Cushing who departed this life | on the 28th day of March 1802 | aged 4 months and 18 days. | Caleb Cushing who departed this life | on the 8th day of October 1804 | aged 13 months. | Also Captain John Cushing | who died on Sunday evening | the 19th day of May 1833, | aged 36 years 7 months and 19 days. | Also Margaret Cushing | Died July 18th 1847 | aged 69 years."

On another stone :

" In | memory of | Eliza Cushing | daughter of | Caleb and Margaret Cushing | who departed this life | July 31st 1795 | aged 6 years and 9 months. | Also Mary Cushing | departed this life March 28 1801 | aged 4 months and 18 days | also Caleb Cushing | departed this life October 22^{d} 1804 | aged 15 months and 12 days.—Also of Geo^{e} L Eyre Jr. | son of George L and Ann C Eyre who departed this life May 6th 1827 | aged 2 years 1 month & 19 days."

In the record of burials kept by the pastor of the " Old Swedes Church," is found the following :

" Aug 1, 1795 Elizah, 6 months old, died of hives. Par. Caleb and Marget Cushing. She is daughter of John Hoover whose wife Latitia Their right is come by the Morton* family."

Under heading " members children " :

" 30 March 1802. Mary daughter of Caleb and Margret Cushing aged 4 months and 18 days."

" 11 October 1804. Caleb son of Caleb and ———— Cushing, b. 8 July 1803."

Under heading " Adult members " :

" 6 December 1820. Caleb Cushing ag. 48. Disease consumption and probably other internal. He had been unwell for 3 years, but confined for —— months. He was a native of Massachusetts, got married by me in 1793 to a d. of John Hoover."

" 1827, 7 May. George son of George L and Ann C. Eyre aged two years. Note. The mother is a daughter of the late Capt. Cushing and his relict Margret."

" 1829, 9 Oct. Ann, wife of George Eyre in S. W. ag. 28 & 2 mos. Phrenitis. Her father was Capt. Cushing."

The record of the marriages at " Old Swedes " Church is fully published by the state of Pennsylvania, and doubtless shows the marriages of such of the above as were married.

———

LONGFELLOW AND TOMPSON.—In Sibley's Harvard Graduates, vol. iii. page 309, it is stated that Abigail, daughter of Rev. Edward Tompson (H. U. 1684) " married Judge Longfellow of Gorham, Maine." This is an error. She married Stephen Longfellow, who was the grandfather of Judge Longfellow.

In vol. 86, page 159, of Deeds recorded in Essex County, Mass., is recorded a deed from the children of Edward Tompson (H. U. 1684), of which the following is an abstract :

Edward Tompson of Gloucester, William Tompson of Newbury, John Tompson of New London, Joseph Tompson, Stephen Longfellow and wife Abigail Longfellow, of Newbury, all in New England ; " all of us being children and heirs of Mr Edward Tompson late of Marshfield, deceased ; " quitclaimed to William Sawyer and Daniel Morse of Newbury, yeomen, one freehold lot lying in the township of Newbury, above Artichoke river, on the South side of the road leading to Bradford, by land of Bartlett Rawlins, &c. Date of deed April 28, 1726.

———

* The Morton family is an old and well known Philadelphia family descended from one of the original Swedish settlers, whose coming antedated that of the Penn emigrants many years.

Acknowledged by Doct: Edward Tompson and Rev: William Tompson, at Gloucester May 24, 1726; Stephen Longfellow and wife Abigail Longfellow and Joseph Tompson, before J. Dummer, Oct: 31, 1726; John Tompson before J. Gerrish Jan: 13, 1728-9.   C. W.
Cambridge, Mass.

GERMAN IMMIGRANTS, 1752.—The following item, taken from "The Boston Weekly News-Letter," Thursday, September 21, 1752, refers to the German settlement at Quincy, Mass.   S. A. G.
"Last Tuesday arrived here a Ship from Holland, in which came Mr. Crellius, with near 300 Germans, Men, Women and Children, some of whom are to settle at Germantown, and the others in the Eastern Parts of this Province.—'Tis said that near 50 children have been born on board the Vessel during their Passage."

ELLIS—MASON.—Among the few County records left in the C. H. of Stafford Co., Va., by the soldiers during the war between the States, there is a power of attorney dated July 29, 1704, from "Francis Ellis, mariner of Salem, in New England," given to "my loving friend and *cousin* George Mason of Stafford County, Virginia, Gentleman," to dispose of all lands of said Ellis in said County. In Bishop Meade's account of the Ellis family of Va. (Families and Churches of Va., ii. 460) no mention is made of the Masons as connected, nor are these Ellises recorded as living in Stafford Co.   HORACE EDWIN HAYDEN.

QUERIES.

BRADLEY.—The records of Tolland, Conn., show that George Bradley married May 7, 1717, Hannah Brown, and afterwards had a wife Mercy. His children were (1) George, born 1718; (2) Hannah, born 1718, married 1743, Robert Styles; (3) Mary, born 1721; (4) Jane, born 1723; (5) Jabez, born 1727, married 1749, Hannah King, and had four daughters and son Capt. Jabez, who married Hannah Lathrop, 1771; (6) Henry, born 1729, married Silence ——; (7) Josiah, born 1730; (8) Jonah, born 1733; (9) George, born 1742; (10) Elijah, born 1744; (11) Jonah, born 1747; (12) Mercy, born 1750; (13) Tryphena, born 1752; (14) Sarah, born 1755; (15) Eunice, born 1757. From these children sprang a numerous and distinguished posterity. I will be much obliged for assistance in ascertaining the ancestry of this George Bradley. Where are the records of the town out of which Tolland was formed?   WM. H. UPTON.
Walla Walla, W. T.

JONES.—I wish to learn the ancestry of Nathan Jones, born April 21, 1753, but whose parentage and place of birth are unknown. He lived in Princeton, Mass., and the births of his children are recorded there. An elderly lady informs me that Nathan was one of fifteen children, some of whose names were Ebenezer, Farwell, Thankful and Timothy. Ebenezer and Timothy at one time did business in Boston. The former died at Charleston, S. C., and the latter in the West Indies. Thankful married, and is said to have died in Bolton, Mass.   F. JONES, M.D.
New Ipswich, N. H.

THE EAGLE AS A SYMBOL OF AMERICA.—Who first suggested the *eagle* as a symbol of English America? Was it Chief Justice Samuel Sewall? In his "Phænomena quædam Apocalyptica" (Boston, 1697), p. 8, he remarks, in commenting on Rev. vi. 8:
"The Four Quarters of the World seem to be represented by Four Animals; Asia, by the Lion; Africa, by the Calf; Europe, by the Man, and America, by the Eagle. [See Rev. iv. 6 & 7.] .... America is fitly represented by an Eagle, which Royal Bird is very frequent there, and was once the Standard of the *Mexican* Empire."   A. H. HOYT.

MUNSON.—April 3, 1640, Bro. Mounson was appointed by New Haven to view the grounds of difference between Mr. Malbon and Thomas Moulender. There is scarcely a particle of doubt that the same Thomas Munson had removed to New Haven the preceding year, especially as his name is sixth among the *autograph* signers of the "Fundamental Agreement," which was adopted in Mr. Newman's barn, June 4, 1639. Previously, according to the earliest records of Hartford, he had owned four pieces of real estate in that place.

Queries.—1. Is there positive evidence that Thomas Munson was a soldier in the Pequot war? 2. Do the antiquarians of eastern Massachusetts find any trace of his earlier residence in either of the ancient towns of that region? 3. Is there in anybody's possession any clue to his parentage or his transatlantic home?

He became very prominent in public affairs, and died in 1685, at the age of 73.

New Haven, Conn. MYRON A. MUNSON.

WOOD.—In the genealogy of the descendants of Robert Williams of Roxbury (REG. xxxvi. 277), the compiler states that Mary, the daughter of Robert,[1] "married Nicholas Wood." Savage (iv. 628) says that Nicholas Wood (of Braintree, Dorchester and Medfield) "m. Mary, d. of Robert Williams of Roxbury, as Mr. Clapp assures me, had Mary and Sarah, tw. b. 25 Dec. 1642."

But Savage also says (iv. 566) that Robert Williams, Roxbury, 1637, came with wife "and children Samuel, Mary, if not more, as that child was five years old." Mary Williams therefore was only ten years old when Nicholas Wood's twin daughters were born. In Rev. John Eliot's Church Records we find (Report Record Commissioners, 1880, "Roxbury, p. 114"), "1642 25, 10, Mary Wood, Sarah Wood, twins: daughters of —— Wood of the church of Brantree who maryed oʳ bro. Pig's daughter and she lying in childbed in this towne they were baptized here by comunion of churches."

Thomas Pig, Pigge or Pidge, was in Roxbury 1634, and his daughter Mary was mentioned in his will, proved Sept. 12, 1644 (REG. iii. 78). Mary, wife of Nicholas Wood (whose youngest child Eleazer was born 1662) died Feb. 19, 1663, and her husband married, Nov. 16, 1665, Hannah, widow of William Page of Watertown. It is possible that Mary Pigge may have died and Mary Williams have taken her place some time between 1642 and the birth of "Jonathan Wood son of Nicholas and Mary Jan. 3 1651." [Medfield Record.] Is there any proof of this marriage?

E. F. WARE.

GARDNER.—"T. C. A." states (REG. xxv. 48) that the first Thomas Gardner (of Cape Ann) died 1635, thus making him the father of the Thomas Gardner who with his wife Damaris died in 1674. Other authorities make no mention of the date 1635, but make these two Thomas Gardners one and the same person. What is the authority for "T. C. A."'s statement? E. F. WARE.

KING.—The Hon. William Rufus King, vice-president of the United States, was born in Sampson Co., N. C., in 1786, and died at his home near Cahawba, Dallas Co., Alabama, in 1853. Pickett's "History of Alabama," in a biographical sketch written during Mr. King's life-time, states that he was the son of William King, a planter in independent circumstances, whose ancestors came from the North of Ireland, and were among the early settlers on the James River, in the Colony of Virginia.

Beyond this incomplete account of Mr. King's family I have been unable to learn anything, and shall feel greatly obliged for any further particulars relating to the early King settlers of Virginia. RUFUS KING.

Yonkers, N. Y.

LOYALISTS.—Can any reader of the REGISTER tell anything about the Assembly of Associated Loyalists supposed to have been held at Newport, R. I., in the spring of 1779, and who issued in that year the "Declaration and Address of His Majesty's Loyal Associated Refugees assembled at Newport, Rhode Island"?

New York City. HAMILTON B. TOMPKINS.

SHEPARD—GLEASON—FITCH.—Noah Shepard, son of Isaac and Elizabeth [Fuller] Shepard of Norton, Mass., born Feb. 22, 1717, married 1st, Margaret, daughter of John and Lydia [Hyde] Stone, born Oct. 12, 1718, and had *Benoni*, born Dec. 10, 1739, died at Tolland, Ct., Jan. 16, 1808, a. 68—*Noah*, born at Weston, Mass., Sept. 8, 1742—*Lydia*, born March 8, 1744.

Mrs. Margaret [Stone] Shepard died March 1, 1746, and Noah Shepard married March 9, 1747, Abigail Gleason, by whom he had *Margaret*, born Feb. 6, 1748—*Mary*, born April 4, 1749—*Jacob*, born Oct. 4, 1750, and married at Enfield, Conn., Aug. 3, 1775, Harriet Fairman, and resided at Somers, Conn.—*Abigail*, born May 18, 1752—*Mehitable*, born Oct. 5, 1753, married at Enfield, Conn., Sept. 5, 1874, Benjamin Meacham—*Eunice*, born Oct. 8, 1755—probably *Isaac*, who married at Somers, Conn., April 26, 1781, Elizabeth Brace, and died at Somers, Conn., Jan. 26, 1805, a. 49—and perhaps others. This Abigail [Gleason] Shepard died at Somers, Conn., Feb. 3, 1819, a. 91. Whose daughter was she? Noah Shepard was the direct ancestor of *Burritt Shepard*, U.S.N., of New York city, and *Fitch Shepard*, *Pres.* of the *American Bank-Note Co.*, whose father, *Noah Shepard*, was born at Somers, Conn., and married Irene, daughter of Ebenezer and Lydia [Johnson] Fitch, of Wallingford, Conn. Wanted, the parentage of *Abigail Gleason* and *Ebenezer Fitch*. The latter may have been a son of Ebenezer Fitch, of Windsor, Ct.

649 *Jersey Ave., Jersey City, N. J.*   E. N. SHEPPARD.

DIARIES OF THE REV. THOMAS PRINCE.—When Dr. Wisner prepared his Historical Discourses on the Old South Church, he had before him the manuscript diaries of the Rev. Thomas Prince, kept during the period of his pastorate. These diaries cannot now be found in any of our historical collections. Information is desired concerning them, if they are still in existence. Address   JOHN WARD DEAN.

TERRY.—Capt. Samuel Terry, of Enfield, Mass. (now Conn.), married in Wethersfield, Conn., Jan. 4, 1697-8, Martha, widow of Benjamin Crane, Jr. Who was she? Address   STEPHEN TERRY.
Hartford, Conn.

STEVENS.—Lydia Stevens, born in 1746, who became the wife of Hon. Jacob Abbott of Brunswick, Me., and grandmother of the authors Jacob Abbott and John Stevens Cabot Abbott, was daughter of John and Lydia Stevens, presumed to be the same who were members of the South Church, Andover, Mass. Who were their parents?   L.
Portland, Me.

LATHAM.—Can any one inform me who were the parents of "Deliverance," the wife of James Latham, son of Robert and father of Thomas and Joseph Latham?
Nevada, Iowa.   R. H. MITCHELL.

REPLIES.

JOHN WING.—I have to-day first noticed the note on John Wing in the REGISTER for April, 1885. I find in Steven's "History of the Scottish Church, Rotterdam," in my possession, the following facts noted about the man, which I send, if they may be of any service.

He was "a pious man and an edifying preacher, was first of Sandwich [Eng.], but had latterly been chaplain to the merchant adventurers of England resident at Hamburg. He exerted himself much for the good of his people here till he was removed to the Hague in 1627." [P. 302.]

This "here" was Flushing, where, 19 June, 1620, Mr. Wing was chosen as pastor of the "renewed English Church." [*Ibid.*]

He went to the Hague—the Scotch Presbyterian Church—11 May, 1627; where [p. 311] he died in office after two years service—which would be in the summer of 1629.

The following publications of his are noted here and in Watt, viz. :

1. The Crowne Conjugall : in two Sermons on Prov. xii. 4. Middleburg, 1620, 4° pp. 146.

2. Abel's Offeringe : a Sermon preached at Hamburgh in Nov. 1617, and now published at the instant entreaty of a godly Christian. By John Wing (then) Pastor to the English Church there. Flushing, 1621, 4° pp. 71.

3. Jacobs Staffe to beare up the Faithfull, and to beate doune the Profane. Formerly preached at Hamburgh by John Wing, late Pastor to the English Church

there, as his farewell to the famous fellowship of Merchant Adventurers of Engglish resident in that City. And now published and dedicated to the honour and use of that worthy Society there, or wheresoever being. Flushing, 1621, 4° pp. 216.

4. The Best Merchandize: or certain Sermons on Prov. iii: 14, 15. Flushing, 1622.

HENRY M. DEXTER.

UPHAM (xl. 80).—With a view to eventually finding the ancestry of John Upham, who came with the Hull Colony to Weymouth in 1635, it is desirable to record the following notes in the REGISTER.

In Helbridge pedigree, of East Coker, Somerset, occurs: "Richard Helmbridge, married Elizabeth, d. of Vpham." This apparently about 1560.

In Warham pedigree of Compton, Devon, and Osmington, Dorset, occurs: "Edw: Warham of Osmington in Com. Dorset, married Phillipa, da. of Upham of —— in Com. Som'set." This about 1569.

(Similar notes in same connection in "Notes and Queries," January, 1885, REGISTER.)

FRANK KIDDER UPHAM.
Fort Custer, Montana.

HISTORICAL INTELLIGENCE.

GUIDE TO ENGLISH AND FOREIGN HERALDRY.—A book entitled "A Guide to Printed Books and Manuscripts relating to English and Foreign Heraldry and Genealogy, being a Classified Catalogue of Works of those branches of Literature," has been prepared by George Gatfield, 111 Gloucester Road, Regent's Park, London, and will be put to press as soon as 200 subscribers have been obtained. It will make a volume of nearly 600 pages, and will comprise about 12000 titles. It will be issued in two sizes, namely, 8vo. at one guinea, and 4to. or large paper (of which only fifty copies will be printed) at two guineas. Orders may be sent to Mr. Gatfield, at the above address, or to Alfred Russell Smith, publisher, 36 Soho Square, London.

HEREFORDSHIRE PEDIGREES.—The Rev. F. W. Weaver, M.A., member of the Harleian Society, and editor of the Visitations of Somerset in 1531, 1573, which we commended to our readers in our issue of October last, is preparing for publication the Visitation of Herefordshire of 1569, the first taken. It will be fully annotated. None of the Heralds' Visitations of this county have yet been printed, and we are pleased to learn that this present Visitation is to be given to the public under the editorship of one so well qualified for the work. The issue will be limited to 250 copies, the price of which will be fifteen shillings, post free. Intending subscribers should send their names to the Rev. F. W. Weaver, Milton Vicarage, Evercreech, Bath, England.

RECORDS OF BRAINTREE, MASS.—The records of marriages, births and deaths, and also the proceedings at the town meetings and other records of the town clerk of Braintree, from 1640 to 1793, are printed and will soon be ready to issue. They make a handsome octavo volume of nearly 1000 pages. The records themselves make about 900 pages, and the indexes, which are very thorough, fill the rest. The limits of ancient Braintree contained the present towns of Braintree, Quincy, Randolph and Holbrook, and these four towns unite to pay the expense of printing this volume. All these towns have an interest in these records to the year 1792, when Quincy was taken from the parent town. The next year, 1793, Randolph was incorporated, and the committees of the several towns in charge of this work have decided to include that year's records. The work is printed under the superintendence of the efficient town clerk of Braintree, Samuel A. Bates, Esq., whose familiarity with the history of that town and his well known accuracy ensure a thorough reliable transcript of the records. He has taken particular pains with the indexes.

RECORDS OF DEDHAM, MASS.—The records of marriages, births and deaths of this town are also in press. The two towns, Braintree and Dedham, are hives which from an early date have sent out swarms of people to settle other parts of New England. Their descendants are found in every part of the union. These printed records will therefore be prized by hosts of people who have never visited the towns. The first two volumes of the vital statistics of Dedham, extending from the settlement of the town in 1635 to the year 1845, will be printed. For the first 150 years the records are remarkably full. The work will make an octavo volume of about 350 pages, which will contain a good classified index. The printing is under the charge of Don Gleason Hill, Esq., the town clerk, who is determined to use the utmost care in copying the records and reading the proof. The book will probably be completed in the early fall. The price at which it will be sold is not fixed, but it will probably be between three and four dollars.

GENEALOGICAL GLEANERS.—Under this heading, F. H. Hosford, city editor of the *Detroit Free Press*, publishes in that newspaper, Sunday, Feb. 21, 1886, an interesting article on the devotees of family history in that city, and the manner in which they proceed to collect data. He names among those compiling genealogies, Dr. E. R. Ellis, who has in press a volume of about 800 pages on the descendants of Richard Ellis, of Ashfield, Mass.; James E. Scripps, who has issued a privately printed volume on the Scripps family, and Theodore P. Hall, of the Board of Trade, who is said to have a complete line of his descent, paternal and maternal, in eight lines. Mr. Hall intended to have had printed in book form at his own expense the complete records of the old St. Anne's Church. The work was to have been compiled by his niece, Mrs. Caroline Watson Hamlin, author of "Legends of Detroit," but her death put a stop to the undertaking. The work, however, may one day be issued.

"The students of genealogy," says Mr. Hosford, "are ordinarily persons who find a keen enjoyment in developing facts concerning ancestry which were supposed to be forever lost. They find in this study great pleasure. These genealogists do not seek to prove themselves descended from European nobility, but trace back their origin for love of the investigation, and are proud if they find their ancestry, though humble, has been respectable."

VIRGINIA NEWSPAPERS AND POSTAGE, 1607–1886.—R. A. Brock, Esq., of Richmond, Va., contributes under this title to the *Richmond Dispatch*, May 23, 1886, in reply to an inquiry by a correspondent of that newspaper, an account of the earliest Virginia newspapers, and a history of the changes in postage to the present time. The first newspaper published in Virginia was the *Virginia Gazette*, issued weekly by William Parks, proprietor. The first number appeared July 1, 1736, price 15s. per annum. Mr. Parks died in 1750, and some months after his death the paper was discontinued. It was revived by William Hunter in 1751, No. 1 appearing in February. Mr. Hunter is said to have died in 1761, but the paper was enlarged to demy size and published at 12s. 6d. by Joseph Boyle. After his death it was carried on successively by John Dixon, William Hunter, Alexander Purdie & Co. and Purdy & Dixon, who published it till the commencement of the revolutionary war. Mr. Brock's history of the postage laws under the colony, state and nation is interesting. The fluctuations in the rates of postage, even under the United States government, have been great.

WESTON.—Joseph Weston[4] was born in Concord, Mass., in 1732. He emigrated in 1772 with his family, consisting of his wife, seven sons and two daughters, to the District of Maine, and located on the Kennebec river at what is now Skowhegan. His wife was the daughter Aaron Farnsworth, of Groton, Mass. Their sixth child, the late Deacon Benjamin Weston,[5] of Madison, Me., purchased land for a farm on which he settled in 1786. It is located on the east side of the Kennebec river, about two miles above Indian Old Point (the scene of the massacre of Father Rale in 1724), and less than that distance above the present thriving manufacturing village of Madison. Here he always resided—he died in 1851, aged eighty-six years. His wife was Anne, daughter of Levi and Mary (Chase) Powers, of Canaan, now Skowhegan, Me. They had eleven children; their descendants have become very numerous, and are settled in New England and the western states and in California.

Preparations are now in progress for the observance of the Centennial Anniversary of the settlement of Dea. Weston on his farm at Madison, by holding a Family

Reunion at the old homestead there in September of this year ; also to celebrate the ninetieth birthday of Mr. Nathan Weston, the present owner and occupant of the place, who is the only surviving child of Dea. Benj. and Anne Weston.

A Genealogy of the family will be published soon after the Reunion, which will also include full records of all the descendants of Joseph,[4] father of Benjamin.[5]

A. C. P.

TOWN HISTORIES IN PREPARATION—Persons having facts or documents relating to any of these towns are advised to send them at once to the person engaged in writing the history of that town.

Hull, Mass.—The history of Nantasket—Hull from 1621—with all the inscriptions now left in the cemetery ; genealogies of the old settlers and others, old houses, public houses, births, deaths, marriages, &c. It is now in manuscript, and will make an 8vo. book of about 400 pages. The author is desirous of obtaining a publisher for it on some terms at the subscription of $3 a copy ; or he would dispose of the MSS.—he correcting proofs, &c., and furnishing some views. Apply to J. W. Dean, librarian N. E. H. Genealogical Society, 18 Somerset Street, or C. J. F. Binney, Binney Street, Roxbury District, Boston, Mass.

GENEALOGIES IN PREPARATION.—Persons of the several names are advised to furnish the compilers of these genealogies with records of their own families and other information which they think may be useful. We would suggest that all facts of interest illustrating family history or character be communicated, especially service under the U. S. government, the holding of other offices, graduation from colleges or professional schools, occupation, with places and dates of births, marriages, residence and death. When there are more than one christian name they should all be given in full if possible. No initials should be used when the full names are known.

Binney. By Charles J. F. Binney.—This book is now being printed by Joel Munsell's Sons, Albany, N. Y. The edition will be limited to 300 copies, at the subscription price of $4 and the postage, about 20 cents, if by mail. There will be some illustrations. A few more subscribers are desired to help pay the cost of publication, notice of which may be sent to Messrs. Munsell's Sons, Albany, N. Y., C. J. F. Binney, Roxbury District, Boston, Mass., or to J. W. Dean, librarian of this society, 18 Somerset Street, Boston, who has a few copies of the nearly exhausted edition of the Prentice–Prentiss Family by the same author, for sale at the same price.

Carter. By Mrs. C. W. Carter, of Leominster, Mass.

Goodwin.—The undersigned is collecting material for a history of the descendants of Ozias Goodwin, a resident of Hartford, Conn., in 1639. All persons having any information, records, or papers of any kind concerning the family, are requested to communicate with Frank F. Starr, Middletown, Ct.

Guild, Guile or Gile.—By Charles Burleigh, of Portland, Me. He is a descendant of the Guile Family of N. H., and is now engaged in the preparation of a second edition of the Guild Family. It is intended to embrace persons of the name of Guild, Gild, Guile or Gile ; and all such are requested to correspond with him in regard to information concerning them. Blanks will be furnished upon application.

Lee. By William Lee, M.D., 2111 Pennsylvania Avenue, Washington, D. C.— This work, which will be entitled, " Genealogical History and Biographical Sketches of the Descendants of John Lee of Agawam (Ipswich), Massachusetts, in 1634, including Notes on Collateral Branches," is ready for the press to the year 1877. It only waits the assurance of sufficient money to defray the expense of publication. Members of the family are invited to send facts to the compiler, particularly births, marriages and deaths in the past nine years. The book will be handsomely printed. Subscription prices, on extra paper, bound in muslin, $5 ; on ordinary paper, unbound, $3.

Paca. By John S. Hughes, 53 St. Paul Street, Baltimore, Md.—Mr. Hughes has nearly completed a genealogy of this family, of which Gov. Paca, the signer of the Declaration of Independence, was a member.

SOCIETIES AND THEIR PROCEEDINGS.

New-England Historic Genealogical Society.

Boston, Massachusetts, Wednesday, Feb. 3, 1886.—A stated meeting was held at 3 o'clock this afternoon, the president, the Hon. Marshall P. Wilder, Ph.D., LL.D., in the chair.

The Rev. Edmund F. Slafter, the corresponding secretary, announced some important donations.

William B. Trask and John Ward Dean were appointed a committee to prepare resolutions on the death of Frederic Kidder.

S. Brainard Pratt, of Boston, read a paper on "The Bible in New England."

Resolutions were passed approving the plan of B. F. Stevens, of London, for printing and rendering accessible the vast collection of manuscripts in the archives of England, France, Holland and Spain, relating to this country, covering a period from 1772 to 1784; and Abner C. Goodell, Jr., Albert H. Hoyt, Rev. Edmund F. Slafter, Hon. Charles L. Flint and John Ward Dean, were appointed a committee to take such measures as they deem expedient to forward this undertaking.

The corresponding secretary reported letters accepting resident membership to which they had been elected, from Hon. Lyman D. Stevens, W. Hapgood, Nathan Allen, LL.D., Benjamin C. Hardwick and the Rev. B. M. Fullerton.

The Rev. Increase N. Tarbox, D.D., the historiographer, reported memorial sketches of six deceased members—Ashbel Woodward, M.D., Ariel Low, Nahum Capen, LL.D., Francis W. Bacon, Edmund B. Dearborn and Henry P. Kidder.

John Ward Dean, the librarian, reported as donations in January, 18 volumes and 34 pamphlets.

March 3.—A stated meeting was held this afternoon, President Wilder in the chair.

William B. Trask reported resolutions on the death of Frederic Kidder, and Hon. Nathaniel F. Safford reported resolutions on his bequest to the society of $2500 in stock of the Cabot Manufacturing Company as a fund for the purchase of books. Both series of resolutions were adopted.

The corresponding secretary announced donations. The Rev. A. P. Marvin, of Lancaster, read a paper on "The Puritans of Massachusetts Bay."

The corresponding secretary reported the acceptance of Hezekiah S. Sheldon as a resident member.

The librarian reported as donations in February, 61 volumes and 36 pamphlets.

The historiographer reported a memorial sketch of William E. Johnston, a deceased member.

New Hampshire Historical Society.

Concord, June 9, 1886.—The sixty-fourth annual meeting was held in the society's building, President Bell in the chair.

The reports of officers were presented, by which it appeared that the funds of the society amount to $8,739.24; and the volumes in the library number 10,385.

Various gifts were received and acknowledged; among which were the correspondence of the late Dr. John Farmer and a series of biographical sketches in MS., composed by the late Gov. William Plumer.

A resolution of approval of the proposal of Mr. B. F. Stevens, of London, to copy for publication the manuscripts in the archives of Europe relating to the American Revolution, and recommending that the same be undertaken by the government of the United States, was adopted.

The following is the list of officers chosen for the coming year.

President.—Charles H. Bell.
Vice-Presidents.—J. E. Sargent and John M. Shirley.
Recording Secretary.—Amos Hadley.
Corresponding Secretary.—John J. Bell.
Treasurer.—William P. Fiske.

Librarian.—Samuel C. Eastman.
Necrologist.—Irvine A. Watson.
Library Committee.—Amos Hadley, Edward H. Spalding, J. E. Pecker.
Standing Committee.—Joseph B. Walker, Sylvester Dana, J. C. A. Hill.

The annual address was delivered by the Hon. Amos Hadley, upon the subject of "New Hampshire in the historical Van and Brunt," and was a very able and scholarly production.

It was voted to hold the annual Field Day of the Society at Charlestown " No. 4," at such time as the president should fix.

OLD COLONY HISTORICAL SOCIETY.

Taunton, Mass., Tuesday, Jan. 19, 1886.—The annual meeting was held in the City Hall this evening, the Rev. S. Hopkins Emery presiding.

The Rev. Mr. Emery delivered an address in which he sketched the history of the society since its incorporation thirty-two years previous, and reviewed the doings of the year. The address is published in the *Bristol County Republican*, Jan. 22.

Rev. William L. Chaffin, of North Easton, read a paper on " The North Taunton Purchase."

A memorial of the late Hon. John Daggett, president of the society, prepared by the historiographer, Judge Fuller, detained by sickness in his family, was read by James H. Dean.

E. C. Arnold, the librarian, reported that over 50 volumes and pamphlets had been received the past year as donations.

The annual election of officers took place with the following result :

President.—Rev. S. Hopkins Emery of Taunton.
Vice-Presidents.—Hon. Edmund H. Bennett of Boston, Rev. William L. Chaffin of Easton.
Corresponding and Recording Secretary.—Hon. Charles A. Reed of Taunton.
Librarian.—E. C. Arnold, Esq., of Taunton.
Treasurer.—Dr. E. U. Jones of Taunton.
Historiographer.—Hon. William E. Fuller of Taunton.
Directors.—Capt. J. W. D. Hall of Taunton, Edgar H. Reed, Esq., of Taunton, Gen. E. W. Peirce of Freetown, James H. Dean, Esq., of Taunton, Hon. John S. Brayton of Fall River, Timothy Gordon, Esq., of Taunton.

Resolutions on the death of the late President Daggett, prepared by his successor, the Rev. Mr. Emery, were adopted.

April.—Rev. Mr. Emery, the president, writes that a meeting was held this month, when " the Rev. C. A. Snow, of Taunton, read a paper on the early meeting-houses of the Baptist Churches in this part of the Old Colony, and Capt. J. W. D. Hall read an article prepared by Elisha C. Leonard, Esq., of New Bedford, a supplement to a former elaborate paper on the Leonard family.

" The prospect is good for the purchase of one of the finest stone buildings in Taunton, as near fire-proof as anything can be, to be the property of the society, in which to store its treasures for all future time."

RHODE ISLAND HISTORICAL SOCIETY.

Providence, Tuesday, Jan. 12, 1886.—The annual meeting was this evening held at the society's Cabinet in Waterman Street, the president, Prof. William Gammell, LL.D., in the chair.

Mr. Richmond P. Everett, the treasurer, made his report. The annual receipts were $888.41; expenditures, $888.40. The life-membership fund amounted to $1292.40, and the publication fund was $166.39.

Hon. Amos Perry, the secretary, made a report of papers which had been promised.

Mr. Isaac H. Southwick reported for the committee on building and grounds, that the annual expenditure had been $42.65.

President Gammell then delivered his annual address, which is printed in full in the Providence *Evening Bulletin*, Jan. 13, 1886.

The election of officers then took place with the following result :

President.—William Gammell.
Vice-Presidents.—Francis Brinley, Charles W. Parsons.
Secretary.—Amos Perry.
Treasurer.—Richmond P. Everett.

Standing Committees.—On Nominations—Albert V. Jencks, William Staples, W. Maxwell Greene. On Lectures—Amos Perry, William Gammell, B. B. Hammond. On Building and Grounds—Isaac H. Southwick, Henry J. Steere, Royal C. Taft. On the Library—Charles W. Parsons, William B. Weeden, Stephen H. Arnold. On Publications—George M. Carpenter, Prof. E. B. Andrews, W. F. B. Jackson. On Genealogical Researches—Henry E. Turner, Horatio Rogers, John O. Austin. Audit Committee—John P. Walker, Lewis J. Chace, Edwin Barrows.

Procurators.—George C. Mason, Newport; Erastus Richardson, Woonsocket; Charles H. Fisher, Scituate; Emery H. Porter, Pawtucket; David S. Baker, North Kingstown; George H. Olney, Hopkinton; James N. Arnold, Hamilton; Lewis H. Meadow, Warren.

It was voted that five hundred copies of the Proceedings be printed, and that the papers of President Gammell on the "Revocation of the Edict of Nantes," and Esther Benson Carpenter on "The Huguenots of Rhode Island," be included, if the committee on publication so decide.

CONNECTICUT HISTORICAL SOCIETY.

Hartford, Monday, May 24, 1886.—The annual meeting was held this evening, and was well attended.

The report of the secretary showed that there had been nine regular meetings during the year, with an average attendance of ten members. Nine resident and two corresponding members have been elected, and there have been two deaths. The accessions have been 97 bound volumes, 28 manuscripts and 426 pamphlets. The use of the library has been double that of last year, and the interest in the society's meetings shows a marked increase. The officers were elected as follows:

President.—Dr. J. Hammond Trumbull.

Vice-Presidents.—The Hon. Henry Barnard, for Hartford County; Prof. Franklin B. Dexter of Yale College, for New Haven County; Judge J. P. C. Mather of New London, for New London County; Col. L. N. Middlebrook of Bridgeport, for Fairfield County; the Hon. J. W. Stedman, for Windham County; the Hon. Robbins Battell of Norfolk, for Litchfield County; Judge James Phelps of Essex, for Middlesex County, and Judge Dwight Loomis of Rockville, for Tolland County.

Treasurer.—J. F. Morris.

Recording Secretary.—Frank B. Gay.

Corresponding Secretary.—Charles J. Hoadly.

Committee on Membership.—Charles J. Hoadly, Sherman W. Adams, F. F. Starr, Rowland Swift, J. F. Morris, Stephen Terry, J. H. Trumbull.

Committee on Library.—Charles J. Hoadly, J. H. Trumbull, Samuel Hart.

Committee on Publications.—The Rev. Dr. George Leon Walker, the Hon. J. W. Stedman, Charles Hopkins Clark.

Mr. F. B. Gay was reëlected librarian. It was voted to have the next regular meeting on the first Tuesday of October.

A request was received to send to the Springfield quarter millennial celebration on the 25th, the shirt of Col. Ledyard to be exhibited. This peculiarly valuable historic relic has never been taken from its case save on the one occasion when Dr. Trumbull personally took it to Groton.

CHICAGO HISTORICAL SOCIETY.

Chicago, Ill., Jan. 19, 1886.—A quarterly meeting was held in the society's Hall, the Hon. E. B. Washburne, the president, in the chair.

Mr. E. G. Mason read a paper "On the March of the Spaniards across Illinois," which was listened to with great interest. By vote the paper is to be published.

Hon. George H. Harlow presented an oak cane made from the unfinished ship "New Orleans," built at Sackett's Harbor in 1813–14.

It was voted that the records of the society, previous to the fire of 1871, so far as they have been collected from contemporaneous newspapers, &c., be published by the society.

VIRGINIA HISTORICAL SOCIETY.

Richmond, Friday, May 28, 1886.—A meeting of the executive committee was held this evening, Col. Henry Coalter Cabell in the chair.

R. A. Brock, Esq., the librarian, reported valuable donations of books, etc.

Letters were read, among them one from W. W. Corcoran, Esq., presenting to the society the stereotype plates of the Madison State Papers, a valuable work long out of print; and another from the Historical Society of Anne Arundel County, Md., which society intend to celebrate at Annapolis, on the 11th of September next, the one hundredth anniversary of the Annapolis Convention of 1786, an event held by statesmen to be one of the most important assemblies in the constitutional history of our country. This society was invited to send representatives. Thanks were voted to Mr. Corcoran for his generous gift.

NECROLOGY OF THE NEW-ENGLAND HISTORIC GENEALOGICAL SOCIETY.

Prepared by the Rev. INCREASE N. TARBOX, D.D., Historiographer of the Society.

THE historiographer would inform the society, that the sketches prepared for the REGISTER are necessarily brief in consequence of the limited space which can be appropriated. All the facts, however, he is able to gather, are retained in the Archives of the Society, and will aid in more extended memoirs for which the "Towne Memorial Fund," the gift of the late William B. Towne, A.M., is provided. Four volumes, printed at the charge of this fund, entitled "MEMORIAL BIOGRAPHIES," edited by the Committee on Memorials, have been issued. They contain memoirs of all the members who have died from the organization of the society to the year 1862. A fifth volume is in preparation.

ROBERT KENDALL DARRAH, Esq., of Boston, a resident member, admitted Feb. 8, 1883, was born in the year 1818, in the town of Charlestown (No. 4), N. H. His father Joseph Darrah and his mother Lefe Putnam were Massachusetts people, of the real Puritanic type; somewhat stern, but with their faces set to walk in the right way if they could find it, no matter how narrow or how difficult. Their boy, the seventh of nine children, was brought up therefore with an educated, as well as an inherited, sense of truthfulness and honor. These qualities were combined in him with a singular simplicity of disposition and boyishness of temper which never left him, and which might be called his dominant characteristics.

His sister writes: "My dear brother received what little education he had in a district school, which he left at the age of fourteen to go into a store in his native village, where he remained until he was eighteen. Robert often said this was an education in a certain way." The fact is very interesting viewed from the standpoint of his later life. Few men knew English literature so well as he. He was full of good reading, and when his health failed and he was left alone, he still found in good books a delightful and consoling companionship.

At the age of eighteen Mr. Darrah came to Boston and entered mercantile life, though he never lost his fondness for his native place, nor drifted away from his old home loves.

He was not destined for a successful business career, but his probity and patriotism fitted him admirably for public service. In 1861 he was appointed by Governor Andrew as appraiser in the Boston Custom House, an office which he filled acceptably for the almost unprecedented term of twenty-two years in spite of changing administrations.

In 1846 he married Sophia Towne, of Philadelphia, a lovely woman possessed of uncommon character and talent. They had no children, therefore she was enabled to devote herself to painting, cultivating her gift with peculiar energy and devotion, and winning at the last an honorable place in the great world of art. They were deeply attached to each other; what was the wish of one was the will of the other; and they continued to live in the closest union and sympathy to the end. No account of his life, however brief, would be possible without some record of his life-long companion.

It was not many years after coming to Boston that Mr. Darrah injured himself at a gymnasium. Naturally strong and athletic, the loss of health, combined with failure in business, could not fail to depress him for a season. He soon rallied, however, and tried to accommodate himself cheerfully to new ways of life. These were necessarily monotonous, as he was no longer able to walk much nor to take active exercise of any kind, but he was seldom to be outdone in good cheer. He made a new life for himself in books. Every day, whether he was by the sea-side in summer, or in town in winter, he would go to the custom-house at nine o'clock in the morning, would dine frugally upon his return, and would then occupy himself in reading for the remainder of the day, except for occasional visits received or made. There was very little variation from this method of his life during thirty years.

Meanwhile Mrs. Darrah's industry was gathering in its harvest. After her death a very large number of pictures were sold in accordance with her will, and the sum of ten thousand dollars was presented to the Society for the Prevention of Cruelty to Animals. Mr. Darrah survived his wife only two years, two years of beneficent kindliness to every one within his reach. From a letter written to his sister by his former business partner after his death, a relation which tries the spirit of the best man, we read : " When you consider an uninterrupted friendship of nearly fifty years without even an unpleasant word, and on my side not even a hard thought, and I am sure of the same on his part, it is an unusual occurrence. We were in business together for years, where very few men get along without some differences."

Mr. Darrah was a loyal American. He was always profoundly interested in the politics of the day, and always a Republican. Like many New England people he was a theorist in government, a position which is hardly tenable for more active men. We have at length learned that government is not an Idea alone, but a power of acting in response to the needs of a people. He was of such gentle nature that even if he not been disqualified for active service by physical weakness, it is doubtful if he could have borne the strain of public affairs.

He was especially fond of little children and of homely ways and scenes, and his kindliness was ever on the alert for others. When various forms of benevolence were presented to his consideration in the city, his mind would first revert to his beautiful home in New Hampshire, and he would satisfy himself that he had done what he could for those who needed his help at home before he could willingly turn to other objects.

His nature was deeply religious ; he " put his creed into his deed ;" he was enthusiastic, and eager, and affectionate. It is not wonderful that with such a character he was ready, when the moment came, to follow his beloved one ; nor, however brief we make the written record of his life, that he should live long among the tenderest memories in the heart of those who knew him.

By Mrs. James T. Fields, of Boston.

Hon. Edward Ashton Rollins, A M., of Philadelphia, a life member, admitted Jan. 26, 1884, was born at Wakefield, N. H., Dec. 8, 1828, and died in Hanover, N. H., Sept. 7, 1885. His father was Hon. Daniel Gustavus Rollins, of Great Falls, N. H., born in Maine ; and his mother was Susan Binney. Mr. Rollins's earliest American ancestor was James[1] Rollins, born in England in 1605, who came to Ipswich, Mass., in 1632, and was settled in Dover, N. H., in 1634. His son, Ichabod[2] Rollins, was born in Dover before 1640, was taxed in that town in 1665, and was killed by the Indians, May 22, 1707. His son, Jeremiah[3] Rollins, lived in what is now Rollinsford, N. H., and was one of the petitioners for the organization of the parish of Somersworth, N. H., in 1729. His son, John[4] Rollins, was born April 2, 1745, in what is now Rollinsford. He was representative to the General Court of New Hampshire. His son, John[5] Rollins, was born in 1771, in what is now Rollinsford, and moved to Maine in 1792. His son, Daniel G.[6] Rollins, was born as above. The subject of this sketch was therefore of the seventh generation from the American founder of the Rollins family.

When young Rollins was seven years old, in 1835, his family removed to Great Falls, N. H., and the boy's early education was gained in the common schools of that village. He was fitted for college at Rochester and Gilmanton Academies, N. H., and in 1847 was entered as a member of the freshman class at Dartmouth College, and was graduated in due course in 1851.

Immediately after graduation he commenced the study of law at Baltimore, with the firm of G. W. Brown and F. W. Brune. There he remained a year, and then spent a year with Hon. Nathaniel Wells, and Hon. Charles H. Bell of Great Falls. He gave a third year to law partly with his wife's father, Hon. Josiah H. Hobbs, and partly in the Harvard Law School. After practising law for some years, he was appointed in 1862, by President Lincoln, cashier of the Internal Revenue Department at Washington. In 1865 he was made Commissioner of Internal Revenue. In 1869 he was elected vice-president, and afterwards president, of the National Life Insurance Company of the United States. He held the office of president until 1874, when the stock was sold and transferred to Chicago. In 1876, in connection with the Centennial Exhibition, he established and was made president of the Centennial National Bank of Philadelphia.

Mr. Rollins was united in marriage, Sept. 27, 1855, with Miss Ellen Hobbs, daughter of Hon. Josiah Hobbs, of Wakefield, N. H. Mrs. Rollins died May 29, 1881.

Of the six children from this marriage two died in infancy and one in boyhood. Two daughters and a son survive.

Mr. Rollins is publicly known for his very generous gifts to Dartmouth College. Rollins Hall, dedicated at last Commencement, was named from him.

Hon. EDWARD LAWRENCE, a life member, admitted March 25, 1869, was born at Harvard, Mass., June 21, 1810, and died at Charlestown, Mass., Oct. 17, 1885. His father was Stephen Lawrence, born in Littleton, Mass., Oct. 27, 1764, and his mother was Lucy Bigelow, born in Harvard, Mass., Oct. 27, 1783.

His early education was gained in the country schools, and in 1825, at the age of fifteen, he came to Charlestown, which has since been his home, and entered into the service of Mr. Charles Foster, a cabinet manufacturer. In 1833, after eight years of faithful service, he became associated with Mr. Foster in the business. In 1856 he succeeded him and enlarged the operations of the house. He employed from one hundred and fifty to three hundred men in the business, a large portion of whom were convicts in the State Prison. He continued in his business of cabinet manufacture until the breaking out of the war of the rebellion in 1860. The firm then took the name of Braman, Shaw & Co., and now bears the name, Shaw, Applin & Co.

He was united in marriage, Feb. 28, 1839, with Miss Mary Thomas Baker, eldest daughter of Capt. Richard and Jerusha Baker, of Charlestown. His wife died Feb. 14, 1867, aged 48 years. He leaves four children, two sons and two daughters. His sons are Edward Lawrence, Jr., engaged in the shipping business in Boston, and Charles R. Lawrence, cashier of the Bunker Hill National Bank. His daughters are Mrs. John Kent, of Charlestown, and Mrs. John Chandler, of Concord, N. H.

He has served in the public affairs of Charlestown quite largely—two years as selectman, and one of those years chairman of the board ; six years as alderman ; two years he represented the city of Charlestown in the legislature. He was chairman of the board of commissioners for introducing water from Mystic Lake into Charlestown. He was a director and afterwards president of the Bunker Hill National Bank, president of the Warren Institution for Savings, and director of the Bunker Hill Association. He has also been one of the leading men of the First Universalist Society of Charlestown. In all these and in other public stations he has been an honored and trusted citizen, and has left behind a good name.

Rt. Rev. CHARLES FRANKLIN ROBERTSON, D.D., LL.D., of St. Louis, Episcopalian bishop of Missouri, a corresponding member, admitted Sept. 8, 1884, was born in New York city, March 2, 1835, and died in St. Louis, Mo., May 1, 1886. His father was James Robertson, born in New York city, Sept. 20, 1812. His mother was Mary Ann Canfield, born in Putnam Valley, N. Y. His grandfather was Albert Robertson, born September, 1780, in Bremen, Germany, and his great-grandfather, also named Albert, was born in the same city. His maternal grandfather, Gold Canfield, was born in South Salem, Westchester Co., N. Y., Sept. 23, 1770.

The subject of this sketch was educated at private schools in New York city, and was graduated at Yale College in 1859, in a class of 105. Among his classmates we find such names as William Kittredge Hall, S.T.D., Prof. John Haskell Hewitt, Prof. George W. Jones, Eugene Schuyler, LL.D., Thomas Bucklin Wells, S.T.D., and Prof. Arthur W. Wright, Ph.D.

Dr. Robertson was united in marriage, Sept. 14, 1865, with Miss Rebecca Duane, daughter of James and Harriet (Constable) Duane, and great-grand-daughter of Joseph Duane, first mayor of New York after the Revolution. From this marriage there were four children, whose given names in their order are—James Duane, Charles Canfield, Frances Constable, and Edward Livingston Hilliker.

Bishop Robertson was educated theologically at the General Theological Seminary in New York, and was admitted to Deacon's and Priest's orders in the Protestant Episcopal Church, in New York in 1862. He was consecrated Bishop of the Diocese of Missouri, Oct. 25, 1868. He became a Trustee of the General Theological Seminary in New York, and president of the Board of Trustees of Racine College and Nashotah Theological Seminary. Previous to his election to the Bishopric he had been Rector of St. Mark's Church, Malone, N. Y., and St. James Church, Batavia, N. Y.

His miscellaneous publications on religious and church matters, as well as on historical subjects, have been numerous. Besides his connection with our society, he was a member of the Historical Societies of Missouri and Virginia, the Southern Historical Society, and corresponding member of the Historical Societies of Wisconsin, Georgia and Long Island. He received the degree of D.D. from Columbia College in 1869; and from the University of the South. That of LL.D came from the University of the State of Missouri in 1883.

BOOK NOTICES.

THE EDITOR requests persons sending books for notice to state, for the information of readers, the price of each book, with the amount to be added for postage when sent by mail.

Life and Letters of Joel Barlow, LL.D., Poet, Statesman, Philosopher. With Extracts from his Works and hitherto Unpublished Poems. By CHARLES BURR TODD. New York and London. G. P. Putnam's Sons. The Knickerbocker Press. 1886. 8vo. pp. iv. & 306. With a Portrait. Price $2.50.

We gladly welcome this biography, and yet we regret that it is so brief. The author had access to the papers left by Mr. Barlow, and to the materials collected and preserved by his relatives. Hence it is obvious that the volume might have been extended so as to include more of the interesting incidents of Barlow's life,— of his college career, his experience in the army of the Revolution, his early literary work in New Haven and Hartford, and especially of his long residence in Europe, from 1788 to 1805, where he witnessed many memorable events, and made the acquaintance of many notable men. But the volume is not destitute of interesting incidents and details. It certainly enables the reader to gain a far more complete and accurate knowledge of the subject and of his eventful life than can be obtained from the comparatively meagre sketches heretofore published.

Barlow was a voluminous writer of poetry, but he was more than this; he was, in an eminent sense, a man of affairs. The biographer has devoted the most of his pages to the latter aspect of his subject. It might well have been anticipated that a due proportion of space would be given to literary criticism. Let us be thankful, nevertheless, for having at last a biography of this interesting character.

As is well known, Barlow began to write verses in his youth, and he continued to write when leisure permitted almost to the last hour of his life. His long poem —one of the longest ever written in the English Language—the "Columbiad," 1808, was an expansion of his "Vision of Columbus," 1787. These and his "Hasty Pudding" constitute his chief poetical works. It is the fashion of certain critics, who presumably have never read Barlow's productions, to speak in contemptuous terms of the "Columbiad." Notwithstanding this, the thorough student of American Literature must and will read the poem, and form his own judgment. We may wonder how it was possible that a man of such abilities and good sense, displayed in other fields of activity, could have had the patience to write and rewrite so many verses on that theme, and could have so unwisely cast his poem in the inartistic form it bears. But Barlow was not the first, nor the latest, poet who has misconceived the limitations of his powers, or blundered in the execution of his purpose. One of his contemporaries, Dr. Dwight, is scarcely less open to a similar criticism. And yet it cannot be denied that Barlow, as well as Dwight, did write not a little poetry, and that some of it is of no mean character. Whoever would get a fair estimate of Barlow's poetical work, will consult Duyckinck and other well-informed and candid literary critics. He will take into consideration the state of society and the literary poverty of this country at the time Barlow wrote, and will compare his productions with those of his chief literary contemporaries—Trumbull, Dwight, Hopkins, Humphreys, Freneau, Brackenridge, Parke, Alston, and others. He will also recall the remark of Stedman, one of the most competent of our living critics : "The author of the Columbiad and the Hasty Pudding was a man of might in his day, and will not pass out of literature or history." It is well to remember, too, that Barlow was a patriot, and that, like the other writers named, he sought by his poetical writings to inspire his countrymen with noble thoughts and impulses, and to glorify his native land. They did inspire the soldiers in the field, as well as their wives and children,—and so helped beyond all question and all computation to strengthen and encourage the patriots of the Revolutionary era.

But, as we have already remarked, Barlow was more than a writer of poetry. After reaching manhood, he passed the greater portion of his life in Europe. When he took up his residence in France he found the people of that land in the early stages of their Revolution. He earnestly espoused the cause of those leaders who desired and endeavored to establish republican institutions ; and by his pen and personal influence he labored to impress upon leaders and people the example set by the people of the United States in their struggle for independence and in the process of establishing a constitutional government. As the agent of the United States Mr. Barlow went on a hazardous and difficult mission to the Barbary Powers, and by his skill and energy was able to put a stop, for a time at least, to their depredations on our commerce, and to their inhuman treatment of American citizens captured by their piratical vessels on the high seas.

It is proper to recall the interesting fact that Barlow was one of the first, if not the first, of Americans to recognize the merits of Fulton, and to see the vast possibilities of usefulness in the inventions of that remarkable man, in the interest of commerce, agriculture, and the industrial arts. At a time of need he aided Fulton with money, influence and practical suggestions,—all of which bore fruit in after years.

Barlow's political writings also deserve consideration. His letters to the French people and to the American people show at least that he had made a careful and intelligent study of the matters discussed ; that he possessed a clear, logical mind and a rare power of argumentative and persuasive statement. They show, moreover, that he had the instinct of statesmanship, and many qualifications for public life.

After an absence of seventeen years, Barlow returned to the United States, with the intention of devoting the residue of his life to historical and other literary work, and to aiding his countrymen in developing useful industries and civilizing institutions. He went abroad with the tastes and ideas, political and social, which he had acquired by his education and associations among those people of Connecticut who then, and for many years afterwards, constituted the ruling class in politics, in society and in religious circles. He returned, not as a Federalist, but as a Republican. In his early years he enjoyed the affectionate regards of such men as Trumbull, Dwight, Buckminster, and Noah Webster. In England and in France he had the respect and companionship of scholars, philanthropists, and statesmen. On his return to America, he was welcomed to the confidence and friendship of Jefferson, Madison and Monroe. His two distinguished brothers-in-law, Abraham Baldwin, Senator from Georgia, and Henry Baldwin, justice of the United States Supreme Court, were then living. He had abundant means. There was not even a shadow on his character as a man of integrity and honor. As President Stiles had written to him, he had acquired " celebrity and fame " by his writings. Like Washington and Hamilton, he had had conferred upon him the privileges of French citizenship. But he never ceased to be an American, and a devoted friend of his own country and its people. He was the most accomplished man of his day in the States.

In 1811, the relations of the United States with France had reached a state so strained and critical that an immediate diplomatic intervention, requiring great skill and special fitness in the minister, became necessary. Hence it is not surprising that of all the able men then living, President Madison selected Mr. Barlow for this delicate and important duty. While engaged in this mission, and when as he hoped and believed he was about to accomplish its object, he was suddenly removed by death.

We may not all read the " Columbiad," but it would be both unjust and uncandid not to think kindly and speak respectfully of this eminent son of America, who gave his life in devotion to the service of his native land.

By Albert H. Hoyt, A.M., of Boston.

Some Account of the Ancient Chapel of Toxteth Park, Liverpool, from the year 1618 *to* 1883, *and of its Ministers, especially of Richard Mather, the first Minister.* By VALENTINE D. DAVIS, B.A., Liverpool [England]: Henry Young. 1884. 12mo. pp. 56. Price one shilling.

We learn from this account of the "Chapel," that Toxteth Park was the property of the Crown, from the reign of King John, until the year 1604, or nearly 400 years. About this period a number of farmers, or cultivators of the soil, of Puritan proclivities, settled on the land. These inhabitants soon gave a tone and character to the whole district, the influence of which was perpetuated. One memorial of this olden time remains, namely, the "Ancient Chapel," built for those Puritans, "the first chapel," says Mr. Davis, "connected with Dissent in the neighbourhood of Liverpool." The present structure, built a century or more ago, stands on the site of the original chapel, some of whose important characteristics are preserved, while the burying ground remains intact. These early settlers in the Park, though Puritan in their principles, did not formally absolve themselves from allegiance to the mother Church, the time for this open dissent not having then arrived. Sir Richard Molyneux, a Roman Catholic, created a baronet in 1611, had purchased Toxteth Park, and with a liberality worthy of commendation, so unusual in his day, granted land to these Puritans whereon to set a chapel, which was built, probably, in 1618, or about the time of the settlement of the Rev. Richard Mather, their first minister. After the "ejection," the chapel continued to be held by the Dissenters as a Presbyterian meeting-house. Eventually the members became Unitarian in their sentiments. It is somewhat remarkable that the Society at Toxteth Park, over which the Rev. Richard Mather was settled as the first minister in 1618, and the Church at Dorchester, in New England, where he was installed in 1636, as the first minister of the Church after its re-organization, should have become and still remain Unitarian in their views.

Mr. Davis gives an extended account of Rev. Richard Mather, obtained chiefly from American sources, with which we are familiar, as also in his notes concerning the family, but the names of Thomas, father of Rev. Richard, and of John, his grandfather, are not introduced. See REGISTER, xxxiii. 101, for information concerning them.

In sketching the character of Mr. Mather, Mr. D. says:—"If we cannot count Richard Mather among the most distinguished men of his time, we must yet acknowledge that his force of character, his earnest and truly devout disposition, his genial temper, blended as they were with a life-history by no means unremarkable, deserve to be remembered. He was one of many noble-hearted Puritans of that day, who stood bravely for the truth as they conceived it; and if there were others more remarkable for intellectual gifts and of wider influence, there were none whose record was more blameless, and over whose story we can linger with more unalloyed pleasure."

There is one thing to be borne in mind in relation to this criticism of Mr. Mather. Good as it is, his character and principles were doubtless not so fully developed as they subsequently were in his Dorchester ministry and pastorate, where he was the third minister, succeeding so ably Maverick and Warham. We are inclined, therefore, to follow out, more strictly, the line of thought suggested by an anagram, entered in the Dorchester Church Records. "Richard Mather. Anagram. A Third Charmer." The Record continues:—

"Third in New Englands Dorchester
Was This Ordained Minister
Second to None, for Fruitfulnesse
Abilitys, & Usefullnesse," &c.

In regard to his "abilities and usefulness," as furnished by his own history and by his contemporaries, the above description seems to our mind singularly just. He may not have had the reputation which Cotton, Hooker and Davenport attained in England, but his New England contemporaries evidently considered him their peer. Two lines from the epitaph that follows, in the Church Records, may here be appended:—

"Hard to Discern a Difference in degree
'Twixt His bright Learning & High Pietie."

We are informed that "his people at Toxteth were devoted to him, and very loath to let him go," but duty seemed clear to them, and to him, and he departed. "After the establishment of the Commonwealth, when the Puritans once more had liberty," in England, " they urgently begged him to return," but, as is well known, their entreaties did not prevail. After a ministry in Dorchester of about four and thirty years, he died, April 22, 1669, aged 73.

The successors of Mr. Mather at Toxteth Park were, Thomas Huggins, Thomas Crompton. Michael Briscoe, Christopher Richardson, John Kennion, Mr. Gellibrand, William Harding, Hugh Anderson, John Porter, John Hamilton Thom, Henry Giles (the well known essayist and lecturer), John Robberds, James E. Odgers, and Valentine D. Davis, the present incumbent.

Rev. James Edwin Odgers, the predecessor of Mr. Davis, in 1882, wrote a pamphlet, which was published, concerning Richard Mather and his connection with Toxteth Park Chapel.

By William B. Trask, Esq., of Boston, Mass.

The Imperial Island. England's Chronicle in Stone. By JAMES F. HUNNEWELL, Author of " The Lands of Scott," " The Historical Monuments of France," etc. Boston : Ticknor & Company. 1886. 8vo. pp. xiii.+433. With Illustrations, Maps, Notes and Index. Price $4.

Whoever wishes to read the history of England thoroughly and completely, must read it partly through its castles, palaces and cathedrals. It is not enough that the philosophical reasoning of Macaulay and of Hume gives us a keen insight into the motives, the reasoning and the character of the temporal and spiritual leaders of England's past. Through these authors we gain a knowledge that is valuable and necessary to a proper study of history, it is true, but we still seem to be remote from the events recorded. It is like gazing upon a beautiful picture seen through a dim light or a great distance.

> " The cloud-capped towers, the gorgeous palaces,
>   The solemn temples " ....

seem to

>   .... " Melt away,
> And, like the baseless fabric of a vision,
> Leave not a rack behind."

We miss the opportunity of a close inspection of the *localities* of history wherewith to make us more in sympathy with its events, and to photograph them more indelibly upon the tablets of the mind.

Such an opportunity is offered us by the excellent volume now under notice. The author has covered the whole period from the Stonehenge of the ancient Britons down through Roman, Saxon, Norman, Plantagenet, Tudor, Stuart and Hanoverian eras to the present time. The stone history of England is here given in a most faithful manner. The pen pictures and illustrations are presented in such an accurate, minute and careful method, that we seem to be with and of the objects and characters represented ; and as we wander, in imagination, through the cloistered abbeys, the lofty cathedrals and the turreted castles which have echoed to the tread of the sceptred sovereign, the mail-clad warrior or the mitred priest, we feel more closely associated with the deeds of the Edwards, the Henrys and the Richards, who swayed the destinies of England before our own country was known. Magna Charta is nearer to us. The Wars of the Roses read no longer like a romance, but broaden out into the realms of fact ; while the Richard and Richmond of Shakespeare step out from that great author's pages and stand, historically correct, before us. Even the more remote ages, the Druid temples, the Roman walls, and the works of the great Saxon Alfred appear in bolder relief, and Westminster Abbey, the Tower of London, the battlements of Warwick and the Cathedral of St. Paul, seem invested with a new interest.

Nor is this volume of much less value as a means of education in architectural art. By its illustrations we are enabled to study the changes and note the contrasts between the mediæval and the modern ages. Most of these illustrations are very fine, and gratify the visual as well as the mental eye. Among the most notable of them are a view of the Poet's Corner in Westminster Abbey, looking southeast, Durham with its cathedral and castle, the west front of Canterbury Cathedral, two views of York Cathedral, the Dome of St. Paul's, the ruins of Middleham Castle, the great Roman Walls, the tomb of Henry III. and the Chapel of Henry VII. at Westminster Abbey, and the series of views of the Tower of London and Windsor Castle.

Mr. Hunnewell's literary style is excellent, and while he may not have added much new matter to the domain of history, he has brought much valuable material within easy reach which would else have been difficult of access, and he has enabled those whose means will not permit them to visit England, to make a close acquaintance with and study its monuments of the past. The book is well printed on good paper, and will prove a welcome addition to all historical libraries.

By Oliver B. Stebbins, Esq., of South Boston.

Memorial of Rev. Simeon North, D.D., LL.D., Fifth President of Hamilton College. Utica, N. Y. : Ellis H. Roberts & Co., Printers, 60 Genesee St. 1884. 8vo. pp.

Dr. North was born in Berlin, Conn., Sept. 7, 1802, and died Feb. 9, 1884. In this sketch we have the record of a long and well-spent life. The book has the merit of being short. It also has a great defect in that it is not a concise and clear cut account of the life of Dr. North. The reader is left to gather, for the most part, what he can from a collection of letters, many of them written about other persons than the subject of this biography. Now this is an unsatisfactory way of getting at the life of a man, even when the account is a long one, although it may throw an occasional ray upon it. But it is more unsatisfactory when the sketch is as short as the one before us. The volume fortunately, however, contains a funeral sermon by Dr. North, in which he presents a strong argument for one of the great truths of the Faith—an argument needed in this agnostic age. I venture to give a short extract. He says: " In the ceaseless round of nature, which through successive years he (man) has watched, he has seen decay and death but the precursors of renewed life. Suns and stars have set in darkness, but he has seen them rise again with undiminished light. The face of nature has been made bare and desolate by the approach of winter, but in turn he has seen the coming of spring with its covering of flowers, and of autumn with its harvest of fruits. The seed which he has committed to the earth has become disorganized and sunk to decay ; but he has seen the germ of a new plant or a new tree survive, striking downward its roots, and upward its branches, and thus rising to the beauty and glory of a new existence.

" Now the Bible has taught him that he himself is not destined to be an exception to this law of reanimation and of renewed life, which he has seen pervading the universe. In the school of Christ he has learned that the noblest of God's works —this complex nature of matter and mind, of body and of spirit—though subject to death, shall yet survive the corruption of the grave, and shall rise to a new and more glorious existence. He has heard the apostle exclaim, in the conclusion of his triumphant argument for the resurrection of the dead, ' Behold I show you a mystery. We shall not all sleep, but we shall all be changed. In a moment, in the twinkling of an eye, at the last trump : for the trumpet shall sound, and the dead shall be raised incorruptible, and we shall be changed. For this corruptible must put on incorruption, and this mortal must put on immortality.' With this assurance, founded upon the united testimony of nature and revelation, the Christian believer can no more doubt, when he lies down in the darkness of the grave, that he is destined to a renewed and more glorious existence, than he can doubt that when he sees the sun going down at night it will again rise on the morrow. Such a doubt he cannot harbor without distrusting the voice of universal nature, and without denying the truth of Him who cannot lie. This is his consolation and support in the hour of death ; and thus to him is reserved the blessed termination of a faithful and useful life."

By Daniel Rollins, Esq., of Boston, Mass.

In Memory of Edwin Channing Larned. Chicago : A. C. McClurg and Co. 1886. Sm. 8vo. pp. 130.

This is a carefully prepared memorial of the life of Edwin C. Larned, who was born in Providence, R. I., July 14, 1820, and died at Lake Forest, Ill., September 18, 1884.

He was graduated at Brown University in 1840, and in 1847 settled in Chicago, and for many years was prominent as a philanthropist and abolitionist. During the eventful period of the war his name became well known as an able and earnest supporter of Lincoln, and he attained the highest rank in his profession, that of the law. The only public office he held was that of district attorney in the years 1861–65, but he took a most active part in several political campaigns, and gained an enviable reputation as a speaker on political questions.

The book contains memorial tributes from Bishops Harris of Michigan and Whipple of Minnesota, Mr. Larned having been a devoted and sincere churchman, and noted for his benevolence and liberality. There are also addresses by Daniel Goodwin, Jr., Judge Henry W. Blodgett and Hon. Franklin MacVeagh. The last fifty-seven pages of the memorial are devoted to Mr. Larned's argument before the U. S. District Court for the Northern District of Illinois, March 12 and 13, 1860, on the trial of Joseph Stout, indicted for rescuing a fugitive slave from the United States deputy marshall at Ottawa, Ill., Oct. 20, 1859.

The typographical work is done in the best manner, and the book is most creditable to all concerned.

By George K. Clarke, LL.B., of Needham, Mass.

Portland in the Past, with Historical Notes of Old Falmouth. By WILLIAM GOOLD. Sixteen Illustrations. Printed for the Author by B. Thurston & Co., Portland, Maine. 1886. 8vo. pp. 543.

It is now over twenty years since a history of the city of Portland has been offered to the public, the last being the second edition of William Willis's well known work which appeared in 1865, the first edition of which was issued in 1832. It was therefore with great satisfaction that the announcement made by Mr. Goold in 1883 of his intention to prepare a history of Portland was received by the people of that city, and his large subscription list of nearly five hundred names, is ample testimony of the interest which his prospectus excited. Nor was this interest in his work founded on any superficial knowledge of the author's qualifications. Mr. Goold has been the "oldest inhabitant," historically speaking, for years, and to him is Portland indebted for a series of sketches of persons and events, famous in her annals, which he has contributed to the local press and antiquarian societies during the last two decades. He is an antiquary by natural selection, and ever since his youth has been collecting the tales of our forefathers as they fell from the lips of the remnants of a previous generation, until he has become the repository of all the interesting phases of social and political life in Portland as it existed for the last hundred years. Thus equipped Mr. Goold presents to the public for favor a handsome volume entitled "Portland in the Past." In his treatment of the work in hand, it seems to us and to others with whom the matter has been discussed, that the author has occupied too much space in the first half of the work with the more than "twice told tales" of the early settlements of Portland, without adding anything new to the information already known by heart to the people of the city. Nearly fifty pages are devoted to the Trelawny plantation at Richmond Island, principally extracts culled from the volume of Trelawny Papers, edited by Mr. J. P. Baxter, and noticed in the January, 1885, issue of this publication. Half as many more pages are taken up with the settlement of Christopher Levett in Portland harbor, containing nothing new except a new theory as to the island selected by Levett for his "fair stone house." Mr. Baxter inclined to the belief that House Island is the place ; Mr. Sargent, in his monograph on "Cushing's Island," noticed in the April number of this periodical, made a strong plea for that particular spot, while Mr. Goold strenuously labors on behalf of Great Hog Island, giving evidence of his faith by a picture of Levett sailing into Hog Island Roads as a frontispiece for the volume. His theory is as good as these or any others could be without facts to support them ; but it is only just to say that Mr. Sargent's claim is fortified by a well deduced chain of title from assignees of Levett, and gives us the best ground for basing an opinion on the question. It seems to us, too, that the author makes a somewhat unnecessary detour to Norridgewock to devote twenty pages to the capture of Fr. Sebastian Rale ; but it may be explained, perhaps, on the ground that it is an interesting story, and because he is able to show to us for the first time pictures of that prelate's "strong box" and the chapel bell of his church in the woods. After passing two more chapters on extraneous subjects (Fort Halifax on the Kennebec and the Pepperell expedition to Louisburg) we come to the meat of the book, the reminiscences. In this portion Mr. G. carries us with him easily for three hundred pages with a story of fascinating interest, told with all the charming tid-bits of personalities that make these figures of the past stand out like *bas-reliefs.* The Tyng family, so prominent in early Portland annals, are presented to us with new and enjoyable stories of their social life and relations, and to our great pleasure portraits of Commodore Edward, Colonel William and their wives are here first published, Mr. Goold having found them in the possession of descendants in Bangor. The Revolutionary period is dealt with in an interesting manner, and with new light shed upon many of the local actors, which had been gleaned from them or their descendants. In the chapters on

Commodore Edward Preble and his famous naval exploits, we are again thoroughly imbued with the subject in hand, and when the war of 1812 is reached and the story of the privateers is told, Mr. Goold is in his element. With many of these daring seamen he was personally acquainted, and the tales of their dashing adventures in the sea-chase rival the fiction of Clark Russell. Mr. Goold has transferred to these pages the very words of these vikings as they fell from their lips, and no one interested in the local history of Portland can fail to thank the author for giving us the stories of men who made riches and renown for themselves and their city, on the high seas, in the exciting times of 1812. The religious history is well told, and many reminiscences add to the value of the matter. The passages on Mowat's bombardment are reprinted from Mr. Goold's article which appeared in the REGISTER, July, 1873, while several of the minor topics (Enterprise and Boxer Fight, Fort Halifax, County Buildings, etc.) have been read before societies or appeared in local prints. The last chapter is not finished according to the head-lines on account of " lack of time and space," much to our regret, especially as the time and space were used up in the manner already noted in the early part of the book. The book closes in its most interesting portion, and were it not that a saving clause in the last line reads—" the deferred matter will subsequently appear in another connection," we should feel that he had not fulfilled the expectations of his subscribers. We hope that the author will give us a second volume devoted entirely to reminiscences, leaving the earlier annals of the seventeenth century to others who have had facilities for original investigation. A fair index ends the volume, although we miss many important names that should appear there. The names of Trelawny, Rale, Flucker, and some others are misspelled, and the name of Richmond Island is said to have been derived from the Duke of Richmond, for which there is no authority. Many other minor errors of this kind appear in the volume, but they have only a local significance, and do not seriously affect the value of the volume. The illustrations inserted are of positive importance as contributions to the history of the city, and are in general well executed wood blocks. The ideal picture given as a frontispiece ought to have some designation, showing its modern design as a fancy sketch.
By Charles Edward Banks, M.D., of Chelsea, Mass.

London of To-day. An Illustrated Handbook for the Season. By CHARLES EYRE PASCOE. Second Year of Publication and Third Edition. Boston : Roberts Brothers. 1886. 16mo. pp. 384. Profusely Illustrated. Flexible covers. Price $1.50.

As a reliable and practical guide to show the stranger in London the way he should go and what he should do, this little volume equals if not surpasses all its predecessors in this line of information. The various departments are well arranged, and all the attractions, places of historic interest and methods of comfortable living in this greatest of cities, are indicated with simplicity and directness. The illustrations are excellent ; and altogether the work is a very attractive and entertaining volume alike to the general reader and the tourist.
By Oliver B. Stebbins, Esq., of South Boston, Mass.

Pennsylvania Genealogies, Scotch, Irish and German. By WILLIAM HENRY EGLE, M.D., M.A. Harrisburg : Lane S. Hart, Printer and Binder. 1886. Sq. 8vo. p. viii.+720. Edition 250 copies. $5.00 to subscribers, $10 to all others.

This is one of the most interesting volumes of genealogy that it has been our pleasure to examine. It is handsomely printed, and arranged according to the New England Historic Genealogical Society plan of notation. It contains sixty distinct pedigrees, including seventy families, with many excellent and modern biographical sketches. Forty-five of these pedigrees are those of Scotch Irish families, and the rest of German and Swiss families. The Scotch Irish lines are those of Ainsworth, Andrews, Allen, Anderson, Awl, Ayres, Burnett, Beatty, Boyd, Crain, Cowden, Dixon, Elder, Espy, Ferguson, Fleming, Foster, Galbraith, Gregg, Curtin, Hamilton, Hays, Linn, Lyon, Maclay, McCormick, McNair, Murray, Neville and Craig, Parker and Denny, Roan, Robinson, Rutherford, Stewart, Swann, Wallace, Wiggins, Wilson, Wyeth. The other lines are those of Alrichs, Boas, Bomberger, Bucher, Egle, Greenwalt, Keller, Kendig, Kunkel, Müller, Lobingier, Orth, Wiestling and Byers.

What is noticeable in this volume is the absence of that homage usually paid to TRADITION by works of genealogy. Few if any of the families in this volume lay any claim to European connexions beyond the fact of emigration from the fatherland.

And yet the honored positions attained by many of the descendants of these emigrants—the intelligence, enterprise, strength of character and social position of the various families recorded in the book, are proof of an ancestry marked by similar characteristics.

There is no better stock in America, distinguished as it is by good sense, religious fervor, strong convictions, steadiness of purpose, than the Scotch Irish. To them as much as to any others Pennsylvania owes her prominence among the States of the Union. In that State the author, Dr. Egle, has a reputation that is a guarantee of thorough and satisfactory work. He is, " par excellence," the *genealogist* of the State. Laborious and painstaking, devoting his life to the development of the history of his State, and especially of the central portion thereof, he is doubtless the most extensive writer on these subjects within the limits of the State. His history of Lebanon Co., Pa., which escaped the usual fate of such county histories, of being tampered with by the publishers, is a most valuable and accurate work, and his History of Pennsylvania is the standard history of the State.

In looking over the present volume one wonders that so much has been gleaned in a field where so little has been done to preserve family history. But one wonders still more when told that Dr. Egle has another similar volume nearly ready for the press.

The present work was published only for subscribers, and not being stereotyped may be considered as already out of print. It is a reflection on the people of the state of Pennsylvania that although well advertised, a work of such a character should command only 250 subscribers, that number of copies being the extent of the edition.

By the Rev. Horace Edwin Hayden, of Wilkes-Barre, Pa.

Southern Bivouac. A Literary and Historical Magazine. Published Monthly at Louisville. By B. F. Avery & Sons. Two Dollars per Annum. New Series. Nos. 10, 11, 12, of Vol. 1, and No. 1 [June, 1886] of Vol. 2.

The editorial conductors of this magazine, Messrs. Basil W. Duke and Richard W. Knott, give every indication needed to show that they intend to furnish for their readers a literary and historical publication that is both attractive in dress and well worthy of patronage. Original articles, by able and graceful writers, in prose and poetry, romance, sketches of battles, biographies of conspicuous chieftains, and incidents of the civil war, are among the contents. In addition to these papers, there are other well written articles, such as the " Virginia Cavaliers," with portraits ; a sketch of the life and character of Charles Gayarré, the distinguished historical writer and publicist, of Louisiana ; and papers on the leading industries of the Southern States, also illustrated. One of the most important of recent contributions to our political history will be found in three papers on the (Kentucky) " Resolutions of 1798 and 1799." Here is now given for the first time a correct history of the origin of these famous resolutions, and the exact text of the same as they passed the legislature, and not as, in some important respects, they have since been misprinted, misquoted, and often misunderstood. These papers deserve to be published in book form. We hope the *Bivouac* will have all the patronage and encouragement it so well merits.

By Albert H. Hoyt, A.M., of Boston.

The History of the Parish and Manor of Wookey; being a Contribution towards a future History of the County of Somerset. By Thomas Scott Holmes, M.A., Vicar of the Parish. Bristol: C. T. Jefferies and Sons, Printers. 1886. 8vo. pp. 164.

The parish of Wookey has an interest for our New England people from the fact that the Buxton or Buckstone family of Salem emigrated from it. A family of Illarie, which is the same as our Ellery, is said to have left Wookey for New England, but they have not been identified with the Ellery family (REG., viii. 317-20) from which the signer of the Declaration of Independence descended. It is possible that other early settlers of this country came from this place.

Wookey is a small parish in the vicinity of Wells, and " derives its name from the great natural cave in the southern slope of the Mendip hills from which issue the waters of the river Axe," which flow into the Bristol Channel. The handsome volume before us gives a full and interesting history of the place. The parish, the manor and manor house, the church and church bells, the rectory and rectors, the vicarage and vicars, the church registers, churchwardens and clerks, and the ecclesiastical and parochial endowments, are all satisfactorily treated. Lists of the rectors and vicars are given, with notices of many of the incumbents. Appended are pedigrees of the more prominent families of that locality, while full indexes make the contents of the volume easily accessible. The author, who is a son-in-law of Dr. Freeman, the English historian, displays here much literary ability as well as antiquarian research.

Documents chiefly unpublished relating to the Huguenot Emigration to Virginia and the Settlement at Manakin-Town; with an Appendix of Genealogies, presenting data of the Maury, Dupuy, Trabue, Marye, Chartain, Cocke and other Families. Edited and Compiled for the Virginia Historical Society. By R. A. BROCK, Corresponding Secretary and Librarian of the Society. Richmond, Virginia: Published by the Society. 1886. 8vo. pp. xx.+245.

The basis of this volume is a collection of records relating to the Huguenot emigration to Virginia in 1700, which our valued correspondent, G. D. Scull, Esq., now of London, England, found in the Bodleian Library. These he copied and presented the transcripts to the Virginia Historical Society. Mr. Scull found them in "a vellum-bound volume of manuscripts endorsed 'Original Papers relating to the French Plantation in the West Indies.' They are undoubtedly the original documents emanating from the Provincial Government of Virginia under Francis Nicholson, as they have the official signature of Dionisius Wright, who, it would appear, was secretary of the Council. When the emigration of the French was completed and the necessary papers connected with it collected, they were no doubt sent over to England for the inspection of Dr. Daniel Coxe, who had been the principal promoter of the enterprise. He was one of the Court Physicians to Queen Anne and also in the preceding reign, and had some influence with royalty in directing the exodus of the French towards Virginia, where he had large grants of territory. He was a zealous churchman, a supporter of Christian missions, and sought to promote the spiritual and temporal welfare of the Huguenot refugees at the same time that he colonized his own lands. At his death his manuscripts were dispersed, and some of them fell into the hands of Rawlinson, the ardent and indefatigable collector, and were by him bequeathed to the Bodleian Library."

To these valuable records discovered by Mr. Scull, which furnish an interesting chapter in the history of Virginia, Mr. Brock, the learned secretary and librarian of the Virginia Historical Society, has added, from his own collection and from other sources, important matter relating to the Huguenot emigration. He has enriched the whole by an historical introduction and very full historical and genealogical notes which no other person could have written. In an appendix of nearly one hundred pages, Mr. Brock gives wonderfully exhaustive genealogies of the descendants, of all names, of John de la Fontaine, Bartholomew Dupuy, the Rev. James Marye and Mary M. Chartain, wife of James P. Cocke. A full index adds to the usefulness of the work.

This is the fifth volume of the new series of the publications of the Virginia Historical Society. The volumes are printed for distribution to the life and resident members of the society, who receive them free of charge.

The fee is fifty dollars for life membership, or five dollars a year for annual members. It is not required that contributing members shall be residents of Virginia.

Admissions to the College of St. John the Evangelist in the University of Cambridge. Part 1. Jan. 1629–30 *to July,* 1665. Cambridge: Printed for the College of the University Press and Sold by Deighton Bell and Co. 1882. 8vo. pp. 172.

On the 21st of January, 1629–30, Dr. Owen Gwyn, master of St. John's College, and the senior fellows made an order that a book should be provided for the Register in which he should from time to time enter "the names, parents, country, school, age and tutor of every one to be admitted into the college before their enrolling into the buttery tables." The first entry in the book here published was made nine days afterwards. A "former book" is cited in this register, but no such book has been found.

This admission book has been transcribed and edited by the Rev. John E. B. Mayor, M.A., a voluminous author and editor, whose reputation for learning is well known. He was the editor of Thomas Baker's "History of St. John's College," published in two volumes in 1869. In performing in so thorough manner the work on the volume before us, he conferred a favor not only on the graduates of his own college, but also upon genealogists in England and in America. The details concerning the individuals are unusually full. The editor remarks that he believes that few colleges have registers containing so full particulars as this, the result of " the wise regulations of Dr. Gwyn."

The Life of Admiral Sir Isaac Coffin, Baronet. His English and American Ancestors. By THOMAS C. AMORY. Boston : Cupples, Upham and Company. 1886. 8vo. pp. 141. Price $1.25.

Mr. Amory, the writer of this work, is also the author of The Life of Gov. James Sullivan, 2 volumes, 1859, The Transfer of Erin, 1877, and several other works which have been received with favor by the public. He has chosen for his subject in this volume the life of Admiral Coffin, a native of Boston, whose achievements as an officer of the British Navy won for him the highest naval honors and a baronetcy. Mr. Amory is a near relative of Sir Isaac, that distinguished officer having been a first cousin of the author's father, Jonathan Amory. Mr. Amory also has the advantage of having had a personal acquaintance with his hero, and has preserved in these pages many interesting incidents in the life of one of whom New England his native land, and Old England his adopted country, may well be proud.

Portions of the present work were read as a paper before the New York Genealogical and Biographical Society, and these portions somewhat extended were printed in the *Record* issued by that society for January last. Besides the biography of Admiral Coffin, we have in this book much material relating to the Coffin and Gayer families, but the volume has reached us while the closing pages of this number are in type, and we have not time for such an extended notice and a critical examination of the contents as the work deservedly merits.

The book is elegantly printed, and is illustrated with a portrait of Sir Isaac.

Memoir of the Hon. David Sears. Prepared agreeably to a Resolution of the Massachusetts Historical Society. By ROBERT C. WINTHROP, Jun'r. Cambridge : John Wilson & Son. 1886. 8vo. pp. 31.

This memoir presents to the reader a truthful picture of the late Hon. David Sears, a wealthy and benevolent citizen of Boston, who, from 1857 to 1862, held the office of vice-president of the Massachusetts Historical Society. His life was not what would be called an eventful one, and yet Mr. Winthrop has woven into his narrative many matters of public interest. The author wields a ready pen, and the reader's interest in the subject is sustained to the end.

Eighteenth Century Baptisms in Salem, Massachusetts, hitherto unpublished. Compiled from the Original Records and Alphabetically Arranged. By JAMES A. EMMERTON, A.B., M.D. Salem Press. 1886. 8vo. pp. 126.

Dr. Emmerton, the compiler of this work, who is an accomplished genealogist and antiquary, has had much experience in work like this. He is the author of the History of the Twenty-Third Massachusetts Regiment, and of the Emmerton, Sillsbee and Prince Genealogies. He is joint author of the Emmerton and Waters Gleanings. He has bestowed much care and labor on the copying and arranging of the present work. " The lists were," he informs us in his introductory remarks, " in every case made from the original records, and, in most cases, with the valuable assistance of Mr. Henry F. Waters, who proof-read mine with the original manuscripts." We have here all the unpublished baptisms in the eighteenth century in Salem proper that were accessible. The baptismal record of the First Church from 1636 to 1765, has been printed in the Historical Collections of the Essex Institute by Dr. Henry Wheatland, and the baptisms in Salem Village (now Danvers Centre), and the Middle Precinct (now Peabody), then parishes of old Salem, have been printed in the same periodical, where the present work originally appeared. The book will be of much assistance to genealogists.

A Chronicle, together with a Little Romance regarding Rudolf and Jacob Näf of Frankford, Pennsylvania, and their Descendants; including an Account of the Neffs in Switzerland and America. By ELIZABETH CLIFFORD NEFF, of Gambier, Knox County, Ohio, U.S.A. Press of Robert Clarke & Company, Cincinnati, Ohio. 1886. Sm. 4to. pp. 352. Price $4 including postage.

William Hobart, his Ancestors and Descendants. By L. SMITH HOBART, A.M., Springfield, Mass. 1886. 12mo. pp. v.+182.

A Brief Study in Genealogy. Connin, Conny, Cony, Coney, Cony. By ONE OF THE FAMILY. Cambridge : John Wilson and Son. 1885. Royal 8vo. pp. 39. Fifty copies printed for Private Distribution.

Memoranda relating to Nathaniel Souther, the First Secretary of the Plymouth Colony, and the Descendants of Joseph Souther of Boston. Springfield, Ill. : H. W. Rokker, Printer. 1886. 8vo. pp. 41.

Genealogical Notes of the Descendants of Eber Stebbins of Wilbraham (1773–1826), *and his wife Elizabeth Bliss* (1781–1831), *also of other Families connected by Marriage.* Compiled by SOLOMON BLISS STEBBINS. Boston : Printed by Nathan Sawyer & Son. 1886. 4to. pp. 16.

The Rainborowe Family. Gleanings by Henry F. Waters, A.M. With Annotations by ISAAC J. GREENWOOD, A.M. New York. Fifty copies Privately Printed. 1886. 8vo. pp. 16.

Descendants of Josiah and Catherine Upton of Charlemont, Mass. By WILLIAM H. UPTON, B.A., LL.M. 8vo. pp. 11.

We continue our quarterly notices of recent genealogical publications.

The book at the head of our list is devoted to the history of Rudolph and Jacob Näff and their descendants. The latter now bear the surname of Neff. The two brothers, Rudolph and Jacob, natives of Zurich, Switzerland, sailed, on their way from their native canton to this country, from the port of Rotterdam in Holland, in 1749, and reached Philadelphia on the 11th of September in that year. They settled at Frankford, Pennsylvania, near Philadelphia. After a brief history of the name, an interesting narrative of the lives of the two immigrants is given, followed by a genealogical account of their descendants. The arrangement of the genealogy is peculiar, but there is a good index, by the aid of which the several members of the family can easily be found. The book is handsomely printed on fine paper and neatly bound. The compilation must have cost the author much labor, and she is to be congratulated on bringing out so useful a book in so handsome a style.

The next book is devoted to the ancestry and descendants of William[6] Hobart, who was born at Groton, Mass., May 23, 1751, was graduated at Harvard College in 1774, and died in Potter, Yates County, N. Y., Jan. 1, 1801. He was a descendant in the sixth generation from Edmund[1] Hobart, an early settler of Hingham, Mass., through Rev. Peter,[2] Rev. Gershom[3] (H. C. 1667), Shubael,[4] and Israel,[5] his father. The book was compiled by his grandson, Rev. L. S.[8] Hobart, a graduate of the New Haven Theological Seminary. A full genealogy of the descendants of Edmund[1] Hobart in one line to William[6] is given, after which all lines are included. It is evidently compiled with care.

The next book is by the Hon. Joseph H. Williams, of Augusta, Me., who terms it "A Coñy Brochure." The author is a grandson of the Hon. Daniel[3] Cony, of whom a memoir will be found in North's History of Augusta, pp. 170–3. Judge Cony's father Samuel[2] was a son of Nathaniel[1] Cony, who settled in Boston at the close of the seventeenth century, whence he removed to Sudbury, then to Rehoboth, and finally to Stoughton, where he probably died about 1745. Besides a genealogy of the descendants of Nathaniel Cony, there is much information relative to the English family of Conny, between which and the American family no connection, however, has been proved, though it is possible that a Nathaniel, baptized Aug. 27, 1665, may have been the immigrant. A tabular pedigree carries the name back to the time of Edward II. The book is well compiled and handsomely printed.

The Souther pamphlet contains accounts of the early settlers of the name in New England, particularly Nathaniel Souther, the first secretary of the Plymouth colony, and Joseph Souther who settled at Boston as early as 1657. The descendants of Joseph are very fully carried out. The author, George Howard Souther, Esq., of Springfield, Ill., has done a commendable work in preparing this genealogy.

The author of the next work is the Hon. Solomon B. Stebbins, of Boston. He has preserved in a handsome form the ancestry of himself and other relatives. One line each of four families, Stebbins, Bliss, Bradford and Rogers, is here traced, Stebbins to Rowland Stebbins of Northampton ; Bliss to Nathaniel Bliss of Springfield ; Bradford to Gov. William Bradford of Plymouth, and Rogers to the Rev. John Rogers of Dedham, England, whom some have erroneously supposed to be a descendant of the Marian martyr. (See REGISTER, xvii. 43, 93.) The Stebbins genealogy, printed in 1771, and reprinted by this society in 1879 (REG. xxxiii. 375), is the earliest known genealogy published in New England.

The Rainborowe and the Upton pamphlets are reprints from the April number of the REGISTER.

RECENT PUBLICATIONS,

Presented to the New England Historic Genealogical Society, to June 1, 1886.

I. *Publications written or edited by Members of the Society.*

Memoir of The Rev. William Stoodley Bartlet. By the Rev. Edmund F. Slafter, A.M. Boston: Privately printed. 1886. 8vo. pp. 8.

Population for 1875 and 1885, Massachusetts. Increase and decrease by towns. 8vo. pp. 181. [By Col. Carroll D. Wright.]

Bar Harbor and Mount Desert Island. Press of Liberty Printing Company, 107 Liberty Street, New York. 8vo. pp. 44. [Compiled by W. B. Lapham, M.D.]

Portland in the Past, with historical notes of Old Falmouth. By William Goold. Printed for the author by B. Thurston and Company, Portland, Maine. 1886. 8vo. pp. 543.

Early Spanish and Portuguese Coinage in America. By J. Carson Brevoort. Boston: Privately printed. 1885. Quarto, pp. 28.

Philip H. Wentworth 1818–1886. Memorial Sermon and address by Samuel J. Barrows. Boston: Press of George H. Ellis, 141 Franklin Street. 1886. 8vo. pp. 21.

Battle of the Bush, Dramas and Historic Legends, illustrated. Elaborated from the startling events of the New England wars of a hundred years—Tragic, Comical, Progressive, and Divine. By Robert Boodey Caverly. Boston: Published by B. B. Russell. 1886. 8vo. pp. 346.

Groton Historical Series, No. X. The earliest Church Records in Groton. Groton, Mass. 1886. 8vo. pp. 42. [By Hon. Samuel A. Green, M.D.]

The Loss of the Oregon. R. B. Forbes. [1886.] 8vo. pp. 78.

Memoir of the Hon. David Sears, prepared agreeably to a Resolution of the Massachusetts Society. By Robert C. Winthrop, Junr. Cambridge: John Wilson and Son, University Press. 1886. 8vo. pp. 31.

Brigadier General Robert Toombs. An address delivered before the Confederate Survivors Association in Augusta, Georgia, at its Eighth Annual Meeting, on Memorial Day, April 26th, 1886. By Col. Charles C. Jones, Jr., LL.D., President of the Association. Augusta, Ga.: Printed at the Chronicle Office. 1886. 8vo. pp. 19.

II. *Other Publications.*

Horace B. Claflin, Born December 18th, 1811, Died November 14th, 1885. Quarto. pp. 161.

Proceedings at the unveiling of the Soldiers' Monument on the site of Fort Stephenson, Fremont, Ohio. Fremont, O.: The Democratic Messenger. 1885. 8vo. pp. 123.

Catalogue of the Officers and Students of Brown University. 1885–6. Providence: E. A. Johnson and Co., Printers, 57 Weybosset St. 1885. 8vo. pp. 64.

Twenty-eighth Annual Report of the Board of Directors of the Brooklyn Library. Presented March 25, 1886. Brooklyn, N. Y. Printed for the Library. 1886. 8vo. pp. 24.

Transactions of the Literary and Historical Society of Quebec. No. 18. Sessions of 1883 to 1886. Quebec: Printed at the "Morning Chronicle" Office. 1886. 8vo. pp. 56.

Dummer Academy. Address of Major Ben. Perley Poore, and the report of Hon. George F. Choate, Chairman of the Building Committee, at the Dedication of the New Dormitory, October 22, 1885. Newburyport: William H. Huse & Co., Printers, Herald Office. 1886. 8vo. pp. 23.

The Delaware State Medical Society and its founders in the Eighteenth Century. Presented at the annual meeting of the American Academy of Medicine, held at New York, October 28 and 29, 1885. By L. P. Bush, A.M., M.D., Wilmington, Delaware. New York. 1886. 8vo. pp. 16.

Proceedings of the Society of Antiquaries of London. November 27, 1884, to July 2, 1885. Second Series, Vol. X. London: Printed by Nichols and Sons, for the Society of Antiquaries, Burlington House. 8vo. pp. 145–364.

The Two hundred and Forty seventh Annual Record of the Ancient and Honorable Artillery Company, 1884–85. Sermon by Rev. William Lawrence of Cambridge. Boston: Alfred Mudge and Son, Printers, 24 Franklin St. 1885. 8vo. pp. 205.

Proceedings of the Twentieth session of the American Pomological Society, held in Grand Rapids, Michigan, September 9th, 10th, and 11th, 1885. Published by the Society. 1886. Royal quarto, pp. 171—lix.

Library of Harvard University. Bibliographical Contributions. Edited by Justin Winsor, Librarian. No. 21. A list of the publications of Harvard University and its officers, with the chief publications on the University, 1880–1885. Cambridge, Mass.: Issued by the Library of Harvard University. 1886. 8vo. pp. 62.

The History of the Parish and Manor of Wookey, being a contribution towards a future history of the County of Somerset. By Thomas Scott Holmes, M.A., Vicar of the Parish. 1886. Bristol: C. T. Jeffries and Sons, Printers. 8vo. pp. 164.

Proceedings of the Davenport Academy of Natural Sciences, Volume IV., 1882-1884. Davenport, Iowa: Published by the Academy of Natural Sciences. 1886. 8vo. pp. 347.

Arnold's Expedition to Quebec, 1775-1776. The Diary of Ebenezer Wild, with a list of such Diaries, by Justin Winsor. Privately Reprinted, 75 copies, from the Proceedings of the Massachusetts Historical Society. Cambridge; John Wilson & Son. 1886. 8vo. pp. 12.

The Mountain Campaigns in Georgia, or War Scenes on the W. and A. 1886. Quarto. pp. 52.

Exercises commemorative of the one hundred and fiftieth anniversary of the West Congregational Church, Haverhill, Mass., including historical addresses, poems, reminiscences, and letters from former pastors. October 22, 1885. Haverhill, Mass.: C. C. Morse and Son, Book and Job Printers. 1886. 8vo. pp. 59.

Proceedings of the Rhode Island Historical Society, 1885-86. Providence: Printed for the Society. 1886. 8vo. pp. 97.

Eightieth Anniversary Celebration of the New England Society in the City of New York, at Delmonico. Dec. 22. 1885. 8vo. pp. 97.

The addresses and proceedings connected with the Semi-Centennial Celebration of Marietta College, June 28—July 1. Marietta, Ohio: E. B. Alderman and Sons. 1885. 8vo. pp. 232.

Catalogue Marietta College. 1885-86. Marietta, Ohio: E. R. Alderman and Sons, Printers. 1886. 8vo. pp. 44.

DEATHS.

SAMUEL WARD FRANCIS, M.D., died at Newport, R. I., March 25, 1886, aged 49. He was the youngest son of John Wakefield Francis, M.D., LL.D., of New York City, of whom a memoir will be found in the "Memorial Biographies of the New England Historic Genealogical Society," vol. iv. page 181.

He was born in New York, Dec. 26, 1836, and was grad. at Columbia College in 1857. He studied medicine, and commenced its practice in his native city. About the year 1859 he married Miss Harriet McAllister, and soon after relinquished his profession and removed to Newport. He resumed practice about fifteen years ago. His wife died before him, but two sons and three daughters survive. He published several works on medical and other subjects. In 1857, while in college, he invented what is now called the type-writer and took out a patent for his invention. See an account of this in the *Historical Magazine* for December, 1857, page 378.

TUTHILL KING, a prominent citizen of Chicago, died on 16th March. He was a descendant of William[1] and Dorothy Kinge, who settled in Salem, Mass., in 1635. Samuel,[2] the second son, removed to Southold, Suffolk Co., N.Y., and from him, in the line of Samuel,[3] Jr., John,[4] John,[5] Jr., and Joseph,[6] Mr. Tuthill[7] King descended. His father, Joseph King of Southold, married Elizabeth Tuthill, and removed to Genesee County, N. Y.

Tuthill King was born there in 1804. At the age of 20 he went to Buenos Ayres, where he remained for ten years, and was successful as a merchant. In 1834 he returned and settled in Chicago, where he remained to the time of his death. He invested largely in real estate in that city, and amassed a fortune of more than a million dollars. He was closely identified with the interests of Chicago, and among his many charities was the endowment of a Chair of Biblical and Ecclesiastical History in the Presbyterian Seminary, by a gift of twenty thousand dollars. He left three daughters, all of whom are married, and a widow.

HENRY STEVENS, F.S.A., of London, England, died in London, Feb. 28, 1886, aged 66. He was a son of the Hon. Henry Stevens, at one time president of the Vermont Historical Society, and was born at Barnet, Vt., Aug. 11, 1819. His descent is traced in Saunderson's History of Charlestown, N. H., from Thomas[1] of London, through Cyprian[2] of Lancaster, Joseph,[3] Capt. Phineas,[4]

Hon. Samuel,[5] Hon. Enos,[6] and Hon. Henry[7] Stevens of Barnet. Henry[8] Stevens was grad. at Yale College in 1843. In 1845 he went to London, and commenced business as a dealer in rare historical and antiquarian books. He assisted the Trustees of the British Museum in completing their collection of American books, and supplied many American collectors with rare Americana. He was also distinguished as an antiquary and bibliopolist, and published a number of valuable books, among which his Historical Nuggets, 2 vols., 1862, Historical and Geographical Notes on the Earliest Discoveries in America, 1869, and The Bibles in the Caxton Exhibition, 1878, are deserving of particular notice. He commenced last year a new series of his Historical Nuggets, and a Catalogue of Rare Books relating to America, both as serials. See REGISTER, xxxix. 407.

ROBERT RIDDLE STODART, of Edinburgh, Scotland, died there April 19, aged 59. He was the eldest son of John Riddle Stodart, W.S., and was born Nov. 16, 1827. He received his education at the High School of Edinburgh and the Edinburgh University. At the age of 18 he went to Ceylon, and took charge of a coffee plantation belonging to his father. In 1863, ill health obliged him to return home, and in April, 1864, he was appointed Lyon Clerk Depute, a post which he held with distinction till his death. He early developed a taste for local and family history, and even while in India he was an ardent student of these subjects. He published in 1880, "Scottish Arms," in two large folio volumes; the first consisting of a collection of arms, beautifully fac-similed in colors from ancient manuscripts; and the second, of heraldic and genealogical notes illustrative of these arms. This work has been called "the most important contribution to Scottish historical heraldry since the days of Nesbet." It established their author's position "as one of the ablest genealogists of the day." A biographical sketch will be found in *The Scotsman,* Edinburgh, April 20, 1886.

Prof. EDWARD TUCKERMAN, LL D., died at Amherst, Mass., March 15, 1886, aged 68. He was the eldest child of Edward and Sophia (May) Tuckerman, and was born in Boston, Dec. 7, 1817.

He prepared for college at Ingraham's School and the Boston Latin School; entered the sophomore class at Union College in 1834, graduating in 1837. From thence he proceeded to Cambridge, and was graduated at the Harvard Law School in 1839. He remained in Cambridge till 1841, continuing his studies at the law school, and then went abroad and studied several years in Germany, devoting himself particularly to philosophy, history and botany. Returning to this country, he joined the senior class at Harvard College in 1846, graduating the following year. In 1852 he completed the course at the Harvard Divinity School. While a student at Union College he was appointed Curator of the Museums. In 1854 he left Cambridge and removed to Amherst. His connection with Amherst College covers a period of thirty-two years. He held the position of Lecturer in History from 1854-55, and again from 1858-73; was Professor of Oriental History from 1855-58, and Professor of Botany from 1858 till his death. In 1875 he received the degree of LL.D. from Amherst College. He married, May 17, 1854, at Boston, Sarah Eliza Sigourney, daughter of Thomas P. Cushing, Esq., of Boston, and leaves no children. One brother, Dr. S. Parkman Tuckerman, who has resided abroad for many years, survives him.

His literary work began at the age of fifteen, while a boy at the Latin School. In 1832 he wrote several minor articles on matters of antiquarian interest, for the *Mercantile Journal* and *Boston Transcript.* In 1833 he assisted the late Mr. Samuel G. Drake, the celebrated antiquary, in annotating two tracts on Philip's War. From 1834-41 he contributed to the *New York Churchman* a series of fifty-four articles entitled "Notitia Literaria" and "Adversaria," covering a wide range in criticism, history, biography and theology. He edited Josselyn's "New England Rarities," published in 1860 in the Transactions of the American Antiquarian Society, which in 1865 was revised and issued in a separate volume. He was an occasional writer in the *Church Eclectic.* During the latter part of his life he devoted himself to the study of botany. On the subject of Lichens he had been for many years the recognized authority in America. He published a number of botanical books and articles.

The early home of JOHN HARVARD'S mother.

THE

HISTORICAL AND GENEALOGICAL REGISTER.

OCTOBER, 1886.

PETER OLIVER,

The last Chief Justice of the Superior Court of Judicature of the Province of Massachusetts Bay.

By Thomas Weston, Jr., Esq., A.M.

Read before the New England Historic Genealogical Society, September, 1885, and before the Bostonian Society, November, 1885.

[Concluded from page 252.]

IN 1769, when Chief Justice Hutchinson left the bench for the position of governor of the Province, Judge Oliver's friends supposed as a matter of course he would succeed to that office. But strong political and other influences secured that position for Mr. Justice Lynde, and it was not until his resignation in 1772 that Judge Oliver was appointed chief justice.

At this time no position in the Province was more important or more embarrassing. The time was at hand when every man of influence and position must show his colors. The popular tide was beginning unmistakably to set strongly in one direction. With Judge Oliver's high social and official position, his popularity, his great wealth, his ability, his scholarship, his many friends, that current would surely bear him to the top. In the other direction was the love he bore to his King, his conscientious views of the relation of the colonies to the mother country, and of the rights of the Crown. The choice involved the probable loss of everything dear to him in the land of his birth. He hesitated not for a moment; conscientiously yet fearlessly he assumed the duties of his high office, resolving that he would faithfully perform them at all hazard, even if thereby he should lose everything and suffer the ignominy which coming generations might heap upon him. He as well as the patriot leaders counted the cost of the decision.

Upon assuming the duties of his office, popular prejudice and passion were running higher than ever before in the history of the colonies. The spirit of liberty and desire for independence were overriding all established precedents.

Events followed each other in rapid succession. Never before had there been such intense excitement in all parts of the province. Matters could not thus long continue without open resistance on the part of the people to the lawful authority of the Crown. It seemed evident to him that the leaders of the patriot party were not careful to allay this excitement, and that every official act of the officers of the King was in some way construed as inimical to their cause. Certain it is, that under other circumstances many of these acts which were so bitterly denounced would have been entirely overlooked. Those who had been sworn to execute the laws of the land could not but regard with jealous eye the course of the patriot leaders in so often ignoring the well-established law and precedent of colonial rule. They never seemed to comprehend how strong and deep was the desire for independence, and how oppressive and unjust were the measures that the British ministry were endeavoring to force upon a people whose ancestors and whose whole training for generations all so thoroughly embued them with a spirit of liberty.

The legislature, too, always heretofore conservative, was now most radical in its opposition to everything that seemed to be encroaching on the part of the Crown upon the liberties of the people, and in the exercise of powers authorized although seldom heretofore exercised by the royal officers, and at the same time quite willing to overlook usurpations by themselves of any rights and privileges on their part, as established by statute and precedent, if thereby they might further the cause which now the people seemed to have so much at heart.

Never was there a parliamentary body which more accurately reflected the advanced thought and opinion of the masses in opposition to the odious measures of his majesty's ministry, than the house of representatives during these years. The turbulent spirit of the times was nowhere more strongly manifested than here. The subject-matter of much of the legislation, as well as the spirit in which it was debated and passed, clearly pointed out the breach between the King and the Province which must sooner or later come. Undoubtedly the General Court of Massachusetts, for these years, was one of the most potent forces of the patriot party, which led to Lexington and Bunker Hill, and July 4, 1776.

Notwithstanding the political excitement of the times, the province was never more prosperous in its financial condition than now, and was in this respect the envy of the other colonies.* Its treasury was full, and this too without the income brought by the obnoxious Stamp Act and other expediencies for increasing the revenue. The people seemed fully to realize that there was no occasion for the passage of these most obnoxious and unjust measures to help swell the coffers of a profligate ministry. The temper of the legislature

* Hutchinson, Vol. 3, p. 350.

was such towards those who were known to be in sympathy with the ministry, that the minority, fearing they would withhold the customary grants for the salaries of the public officers, recommended to the ministry, that there should be a modification of the charter by which salaries of such officers, which had heretofore been voted by the General Court and paid by the province, should hereafter be paid by the King. The salary of the chief justice, which had been only two hundred pounds per annum, was wholly inadequate to meet his personal expenses.* The payment of this small sum even had been delayed until the legislature should choose to vote it. This most unfortunate recommendation on the part of the minority was adopted by the ministry, and by this change the salary of the chief justice was raised to four hundred pounds. The fact that the justices of the highest court in the land should thus be made dependent on the Crown, provoked the most bitter indignation on the part of the legislature, and to the leaders of the patriot party no measure thus far in the history of the times met with such determined resistance.

When the change in the charter affecting the salaries of the governor and justices of the Superior Court was first promulgated, the legislature was not in session. But immediately a petition was presented to the selectmen of Boston praying for a public meeting to consider this most odious measure. Mr. Hancock opposed it, and it was not granted by them. This seemed to excite suspicion in the minds of the people, and the news of the change in the charter was widely disseminated and provoked the most bitter opposition. Several addresses to the governor were made regarding it, and his reply exasperated the patriot party more than ever. Town meetings were called all over the province to protest against the obnoxious grants, and sharp and bitter were the debates thereon. It was brought into the legislature, but for various reasons postponed until its next meeting.

Upon the coming in of the legislature in February, 1774, it was evident that this question would be the most important one to be considered during the session. The previous legislature, aware of the action that the ministry would probably take, had raised the salary of the justices of this court one hundred pounds more than they had formerly received. Early in the session they had voted that the justices of the court give to the Assembly their decision upon the question whether or no they would receive their salaries from the Crown. The Court met, and agreed that they would give no separate answer, but would carefully consider the subject-matter, and then would give such reply, as a whole, as should to them seem proper. During the recess, however, Judge Trowbridge had been persuaded to refuse the salary from the King and accept it from

---

* Hutchinson, Hist., Vol. 3, p. 388.

the legislature, and addressed a note to the speaker informing him of his action, without consulting with his associates. Judge Oliver, on being informed of this breach of faith on the part of so eminent a man as Mr. Justice Trowbridge, determined to render himself unable to comply with what seemed to him an improper and unreasonable demand of the house of representatives made under such implied threats, and formally accepted the full amount of the salary granted by the Crown.*

The Assembly on coming together resolved that the conduct of Judge Trowbridge was satisfactory, and the next day passed a resolve, "that unless the other justices shall within eight days inform the house whether they had received in full the grants made by the assembly for last year's salary, and shall also explicitly declare that for the future, according to invariable usage, they will accept the grants of the general assembly without accepting any grant from the Crown for the same time, the house will then have further proceedings on their conduct."

Three of the justices gave such answers as were satisfactory. Judge Oliver felt that the course of the house of representatives in this matter was an insult to his dignity and to the Court over which he presided, and declared if need be he would stand alone rather than yield to such an impertinent demand.

In his answer he set forth, "that he had been a justice of the Superior Court for 17 years : that his salary had been insufficient for his support : that he had thrown himself on former assemblies for the redress which he could not obtain : that his estate was much impaired by neglect of attendance upon his private business : that he had repeatedly intended to resign his office, but had been dissuaded from so doing by respectable members of the Assembly, who encouraged him to hope for better support : that when his Majesty, in his great and good name, granted him a salary as he had done to others in like station in other colonies, he thought himself bound to take it, for the time which is past, and that he should not dare refuse it for the time to come."†

This bold and fearless answer of the chief justice was unexpected, and as it was read in the house produced a profound sensation. Upon receiving this answer from him they sent a remonstrance to the Governor and Council, declaring that by such conduct " the Chief Justice had perversely and corruptly done that which hath an obvious and direct tendency to the perversion of law and justice ; that he thereby had proved an enemy to the constitution of the province, and placed himself under bane and detached himself totally from his connections with the people and lost their confidence ; and rendered himself totally disqualified any longer to hold and act in the office of a Justice of the Superior Court, and they therefore pray that he may be forthwith removed."‡

---

* Hutchinson, Vol. 3, p. 442.   † Hutchinson, Vol. 3, p. 443.   ‡ Ibid.

Upon presenting this remonstrance an order was soon after passed, that it was improper for the chief justice to sit in Court while these proceedings were pending before the governor. The house also asked that the term of the Court which came in on the 15th of February might be adjourned. The majority of the Court came in, but the chief justice, advised by his friends not to be present lest he should meet with bodily harm from the populace, so great was the feeling against him, did not attend. The grand jury refused to act, and the Court finally adjourned without further action.*

Never before had there been such excitement, not only in the streets of Boston but even in the General Court itself. The chief justice was hung in effigy,† and subject to such insult whenever he appeared in public that he was forced to avoid the public thoroughfares of the town.‡

On the 24th, the house of representatives voted to impeach the chief justice before the Council. The measure had been advised by John Adams, who was chairman of the committee. But Samuel Adams was the actual leader in all these bold proceedings.§ The committee, with John Adams at their head, waited upon the governor, desiring him to be in the chair with the Council, that he might hear them as they presented the impeachment.‖ His Excellency refused to act upon the articles of impeachment, as in his opinion he had no jurisdiction over the matter.

The house, upon receiving the answer of the governor, after a stormy debate, decided to make no reply, but soon after framed and passed a new order impeaching before the General Court of the Provinces, Peter Oliver, Esq., Chief Justice of the Superior Court, of certain high crimes and misdemeanors, and ordered the committee to prepare the articles of impeachment.¶ His official conduct for seventeen years was most critically examined—his public and private life underwent the most rigid scrutiny, in the hope that something might be discovered upon which additional charges might be framed against him.** His bitterest enemies could not discover the faintest indication of a single blemish to mar his character; and these new proceedings only embodied the same charge of receiving a salary from the King, with an additional count that in the reply to the house he had said that the salary granted by the Assembly had been inadequate to his support, which they alleged was ungrateful, false and malicious, and tended to bring scandal upon his Majesty's government in the province, and was sufficient cause alone for his removal. The house of representatives in their haste seemed to for-

---

* Hutchinson, Vol. 3, p. 444.
† John Adams's Works (Diary), Vol. 2, p. 334.
‡ Hutchinson (Diary), pp. 146, 147.
§ Life of Samuel Adams, Vol. 2, p. 135.
‖ Their Articles of Impeachment are still extant in the hand writing of John Adams.
¶ Hutchinson, Vol. 3, p. 445.
** Hutchinson (Diary), p. 146.

get that his salary had only been two hundred pounds per annum, with great delays in its payment, and that it was not until after the grant made by the Crown of four hundred pounds that they had raised it to three hundred per annum. He had been repeatedly assured by leading members of the house that his salary, being inadequate, should be raised, and after the change by thus increasing it to this amount, they seemed to confess that it had been altogether too small.

The governor again declined to hear the committee, avoiding the issue by saying that he was about to leave the provinces for England, and had not time to consider it, and recommended the despatch of the necessary business before them. The council and house were most diligent in discovering ways by which the governor would be compelled to appoint a time for the consideration of the impeachment. The governor concluded that the wisest course for him was to dissolve the assembly, and had prepared a long message to that effect. While this message was being read before the council, the house, hearing of its purport, closed its doors, refused admission of the secretary to deliver the message and thus prorogue them, until they had voted their salaries and passed a resolve that they had done all that in the capacity of representatives of the people in this court could be done for the removal of Peter Oliver, Esq., the chief justice, from his seat in the Superior Court, and that it must be presumed that the governor refusing to take any measures therein is because he also received his support from the Crown,"[*] and after attending to a few minor matters they opened their doors and allowed the secretary to enter and deliver the governor's message proroguing them.[†]

The odium which the chief justice incurred in thus defying the sentiment of the house of representatives soon spread throughout the province. The other justices, although sharing the same political opinion as Judge Oliver, having so shaped their course as to incur no censure on the part of the General Court, were allowed to proceed with their duties without the chief justice. But jurors refused to appear while the chief justice was yet in office, and early in 1774 the whole course of judicial proceedings had stopped.[‡]

To add to the opprobrium now so generally heaped upon Judge Oliver[§] while the stormy proceedings of his impeachment were going on, news arrived in Boston that Gov. Hutchinson, the chief justice and others had written letters to his Majesty's ministers in London, giving them false accounts of the affairs in the colonies,

---

[*] Hutchinson, Hist., Vol. 3, p. 454.
[†] Life of Samuel Adams, Vol. 2, p. 137.
[‡] Hutchinson, Hist., Vol. 3, p. 454. John Adams's Works, Vol. 2, p. 332; Vol. x. p. 240.
[§] John Trumbull, then a student in John Adams's office—the author of M'Fingal—thus referred to him:

> " Did Heaven appoint our Chief Judge Oliver,
> Fill that high place with ignoramus,
> Or has it covals by mandamus ? "

and advising extreme measures for their complete subjugation. These letters had been intercepted by Franklin and by his agents, sent to Holland, and from there returned to Boston. They were publicly read in Faneuil Hall to a large assembly of citizens, and the contents published and widely scattered throughout the country. Their contents set the whole province in a blaze. They proved to be the spark that was only wanting to fire the hearts of the patriots of the Revolution. From every part of the province came loud and bitter denunciations against the infamous ministers of the Crown. Whoever questioned the measures of the patriot party was regarded with suspicion. To be in sympathy even with his Majesty's officers of the province was beginning to be regarded as hostile to the liberties of the people. In a few months more the chasm had become too wide to cross, and the conflict was ready to begin.

The chief justice had always been a most zealous supporter of the royal prerogative. He was known to be in full sympathy with his Majesty's ministry in their policy towards the American colonies, and the people at once assumed that he was one of the authors of these infamous letters. He regarded it as beneath his dignity to make denial of this groundless charge, and while he may have known that such letters had been sent abroad by some of the unscrupulous officers of the Crown, there is no proof that he was the author of any of them.

Boston was now under military rule, and the war for independence had begun. The General Court never again assembled under the charter. Now other matters were more important than the trial of the chief justice upon the articles of impeachment, and no further action was ever taken upon them. Certain it is in the history of the country no judicial officer was ever threatened with impeachment upon such trivial charges, and which, under less exciting times, would never have been entertained by a legislative assembly. It illustrates the temper of the times, and how even deliberative bodies are sometimes swayed by the prejudice and excitement of the hour.

The position in which Judge Oliver now found himself was painful in the extreme. He had dared to resist the known will of the legislature of the province. He had been impeached by the representatives of the people in his high and dignified office; his friends had forsaken him; public confidence in him was lost; his influence destroyed; his usefulness at an end. He had been insulted by the mob and hung in effigy. Fears for his personal safety even were entertained by the few friends who still adhered to him. It was deemed unsafe for him to attend the death-bed of his only brother, Lieut. Gov. Oliver, or even to be present at his funeral.* No man of the time encountered such obloquy and reproach.

Tradition has it, that while the English ships were in the harbor

---

* Hutchinson (Diary), Vol. 1, p. 147.

to take Lord Howe and his troops from Boston, in the edge of the evening Judge Oliver was seen coming on horseback up the hill upon which stood Oliver Hall in Middleborough. He had come in this way from Boston. No one would have recognized him as the chief justice. He was alone and covered with mud; his face haggard and careworn. He did not stop to eat or rest. Hastily entering the doorway of the Hall, he went directly to a secret closet in the great parlor where he kept his valuables, unlocked the door, took his money and such articles of value as his saddlebags would hold, cast a long, sad look into his library, hurriedly glanced from room to room in what had been to him so delightful a home, hastily bade the housekeeper good-bye, and galloped out into the darkness of the night, never more to see the place where he had spent so many happy years and enjoyed so much with friends and neighbors.* The next morning he embarked with Lord Howe, and never after saw the land of his birth.†

Oliver Hall remained for some years after, with most of its furniture and adornments. But the populace were becoming more and more enraged against the tory traitors to their cause. Their fathers, their husbands and sons had been at Bunker Hill and never returned; others had come back to tell of the hardships and sufferings at Long Island and Monmouth. The cause of liberty and independence was the absorbing theme. The tory was the most hated and despised of all men. Every reminder of him was hateful. The patriots began to contrast the wealth and sumptuous living of the officers of the Crown with their own plain habits and customs. Every mark which their tory rulers had left seemed to cause fresh smarts to the wounds received at the hands of the mother country. No monument of British influence remaining was so conspicuous as Oliver Hall. About midnight, after some of the soldiers of the town had returned from a hard-fought campaign, an unusual number of people seemed to be about the village, when suddenly the Hall was discovered to be on fire. No effort was made to extinguish it. It was a long time in burning.‡ The contents were taken out by whoever desired them, and to-day many relics of its former splendor may be found in the old houses and families of the place. The doors were taken off and may now be seen in a house some five miles away.§ The women tore off the paper-hangings, and for years afterwards used the sprigs of gold leaf as ornaments for their hair when they were to grace with their presence the fashionable parties in that or neighboring towns.

After the Hall had been burned its grounds were entirely neglect-

---

* Mrs. Mary Norcutt, account of the last time Judge Oliver was in Middleboro'.
† He, with certain other loyalists, was by act of General Court of Massachusetts, passed October, 1778, banished from the country.
‡ This is from Mrs. Norcutt's description of the burning of Oliver Hall. The Hall was burned about the year 1780.
§ House of Sprague Stetson, Esq., in Lakeville.

ed, and passers-by seemed to take especial delight in destroying what
the flames had left belonging to the hated tory. Some of the seats
in the groves and the summer house on the banks of the pond
remained for a few years, but finally rotted away and fell in
pieces. The trees, many of them of the first growth of the forest,
were cut by such of the neighbors as wanted wood, and in a few
years but little was left to indicate what Judge Oliver's residence
had once been. The estate was confiscated and afterwards sold by
the commissioner appointed to sell the property of royalists.*

There has always been a bitter prejudice against the loyalists who were on the bench at the beginning of the Revolution,
which did not attach to the members of the bar, a large majority
of whom were loyalists, and that prejudice has shown itself all
through the history of the times. Most writers of this period
have been content to accept the estimate of those men as gathered
from the utterances of their cotemporaries, who were not in political
sympathy with them, during the turbulent times immediately preceding the open rupture between the colonies and the mother country. The justices of both the Superior Court and the Court of Common Pleas, were conscientious and fearless men. Most of them had
passed far beyond that period of life when opinions on political
subjects would be likely to be changed. On the other hand, the
leaders of the patriot party for the most part were in the flush of early
manhood, of ardent temperament, keen to the oppressive acts of the
Crown and zealous for the liberties of the people. Their measures and
their methods were not calculated to change the convictions of the
grave and thoughtful men on the bench. Neither could they be neutral at such times. They were bound to act in their official capacity
according to their convictions, which they were not careful to conceal. Moreover, they thoroughly believed in the Crown and the
principles of government on which it rested. All of their official
surroundings served to make their convictions permanent. They
had been trained either at the bar or by long experience on the bench,
to adhere with great tenacity to the forms and precedents of the
English law and of the English constitution. The form of government and its administration was to them a sacred thing. They had
taken their solemn oaths faithfully to administer and maintain the
constitution and laws of the realm. Such men could not have been
true to themselves, and approved or even done otherwise than
condemn the measures brought forward by the patriot leaders
under such exciting circumstances, and necessarily in their judgment
of doubtful expediency and tending to overthrow the very foundations
upon which the government rested.

It is worthy of remark, in making our estimate of the character of
Judge Oliver, that notwithstanding his love for his King and the laws

* See Acts of Gen. Court of Massachusetts, passed October, 1779.

and institutions of the mother country ; notwithstanding the many public insults he had received, and the strong provocations constantly thrust upon him by his political enemies, not a judicial act, during all of these stormy times, has come down to us which was hasty or inconsiderate, or where any trace of personality was manifested. His most bitter enemies could bring no complaint against him personally. His conduct was always open. There was no guile or deceit in his nature. He was always dignified, yet courteous, polite, patient. He cared nothing for personal vindication of his honor or for criticisms upon the correctness of his views upon government and public affairs. He seemed to carry with him the consciousness that in his official capacity he was in the discharge of his sworn duty, and was not careful as to what the consequences to him while acting in that capacity might be, or what would be the estimate that might be put upon them by others. While guarded in his public utterances concerning the leaders of the patriot party and their cause, his notes in his diary show that he regarded them as men of desperate fortune, unbounded ambition, and who were bringing ruin on their own happy and prosperous country. Undoubtedly many of his associates who espoused the cause of the Crown were actuated by the general belief among them that the rebellion would soon be suppressed and they rewarded for their loyalty and the patriot leaders punished ; but with him, his course was a matter of principle, conscientiously and deliberately taken.

The offence of which Judge Oliver was guilty was that of being true to his convictions, in opposition to that of a very large majority during the most exciting period of the history of the province. It was, however, then, in the estimation of the country, an offence of the greatest enormity. His position, his great ability as a jurist, his high sense of honor, his cultivated tastes, his learning, his zeal in guarding the rights of the people and of the government in times past, his just and impartial interpretation of the laws of the province as they had come down from their earliest settlements, his correct application of the preambles of the common law which the colonists had brought with them from the mother country, as applied to the new and varied condition of affairs here existing, his keen legal perceptions, his logical mind, his fearlessness in the discharge of what he believed to be his duty, his generosity, his irreproachable character, his many friends and associations with men of letters, what he had done by his personal exertions to promote the welfare of his town and county, were all forgotten.* It was enough that when the struggle for independence was approaching he was found to be a loyalist, an officer under the Crown who had received his salary from the King and not at the hands of the legislature ; and this was sufficient to brand him with the opprobrium of the times.

---

* See John Adams's estimate of Judge Oliver, Vol. 2, pp. 134–328; also, see Dr. Eliot.

After leaving Boston he went to Halifax, and soon after removed to Burmington, England, where he died in 1797. After his death a tablet to his memory was placed in St. Philip's Church, where it is still to be seen. He lived there a quiet and happy life, beloved and respected by all who knew him.* He was always a welcomed guest in the choicest circles of rank and culture of English society. He had no regrets for the sacrifices he had made or for the course he had taken. Nor did he even manifest any bitterness of feeling towards those who seemed to be his personal enemies or the many former friends who had deserted him. His letters to his children in this country were models of composition, showing the culture of the scholar as well as the tender solicitude of the parent, often expressing the wish that their lives and character might be irreproachable and the world better for their living. One of them closes with this quotation from his favorite poet, "That life is long that answers life's great end."

Note.—Judge Oliver married, as has been already stated, Mary, a daughter of William Clarke, Esq. He left issue—1. *Elizabeth*, who married Major George Watson, one of whose daughters married Martin Brimmer, Esq., and another Sir Grenville Temple; 2. *Daniel*, born October 8, 1738, H. C. 1758, died s. p.; 3. *Peter*, born June 17, 1741, H. C. 1761, M.D., married Nellie, eldest daughter of Gov. Hutchinson, and died at Shrewsbury, England, July 30, 1822, leaving issue; 4. *William*, born May 23, 1743; 5. *Andrew*, born Sept. 15, 1746, H. C. 1765, married Phebe Spooner, and died at Middleboro', January, 1772. His daughter married Dr. Waterhouse of Cambridge. 6. *Mary*, born June 22, 1751, and died young.

CHURCH RECORDS OF FARMINGTON, CONN.

Communicated by Julius Gay, A.M., of Farmington, Conn.

[Concluded from page 157.]

Deaths.

Jany. 5, 1781	Departed this life Wid: Mary Bull.
Jany. 11, 1781	Departed this life Daniel Gridley.
Jany. 24, 1781	Departed life a Child of Salmon Root.
March, 1781	Departed life a Child of Willm Portter.
April 5, 1781	Departed life a Babe of Gad Woodruff.
April 15, 1781	Departed this life Lucretia Merrell.
April 16, 1781	Departed this life Stephen Hart.
April 27, 1781	Departed this life Samuel Stedman.

* Soon after his arrival in England he compiled a Scripture Lexicon, which went through several editions. It was a text-book at Oxford for some time, from which University its author received the degree of Doctor of Laws. While a resident of Burmington he formed an acquaintance with Lord Lyttleton, which afterward ripened into intimacy.—*Dr. F. E. Oliver.*

May 9, 1781	Departed this life Timothy Portter.
May 16, 1781	Departed this life the Wife of Tim° Woodruff.
June 10, 1781	Departed this life Charles son of Lieut. Isaiah Thomson.
August 4, 1781	Departed this life a Babe of Luke Thomson.
August 9, 1781	Departed this life Lieut. Elnathan Gridley.
August 18, 1781	Departed this life the Wife of Eli Andruss.
August 30, 1781	Departed this life Erastus son of John Thomson.
August 31, 1781	Departed this life the Widow Pratt. [ter.
August 31, 1781	Departed this life Noah son of Deaᶜⁿ Noah Port-
January 12, 1782	Departed this life Capt. Ephraim Treadwell.
January 19, 1782	Departed this life Cornelius Dunham.
Feby. 11, 1782	Departed this life Gad Woodruff.
Feby. 15, 1782	Departed this life the Wife of Joseph Woodruff, Jr.
Feby. 18, 1782	Departed this life a Babe of Solomon Cowles Junʳ.
March 9, 1782	Departed this life Wid° Elizabeth Hawley.
March 11, 1782	Departed this life Mr. Robert Portter. [tiss.
March 24, 1782	Departed this life the Wife of Lieut. Abner Cur-
April 29, 1782	Departed this life John son of Rhoda Smith.
June 7, 1782	Departed this life John Clarke.
July 20, 1782	Departed this life William Hooker.
July 31, 1782	Departed this life Patty Daugʳ of Jacob Byington.
Septr. 25, 1782	Departed this life a Babe of Isaac Ingham.
Septr. 30, 1782	Departed life Catherine Daugʳ of Martin Bull.
December 14, 1782	Departed this life Reuben son of John Portter.
Decbr. 15, 1782	Departed this life John Carronton.
Decbr. 17, 1782	Departed this life London a negro man.
Jany. 28, 1783	Departed this life Wid: Rebecca Woodruff.
March 9, 1783	Departed this life Thomas Warner.
[Torn off] 1783	Departed this life a Child of John North.
[Torn off] 1783	Departed this life Joseph Brownson.
July 10, 1783	Departed this life Sarah Pratt young woman.
Septr. 10, 1783	Departed this life John Pratt.
Septr. 14, 1783	Departed this life the Wife of Samuel North.
Septr. 17, 1783	Departed this life a Child of Charles Stedman Jun.
Octr. 10, 1783	Departed this life a Child of Samuel Root Senʳ.
Octr. 12, 1783	Departed this life a Child of Lieut. John Mix.
Octr. 13, 1783	Departed this life Sarah Hosmer—young woman.
Novr. 4, 1783	Departed this life Joseph Root.
Novr. 10, 1783	Departed this life yᵉ Wife of James Hickcox.
December 4, 1783	Departed this life the wife of Thos. Parsons Junʳ.
February 7, 1784	Departed this life the Wife of Amos Shepard.
Febry. 10, 1784	Departed this life the Wife of Eneas Cowles.
March 23, 1784	Departed this life Daniel North.
April 26, 1784	Departed this life the Wife of Doct. Asa Johnson.
April 29, 1784	Departed life a Child of Alexander Dorchester.
May 6, 1784	Departed this life Josiah North.
June 23, 1784	Departed this [life] the Wid° Mary Gridley.
June 30, 1784	Departed this life Temperance Brownson—a Child.
Octr. 20, 1784	Departed this life a Babe of Chauncey Deming.
December 18, 1784	Departed this life John Stedman.
May 5, 1785	Departed this life Widow Izabel Luske.

After Dismission.

July 20, 1785	Departed this life a Babe of Chauncey Deming.
August 7, 1785	Departed this life a Babe of Jesse Curtiss.
August 29, 1785	Departed this life a Child of Danl Gridley.
Septr. 2, 1785	Departed this life a Child of Danl Gridley.
Novr. 2, 1785	Departed this life two Children of Benjn Welton.
Novr. 14, 1785	Departed this life Hannah Stedman.
Novr. 15, 1785	Departed this life the wife of Matthew Clarke.
Novr. 16, 1785	Departed this life a Child of Martin Hart.
Decbr. 16, 1785	Departed this life James Thomson.
Jany. 19, 1786	Departed this life Elisha Deming.
Febry. 3, 1786	Departed this life William Smith.
Febry. 15, 1786	Departed this life Ebenezer Carrington.
March 31, 1786	Departed life a Child of Luke Thomson.
May 3, 1786	Departed this life John Portter.
July 2, 1786	Departed this life Josiah Clarke.

Admissions to the Church.

Febry. 10, 1765	Benjn Andruss.
Eodem Die	Oliver Newell.
April 14, 1765	John Pratt Junr.
October 13, 1765	Noadiah Hooker.
October 27, 1765	Zadoc Orvis.
Novr. 10, 1765	Ezekiel Hosford.
March 30, 1766	The Wife of Solomon Curtiss.
July 20, 1766	Joseph Loomis.
August 3, 1766	Caleb Hopkins.
Octr. 12, 1766	Ichabod Andruss.
Novr. 9, 1766	Tim° Marsh Jr.
Nov. 16, 1766	Allan Merrill.
Novr. 23, 1766	Thomas Lewis.
Novr. 30, 1766	Tim° Portter Junr.
Novr. 30, 1766	Wid. Huldah Mather.
October 4, 1767	Elisha Scott.
Novr. 1, 1767	Eli North.
Novr. 8, 1767	Oliver Elsworth.
December 27, 1767	Elijah Woodruff.
January 3, 1768	William Wadsworth Junr.
January 24, 1768	Asahel Woodruff.
Febry. 7, 1768	Jesse Judd.
May 22, 1768	Micah Woodruff & Baptized.
July 30, 1768	Joseph Bird.
July 30, 1768	Wid° Sarah Hart.
August 21, 1768	Amos Cowles.
February 12, 1769	Asahel Wadsworth.
February 12, 1769	Eneas Cowles.

[*Election of Deacons.*]

October 26, 1753	William Wadsworth.
Novr. 9, 1769	Seth Lee & Stephen Dorchester.
December 29, 1775	Noah Portter.

JOHN HARVARD AND HIS ANCESTRY.

PART SECOND.

Communicated by HENRY F. WATERS, A.M., now residing in London, Eng.

IN the article in the REGISTER for July, 1885 (xxxix. 265), entitled "John Harvard and his Ancestry," which formed the ninth instalment of his "Genealogicial Gleanings in England," Mr. Waters conclusively established the fact that John Harvard was one of the sons of Robert Harvard of the Parish of St. Saviours, Southwark, London, and Katherine (Rogers) Harvard, his wife, and that he was baptized in that parish, Nov. 29, 1607. In support of this statement he published, among others, the wills of Harvard's father, mother, brother, uncle, aunt, two step-fathers and father in law.

In the present paper he continues still further the investigations so successfully begun. He here gives us, with other new and important matter now for the first time published, the probate of the will of Thomas Rogers of Stratford-on-Avon, Harvard's maternal grandfather, the wills of Rose Reason, his aunt, and Thomas Rogers, Jr., his uncle, both on his mother's side, with extracts from the Parish Registers of Stratford, setting forth the baptisms, marriages and burials of the Rogers family. Harvard's grandfather, Thomas Rogers, was, at the time of his death, an alderman of Stratford, and the house which he built there in 1596 is still standing. From it John Harvard's father and mother were married in 1605. It is one of the oldest and certainly the best remaining example of ancient domestic architecture in Stratford. The illustration in this number is a heliotype copy, slightly reduced, of an excellent photograph just taken.

When it is remembered that the late Hon. James Savage, LL.D., the author of the "Genealogical Dictionary of New England," made a voyage to England for the express purpose of ascertaining what could be learned of the early history of John Harvard, and that he would gladly have given, as he himself tells us, five hundred dollars to get five lines about him in any capacity, public or private, but that all his efforts were without avail, the accumulation of material now brought to light by the perseverance of Mr. Waters is certainly most surprising. From being almost a semi-mythical figure in our early colonial history, John Harvard bids fair to become one of the best known of the first generation of settlers on these shores. The mystery which surrounded him is now dispelled. No better illustration could be given of the importance of the work Mr. Waters is doing in England, no more striking instance could be found of the extraordinary success which is attending his labors there.

The Committee earnestly hope that funds sufficient to carry on still further these valuable investigations may be speedily raised.

JOHN T. HASSAM.

MENSE APRILIS 1611.

Thomas Rogers   Vicesimo Septimo die probatum fuit testīm Thome
Sen.   Rogers señ nup de Stratford sup Avon in Cofñ Warwici
def heñts etc.   Juramento Thome Rogers filii dicti def et
exr̄is etc. cui etc de bene etc iurat.   Probate Act Book.

[The will of which the above is the Probate Act, does not seem to have been co-pied into the Register, which I examined leaf by leaf, with hopes to find it. My friend J. C. C. Smith, Esq., then hunted through the bundle of original wills for that year, but in vain. That the testator was the father of Mrs. Harvard, and grandfather of our John Harvard, there can be no doubt. The extracts from the Parish Register of Stratford upon Avon, together with the wills of his daughters, &c., prove that. Among the Feet of Fines of the Easter Term, 23d Elizabeth (1581), I find a conveyance made to him by one Henry Mace, of two messuages and two gardens with their appurtenances in Stratford upon Avon. He seems to have been a prominent citizen of that borough, as will appear from the extracts I shall give from the records, and, in 1596, while he was holding the office of Bailiff, built the house still standing in High Street, now known as " Ye Ancient House," the best specimen now left in that street, or perhaps in the borough. On the front, under the broad window of the second story, appear these characters :

T R   1596   A R

In this house, therefore, Katharine Rogers lived from 1596 until her marriage to Robert Harvard, and to it she may have come with her little son John to attend the obsequies of her father. A heliotype of this house illustrates this number.
—H. F. W.]

The Parish Registers of Stratford upon Avon commence Anno 1558. By the kind permission of the Vicar, the Rev. George Arbuthnot, M.A., I was enabled to devote the whole of one day, from the close of the morning service to the beginning of the afternoon service, to an examination of them. I took notes of the following marriages :

1562   January 31, Thomas Rogers and Margaret Pace.
1563   November 27, Henry Rogers and Elizabeth Burback.
1566   July 6, Edward Huntington and Matilda Rogers.
1570   October 15, John Rogers and Anne Salsbury.
1579   July 20, William Rogers and Elizabeth Walker.
1581   October 30, Richard Rogers and Susanna Castell.
   "   November 5, Richard Rogers and Ales Calle.
1592 (?3)   December 30, Antherin Russell and Joyce Rogers.
1596   November 21, William Rogers and Jone Tante.
1600   October 28, John Nelson to Elizabeth Rogers.
1602   April 13, Lewes Rogers to Joane Rodes.
   "   October 12, Francis Rogers to Elizabeth Sperpoint.
1603 (4)   January 1, William Smith to Ales Rogers.
1605   " Apriell 8, Robertus Harwod to Katherina Rogers."
1608 (9)   February 6, Henry Stanton to Phillip Rogers.
1609   July 18, Thomas Chestley to Margaret Rogers.

I looked through the record of the marriages down to 1637 inclusive, and found a few other Rogers marriages, which it hardly seems worth the while to print. Thomas, Henry, John, William and Richard Rogers had numerous children baptized and buried. Of these I pick out the children of Thomas.

Baptized.	*Buried.*
Margaret, September 26, 1562.	Margaret, December 1, 1562.
Elizabeth. October 28, 1563.	Johanna, February 21, 1566 (7).
Charles, March 28, 1565.	Alice, October 3, 1568.
Johanna, January 24, 1566 (7).	Anne, July 24, 1581.
Alice, September 2, 1568.	Thomas, August 13, 1584.
Joanna, October 14, 1571.	" Infant," January 15, 1591.
Joyce, February 9, 1572 (3).	Charles Rogers, " homo " March 30,
Ales, September 11, 1574.	1609 (10).
Richard, November 10, 1575.	Thomas Rogers, August 31, 1639.
William, June 8, 1578.	
Edward, February 18, 1579.	
Thomas, July 22, 1582.	
Katherin, November 25, 1584.	
Thomas, June 11, 1587.	
Rose, March 29, 1590.	
Frances, March 10, 1593.	

The burial of Margaret, the wife of Mr. Rogers, I did not find. He evidently married again; for I found the burial of "Alice wyf to Mr Thomas Rogers," August 17, 1608. His own burial is thus given :

1610 (11) February 20, Thomas Rogers, one of the Aldermen.

THOMAS ROGERS of Stratford upon Avon in the County of Warwick yeoman 27 Aug. 1639, proved at Worcester 21 May 1640. To Anne my beloved wife all that my messuage or tenement wherein I now dwell, with the appurtenances, and all other my lands and tenements whatsoever situate & being in the said town of Stratford &c. to have and to hold for life or until marriage, and, after her decease or day of marriage, to my four daughters Lydia, Alice, Ruth & Hannah & their assigns until Edward Rogers my son shall well & truly pay unto my said four daughters the sum of twenty pounds apiece, and after such payment, then to the said Edward & to the heirs of his body Lawfully to be begotten ; failing such to my right heirs forever. To the poor of Stratford twenty shillings. Towards the repair of Stratford church twenty shillings. John Whinge of Blackwell in the county of Worcester, yeoman to be the executor and my loving kinsman John Woolmer the younger and Henry Smyth of Old Stratford, yeoman, to be the overseers of this my will.

The Inventory of his goods, &c. was taken 1 October 1639 by John Wolmer the younger, gentleman, John Wynge and Henry Smith. The sum total was 86^{li} 13^s 0^d.

The widow Anna Rogers was appointed administratrix with the will annexed and gave her bond 23 May 1640, with Francis Baggott of Witley Parva in the parish of Holt in the County of Worcester, as her surety.

WILLIAM SMYTHE of Stratford upon Avon in the County of Warwick mercer, 30 March 1626, proved at Worcester 10 May 1626. To Thomas, my eldest son my shop & the cellars lying in the Middle Row & now in the tenure of William Ayng, butcher, and also my three tenements in the Henley Street, now in the tenures of Thomas Alenn & Thomas Woodwarde and that I late did dwell in, &c. &•for want of lawful issue then to Francis my son & to his lawful issue & for want of such issue to my two daughters Mary & Alice (equally). To daughter Mary twenty pounds to be paid to her within two years after my decease by my son Francis, and in consideration thereof I give to my son Francis the lease of the house wherein I now dwell, &c. To my daughter Alice Smythe all my household stuff, &c. &c. and I make Alice Smyth my said daughter executrix of this my last will & testament, and I make my brother Henry Smythe and John Wolmer overseers, &c.

The Inventory of his goods & chattels was taken 28 April 1626.

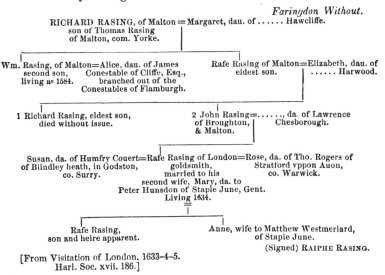

Faringdon Without.

RICHARD RASING, of Malton = Margaret, dau. of . . . . . . Hawcliffe.
son of Thomas Rasing
of Malton, com. Yorke.

Wm. Rasing, of Malton=Alice, dau. of James   Rafe Rasing of Malton=Elizabeth, dau. of
second son,   Conestable of Cliffe, Esq.,   eldest son.   . . . . . . Harwood.
living aᵒ 1584.   branched out of the
                 Conestables of Flamburgh.

1 Richard Rasing, eldest son,   2 John Rasing=. . . . . ., da. of Lawrence
    died without issue.   of Broughton, | Chesborough.
                                         & Malton.

Susan, da. of Humfry Couert=Rafe Rasing of London=Rose, da. of Tho. Rogers of
of Blindley heath, in Godston,   goldsmith,   Stratford vppon Auon,
        co. Surry.   married to his   co. Warwick.
                              second wife, Mary, da. to
                         Peter Hunsdon of Staple June, Gent.
                                  Living 1634.

Rafe Rasing,   Anne, wife to Matthew Westmerlard,
son and heire apparent.   of Staple June.
                                      (Signed) RAIPHE RASING.

[From Visitation of London, 1633-4-5.
Harl. Soc. xvii. 186.]

Mense Junii 1647. Undecimo die emᵗ Comᵒ Rose Reason Relce Radulphi Reason nup̃ p̃oe Ste Bridgitte als Brides prope Fleetstreete Civitat London deft haben & ad adstrañd bona iura et credita dict deft de bene &c. iurat.   Admon. Act. Book. Fol. 76.

[The two forms of spelling this surname are interesting for two reasons; first, as showing the loss of the guttural final *g* sound in Rasing (in connection with which it may be well to note that the crest of this family was a hand grasping a bunch of *grapes*), and, secondly, as illustrating the sound of the diphthong *ea* in *Reason*. I have seen many similar instances showing that in Shakspeare's time the word was pronounced like *raisin*. Recall Fallstaff's play on the word in Henry IV. Part I. Act ii. Sc. 4 : " Give you a reason on compulsion ! If reasons were as plenty as blackberries I would give no man a reason upon compulsion."—H. F. W.]

IN THE NAME OF GOD AMEN. I Rose Raysings of the Parish of Saint Bride London Widdowe being weake in bodie but of sound and perfect memorie thankes be to God doe make this my last Will and Testament in manner and forme following (videlicet) ffirst I bequeath my soule to Almighty God who gaue it me and my bodie to the Earth from whence it Came to be buried in Saint Brides Church London in Christian decentlike manner as my Executor hereafter named shall thinke fitting. Item I giue to my daughter Rose Haberly the Wife of Anthony Haberly the summe of Tenne poundes and alsoe my best Gowne and petticoate and a payre of Hollande sheetes and one douzen and to her husband twentie shillinge. Item I giue to the Children of my daughter Rose Haberley (that is to say) to Anthonie John Mary and Rose I giue fiue poundes apeece But to my Grandchild Elizabeth Haberley who is my God daughter I giue Tenne poundes. Item I giue to Katherine Wilmour my Executors Wife here after named fiue poundes. Item I giue to Joane Wilmour her Kinswoeman fiue poundes. Item I giue to John Wilmour the younger my sisters Grand-

Child fiue poundes. Item I giue to my Cousin Brockett's sonne Joseph Brockett in Southwarke fiue poundes and to his Mother twenty shillings to buy her a Ring. Item I giue to Marie Right That Tends me in my sicknes fiue pounds. Item I giue John Corker my Godsonne Twenty shillings and to his Mother and his brother Tenne shillings a peece. Item I giue to William Suthes the sonne of James Suthes twenty pounds to be paid att his age of one and twentie yeares. Item I giue to Master James Palmer formerly the Viccar of Saint Brides London fiue poundes. Item I giue to Master Alexander Baker of Cliffords Inne London Gentleman that Bond wherein Master Morgan and Master Powell stands bound unto my late husband Ralph Raysing which is now in suite in the upper Bench and in the Chancerie and I doe hereby giue power to the said Master Baker to sue in my Executors name for the same provided alwaies That if the said James Suches shall att anie time hereafter trouble my Executor hereafter named for any concerning mee or my late husband Ralph Raysing That then my Legacie to the said Williā Suthes his sonne shall be absolutely voyd. Item I giue to Thomas Smith the sonne of my sister Alice Smith in Warwickshire the summe of fiue pounds. And last of all I make my loueing Kinseman Master John Wilmour of Stratford upon Avon in the Countie of Warwick my full and sole Executor of this my last Will and Testament desireing him to doe all things accordingly as I haue by this my last Will required him. And the remainder of all my goods and Chattells not formerlie bequeath I doe hereby give and bequeath to my said Executor and I doe hereby renounce all former Wills and Testam^{ts} whatsoever and doe hereby revoake the same and publish this to be my last Will and Testament and desire that none may stand for my last Will but this and I doe alsoe giue and bequeath to Mistris Susan Annyon Widdowe the summe of Thirtie shillings to buy her a Ring. In Witnes whereof I haue to this my last Will and Testament sett my hand and seale dated This first Day of December in the yeare of our Lord One Thousand six hundred fifty and fower. Rose Raysings Signed sealed published and delivered as her last Will and testam^t Theise words (videlicet) and alsoe my best gowne and petticoate and a payre of Holland sheetes and one douzen of Napkins and my Bible Kinsewoeman to be paid att his age of one and twenty yeares Avon in the Countie of Warwicke being first interlined in the presence of us Susan Annyon Alex Barker.

THIS WILL was proved in London the twentith Day of June in the yeare of our Lord God One Thousand six hundred fiftie and fiue before the Judges for probate of Wills and granting Administrations lawfully authorized by the oath of John Willmour The Sole Executor named in the aboue written Will To whome Administration of all and singular the goods Chattells and debts of the said deceased was Committed he being first legally sworne truly and faithfully to administer the same. 291, Aylett.

JOH. SADLER clerk M.A. adm., on the resignation of Simon Aldriche, to the Vicarage of Ringmer, 6 October, 1626.

Archbishop Abbot's Reg. p. 2, f. 349^b.

JOHN SADLER was inducted into the possession of ye vicaridge of Ringmer Octob^r xij^{th} 1626.

1640 Oct. 3 buryed Mr John Sadler minister of Ringmer.

Ringmer Parish Register.

Sussex, Ringmer Vic. John Sadler 14 Nov. 1626 (to Nov. 1628), William Thomas of Lewes and William Michelborne of Westminster (his sureties). Compositions for First Fruits.

EDWARD FENNER of Auburne in the County of Sussex (13 July 1603 proved 9 October 1605) wishes his body to be buried in the parish church of Auburne and leaves all to his wife Mary whom he appoints executrix & entrusts the children to her care. 69, Hayes.

License granted 12 May 1613 to the Rector, Vicar or Curate of Stepney in the county of Middlesex to solemnize the marriage between John Sadler, clerk, and Mary Fenner, widow, late the relict of Edward Fenner, while he lived of Auburne in the County of Sussex, gen. dec'd.
Vicar General's Book.

[Albourne is a parish in Sussex near Cuckfield.—H. F. W.]

MARY SADLER of Mayfield in the County of Sussex, widow, 16 January 1645, proved 13 November 1647. " My Corpes to bee interred where ever ytt shall please God by my surviving freindes to dispose of ytt." I do nominate & appoint my daughter Elizabeth James to be my sole Executrix. And I bequeath and give unto her one hundred pounds of money which is in her husband's hands, and such bedding and chests and wearing clothes as I have (saving one chest which is full of linnen and pewter, and other small things). My will is that she shall buy & give to my grandchild Mary Russell two silver spoons of ten shillings apiece price and to Thomas Russell my grandson ten shillings of money. I will & bequeath unto my son John Sadler the money which I have in Mr William Michilborne's hands. Item I give unto my grandchild Mary James one chest of linen and pewter except two pair of the sheets and one pair of pillowcoats therein, which I give unto Anne James, and one other pair of sheets which are also in the said chest, which I give unto Elizabeth James my grandchildren. Item I give to each of my son Russell's children not before named in this my will one shilling apiece for the buying them gloves. Item I give unto my daughter Mary Sadler and to each of her children which I suppose to live in "newe" England one shilling apiece. Item I give unto my daughter Anne Allin and to her daughter Mary one shilling apiece, and this I do appoint and intend my last will and testament. 231 Fines.

ALLEN.—THOMAS, son of John Allen, dyer, of Norwich. At school under Mr Briggs eight years. Age 15. Admitted sizar litt. grat. July 6, 1624. Surety Mr Moore. Admissions Caius Coll. Cambridge.

THOMAS HERVY, citizen & " Bocher " of London, 16 June 1505, proved at Lambeth 3 October 1505. " I bequeth my soule to god to our blissed lady Virgyñ Mary his moder and to all the holy company of heveñ And my body to be buried in the churchyerd of Seynt Clementes in Candilwykstrete of London on the Northside of the same Churchyerd where the body of William more late Citezein and bocher of London my graundfader lyeth buried. And if it fortune that I dye or decesse owte of Londoñ thañ I will that my body be buried where as it shall please god for it to dispose. Item I bequeth to the high aulter of the said churche of Seynt Clementes for myñ offerynges forgoten or negligently w'draweñ in dischargyng of my soule iij^s iiij^d. It I bequeth unto Margarete my wife for hir parte purparte and porcioñ of all my goodes moevable and unmoevable in redy money xl^{li} sterl and all my stuff of household and plate hole as it

shalbe the day of my decesse.   It I bequeth unto my sonnes Thomas Hervy and Nicholas Hervy and to the Infaunte beyng in my wiffs wombe if she
now be w^t childe in redy money xl^{li} evenly to be devided and departed
amonges theym and to be deliūed to theym and eūry of theym whañ they
or eny of theym shall cõme to their laufull ages or mariages the which
money I will my moder mawde Hoppy haue the keping to the use of my
said childerñ till they shall cõme to their laufull ages or mariages.   And if
it fortune any of my said sonnes or the Infañt in my wiffes wombe for to
dye or decesse afore they or any of theym shal cõme to their laufull ages
or mariages, thañ I will that the parte of hym or theym so decessyng remayne
to hym or theym beyng on lyve.   And if it fortune all my said childerñ to
dye afore they cõme to their laufull ages or be maried thañ I will that my
said moder dispose the same xl^{li} to my said childerñ before bequethed for
my soule my faderes soule my childerñ soules and for all my goode frendes
soules in deedes of almes and of charitie as she shall thinke best for the helth
and saluaciõ of my soule.   It I will that my saide moder haue the keping of my said childreñ duryng their noonage It I will that the saide Mawde
my moder take haue & receyve the proffittes and revenues coñmyng and
growying of my fermes called Gubbons and Waltoñs in the Countie of
Essex and of my ferme in Madebrokes long mede and Wottons croftes lying in the p̣isshe of Retherhith in the Countie of Surrey towardes the sus-
tentaciõ and fynding of my said childerñ duryng their noonage and the sur-
plusage of the same revenues and proffittes cõming & growyng of the same
fermes I will it be evenly devided and dep̣ted amonges my said childerñ
and Infaunt by the said Mawde my moder.   It I bequeth to my suster Elyñ
fflynte the wif of Johñ fflynte all my state and Tñme of years which I haue
to cõme of in my ferme called preestes ñshe sett and lying in the p̣isshe
of Retherhed aforesaid.   And I will that thendentur of the same ferme be deliūed unto my said suster incontinent aft^r my decesse.   Itñ I bequeth unto
my cosyñ Thomas Hervy myñ state and termes of yeres which that I haue
to cõme of and into the tenementes called the Dogge and the Shippe in Est-
chepe in the p̣isshe of Seynt Clementes aforesaid and in seynt Leonardes.
And I will that thendentures of the same houses be deliūed unto my said
cosyñ Thomas assone aft^r my decesse as is possible.   It I bequeth unto my
sūnt William Anderby xx^s in money.   It I bequeth unto Johñ ffelix xx^s.
It I bequeth unto Richard ffelix xx^s.   It I will that my moder or hir Ex-
ecuto^rs fynde the said Johñ ffelix to gram^r scoole and to writting scole by the
space of a yere aft^r my decesse.   The Residue of all my goods moevable
and unmoevable aft^r my dettes paid my burying done and this my p̣^rsent testament in all thinges fulfilled I geve and bequeth unto the forsaid Mawde my
moder she therew^t to doo ordeyne and dispose hir owne freewill for eūmore.
Which Mawde my moder I make and ordeyne executrice of this my p̣^rsent
testament.   In witnesse wherof to this my p̣^rsent testament I haue setto my
seale.   Youeñ the day and yeř aforesaid."   36 Holgrave.

IN THE NAME OF GOD AMEN   The xxixth day of the moneth of July In
the yere of o^r lord god m^t v^c and viij.   I Thomas Hervy bocher of the p̣isshe
of seynt Oluff in Suthwerk in the diocise of Winchester beyng hole of
mynde and memory thanked be almighty god sett make and ordeyne this
my p̣^rsent testament and last will in man^r and fo^rme folowing ffirst I bequeth and recoñmend my soule unto almighty god my creato^r and savio^r, my
body to be buryed in the church of seynt Oluff aforesaid And I bequeth unto
the high aulter of the same churche for my tithes & oblaciõs here before

necligently paid or forgoteñ ij⁸. Also I bequith to my moder church of Wynchestre iiij^d And I geve and bequeth to the aulter of our lady in the said pisshe church of seynt Orluff iiij^d. Also I bequeth to the ault^r of seynt Anne there iiij^d. Also to the aulter of seynt Clement iiij^d. The Residue of all my goodes and catalles not bequethed nor geven after my fuñall expences dooñ and my dettes paied I will and geve unto Guynor my wif she to dispose theym after hir discrecioñ as she shall thinke moost convenyent. And of this my present testament and last will I make and ordeyne myñ executrice my said wif Thiese witnesses Sr William Priour Curat of seynt Oluff aforeseid William Bulleyñ grocer William Symsoñ and other.

Probatum fuit suprascript testm corā Dño apud Lamehith xv° die mens Augusti Anno Dñi Milliñio quingētesimo octauo Jur Guynoris Relicte et executricis in huiõi testõ noiāte Ac approbat & insinuat Et cõmissa fuit adm̄istra° om̄ bonorum & debit dicti defuncti prefate executrici de bene & fidelit adm̄istrand Ac de pleno & fideli Inuētario citra p^rimũ diem Septembr̄ p̄x futur exhibend necnõ de plano et vero cõm̄pto reddend ad sca dei euñg in debita iuris forma iurat.   4 Bennett (P. C. C.)

William Herford citizen & tallowchandler of London, 31 August 1518, proved 10 Nov. 1518. My body to be buried in the parish church of St Olave in the old " Jure " of London in the same place where my late wife Johan resteth buried. " And I haue bought & payed for the stone that lyeth on her. And therefor I woll haue the same stone layed on my body & I woll have a scripture graveñ & fyxed yn the same stone makyng mension off the tyme off my deceasse requiryng the people to pray for me." To the high altar of the same church for tythes & oblations forgotten or negligently withholden iij⁸ iiij^d. Towards the gilding of the tabernacle of St John the Baptist at the south end of the high Altar of the same church xx.⁸ Towards the maintenance of Olave's Brotherhood within the same church xij^d. To the company & brotherhood of Our Lady & St John Baptist Tallowchandlers of London my silver pot. To John Hone my best dagger the sheath garnished with silver as it is. To Richard Chopyn my purse garnished with silver. " It I beqweth to Nicholas Pynchyn my best Jaket." Touching the disposition of my lands & tenements in the parish of St. Stephen in Colemanstreet I will that my wife Agnes Herford shall have them during her life and after her decease they shall remain to my children and to the heirs of their bodies lawfully begotten & for lack of such issue they shall remain to the company of Butchers of London forever, they finding forever in the same church of St. Olaves the day of my decease dirige " on nyght and masse of Requiem on the morne by note dispendyng at eūry such obyte amongyst prestes and clerkes wex Ryngyng off belles & poū people 20⁸ foreu^r. And if the same Company of Bouchers make defaute of and yn kypyng of the same obyte yn man^r & forme a bouesayd then I woll that the same landes and tenūtes shall full & hole remayne to the cõ-pany & felyshippe of Talow chaundelers of London foreū they doyng and dyspendyng yerely therfore at an obytt yerly yn man^r and forme as the forsayd cõpany off Bouchers ar bounde to doo yn kepyng of the forsayd Obyte as they wyll answere before God." ———— To my cousin Richard Baynbery my tawney gown furred with black, to John Kyttelwell & Robt Kyttelwell either of them my single Ray gowns, to John Ryve my best dublett to William Knott my second Dublet, to William Pyper, George Chelsey & James Quick mine apprentices, so that they continue & serve out their terms well & truly to my wife their mistress, to either of them vi⁸ viij^d. when their terms of prenticehood shall be finished. To my god children that at time of my decease shall be living xii^d. The residue shall be divided amongst my wife & children accordinge to the laws & custōms of the city of London. And Executors of this will &c. I make & ordaine my said wife Agnes & the said Nicholas. To Robert Whetecroft my riding coat.

102 Bennet (Commissary Court of London).

CRISTIANA HARVYE of Shenley in the County of Hertford widow, and John Harvye, son and heir apparent of the said Cristiana, give a bond 30 June 10 Elizabeth, of one hundred pounds, to Lawrence Greene, citizen and cutler of London, that they will carry out an agreement specified in a pair of Indentures bearing date 30 June 10 Elizabeth.

Claus Roll 10 Elizabeth, Part 13.

THOMAS HARVARD of the precinct of St Katherine's near the Tower of London, butcher, conveys to Henry Rawlins of Lee in the county of Essex, mariner 29 January 1621, for the sum of one hundred and fifty pounds already received, all those three several messuages and tenements, with all shops, cellars, rollers, warehouses, backsides, entries, lights, easements, commodities and appurtenances whatsoever to the said three several messuages or tenements, or any of them, belonging, situate, &c. at the North end of Bermondsey Street, near Battle Bridge, it the parish of St Olaves, *als.* tooles in Southwark, &c. now or late in the several tenures or occupations of William Pilkington, William Hatcham and William Fells or their assigns, &c. to be delivered up the 2^d day of July next. His wife Margaret unites. (What follows seems to indicate that this conveyance is a mortgage.)

Claus Roll 20 Jac. I. Part 37.

HILL. 6 H. viij (1514) Apud Westm̃ a die Sci Martini in quindecim dies. Int^r Johēm Kyrton Nichū Tycheborñ Henr̃ Tyngylden & Johem Fowler quer. et Ricū Harvy & Cristinam uxem̃ eius deforc de uno mesuagio & uno gardino cum p̃tin in Southwerk Et preterea iidem Ricus & Cristina concesserunt pro se & hered ipius Cristine qd ipi warant pdcis Johi Nicho Henr & Johi & hered ipius Johis Kyrton pdca ten cum p̃tin contr̃ Johem Abbem monastri Sc Petri Wes̃m̃ & successores suos &c. &c.

The consideration was twenty marks of silver.

Feet of Fines. Surrey.

Trin. 10 Elizabeth (1568). Hec est finalis concordia fc̃a in cur Dñe Regine apud Westm̃ in crastino Sc̃e Trinitatis anno regni Elizabeth dei grã Anglie ffranc & hibñie Regine fidei defensoris etc a conqu decimo, coram (&c.), Int Laurenciū Grene quer et Cristianam Harvye viduam & Johem Harvye geñosum deforc de septem messuagiis septem gardinis & una acra trē cum p̃tin in p̃ochia Sc̃i Georgii in Southwarke etc. Consideration eighty pounds sterling.

Feet of Fines, Surrey.

Trinity Term 37 Elizabeth, Essex. Oliver Skinner quer. and Thomas Harvard and Johann his wife, Hugh Gullifer and Anne his wife, William Smarte, Henry West and Margaret his wife and William Spalding and Elizabeth his wife deforc,—for one acre of pasture with the appurtenances in Westham. Consideration 40^{li} sterling.

Feet of Fines.

Hillary Term 37 Elizabeth, Surrey. Thomas Harvard & Johan his wife quer. and John Leveson mil. deforc,—for three messuages with the appurtenances in the parish of St Olave alias St Toolyes in Southwark. Consideration 160^{li} st.

Feet of Fines.

Easter Term 38 Elizabeth, Essex. Christopher Poyner gen. quer. and Thomas Harvey & Johan his wife deforc, for one messuage with the appurtenances in Foxyearth & Pentrowe. Consideration 80^{li} st.
Feet of Fines.

Easter Term 38 Elizabeth, Essex. John Jefferson and Thomas Smyth quer. and Thomas Harvard & Johan his wife & Henry West & Margaret his wife deforc, for three parts of one messuage, one barn, one garden, one orchard and twelve acres of arable land with the appurtenances, into four parts to be divided, in Westham & Stratford Langthorne. Feet of Fines.

Mich. Term 39–40 Elizth (1597) Surrey. Thomas Harvard quer. and John Anwyke and Alice his wife and William Crowcher (Crowther?) and Agnes his wife deforc ; for two messuages, two gardens with the appurtenances in the parish of St Olave, Southwark. Consideration 80^{li} st.
Feet of Fines.

Easter Term 40 Elizabeth, Essex, David George quer. and Thomas Herverd and Johan his wife and William Spaldinge and Elizabeth his wife deforc,—for one messuage, one barn, one garden, one orchard, twenty acres of land (arable), four acres of meadow and six acres of pasture with the appurtenances in Westham. Consideration 100^{li} sterling. Feet of Fines.

Mich. Term 22 James I. Surrey. Robert Harverd quer. and Thomas Harverd deforc,—for three messuages, with the appurtenances in the parish of St Olaves in Southwark. Consideration 240^{li} sterling.
Feet of Fines.

THOMAS ROWELL of the Parish of Westham in the County of Essex yeoman, 12 August 1583, proved 23 August 1583. My body to be buried in the churchyard of Westham.

"Also I doe giue unto my sonne in Lawe Thomas Harford butcher dwellinge in London one redd cowe and he havinge the said Cowe to giue unto his mother in Lawe the some of xl^s." To John Bestone my wife's son all my wearing apparell. To Joane my wife all the rest of my goods & I make her Executrix.

Wit. John Hall curate, John Rowell yeoman Richard Cannon yeoman Isabell Spike widow.   306 Bullocke, Consistory Court of London."

Married, 1582, Nov. 19, Thomas Harvarde & Jane Rowell.
Register of St Saviour's Parish, Southwark.

JONE HARVARD wife of Thomas Harvard buried June 10, 1599.
Register of St Savior's Parish, Southwark.

RICHARD YEARWOOD and Katherine Ellettsone were mar^d xxviiith of May 1627.   Parish Register of Wandsworth, Surrey.

[This is the third marriage of John Harvard's mother. I am indebted to J. T. Squire, Esq., for his kind permission to extract the above from his MS. copy of this Register, and to my friend J. C. C. Smith, Esq., who discovered this important entry.—H. F. W.]

PETER MEDCALFE of the parish of St Olave's in Southwark in the County of Surrey clothworker 24 August 1592, proved 6 September 1592. To Mr Richard Hutton Deputy of the Borough of Southwark my best gown faced with Foynes. To my very friend Mr Thomas Lynne in Pater Noster

Rowe my best gown faced with satin. To Richard Barker my gown faced with Budge or Damask at his choice. To Peter Keseler one of my gowns faced with budge. To the poor of St Olave's in Southwark forty shillings To the poor of Redderiffe in the County of Surrey twenty shillings. To my very good friend Mr John Nokes a ring of gold with an agate cut. "Item I giue and bequeathe unto Robert Harvey a boye which I keepe the somme of ffyue poundes lawfull money of Englande to be paied unto hym at his age of one and twentie yeres. So that he be ordered and ruled by my executrix and that he do liue to accomplishe the age of one and twentie yeres aforesaied." To Symon Harvye my servant my great anvil & two of my best vices with the bellows thereunto belonging. To my other servants viz Francis, Thomas & Peter being my household servants each of them 20 shillings. Others mentioned. Wife Margaret Medcalfe to be executrix.

71 Harrington (P. C. C.)

Admon de bonis non was granted 26 (September) to Christopher Medcalf, the next of kin.

JOHN GUY of the parish of St Saviour in Southwark, in the County of Surrey, brewer (17 June 1625, proved 28 June 1625) bequeaths to Richard Harford citizen & brewer of London the sum of thirty shillings to make him a ring for a remembrance. 64, Clarke.

ROBERT GREENE of the parish of St. Savior in Southwark in the county of Surrey, yeoman (8 November 1645, proved 19 January 1645) appoints as one of the overseers of his will Mr Thomas Harvard of the said parish Butcher, calling him friend & neighbor, and gives him five pounds. In a codicil, made 11 January 1645, he bequeathes unto Robert Harvard son of Thomas Harvard (above) the sum of ten shillings. The testator had a sister Jane Marshall of Billerica, Essex. 3, Twisse.

RAPH YARDLEY citizen & merchant tailor of London. 25 August 1603, proved 27 February 1603. After my debts paid and my funerals discharged I will that all and singular my goods chattels & debts shall be parted & divided into three equal parts & portions according to the laudable use and custom of the city of London. One full third part thereof I give and bequeath to Rhoda my wellbeloved wife, to her own use, in full satisfaction of such part and portion of my goods, chattells & debts as she may claim to have by the custom of the same city. One other full third part thereof I give & bequeath unto and amongst my children, Raphe, George, John, Thomas and Anne Yardley and to such other child or children as yet unborn as I shall happen to have at the time of my decease, to be equally parted, shared & divided between them, and to be satisfied and paid to my said sons at the accomplishment of their several ages of one and twenty years, and to my said daughter at the accomplishment of her age of one & twenty years or marriage, which shall first happen, &c. &c. And the other third part thereof I reserve to myself therewith to perform & pay these my legacies hereafter mentioned, that is to say, Item I give & bequeath to the poor of the parish of St Saviours in Southwark where I now dwell twenty shillings, to be divided amongst them by the discretion of the overseers of the poor there for the time being, and to such of the bachelors and sixteen men of the company of merchant tailors London as shall accompany my body to burial twenty shillings for a recreation to be made unto them, and to the Vestrymen of the same parish twenty shillings more for a recreation to be made unto them. Item I give and bequeath to my sister Palmer a ring of gold to the value of six shillings eight pence, and to my cousin John Palmer her husband a like ring to the like value, and to my daughter Earby my first wife's wedding ring, and to my son Erbye her husband my best cloak, and to my cousin Richard Yearwood my black cloth gown of Turkey fashion. The rest & residue of all & singular my goods &c. I wholly give unto my said children &c. &c. Item I give & bequeath to my brother Thomas Yardley a ring of gold to the value of six shillings eight pence. And I ordain & make the said Raph Yardley my son to be the Executor &c. and the said Richard Yerwoode and my son Edward Earbye overseers.

As to my freehold lands tenements & hereditaments I will demise give & bequeath my messuages, lands &c in Southwark or elsewhere unto my said children &c.   24, Harte.

John Hall, Not. Pub., one of the witnesses.

AGNES PARKER of London, spinster, 27 November 1617, proved 9 January 1617. Brother in law Edward Smyth and sister Julian, his wife, Sister Margery, the wife of Thomas Flinte of Litterworth in the County of Leicester, glazier. To M^{ris} Elizabeth Bygate, sometime my M^{ris} the sum of twenty pounds &c. To Anne the wife of William Hughes, Elizabeth Turner, the daughter, and Elizabeth Turner, the wife, of James Turner citizen & haberdasher of London. To the poor of all Hallows Barking London where I am now inhabiting. Item I do bequeath to Mr John Ellatson & his wife for a remembrance a piece of gold of five shillings & six pence. And likewise to Mr William Bygate & his now wife a like piece of gold. And to Mr William Turner & wife another piece of gold. To Sarah the wife of Thomas Skinner ten shillings. The residue to James Turner whom I hereby make ordain & constitute my full & sole executor.

122, Vol. 23, Commissary Court of London.

ANN PALMER of London widow, 30 January 1621 proved 31 December 1624. My body to be buried in the parish church of St. Olaves in Southwark in the county of Surrey, where now I am a parishioner, as near the place where my late deceased husband was buried as conveniently may be. I give & bequeath to my son Michael Palmer all such debts duties sum & sums of moneys as are and shall be due & owing unto me at the time of my decease by Jacob Manninge Percival Manninge or either of them or by any other persons by or for them or either of them, all which debts do amount unto the sum of three score and five pounds and twelve shillings or thereabouts principal debt besides all the interest long due, the which money he caused me to lend. Item I give to John Palmer son of my son Michael Palmer three hundred pounds of lawful English money besides I have given to his master the sum of thirty pounds of like money, and unto Andrew Palmer one other son of my said son Michael Palmer twenty pounds &c. and unto Mary Palmer daughter of my said son Michael Palmer one hundred & fifty pounds of like money, and unto Thomas Palmer one other son of my said son Michael twenty pounds &c. & unto Elizabeth Palmer one other daughter of my said son Michael Palmer twenty pounds of like money. To my son William fifty pounds besides I have heretofore given him two hundred pounds and one hundred & fifty pounds before hand, which sums were intended to have been given him for a legacy; of both which sums I do discharge him, the which may appear partly by his bond of three hundred pounds, dated 19 July 14 James &c. and partly by other writings, and I give him his plate remaining in my hands as a pledge for twenty pounds more, which twenty pounds I forgive unto him also. To John Palmer, son of my said son Michael (*sic*) two hundred pounds, besides I have given with him to his master the sum of forty pounds. To the said John Palmer, son of my said son William, the lease of my now dwelling house situate upon London Bridge, &c. &c., provided that the said William Palmer, his father, shall, from and after the end of two months next after my decease, until the said John Palmer his son shall accomplish his full age of four & twenty years, have hold & enjoy my said dwelling house, given unto his said son, paying & discharging the rent to be due for the whole to the Bridgehouse and one pepper corn yearly at the Feast of the Birth of our Lord God unto his said son if he lawfully demand the same. Reference made to the will of John Palmer, the late husband of the testatrix, and legacies to John and Mary Palmer, children of Michael, and John Palmer, son of William.

Item I give and bequeath unto my daughter Anne Faldo, late wife of Robert Faldo Esquire, deceased, two hundred and three pounds of lawful money of England and my chain of gold, and unto Thomes Faldo, her son, forty pounds, and unto Francis Faldo, her son, forty pounds, to be paid to my said daughter their mother, and by her to be paid to the said Thomas & Francis when they shall accomplish their ages of two & twenty years. To Anne Faldo, her daughter, forty pounds, and to Jane Faldo, one other of her daughters, twenty pounds, and to Elizabeth Faldo, one other of her daughters, forty pounds, at their several ages of one and twenty years or at the days of their several marriages &c.

To my daughter Elizabeth Fawcett, wife of William Fawcett, gentleman, two hundred pounds, besides four hundred pounds to them formerly given &c. and my bracelets and all my rings of gold &c.

Reference to an Obligation wherein the said John Palmer deceased (former husband of the testatrix) stood bound with the said Michael Palmer (the son) to Mr Jacob Vercelin in the sum of twelve hundred pounds, with condition thereupon endorsed to leave Mary, then wife of the said Michael Palmer & daughter of the said Jacob, if she survive the said Michael, worth in goods & chattels the sum of one thousand pounds &c.

Item I give and bequeathe unto my cousin Anne Streate and to my cousin Ellen Yarwoode twenty shillings apiece to buy them rings to wear in remembrance of me. As touching blacks to be worn at my funeral I dispose them as hereafter followeth, that is to say, I give and bequeathe unto my son Michael Palmer & William Palmer and unto my son-in-law William Fawcett and unto John Fawcett, husband of Jane Faldoe, and to my loving friends & cousins Stephen Streate and Richard Yarwoode and John Grene and Ralphe Yardley, to every of them a cloak of brown blue cloth containing three yards and half quarter in every cloak at twenty shillings every yard or thereabouts. I give and bequeathe unto my cousin Robert Poole a cloak cloth of forty shillings price, to my cousin Richard Hinde a cloak cloth, about forty shillings price and unto his wife a piece of stuff about fifty shillings price to make her a gown. Similar bequests to "my" cousin Nicholas Cowper and his wife, and cousins Anne Streate and Ellen Yarwood, and to Elizabeth Blinkensopp and Margaret Kinge and to Christopher Blinkensopp and Nicholas Kinge their husbands. Other bequests.

And I do ordain and make the aforesaid Richard Yarwoode & Stephen Streete grocers, "my cosens," full executors &c. and I appoint my loving friends John Grene Esq. and "Richard (*sic*) Yardlye Pottecary my cosen" overseers of this my will and testament, and I give and bequeath unto the said John Grene and Ralphe Yardeley for their pains therein to be taken twenty nobles apiece &c.

In a codicil dated 17 June 1624 the testatrix refers to her daughter Anne Faldoe as since married to Robert Bromfield.   111, Byrde.

Inquisition taken at St Margaret's Hill, St Savior's Southwark in the County of Surrey, 11 March 22 James I. *post mortem* Ralph Yardley, lately citizen and merchant taylor of London Deceased, who was seized, before death, in fee of one capital messuage with the appurtenances called the Horn, lately divided into two several messuages, and situate lying and being in the parish of St Savior in the Borough of Southwark, in the County of Surrey, now or late in the several tenures or occupation of George Fletcher, fisherman, and Lawrence Lunde, or their assigns; and the said Ralph Yardley, being so seized, did on the 25th day of August 1603, 1 James, by his last will in writing, give and bequeath all and singular these premises, in English words, as follows (then follows an extract from the will). And he died, so seized, the 1st day of July 1618, and Ralph Yardley, named in the will, is son and next heir, and was aged at the time of the death of the said Ralph Yardley the father, twenty one years and more ; and the said capital messuage, into two separate messuages divided (as above) with the appurtenances, is held and, at the time of the death of the said Ralph Yardley, was held, of the Mayor, Commonalty and Citizens of the City of London in free soccage, as of their manor of Southwark, in Southwark aforesaid, by the annual rent of two shillings per annum, and is worth clear per annum, during a certain lease made by the said Ralph Yardley to a certain Richard Yerwood, citizen and grocer of London, bearing date 10 July 1603, and during the term of one hundred years, one peppercorn, and after the determination of the said lease will be worth clear and in all events and beyond reprise, three pounds per year.

Chancery Inq. p. m., Miscel., Part 4, No. 130.

[These Yardley items are interesting as showing the connection of Sir George Yardley, the governor of Virginia, to Richard Yerwood, one of John Harvard's step-fathers. I believe a little research would show that these Yardleys were of the Warwickshire family of that name. Richard Yerwood and his kinsman Stephen Street were of Cheshire, I have no doubt.—H. F. W.]

RICHARD BOWMER of the parish of St Saviours in Southwark in the county of Surrey Innholder, 7 January 1593 proved 20 March 1593. My body to be buried in the parish church of St Saviours. To the poor people of the said parish forty shillings and to the poor of the parish of St George in Southwark twenty shillings. For a sermon made at the time of my burial for me (by Mr Ratliffe if it please him) ten shillings. To the three daughters of Agnes Lackenden widow, vizt Joane, Alice and Mary, twenty shillings apiece. To Stephen Lackendon ten shillings, and to my godson, his son, five shillings. To my godson Richard Smyth of Plumpstede in the county of Kent five shillings & to my godson William Cleere of Walworthe five shillings. To my goddaughter Ellyn Beech five shillings. To Thomas Vaugham five pounds and to Henry Vaugham, brother to the said Thomas, three pounds six shillings & eight pence. To Cisly Vaugham, their sister, four pounds. To Richard Emmerson, son of William Emmerson, five shillings. To Richard Emmerson son of Humfrey Emmerson, five shillings. To Robert Rodes, youngest son now living of Roger Rodes of said parish of St Saviours, goldsmith, three pounds six shillings and eight pence, and to Elizabeth Rodes mother to the said Robert five pounds. To my kinsman

Peter Bowmer of Sevenocke in Kent, sadler, ten pounds. To Elizabeth Mitchell wife of Abraham Mitchell feltmaker dwelling at Horseydowne near Southwark, thirty shillings, and to my godson, her son, ten shillings. To Lambert Bowmer of the parish of St Ollifes twenty pounds, and to Robert Bowmer, his son, twenty pounds, also to the two daughters of the said Lambert now living five pounds apiece. To Henry Yonge twenty shillings, to John Yonge twenty shillings, to Gregory Francklyn twenty shillings, to Abraham Allyn twenty shillings, and to every one of their wives twenty shillings apiece to make every of them a ring of gold withall. To Richard Cuckowe ten shillings and to Peter Holmes scrivener ten shillings (for rings) and to Isaac Allen twenty shillings.

" Allso my full intente will and mynde ys : and I doe herebye giue and graunte the lease of my nowe dwellinge house called the queens heade scituate in the sayd parrishe of St. Saviors wythall my Intereste and tytle therein after my decease unto Rose my wife duringe all the yeares therein to come. Provided allwayes and my will and mynde is that the sayd Rose my wife shall haue one years respitte after my decease to pay and dischardge my legacyes herein bequeathed, and therefore I doe appoynte hereby that shee the sayd Rose shall wythin one month nexte after my decease become bounde in good and sufficyente bonde in lawe unto my ouerseers here after nominated in the some of two hundred poundes of lawfull money of Inglande that shee the sayd Rose or her assignes shall well and truly performe fulfill and keepe the tenor of this my will : and pay and discharge : all legacyes and other duetyes by me hereby given and appoynted accordinge to the tennor and true meaninge of this my last will and Testamente."

To the Society of the Vestry of St. Saviors thirteen shillings & four pence. The residue to Rose my well beloved wife whom I make & ordain my full & sole executrix. Thomas Jackson, merchant Tailor, & Miles Wilkinson, Baker, to be overseers.   23, Dixey.

ROSE BOOMER of the parish of Saint " Savyoure " in Southwark in the County of Surrey, widow, 29 March 1595, proved 9 August 1595. My body to be buried in the parish church of St Saviour's where I am a parishioner. To the preacher that shall make a sermon at my funeral ten shillings. To the poor people of the said parish forty shillings, to be distributed amongst them at the discretion of my Executor & the Collectors for the poor there for the time being. To the poor people of the parish of Bossham in the County of Sussex, where I was born, the sum of forty shillings, whereof I will that ten shillings shall be paid to Alice Reade, the widow of Richard Reede (if she be then living) And if she be then deceased then the same ten shillings to be paid to Richard Chapman. To the poor people of St John's house in the city of Winchester forty shillings. To Richard Braxton, son of Cornelius Braxton, the sum of six pounds thirteen shillings and four pence, which I will shall remain in the hands of such person as shall keep him towards his education until he shall be bound apprentice and then delivered over to use for the best profit of the same Richard and the same, with the interest, to be paid him at the expiration of his apprenticeship. And if he happen to decease before the said sum shall come unto his hands then I will to his half brother Edmond Braxton ten shillings & to his sister ten shillings, and the residue to his other two whole brethren both by father and mother, equally. To Richard Mapcrofte six pounds thirteen shillings & four pence, or if he dies to his children (in hands of his wife). To Matthew Barnard the younger, dwelling in Yorkshire three pounds. To Matthew Barnard the elder ten shillings. To William Hildrop a piece of gold of ten shillings, for a remembrance. And a similar bequest to his brother Barnabie & his brother Richard and to John Hildrop and their sister ——, also to Johane Hoskyns, widow, and to her sister the daughter of Edward Hildroppe, and to William Braxton and —— Hardam of Chichester, son of Margery Braxton, and to Richard Wallys of Winchester, to Margaret Bathe, to John Homeade's wife of Winchester and to Richard Homeade her son, to Mrs Bird, to Mistress Denham, to Mr Thomas Thorney, of Portsmouth, to John Androwes, to Robert Boomer, to Thomas Vaughan, to his sister Cicely, to Robert Roades, & his brother Henry Clarke, and to my servant that shall attend upon me at the time of my decease, ten shillings. To Johane Allen, my daughter, fifty pounds (and certain household stuff). To Isaacke Allen, her son, & to Rosanna Allen the sum of twentie five pounds each. To my daughter Alice Francklin (certain household stuff).

" Item I will and bequeathe unto Gregorye ffrancklyn my sonne in lawe and the sayed Alice his wife (yf she the same Alice shalbe living at the tyme of my decease) all my Righte title and interest of and in so muche and suche partes and parcells of the mesuage or Inne called the Quenes hed in the parishe of Sainct Savyoure in Sowthwarke aforesayed as I lately demised by Indenture of Lease unto one Oliuer Bowker and of in and to the gatehouse of the sayed Inne nowe in the occupacõn of Bryan Patteson : The Interest of which premisses I haue and hould by vertue of a Lease heretofore made and graunted by one John Bland unto Richard Boomer my late husband deceased and me the said Rose for diuers yeres yet to haue contynewance. Except allwayes and my meaning ys that the sayed Devise by me as aforesayed made shall not extend to certeyne garden plottes lying on the East syde of the Dytche or Common Sewer extending and passing by the Tenter yard and the garden behinde the sayed mesuage. Prouided allwayes that yf the sayed Gregory and Alice shall not permitt and suffer Abraham Allen and Jone his wife Isaacke Allen and Rosanna Allen and theire assignes peaceablye and quietly to hould and enioye the sayed excepted garden plottes according to the tenure of suche graunte and assuraunce as I haue lately made unto them That then and from thencefourthe the Devise made to the sayed Gregorye and Alice as aforesayed shall cease and be utterlie frustrate and voyde (any thinge before expressed to ye Contrary notwithstandinge)."

To my daughter Anne Younge the lease of my now dwelling house and of certain grounds at Wallworth and one hundred pounds (and certain household stuff). To my son in law John Younge and Anne his wife towards the buying of their blacks for my funeral four pounds. The same to Gregory Franckling & Alice his wife & to Abraham Allen & Johane his wife. Bequests to others. John Younge to be executor and Thomas Jackson & Myles Wilkenson supervisors.   53, Scott.

GREGORY FRANCKLIN of the parish of St Savior in Southwark in the County of Surrey, citizen & sadler of London, 11 September 1624, proved 22 September 1624. My body to be buried within the church of the parish of St Savior, at the discretion of Katherine my wife & sole executrix. To the poor of the said parish forty shillings. To the Wardens of the Company of Sadlers in London four pounds to make them a supper withall.

" Itm̃ whereas I the said Gregory ffrancklin by my deede indented bearing date the Second day of ffebruary in the Thirteenth yeare of the Kings

Ma^{ts} Raigne aforesaid of England ffraunce and Ireland, And of Scotland the Nyne and ffortieth (ffor the Consideraçons in the said deede expressed) did graunte enfeoff and confirme unto Gilbert Kinder Cittizen and Mercer of London All that Capitall Messuage or Inne called or knowne by the name of the Queenes head Scituat and being in the pish of St Savio^r in the Borrough of Southwark in the County of Surr. and one garden to the same belonging To certen severall uses in the said deede expressed As by the same more plainly may appeare, I the said Gregory ffrancklin doe hereby publish and declare that the only cause and consideraçon wch moved me to Seale unto the said deede was for that at the tyme of the making and sealing thereof I was a widdower and a sole pson, not having any yssue of my body then living nor then intending to marrye. Nevertheles wth a Res^{r}uacoñ unto myselfe in case I did marrye and had yssue, That not wthstanding the saide deede, or any estate thereupon executed, the power should remaine in me to giue and dispose of the said Inne and p^{r}imsses at my owne will and pleasure, In such manner as I should thinck fitting. And therefore for significaçon of my will intent and meaning concerning the same, And forasmuch as it hath pleased God that I have marryed the said Katherine my nowe wiffe by whome I have yssue Gregory ffrancklin my sonne and heir who is very young and of tender yeares, unto whome I have but small meanes to conferre and settle upon him both for his educaçon and bringing upp and otherwise wch wth care I would willingly provide for after my decease, And not minding or intending that my said sonne should be disinherited or deprived of his lawfull right of and to the said Messuage or Inne doe hereby renounce and frustrate the said deede and all thestate thereupon had Togeather wth the severall uses and limitaçons therein expressed, And doe declare the same to be of noe force or vallidity at all. And doe hereby giue deuise and bequeath the said Messuage or Inne and garden wth thapp^{r}tenñces to the said Gregory ffrancklin my sonne and the heires of his body lawfully to be begotten, And for default of such yssue unto Gilbert Kinder and Margarett his wife and unto theire heires for ever."

Reference made to a deed indented dated the last day of August 1616 for the jointure of the said Katherine (if she should happen to survive), conveying certain tenements in the parish of St Savior in Southwark & in the parish of St Sepulchre without Newgate London and confirmation of that deed. Also to the said Katherine the moyty or one half part of the Rents Issues and Profits, when and at such time as the same shall grow due and payable of all and singular those gardens or garden plots with the Alley way or passage to the same leading and used with all the appurtenances thereunto belonging lying and being on the backside of the Messuage or Inne commonly called &c. the Queen's Head &c. now in the tenure or occupation of Isaac Allen Gen^t or his assigns. And the other moiety or half part of the Rents &c. of the same gardens and premisses I give, will and bequeath to the said Gregory Francklin, my son, at such time as he shall accomplish his full age of one & twenty years. And after the decease of the said Katherine, my wife, I give will & bequeath all the said premisses unto the said Gregory my son & the heirs of his body lawfully begotten. If my son shall happen to depart this transitory life before his said age &c. (having no issue of his body living) then the said Katherine, my wife, shall freely have, hold, possess & enjoy all & singular the same gardens & premisses &c. for & during her natural life, and from & after her decease then to the Wardens or keepers & Commonalty of the mystery or Art of Sadlers of the City of London & to their Successors forever the moiety or half part of the said gardens &c., And the other moiety &c. to the Governors of the Free School of the Parish of St Saviour in Southwark, aforesaid, and to their successors forever, to this use, intent and purpose only (that is to say) for & towards the maintaining & bringing up of some one child or youth, which shall from time to time forever hereafter be born within the said parish. And I hereby will that such one always may be first taught learned and instructed sufficiently in the said free school and afterwards by them the said Governors and their successors for the time being put forth and brought up in learning, during the term of eight years, so that from time to time such one scholar may attain to the degree of M^r in Arts in one of the Universities of Oxon or Cambridge if such one scholar shall so long continue both scholar and student in either of the same, as by their discretions shall be thought most meet and convenient, whereunto I refer myself.

To the said Katherine, my wife, the lease which I hold of & from the Wardens &c. of the said mystery or Art of Sadlers &c. of all that Messuage or Tenement with the appurtenances &c. called or known by the sign of the Three Kings set, lying and being upon Snowe Hill near the Conduit there, within the parish of St Sepulchre without Newgate London, now in the Tenure or occupation of Josias Curtis, tailor &c. If she die before the expiration of the term granted by the same lease, then to the said Gregory Francklin, my son, for the time &c. unexpired. To my said son Gregory my gold seal ring (and other personal property).

Item my special will & meaning is that the said Katherine my wife shall within the space of six months next after my decease well & truly satisfy & pay or cause to be paid unto Ann Parkhurst & Katherine Parkhurst, daughters of Edward Parkhurst, late citizen & merchant tailor of London deceased & of the said Katherine my wife, the sum of one hundred pounds of lawful money of England for the redeeming of the said Gardens or garden plots, and two tenements with the appurtenances thereupon erected, which I mortgaged and stand engaged to pay the said sum by my deed as thereby appeareth.

A bequest is made to John Parvish, "my old servant," and the residue is bequeathed to wife Katherine who is made sole Executrix, and friends Richard Yerwood grocer and Robert Bucke glover are appointed supervisors, and to either of them, for their pains, a ring of gold of twenty shillings apiece is bequeathed.

Witnesses Richard Harrison, Richard Haukins, Antho: Rogers Scr., John Dodsworth, servant to Edr^d Jackson Scr.

Probate granted to the widow 22 September 1624.

Decimo quinto die mensis Junii An^o Dñi 1637° Emanavit Comissio Henrico Creswell p͞oe St Bothi extra Aldersgate London aurifabr̃ ad administrand bona iura et cr͞ed dc̃i Gregorii ffranncklyn def iuxta tenorem et eff͞cum testĩ pr͞ed p Cather̃inam Creswell al̃s ffrancklyn al̃s Blackleech nup̃ relcam et execũt testĩ dc̃i Gregorii (iam etiam demort.) non plene adm̃istrat de bene etc iurat.   73, Byrde.

ANNE WHITMORE of Lambehith in the county of Surrey, widow, 9 August 1624, proved 12 October 1624. I give all my worldly goods, money, jewells, plate and household stuff whatsoever unto my grandchild· Martha Smith and to the heirs of her body, lawfully begotten, provided always that if the said Martha shall happen to die and depart this life without such issue of her body lawfully begotten then my will is and I bequeath unto my grandchildren Gregory Francklin, Anne Parkhurst & Katherine

Parkhurst, the son and daughters of Katherine Francklin, wife of Gregory Francklin, to every of them the sum of ten pounds; also I give and bequeath unto Richard Smith and Thomas Bradbridge, the sons of Anne Bradbridge, my daughter, of Lambehith aforesaid, widow, the like sum of ten pounds and also to the said Anne Bradbridge the sum of forty pounds. And I nominate appoint and ordain the said Martha Smith to be sole executrix &c. And my will is that she shall within six months after my decease give unto her Aunt Katherin Francklin the sum of three pounds sterling to buy her a cup or bowl, in token of my love unto her, and I do appoint my loving friend Mr William Childe to be overseer &c.　118, Byrde.

GREGORY FRANCKLYN 19 February 1635. I do bestow all the estate that is or shall be mine upon my sister Ann, conditionally that she shall help, succor & relieve my mother in all her wants and necessities so far as she is able. And to my sister Kate I give a pair of sheets, a dozen of napkins and a towel, and to my cousin Mrs Martha Marshall a pair andirons, and to Thomas Day a piece of gold of five shillings.

Administration was granted 1 March 1635 to Anne Parkhurst natural & lawful sister of the said Gregory Francklyn of the Parish of St Buttolph without Aldersgate London deceased.　32, Pile.

LORD TIMOTHY DEXTER.

By WILLIAM CLEAVES TODD, A.M., of Newburyport, Mass.

THE writer lost years ago much of his faith in history and tradition. Events are misstated; good and wise men are represented as wicked and foolish, and virtue and greatness bestowed on the undeserving. After centuries, often, men and actions are shown to have been entirely misjudged, and, in some cases, as in that of William Tell, history becomes pure fiction.*

Timothy Dexter, or Lord Timothy Dexter, as he was generally called, had a peculiar and enduring celebrity. Many distinguished men have lived in Newburyport, yet the home of no one else is so frequently asked for by strangers in that city, and in all parts of the country when the writer has spoken of residing there, the first exclamation has been, "Ah! that was the home of Lord Timothy Dexter!" He has been regarded as the most marked example of a man of feeble intellect gaining wealth purely by luck. However unwise seemed the speculation into which he was drawn by his own folly, or by suggestions from others made in joke, it always resulted in large gains, and the stories are still fresh and often repeated, four

---

* An amusing illustration of one of these persistent and popularly cherished fictions has recently come to the knowledge of the writer. According to all histories of the United States, Ethan Allen demanded from the British commander the surrender of Ticonderoga "In the name of the Great Jehovah and the Continental Congress." Prof. James D. Butler, of Madison, Wisconsin, has informed me that his grandfather Israel Harris was present, and had often told him that Ethan Allen's real language was, "Come out of here, you d—d old rat."

score years since his decease, of his sending warming-pans and bibles to the West Indies, &c. &c. These stories have been received, too, without a question of their truth, even in the place where he lived, and have been endorsed by every history of Newburyport. It may be well, then, at a time when the credibility of so much in the past, important and unimportant, is subjected to criticism, to examine the correctness of the popular estimate of this man, whose name is so familiar when so many distinguished men of his time have been forgotten. So prominent was he that Samuel L. Knapp, a well-known literary man, author of the first life of Daniel Webster, who came to Newburyport to reside two years after Dexter's death, and had often seen him, thought fit to write his life, now a rare book, though several times republished.

Timothy Dexter was born in Malden, Mass., January 22, 1747. He learned the trade of a leather dresser, an occupation then popular and profitable, and at the age of twenty-one commenced business for himself in Charlestown, where leather-dressing was much carried on, and by his industry and economy was from the first successful. He early married the widow of a glazier, nine years his senior, whose husband had left her considerable property. She was Elizabeth Lord, daughter of John Lord, of Exeter, N. H., and her first husband was Benjamin Frothingham, of Newbury, who was born April 30, 1717, and died June 1, 1769. She was an industrious and frugal woman, and by keeping a huckster's shop added to her husband's income, so that Dexter soon had several thousand dollars in specie at his command, which he was anxious to invest profitably. It was when continental money was so depreciated, and he had learned that Gov. Hancock and Thomas Russell, a noted merchant, had been buying up this paper at a small part of its face value, and in imitation of them he began to do the same. He probably made better bargains, too, because he bought in small quantities, of poor holders, obliged to sell for what they could get. He was fortunate in his purchase, as were all others of that day, and during our late war, who had faith in the government. The funding scheme of Hamilton gave this depreciated paper its par value, and he soon found himself a rich man for that period, and became an operator in the stocks of the day, which were constantly advancing.

With wealth came different and large ideas. As he had become rich like Hancock and Russell, his vanity led him to think himself their equal and entitled to the same consideration. Finding that he was not received into the best society as they were, he sought another home where he would be better appreciated, and finally fixed upon Newburyport. His wife's associations with the place probably also influenced his decision. This was at that time a town of much wealth and commercial importance, the third in the state in population, occupying a very different position relatively from its present rank. John Quincy Adams, a law student then with the celebrated

Theophilus Parsons, used to say that he found better society there than at Washington. Harrison Gray Otis, who was often there when a young man, bore similar testimony ; and Talleyrand and other distinguished strangers who visited it, praised warmly its generous hospitality, its air of wealth and refinement, and the beauty of its long High Street.

Real estate was low, as several large failures had occurred, and Dexter bought and occupied one of the best houses in the town, that now used for the public library, but he soon removed to another house on High Street, with ten acres of land, which he fitted up in a manner worthy of his estimate of himself. He laid out the grounds after what he was told was the European style, and had fruits, flowers and shrubbery of many varieties planted in them. He put minarets on the roof of the house, surmounted with gilt balls, and in front placed rows of columns fifteen feet high—about forty in all—each having on its top a statue of some distinguished man. Before the door were two lions on each side, with open mouths, to guard the entrance. On an arch, and occupying the most prominent position, were the statues of Washington, Adams and Jefferson, and to the other statues he gave the names of Bonaparte, Nelson, Franklin, and other heroes, often changing them according to his fancy. In a conspicuous place was a statue of himself, with the inscription, "I am the first in the East, the first in the West, and the greatest philosopher in the Western world." All these statues were carved in wood by a young ship-carver, Joseph Wilson, who had just come to Newburyport. They were gaudily painted, and though having but little merit as works of art, and less as likenesses, gave the house a strange appearance, and attracted crowds, whose curiosity deeply gratified the owner, and he freely opened his grounds to them. Knapp says these images cost $15,000, but an old gentleman, who remembered Dexter and knew the artist, has told me the price was $100 for each, and that Dexter made as sharp a bargain as he could with the artist, as he did with every one. Wishing his house to be in all respects equal to those of Hancock and Russell, he imported from France expensive furniture and works of art, as they had done, and bought many costly books, as he knew they had fine libraries. Having made himself a "Lord" he bought good horses and an elegant coach, on which he caused to be conspicuously painted a coat of arms taken from a book of heraldry, in imitation of European lords. Ranking himself with the nobility, he showed much commiseration for the sufferings of the higher classes during the French Revolution, caused the bells to be tolled on the death of Louis XVI., and sent out an invitation to the survivors of the royal family to become his guests. In expectation of their acceptance he laid in a large stock of provisions which rose on his hands, an act of Providence, as he said, to reward him for his good intentions, but according to the popular idea, another instance of his unfailing good luck.

He had a tomb constructed in his garden, and having heard that some great man had had his coffin made during his life, he also caused a coffin to be made of mahogany, with silver handles, expensively lined, which he kept in his house and used to exhibit to his guests. An old gentleman has told me within a few days that he remembers when a boy looking in at the window to see it.

With no regular business and restless, Dexter gave himself up to his whims, was much of the time in a state of intoxication, and was constantly doing strange things, of which many instances are given. Acting on some impulse, he had a mock funeral. Some one was procured to officiate as clergyman, cards were sent out to invite the mourners, and Dexter watched the people to see how they were affected. He was satisfied with all except that his wife did not shed so many tears as he thought were becoming, for which, as the story is, he caned her severely after the ceremony. Persons would go to his house professing to be lords, and saying they were desirous of paying their respects to one whose fame had become so worldwide, whom he would receive with consideration, and offer them the best he had to eat and drink. Mr. Ladd, the well-known peace advocate, of Portsmouth, used to describe such a visit. One of the party told Dexter that this gentleman was one of the first lords of England, and Dexter wished to know what the king had said about him lately. A gentleman told me recently he had often heard his father speak of a visit made to Dexter with other young men, who asked for the honor of crowning him. He consented, and they placed him on a table full of liquor, and all had a carousal. Only a few days ago a gentleman said to me that one of his ancestors, a clergyman, called on him, and after some conversation wished to offer a prayer, for which permission was given. At the close Dexter turned to his son and said, "That was a d—d good prayer, was n't it, Sam?"

Wishing to extend his fame, he bought a country seat in Chester, N. H., on which he spent considerable money in ways to make a show, and called himself "Lord of Chester." He often visited Hampton Beach, then as now a favorite resort, and was delighted with the sensation he made. At one time he was sent to the county jail, at Ipswich, for attempting to shoot a man in a drunken frolic, and rode thither in his coach, boasting that no one else had ever been carried there in that style. He was accustomed to walk through the streets wearing a cocked hat and long coat, and carrying a cane, followed by a peculiar looking black dog with no hair; and boys knowing his vanity would follow him and salute him as "Lord Timothy Dexter," whom he would reward by money, a scene which a few now living can remember.

Newburyport at that time was a large market town, and countrymen came from far with their market wagons to buy and sell, and they all carried home wonderful stories about Dexter, his great wealth, his house decorated with images, and his many strange acts. With but few newspapers, and so much less than now to discuss, it is not to be wondered at that his eccentricities should have been so much talked about, and that people came from a great distance simply to see him and his images.

Persuaded of his own greatness, and that he was equal to any undertaking, like other eminent men, he thought he must become an author, and so he wrote a book called "Pickle for the Knowing Ones." It was a small volume, with some sense and much nonsense jumbled together. There were no punctuation marks, and as this was commented upon, in the second edition he placed at the end a page of different punctuation marks with this note:

"Mister printer the Nowing ones complane of my book the first edition had no stops I put in A Nuf here and thay may peper and solt it as they plese."

He had thousands of copies printed, and gave them away, and this, perhaps, more than any other one thing increased his notoriety. Even now there is a demand for this little work, and though it has been reprinted several times, a short time ago its market price was a dollar for what had cost but a few cents. He expresses his views on many topics, and some of his remarks indicate shrewdness. He condemns the folly of Newburyport in being set off from Newbury with an area of only six hundred acres, and within a few years it has been reannexed to a large part of Newbury, from Dexter's advice, or for some other reason. In speaking of the ministers he says: "I suppose they are all good men, but I want to Know why they do not agree better. They are always at swords' points, and will not enter each other's houses, nor hardly nod to each other in the street." This remark certainly would not indicate a want of sense.

Having heard that the kings of England had a poet laureate to sing their praises, Dexter thought he also should have one, and he found him in the person of Jonathan Plummer, a young man who had been a peddler of fish, then of sermons, songs, and sheets on which were printed horrible events, and who in the end turned poet and sold his own verses. Dexter took him into his service, gave him a suit of black livery ornamented with stars, and crowned him with parsley, and, thus equipped, the bard travelled around selling verses in praise of his patron. A few stanzas from a long poem will illustrate the character of his productions:

Lord Dexter is a man of fame;
Most celebrated is his name;
More precious far than gold that's pure,
Lord Dexter shine forever more.

His noble house, it shines more bright
Than Lebanon's most pleasing height;
Never was one who stepped therein
Who wanted to come out again.

> Lord Dexter, thou, whose name alone
> Shines brighter than king George's throne ;
> Thy name shall stand in books of fame,
> And princes shall thy name proclaim.
>   *   *   *   *
>
> Lord Dexter like king Solomon
> Hath gold and silver by the ton,
> And bells to churches he hath given—
> To worship the great King of heaven.
>   *   *   *   *
>
> In heaven may he always reign,
> For there's no sorrow, sin, nor pain ;
> Unto the world I leave the rest
> For to pronounce Lord Dexter blest.

Dexter was superstitious, had a collection of dream books, and was much governed by the advice of others. He used often to consult a fortune-teller, Madam Hooper, and, after her decease, Moll Pitcher, a fortune-teller celebrated in the whole region around Lynn, her home, both of whom knew how to make money out of him. The one who had the most influence over him, however, was Lucy Lancaster, a colored woman, whose father was said to have been the son of an African prince. She was shrewd, well informed, well disposed, and used her power over him to restrain his excesses. She gave him more credit for intellect than did most others, saying that he was honest, and that his follies sprang in a great degree from his uneasy nature and want of regular employment.

But the great notoriety of Dexter, as has been stated, is as a man who with poor judgment gained his wealth by luck. Did he so gain it?

There is no doubt that his first wealth was gained by the exercise of his trade, in competition with skilled workmen, and without ordinary business capacity it is hard to understand how he could have succeeded. He added to his wealth by marriage, and as this union is the result of luck, or calculation, or love, which decided it in his case is unknown. He certainly made a large sum by his speculation in continental money, as did all who bought it. In the case of Hancock and Russell, this would be called shrewd foresight; in Dexter it was regarded as his luck. After he gave up his trade he seems to have speculated in many ways, generally or always, as is supposed, taking hints from others, as all speculators do ; but it is hardly credible, from his early history and constant success, that he did not reason about his ventures. Knapp says : " Many who attempted to take advantage of him got sadly deceived. He had no small share of cunning, when all else seemed to have departed from him. He by direct or indirect means obtained correct opinions upon the value of goods and lands, and seldom made an injudicious speculation." He was in the habit of finding out what articles were scarce, thus making what would now be called in Wall Street parlance a " corner." The shrewdest Wall Street operators fail—Dexter seems never to have made a mistake. He would transact no business when intoxicated, and made his appointments for the forenoon, saying he was always drunk in the afternoon. In buying he gave the most foolish reasons to blind the seller, who thought he was deceived when deceiving. He bought up such articles as opium, of which it was easy at that period of limited supply to secure most in the market. Knapp says : " It often happened that shrewd merchants were suspicious of selling him an article, apprehensive that it was almost a sure sign that it was going to rise, although they could see no reason for it."

Dexter's ostentation in so many foolish ways naturally caused a high estimate of his wealth, and much curiosity how a man of his capacity could have gained it. He seems to have been often questioned about it, and in the "Pickle for the Knowing Ones," gives his answer, which is quoted in full as a good illustration of the style of the book.

" How Did Dexter Make his Money ye says bying whale bone for staing for ships in grosing three hundred & 40 tons bort all in boston salum and all in Noue york under Cover oppenly told them for my ships they all laffed so I had at my own pris I had four Counning men for Rounners thay found the horne as I told them to act the fool I was full of Cash I had nine tun of silver on hand at that time all that time the Creaters more or less laffing it spread very fast here is the Rub in fifty days they smelt a Rat found where it was gone to Nouebry Port spekkelaters swarmed like hell houns to be short with it I made seventey five per sent one tun and halfe of silver on hand and over one more spect Drole a Nuf I Dreamed of warming pans three nites that thay would doue in the west inges I got no more than fortey two thousand put them in nine vessels for difrent ports that tuck good hold I cleared sevinty nine per sent the pans thay made yous of them for Coucking very good masser for Couckey blessed good in Deade missey got nice handel Now burn my fase the last thing I Ever see in borne days I found I was very luckky in spekkelation I dreamed that the good book was Run Down in this Countrey nine years gone so low as halfe prise and Dull at that the bibel I means I had the Ready Cash by holl sale I bort twelve per sent under halfe pris they Cost fortey one sents Each bibbel twentey one thousand I put them into twenty one vessels for the west inges and sent a text that all of them must have one bibel in every family or if not thay would goue to hell and if thay had Dun wiked flie to the bibel and on thare Neas and kiss the bibel three times and look up to heaven aunest for forgivness my Capttains all had Compleat orders here Comes the good luck I made one hundred per sent & littel over then I found I had made money enuf I hant spekalated sence old time by government securities I made or cleared forty seven thousands Dolors that is the old afare Now I toald the all the sekrett Now be still let me A lone Dont wonder Noe more houe I made my money boas."

It would be difficult to condense into the same space more improbable statements than are found in this explanation of how Dexter made his money, as a little examination will show.

The first speculation named is that of whalebone. The year is not stated, so that it is not possible to give the amount in the country and the price at that date, which have greatly varied at different periods. The amount in the country in 1830 was 120,000 lbs.; the maximum quantity was 5,652,300 lbs. in 1853. The price is now $2 a pound; within three years it has been $3 a pound; and I have heard of sales as low as eight cents—the price of course varying with the demand and supply. Three hundred and forty-two tons would be in the old reckoning 761,600 lbs., costing at the highest price given over two millions of dollars, and at the lowest over $60,000 dollars. It is not probable that this quantity was in the country nearly a century ago, nor that it could have found a market, as the demand for it has always been limited. Dexter never could have bought this quantity except at the lowest price, and even that is doubtful, as will be shown later. The tradition is that as soon as he had purchased it the fashion for broad skirts was introduced, and it was all in demand. How far a ton of whalebone would go in satisfying the expansive desires of the ladies of that time, the writer has no data for a calculation. Most of them, however, were practical, hard-working and economical, from necessity; merely fashionable ladies were rare, and visits to Newport and Saratoga unknown. As to the foolish reason for the purchase, it was characteristic in him to give it if he wished to buy.

He says he had nine tons of silver on hand, which would be worth in round numbers $300,000, a sum which he never could have commanded, as will be shown farther on. It was just after the commencement of our government, when hard money was scarce, and most of it foreign, as we had coined but little before the day of safety vaults, and banks were few. If one had had such a large amount of coin, where could he safely have deposited it? Who ever dared to keep such an amount in a private house?

His next most noted speculation was in sending 42,000 warming-pans to the West Indies. No hard-ware was made in this country until a little more than half a century ago, and all the warming-pans in use came from Great Britain. The amount named would have cost about $150,000, to be paid for in hard money, as bills of exchange were then but little used. Such an importation and exportation would have required months of time, and would have made a sensation indeed, for, though common, a large part of the families had none, and they are now rare as old curiosities. Is it possible, rating his intelligence very low, that, if he had attempted such a speculation, he would not have been persuaded of its folly long before he could have executed it? Except for the purpose for which they were made, they are of no value. Dexter says they were sold in the West Indies as cooking utensils, but a glance shows how inconvenient they would be for such use. The tradition is that they were sold to dip and strain molasses, but they are poorly adapted to this, and nearly a century ago, when sugar plantations were few in the West Indies, but a small part of 42,000 would have satisfied any such demand. Did any visitor to the West Indies ever see or hear of one of these 42,000 warming-pans?

Of all his speculations the bible venture seems most improbable. If there was an over supply, they would be English bibles, sent to a Roman Catholic country where bibles are but little circulated, to a Spanish talking people that could not read them, and, of course, could not be made to understand their terrible destiny if they did not buy one.

There is another speculation often spoken of, and mentioned by Mrs. Smith in her History of Newburyport, but which Dexter does not give in his "Pickle for the Knowing Ones"—a consignment of mittens to the West Indies, which were bought at a large advance by a vessel bound for the Baltic. It is enough to say of this that wool and labor have always been cheaper in the North of Europe than here, and there has never been a time since 1492 when mittens could have been shipped there from America at a profit. The sale of this article is limited everywhere, as the supply from lady friends usually equals every demand. If one consignment of mittens, or of any other article in which Dexter was so fortunate, could yield such a return, why did not some other Yankee, taking the hint, repeat the venture?

All these professed importations and exportations would naturally have been made at Newburyport, where Dexter lived, and which had a large trade with the West Indies; yet the collector of customs of that place has told me that the books of the custom house contain no evidence of any such transactions. Every old person in Newburyport with whom I have conversed, has accepted all these stories, yet could give no foundation for them except the common belief. If Dexter dealt in warming-pans and the other articles named at all, it was probably in small quantities, as he would have dealt in other articles in common demand, to make a little " corner," and, to conceal his object, he would give the most foolish reason. The only direct evidence I can find is Dexter's own word, and he professes to tell a " secret," when such large and unusual speculations could not have taken place without general knowledge and discussion. Knapp says: "Tricks without malice made up the great amusement of his latter days. He devised it in the morning and cherished it at night, and no doubt it filled his dreams." The only satisfactory explanation, then, of these stories which Dexter tells to those inquiring minds so anxious to learn the secret how he made his money, is that they were the creation of his own brain, a great joke worthy of Mark Twain, successfully imposed on the community—that instead of being the fool he is commonly regarded, he fooled others.

The inventory of Dexter's estate, taken from the Probate Office, is as follows:

Real Estate	.	.	.	.	.	12,000.
Personal Estate	.	.	.	.	.	15,500.
Goods .	.	.	.	.	.	7,527.39

$35,027.39

This small estate shows how largely Dexter's wealth was over-estimated, and how improbable are the statements of transactions calling for such large sums as have been named. He was sharp in all his business affairs, and spent but little except to gratify his vanity and his passion for drink. A little money in those days of small means and great economy made much show, and it is doubtful if he ever could have been worth as much as $75,000. There is no reason to believe he ever made any serious losses ; this would be contrary to the tradition that he was always a lucky fool. All the business operations of which we have any knowledge seem to have been marked by good sense. He was interested in public affairs, and gave judiciously, but not largely, to objects of charity. He took one hundred shares and was the largest stockholder in the new bridge over the Merrimack, at Deer Island, now the attractive home of Richard S. and Harriet Prescott Spofford, and at its opening, July 4, 1793, delivered an oration which one of the newspapers of that day, thrusting greatness on Timothy Dexter as they have done on many a Dexter since, pronounced "for elegance of style, propriety of speech, and force of argument, truly Ciceronian." And it may be stated, that these shares are all the stocks named in his will, or in the inventory of his estate. It has been said that his motive for putting up the images was to make the new bridge a paying investment by drawing travel over it and past his house, and he wrote some newspaper articles against other proposed bridges. He gave a bell to one of the churches, and sums to the other churches to be used in benevolence. A gift was made to St. Paul's Church on condition that a tablet should perpetuate it, and there it hangs to-day with gilt letters, a monument of his vanity and of his shrewdness in so ingeniously perpetuating his name. He offered to pave High Street if it should be called by his name, and to build a market house for the use of the town with a similar condition. Both objects were much needed, and he showed far better judgment in the offer than did the town in its rejection.

If the view here taken is correct, the Dexter of tradition and common belief disappears, and in his place is a vain, uneducated, weak, coarse, drunken, cunning man, low in his tastes and habits, constantly striving for foolish display and attention, but, with all his folly, having business shrewdness, to which, and not to luck, he owed his success.

His family, mainly his own fault, was not a happy one. His only son was allowed to spend money as he pleased, was sent to Europe, and had every opportunity for improvement; but, as might be expected, he became dissipated, a prodigal, and died a drunkard one year after his father. His only daughter, with some beauty, but a feeble intellect, was sought on account of her reputed wealth, and married a judge, who soon became tired of her, and obtained a divorce, with or without reason, and sent her home an imbecile, with confirmed habits of intoxication. A child of this daughter married respectably, but died early, and with the death of the daughter, about 1850, the family became extinct.

A lady in Newburyport has a portrait of Dexter, taken by an artist in New Haven, where his daughter had married. He is represented dressed as a gentleman of that day, wearing a wig, a ruffled bosom and ruffled wristbands, and his face certainly indicates no lack of intelligence.

He died October 26, 1806; his death caused or hastened by intemperate habits. His will was judicious. He provided carefully for his family and others having natural claims on him, and made some sensible bequests, among them $2,000 to Newburyport, the income to be expended for the poor, and $2,000 for the support of the gospel, and $300 for a bell to his native town, Malden. He requested to be buried in the tomb he had constructed in his garden, but the board of health interfered, and he rests with his follies in the cemetery close to the beautiful mall. On the plain stone over his grave is the following inscription:

> "In memory of Timothy Dexter who died Oct. 26, 1806,
> Ætatis 60.
> He gave liberal Donations
> For the support of the Gospel;
> For the benefit of the Poor,
> And for other benevolent purposes."

Near his grave are those of his wife, who died July 3, 1809, aged 72, and of his son, who died July 20, 1807, aged 36.

The images remained as at Dexter's decease until the great gale in 1815 blew down most of them, which were sold by auction for a small sum. The three presidents on the arch, however, occupied their place till about 1850, attracting much attention, and keeping alive the old curiosity about the former eccentric owner.

The house was used as a hotel and the home of the daughter till her death, and with the grounds was neglected. It was then bought by a gentleman of good taste, the late Dr. E. G. Kelley, who greatly improved the buildings and grounds, and sold it to the Hon. George H. Corliss, who has made it one of the most attractive homes of the city. The eagle on the top remains, the last of Dexter's images.

SOLDIERS IN KING PHILIP'S WAR.

Communicated by the Rev. GEORGE M. BODGE, A.M., of East Boston, Mass.

[Continued from page 320.]

No. XVI.

CAPT. SAMUEL WADSWORTH AND THE SUDBURY FIGHT.

IT is proper to close the account of affairs at the garrison at Marlborough during and immediately after the fight at Sudbury, as given in the following letters of Lieut. Richard Jacob, upon whom the command of the garrison devolved after Capt. Brocklebank's death. And it is well to bear in mind that, between the time of the requests of Gen. Denison and Capt. Brocklebank that the garrison might be relieved to go home, &c., and these letters of Lieut. Jacob, the new army under Major Savage had marched out from Marlborough to the Connecticut River, driving the main body of the hostile Indians beyond that river, as was supposed, but as was found afterwards, leaving a great number gathered near Mount Wachuset. After operating till about March 28th in defence of the western towns, he was ordered to leave one hundred and fifty men under command of Capt. Turner, and return home as far as Marlborough, and await further orders. By an order of the Council, passed April 10th, 1676, Major-Gen. Denison was to meet and dispose the returning troops at Marlborough.

In the mean time the Indians, closely watching the movements of our forces, and alert to strike at every exposed point, on Sunday, March 26th, attacked Marlborough, as we see by Capt. Brocklebank's letter, and burned a large part of the town. The garrisons were unable, or feared, to attack them in force; but that night Lieut. Jacob of Capt. Brocklebank's company, with twenty of his men and twenty volunteers coming up from Sudbury, followed and surprised the Indians sleeping by their fires, and killed some of them, though it is not known how many. Mr. Hubbard says they wounded thirty, fourteen of whom died the same day or soon after, and popular rumor, as usual, exaggerated the number, and in this case made it seventy.

These letters show the situation of Marlborough.

Lieut. Richard Jacob's First Letter.

from Malbary ye 22 April 1676.

Hono'rd Sirs This morning aboute Sun two hours high ye Enimie Alarmed us by firing & Shooting towards ye Lowermost Garason Next Sudbury, which made us feare y^t Garason to be in Danger which shooting we afterward understood was ye Enimie killing off Cattle. Some after they gave a shout & Came in sight upon ye Indian hill great Numbers of them & one as

theire accustomed maner is after a fight, began to signifie to us how many were slaine. They Cohoop'd seventy-four times, which we hoped was only to affright us seing we have had no intelegence of any such thing, yet we have Reason to feare the worst Considering Theire Numbers which we aprehended to be five hundred at ye least others Thinke a thousand y^o most of y^{em} hasted toward ye Northwest side of ye towne firing ye Remainder of ye Garason houses & others y^t were deserted as they went: they have been hunting in al quarters of ye towne to kill & take what Cattle were without Comand of ye four Garasons That yet Remain.   Severall of ye furthermost houses of this town next Sudbury have bin fired now toward Night which gives Reason to Thinke that ye Enimie is not yet Departed from us :   Thus I thought it my Duty to give a briefe account of ye present proceedings of ye Enimie: to your Honours Leaving itt with your wisdoms Consideration.
   Beging pardon for This my Bouldnes I Remaine your Honoures
Humble Servant   RICHARD JACOB.

[Attached to the above letter is Secretary Rawson's Copy of an Order of the Council, as follows :]

   Leftenant Jacob, yesterday upon the Councils having the sad intelegence of y^{or} Capt. & Capt. Wadsworths death ordered your taking the charge of the souldgers at Malborough since wch I received your of 22 Apr. giving intelegence of the enemyes infesting y^{or} quarters & apearance in a boddy of at least 500 & these wasting by fyers what they can come at so driving cattle, yesterday was ordered eighty troopers to advance to observe the motions of the enemy y^{or} twoe souldgers returne wth a p^{ty} of horse to Sudbery & so with these to you I desyer your vigilance & care for the preserving your men & what is under your charge & you shal have ffurther orders so soone as the Councell meete, desyring Gods presence with and assistance of you,   23, 2, 76.
Mass. Archives, Vol. 68, p. 223.

Lieutenant Richard Jacob's Second Letter.
Marlborough 24. Aprill 1676.

   Honoured Sirs,   Having now Received Information of God's ffurther frowns on ye Country In Suffering two Such worthy Captaines to fall before ye Enimie whome we might have hop^t to have bin Instruments of more good in these troublous times : But In this God's will is Done.
   Receiving an Order from your Honours wherein your Honours are pleased to Devolve ye charge and betrustment of our late Capt. Brocklebanke upon me, for which I am sensible of my Inefficiency & Incapacity, yet Since tis your Honours pleasure, to Require me to Certifie your Honours of ye state of ye soldeirs & of ye place. That I shall Readyly, here is Remaining of our Company about fourty-six, Several whereofe are young soldiers left here by Capt Wadsworth being unable to march. The Towne is wholy consumed Excepting four Garasons that were man'd when the Enimie was last with us, all ye cattle without Reach of The garasons are Lost : one of ye Garason Houses which was Judg'd to be most fitt by our Captaine : who your Honours did apoynt to order according to his Discretion for a stated garason now burnt by Reason off ye Inhabitants not attending thereunto Every one being Carful to Secure his private Interest, here is only Remaining These two houses where the Magazine Lyes That are in a Capacity to assist each other. ye other two Lying att a greater Dis-

tance with other Inconveniences. May it please your Honours further to Order of ye state of our Company being Generally such as live upon Husbandry & seed time being now far spent which may be prejudiciall to ourselves & others if ye season so slipt. But I shall leave that to your Honours Consideration only begging pardon for my bouldnes I Rest your Honours Servant to my utmost ability   RICHARD JACOB

Postscript: Some of ye principle of ye Towns men In the behalfe of ye Rest y^t are yet Remaining which are but few Would Desire your Honours to Consider their present Condition being altogether incapable for Remaining without assistance both with Carts & a Guard They are destitute of Carts Their Teames being at Sudburie & not Daring to Returne. Removing of theire goods if your Honours see meete to Grant it or otherwise willing to refer their loss to your Honours further Consideration.

Mass. Archives, Vol. 68, p. 227.

CAPT. WADSWORTH AND HIS MEN AT NARRAGANSET, MARLBOROUGH AND LANCASTER.

Capt. Samuel Wadsworth was the son of Christopher, who came from England in the ship Lion; was settled in Duxbury in 1632 with wife Grace, and had four children, who in their mother's will, 1688, are named in the order—Joseph, Samuel, Mary and John, and the last was born 1638.

Capt. Samuel moved to Milton about 1656 and selected a large tract of land in the centre of that town, and settled there with his wife Abigail, daughter of James Lindall, of Duxbury. Their children, born between 1659 and 1674, were Ebenezer, Christopher, Timothy, Joseph, Benjamin, Abigail, whose descendants have honored the name in their generations.

Agreeably to the order of the Commissioners of the United Colonies to raise one thousand men to continue the war against the Indians, passed at Boston, December 25th, Massachusetts on the 28th issued orders for impressing three hundred men forthwith; Essex 105, Middlesex 83, Suffolk 112. See Mass. Archives, vol. 68, p. 107—the time and place of rendezvous being January 5th, at Dedham, as we learn from the Archives, vol. 68, p. 112.

Of the recruits that were sent out at this time, Capt. Samuel Brocklebank, of Rowley, was in command of one company, the account of which was in the last chapter; and Capt. Samuel Wadsworth, the subject of the present chapter, commanded another. There is no published reference to such service by these officers, and only the casual mention in Gen. Gookin's account of the "Praying Indians," and by the writer of the pamphlet "News from New Enggland," to the effect that, when the army returned to Marlborough, and the rest of the forces were dismissed, "Capt. Wadsworth with his company was left at Marlborough." The garrisons from all the frontier towns, save such as the inhabitants furnished, had been withdrawn by an order of the Council, January 14th.

There is no mention of either of the above officers until the return to Marlborough, and therefore our account of Capt. Wadsworth and his company must begin there; they having taken part in the "Hungry March" from Narraganset, were now left to bear the brunt of any attack the Indians might make upon the frontiers.

On February 6th the Council issued an order to Major Appleton, then at Marlborough with the returned army, to dismiss the soldiers to their several homes, "as soone as the Sabbath is past." But it will be remembered that Gen. Winslow, now in command of the army, and under the pressure of the lack of provisions, would scarcely wait for this order, and probably marched to Boston on February 5th, with at least a large proportion of his army. Rev. Increase Mather, living in Boston at the time, and deeply interested in all these affairs, writes in his history : " Feb. 5th, the Army returned to Boston not having obtained the end of their going forth ;" while the anonymous contemporary writer of the pamphlet above mentioned, states that " Major Gen. Winslow only with his Troops (marched) to Boston, leaving the Foot at Malbury and South-bury, who came home on Munday following and were all dismist to their several Habitations except Capt. Wadsworth, who was left at Malbury in pursuit of the Enemy of whom he destroyed about 70 Old Men Women and Children, who wanted strength to follow the fugitive Army."[120] Hull's treasury accounts agree with this date of the disbanding of the army, so that Capt. Wadsworth's operations on the frontiers with his headquarters at Marlborough, began doubtless on the same day.

On February 10th a large body of Indians fell upon Lancaster and burned near half the town, consisting of about fifty families, but succeeded in capturing only one of the garrison houses, of which there were several. The one captured was that of Rev. Joseph Rowlandson, who was himself absent at the time in Boston, seeking assistance from the Council for the threatened town. The house was sufficiently garrisoned, but the enemy succeeded in setting fire to the rear portion, and forced all within to surrender or die, as the house was quickly burnt to the ground. Forty-two persons were thus made prisoners, most of whom were women and children. As soon as the news of this attack upon Lancaster reached Marlborough, Capt. Wadsworth mustered a company of about forty men of his garrison and hastened to the rescue of the remaining part of the

---

[120] This writer is unreliable in his account of the war, and in attributing this last exploit to Capt. Wadsworth undoubtedly confuses things in mixing the rescue of Lancaster by him with the midnight surprise of Indians March 27th, by Lieut. Jacob. But while his direct statements are to be received with caution, his casual references are valuable as hints of existing facts which others do not mention, and many of which, confirmed by evidence gleaned from the Archives, throw light upon things which have hitherto been entirely unknown in history ; for instance, this reference to Capt. Wadsworth, together with Major Gookin's mention, is the only hint, in published accounts, that connects him with the Narraganset campaign, and in these references there is only inferential evidence, and in regard to Capt. Brocklebank there is absolutely no reference until the present investigations based upon Treasurer Hull's accounts; but following up the clues, there is plenty of evidence in the Archives of these officers and others having had part in this campaign, that have never been mentioned in connection with it.

town.   On one side the Indians had cut off the approach of assistance, as they supposed, by tearing off the planks from the bridge;
but the English readily repaired this and passed over, and by a
secret way were led into the town, where they succeeded in driving
off the enemy.

During the rest of this month Capt. Wadsworth and his men
were employed scouting along the frontiers, with head-quarters
chiefly at Marlborough, I think, where Capt. Brocklebank was in
command, whose company, dismissed on February 5th, had been
called again into service upon the news of the assault upon Lancaster.   An order of the Council, dated February 11th, appoints Capt.
Samuel Wadsworth; Robert Badcocke, Sergeant; and "those that
are at present selectmen" a council of militia for Milton; and this
would seem to indicate the design of the Council to keep Capt.
Wadsworth upon the home frontiers, as will further appear.

When, on the first of March, the newly levied army was being organized at Marlborough for operations in the west, Capt. Wadsworth was there with his company, and was sent out by the General
to recall Job Kattenanit upon the occasion detailed in the last
chapter.

In making up the army the General made a selection of the best
soldiers out of all at his disposal, and among other changes, transferred a part of Capt. Wadsworth's company to Capt. William Turner, who led out a company in this expedition to the west.

A letter from William Torrey to the Council, dated March 7th,
expresses gratitude for the assistance rendered by the Council in defence of the towns of Milton, Braintree, Weymouth and Hingham,
and says that the Major General has "ordered the remaynder of Capt.
Wadsworth and Capt. Jacobs forces to be a guard to our townes,"
&c.; and that Capt. Wadsworth and his men shall be a guard to
Milton, Braintree, &c.

The credits in Hull's account indicate the discharge of the remainder of the company about the 7th or 8th of March, and thereafter
they were employed as home-guards, and supported by their respective towns, and there is no further mention of service by Capt.
Wadsworth during the next month, the operations in the western
towns engrossing all the energies of the colonies and all the attention of the people.   The soldiers are credited with service up to this
time, and thus properly the names and credits are given in this place.

Credited under Capt. Samuel Wadsworth.

February 29, 1675–6.			Nathaniel Jewett	02 02 02
Henry Pellington	00	12 00	John Hunt	04 02 03
Robert Miller	01	01 04	James Hadlock	03 04 00
John Rowlston	01	01 04	Thomas Vos, *Lieut*	07 10 00
Stephen Fielder	01	01 04	Ebenezer Williams	02 11 00
March 24th 1675–6.			Richard Evans	02 14 10
John Starr	02	08 00	William Scant	02 14 10

John Horsington	02	14	10	James Badcock	03 03 00
John Trescott	00	18	10	Thomas Beetle	02 04 10
Timothy Wales	02	04	06	Thomas Mory	02 08 00
William Deane	03	12	00	Thomas Lawrence	02 03 08
Martho Hurley	02	07	02	John Baker	03 18 08
James Stuart	03	15	09	Thomas Williams	02 08 10
Thomas Woods	02	10	06	John Poole	02 09 08

April 24th 1675.

			Joseph Bosworth	02 15 08
James Dolvine	02 07 02	Robert Milton	02 15 08
Jacob Leonard	02 09 08	Isaac Lobdell	02 15 08
Robert Braine	02 14 00	William Hooper	02 15 08
Samuel Wadsworth, *Capt*	15 00 00	William Lyon	01 10 00
James Ford	02 15 08	James Badcock	00 09 00
Peter Roberts	01 18 06	John Thare	02 14 10
Robert Corbett	02 06 02	July 24th 1676.
Henry Ledebetter	02 11 00	Paul Gilford	02 09 06
Robert Parker	02 14 10	Joshuah Lane	05 14 00
Timothy Tilston	02 05 00	John Alger	02 08 00
John Sharp	03 15 00	Jeremiah Hood	02 08 00
June 24th 1676.		Robert Mutson	02 08 00
George Ripley	02 06 02	Samuel Gill	02 09 06
Robert Munson	03 06 00	August 24th 1676.
Robert Judd	01 11 06	John Angell	03 12 00
John Hands	02 07 00	Jonathan Dunning	08 19 00
John Adis	02 08 00	Edward Mortmore	02 08 00
Ephraim Pond	02 08 00	Samuel Nicholson	01 07 04
Jonathan Gray	02 08 00	Edward Samson	02 08 00
Abraham Hathaway	02 08 00	Sept. 23d 1676.
Richard Evans	01 14 02	John Tuckerman	00 12 00
John Redman	02 14 10		

THE SUDBURY FIGHT.

Upon the disbanding of the army under Gen. Winslow, as noted in the first of this chapter, the Indians began to gather in towards the frontier towns in large numbers, evidently elated at the apparent inability and supposed discouragement of the English. Upon April 18th they came upon Marlborough again, and burned the houses they had left in the former attack. They hovered about the town for two days, evidently seeking to draw out the soldiers from the garrisons and away into an ambush, according to their usual mode of warfare. They did not dare to engage the garrisons, however, or to come within range of the guns, but having invested the town with small parties set in ambush to guard the roads and prevent messengers or relief passing to and fro, they began to creep slowly in about Sudbury upon Thursday, April 20th. In the mean time, according to the best evidence of the best accounts from contemporary sources (always excepting the very evident mistake of Mr. Hubbard in regard to the date), Capt. Wadsworth, with a company of some fifty or more men, marched out of Boston towards

Marlborough upon the same day, expecting to make up the company to one hundred with the quotas of the Middlesex towns, but did not have over seventy probably on his arrival at Marlborough, which it was the design that he should relieve with the company of one hundred men impressed[121] for the purpose, of whom not more than seventy appeared, and these, many of them, mere boys. They marched through Sudbury in the evening of the 20th, and without any sign of attack from the great body of Indians lying about the town and its approaches, arrived in Marlborough near midnight, where, learning that the enemy had gone towards Sudbury, Capt. Wadsworth, after a brief stop and slight reorganization of his company, leaving some of the boys that were unable to march at the garrison, and doubtless taking some fitter men in their places, and being joined by Capt. Brocklebank, who apparently started for Boston, being relieved of his charge at the garrison by the coming of Capt. Wadsworth, with this company he marched hastily back towards Sudbury.

While this company were thus marching to and from Marlborough, the enemy were gathering more closely about Sudbury, as the following account, contained in the petition of the inhabitants who suffered loss in the attack, shows. The paper has been buried in the old court files for more than two hundred years, and was discovered by the writer just in time for insertion in this chapter. This paper gives much new material in regard to the fight, and incontrovertible contemporary testimony that the fight occurred on the 21st of April.

To ye Honble Governour Dept Govern^r Magistrates and Deputies of ye Gen^ll Court assembled at Boston ye 11th Octo'ber 1676

The hum^ble Petition of ye poore distressed Inhabitants of Sudbury Humbly Sheweth. That Whereas yor impoverished Petition^rs of Sudbury have

---

[121] Upon the alarm from Marlborough on the 18th, the Council immediately ordered a company of men impressed, forty-six of whom were to be furnished by the Major of Suffolk, Thomas Clarke, as shown by the following paper:

"Whereas there was a warrant issued forth By the Honor^d Major Clarke for the Impressing of fforty-six men wth fire arms and ammunition and directed to the Committee of Militia of Boston and the Comittee ordered 5 men out of Capt. Thomas Clarke his company in order thereunto there were Impressed on ye 19th of Aprill 1676

(1) Aaron Stephens who sliped aside as soon as ever spoken to and could not be found any more.

(2) Philip Cain who said he would go to the Governour to be cleared but afterwards could not be found.

(3) James Burges who could not be seen by us after notis given that he should attend ye countreys servis.

(4) Thomas Wats who pretended to goe home to put on his clothes and came not again neither could he be found though there were severall messengers to seek him.

(5) Thomas Smith who marched according to order.

As Attesteth   Thomas Clarke Capt.   (Mass. Archives, Vol. 68, p. 234.)

Another paper is preserved relating to the same matter:

"19th 2mo 1676 Impressed by virtue of an ord^r from Maj^r Tho : Clarke for ye countreys servis

John Pittam } who sayde they would be hanged drawne and quartered Rather then
Robt Miller }   goe or words to thatt effect

                                        Francis Hudson Clerk
Mass. Archives, Vol. 68, p. 216.   Jacob Feriside."

received intelligence of a large contribution sent out of Ireland[122] by some pious & well affected p'sons for ye releife of their brethren in New England distressed by ye hostile intrusion of ye Indian Enemy, and that upon this divers distressed townes have presented a list of theire losses sustained by fireing and plundering of their Estates. Let it not seeme presumption in yor poore petitioners to p'sent a list of what damages we sustained by ye Enemyes attempts hopeing that o^r lott will be to be considered among our brethren of the tribe of Joseph being encouraged by an act of our Honble Gen^ll Court that those who have sustained considerable damage should make address to this p'sent Session. And is there not a reason for our re- leife? Not only by reason of Our great losses but alsoe for Our Service p'rformed in repelling ye Enemy ! Let ye Most High have ye high praise due unto him ; but let not ye unworthy Instruments be forgotten. Was there with us any towne so beset since ye warre began, with twelve or fourteen hundred fighting men various Sagamores from all Parts with their men of Armes & they resolved by our ruin to revenge ye releife which Our Sudbury volunteers afforded to distressed Marlborough in slaying many of ye Enemy and repelling ye rest. The strength of our towne upon ye En- emy's Approaching it consisted of Eighty fighting men. True many houses were fortified & Garrison'd, & tymously after ye Enemy's invasion, and fire- ing some Volunteers from Watertowne, & Concord & deserving Capt: Wadsworth with his force came to Our releife, which speedy & noble ser- vice is not to be forgotten. The Enemy well knowing our Grounds, passes, avenues, and Scituations had neare surrounded Our towne in ye Morning early (wee not knowing of it) till discovered by fireing severall disserted houses : the Enemy with greate force & fury assaulted Deacon Haines House well fortified yet badly scituated, as advantageous to ye Enemys ap- proach & dangerous to ye Repellant, yet (by ye help of God) ye garrison not onely defended ye place from betweene five or six of ye clock in ye Morning till about One in ye Afternoon but forced ye Enemy with Consid- erable slaughter to draw-off.

Many Observables worthy of Record hapned in this assault, Viz^t That noe man or woman seemed to be possessed with feare ; Our Garrison men kept not within their garrisons, but issued forth to fight ye Enemy in theire sculking approaches: Wee had but two of our townesmen slaine, & y^t by indiscretion, none wounded ; The Enemy was by few beaten out of houses which they had entered and were plundering ; And by a few hands were forced to a running flight which way they would ; The spoyle taken by them on ye East side of ye river was in greate p^te recovered.

Furthermore p'mitte yor humble Petition^rs to present a second Motion, And let it be acceptable in ye eyes of this our Grand Court Vizt. That whereas by an Act of Our late Gen^ll Court Tax rates are leavied upon Our towne amounting to £200 (as appeareth p^r Warrant from Our Treasurer, which said sum was leavied by Our Invoice taken in ye yeare before Our greate damage susteyned. It is ye humble & earnest request of yor Petition^rs to commiserate Our Condition in granting to us some abate- ment of ye said sum, for ye ensueing considerations, Viz^t ffirst Our towne to pay full for their Rates then taken, which in greate p^te they have now lost by the Enemys invasion may seeme not to savour of pitty no not of equity. Secondly if ye Service p'formed at Sudbury (by ye help of ye Al- mighty) whereby ye Enemy lost some say 100, some 105, some 120,

---

[122] See article on " The Irish Donation of 1676," by Charles Deane, LL.D., in the Reg- ister, vol. ii. pp. 245-50.

and by that service much damage prevented from hap'ning to other places whereby ye Country in generall was advantaged, reason requires some favorable consideration to yor Servants of Sudbury. For if it be considered what it hath cost Our Country in sending out some forces some of which p^ties have not returned with ye certaine newes of such a number slaine as with us, is it not reasonable that this service soe beneficiall should not be considered with some reward which may most easily be effected by issueing forth an Act of your grace in a sutable abatem^t of ye said Sum leavied, with ye conferring of a Barrill of Powder & sutable shott in regaurd that yor Petitioners have spent not onely theire owne stock of either, but much of ye Towne stock. To which humble and Equitable Motions if Our hon^ble Court shall benignely condescend, You will deeply oblidge yor humble petitioners not onely to pray for ye p^rsence of ye Lord to be with yo^u in all yor arduous affaires with the blessing of The Almighty upon all yor Undertakings but shall for Ever remaine   Yo^r humble servants

Edm: Browne	Benjamin Crane	Tho: Walker
Edm: Goodnow	Zacriah Maynord	John Blanford
John Groutt	Joseph Moore	John Allen
John Haines	John Parminter	Henry Curtis
Josiah Haynes	Joseph Parmenter	John Brewer
Thomas Veal	Peter Noyes	James Ross
Peter King	Jonathan Stanhope	Richard Burk
John Loker Senr	Edward Wright	John Smith
Joseph Noyes	Jabez Browne	Thomas Brewes?
John Goodenow	John Grout jun^r	Samuell How
Mathew Gibs	Joseph Graves	Henry Loker
Thomas Wedge		

In Ans^r to the Petion^rs for Abatement in their last Ten Country Rates by reason of their losses in Estates by the Common Enemy ; Wee uppon examination finde y^t in their last Assm^t their estates falls short 4^l. 9^s. in their single County Rate, doe therefore judge meet, s^d Towne of Sudbury be Allowed 44, 10, 0 out of their whole sum to them pr Rates & Referring to their request for a Barrell of Powder &c wee refer it to ye Courts determination.   WILLIAM PARKER ?
                                    HUGH MASON
                                    JOHN WAYTE

The deputyes approve of the ret. of this Committee in answer to this p^te O^r Hono^rd Magis^tts Consenting thereto   WILLIAM TORREY, Cleric

25 October 1676   Consented to by ye Magis^ts   EDW^d RAWSON,
                                                        Sect'y.

An Accompt of Losse sustained by Several Inhabitants of ye towne of Sudbury by ye Indian Enemy ye 21st Aprill 1676.

Mary Bacon formerly ye Relict		Edward Wright	100 00 00
of Ensigne Noyes	£140 00 00	Elias Keyes	060 00 00
Thomas Plympton	130 00 00	John Smith	080 00 00
Deacon John Haines	130 00 00	Samuell How	140 00 00
Serj: Josiah Haines	190 00 00	Mr Pelham	050 00 00
Capt: James Pendleton	060 00 00	Mr Thomas Steevens	015 00 00
John Goodenow	150 00 00	Corporall Henry Rice	180 00 00
William Moores	180 00 00	John Allen	060 00 00

James Rosse	070 00 00	Peter King	040 00 00
John Grout Junr	060 00 00	Widd. Habgood	020 00 00
Thomas Rice	100 00 00	Benjamin Crane	020 00 00
Widd. Whale	024 00 00	Thomas Wedge	015 00 00
Henry Curtice	200 00 00	John Blanford	010 00 00
John Brewer	120 00 00	Thomas Brewes	010 00 00
Jacob Moores	050 00 00	Richard Burt	010 00 00
Henry Loker	100 00 00	Thomas Reade	003 00 00
Joseph ffreeman	080 00 00		
Joseph Graves	060 00 00	Totall Sum	2707 00 00

Besides ye uncovering of many houses & Barnes & some hundreds of
Acres of land which lay unimproved for feare of ye Enemy to our greate
loss and Damage.
(Endorsed)
Sudbury's Accompt of Losses (and also) Sudbury's Losses—76

This paper, never before published, gives a new phase of the
fight. (Mass. Arch., Vol. 30, p. 205.)

The deposittion of Edward Cowell Aged About —— years—
This deponantt upon oath testifieth that I being upon the Counteries
Searvis in Aprill last and haveing under my Conduct Eighteen men;
Upon our Returning from Mallberough to Boston; and About three
Milles From Sudbeury Wee ware surprised with divers Hundred of In-
dians; Wheere of this Indian Tom was one (—) by a grombling signe
or Noyse thatt hee Mayde; as in My Judgement was the Cause of our be-
ing ffiored upon; at which tyme fower of my Company was killed and one
Wounded; beside ffive horses ware disenabled they Being Shott upon
Capt. Wadsworths Ingadgine with the Indian I wentt Backe and Beuryed
the fower men which were killed whereof (Lt. ?) Thomas Haw[le]y, and
Hopkinsies son both of [Edmund Rice[123]] Roxbeury; Goodman [Baker's?]
son and Robert Wayle[s] of Dorchister.
Sworn to before the Council 19 June 1676.

EDWARD RAWSON, Secretary.

OTHER CORRESPONDENCE, &c., ABOUT THE SUDBURY FIGHT.

Letter of the Massachusetts Council to the Governor of Plymouth.

Hon^d Sr Since o^r last to you It pleaseth the holy God to give still further successe to the Enemye in this Colony by killing two men the one in
Hingham, & the other in Weymouth aboute the same tyme At Marlborough
also upon Tuesday and Wednesday last they burned the remainder of the
Houses, so that now but three are standing that we know of but two or three
garrisons; This day we have intelligence in the general that Sudbury was
this morning assaulted and many houses burnt down, particulars and the more
full certainty of things is not yet come to hand whilest we are consulting
what to doe, earnestly we are moved to settle some of o^r faithful Indians at
Meadfield or Punquapoag, & others at Woodcocks & we desire that yor Colony would send such a number of yor Indians as may be convenient to be
joyned in the same service whose work shall be constantly to scout abroad

---

[123] The name Edmund Rice is in the margin. He was probably one of those of Sudbury
killed, and his name was inserted by some one in the margin of Cowell's note. Only the
letter *a* in Baker is present. The paper is badly torn.

between Seaconck and Meadfield & Dedham wch is thought to be a very probable way Either to prevent the enemies coming in upon yor Colony and ours that way, or at least to give speedy notice of their motions and dissapoynt theire mischievous designes. This motion proceeds from some of the cheef of our Indians William Ahaton & Capt. John who are very willing to be imployed and much persuaded, that there may be good therein. o^r present thoughts are to indeavor and incourage this matter with all speed and in order hereto we have sent our Corporall Swift the bearer hereof to yo^rselfe from whome you may understand things more fully & by him acquaint us with yor view of the matter and further advise for the better perfecting of the designe & that we may also know whether you can furnish out any sufficient number of Indians from yor parts & how soone.

O^r General Court of Elections is to sit upon Wednesday come sevennight, & then full order may be taken.

Commending you to the God of Councell & Protection

we remain   E. R. S:

past & signed   21 Ap^r 76

Directed to the Honble Josia Winslow Govr
of his maj^sty Colony at New Plymouth. (Mass. Arch., Vol. 68, p. 220.)

Petition of Daniel Warren and Joseph Peirce.

To Inform the Honoured Counsel of the Service don at Sudbury by severall of the Inhabatance of Watertowne as our honoured Captain Mason hath Allready informed a part thereof in the petion: but we who wear thear can moer largely inform this honoured Councel: that as it is said in the petion that we drove two hundred Indians over the River; wee followed the enimie over the river and joyned with som others and went to see if wee could relieve Captain Wadsworth upon the hill and thear we had a fight with the Indians but they beinge soe many of them and we stayed soe long that we wear allmost incompassed by them which cased us to retreat to Captain Goodanous Garrison; and their we stayed it being ner night till it was dark and then we went to Mr Noices Mill to see if we could find any that were escaped to that place all though thear wear noe persons dwelling there; but thear we found :13: or :14: of Captain Wadsworths men who wear escaped some of them wounded and brought them to Sudbury towne;

On the next day in the morning soe soon as it was light we went to looke for — Concord men who wear slain in the River middow and thear we went in the colld water up to the knees where we found five and we brought them in Conus to the Bridge fut and buried them thear; and then we joyned ourselves to Captain Hunton with as many others as we could procuer and went over the River to look for Captain Wadsworth and Captain Brattlebank and the soldiers that wear slain; and we gathered them up and Buried them; and then it was agreed that we should goe up to Nobscut to bring the Carts from thence into Sudbury-Towne and soe returned Hom againe; to what is above written we whos nams are subscribed can testifi:

dated the :6: of march :78:   DANIEL WARRIN
:79:   JOSEP PEIRCE

Our request is to the much Honoured Counsel that they would be pleased to consider us in reference to our Request; their being 2 troops of hors

appointed to bury the dead as we wear informed whos charg was spared
and we as yet not allowed for what we did;

    Your most Humb^le Servants to Command to the utmost of our poor S
for our selves and in the behalf of the rest   Daniel Warrin

    Mass. Arch., Vol. 68, p. 198.   Josep Peirce

Of other contemporary accounts of the fight and its consequences
there are several from eminently reliable authorities. Treasurer
John Hull wrote a letter on April 29th, 1676, concerning the sad
state of affairs in the colony, giving details of successive casualties,
and says : "On ye 21st valiant Captains Wadsworth and Brocklebank wth about 50 valiant souldiers were slain by ye Indians."

The letters of the "Anonymous writer," published in London,
which have been several times referred to above, give a very concise account, as follows : "April 20th Capt. Wadsworth of Dorchester, being designed with an 100 men to repair to Marlborough to
strengthen the garrison, and remove the goods &c. there; did accordingly this evening march with about 70 men from Sudbury, the
rest of his men not appearing. The Enemy who were about 1000
strong lay near his Passage, but kept themselves undiscovered and
permitted him to passe them in the night but in the morning assaulted and burned most of the Houses in Sudbury (save those that
were ingarrisoned)." The writer goes on to tell that twelve volunteers
from Concord came down to lend assistance, and eleven of the number were slain, and that Capt. Wadsworth with his tired troops, that
had marched all the day and night before, marched promptly back
from Marlborough, being joined by Capt. Brocklebank and a few of
the garrison soldiers, making a company of not more than eighty
men miserably tired for want of rest and sleep. This company was
drawn into ambush and encompassed by many hundred Indians,—
our authorities say a thousand or more,—fought them from a hill for
four hours with the loss of only five men, till the Indians set fire to
the woods at the windward of them, and thus forced them from their
strong position, and in their retreat waylaid and destroyed all but a
few of the men who escaped to a mill where they defended themselves till night, when rescued by Capt. Prentice's troopers, who
themselves had just been rescued by Capt. Cowell and his dragoons.

Rev. Increase Mather, of Boston, who published a history of this
Indian war at about the same time with Mr. Hubbard, writes—
"April 20th, a day of humiliation was observed at Boston. The
next day sad tidings came to us. For the enemy set upon Sudbury and burnt a great part of the town; and whereas Capt. Wadsworth and his Lieutenant Sharp, also Capt. Brocklebank (a godly
and choice spirited man) was killed at the time."

Major Daniel Gookin, the commanding officer of Middlesex
forces and superintendent of the "Praying Indians" in the colony,
writes :

"Upon April 21, about midday tidings came by many messengers that a great body of the enemy not less as was judged than fifteen hundred .... had assaulted a town called Sudbury that morning ..... Indeed (thro' God's favor) some small assistance had already been sent from Watertown by Capt. Hugh Mason, which was the next town to Sudbury. These with some of the inhabitants joined and with some others that came in to their help, there was vigorous resistance made and a check given to the enemy. .... But these particulars were not known when the tidings came to Charlestown."

Major Gookin gives a very full account in his history of the "Praying Indians," his object being to vindicate the Indians from the charges of treachery and inefficiency made against them by popular clamor. His account was necessarily accurate, and it agrees closely with the records. From him, and also from the Archives, we learn that a company of Indians was being organized at this time, and the letters of the Council show that the design of this company was to fortify the fishing places upon the Merrimac, in conjunction with a company of English, and under command of Capt. Samuel Hunting, of Charlestown. This Indian company, it seems, was at Charlestown when the news of the attack upon Sudbury came, and without waiting for particulars, Major Gookin immediately despatched "a ply of horse" from Capt. Prentice's troop under Corporal Phipps, and forty Indians under Capt. Hunting, which force arrived at Sudbury that evening, the troopers in time to rescue the remnants of Capt. Wadsworth's company from the mill where they had taken refuge and had defended themselves against the enemy.

All the above accounts are of contemporaries, and all agree in the main particulars and confirm each other in the matter of the date. Rev. Mr. Hubbard, of Ipswich, whose history of this war is most complete, and, in the main, the most reliable, agrees mostly with the others, but seems to have known less of this fight than usual, and less of the details than the others, and in the matter of the date was unquestionably wrong.

From all the above authorities, the true account in brief seems to be, that the English had no suspicion of the great numbers of the Indians that were gathering about Marlborough and Sudbury, or of the vicinity of any until early in the morning of the 21st, when several deserted houses were burnt with the evident purpose of drawing out the garrisons into an ambuscade. Then Deacon Haines's garrison-house was attacked with fury by large numbers, but was successfully defended from six o'clock in the morning until one o'clock, P.M., when the assault was abandoned. Twelve volunteers coming from Concord upon the alarm, to aid the garrison, were lured into the river meadow, and all slain save one. Mr. Edward Cowell, with a body of eighteen mounted men, coming from Brookfield by way of Marlborough, and by a different way from that taken by Capt. Wadsworth, became sharply engaged with an outlying party of the enemy, and lost four men killed, one wounded, and had five of his horses disabled.

While the attack upon Cowell's party was still going on, Captain Wadsworth and his company came upon the scene, and seeing a small party of Indians, rushed forward with the usual impetuous haste, and were caught in the usual ambuscade, for when within about a mile of Sudbury they were induced to pursue a body of not more than one hundred, and soon found themselves drawn away about one mile into the woods, where on a sudden they were encompassed by more than five hundred, and forced to a retreating fight towards a hill where they made a brave stand for a while (one authority says four hours), and did heavy execution upon the enemy, until (Mr. Hubbard says) the night coming on and some of the company beginning to scatter from the rest, their fellows were forced to follow them, and thus being encompassed in the chase by numbers, the Captains and most of the company were slain. The anonymous writer above referred to, says the Indians set fire to the woods and thus forced the disastrous retreat. Thirteen only out of the company escaped to "Noyes's mill," and there held the enemy in check. In the mean time Cowell withdrew his party from their dangerous situation, went back and buried their dead comrades, and then rode around into the town by another way in time to rescue Capt. Prentice's troopers, and afterwards, with others in company, the men at the mill. It was probably about noon when Capt. Wadsworth became actively engaged with the Indians, and thus withdrew their attention from both Cowell and Haines's garrison. The Watertown company arrived at about the same time, followed the Indians over the river, and made a brave fight to get to the hill where Capt. Wadsworth was engaged in his desperate struggle, but such fearful odds were against them that they were forced to fall back to Goodenow's garrison, "it being ner night." After dark they went to the "mill," probably with the troopers and Cowell's men, and brought off the soldiers there. The troopers sent from Charlestown, with the Indian company under Capt. Hunting, must have arrived quite late in the afternoon. These are the main facts, in brief, of the Sudbury fight. The next day the Watertown company, with Capt. Hunting's Indians, buried the dead. The site of the battlefield where Capt. Wadsworth so long held the Indians at bay, is upon what is now called "Green Hill." Here in 1730, fifty-four years after the battle, Rev. Benjamin Wadsworth, fifth son of Capt. Samuel, and at that time president of Harvard College, erected a monument to the memory of his father and those that fell with him. It is to be regretted that President Wadsworth accepted the erroneous date given by Mr. Hubbard,[124] which has been perpetuated upon the new monument erected in 1852.

---

[124] The investigations of Mr. Drake first exposed the error which Mr. Hubbard made in his history, and his discussion of the question is contained in Reg., vol. vii. p. 221. Gov.

It is a regret that we are unable to know positively the numbers of English engaged. The number with Capt. Wadsworth upon the " Hill" was probably near fifty. The most definite statement is that of Major Gookin, who puts the number of those slain, besides the two Captains, as "about thirty-two private soldiers." Cowell had eighteen, and the Concord men were twelve. The Watertown company was not probably over forty, while the garrisons of Sudbury amounted to but eighty. Thus about two hundred men were actively engaged with, and holding in play, probably more than a thousand Indians one whole day, and finally defeated their intention of capturing the town, sending them away with fearful loss.

Unfortunately we are not as yet able to find any list of the names of those killed on that day, and Mr. Hull's accounts do not show any credits referable to that service; only here and there are we able to glean from probate and town and church records a few names of those killed.

From the Roxbury Records we find that

" Samuel Gardner, son of Peter William Cleaves
Thomas Baker Joseph Pepper
John Roberts John Sharpe
Nathaniel Sever Thomas Hopkins
Thomas Hawley Sr Lieut Samuel Gardner

were all slain att Sudbury under command of Capt. Sam^ll Wadsworth upon 21 Aprill 1676."

Of the Concord men killed in the meadow near " Haynes's Garrison," but five bodies were recovered, and but seven names of the killed are preserved in the records.

James Hosmer Samuel Potter John Barnes
Daniel Comy Joseph Buttrick Josiah Wheeler
William Heywood

Three of Cowell's men that were killed are in the Roxbury list above. The fourth was Robert Wayles, of Dorchester. The Suffolk Probate Records give an additional name, Eliazer Hawes, of

George S. Boutwell, who delivered the historical discourse at the dedication of the new monument, Nov. 23, 1852, and at that time assigned the date April 18, replied in 1866 (see REGISTER, vol. xx. p. 135) to Mr. Drake's article, and contended that the date given in his discourse was the true one. The Historic Genealogical Society then took the matter in hand, and appointed a committee, Gen. A. B. Underwood and Frederic Kidder, who made a thorough and exhaustive report at the society's meeting, October, 1866, which was published in the REGISTER, vol. xx. p. 341, proving beyond question that the date April 21st is the true date of the fight. Contemporary Official Records, the highest evidence of all, testify in every case to this date, while the evidence for the 18th is only found in Mr. Hubbard's history and in several books of remarkable events kept by some prominent men of the colony, who, it is evident, not unfrequently made their entries some time after the occurrence of the events, and who, in this case, probably adopted the date of Hubbard. John Hull, for instance, whose letter-extract above, written within a few days, gives the date the 21st, in his diary of notable events puts it down as on the 18th. Major Daniel Gookin, Rev. Increase Mather, the writer of the " Present State of New England," and other authorities, agree with the official Records in giving the 21st. Subsequent historians, until Mr. Drake, simply quote Hubbard's date.

It is a great satisfaction to the present writer to add the new testimony of the petition of the inhabitants of Sudbury.

Dorchester. These, with Capts. Wadsworth and Brocklebank, make in all but twenty-one. It is hoped that a more complete list of those who fell with Capt. Wadsworth may be made before the close of this series of articles, and any assistance in that direction will be gratefully received.

NOTES AND QUERIES.

NOTES.

FORTY YEARS OF THE REGISTER.—The October number now issued completes the fortieth annual volume of the NEW ENGLAND HISTORICAL AND GENEALOGICAL REGISTER. Two historical sketches of this periodical have been printed in its pages, namely, one by the present editor in the preface to vol. xvii. for 1863, with additions in vol. xviii. p. 88; and the other by Col. Albert H. Hoyt in the number for April, 1876, vol. xxx. pp. 184–8. Notices of the several Editors are found in the preface to vol. xxxiii. for 1879. Such a periodical as this was contemplated when the society was formed; and in a little more than two years from its organization, Feb. 5, 1847, the first number of the REGISTER was issued.

The writer of this note has been an editor of the work for fourteen years and three quarters, in the aggregate, or more than one-third of the time since the REGISTER was commenced. He has had the sole editorship for twelve years and three-quarters, and has been a member of the Publishing Committee continuously for thirty-two of the forty years that the work has been published.

JOHN WARD DEAN.

CAPT. JOHN TUFTON (Com. by William B. Trask, Esq.).—The following document is on file in the Suffolk Probate Office, Boston, Mass.:

This may Certifie Whome itt may Concearn That Whereas Capt John Tufton wass Taken in the Sloop Tryall in march Lasst Coming from Surenam And Ransomed said Sloop And Cent his matte John Westlake Hostedg I haue Receiued of said Tufton The Said Sloope And Cargoe & doc Oblidge myselfe To Redeem The Hostedg ass Wittnes my hand this 1th of may 1712.   JOHN COLMAN.

Wittnised
  Nich Andrews
  Elizabeth × Craftes
      her marke

This is a Trew Coppy of The Oridgnale Obligation from m^r John Colman To Capt Tufton.

[Capt. John Tufton was a shipmaster in Boston, and died in 1718 in Havana. He was the father of John Tufton born at Boston April 29, 1713, died at Buckden, England, Aug. 8, 1787, who added the surname Mason, and in 1746 sold to the Masonian Proprietors the right to lands in New Hampshire, which he inherited from his great-great-grandfather, Capt. John Mason, the founder of that colony.—EDITOR.]

BURCHAN FAMILY.—I send a fragment of the Genealogy of the Burchan Family, which may be valuable enough to be preserved. It was communicated to me in part by an aged relative during my researches in preparation of the genealogy of my own family.

ROBERT BURCHAN, died in Philadelphia; married Ann ——, who died June 28, 1811, aged 80, in Washington, D. C. His son was Robert George.

Robert George Burchan, born 1758 in Philadelphia; died May 25, 1796, in New York city. Captain of a sailing vessel. Married Mary Young (daughter of Mehitabel Young, who died in Boston, Oct. 7, 1797, aged 70), born in Boston, 1762, died in New York city, May 1, 1796. Six children:

1. Richard, b. Oct. 23, 1779, in Boston, Mass.; d. Sept. 23, 1828, New York city; m. Catharine Ward, May 3, 1800, in New York city. [Rev. Samuel

Miller.] (She was daughter of Mary Ward, who d. in Newark, N. J., Sept. 27, 1803, aged 63 years. She was b. Aug. 12, 1783, in Newark, N. J., and d. May 29, 1860, in Hackinsack, N. J.)

2. Ann, b. Aug. 12, 1781, in Boston; d. June 15, 1822, in New York city; m. Nathaniel L'Hommedieu. (He was captain of a sailing vessel, and m. 1st, Lydia Moore, 2d, Lydia Peck, 3d, Christina ———, 4th, Ann Burchan, and 5th, Catharine Rose.)

3. George Young, b. May 18, 1784; d. March 5, 1810, N. York city. A sailor.

4. Mehitable, b. Boston; d. in Philadelphia.

5. John, b. Aug. 29, 1790, in Boston; d. Oct. 26, 1819, at quarantine, New York city. A sailor.

6. Andrew, b. May 18, 1794, in Philadelphia; d. July 4, 1794, in Philadelphia.

Following are the nine children of Richard Burchan and Catharine Ward:

1. Catharine Ann, b. May 18, 1801, New York; d. Sept. 9, 1837, New York; m. Isaac Ferris, D.D., LL.D., chancellor of the University of the City of New York, Dec. 30, 1820 (Rev. C. Bourk officiating).

2. Lydia, b. Feb. 13, 1803, New York; d. June 22, 1804.

3. Laura, b. March 26, 1805, New York city.

4. Alexander Young, b. Feb. 15, 1807, New York; d. Jan. 16, 1821.

5. Gertrude, b. Oct. 2, 1809, New York city.

6. Ward, b. Feb. 13, 1812, New York city; d. May 15, 1836, Florida.

7. Lydia Bruckman, b. Aug. 16, 1814, New York; d. Oct. 3, 1826.

8. Eliza Monroe, b. June 10, 1817, New York; d. Nov. 11, 1822.

9. Peter Stanford, b. Sept. 7, 1819, New York; d. March 31, 1859, Williamsburg, N. Y.; m. Hannah ———.

10. Richard, b. Jan. 16, 1822, in New York; d. March 11, 1822.

11. Frances, b. Jan. 10, 1823, in New York; d. Oct. 20, 1826.

Four children of Peter Stanford Burchan and Hannah ———:

1. Ward.

2. Catharine, m. Philip Ramée.

3. Lily, d. March, 1884; m. Lyman.

4. Joseph.

Query. Is the Burchan family descended from the same source as the Buchan family?   ALBERT W. FERRIS, A.M., M.D.
Sanford Hall, Flushing, N. Y.

QUERIES.

D'WOLF.—Can any one give the parentage of Jehiel, Nathan and Simeon D'Wolf, who went in 1760-2 from Connecticut to Nova Scotia?

Does any member of the Kirtland family of Connecticut know the names of the parents of Phebe D'Wolf, who, 22 August, 1716, married (as his second wife) Nathaniel Kirtland of Saybrook, born 24 October, 1690?

WILCOX.—Whose son was Sylvanus Wilcox, who about 1760 went from Simsbury, Ct., to the "Nine Partners" in Dutchess Co., N. Y., and settled finally in Alford, Mass.?

He was in the revolutionary war as an officer. His tombstone at Alford has "Capt." on it. He owned property in Simsbury, and in 1760, together with Ephraim Willcocksun, deeded it to Daniel Willcocksun. His own name was spelled Willcocksun. I think he had a brother Adijah, who settled and died in Peterboro', New York.   S. P. MERRILL.
Rochester, N. Y.

GREEN, &c.—Information wanted concerning the following persons:

Mr. Green, who led the Boston ship carpenters April 18, 1689, took the commander of the frigate Rose prisoner, and began an insurrection which "made a great noise in the world." Bancroft's U. S., II. 445.

William Green.—Date of birth and parentage. He married Desire Bacon at Barnstable, Mass., 25 March, 1709, and died 1756, aged over 70.

Col. Joseph Spencer (East Haddam, Conn., April, 1775) went to Boston with 43 men. What were some of their names?

John Marshall, born at Freetown, 1702-3, married Elizabeth Winslow. Who were his parents?   R. C. GREEN.

STRIDE.—Mr. E. E. Stride, of the British Museum, London, wishes for information respecting *Stride*, mentioned by Bowditch in his "Suffolk Surnames." Mr. Stride has a tradition that he himself is descended from the Huguenots through his father (as he is through his mother), and would be most thankful for any advice relating to the origin of the name.

MOULTHROP.—I wish to ascertain any facts that readers of the REGISTER can furnish regarding the genealogy of the surname "Moulthrop." Address 107, 109 and 111 *Main St., Rockford, Ill.* L. MOULTHROP.

HISTORICAL INTELLIGENCE.

THE DOMESDAY CELEBRATION.—The Royal Historical Society of London, England, will commemorate the present month (October) the Eight Hundredth Anniversary of the completion of the Domesday Survey of England. The proceedings will be under the charge of a committee of which Lord Aberdare, the president of that society, is chairman. Other members are the Minister of the United States, the Master of the Rolls, the Dean of Westminster, Dr. Bond, the Principal Librarian of the British Museum, the Rev. Dr. Bright, Master of University College, Oxford, Mr. Madan, the sub-librarian of the Bodleian Library, Mr. Walford, the editor of *Walford's Antiquarian*, Mr. Selby, editor of *The Genealogist*, Mr. Lyte, Deputy Keeper of the Public Records, and other persons of distinction. Delegates from kindred societies will attend. Communications should be addressed to P. Edward Dove, F.R.A.S., 23 Old Building, Lincoln's Inn, London, the honorary secretary.

The *Academy* of July 17th, says that the commemoration " will take three forms : (1) a series of meetings for the reading of papers ; (2) the compilation of a Domesday bibliography ; and (3) an exhibition of MSS. &c., at the British Museum and at the Public Record Office.

" With regard to the papers to be read, it is proposed that they should deal with Domesday Book as a whole, without excluding local inquiries or later surveys that may lead by comparison and inference to results of general application. In the bibliography it is proposed to include brief descriptions of the several Domesday MSS. with reference to their places of deposit ; the titles of all separate works dealing with any portions of Domesday Book ; and the titles of all papers and pamphlets on the subject. The exhibition at the British Museum will comprise the Survey of Lindsey, monastic chartularies containing surveys, Inquisitio Eliensis, the transcript of the original Domesday return for Cambridge, printed editions of the survey and translations, and (it is hoped) loan contributions from other libraries. The exhibition at the Public Record Office will comprise the MS. of Domesday Book (2 vol.), the abbreviatio, the Breviate, a copy of the Bolden Book, the Red and Black Books of the Exchequer, the two volumes entitled 'Testa de Nevil,' early Hundred Rolls, Book of Aids of Edward III., &c." All offers of help towards the bibliography should be addressed to Mr. Dove, the honorary secretary.

NEW BUILDINGS FOR THE ESSEX INSTITUTE AND THE OLD COLONY HISTORICAL SOCIETY.—Both of these societies have recently secured better accommodations for their libraries and meetings. The Essex Institute, Salem, Mass., has purchased the Deland estate, a very desirable property adjoining Plummer Hall, its present quarters, and "at last has a home of its own." A circular has been issued in relation to the society and its plans. It solicits from its friends donations for a fund of $15,000 to fit the building for the uses of the society and to provide for its increased running expenses for the next three years. Contributions, large or small, may be sent to G. D. Phippen, treasurer of the fund, Salem, Mass.

The Old Colony Historical Society, Taunton, Mass., has purchased for its use the Cedar Street Chapel, a beautiful stone edifice 80 feet long and 40 feet wide. The owner, Mr. Joseph Dean of that city, reduced the price from eight thousand dollars, its estimated value, to seven thousand dollars, and subscribed himself five hundred dollars toward the purchase. This liberality was responded to by others, and the sum required has been raised, and the building has been purchased. Forty-three of the contributors, representing $4000, were residents of Taunton. Other subscriptions are solicited to carry on the work of the society. The building will furnish ample room for the library and museum. The hall and gallery will seat five hundred people.

We congratulate these two societies on their enterprise and success.

BANCROFT'S CALIFORNIA.—The fifth volume of California, "Bancroft's Works," will soon be issued; the terrible loss suffered by the author in the fire of April 30 having checked the publication of his work only temporarily. The volume referred to covers the period of gold discovery in 1849, and will be of very great general, as well as local interest.

———

DENNYSVILLE CENTENARY.—The one hundredth anniversary of the settlement of Dennysville, Maine, was celebrated on the 17th of May last. The historical oration was delivered in the forenoon by George F. Talbot, Esq., of Portland, followed by a poem, the Century Plant, by Mrs. Ida S. Woodbury. In the afternoon addresses were made by Rev. Mr. Whittier, Peter E. Vose, Esq., William H. Kilby and others. Mr. Whittier's subject was "The Church and Schools," and Mr. Vose's "The Municipal History of Dennysville." The latter concluded his speech with a poem on the Founders of Dennysville, in which he referred to the several founders by name.

———

COAL AND IRON IN VIRGINIA.—R. A. Brock, Esq., of Richmond, the able secretary of the Virginia Historical Society, has prepared with great care for the commercial organizations of that city, two important papers giving much information on the Coal and Iron industries of that state, abstracts of which are printed in the *Richmond Dispatch*, June 25, 1886. One of these papers gives an account of the Iron Manufacture in Virginia, Past and Present, and the other is on the Discovery of Coal in Virginia, and the Coal Trade in Richmond in 1885.

———

GENEALOGIES IN PREPARATION.—Persons of the several names are advised to furnish the compilers of these genealogies with records of their own families and other information which they think may be useful. We would suggest that all facts of interest illustrating family history or character be communicated, especially service under the U. S. government, the holding of other offices, graduation from colleges or professional schools, occupation, with places and dates of births, marriages, residence and death. When there are more than one christian name they should all be given in full if possible. No initials should be used when the full names are known.

Brown. By William Cutter Brown, P. O. Box 2684, Boston, Mass.—Mr. Brown is compiling a genealogy of the descendants of Bartholomew and Sarah (Rea) Brown, and asks assistance from the readers of the REGISTER. Bartholomew Brown was born at Danvers, Mass., about 1721, married Feb. 26, 1745, Sarah, daughter of Zerubbabel and Margaret (Rogers) Rea, and died about 1752. His widow Sarah, born July 17, 1727, married March 27, 1755, Benjamin Porter, their eldest son being Gen. Moses Porter.

Nason. By the Rev. Elias Nason, M.A., of North Billerica, Mass.—The Rev. Mr. Nason, well known as an author and lecturer, and as the editor of the REGISTER, 1866-7, has in preparation a genealogy of the Nason Family, descendants of Willoughby and Ruth Nason, of Ipswich, Mass., 1712. Thomas, their son, the great grandfather of the Rev. Mr. Nason, removed to Walpole, Mass., prior to 1712. The merest item concerning any descendant of Willoughby Nason, will be gratefully welcomed. A prompt response is desired. The Nason Genealogy will consist of about 200 pages, Royal 8vo., handsomely printed and illustrated. The price will be, in paper, uncut, $2 a copy; in cloth, $2.50; in calf, $3. For $6, a portrait of a person or a view of a building will be taken from a photograph and inserted in the book. Address, Rev. Elias Nason, North Billerica, Mass.

Perham.—The Genealogical history of the Perhams is being compiled by Joel Perham, of Boston, Mass. The book will contain about 400 pages, and be published as soon as the necessary information can be obtained, and give the descendants (in both male and female lines) of John and Lydia (Shepley) Perham, who married and settled in Chelmsford, Mass., in 1664. All the descendants who have not already perfected their family records should attend to it at once by corresponding with Mr. Perham.

Raymond. By Samuel Raymond, 842 Fulton Avenue, Brooklyn, N. Y.—Mr. Raymond has for more than three years been engaged on a genealogy of the descendants of the immigrants Richard, John and William Raymond of Salem and Beverly,

Mass., and has the record of 1061 families, or 5100 individual descendants. He will print the work in a volume of about 360 pages at $5 a copy, provided 200 copies are subscribed for. The edition of 200 copies, it is estimated, will cost him, including all expenses, near $1000, or the whole amount received from subscribers.

NECROLOGY OF THE NEW-ENGLAND HISTORIC GENEALOGICAL SOCIETY.

Prepared by the Rev. INCREASE N. TARBOX, D.D., Historiographer of the Society.

THE historiographer would inform the society, that the sketches prepared for the REGISTER are necessarily brief in consequence of the limited space which can be appropriated. All the facts, however, he is able to gather, are retained in the Archives of the Society, and will aid in more extended memoirs for which the "Towne Memorial Fund," the gift of the late William B. Towne, A.M., is provided. Four volumes, printed at the charge of this fund, entitled "MEMORIAL BIOGRAPHIES," edited by the Committee on Memorials, have been issued. They contain memoirs of all the members who have died from the organization of the society to the year 1862. A fifth volume is in preparation.

FRANCIS MERRILL BARTLETT, Esq., a benefactor, died at his residence, 121 Oxford street, Cambridge, Mass., December 21, 1885, aged 63. He was born in Boston, July 6, 1822. His father James Bartlett, Esq., the owner of Bartlett's wharf and other real estate in Boston, was b. March, 1779, and d. April 6, 1847. His grandfather was Daniel Bartlett, of Newbury, b. June 28, 1744, d. 1818, who married Priscilla, daughter of Dea. Roger and Mrs. Mary (Hale) Merrill, of Newbury. A brother of Priscilla Merrill, our benefactor's grandmother, was Ezekiel Merrill, Esq., the first settler of Andover, Me., and their sister, Edna, was the first wife of Dr. James Brickett of Haverhill, a brigadier general in the revolutionary war. Mr. Bartlett's mother was Sarah Thayer, daughter of Benjamin and Sarah (Vesey) Thayer. She was born in Braintree, Dec. 4, 1779, and died in Boston, Jan. 15, 1835. The emigrant ancestor of this family was *Richard*[1] *Bartlett*, of Newbury, of whom an account was printed in the April REGISTER, pp. 192–204. From him Mr. Bartlett was the eighth in descent, through *Richard,*[2] of N., born Oct. 31, 1621, whose wife Abigail died March 1, 1687; *Richard,*[3] of N., born Feb. 21, 1649, died April 17, 1724, whose wife Hannah, a daughter of John Emery, of N., was a sister of Rev. Samuel Emery, of Wells, Me.; Deacon *Daniel,*[4] of N., born August 8, 1682, died May 14, 1756, whose wife Abigail was a daughter of William Moulton and Abigail his wife, sister of Rev. Nicholas Webster; *Daniel,*[5] of Newburyport, born March 22, 1706, died September 28, 1786, whose wife Alice was a daughter of Jacob Davis, of Amesbury; *Daniel,*[6] as above, *James*[7] and *Francis M.*[8] Bartlett.

Mr. Bartlett evinced at an early age a love of reading which he retained through life. His favorite studies were history, biography and genealogy as well as general literature. He loved to own books as well as to use them, to have these unobtrusive friends at his side, so that he might converse with them when he was in the mood to do so. For this purpose he collected, as his means and opportunities permitted, a very select library upon the subjects to which his tastes inclined him, which library at his death amounted to nearly sixteen hundred volumes, besides many pamphlets. His reading extended over a wide range of literature, but he found his chief pleasure in American and English family and local history.

At his death he bequeathed to the New England Historic Genealogical Society his entire library, which contained many rare and valuable books in its specialties, not then on its shelves. In the objects of this society he took a deep interest, and loved to visit and use its library. He was, from an early day, a subscriber to the REGISTER, and made valuable contributions to its pages.

He was of exemplary character, kind hearted and genial in his manners. The writer of this sketch and other members of this society, can testify that we found him an agreeable companion and one on whose friendship and good offices we could always rely. He made himself familiar with the contents of the books in his library, and though modest and averse to making a display of his learning, he was ever ready to impart his knowledge to those, and they were not few, who sought it. He had prepared a genealogy of the Bartletts, which remains in manuscript.

At a meeting of the society, held June 2, 1886, the Rev. Artemas B. Muzzey, chairman of a committee appointed for the purpose, reported the following resolutions, which were unanimously adopted :

"Resolved, That the New England Historic Genealogical Society accepts with high appreciation and profound gratitude, the valuable bequest of the late Francis Merrill Bartlett of Cambridge, a zealous student of history. Mr. Bartlett, in the course of his quiet life, had collected, and in his will has bequeathed to this society, a valuable library of over 1500 volumes, mostly relating to history and genealogy, and including some English County histories, which will be of special value as acquisitions to our library. Though his modest and retiring disposition prevented his becoming a member of this society, he has thus given the most unquestionable evidence of his interest in its work ; and he will be remembered as one of its honored and distinguished benefactors.

"Resolved, That a copy of this resolution be sent to the family of Mr. Bartlett."

The library was received, from Mr. Bartlett's sister and executrix, Mrs. Eliza B. Seymour of Cambridge, on the 21st of April, 1886. Mrs. Seymour has, in every way, shown an earnest desire to carry out the wishes of her brother, in this respect, as he expressed them to her personally while living, and as he provided for in his will.

By John Ward Dean, A.M.

GEORGE HAYWARD ALLAN, Esq., a resident member, admitted March 4, 1876, was born in Boston, Mass., June 16, 1832, and died in same city, March 15, 1886. His father, George Washington Allan, was born in Lubec, Me., Sept. 25, 1802, and his mother, Mary Ann Bowdoin Rotch, was born in Boston, July 17, 1810. His grandfather was William Allan, born in Halifax, Nova Scotia, July 23, 1768, and his great-grandfather was Col. John Allan, born in Edinburgh Castle, Scotland, Jan. 3, 1746. The father of this Col. John was William Allan, born in Scotland in 1720.

Mr. Allan's early education was obtained in the schools of Boston. In the Dwight Grammar School, in July, 1847, being then fifteen years old, he was the first Franklin Medal scholar. After leaving the Boston schools he was for some time connected with Comer's Commercial College, engaged in the studies pertaining to a mercantile education. After that he removed to New York, and was in mercantile business. From 1859 to 1865 he was the Western Agent of the New York Juvenile Asylum. In 1865 he was the General Relief Agent for the New York American Union Commission. In 1866 he was the General Assistant of the Freedmen Union Commission for Schools and relief work in Florida and Alabama. In 1867 he was Assistant Treasurer of the Woodlawn Cemetery. From 1869 to 1875 he was Secretary of the New York Gas-Saving Meter Company. His later years have been passed in Boston. He visited Europe in 1867, and again in 1875. In these visits two years were spent in travel and study, devoting himself especially to languages and to the antiquities of London. The knowledge which he gained in this European life made him quite familiar with persons and places abroad, and was often shown in the remarks made by him in the monthly meetings of our society, in his comments on the papers read.

He was accustomed to use his pen, and among his other writings was a memoir of his great-grandfather, entitled "Memoir of Col. John Allan, with a Genealogy," 8vo. Albany, 1867, pp. 32. This work is also printed in Kidder's Revolutionary Operations in Eastern Maine.

The following article by his teacher at the Dwight School, James Alfred Page, Esq., was printed in the *Boston Evening Transcript*, Monday, May 3, 1886 : "The many friends of Mr. George H. Allan were painfully surprised at hearing of his death, which took place in this city, March 15, 1886. Mr. Allan was a Boston boy, and the boy was emphatically the father of the man. He was a graduate of the public schools, and felt a loving pride in them. He obtained a Franklin medal as the result of prompt, active and continued effort, and he carried the same qualities into and through his whole life. He had travelled widely in the West as the trusted agent of great institutions, and at different times had been abroad. He availed himself fully of the opportunities thus given him, but he gladly returned to Boston and spent all the latter part of his life in this city of his birth. Her history interested him. Every old house and tree that had a story to tell was known to him, and while yet young he was better informed in certain lines of study, than most well read people in the city. He knew not only all the details of Bunker Hill and Dorchester Heights, of Lexington and Concord (we are all supposed to retain something of these), but the windows in the Old State House and every British station at the South End were as familiar to him as household words. His natural energy and decision of character were united with many genial and kindly qualities. These were all tested by a painful and harassing complaint, which for years he was never able to throw off, and which finally ended his life. He bore everything, however, with a placid courage and a sustained cheerfulness, that makes life under such circumstances heroic. 'They serve who only wait.' Mr. Allan was never married, but lived with his aged parents in this city, who have the tender sympathy of many friends at the loss of such a son."

CHARLES OCTAVIUS WHITMORE, Esq., of Boston, a life member and benefactor, admitted Nov. 10, 1863, was b. in Bath, Me., Nov. 7, 1802, and died in Boston, Nov. 14, 1885, at his home, No. 14 Beacon Street. He had enjoyed good health till about a month before his death, when he had a slight stroke of paralysis, but was not confined till a few days before his death. His father was William D. Whitmore, of Bath, Me., and his mother was Rhoda Woodward. His earliest American ancestor was Francis Whitmore, of Cambridge, 1659, whose wife was Isabel Park. From him the line ran through John[2] Whitmore, of Medford, whose wife was Rachel Eliot, niece of Rev. John Eliot. Their son was John[3] Whitmore, who married Mary Lane. Next came Francis[4] Whitmore, of Medford, whose wife was Mary Hall, followed by John[5] Whitmore, of Bath, Me., who was born in the year 1754, and whose wife was Huldah Crooker. We then reach William D.[6] Whitmore, of Bath, father of the subject of this sketch.

Charles Octavius[7] Whitmore was therefore of the sixth generation from the American founder of the family. His early education was secured in the schools of Bath, which, from the size and business activity of the place, were probably of a higher order than the average. In 1821, being then at the age of 14, he came to Boston as clerk in the store of Fife & Brown, West India merchants. About 1830 he entered into partnership in the grocery business with Mr. Israel Lombard, and in this connection he continued, 1830-1855.

After this business connection closed, Mr. Whitmore associated with himself his son Charles J. Whitmore, and afterward his son William H. Whitmore, and they continued business under the firm name of C. O. Whitmore & Sons until the year 1860. In 1862, Mr. Whitmore, with others, built the Union Sugar Refinery in Charlestown, which about ten years later was sold to the Eastern Railroad Company, that they might occupy the ground with their freight depot. Mr. Whitmore then retired from general business, but remained president of the Market National Bank, to which office he was elected in 1860, and which he kept till his death.

Mr. Whitmore was united in marriage with Miss Lovice Ayres, daughter of John and Rebecca (Lombard) Ayres, of Brookfield, Mass., who died Sept. 27, 1849, leaving five children. These children, two sons and three daughters, are still living, one daughter being the widow of the late Philip L. Van Rensselaer, of New York.

WILLIAM TEMPLE, Esq., of Woburn, a resident member, admitted April 19, 1870, was born in Reading, Mass., Sept. 15, 1801, and died in Woburn, Mass., March 18, 1886. His father, William[4] Temple, was born in Reading, Mass., Jan. 5, 1773, and his mother, Zerviah Richardson, was born in Woburn, Mass., August 30, 1780. His remoter ancestors on his father's side were William[4] Temple, his grandfather, born in Reading, Jan. 13, 1745, who married Rebecca Weston; John[3] Temple, born in Reading, Oct. 21, 1704, who married Rebecca Parker; Richard[2] Temple, who lived in Saco, Me., in 1668, and whose wife was Deborah Parker; Robert[1] Temple, of whom the tradition is that he was killed by the Indians in 1675.

After a common school education in his native town, at the age of fourteen he went as an apprentice to learn the trade of a blacksmith. In 1819, being then eighteen years of age, he went to live in Boscawen, N. H., where he remained forty-six years, or until 1865, steadily following his trade.

After fixing his home at Boscawen, he was united in marriage, June 12, 1823, with Susanna Noyes, daughter of Tristam and Miriam (Eastman) Noyes, of Newbury. From this marriage there were no children. Mr. Temple, though not a public writer, was deeply interested in the questions which came up for consideration before our society. Hardly any member was more constant at our monthly meetings, though he seldom spoke at them. He was of a gentle, sincere nature, true to all the duties and trusts imposed on him. He was for many years deacon of the Congregational Church in Boscawen. He has passed away in a peaceful and ripe old age.

HENRY PURKITT KIDDER, Esq., of Boston, a life member, admitted Nov. 3, 1859, was born in Cambridge, Mass., Jan. 8, 1823, and died in New York city, Jan. 28, 1886. His father was Thomas Kidder, born in Cambridge, May, 1783, and his mother was Clarissa Purkitt. His paternal grandfather was John Kidder, whose wife was Mary Jackson.

Seldom does a death occur which leaves behind a wider sense of public loss. Mr. Kidder was a man of a quiet and gentle nature, friendly and accessible, and yet of strong and matured opinions and of large business capacities. Among the many generous givers of Boston, he has been known for years as one of the most charitable and generous. His public and private gifts would amount to a large fortune. In reference to this trait of character the Boston Evening Record of Jan. 29, 1886, says : "His charities have been almost unlimited, and there is hardly his peer to be found. He was always among the first to offer assistance in time of fire or plague in sister cities where help was needed, and was always ready to lend a helping hand to those in distress."

In his business training he has, almost from the first, been connected intimately with the chief bankers and moneyed men of Boston. At the age of eighteen he became a clerk in the office of Coolidge & Haskell. In 1847 commenced more particularly his education as a banker in the well known house of John E. Thayer & Bro. Here he so conducted himself and made himself so useful to the firm, that in a few years he became a member of it. In the changes taking place by death and the succession of events, it came to pass years ago that Mr. Kidder's name moved to the front, his chief partner being Mr. Francis H. Peabody. This house stands connected with the great banking houses of the world. The errand that called him to New York on the 13th of January last (where he sickened and died) was a dinner given to Mr. Thomas Baring, who had been taken in as a partner in the firm of Kidder, Peabody & Co.

The Evening Record, from which we have already quoted, gives the following facts touching Mr. Kidder's domestic life. "Mr. Kidder was twice married, his first wife being a Miss Archibald, who died several years ago, leaving three sons, the oldest of whom, Henry, lately married, is now in Europe, and the two younger were with their father at the time of his death. A few years ago Mr. Kidder married Miss Elizabeth Huidekoper, of Meadville, Penn., who survives him."

WILLIAM EDWARD JOHNSTON, M.D., of Paris, France, a corresponding member, admitted March 25, 1859, was born in Wayne County, Ohio, February 16, 1821, and died in Paris, Feb. 15, 1886. His father was Robert Clark Johnston, M.D., born in Beaver County, Pa., in the year 1800. His mother was Mary Wilson, born in Beaver County, Pa., in 1794.

After his early academic education in Latin and mathematics was completed, he studied medicine at the University of the City of New York, finishing his course in 1847. He then returned to Ohio to join his father in the practice of medicine, in which connection he remained five years. In 1852 he went to Paris to accomplish himself in medical and surgical knowledge, with an intention, on his return, of establishing himself in the city of New York. But after continuing in Paris some years, he concluded to make that city itself the field of his professional labors, and at the time of his death he had been a resident of Paris for thirty-four years. During his life there he made two campaigns with the French army as volunteer surgeon, one in Lombardy in 1859, in the war against Austria, and the other during the siege of Paris in 1870-71.

He was united in marriage at Frankfort on the Main, in the year 1866, with Elizabeth Matteson, a native of Chicago, Ill. She was a daughter of Joseph Matteson, and was born in 1845. From this marriage there was one child, Robert Johnston.

Since living in France he has had many important trusts. He was president of the American Medical Society in Paris ; was appointed Commissioner from Ohio to represent that state in the Universal Exhibition at Paris in 1855 ; was honorary

Commissioner of Ohio in the like Exhibition at Paris in 1867; represented the United States at the Universal Geographical Congress and Exhibition in Paris, 1875. He was the "Malakoff" correspondent of the New York Tribune, from the Crimea, for two years, 1853–1855, during the war between Russia and the Allies, and for a long course of years has been the French correspondent, with the same nom de plume, of the New York Times. For his various services he received the Decoration of Chevalier or Knight of the French Legion of Honor, in 1871; the Decoration of Officer in the Order of the Crown of Prussia, signed by the emperor of Germany, 1872; and the promotion to the rank of Officer in the French Legion of Honor, 1876.

His wife, and son above named, now nineteen years old, survive him.

Rev. NICHOLAS HOPPIN, D.D., of Cambridge, a resident member, admitted Sept. 24, 1862, was born in Providence, R. I., Dec. 3, 1812, and died in Cambridge, Mass., March 8, 1886. The Hoppins of this country are all supposed to be descended from Stephen Hoppin, of Dorchester, who was born in England in 1626.

The subject of this sketch enjoyed excellent advantages for early education, and was graduated at Brown University at the age of nineteen, in the class of 1831. It was a small class of only thirteen members, but he had among his classmates William Gammell, LL.D., Professor of Rhetoric, History and Political Economy from 1835 to 1864, Henry Waterman, D.D., and David King, M.D., president of the Rhode Island Medical Society. He studied theology, and was graduated from the General Theological Seminary of New York in 1837. As a youth he had grown up in St. John's Church, Providence, under the ministry of Nathan B. Crocker, D.D., and was one of several young men who had been influenced by the Doctor to study for the ministry. He began his work of the ministry in Bangor, Me., in 1837, in St. John's Church, and in 1839 was ordained to the priesthood. In that year (1839) he was called to Christ Church, Cambridge, where he remained twenty-five years, till 1874.

Dr. Hoppin was a man of choice culture and scholarly habits. He was accustomed to use his pen freely, not only in the direct line of his profession, but in the broader ranges of literary and philosophical studies. Besides his membership in our own society, he was a member also of the Massachusetts Historical Society and of the American Oriental Society. He was a man of pleasing address and winning manners, affable, and easily approachable.

Dr. Hoppin's more immediate ancestors were as follows. His father was Richard Hoppin, of Providence, R. I., born in 1783, and his mother was Abby Spears, born in 1805, who died in 1819, leaving six children, of whom Dr. Hoppin was the fourth child and the second son. By a second marriage Richard Hoppin had three children. His grandfather was Nicholas Hoppin, who died in Providence, 1827, at the age of 78. The wife of this Nicholas was Hannah Lewis, who died in 1828. His great-grandfather was William Hoppin, of Charlestown, Mass., who died about 1773.

Dr. Hoppin was united in marriage in November, 1838, with Miss Elizabeth Mason Parker, of Boston, daughter of Mr. Samuel Dunn Parker and granddaughter of Bishop Parker. From this marriage there were three children, of whom one, Robert Lewis, died in infancy. His son, Henry Parker Hoppin, resides at St. Paul, Minn., and the daughter, Eliza Mason Hoppin, resides at Cambridge. Their mother survives.

Hon. GEORGE CARTER RICHARDSON, of Boston, elected a member in 1863, and made life member the same year, was chosen vice-president in 1875, and held the office till his death. He was born in Royalston, Mass., April 27, 1808, and died in Boston, May 20, 1886. He was a generous benefactor of this society, and a liberal giver to all worthy institutions and objects. His earliest American ancestor was Thomas Richardson, who with Mary his wife was in Charlestown as early as February, 1635–6, when his wife joined with the Charlestown Church. From Thomas[1] the line ran through Nathaniel,[2] James,[3] James,[4] Luke[5] and Thomas.[6] His father Thomas was a physician, and his mother was Jane Brown.

His training for mercantile life began when he was fifteen years old, in his native town, and in the store of Gen. Franklin Gregory. When about eighteen years old he began to visit Boston in the interest of the country trade, taking down country produce and bringing back such goods as were wanted by the customers of the store. When twenty-two years of age he became a partner with Gen. Gregory, and continued in this connection five years. He then formed a partnership with Henry Earle, and they opened a dry-goods store in Boston under the firm name of Richardson & Earle. This was in 1835. In 1837 this firm was dissolved, and he associated himself with George D. Dutton (who had been a partner with Daniel Denny), and so in the firm name of Dutton & Richardson, and afterward Dutton, Richardson & Co., they became the successors of Daniel Denny & Co. In this firm his business went on for seventeen years, or until 1855. Then for a time he was in the firm of James M. Beebe, Richardson & Co. He was afterwards in the firm of Richardson, Deane & Co. Here he continued till 1864, when his firm was made that of George C. Richardson & Co. As a merchant he was prosperous, and bore a name of dignity and honor through the whole of his long life.

Mr. Richardson was united in marriage, Feb. 2, 1832, with Miss Susan Gore Moore. She died Nov. 18, 1845. He was again married, Nov. 5, 1850, to Miss Ellen Gregory, daughter of Stephen Gregory, of Guilford, Vt. By his first marriage there were four children—George Elliot, Henry Augustus, Charles Howard and Edward. Of these the first died in 1861, aged 28, a member of the firm of Tilton, Gregory & Richardson; his second son, a graduate of Harvard College and Harvard Medical School, died as a surgeon in the navy, 1863. His third son, a partner with his father, died in 1867, and Edward, the fourth, is also dead. All the children of the first marriage are dead. The second wife and her son Arthur Gregory survive.

Mr. Richardson was a man greatly honored and beloved among the merchants of Boston, and was called to act in many conspicuous positions.

Hon. JOHN JAMES BABSON, of Gloucester, a corresponding member, admitted Feb. 9, 1847. was born in Gloucester, Mass., June 15, 1809, and died in same place, April 13, 1886. His father was William[6] Babson, born in Annisquam Village, Gloucester, June 7, 1779, and his mother was Mary Griffin, born in the same village, March 31, 1779. The American founder of his family was James[1] Babson, who died Dec. 21, 1683. From him the line ran through John,[2] born Nov. 27, 1660, died 1737; John,[3] born Dec. 14, 1691, died June 1, 1720; William,[4] born Nov. 4, 1719, lost at sea 1750; William,[5] born Sept. 5, 1749, died Dec. 30, 1831; William,[6] father of the subject of this sketch, as given above.

In the brief account which Mr. Babson has given of his own early life, he says: "The only systematic education I ever received was obtained at the public schools of Gloucester, which I left before the age of fourteen to go into my father's store, where I found ample leisure for reading, to which I was strongly inclined. .... Scott's novels and the early volumes of the Mass. Historical Collections were equally acceptable, and devoured with equal relish, and I feel quite sure that it was to the latter that I can trace the beginning of the pleasure which historical and genealogical pursuits have afforded me through manhood to old age."

Mr. Babson was united in marriage, June 17, 1832, with Miss Mary Coffin Rogers, daughter of Timothy Rogers. From this marriage there were five children, four sons and one daughter. This daughter and two of the sons died in early life. The oldest son William is cashier of the Gloucester National Bank, and the third son, Robert Edward, is a graduate of Harvard College in the Class of 1856, and has been a Master in the English High School, Boston.

The first wife died Dec. 5, 1842, and he was again united in marriage, June 14, 1851, with Miss Lydia Ann Mason, daughter of Alpheus Mason. From this marriage there was one son, John James, now in business in Gloucester.

Mr. Babson was for nineteen years cashier of the Gloucester Bank, selectman of Gloucester one year, member of the school committee twenty-eight years, and chairman of the same twenty-five years. He was representative to the General Court five years, and was State Senator two years. He was bank commissioner two years. He wrote the History of Gloucester, published in 1860, and is now out of print; and Notes and Additions to the History of Gloucester, published in 1876. He has been preparing a new edition of his history, which, as we have understood, was drawing near completion. By his death the city of Gloucester loses one of its oldest and best citizens. In respect to intelligence and excellence of character, few men were before him. Our society loses one of its early members thoroughly in sympathy with its objects and aims. His wife survives him.

JOHN GERRISH WEBSTER, Esq., of Boston, a life member and benefactor, admitted Dec. 21, 1883, was born in Portsmouth, N. H., April 8, 1811, and died in Boston, Feb. 7, 1886, at 188 Boylston Street. His father was David Webster, born in Rye, N. H., Sept. 23, 1784, and his mother Eunice Gerrish Nowell, of York, Me., born May 23, 1784.

His early education was in the public schools of Portsmouth, and afterwards, as he himself described it, "at a large school of some five or six hundred boys, all occupying one large room, and arranged and conducted under a monitorial system, devised by an Englishman named Lancaster. The principal of the school was Mr. Henry Jackson, who was a good-hearted gentleman of the old school, whom all the boys loved. We called him Master Jackson. The school was called after the name of its founder, the Lancasterian School." After this he passed to the Portsmouth High School, where he remained two years. At the age of twelve he went to the South Berwick Academy, Me., and commenced a course of study preparatory to college. In consequence of ill health, his purpose of obtaining a collegiate education was not carried out.

In 1838 he left his native town and came to Boston, to be associated in business with his brother, David Lock Webster, who had established in Boston five years before a leather manufactory. This firm has remained until now, that of Webster & Co., and is one of the oldest in the city in this department.

He was united in marriage, Oct. 15, 1842, with Mary Moulton, daughter of Jeremiah Moulton, of Sebec, Me. From this marriage there were five children, the eldest of whom was Frederick Hedge Webster, who was a lieutenant in Col. Shaw's colored regiment, the 54th, and died at Beaufort, South Carolina. The other four children were daughters.

Mr. Webster has occupied many positions of trust and responsibility. He was one of the incorporators and was president of the Malden Bank ; was treasurer and director of the Suffolk Railroad Co., now a part of the Metropolitan Railroad ; member of the Common Council of Boston ; member of the Massachusetts Legislature in 1857, and again in 1880 and 1881 ; director and treasurer of the Boston, Revere Beach and Lynn Railroad. He passes away leaving an honorable name and record.

GEORGE SHEFFIELD, ESQ., of Cambridge, a resident member, admitted Sept. 20, 1883, was born in Lyme, Huron County, Ohio, August 11, 1849, and died in Cambridge, Dec. 30, 1884, aged thirty-five years, four months and nineteen days. The name of his father was George Woodward Sheffield, who was born in New London, Conn., Nov. 18, 1814. His mother was Lucy Woodward, born in Lyme, Ohio, Jan. 7, 1820, the daughter of Gurdon Woodward, born in New London, Ct., Feb. 21, 1795, removing thence to Lyme, Ohio. His grandfather was George Sheffield, born in New London, Ct., Apr. 4, 1786. His great-grandfather was George Sheffield, born in South Kingston, R. I., Jan. 9, 1744, and his great-great-grandfather was of the same name, born in South Kingston, R. I., July 12, 1718.

His early education was obtained in the public schools of Lyme, Ohio. This was supplemented by attendance upon the High School of Bellevue, Ohio, and afterwards by private instruction under a tutor. Thus prepared he entered the Harvard Law School, Cambridge, where he was graduated in 1876, and received the degree of LL.B. He was united in marriage, June 15, 1881, with Miss Mary Gertrude Parker, daughter of Hon. Joel Parker of Cambridge.

He had established himself in the practice of law, at 85 Devonshire St., Boston, but so little time had passed since the close of his law studies, that he had hardly entered upon his professional career when his plans were cut short by death. He was a man of excellent character and promise. One of our members, J. Gardner White, Esq., writing to Mr. Dean says : "It occurred to me that it may be important to secure material for George Sheffield's life while his personality is fresh in the remembrance of his friends, as after a few years there may be but little recalled, except that he was born, married and died. He was a young man of noble character and much intellectual ability and energy, and seemed to have a valuable and useful career before him ; but he had not lived long enough to make incidents and points for the biographer."

BOOK NOTICES.

The Memorial History of Hartford County, Connecticut, 1633—1884. Edited by J. HAMMOND TRUMBULL, LL.D., President of the Connecticut Historical Society. In two volumes. Projected by Clarence F. Jewett. Boston : Edward L. Osgood, Publisher. 1886. 4to. Subscription Price $15 for the set. Vol. i. pp. 704 ; vol. ii. pp. 570.

This large and important work, which was projected and begun some years since, has been subject to the delays and hindrances often incident to such extended enterprises. It appears now, however, with a larger wealth of pictorial illustrations than if it had been finished in the time originally named. It is modelled in general after the Memorial History of Boston, that being in four quarto volumes, and this in two.

Hartford County holds a peculiar place in our history, as being one of the four early centres of English life in New England. Two hundred and fifty years ago, our fathers talked of the four Colonies, Massachusetts, Plymouth, Connecticut and New Haven, as we now speak of the six New England States. They were separated from each other by wide tracts of wilderness, but were bound together in close alliance, for mutual help and defence, and were often in conference, one with another. The three towns, Windsor, Hartford and Wethersfield, planted in the Connecticut Valley in 1635-36, were the beginnings of Hartford County and of the State of Connecticut.

If one will turn back and trace the early boundaries, he will discover that what is now Hartford County, with its twenty-eight towns and one city, was largely included in the three original townships. Out of the ancient Windsor, nine of these townships have been formed, and Wethersfield has been the mother of nearly as many more. Hartford, the county town and chief in population, was the smallest in extent, in the original distribution. There were fringes of territory on the southern, western and northern borders of the present County, that did not belong to the three ancient towns.

Of the two volumes composing this work, the first is occupied with things in general: the Indian Tribes occupying the soil at the time our fathers came over; topography and natural features of the country; the previous discovery and occupation of the Connecticut Valley by the Dutch; the motives which led to the removal of colonies from the Massachusetts Bay to plant these river towns; the organization and history of Hartford County as a county, as also the history of Hartford as a city. Then in this first volume come up in extended review, the public institutions of the county, and its great leading enterprises and interests; the courts, schools, churches, literary and charitable foundations, and all that goes to make up modern civilized and christian society. A large corps of writers, specially qualified for their work, have been employed in the treatment of these various topics; and among them we notice the names of Rev. Increase N. Tarbox, D.D., ex-President Noah Porter, Charles Dudley Warner, Esq., Sherman M. Adams, Esq., H. S. Sheldon, Hon. Henry Barnard, Miss Mary K. Talcott, and Rev. Dr. George L. Walker.

The second volume is wholly devoted to the histories of the twenty-eight towns, which, with the city of Hartford, make up the county. Not far from thirty different writers have wrought in this part of the general work.

The whole has been under the editorial supervision of J. Hammond Trumbull, LL.D., of Hartford, President of the Conn. Historical Society, and no man could be found more thoroughly at home in all the details of Connecticut history than he.

This work will take its place among the various County Histories which have already appeared, and will be a truly valuable contribution in this department. Year by year new helps and facilities are afforded for tracing minutely the origin and progress of the early New England civilization. Of course, these County Histories have, in the nature of things, to be somewhat fragmentary. But they lead to research among the old records of towns and churches, and a large number and variety of facts are thus brought to light and forever fixed as materials for history.

Volumes like these, so carefully prepared and so copiously illustrated, are alike ornamental and instructive in households, where a great number of them will doubtless find their home. But they are perhaps still more in place in all large libraries, as books of reference for historical students. Clarence F. Jewett, the projector of this work, occupied the same relation to the Memorial History of Boston

Prytaneum Bostoniense. Notes on the History of the Old State House, formerly known as the Town House in Boston, the Court House in Boston, the Province Court House, the State House, and the City Hall. By GEORGE H. MOORE, LL.D., Superintendent of the Lenox Library. Second Paper. Read before the Bostonian Society, February 9, 1886. Boston: Cupples, Upham & Co., the Old Corner Bookstore. 1886. 8vo. pp. 80. Price 75 cts. Address the publishers, 283 Washington St., Boston, Mass.

Dr. Moore's first paper on the Old State House was read before the Bostonian Society May 12, 1885, and was published in pamphlet form the same year. A notice of it will be found in our issue for January last. In the two works, the author has given us much interesting matter concerning the historic halls now in the custody of the Bostonian Society, most of which will be new to his readers. It would be safe to say that no other person could produce two papers on this subject containing such an array of new and interesting matter. Concerning the edifice and its associations, the author says:

"As we review the history of this venerated structure, we cannot fail to recall those men of old whose names are identified with its ancient glories. 'There were giants in those days.' I am not aware that its doors were ever darkened by Kings or Princes of the earth—excepting when the chiefs of native tribes of Indians may have stood here as delegates of their people or as prisoners and hostages. The great names of Massachusetts are of course all written in its visitors' book of remembrance: but even that brilliant record of personal memories and associations is exalted and dignified by other names never to be forgotten in the history of this nation or that of the world, Washington, Lafayette, Franklin, Jefferson, besides a host of other worthies, who are always present or accounted for on the roll-call of History."

Dr. Moore gives interesting incidents in the visits of the eminent men he names to Boston and to the Old State House, and he continues the history of the edifice till it ceased to be a State House and became a City Hall.

An Appendix of 42 pages furnishes documentary and other historical matter illustrating the paper. Appendix No. 3 is an "Examination of the Old State House Memorial and Reply to Mr. Whitmore's Appendix N." Dr. Moore furnishes sufficient evidence to prove that the interior which the committee of the City Government restored was the old City Hall and not the old State House. And yet we think the committee acted judiciously in the premises, nor do we see that Dr. Moore condemns their action. It was better to restore the historic halls of which the architect's plans were preserved than to attempt to restore other halls, even though of greater historic interest, where a great portion of the details would be left to mere guess work.

The History of Medway, Mass., 1713 *to* 1885. Edited by Rev. E. O. JAMESON. Published by the Town. Millis, 1886. Royal 8vo. pp. 534. Price $5.00.

The Biographical Sketches of Prominent Persons and the Genealogical Records of Many Early and Other Families in Medway, Mass., 1713–1886. Illustrated by Numerous Steel and Wood Engravings. By E. O. JAMESON. Millis, Mass., 1886. Royal 8vo. pp. 208. Price $2.50.

The Military History of Medway, Mass., 1745–1885. Illustrated. By E. O. JAMESON. Millis, 1886. Royal 8vo. pp. 110. Price $1.25.

The first title above is that of the long expected "History of Medway." It was prepared by a committee chosen by the citizens of Medway April 4, 1881. Rev. Mr. Jameson, well known as the compiler of "The Cogswells in America," a very elaborate and valuable work, was chosen editor by his associates of the committee, and has ably performed the labor. The opening chapter is devoted to the region and its settlement, and is enriched with several handsome illustrations by George J. La Croix assisted by Messrs. Frank Myrick and F. Childe Hassam. These gentlemen have added much to the volume, and their work is worthy of special mention. Although Medway was not incorporated till 1713, the locality has been settled for two hundred and twenty-five years, and this entire period is covered by the History. Old Medfield, known to historical students in consequence of its experiences during King Philip's war, was the mother town of Medway, and in 1885 that part of Medway included in what was known as the "Old Grant" became a separate town by the name of Millis, a name taken in honor of a prominent citizen, Lansing Millis.

The ecclesiastical, educational, and military history of the town is given with much detail, and seventy pages are devoted to carefully prepared sketches of soldiers from Medway in the Civil War. The book is especially rich in biographical matter, and contains a large number of notices of leading citizens, including some who have been dead for generations, and a record of whose lives is the more valuable for that fact. The manufacturing industries occupy a proper portion of the work, and the buildings are illustrated by the gentlemen before mentioned. Local organizations, such as the lodges of the various societies, the fire companies, and the Grand Army of the Republic, are duly noticed, and a list of the officers given. The genealogies of the Medway families occupy the last eighty-seven pages, and form an interesting and valuable portion of the work, and one in which the citizens may well take pride. The numerous portraits of citizens is a feature which must not be overlooked, and the maps showing the inhabitants in the various localities at different periods is an important addition to the value of the book.

The second book whose title is given above, the Medway Biographies and Genealogies, is a reprint from the first named work with fuller and very satisfactory indexes to that portion of the work. It contains more than one hundred and fifty biographical sketches, and genealogical records of over five hundred families.

The last book, the Military History of Medway, is also reprinted from the larger work. It contains " the names of the inhabitant soldiers in the French and Indian wars ; the Continental soldiers and minute-men in the war of the Revolution ; a mention of the war of 1812 ; the doings of the town in support of the war for the Union ; a record, with biographical sketches, of the Union soldiers and Portraits of Washington, Lincoln and Grant, with other Illustrations."

Those who are not able to procure the entire work of which a very limited edition was printed, will be glad to obtain separately the parts relating to the family and military history of the town, and even those who have the History itself will find these volumes convenient.

The typographical work seems to be well done, and the History of Medway is an addition to the ever increasing number of excellent and reliable town histories. *By George K. Clarke, LL.B. of Needham, Mass.*

Proceedings and Collections of the Wyoming Historical and Geological Society. Vol. II. Part II. Wilkes-Barre, Pa.: Printed for the Society. 1886. 8vo. pp. 164.

An Account of the Various Silver and Copper Medals presented to the North American Indians by the Sovereigns of England, France and Spain from 1600 to 1800. Read before the Wyoming Historical and Geological Society. By Rev. HORACE EDWIN HAYDEN, Curator of Numismatics, Wilkes-Barre, Pa. 1886. 8vo. pp. 26.

This part of the proceedings of the Wyoming Historical and Geological Society completes the second volume of that work. The proceedings of the society here printed commence May 9, 1884, and end Feb. 11, 1886. The several reports presented to the society by its officers and the papers read before it are also inserted in the volume. The papers are Rev. Bernard Page, by Sheldon Reynolds, Esq.; various Silver and Copper Medals, by Rev. H. E. Hayden ; Carboniferous Fossils found near Wilkes-Barre, by Prof. E. W. Claypole ; and Carboniferous Limestone Beds of the Wyoming Valley, by Charles A. Ashburner. The number closes with obituaries of Stewart Pearce, Esq., author of " Annals of Luzerne County " and eight other members of the society, written by the historiographer, George B. Kulp.

The Rev. Mr. Hayden's paper on Indian Medals has been reprinted from the proceedings and the title of the pamphlet is given above. The paper was suggested by the fact that five Indian Medals of George I. of Great Britain are now in the possession of the society and its members. One of these medals belongs to the society, one to the Hon. Steuben Jenkins, two to Mr. Hayden himself, and the other to Master Dennison Stearns. These medals are particularly described and their history is given. Besides the description of these medals a brief but interesting account of the Indian medals of England, and also notices of those of France and Spain, will be found here.

The Record. First Presbyterian Church, Morristown, N. J. Published Monthly. 8vo. 12 pages in each number. Price $1. a year. Single number 10 cts each. Address Mr. James R. Voorhees, or Rev. William Durant, Morristown, N. J.

This periodical was commenced in January, 1880, and was published regularly to the end of 1885, except that its issue was suspended in the year 1882. The work has been noticed twice before this in these pages, namely, in July, 1880, and October, 1881. The *Record* was commenced by the Rev. Rufus Smith Green, who was then the pastor of the First Presbyterian Church in Morristown. He removed to Buffalo, N. Y., in October, 1881, but continued the publication of this work to the end of the year, when it was suspended. The Rev. William Durant was settled as his successor in 1882, and in January, 1883, the publication of the *Record* was resumed under his editorial charge ; and it has been continued by him to Dec. 1885, the close of the fifth volume.

The object of this work is to preserve in print the records and other historical material, relating to the First Presbyterian Church of Morristown ; and we would recommend the example set by this church to other churches in this country, of all denominations. The work performed by the Rev. Messrs. Green and Durant, in this publication, is summed up in the number for Dec. 1885. They have given : " 1st. Historical narratives of the Church and Town from 1742 to 1840 ; 2d. Biographical narratives concerning some of the pastors and leading men of former generations; 3d. Reprints of rare and valuable publications, respecting the Church ; 4th A continuous copy of all names recorded in the Minutes of the Parish, of the Trustees, and of the Sessions, from 1742 down to 1882 : 5th. Complete lists of all names recorded in the various Registers of the Church, viz., those of Baptisms, of Communicants, of Marriages and of Deaths, from 1742, down to 1815 ; together with an alphabetical arrangement, printed nearly through the C's, which includes all names down to 1885."

The publication of the *Record* was discontinued last year with the December number, owing to a lack of subscribers ; but the editor hopes " that it may be possible, before long, to complete the printing of the Combined Registers, and some other matters. In this case it is probable that the monthly form will not be resumed, but that all additional pages will be issued at one time." The Rev. Mr. Durant writes to us that the manuscript of the Combined Registers is nearly completed, and he hopes that the additional pages, above referred to, will be printed within a year or two. He adds, " The aim has been a Church Record, and not primarily a genealogical or town history." The genealogist and student of local history will, however, find valuable materials in these five volumes, which we hope will not be the last.

1830. *H. U. Memoirs.* Boston : Press of Rockwell & Churchill. 1886. 8vo. pp. 145.

The class of 1830, Harvard University, graduated with forty-eight members of whom ten only survive. The survivors appointed Messrs. John O. Sargent, James Dana and Thomas C. Amory a committee to cause memoirs of their " classmates who have passed away to be prepared and printed for private distribution." The memoirs of these thirty-eight Harvard graduates have been prepared by their friends or relatives; and several are by their classmates. Among the memoirs here are those of Hon. Charles Sumner, Hon. Elisha R. Potter, Rev. Samuel B. Babcock, Hon. Thomas Hopkinson, Henry Winthrop Sargent, Rev. Albert C. Patterson, Hon. George W. Warren and Hon. Samuel T. Worcester. The committee deserve thanks both for the excellent memoirs of their classmates which they have procured, and for the creditable manner in which they have brought out the volume.

Milwaukee Under the Charter from 1854 *to* 1860 *inclusive.* Vol. IV. By JAMES S. BUCK. Milwaukee : Swain & Tate, Printers. 1886. 8vo. pp. 465. Price $4. Sold by the author, Milwaukee, Wisconsin, and by G. E. Littlefield, 67 Cornhill, Boston, Mass.

This is the fourth volume of Mr. Buck's History of Milwaukee. The first two volumes, published respectively in 1876 and 1881, give the " Pioneer History " of the place from 1833 to 1846. The two following volumes, issued in 1884 and 1886, give its history " Under the Charter," from 1847 to 1860. The three previous volumes have been noticed in this periodical : namely, Vol. I. in April, 1877, Vol. II. in January, 1882, and Vol. III. in October, 1884. Mr. Buck arrived in Milwaukee in January, 1837, a little more than three years after the arrival of the first English settlers, and he has lived there ever since, a residence which lacks but three months of half a century. He has been a witness and an actor in the events which he narrates in these volumes, and has produced a work that will be highly appreciated by his fellow citizens and will be more highly prized in future years. Much that he preserves would, we feel certain, have been lost if he had failed to record it.

Transactions of the Kansas State Historical Society, embracing the Third and Fourth Biennial Reports, 1883-1885, *Together with copies of Early Kansas Territorial Records, and other Historical Papers, and the Proceedings of the Kansas Quarter-Centennial Celebration, Jan.* 25, 1886. Vol. III. Topeka : Kansas Publishing House, T. D. Thacher, State Printer. 1886. 8vo. pp. 519.

Kansas was admitted as a state into the Union on the 29th of January, 1861. On the completion of a quarter of a century, on the 29th of January last, the event was commemorated in the Grand Opera House at Topeka. Col. D. R. Anthony, president of the Historical Society, was chairman of the committee of arrangements, and F. G. Adams, secretary of that society, was secretary of the committee. In the various addresses, the progress of the state and country within the last twenty-five years was well presented. The proceedings of this celebration fill 103 pages of the volume before us. The celebration seems to have been in every way a success.

Though one of the youngest of the state historical societies, the Historical Society of Kansas, in the few years—less than eleven—since it was formed, has done much good work in preserving materials for the history of the state. We have commended their work before in these pages, namely, in July, 1881, and July, 1884. Besides the historical material in the two biennial reports for 1883 and 1885, and the Quarter-Centennial Proceedings, there is in this volume a large quantity of material relating to the early history of Kansas, such as the official documentary records of Kansas Territory, consisting of the minutes kept in the office of the Territorial government from Oct. 7, 1854, to Sept. 7, 1856 ; biographical sketches of Governors Reeder and Shannon ; extracts from Gov. Reeder's diary ; a paper by George C. Brackett, and addresses in 1884 by Govs. Stanton and Denver.

The book has an unusual quantity of original historical matter, and is furnished with an excellent index of 49 pages, in double columns and closely printed.

The Musical Record. A Journal of Music, Art, Literature. Edited by DEXTER SMITH. Boston: Oliver Ditson & Co. August, 1886. Published monthly. 32 pages large 4to. in each number. Price $1. a year, or 10 cts. a number.

This periodical maintains the high reputation that it has attained as a musical miscellany. Mr. Smith the editor has marked qualifications for the position which for so many years he has ably occupied. Besides the sheet music furnished, which alone is worth more than the price of the work, there are essays on musical subjects and other matters of interest to the musical world.

The Dearborns; a Discourse Commemorative of the Eightieth Anniversary of the Occupation of Fort Dearborn and the First Settlement at Chicago ; read before the Chicago Historical Society, Tuesday, Dec. 18, 1883, by DANIEL GOODWIN, JR. With remarks of Hons. John Wentworth, J. Young Scammon, E. B. Washburne and I. N. Arnold. Chicago: Fergus Printing Company. 1884. pp. 56. With two Portraits and Index.

Provincial Pictures by Brush and Pen : An Address Delivered before the Bostonian Society in the Council Chamber of the Old State House, Boston, May 11, 1886. By DANIEL GOODWIN, JR., Member of the Chicago Historical Society. Chicago: Fergus Printing Company. 1886. pp. 84. With Appendix, Illustrations and Index.

These two papers form an interesting octavo volume of one hundred and forty pages, handsomely printed, with cloth binding. They carry the reader back to colonial days and "the times that tried men's souls." The first paper describes the career of Major General Henry Dearborn and his almost equally celebrated son, Adjutant General Henry Alexander Scammel Dearborn. General Henry Dearborn was no holiday soldier, but a downright fighting commander ; and no officer of the Revolution has a better record than he. His services at Breed's Hill in the famous First New Hampshire Regiment commanded by Colonel John Stark, in which he led one of the companies, contributed as much as any officer to save the forces under Colonel Prescott from probable destruction ; and it cannot be denied that a portion of the honors awarded to the latter officer should belong to the men who did so much to save his command. General Dearborn's efforts in Canada and in the campaign against Burgoyne were equally creditable, while his operations in a higher station during the war of 1812 were no less worthy of commendation. The efforts of his distinguished son to secure the completion of the great monument on the battle field where his father fought, are also held in high appreciation. A portrait of each of these eminent officers accompanies the paper.

The second article relates mainly to the Pitts family, and the patriotic Councillor, James Pitts, is here conspicuously described. There are also reminiscences of the Bowdoin family, the elder Samuel Dexter, Benjamin Franklin, Professor John Winthrop, the painters Smibert, Blackburn, Copley, Stuart, and other notable characters before and during the Revolutionary period. The proceedings of the council, Gov. Hutchinson presiding, on the 6th of March, 1770, relating to the withdrawal of the troops from Boston, just after the Boston Massacre, are here given in print for the first time. In all these sketches, although the writer is treading on somewhat familiar ground, he has brought to light much historical matter not generally known, and so rendered essential service to the department of our local history.

Mr. Goodwin writes in a remarkably graceful, fluent style, and evidently with a strong personal interest in the subjects of which he treats. He is open to criticism at times for carelessness of statement, such as on page 15 of the second paper, where he describes Governor Jonathan Belcher as a " college-mate " of James Pitts of the Harvard class of 1731. Governor Belcher was of the class of 1699 at Harvard, and was governor of the province in 1731. The writer evidently means the governor's son, Jonathan Belcher, H. C. 1728, one of the first settlers of Halifax, N. S., who was really a " college-mate."

The illustrations of the second paper are a represention of the Old State House, and portraits of Gilbert Stuart and General Arthur St. Clair. The book is finely printed, and altogether is an interesting volume.
By O. B. Stebbins, Esq., of South Boston.

Gray's Inn. Its History and Associations. Compiled from original and unpublished Documents. By WILLIAM RALPH DOUTHWAITE, Librarian. Reeves and Turner. London. 1886. 8vo. pp. xxiii.+283. Price 7 shillings.

This is a well written and valuable history of one of the four famous Inns of Court, all of which were anciently situated in the suburbs of London. Gray's Inn is on the north side of Holborn, and until the present century its surroundings were quiet and rural, and many men of letters other than law students found here attractive places of residence. Gray's Inn stands on ground formerly known as the manor of Portpool, and the Inn itself takes its name from the Lords Grey de Wilton, one of the numerous branches of the great historic house of Grey, which now survives in only one line, that of the Earls of Stamford. For three hundred years the Greys of Wilton were lords of the manor of Portpool, and early in the fourteenth century Gray's Inn was an Inn of Court. The fourth chapter tells of the ancient Constitution and Orders of the Inn, and gives a list of its " Readers " from 1391 to 1675, including such names as Nicholas and Francis Bacon. In the fifth chapter there is a history of the old buildings with illustrations, and later in the book there is an account of the ancient hall built in the Tudor period, and of the numerous armorial bearings, many of them noted in history, which adorn its walls and windows. The chapel of the Inn is described, and there is a list of the preachers from 1574 to 1883. The Library and Gardens receive the author's attention, and he gives us a very interesting list of the eminent persons who have been connected with Gray's Inn. We also learn something of the " Masques and Revels " in the olden time, and of the allied Inns of Chancery, of which Staple and Barnard Inns are illustrated. The greatest men in the kingdom often entered their sons as students at Gray's Inn, and it was a centre of culture and a haunt of scholars for ages.

The book is illustrated by an autotype fac-simile of the Carved Screen in the Hall, and engraved views of South Square, Field Court, the Gate House in Holborn, Barnard's Inn and Staple Inn. It is well printed and indexed, and the author has ably performed his work.
By George K. Clarke, LL.B., of Needham, Mass.

Northern Notes and Queries. Published Quarterly. Edited by the Rev. A. W. CORNELIUS HALLEN, M.A., F.S.A. Scot., &c. Vol. I. No. 1. June, 1886. Edinburgh : Douglas & Foulis.

Notice is taken with pleasure of the first number of this magazine, published at Edinburgh. It will be devoted to the Antiquities, Family History, Local Records, Folk Lore, Heraldry and History of Scotland.

As an antiquarian magazine outside of London, it appears that Edinburgh, with all the advantges of its valuable manuscripts, the Records in the General Register House and at the Lyon Office, is a most suitable place for such a work to emanate from and be successful. The living historical and antiquarian authorities of Scotland will doubtless take a pride in this magazine and give it their full support, and some of their number have already given in it interesting articles. Encouragement should be given to it by the historical and genealogical societies of the United States. This magazine is published quarterly, at 4s. per annum, and is edited by the Rev. A. W. Cornelius Hallen, M.A., F.S.A. Scot., to whom communications and subscriptions can be sent. His address is care of Douglas & Foulis, Castle Street, Edinburgh, Scotland.
By A. D. Weld French, Esq., of Boston.

George Lansing Taylor : a Sketch of his First Itinerant Pastorate at Seymour, Ct., in the New York East Conference in the years 1862, 1863. By WILLIAM C. SHARPE, author of History of Seymour, etc. Record Print, Seymour, Conn. 1886. Sm. 8vo. pp. 94.

This is a reprint from the author's forthcoming " Annals of the Methodist Episcopal Church of Seymour, Ct.," and furnishes some interesting pages in the history of that church during the pastorate of the patriotic and popular minister named in the title-page.

Mr. Sharpe, the author of this pamphlet, is the editor and proprietor of the *Seymour Record*, a weekly newspaper published in that town, at one dollar a year. His taste for local history leads him to preserve in the columns of his paper much valuable historical and genealogical matter relating to the town of Seymour and its vicinity. A series of articles commenced this year is entitled "Industries of Seymour," and is illustrated by views of buildings, etc.

A Bibliography of the Writings of Franklin Benjamin Hough, Ph.D., M.D. By JOHN H. HICKCOX. Washington, D. C. 8vo. pp. 27. Issued in 1886.

Dr. Hough was one of the most voluminous writers in the country, and in his specialties, one of the best. The late Mr. Joel Munsell, of Albany, remarked to the writer of this notice, that he knew of no writer who could perform so much literary labor, so quickly and so well, as Dr. Hough. He was born in 1822, and died in 1885, aged 63. A biographical notice of him is printed in the REGISTER for January, 1886, page 118. We notice that his second christian name is here given as *Benjamin*. In an account of himself, furnished Feb. 3, 1860, to the New England Historic Genealogical Society, he states that he was "originally named Benjamin Franklin Hough, but having a cousin of the same name, he assumed in childhood the name as now written [i. e. Franklin B. Hough], to distinguish him from his cousin. The B." he adds, "is retained without attaching to it any particular significance, and it is invariably written with the initial only."

Mr. Hickcox has done a good service in preparing this bibliography of Dr. Hough's writings, which is surprising from its fulness, especially for the ample and precise details relative to pamphlets and contributions to newspapers and other periodicals.

A History of the Kidder Family from A.D. 1300 *to* 1676, *including a Biography of our Emigrant Ancestor, James Kidder, also a Genealogy of his Descendants through his son John Kidder, who settled in Chelmsford about* 1681. By F. E. KIDDER. Allston, Mass.: 1886. 8vo. pp. 175. Price $1.50, with all the engravings, or $1 without the heliotype portraits.

Genealogical Notes of the Families of Chester of Blaby, Leicestershire, and Chester of Wethersfield, Conn., New England. Compiled by ROBT. EDMOND CHESTER-WATERS, B.A., a Barrister of the Inner Temple, etc. etc. Printed for the Author. Leicester: Clarke and Hodgson. 1886. 8vo. pp. 29. Price 3s. 6d., or post free 3s. 9d. Address the author, 29 The Grove, Hammersmith, London, W., England.

Descent of Comfort Sands and of His Children. With Notes on the Families of Ray, Thomas, Guthrie, Alcock, Palgrave, Cornell, Dodge, Hunt, Jessup. New York. 1886. 8vo. pp. 91.

American Boynton Directory, containing the Address of all known Boyntons, Boyingtons and Byingtons in the United States and British Dominions. Compiled by JOHN FARNHAM BOYNTON. Syracuse, N. Y. 1884. 8vo. pp. 147. Price $2. Address, John F. Boynton, M.D., Highland Place, Syracuse, N. Y.

Memoirs of Major Jason Torrey, of Bethany, Wayne County, Pa. By Rev. DAVID TORREY, D.D. Scranton, Pa.: James S. Horton, Printer and Publisher. 1885. 8vo. pp. 131.

Genealogy of the Fenner Family. By Rev. JAMES P. ROOT. No. 1. Providence. 1886. 8vo. pp. 19.

Origine des familles Brothier, Comtes d'Antioche, anciens seigneurs de Lavaux, Rollière, des Roys, de Chambes etc.; en Poitou, Nivernais, Aunis et Savoie. Broadside 9 by 14 inches.

Some Doubts concerning the Scars Pedigree. By SAMUEL PEARCE MAY. Boston: Printed by David Clapp & Son. 1886. Royal 8vo. pp. 10.

Excerpts from the Hitchcock Genealogy. By H. G. CLEVELAND, of Cleveland, Ohio. 8vo. pp. 3. Price 15 cts. For sale by C. L. Woodward, 78 Nassau Street, New York, and George E. Littlefield, 67 Cornhill, Boston, Mass.

Extracts from the Parish Register of Ardeley, co. Hertford, England. Chauncy, &c. By GEORGE W. MARSHALL, LL.D., F.S.A. 1886. 8vo. pp. 7. Price 20 cts. For sale by Charles L. Woodward, 78 Nassau Street, New York, N. Y., and G. E. Littlefield, 67 Cornhill, Boston, Mass.

We continue our quarterly notices of recent genealogical publications.

The Kidder family, the subject of the first book, is fortunate in being able to trace its ancestry back in an unbroken line to the time of Henry VII. The late Frederic Kidder, Esq., author of the History of New Ipswich, spent much time in collecting the genealogy of his family, and in pursuing his researches entered into correspondence with the late Rev. Edward Turner, of Maresfield, Sussex, England, who was interested in the Kidders of that parish, and in tracing their history had found the name there as early as 1320. By his aid the New England immigrant, James Kidder, from whom most if not all of the name in New England descend, was connected with the Maresfield family, and his ancestry was traced back for seven generations, to 1492. Mr. Kidder printed the English pedigree and his own line of the American family in 1852, in his History of New Ipswich. This is the basis of the present work, which has been much enlarged and has been brought out in a handsome volume from the press of Messrs. David Clapp & Son. The author acknowledges indebtedness to Miss S. B. Kidder. The English history of the name and the early generations of the New England branch are fully given, but in later generations the author has confined himself to the descendants of John Kidder, the second son of the immigrant. Of these he has given us a very full record. The book is illustrated by a steel engraved portrait of Frederic Kidder, and six heliotype portraits and views, besides a number of other engravings. Mr. Kidder deserves credit for the able manner in which the book has been compiled. It is thoroughly indexed.

Edmond Chester-Waters, Esq., of the Inner Temple, London, is well known to the antiquarian world, having published several important genealogical works which have received warm commendation from the best writers on family history. Though suffering for a long period from ill health, he has accomplished more than most of those in good health. The present work, the second on our list, is devoted to the Chesters of Blaby, Leicestershire, one of which family, Leonard Chester, baptized in that parish, July 15, 1610, emigrated to New England and finally settled at Wethersfield, Connecticut. His mother was a sister of the famous Rev. Thomas Hooker, of Hartford, Ct. A genealogical account of Leonard Chester's descendants is printed in the Register, vol. xxii. pp. 338–42, and is reprinted in this book. The Chesters of Blaby are traced to William Chester of Chipping Barnet, Herts, where at his death in February, 1565–6, he held a considerable freehold estate. The family was one of some importance, and ample details concerning the several members are given in the book before us. A number of their wills are given in full, and abstracts of those of others are also printed. An appendix furnishes extracts from parish registers and other records. There is also a folding tabular pedigree. We commend the book to New England genealogists, and particularly to descendants of Leonard Chester.

The book on the Sands family is by Temple Prime, Esq., of Huntington, Long Island, N. Y. Comfort Sands, to whose ancestry and family this work is devoted, was a merchant in New York before and after the Revolution. He was a descendant in the 5th generation from James[1] Sands, the immigrant, who died on Block Island, March 13, 1695, aged 73, through John,[2] John,[3] John.[4] Besides a genealogy of one line of this family, letters and other documents illustrating its history are given, with genealogical notes on the families named on the title page. The compiler expresses a hope that at no distant day he may be able to publish a more complete work. This book is printed to preserve what has already been collected, and to elicit further information.

Dr. Boynton, of Syracuse, N. Y., has been long engaged in preparing a book on the genealogy of the Boynton family in England and America. As a preliminary to the publication of this work, which is far advanced towards completeness, he has issued the next work on our list, a directory to the Boyntons in this country. It will be found very useful, particularly to persons of the name or blood. The arrangement is by states, and under them individuals, both alphabetically.

The next book is a well written life of Major John Torrey of Bethany, Pa., to whose ancestry and descendants, the book by the Hon. John Torrey of Honesdale, Pa., noticed by us in April, is devoted. That genealogy is appended to the memoir. The memoir, which is by the Rev. Dr. Torrey of Honesdale, Pa., a son of Major Torrey, contains some genealogical information.

The first number of the work on the Fenner family, contains a sketch of Capt. Arthur Fenner, of Providence, R. I., by the compiler of the genealogy, Rev. James Peirce Root, read as a paper before the Rhode Island Historical Society. Arthur Fenner was the Myles Standish of Rhode Island. He was the stirps of a distinguished family in that state.

The Brothier family, the subject of the broadside, is of German origin, and established itself in Poitou, towards the close of the eleventh century. The leaf we have received, is from M. Brothier de Rollière, a gentleman resident near Jaulnay, in the department of Vienne, France, who apprehends that a member of this family settled at or near Boston, after the French revolution of 1793. We regret to say that we find no trace of him. The family is spoken of in the Dictionnaire Généalogique du Canada.

The pamphlets on the Sears, Hitchcock and Chauncy families, are reprints from the REGISTER.

RECENT PUBLICATIONS,

PRESENTED TO THE NEW ENGLAND HISTORIC GENEALOGICAL SOCIETY, TO AUG. 1, 1886.

I. *Publications written or edited by Members of the Society.*

Addresses and Speeches on various occasions from 1878 to 1886. By Robert C. Winthrop. Boston: Little, Brown and Company. 1886. 8vo. pp. 620.

The History of the People of the United States. A Review of McMaster's history by Hon. Mellen Chamberlain, LL.D. Cambridge: Printed at the Riverside Press. 1886. 8vo. pp. 19.

The Life of Admiral Sir Isaac Coffin, Baronet. His English and American Ancestors, by Thomas C. Amory. Boston: Cupples, Upham & Co. 1886. 8vo. pp. 141.

Bulletin of the National Association of Wool Manufacturers. A quarterly Journal devoted to the interests of the national Wool Industry, founded Nov. 3), 1864. 1886. Edited by John L. Hayes, LL.D. Boston. 1886. University Press: John Wilson and Son, Cambridge. 8vo. pp. 91.

Andover Theological Seminary. Necrology, 1885–86. Prepared under the direction of the committee. By Henry A. Hazen, Secretary. No. 6. Boston: Beacon Press. Thomas Todd, Printer, No. 1 Somerset Street. 1886. 8vo. pp. 75–84.

Biographical Sketch of the Honorable Major John Habersham, of Georgia. By Charles C. Jones, Jr., LL.D. Privately Printed. The Riverside Press. Cambridge. 1886. 8vo. pp. 30.

Groton Historical Series. No. XIII. A Register of Births, Deaths and Marriages in Groton, 1664–1693, and of Marriages, 1713–1793. As copied from the Middlesex County Records. . . . Groton. 1886. 8vo. pp. 64.

Groton Historical Series. No. XIV. Revolutionary Item, Boston Port Bill, Minute Men, Powder Mill at Pepperell, Rev. Samuel Dana, ... The Presbyterian Controversy in Groton. President Dwight's description in Groton. . . . Groton. 1886. 8vo. pp. 32.

The Pennsylvania Magazine of History and Biography. July, 1886. Philadelphia: Publication Fund of the Historical Society of Pennsylvania. No. 1300 Locust St. Published quarterly. 8vo. Price $3 a year. F. D. Stone, Editor.

Walford's Antiquarian: a Magazine and Bibliographical Review. Edited by Edward Walford, M.A., London. George Redway, 15 York Street, Covent Garden. Published monthly; June, July and August. 1886. Price one shilling a number. J. W. Bouton, Agent for America, 706 Broadway, New York.

Miscellanea Genealogica et Heraldica. Edited by Joseph Jackson Howard, LL.D., F.S.A. London: Mitchell & Hughes, 140 Wardour St. Published monthly; June and July, 1886. Price 1s. a number; annual subscription 10s. 6d.

Education. A monthly Magazine devoted to the Science, Art, Philosophy and Literature of Education. William A. Mowry, Editor. June, 1886. Boston: W. A. Mowry, Publisher, 3 Somerset St. Price $3 a year or 35 cts. a number.

The Name "Columbia." By Albert H. Hoyt. Royal 8vo. pp. 7.

Collections of the Virginia Historical Society. New Series. Vol. V. Documents chiefly unpublished relating to the Huguenot emigration to Virginia, and to the settlement at Manakintown. With an appendix of genealogies. . . . Edited and compiled for the Virginia Historical Society, by R. A. Brock. Richmond, Va. Published by the Society. 1886. 8vo. pp. 247.

II. *Other Publications.*

Collections of the Massachusetts Historical Society. Vol. I. Sixth Series. Boston: Published by the Society. 1886. 8vo. pp. 424.

The Narraguagus Valley. Some account of its early settlement and settlers. By J. A. Milliken. Printed by C. O. Furbush. Machias, Me. 8vo. pp. 24.

General Catalogue of the Massachusetts Agricultural College, including the officers of government and instruction. Sketches of the alumni, occupations and addresses of the non-graduates, and other matters of interest relating to the College. 1862–1886. Amherst, Mass. 1886. 8vo. pp. 128.

Letters and Addresses contributed at a general meeting of the Military Service Institution held at Governor's Island, N. Y. H., February 25, 1886. In memory of Winfield Scott Hancock, Major General in the army of the United States, Commander Second Corps, army of the Potomac, President of the Military Service Institution, Commander in Chief of the Loyal Legion. Published for the Military Service Institution. By G. P. Putnam's Sons. New York. 1886. Large 8vo. pp. 89.

A Remarkable Self-Made Man. By John Langdon Sibley. Reprinted from the Unitarian Review, April, 1875, with remarks by the editor. Cambridge: John Wilson and Son, University Press. 1886. 8vo. pp. 20.

Boston University Year Book. Edited by the University Council. Vol. XIII. Boston University Offices, 12 Somerset Street. Printed by Rand, Avery & Co. 1886. 8vo. pp. 164.

Oceana, or England and her Colonies, by James Anthony Froude. New York: Charles Scribner's Sons. 1886. 8vo. pp. 396.

The Winchester Record. March, 1886. Vol. II. No. 2. Printed for the members of the Winchester Historical and Genealogical Society. 8vo. pp. vi. 199–416.

Catalogus Senatus Academici et forum qui munera et officia Academica gesserunt quique aliquovis Gradu exornate fuerunt in Collegio Yalensi, in Nova-Portu in Republica Connecticutensi in Nova-Portu. Tuttle et Morehouse et Taylor Typoraphis. 1886. 8vo. pp. 168+lxxx.

A Sketch of the Women's Art Museum Association of Cincinnati. 1877–1886. Cincinnati: Robert Clarke & Co. 1886. 8vo. pp. 134.

Memorial. Alpheus Spring Packard. 1798–1884. Printed for Bowdoin College Library. Brunswick, Maine. 1886. 8vo. pp. 95.

Methodist Review. Bi-monthly. Daniel Curry, D.D., LL.D., Editor. July, 1886. New York: Phillips & Hunt. Price $2 50 a year.

The Universalist Quarterly. July, 1886. Thomas B. Thayer, D.D., Editor. Boston: Universalist Publishing House, 16 Bromfield St. Price $2 a year.

American Catholic Quarterly Review. July, 1886. Philadelphia: Hardy & Mahony, 505 Chestnut St. Price $5.

New Englander and Yale Review. New Haven: William L. Kingsley. July and August, 1886. Published monthly. Price $3 a year.

Notes and Queries: a Medium of Intercommunication for Literary Men, General Readers, etc. London: John C. Francis, 22 Took's-court, Cursitor-street, Chancery Lane, E. C. 7th Series, Vol. II. Nos. 27 to 31. July 3 to 31, 1886. Published weekly. Price 4d. a number.

The Narragansett Historical Register. James N. Arnold, Editor. April, 1886. Providence, R. I.: The Narragansett Historical Publishing Co. Price $2 a year.

DEATHS.

ABRAHAM FIRTH, Esq., of Lynn, Mass., died in that city, July 17, 1886, aged 68. He was born in Leicester, Eng., Jan. 2, 1818. He was for many years superintendent of the Boston and Worcester Railroad, and afterwards of the Marginal Freight Railroad, Boston. In 1852 he represented Leicester, Mass., in the legislature, and in 1875 was a member of the Boston Common Council.

Major ALBERT LOUIS RICHARDSON died at his residence, Montvale, Woburn, Mass., April 24, 1886, aged 82. He was a son of Jacob and Sarah (Lewis) Richardson, of Greenfield, N. H., and was born in that town, Oct. 16, 1803. He was the seventh generation in descent from Thomas[1] Richardson, one of the first settlers of Woburn, through Thomas,[2] Nathaniel,[3] Hezekiah,[4] Jacob,[5] and Jacob[6] his father. His early occupation was that of a civil engineer. At the time of his death he was postmaster of Montvale, and had held the office for more than thirty years. He assisted the late Rev. John A. Vinton in the preparation of his Richardson Memorial (*ante*, xxxi. 131), and Mr. Vinton states that "without him it might not have been undertaken."

INDEX OF NAMES.